A People and a Nation

A PEOPLE AND A NATION

A History of the United States

VOLUME I: To 1877

Eighth Edition

ADVANTAGE EDITION

Mary Beth Norton
Cornell University

Carol Sheriff
College of William and Mary

David M. Katzman
University of Kansas

David Blight
Yale University

Howard Chudacoff
Brown University

Fredrik Longevall
Cornell University

Beth Bailey
Temple University

WADSWORTH
CENGAGE Learning

Australia • Brazil • Japan • Korea • Mexico • Singapore • Spain • United Kingdom • United States

WADSWORTH
CENGAGE Learning

A People and a Nation: A History of the United States, Eighth Edition, Advantage Edition

Mary Beth Norton, Carol Sheriff, David M. Katzman, David Blight, Howard Chudacoff, Fredrik Longevall, Beth Bailey

Sponsoring Editor: Ann West

Development Manager: Jeffrey Greene

Assistant Editor: Megan Curry

Editorial Assistant: Megan Chrisman

Senior Media Editor: Lisa Ciccolo

Senior Marketing Manager: Katherine Bates

Marketing Coordinator: Lorreen Pelletier

Marketing Communications Manager: Christine Dobberpuhl

Senior Content Project Manager, Editorial Production: Margaret Park Bridges

Art and Design Manager: Jill Haber

Manufacturing Buyer: Arethea L. Thomas

Senior Rights Acquisition Account Manager: Katie Huha

Text Researcher: Michael Farmer

Production Service: Lachina Publishing Services

Senior Photo Editor: Jennifer Meyer Dare

Cover Design Director: Tony Saizon

Cover Image: King, Samuel (1748–1819). *Ezra Stiles* (1727–1795). 1771. Oil on canvas. Credit: Yale University Art Gallery. Bequest Charles Jenkins Foote/Art Resource, NY.

Compositor: S4Carlisle Publishing Services

Printed in the United States of America
2 3 4 5 6 7 12 11 10 09

For product information and technology assistance, contact us at **Cengage Learning Academic Resource Center, 1-800-423-0563**

For permission to use material from this text or product, submit all requests online at **www.cengage.com/permissions.** Further permissions questions can be e-mailed to **permissionrequest@cengage.com.**

Library of Congress Control Number: 2008928058

ISBN-13: 978-0-547-06036-1

ISBN-10: 0-547-06036-X

Wadsworth
25 Thomson Place
Boston, MA 02210
USA

Cengage Learning products are represented in Canada by Nelson Education, Ltd.

For your course and learning solutions, visit **academic.cengage.com.**

Purchase any of our products at your local college store or at our preferred online store **www.ichapters.com.**

Brief Contents

Contents

Advantage Edition Preface

This Advantage Edition is based on the eighth edition of *A People and a Nation* and reflects its major revisions, while still retaining the narrative strength and focus that characterized its earlier editions and made it so popular with students and teachers alike. In the years since the publication of the seventh edition, new materials have been uncovered, new interpretations advanced, and new themes have come to the forefront of American historical scholarship. All the authors—joined by one new member, Carol Sheriff,—have worked diligently to incorporate those findings into this text.

Like other teachers and students, we are always re-creating our past, restructuring our memory, and rediscovering the personalities and events that have influenced us, injured us, and bedeviled us. This book represents our continuing rediscovery of America's history—its diverse people and the nation they created and have nurtured. As this book demonstrates, there are many different Americans and many different memories. We have sought to present as many of them as possible, in both triumph and tragedy, in both division and unity.

ABOUT A PEOPLE AND A NATION

A People and a Nation, first published in 1982, was the first major textbook in the United States to fully integrate social and political history. From the outset, the authors have been determined to tell the story of *all* the people of the United States. This book's hallmark has been its melding of social and political history, its movement beyond history's common focus on public figures and events to examine the daily life of America's people. All editions of the book, including this Advantage Edition, have stressed the interaction of public policy and personal experience, the relationship between domestic concerns and foreign affairs, the various manifestations of popular culture, and the multiple origins of America and Americans. We have consistently built our narrative on a firm foundation in primary sources—on both well-known and obscure letters, diaries, public documents, oral histories, and artifacts of material culture. We have long challenged readers to think about the meaning of American history, not just to memorize facts. Both students and instructors have repeatedly told us how much they appreciate and enjoy our approach to the past.

As has been true since the first edition, each chapter opens with a dramatic vignette focusing on an individual or a group of people. These vignettes introduce key themes, which then frame the chapters in succinct introductions and summaries. Numerous maps, tables, graphs, and charts provide readers with the necessary geographical and statistical context for observations in the text. Carefully selected illustrations—many of them unique to this book—offer readers visual insight into the topics under discussion, especially because the authors have written the captions. In this edition, as in all previous ones, we have sought to incorporate up-to-date scholarship, readability, a clear structure, critical thinking, and instructive illustrative material on every page.

THEMES IN THIS BOOK

Several themes and questions stand out in our continuing effort to integrate political, social, and cultural history. We study the many ways Americans have defined themselves—gender, race, class, region, ethnicity, religion, sexual orientation—and the many subjects that have reflected their multidimensional experiences. We highlight the remarkably diverse everyday lives of the American people—in cities and on farms and ranches, in factories and in corporate headquarters, in neighborhoods and in legislatures, in love relationships and in hate groups, in recreation and in work, in the classroom and in military uniform, in secret national security conferences and in public foreign relations debates, in church and in voluntary associations, in polluted environments and in conservation areas. We pay particular attention to lifestyles, diet and dress, family life and structure, labor conditions, gender roles, migration and mobility, childbearing, and child rearing. We explore how Americans have entertained and informed themselves by discussing their music, sports, theater, print media, film, radio, television, graphic arts, and literature, in both "high" culture and popular culture. We study how technology has influenced Americans' lives, such as through the internal combustion engine and the computer.

Americans' personal lives have always interacted with the public realm of politics and government. To understand how Americans have sought to protect their different ways of life and to work out solutions to thorny problems, we emphasize their expectations of governments at the local, state, and federal levels; governments' role in providing answers; the lobbying of interest groups; the campaigns and outcomes of elections; and the hierarchy of power in any period. Because the United States has long been a major participant in world affairs, we explore America's participation in wars, interventions in other nations, empire-building, immigration patterns, images of foreign peoples, cross-national cultural ties, and international economic trends.

What's New in This Edition

Planning for the eighth edition began at a two-day authors' meeting in Boston. There we discussed the most recent scholarship in the field, the reviews of the seventh edition solicited from instructors, and the findings of our own continuing research. For this edition, we added a new colleague, Carol Sheriff, who experienced the intellectual exhilaration and rigor of such an authors' meeting for the first time. Sheriff, a member of the History Department at the College of William and Mary, has written extensively on antebellum America, especially in the north, and she has taken on the responsibility for those chapters in the eighth edition.

This edition builds on its immediate predecessor in continuing to enhance the global perspective on American history that has characterized the book since its first edition. From the "Atlantic world" context of European colonies in North and South America to the discussion of international terrorism, the authors have incorporated the most recent globally oriented scholarship throughout the volume. Significantly, the eighth edition includes an entirely new chapter on the American west in the years before the Civil War and the discussion of the west has been expanded throughout. The treatment of the history of children and childhood has been increased, as has the discussion of environmental history, including the devastating impact of hurricanes in North America and the Caribbean from the earliest days of European settlement. As in the seventh edition, we have worked to strengthen our treatment of the diversity of America's people by examining differences within the broad ethnic categories commonly employed and by paying greater attention to immigration, cultural and intellectual infusions from around the world, and America's growing religious diversity. We have also stressed the incorporation of different peoples into the United States through territorial acquisition as well as through immigration. At the same time, we have integrated the discussion of such diversity into our narrative, so as not to artificially isolate any group from the mainstream. We have added three probing questions at the end of each chapter's introduction to guide students' reading of the pages that follow.

As always, the authors reexamined every sentence, interpretation, map, chart, illustration, and caption, refining the narrative, presenting new examples, and bringing to the text the latest findings of scholars in many areas of history, anthropology, sociology, and political science. More than one-third of the chapter-opening vignettes are new to this edition.

"Links to the World"

Each chapter contains one brief feature essay: "Links to the World" (introduced in the seventh edition). "Links to the World" examine both inward and outward ties between America (and Americans) and the rest of the world. The "Links" appear at appropriate places in each chapter to explore specific topics at considerable length. Tightly constructed essays detail the often little-known connections between developments here and abroad. The topics range broadly over economic, political, social, technological, medical, and cultural history, vividly demonstrating that the geographical region that is now the United States has never lived in isolation from other peoples and countries. New to this edition are Links on smallpox inoculations, the Amistad case, Russian Populism, European influence on American workers' compensation, and *National Geographic*. Each Link highlights global interconnections with unusual and lively examples that will both intrigue and inform students.

SECTION-BY-SECTION CHANGES IN THIS EDITION

Mary Beth Norton, who had primary responsibility for Chapters 1 through 8 and served as coordinating author, augmented her discussion of the age of European expansion with new information on Muslim power and the allure of exotic spices; she also expanded the treatment of Spanish colonization and settlements in the Caribbean. She incorporated extensive new scholarship on early Virginia into Chapter 2. In addition to reorganizing part of Chapter 3 to bring more coherence to the discussion of the origins of slavery in North America, she added demographic information about enslaved people (both Indians and Africans) and those who enslaved and transported them, stressing in particular the importance of African women in South Carolina rice cultivation. She added material on transported English convicts, Huguenot immigrants, Acadian exiles, iron-making, land riots, the Stono Rebellion, the Seven Years' War in western Pennsylvania, the experiences of common soldiers in the Revolution, Shays's Rebellion, and the Jay Treaty debates. In Chapter 8 she created new sections on Indians in the new nation and on revolutions at the end of the century, including among them the election of Thomas Jefferson.

Carol Sheriff completely reorganized the contents of Chapters 9, 11, and 12, clarifying chronological developments and including much new material. Chapter 9 now covers politics through 1823 in order to emphasize the impact of the War of 1812 in accelerating regional divisions. It has expanded coverage of popular political practice (including among non-voters), the separation of church and state, the Marshall Court, the First and Second Barbary Wars, and the incorporation of the Louisiana Territory and its residents into the United States. Chapter 11, retitled "The Modernizing North," consolidates information previously divided between two chapters and augments it with new discussions of daily life before commercial and industrial expansion, rural-urban contrasts, children and youth culture, male and female common laborers, and the origins of free-labor ideology. Chapter 12 focuses on reform and politics in the age of Jackson, with expanded attention to communitarian experiments, abolitionism (including African Americans in the movement), women's rights, and religion, including revivalism in general and the Second Great Awakening in particular. The entirely new Chapter 13, "The Contested West," combines material that was previously scattered in different locations with a great deal of recent scholarship on such topics as the disjunction between the ideal and reality of the West, exploration and migration, cultural diversity in the West, cooperation and conflict among the West's peoples, and the role of the federal government in regional development. In all her reorganized chapters she relied on a base created by David M. Katzman, an original member of the author team who had responsibility for this section in the seven earlier editions.

David W. Blight, who had primary responsibility for Chapters 10 and 14 through 16, extensively reorganized Chapter 10 (previously Chapter 13), on the South, in part to reflect its new chronological placement in the book. The chapter now covers material beginning in 1815 rather than 1830 and contains a section on Southern expansion and Indian removal. In his chapters he has added material on the Taos revolt, enslaved children, "Bleeding Kansas," Harriet Scott, Louisa May Alcott, union sentiment in the South, the conduct of the war, and economic and social conditions in the postwar North and South. He has revised Chapter 16 to emphasize economic as well as political change in the era of Reconstruction.

Howard P. Chudacoff, responsible for Chapters 17 through 21 and 24, has increased the coverage of Indians, Exodusters, and Hispanics in the West, and of western Progressivism. His treatment of popular culture now stresses its lower-class, bottom-to-top origins. He added information on the history of childhood, vaudeville, and the movies; and he revised discussions of monetary policy, Progressivism, Populism, and urban and agrarian protests. He also has included more coverage of racism and those who combated it, such as Ida B. Wells, and on women and the Ku Klux Klan. Business operation and regulation receive new attention in his chapters, as do Calvin Coolidge, consumerism, and baseball.

Fredrik Logevall, with primary responsibility for Chapters 22, 23, 26, and 28, continued throughout his chapters to work to establish the wider international context for U.S. foreign affairs. He added considerable new material on the Middle East (especially in Chapter 28) and incorporated recent scholarship on the Vietnam War. He also updated the treatment of the Spanish-American War with new information on the sinking of the *Maine* and on the Philippine insurrection. His discussion of World War I now includes consideration of the antagonistic relationship of Woodrow Wilson and V.I. Lenin; and he has given more attention to American economic and cultural expansion in the 1920s and 1930s. He has furthermore expanded his treatment of American reactions to the Spanish Civil War.

Beth Bailey, primarily responsible for Chapters 25, 27, and 29, added information on women, the left, and popular culture (especially film and the production code) during the 1930s. She expanded coverage of the European front in World War II and of divisions within the United States during the war. In Chapter 29, she thoroughly reorganized the section on civil rights to clarify the chronology and key points of development, and she also included new information on emerging countercultures and the beats, union activities, and the Eisenhower administration.

Bailey and Logevall shared responsibility for Chapters 30 through 33. In Chapter 30 Freedom Summer is given enhanced attention and the section on civil rights has been reorganized to emphasize a clear chronology. These chapters contain new material on the women's movement and the barriers women faced before 1970s reforms, recent immigration, neoconservatism, anti-Vietnam War protests, Nixon's presidency, the Supreme Court, the 1982 Israeli invasion of Lebanon, and the 1991 Iraq War. Chapter 33 in particular has been thoroughly revised to include the latest demographic data on Americans and their families, along with discussions of the struggles over science and religion, hurricane Katrina, the Bush administration's domestic policies, and especially the Iraq War.

M.B.N.

C.S.

D.B.

H.C.

F.L.

B.B.

About the Authors

MARY BETH NORTON

Born in Ann Arbor, Michigan, Mary Beth Norton received her B.A. from the University of Michigan (1964) and her Ph.D. from Harvard University (1969). She is the Mary Donlon Alger Professor of American History at Cornell University. Her dissertation won the Allan Nevins Prize. She has written *The British-Americans* (1972), *Liberty's Daughters* (1980, 1996), *Founding Mothers & Fathers* (1996), which was one of three finalists for the 1997 Pulitzer Prize in History, and *In the Devil's Snare* (2002), which was one of five finalists for the 2003 *LA Times* Book Prize in History and which won the English-Speaking Union's Ambassador Book Award in American Studies for 2003. She has coedited *Women of America* (with Carol Berkin, 1979), *To Toil The Livelong Day* (with Carol Groneman, 1987), and *Major Problems in American Women's History* (with Ruth Alexander, 2007). She was general editor of the *American Historical Association's Guide to Historical Literature* (1995). Her articles have appeared in such journals as the *American Historical Review, William and Mary Quarterly,* and *Journal of Women's History.* Mary Beth has served as president of the Berkshire Conference of Women Historians, as vice president for research of the American Historical Association, and as a presidential appointee to the National Council on the Humanities. She has received four honorary degrees and in 1999 was elected a fellow of the American Academy of Arts and Sciences. She has held fellowships from the National Endowment for the Humanities, the Guggenheim, Rockefeller, and Starr Foundations, and the Henry E. Huntington Library. In 2005–2006, she was the Pitt Professor of American History and Institutions at the University of Cambridge and Newnham College.

CAROL SHERIFF

Born in Washington, DC, and raised in Bethesda, Maryland, Carol Sheriff received her B.A. from Wesleyan University (1985) and her Ph.D. from Yale University (1993). Since 1993, she has taught history at the College of William and Mary, where she has won the Thomas Jefferson Teaching Award, the Alumni Teaching Fellowship Award, and the University Professorship for Teaching Excellence. Her publications include *The Artificial River: The Erie Canal and the Paradox of Progress* (1996), which won the Dixon Ryan Fox Award from the New York State Historical Association and the Award for Excellence in Research from the New York State Archives, and *A People War: Civilians and Soldiers in America's Civil War, 1854–1877* (with Scott Reynolds Nelson, 2007). Carol has written sections of a teaching manual for the New York State history curriculum, given presentations to a Teaching American History grant project, consulted on an exhibit for the Rochester Museum and Science Center, appeared in the History Channel's Modern Marvels show on the Erie Canal, and is serving as a consultant for "The Inland Voyage," a forthcoming television documentary on the Erie Canal. At William and Mary, she teaches the U.S. history survey as well as upper-level classes on the Early Republic, the Civil War Era, and the American West.

DAVID W. BLIGHT

Born in Flint, Michigan, David W. Blight received his B.A. from Michigan State University (1971) and his Ph.D. from the University of Wisconsin (1985). He is now professor of history and director of the Gilder Lehrman Center for the Study of Slavery, Resistance, and Abolition at Yale University. For the first seven years of his career, David was a public high school teacher in Flint. He has written *Frederick Douglass's Civil War* (1989) and *Race and Reunion: The Civil War in American Memory, 1863–1915* (2000). His most recent book is *A Slave No More: the Emancipation of John Washington and Wallace Turnage* (2007). His edited works include *When This Cruel War Is Over: The Civil War Letters of Charles Harvey Brewster* (1992), *Narrative of the Life of Frederick Douglass* (1993), W. E. B. Du Bois, *The Souls of Black Folk* (with Robert Gooding Williams, 1997), *Union and Emancipation* (with Brooks Simpson, 1997), and *Caleb Bingham, The Columbian Orator* (1997). David's essays have appeared in the *Journal of American History, Civil War History,* and Gabor Boritt, ed., *Why the Civil War Came* (1996), among others. In 1992-1993 he was senior Fulbright

Professor in American Studies at the University of Munich, Germany. A consultant to several documentary films, David appeared in the 1998 PBS series, *Africans in America*. In 1999 he was elected to the Council of the American Historical Association. David also teaches summer seminars for secondary school teachers, as well as for park rangers and historians of the National Park Service. His book, *Race and Reunion: The Civil War in American Memory* (2000), received many honors in 2002, including The Bancroft Prize, Abraham Lincoln Prize, and the Frederick Douglass Prize. From the Organization of American Historians, he has received the Merle Curti Prize in Social History, the Merle Curti Prize in Intellectual History, the Ellis Hawley Prize in Political History, and the James Rawley Prize in Race Relations.

HOWARD P. CHUDACOFF

Howard P. Chudacoff, the George L. Littlefield Professor of American History and Professor of Urban Studies at Brown University, was born in Omaha, Nebraska. He earned his A.B. (1965) and Ph.D. (1969) from the University of Chicago. He has written *Mobile Americans* (1972), *How Old Are You?* (1989), *The Age of the Bachelor* (1999), *The Evolution of American Urban Society* (with Judith Smith, 2004), and *Childern at Play: An American History* (2007). He has also coedited with Peter Baldwin *Major Problems in American Urban History* (2004). His articles have appeared in such journals as the *Journal of Family History*, *Reviews in American History*, and *Journal of American History*. At Brown University, Howard has co-chaired the American Civilization Program, chaired the Department of History, and serves as Brown's faculty representative to the NCAA. He has also served on the board of directors of the Urban History Association. The National Endowment for the Humanities, Ford Foundation, and Rockefeller Foundation have given him awards to advance his scholarship.

FREDRIK LOGEVALL

A native of Stockholm, Sweden, Fredrik Logevall received his B.A. from Simon Fraser University (1986) and his Ph.D. from Yale University (1993). He is a professor of history at Cornell University. He is the author of *Choosing War: The Lost Chance for Peace and the Escalation of War in Vietnam* (1999), which won three prizes, including the Warren F. Kuehl Book Prize from the Society for Historians of American Foreign Relations (SHAFR). His other publications include *The Origins of the Vietnam War* (2001), *Terrorism and 9/11: A Reader* (2002), as coeditor, the *Encyclopedia of American Foreign Policy* (2002) and, as co-editor, *The First Vietnam War: Colonial Conflict and Cold War Crisis* (2007). Fred is a past recipient of the Stuart L. Barnath article, book, and lecture prizes from SHAFR and is a member of the SHAFR Council, the Cornell University Press faculty board, and the editorial advisory board of the Presidential Recordings Project at the Miller Center of Public Affairs at the University of Virginia. In 2006-2007 he was Leverhulme Visiting Professor at the University of Nottingham and Mellon Senior Fellow at the University of Cambridge.

BETH BAILEY

Born in Atlanta, Georgia, Beth Bailey received her B.A. from Northwestern University (1979) and her Ph.D. from the University of Chicago (1986). She is now a professor of history at Temple University. Her research and teaching fields include American cultural history (nineteenth and twentieth centuries), popular culture, and gender and sexuality. She is the author of *From Front Porch to Back Seat: Courtship in 20th Century America* (1988), a historical analysis of conventions governing the courtship of heterosexual youth; *The First Strange Place: The Alchemy of Race and Sex in WWII Hawaii* (with David Farber, 1992), which analyzes cultural contact among Americans in wartime Hawaii; *Sex in the Heartland* (1999), a social and cultural history of the post-WWII "sexual revolution"; *The Columbia Companion to America in the 1960s* (with David Farber, 2001); and is co-editor of *A History of Our Time* (with William Chafe and Harvard Sitkoff, 6th ed., 2002). Beth has served as a consultant and/or on-screen expert for numerous television documentaries developed for PBS and the History Channel. She has received grants from the ACLS and NEH, was the Ann Whitney Olin scholar at Barnard College, Columbia University, from 1991 through 1994, where she was the director of the American Studies Program, and held a senior Fulbright lectureship in Indonesia in 1996. She teaches courses on sexuality and gender, war and American culture, research methods, and popular culture.

1

Three Old Worlds Create a New
1492–1600

AMERICAN SOCIETIES

Human beings originated on the continent of Africa, where humanlike remains about 3 million years old have been found in what is now Ethiopia. Over many millennia, the growing population slowly dispersed to the other continents. Because the climate was then far colder than it is now, much of the earth's water was concentrated in huge rivers of ice called glaciers. Sea levels were accordingly lower, and land masses covered a larger proportion of the earth's surface than they do today. Scholars long believed that the earliest inhabitants of the Americas crossed a land bridge known as Beringia (at the site of the Bering Strait) approximately 12,000 to 14,000 years ago. Yet striking new archaeological discoveries in both North and South America suggest that parts of the Americas may have been settled much earlier, perhaps by seafarers. Some geneticists now theorize that three successive waves of migrants began at least 30,000 years ago. When, about 12,500 years ago, the climate warmed and sea levels rose, Americans were separated from the peoples living on the connected continents of Asia, Africa, and Europe.

Ancient America   The first Americans are called Paleo-Indians. Nomadic hunters of game and gatherers of wild plants, they spread throughout North and South America, probably moving as bands composed of extended families. By about 11,500 years ago the Paleo-Indians were making fine stone

1

projectile points, which they attached to wooden spears and used to kill and butcher bison (buffalo), woolly mammoths, and other large mammals then living in the Americas. But as the Ice Age ended and the human population increased, all the large American mammals except the bison disappeared. Scholars disagree about whether overhunting or the change in climate caused their demise. In either case, deprived of their primary source of meat, Paleo-Indians found new ways to survive.

By approximately 9,000 years ago, the residents of what is now central Mexico began to cultivate food crops, especially maize (corn), squash, beans, avocados, and peppers. In the Andes Mountains of South America, people started to grow potatoes. As knowledge of agricultural techniques improved and spread through the Americas, vegetables and maize proved a more reliable source of food than hunting and gathering. Except for those living in the harshest climates, most Americans started to adopt a more sedentary style of life so that they could tend fields regularly. Some established permanent settlements; others moved several times a year among fixed sites. They cleared forests through the use of controlled burning. The fires not only created cultivable lands by killing trees and fertilizing the soil with ashes but also opened meadows that attracted deer and other wildlife. All the American cultures emphasized producing sufficient food. Although they traded such items as shells, flint, salt, and copper, no society ever became dependent on another group for items vital to its survival.

Wherever agriculture dominated the economy, complex civilizations flourished. Such societies, assured of steady supplies of grains and vegetables, no longer had to devote all their energies to subsistence. Instead, they were able to accumulate wealth, produce ornamental objects, trade with other groups, and create elaborate rituals and ceremonies. In North America, the successful cultivation of nutritious crops, such as maize, beans, and squash, seems to have led to the growth and development of all the major civilizations: first the large city-states of Mesoamerica (modern Mexico and Guatemala) and then the urban clusters known collectively as the Mississippian culture and located in the present-day United States. Each of these societies, many historians and archaeologists now believe, reached its height of population and influence only after achieving success in agriculture. Each later declined and collapsed after reaching the limits of its food supply, with dire political and military consequences.

Mesoamerican Civilizations   Archaeologists and historians still know little about the first major Mesoamerican civilization, the Olmecs, who about 4,000 years ago lived near the Gulf of Mexico in cities dominated by temple pyramids. The Mayas and Teotihuacán, which developed approximately 2,000 years later, are better recorded. Teotihuacán, founded in the Valley of Mexico about 300 B.C.E. (Before the Common Era), eventually became one of the largest urban areas in the world, housing perhaps 100,000 people in the fifth century C.E. (Common Era). Teotihuacán's commercial network extended hundreds of miles in all directions; many peoples prized its obsidian (a green glass), used to make fine knives and mirrors. Pilgrims traveled long distances to visit Teotihuacán's impressive pyramids and the great temple of Quetzalcoatl—the feathered serpent, primary god of central Mexico.

CHRONOLOGY

12,000–10,000 B.C.E. • Paleo-Indians migrate from Asia to North America across the Beringia land bridge

7000 B.C.E. • Cultivation of food crops begins in America

c. 2000 B.C.E. • Olmec civilization appears

c. 300–600 C.E. • Height of influence of Teotihuacán

c. 600–900 C.E. • Classic Mayan civilization

1000 C.E. • Ancient Pueblos build settlements in modern states of Arizona and New Mexico

1001 • Norse establish settlement in "Vinland"

1050–1250 • Height of influence of Cahokia
• Prevalence of Mississippian culture in modern midwestern and southeastern United States

14th century • Aztec rise to power

1450s–80s • Portuguese explore and colonize islands in the Mediterranean Atlantic

1477 • Marco Polo's *Travels* describe China

1492 • Columbus reaches Bahamas

1494 • Treaty of Tordesillas divides land claims between Spain and Portugal in Africa, India, and South America

1496 • Last Canary Island falls to Spain

1497 • Cabot reaches North America

1513 • Ponce de León explores Florida

1518–30 • Smallpox epidemic devastates Indian population of West Indies and Central and South America

1519 • Cortés invades Mexico

1521 • Aztec Empire falls to Spaniards

1524 • Verrazzano sails along Atlantic coast of United States

1534–35 • Cartier explores St. Lawrence River

1534–36 • Vaca, Estevan, and two companions walk across North America

1539–42 • Soto explores southeastern United States

1540–42 • Coronado explores southwestern United States

1587–90 • Raleigh's Roanoke colony vanishes

1588 • Harriot publishes *A Briefe and True Report of the New Found Land of Virginia*

On the Yucatán Peninsula, in today's eastern Mexico, the Mayas built urban centers containing tall pyramids and temples. They studied astronomy and created an elaborate writing system. Their city-states, though, engaged in near-constant warfare with one another. Warfare and an inadequate food supply caused the collapse of the most powerful cities by 900 C.E., thus ending the classic era of Mayan civilization. By the time Spaniards arrived 600 years later, only a few remnants of the once-mighty society remained.

Pueblos and Mississippians

Ancient native societies in what is now the United States learned to grow maize, squash, and beans from Mesoamericans, but the exact nature of the relationship of the various cultures is unknown. (No Mesoamerican artifacts have been found north of the Rio Grande, but some items resembling Mississippian objects have been excavated in northern Mexico.) The Hohokam, Mogollon, and ancient Pueblo peoples of the modern states of Arizona and New Mexico subsisted by combining hunting and gathering with agriculture in an arid region of unpredictable rainfall. Hohokam villagers constructed extensive irrigation systems, but even so, they occasionally had to relocate their settlements when water supplies failed. Between 900 and 1150 C.E. in Chaco Canyon, the Pueblos built fourteen "Great Houses," multistory stone structures averaging two hundred rooms. The canyon, at the juncture of perhaps 400 miles of roads, served as a major regional trading and processing center for turquoise, used then as now to create beautiful ornamental objects. Yet the aridity eventually caused the Chacoans to migrate to other sites.

At almost the same time, the unrelated Mississippian culture flourished in what is now the midwestern and southeastern United States. Relying largely on maize, squash, nuts, pumpkins, and venison for food, the Mississippians lived in substantial settlements organized hierarchically. The largest of their urban centers was the City of the Sun (now called Cahokia), near modern St. Louis. Located on rich farmland close to the confluence of the Illinois, Missouri, and Mississippi Rivers, Cahokia, like Teotihuacán and Chaco Canyon, served as a focal point for both religion and trade. At its peak (in the eleventh and twelfth centuries C.E.), the City of the Sun covered more than 5 square miles and had a population of about twenty thousand—small by Mesoamerican standards but larger than any other northern community, and larger than London in the same era.

Although the Cahokians never invented a writing system, these sun-worshippers developed an accurate calendar, evidenced by their creation of a woodhenge—a large circle of tall timber posts aligned with the solstices and the equinox. The city's main pyramid (one of 120 of varying sizes), today called Monks Mound, was at the time of its construction the third largest structure of any description in the Western Hemisphere; it remains the largest earthwork ever built anywhere in the Americas. It sat at the northern end of the Grand Plaza, surrounded by seventeen other mounds, some used for burials. Yet following 1250 C.E. the city was abandoned, several decades after a disastrous earthquake. Archaeologists believe that climate change and the degradation of the environment, caused by overpopulation and the destruction of nearby forests, contributed to the city's collapse.

Aztecs

The Aztecs' histories tell of the long migration of their people (who called themselves Mexica) into the Valley of Mexico during the twelfth century. The uninhabited ruins of Teotihuacán, which by then had been deserted for at least two hundred years, awed and mystified the migrants. Their chronicles record that their primary deity, Huitzilopochtli—a war god represented by an eagle—directed them to establish their capital on an island where they saw an eagle eating a serpent, the symbol of Quetzalcoatl. That island city became Tenochtitlán, the center of a rigidly stratified society composed of hereditary classes of warriors, merchants, priests, common folk, and slaves.

The Aztecs conquered their neighbors, forcing them to pay tribute in textiles, gold, foodstuffs, and human beings who could be sacrificed to Huitzilopochtli. They also engaged in ritual combat, known as flowery wars, to obtain further sacrificial victims. The war god's taste for blood was not easily quenched. In the Aztec year Ten Rabbit (1502), at the coronation of Motecuhzoma II (the Spaniards could not pronounce his name correctly, so they called him Montezuma), thousands of people were sacrificed by having their still-beating hearts torn from their bodies.

The Aztecs believed that they lived in the age of the Fifth Sun. Four times previously, they wrote, the earth and all the people who lived on it had been destroyed. They predicted that their own world would end in earthquakes and hunger. In the Aztec year Thirteen Flint, volcanoes erupted, sickness and hunger spread, wild beasts attacked children, and an eclipse of the sun darkened the sky. Did some priest wonder whether the Fifth Sun was approaching its end? In time, the Aztecs learned that Thirteen Flint was called, by Europeans, 1492.

North America in 1492

Over the centuries, the Americans who lived north of Mexico adapted their once-similar ways of life to very different climates and terrains, thus creating the diverse culture areas (ways of subsistence) that the Europeans encountered when they arrived. Scholars often refer to such culture areas by language group (such as Algonquian or Iroquoian) because neighboring Indian nations commonly spoke related languages. Bands that lived in environments not well suited to agriculture—because of inadequate rainfall or poor soil, for example—followed a nomadic lifestyle similar to that of the Paleo-Indians. Within the area of the present-day United States, these groups included the Paiutes and Shoshones, who inhabited the Great Basin (now Nevada and Utah). Because of the difficulty of finding sufficient food for more than a few people, such hunter-gatherer bands were small, usually composed of one or more related families. The men hunted small animals, and women gathered seeds and berries. Where large game was more plentiful and food supplies therefore more certain, as in present-day central and western Canada and the Great Plains, bands of hunters were somewhat larger.

In more favorable environments, larger groups combined agriculture with gathering, hunting, and fishing. Those who lived near the seacoasts, like the Chinooks of present-day Washington and Oregon, consumed fish and shellfish in addition to growing crops and gathering seeds and berries. Residents of the interior (for example, the Arikaras of the Missouri River valley) hunted large animals while also cultivating maize, squash, and beans. The peoples of what is now eastern Canada and the northeastern United States also combined hunting, fishing, and agriculture. They regularly used controlled fires both to open land for cultivation and to assist in hunting.

Gendered Division of Labor   Societies that relied primarily on hunting large animals, such as deer and buffalo, assigned that task to men, allotting food preparation and clothing production to women. Before such nomadic bands acquired horses from the Spaniards, women—occasionally assisted by dogs—also carried the family's belongings whenever the band relocated. Such a sexual

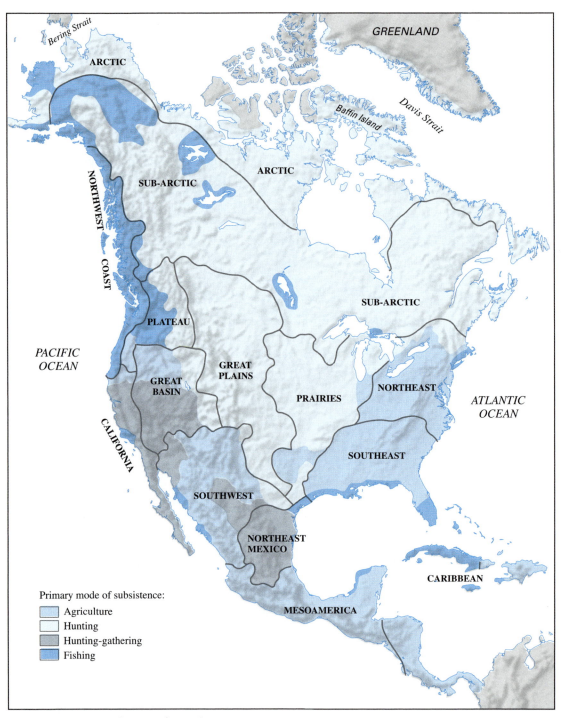

MAP 1.1 Native Cultures of North America

The natives of the North American continent effectively used the resources of the regions in which they lived. As this map shows, coastal groups relied on fishing, residents of fertile areas engaged in agriculture, and other peoples employed hunting (often combined with gathering) as a primary mode of subsistence.

Jacques Le Moyne, an artist accompanying the French settlement in Florida in the 1560s (see page 35), produced some of the first European images of North American peoples. His depiction of native agricultural practices shows the gendered division of labor: men breaking up the ground with fishbone hoes before women drop seeds into the holes. But Le Moyne's version of the scene cannot be accepted uncritically: unable to abandon a European view of proper farming methods, he erroneously drew plowed furrows in the soil. (Collection of Mary Beth Norton)

division of labor was universal among hunting peoples, regardless of their location. So, too, among seacoast peoples women gathered shellfish along the shore while men fished from boats. Yet agricultural societies assigned work in divergent ways. The Pueblo peoples, who lived in sixty or seventy autonomous villages and spoke five different languages, defined agricultural labor as men's work. In the east, large clusters of peoples speaking Algonquian, Iroquoian, and Muskogean languages by contrast allocated most agricultural chores to women, although men cleared the land. In all the farming societies, women gathered wild foods and prepared food for consumption or storage, whereas men were responsible for hunting.

Everywhere in North America, women cared for young children, while older youths learned adult skills from their same-sex parent. Children generally had a great deal of freedom. Young people commonly chose their own marital partners, and in most societies couples could easily divorce if they no longer wished to live together. In contrast to the earlier Mississippian cultures, populations in these societies remained at a level sustainable by existing food supplies, largely because of low birth rates. Infants and toddlers were nursed until the age of two or even longer, and taboos prevented couples from having sexual intercourse during that period.

Social Organization The southwestern and eastern agricultural peoples had similar social organizations. They lived in villages, sometimes with a thousand or more inhabitants. The Pueblos resided in multistory buildings constructed on terraces along the sides of cliffs or other easily defended sites. Northern Iroquois villages (in modern New York State) were composed of large, rectangular, bark-covered structures, or long houses; the name Haudenosaunee, which the Iroquois called themselves, means "People of the Long House." In the present-day southeastern United States, Muskogeans and southern Algonquians lived in large houses made of thatch. Most of the eastern villages were surrounded by wooden palisades and ditches to aid in fending off attackers.

In all the agricultural societies, each dwelling housed an extended family defined matrilineally (through a female line of descent). Mothers, their married daughters, and their daughters' husbands and children all lived together. Matrilineal descent did not imply matriarchy, or the wielding of power by women, but rather served as a means of reckoning kinship. Matrilineal ties also linked extended families into clans. The nomadic bands of the Prairies and Great Plains, by contrast, were most often related patrilineally (through the male line). They lacked settled villages and defended themselves from attack primarily through their ability to move to safer locations when necessary.

War and Politics The defensive design of native villages discloses the significance of warfare in pre-Columbian America. Long before Europeans arrived, residents of the continent fought one another for control of the best hunting and fishing territories, the most fertile agricultural lands, or the sources of essential items, such as salt (for preserving meat) and flint (for making knives and arrowheads). Bands of Americans protected by wooden armor battled while standing in ranks facing each other, the better to employ their clubs and throwing spears, which were effective only at close quarters. They began to shoot arrows from behind trees only when they confronted European guns, which rendered their armor useless. People captured by the enemy in such wars were sometimes enslaved and dishonored by losing their previous names and identities, but slavery was never an important source of labor in pre-Columbian America.

American political structures varied considerably. Among Pueblos, the village council, composed of ten to thirty men, was the highest political authority; no government structure connected the villages. Nomadic hunters also lacked formal links among separate bands. The Iroquois, by contrast, had an elaborate political hierarchy incorporating villages into nations and nations into a confederation. A council comprising representatives from each nation made crucial decisions of war and peace for the entire confederacy. In all the North American cultures, civil and war leaders divided political power and wielded authority only so long as they retained the confidence of the people. Autocratic rule of the sort common in Europe was found only in southeastern chiefdoms descended from the Mississippians. Women more often assumed leadership roles among agricultural peoples, especially those in which females were the primary cultivators, than among nomadic hunters. Female sachems (rulers) led Algonquian villages in what is now Massachusetts, but women never became heads of hunting bands. Iroquois women did not become chiefs, yet clan matrons exercised political power. The older women of each village chose its chief and could both start wars (by calling for the capture of prisoners to replace dead relatives) and stop them (by refusing to supply warriors with necessary foodstuffs).

Religion All the American peoples were polytheistic, worshiping a multitude of gods. Each group's most important beliefs and rituals were closely tied to its means of subsistence. The major deities of agricultural peoples like the Pueblos and Muskogeans were associated with cultivation, and their chief festivals centered on planting and harvest. The most important gods of hunters like those living on the Great Plains and Prairies were associated with animals, and their major festivals were related to hunting. A band's economy and women's role in it helped to determine women's potential as religious leaders. Women held the most prominent positions in those agricultural societies in which they were also the chief food producers, whereas in hunting societies men took the lead in religious as well as political affairs.

A wide variety of cultures, comprising more than 10 million people, thus inhabited America north of Mexico when Europeans arrived. The hierarchical kingdoms of Mesoamerica bore little resemblance to the nomadic hunting societies of the Great Plains or to the agriculturalists of the Northeast or Southwest. The diverse inhabitants of North America spoke well over one thousand different languages. For obvious reasons, they did not consider themselves one people, nor did they—for the most part—think of uniting to repel the European invaders.

AFRICAN SOCIETIES

Fifteenth-century Africa, like fifteenth-century America, housed a variety of cultures adapted to different terrains and climates. Many of these cultures were of great antiquity. In the north, along the Mediterranean Sea, lived the Berbers, who were Muslims, or followers of the Islamic religion founded by the prophet Mohammed in the seventh century C.E. On the east coast of Africa, Muslim city-states engaged in extensive trade with India, the Moluccas (part of modern Indonesia), and China. In these ports, sustained contact and intermarriage among Arabs and Africans created the Swahili language and culture. Through the East African city-states passed waterborne commerce between the eastern Mediterranean and East Asia; the rest followed the long land route across Central Asia known as the Silk Road.

South of the Mediterranean coast in the African interior lie the great Saharan and Libyan Deserts, vast expanses of nearly waterless terrain crisscrossed by trade routes passing through oases. The introduction of the camel in the fifth century C.E. made long-distance travel possible, and as Islam expanded after the ninth century, commerce controlled by Muslim merchants helped to spread similar religious and cultural ideas throughout the region. Below the deserts, much of the continent is divided between tropical rain forests (along the coasts) and grassy plains (in the interior). People speaking a variety of languages and pursuing different subsistence strategies lived in a wide belt south of the deserts. South of the Gulf of Guinea, the grassy landscape came to be dominated by Bantu-speaking peoples, who left their homeland in modern Nigeria about two thousand years ago and slowly migrated south and east across the continent.

West Africa (Guinea)

West Africa was a land of tropical forests and savanna grasslands where fishing, cattle herding, and agriculture had supported the inhabitants for at least ten thousand years before Europeans set foot there in the fifteenth century. The northern region of West Africa, or Upper Guinea, was heavily influenced by the Islamic culture of the Mediterranean. As early as the eleventh century C.E., many of the region's inhabitants had become Muslims. Trade via camel caravans between Upper Guinea and the Muslim Mediterranean was sub-Saharan Africa's major connection to Europe and West Asia. In return for salt, dates, silk, and cotton cloth Africans exchanged ivory, gold, and slaves with northern merchants.

Upper Guinea runs northeast-southwest from Cape Verde to Cape Palmas. The people of its northernmost region, the so-called Rice Coast (present-day Gambia, Senegal, and Guinea), fished and cultivated rice in coastal swamplands. The Grain Coast, the next region to the south, was thinly populated and not readily accessible from the sea because it had only one good harbor (modern Freetown, Sierra Leone). Its people concentrated on farming and raising livestock.

In Lower Guinea, south and east of Cape Palmas, most Africans were farmers who practiced traditional religions, not the precepts of Islam. Believing that spirits inhabited particular places, they invested those places with special significance. Like the agricultural peoples of the Americas, they developed rituals intended to ensure good harvests. Throughout the region, individual villages composed of kin groups were linked into hierarchical kingdoms. At the time of initial European contact, decentralized political and social authority characterized the region's polities.

Complementary Gender Roles

The societies of West Africa, like those of the Americas, assigned different tasks to men and women. In general, the sexes shared agricultural duties. Men also hunted, managed livestock, and did most of the fishing. Women were responsible for childcare, food preparation, manufacture, and trade. They managed the extensive local and regional networks through which families, villages, and small kingdoms exchanged goods.

Despite their different economies and the rivalries among states, the peoples of Lower Guinea had similar social systems organized on the basis of what anthropologists have called the dual-sex principle. In Lower Guinea, each sex handled its own affairs: just as male political and religious leaders governed men, so females ruled women. In the Dahomean kingdom, for example, every male official had his female counterpart; in the thirty little Akan states on the Gold Coast, chiefs inherited their status through the female line, and each male chief had a female assistant who supervised other women. Many West African societies practiced polygyny (one man's having several wives, each of whom lived separately with her children). Thus few adults lived permanently in marital households, but the dual-sex system ensured that their actions were subject to scrutiny by members of their own sex.

Throughout Guinea, religious beliefs stressed complementary male and female roles. Both women and men served as heads of the cults and secret societies that directed the spiritual life of the villages. Young women were initiated into the Sandé cult, young men into Poro. Neither cult was allowed to reveal its secrets to the opposite sex. Although West African women (unlike some of their Native American contemporaries) rarely held formal power over men, female religious leaders did govern other members of their sex within the Sandé cult, enforcing conformity to accepted norms of behavior and overseeing their spiritual well-being.

Slavery in Guinea   West African law recognized both individual and communal land ownership, but men seeking to accumulate wealth needed access to labor—wives, children, or slaves—who could work the land. West Africans enslaved for life therefore composed essential elements of the economy. Africans could be enslaved as punishment for crimes, but more often such slaves were enemy captives or people who voluntarily enslaved themselves or their children in payment for debts. An African who possessed bondspeople had a right to the products of their labor, although the degree to which slaves were exploited varied greatly, and slave status did not always descend to the next generation. Some slaves were held as chattel; others could engage in trade, retaining a portion of their profits; and still others achieved prominent political or military positions. All, however, found it difficult to overcome the social stigma of enslavement, and they could be traded or sold at the will of their owners.

West Africans, then, were agricultural peoples, skilled at tending livestock, hunting, fishing, and manufacturing cloth from plant fibers and animal skins. Both men and women worked communally, in family groups or alongside others of their own sex. They were accustomed to a relatively egalitarian relationship between the sexes, especially within the context of religion. Carried as captives to the Americas, they became essential to transplanted European societies that used their labor but had little respect for their cultural traditions.

EUROPEAN SOCIETIES

In the fifteenth century, Europeans, too, were agricultural peoples. The daily lives of Europe's rural people had changed little for several hundred years. Split into numerous small, warring countries, Europe was divided linguistically, politically, and economically, yet in social terms Europeans' lives exhibited many similarities. In the hierarchical European societies, a few families wielded autocratic power over the majority of the people. English society in particular was organized as a series of interlocking hierarchies; that is, each person (except those at the very top or bottom) was superior to some, inferior to others. At the base of such hierarchies were people held in various forms of bondage. Although Europeans were not subjected to perpetual slavery, Christian doctrine permitted the enslavement of "heathens" (non-Christians), and some Europeans' freedom was restricted by such conditions as serfdom, which tied them to the land if not to specific owners. In short, Europe's kingdoms resembled those of Africa or Mesoamerica but differed greatly from the more egalitarian societies found in America north of Mexico.

Work, Politics, and Religion   Most Europeans, like most Africans and Americans, lived in small villages. Only a few cities dotted the landscape, most of them seaports or political capitals. European farmers, called peasants, owned or leased separate landholdings, but they worked the fields communally. Because fields had to lie fallow (unplanted) every second or third year to regain fertility, a family could not ensure itself a regular food supply unless all villagers shared annually the work and the crops. Men did most of the fieldwork; women helped out chiefly at planting and harvest. In some regions men concentrated on herding livestock. Women's duties consisted primarily of childcare and household tasks, including preserving food, milking cows, and caring for poultry. If a woman's husband was a city artisan or storekeeper, she might assist him in business. Because Europeans kept domesticated animals (pigs, goats, sheep, and cattle) for meat, hunting had little economic importance in their cultures. Instead, hunting was primarily a sport for male aristocrats.

Unlike in Africa or America, where women often played prominent roles in politics and religion, men dominated all areas of life in Europe. A few women—notably Queen Elizabeth I of England—achieved status or power by right of birth, but the vast majority were excluded from positions of political authority. European women also generally held inferior social, religious, and economic positions, yet they wielded power in their own households over children and servants. In contrast to the freedom children enjoyed in American families, European children were tightly controlled and subjected to harsh discipline.

Christianity was the dominant European religion. In the West, authority rested in the Catholic Church, based in Rome and led by the pope, who directed a wholly male clergy. Although Europeans were nominally Catholic, many adhered to local belief systems that the church deemed heretical and proved unable to extinguish. Kings would ally themselves with the church when it suited their needs but often acted independently. Yet even so, the Christian nations of Europe from the twelfth century on publicly united in a goal of driving nonbelievers (especially Muslims) not only from their own domains but also from the holy city of Jerusalem, which caused the series of wars known as the Crusades. Nevertheless, in the fifteenth century Muslims dominated the commerce and geography of the Mediterranean world, especially after they conquered Constantinople (capital of the Christian Byzantine empire) in 1453. Few would have predicted that Christian Europeans would ever be able to challenge that dominance.

Effects of Plague and Warfare   When the fifteenth century began, European nations were slowly recovering from the devastating epidemic of plague known as the Black Death, which first struck them in 1346. The Black Death seems to have arrived in Europe from China, traveling with long-distance traders along the Silk Road to the eastern Mediterranean. The disease then recurred with particular severity in the 1360s and 1370s. Although no precise figures are available and the impact of the Black Death varied from region to region, the best estimate is that fully one-third of Europe's people died during those terrible years. A precipitous economic decline followed—in some regions more than half of the workers had died—as did severe social, political, and religious disruption because of the deaths of clergymen and other leading figures.

As plague ravaged the population, England and France waged the Hundred Years' War (1337–1453), initiated because English monarchs had claimed the French throne. The war interrupted overland trade routes connecting England and Antwerp (in modern Belgium) to Venice, a Christian trading center, and thence to India and China. England, on the periphery of the Mediterranean commercial core, exported wool and cloth to Antwerp in exchange for spices and silks from the East. Needing a new way to reach their northern trading partners, eastern Mediterranean merchants forged a maritime route to Antwerp. Using a triangular, or lateen, sail (rather than the then-standard square rigging) improved the maneuverability of ships, enabling vessels to sail out of the Mediterranean and north around the European coast. Also of key importance was the perfection of navigational instruments like the astrolabe and the quadrant, which allowed oceangoing sailors to estimate their position (latitude) by measuring the relationship of the sun, moon, or certain stars to the horizon.

Political and Technological Change

After the Hundred Years' War, European monarchs forcefully consolidated their previously diffuse political power and raised new revenues through increased taxation of an already hard-pressed peasantry. The long military struggle led to new pride in national identity, which eclipsed the prevailing regional and dynastic loyalties. In England, Henry VII in 1485 founded the Tudor dynasty and began uniting a previously divided land. In France, the successors of Charles VII unified the kingdom and levied new taxes. Most successful of all were Ferdinand of Aragón and Isabella of Castile, who married in 1469, founding a strongly Catholic Spain. In 1492 they defeated the Muslims, who had lived in Spain and Portugal for centuries, thereafter expelling all Jews and Muslims from their domain.

The fifteenth century also brought technological change to Europe. Movable type and the printing press, invented in Germany in the 1450s, made information more accessible than ever before. Printing stimulated the Europeans' curiosity about fabled lands across the seas, lands they could now read about in books. The most important such work was Marco Polo's *Travels*, first published in 1477, which recounted a Venetian merchant's adventures in thirteenth-century China and, most intriguing, described that nation as bordered on the east by an ocean. Polo's account circulated widely among Europe's educated elites, first in manuscript and later in print. The book led many Europeans to believe that they could trade directly with China in oceangoing vessels instead of relying on the Silk Road or the route through East Africa. A transoceanic route, if it existed, would allow northern Europeans to circumvent the Muslim and Venetian merchants who hitherto had controlled their access to Asian goods.

Motives for Exploration

Technological advances and the growing strength of newly powerful national rulers made possible the European explorations of the fifteenth and sixteenth centuries. Each country craved easy access to African and Asian goods—silk, dyes, perfumes, jewels, sugar, gold, and especially spices, such as pepper, cloves, cinnamon, and nutmeg. Spices were desirable not only for seasoning food but also because they were believed to have medicinal and magical properties. Their allure stemmed largely from their rarity, their extraordinary cost, and their mysterious origins. They passed through so many hands en route to London or Seville that no European knew exactly where they came from. (Nutmeg, for example, grew only on nine tiny islands in the Moluccas, in what is now eastern Indonesia.) Avoiding intermediaries in Venice and Constantinople, and acquiring such valuable products directly, would improve a nation's income and its standing relative to other countries, in addition to supplying its wealthy leaders with coveted luxury items.

A concern for spreading Christianity around the world supplemented the economic motive. The linking of materialistic and spiritual goals perhaps seems contradictory today, but fifteenth-century Europeans saw no necessary conflict between the two. Explorers and colonizers—especially Roman Catholics—honestly sought to convert "heathen" peoples to Christianity. At the same time they hoped to increase their nation's wealth by establishing direct trade with Africa, China, India, and the Moluccas.

EARLY EUROPEAN EXPLORATIONS

To establish that trade, European mariners first had to explore the oceans. To reach Asia, seafarers needed not just the maneuverable vessels and navigational aids increasingly used in the fourteenth century but also knowledge of the sea, its currents, and especially its winds. Wind would power their ships. But how did the winds run? Where would Atlantic breezes carry their square-rigged ships, which, even with the addition of a triangular sail, needed to run before the wind (that is, to have the wind directly behind the vessel)?

Sailing the Mediterranean Atlantic   Europeans learned the answers to these questions in the region that has been called the Mediterranean Atlantic, the expanse of the Atlantic Ocean that is south and west of Spain and is bounded by the island groups of the Azores (on the west) and the Canaries (on the south), with the Madeiras in their midst. Europeans reached all three sets of islands during the fourteenth century—first the Canaries in the 1330s, then the Madeiras and the Azores. The Canaries proved a popular destination for mariners from Iberia, the peninsula that includes Spain and Portugal. Sailing to the Canaries from Europe was easy because strong winds known as the Northeast Trades blow southward along the Iberian and African coastlines. The voyage took about a week, and the volcanic peaks on the islands made them difficult to miss even with navigational instruments that were less than precise.

The problem was getting back. The Iberian sailor attempting to return home faced a major obstacle: the very winds that had brought him so quickly to the Canaries now blew directly at him. Rowing and tacking back and forth against the wind were similarly tedious and ineffectual. Confronted by contrary winds, mariners had usually waited for the wind to change, but the Northeast Trades blew steadily. So they developed a new technique: sailing "around the wind." That meant sailing as directly against the wind as was possible without being forced to tack. In the Mediterranean Atlantic, a mariner would head northwest into the open ocean, until—weeks later—he reached the winds that would carry him home, the so-called Westerlies. Those winds blow (we now know, although the seafarers at first did not) northward along the coast of North America before heading east toward Europe.

This solution must at first have seemed to defy common sense, but it became the key to successful exploration of both the Atlantic and the Pacific Oceans. Once a sailor understood the winds and their allied currents, he no longer feared leaving Europe without being able to return. Faced with a contrary wind, all he had to do was sail around it until he found a wind to carry him in the proper direction.

Islands of the Mediterranean Atlantic   During the fifteenth century, armed with knowledge of the winds and currents of the Mediterranean Atlantic, Iberian seamen regularly visited the three island groups, all of which they could reach in two weeks or less. The uninhabited Azores were soon settled by Portuguese migrants who raised wheat for sale in Europe and sold livestock to passing sailors. The Madeiras also had no native peoples, and by the 1450s Portuguese colonists were employing slaves (probably Jews and Muslims brought from Iberia) to grow large quantities of sugar for export to the mainland. By the 1470s

Madeira had developed into a colonial plantation economy. For the first time in world history, a region had been settled explicitly to cultivate a valuable crop—sugar—to be sold elsewhere. Moreover, because the work involved in large-scale plantation agriculture was so backbreaking, only a supply of enslaved laborers (who could not opt to quit) could ensure the system's continued success.

The Canaries did have indigenous residents—the Guanche people, who began trading animal skins and dyes with their European visitors. After 1402 the French, Portuguese, and Spanish began sporadically attacking the islands. The Guanches resisted vigorously, even though they were weakened by their susceptibility to alien European diseases. One by one the seven islands fell to Europeans, who then carried off Guanches as slaves to the Madeiras or the Iberian Peninsula. Spain conquered the last island in 1496 and subsequently devoted the land to sugar plantations. Collectively, the Canaries and Madeira became known as the Wine Islands because much of their sugar production was directed to making sweet wines.

Portuguese Trading Posts in Africa

While some Europeans concentrated on exploiting the islands of the Mediterranean Atlantic, others used them as stepping-stones to Africa. In 1415 Portugal seized control of Ceuta, a Muslim city in North Africa. Prince Henry the Navigator, son of King John I of Portugal, knew that vast wealth awaited the first European nation to tap the riches of Africa and Asia directly. Repeatedly he dispatched ships southward along the African coast, attempting to discover an oceanic route to Asia. But not until after Prince Henry's death did Bartholomew Dias round the southern tip of Africa (1488) and Vasco da Gama finally reach India (1498), where at Malabar he located the richest source of peppercorns in the world.

Long before that, Portugal reaped the benefits of its seafarers' voyages. Although West African states successfully resisted European penetration of the interior, they allowed the Portuguese to establish trading posts along their coasts. Charging the traders rent and levying duties on goods they imported, the African kingdoms benefited considerably from their new, easier access to European manufactures. The Portuguese gained, too, for they no longer had to rely on trans-Saharan camel caravans. Their vessels earned immense profits by swiftly transporting African gold, ivory, and slaves to Europe. By bargaining with African masters to purchase their slaves and then carrying those bondspeople to Iberia, the Portuguese introduced black slavery into Europe.

Lessons of Early Colonization

An island off the African coast, previously uninhabited, proved critical to Portuguese success. In the 1480s they colonized São Tomé, located in the Gulf of Guinea. By that time Madeira had already reached the limit of its capacity to produce sugar. The soil of São Tomé proved ideal for raising that valuable crop, and plantation agriculture there expanded rapidly. Planters imported large numbers of slaves from the mainland to work in the cane fields, thus creating the first economy based primarily on the bondage of black Africans.

By the 1490s, even before Christopher Columbus set sail to the west, Europeans had learned three key lessons of colonization in the Mediterranean Atlantic. First, they had learned how to transplant their crops and livestock successfully to exotic locations. Second, they had discovered that the native peoples of those lands could be either conquered (like the Guanches) or exploited (like the Africans). Third, they had developed a viable model of plantation slavery and a system for supplying nearly unlimited quantities of such workers. The stage was set for a pivotal moment in world history.

VOYAGES OF COLUMBUS, CABOT, AND THEIR SUCCESSORS

Christopher Columbus was well schooled in the lessons of the Mediterranean Atlantic. Born in 1451 in the Italian city-state of Genoa, this largely self-educated son of a wool merchant was by the 1490s an experienced sailor and mapmaker. Like many mariners of the day, he was drawn to Portugal and its islands, especially Madeira, where he commanded a merchant vessel. At least once he voyaged to the Portuguese outpost on the Gold Coast. There he became obsessed with gold, and there he came to understand the economic potential of the slave trade.

Like all accomplished seafarers, Columbus knew the world was round. (So, indeed, did most educated people: the idea that his contemporaries believed the world to be flat is a myth.) But he differed from other cartographers in his estimate of the earth's size: he thought that China lay only 3,000 miles from the southern European coast. Thus, he argued, it would be easier to reach Asia by sailing west than by making the difficult voyage around the southern tip of Africa. Experts scoffed at this crackpot notion, accurately predicting that the two continents lay 12,000 miles apart. When Columbus in 1484 asked the Portuguese rulers to back his plan to sail west to Asia, they rejected what appeared to be a crazy scheme.

Columbus's Voyage Ferdinand and Isabella of Spain, jealous of Portugal's successes in Africa, were more receptive to Columbus's ideas. Urged on by some Spanish noblemen and a group of Italian merchants residing in Castile, the monarchs agreed to finance the risky voyage, in part because they hoped the profits would pay for a new expedition to conquer Muslim-held Jerusalem. And so, on August 3, 1492, in command of three ships—the *Pinta*, the *Niña*, and the *Santa Maria*—Columbus set sail from the Spanish port of Palos.

The first part of the journey was familiar, for the ships steered down the Northeast Trades to the Canary Islands. There Columbus refitted his square-rigged ships, adding triangular sails to make them more maneuverable. On September 6, the ships weighed anchor and headed out into the unknown ocean.

Just over a month later, pushed by favorable trade winds, the vessels found land approximately where Columbus had predicted. On October 12, he and his men landed on an island in the Bahamas, which its inhabitants called Guanahaní but which he renamed San Salvador. (Because Columbus's description of his landfall can be variously interpreted, three different places—Samana, Plana, and Mayaguana—are today proposed as the most likely locations for his landing site.) Later he went on to explore the islands now known as Cuba and Hispaniola, which their residents, the Taíno people, called Colba and Bohío. Because he thought he had reached the East Indies, Columbus referred to the inhabitants of the region as "Indians."

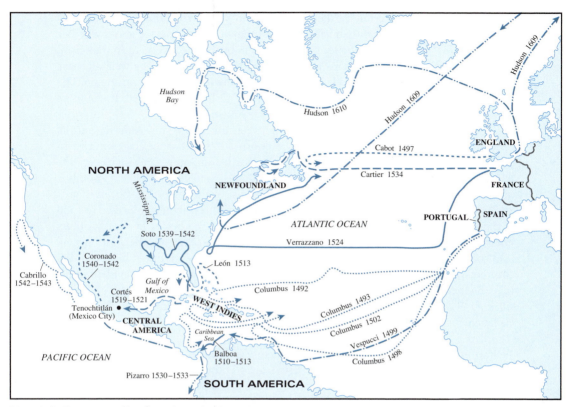

MAP 1.2 European Explorations in America

In the century following Columbus's voyages, European adventurers explored the coasts and parts of the interior of North and South America.

Columbus's Observations

Three themes predominate in Columbus's log, the major source of information on this first encounter. First, he insistently asked the Taínos where he could find gold, pearls, and spices. Each time, his informants replied (via signs) that such products could be obtained on other islands, on the mainland, or in cities in the interior. Eventually he came to mistrust such answers, noting, "I am beginning to believe . . . they will tell me anything I want to hear."

Second, Columbus wrote repeatedly of the strange and beautiful plants and animals. "Here the fishes are so unlike ours that it is amazing. . . . The colors are so bright that anyone would marvel," he noted, and again, "The song of the little birds might make a man wish never to leave here. I never tire from looking at such luxurious vegetation." Yet Columbus's interest was not only aesthetic. "I believe that there are many plants and trees here that could be worth a lot in Spain for use as dyes, spices, and medicines," he observed, adding that he was carrying home to Europe "a sample of everything I can," so that experts could examine them.

Third, Columbus also described the islands' human residents, and he seized some to take back to Spain. The Taínos were, he said, very handsome, gentle, and friendly, though they told him of fierce people who lived on other nearby islands and raided their villages. The Caniba (today called Caribs), from whose name the word *cannibal* is derived, were reported to eat their captives, but today scholars disagree about whether the tales were true. Columbus believed the Taínos to be likely converts to Catholicism, remarking that "if devout religious persons knew the Indian language well, all these people would soon become Christians." But he had more in mind than conversion. The islanders "ought to make good and skilled servants," Columbus declared. It would be easy to "subject everyone and make them do what you wished."

Thus the records of the first encounter between Europeans and America and its residents revealed themes that would be of enormous significance for centuries to come. Europeans wanted to extract profits from North and South America by exploiting their natural resources, including plants, animals, and peoples alike. Columbus made three more voyages to the west, exploring most of the major Caribbean islands and sailing along the coasts of Central and South America. Until the day he died in 1506 at the age of fifty-five, he believed he had reached Asia. Even before his death, others knew better. Because the Florentine Amerigo Vespucci, who explored the South American coast in 1499, was the first to publish the idea that a new continent had been discovered, Martin Waldseemüller in 1507 labeled the land "America," as is evident in his map. By then, Spain, Portugal, and Pope Alexander VI had signed the Treaty of Tordesillas (1494), confirming Portugal's dominance in Africa—and later Brazil—in exchange for Spanish preeminence in the rest of the Americas.

Norse and Other Northern Voyagers Five hundred years before Columbus, about the year 1001, the Norseman Leif Ericsson and other Norse people had sailed to North America across the Davis Strait, which separated their villages in Greenland from Baffin Island by just 200 nautical miles, settling at a site they named "Vinland." Attacks by local residents forced them to depart hurriedly from Vinland after just a few years. In the 1960s, archaeologists determined that the Norse had established an outpost at what is now L'Anse aux Meadows, Newfoundland, but Vinland itself was probably located farther south.

Later Europeans did not know of the Norse explorers, but some historians argue that in the 1480s sailors probably located the rich fishing grounds off the coast of Newfoundland but kept the information secret. Whether or not fishermen crossed the entire width of the Atlantic, they thoroughly explored its northern reaches. Like the Portuguese in the Mediterranean Atlantic, fifteenth-century seafarers voyaged between the European continent, England, Ireland, and Iceland. The mariners who explored the region of North America that was to become the United States and Canada built on their knowledge.

The winds that the northern sailors confronted posed problems on their outbound rather than on their homeward journeys. The same Westerlies that carried Columbus and other southern voyagers back to Europe blew in the faces of northerners looking west. But mariners soon learned that the strongest winds shifted southward during the winter and that, by departing from northern ports in the spring, they could make adequate headway if they steered northward to catch sporadic easterly breezes. Thus, whereas the first landfall of most sailors to the south was somewhere in the Caribbean, those taking the northern route usually reached America along the coast of what is now Maine or the Canadian Maritime Provinces.

John Cabot's
Explorations

The European generally credited with "discovering" North America is Zuan Cabboto, known today as John Cabot. More precisely, Cabot brought to Europe the first formal knowledge of the northern continental coastline and claimed the land for England. Like Columbus, Cabot was a master mariner from the Italian city-state of Genoa. Calculating that England—which traded with Asia only through a long series of intermediaries stretching from Antwerp to Venice to the Muslim world—would be eager to sponsor exploratory voyages, he gained financial backing from King Henry VII. He set sail from Bristol in late May 1497 in the *Mathew*, reaching his destination about a month later. Scholars disagree about the location of Cabot's landfall, but all recognize the importance of his month-long exploration of the coast of modern Newfoundland. Having achieved his goal, Cabot rode the Westerlies back to England, arriving just fifteen days after he left North America.

The voyages of Columbus, Cabot, and their successors finally brought the Eastern and Western Hemispheres together. The Portuguese explorer Pedro Álvares Cabral reached Brazil in 1500; John Cabot's son Sebastian followed his father to North America in 1507; France financed Giovanni da Verrazzano in 1524 and Jacques Cartier in 1534; and in 1609 and 1610 Henry Hudson explored the North American coast for the Dutch West India Company. All of these men were searching primarily for the legendary, nonexistent "Northwest Passage" through the Americas, hoping to find an easy route to the riches of Asia. Although they did not attempt to plant colonies in the Western Hemisphere, their discoveries interested European nations in exploring North and South America.

SPANISH EXPLORATION AND CONQUEST

Only in the areas that Spain explored and claimed did colonization begin immediately. On his second voyage in 1493, Columbus brought to Hispaniola seventeen ships loaded with twelve hundred men, seeds, plants, livestock, chickens, and dogs—along with microbes, rats, and weeds. The settlement named Isabela (in the modern Dominican Republic) and its successors became the staging area for the Spanish invasion of America. On the islands of Cuba and Hispaniola the Europeans learned to adapt to the new environment, as did the horses, cattle, and hogs they imported. When the Spaniards moved on to explore the mainland, they rode island-bred horses and ate island-bred cattle and hogs.

Cortés and Other
Explorers

At first, Spanish explorers fanned out around the Caribbean basin. In 1513 Juan Ponce de León reached Florida, and Vasco Núñez de Balboa crossed the Isthmus of Panama to the Pacific Ocean, followed by Pánfilo de Narváez and others who traced the coast of the Gulf of Mexico. In the 1530s and 1540s, conquistadors traveled farther, exploring many regions claimed by the Spanish monarchs: Francisco Vásquez de Coronado journeyed through the southwestern portion of what is now the United States at approximately the same time Hernán de Soto explored the Southeast. Juan Rodríguez Cabrillo sailed along the California coast; and Francisco Pizarro, who ventured into western South America, acquired the richest silver mines in the world by conquering the Incas. But the most important conquistador was Hernán Cortés, who in 1521 seized control of the Aztec Empire.

Cortés, an adventurer who first arrived in the Caribbean in 1506, landed a force on the Mexican mainland in 1519 to search for rumored wealthy cities. Near the coast, local Mayas presented him with a group of young enslaved women. One of them, Malinche (whom the Spaniards baptized as a Christian and renamed Doña Marina), had been sold into slavery by the Aztecs and raised by the Mayas. Because she became Cortés's translator, some modern Mexicans regard her as a traitor, but others suggest that she owed no loyalty to people who had enslaved her. In her own day, both Europeans and Aztecs accorded her great respect. Malinche bore Cortés a son, Martín—one of the first *mestizos*, or mixed-blood children—and eventually married one of his officers.

Capture of Tenochtitlán   As he traveled toward the Aztec capital, Cortés, with Malinche's help, cleverly recruited peoples whom the Aztecs had long subjugated. The Spaniards' strange beasts (horses, livestock) and noisy weapons (guns, cannon) awed their new allies. Yet the Spaniards, too, were awed. Years later, Bernal Díaz del Castillo recalled his first sight of Tenochtitlán, situated in the midst of Lake Texcoco: "We were amazed and said that it was like the enchantments . . . on account of the great towers and cues [temples] and buildings rising from the water, and all built of masonry." Some soldiers asked, he remembered, "whether the things that we saw were not a dream."

The Spaniards came to Tenochtitlán not only with horses and steel weapons but also with smallpox, bringing an epidemic that had begun on Hispaniola. The disease peaked in 1520, fatally weakening Tenochtitlán's defenders. "It spread over the people as great destruction," as elderly Aztec later remembered. "Some it quite covered [with pustules] on all parts—their faces, their heads, their breasts. . . . There was great havoc. Very many died of it." Largely as a consequence, Tenochtitlán surrendered in 1521, and the Spaniards built Mexico City on its site. Cortés and his men seized a fabulous treasure of gold and silver. Thus, not long after Columbus's first voyage, the Spanish monarchs—who treated the American territories as their personal possessions—controlled the richest, most extensive empire Europe had known since ancient Rome.

Spanish Colonization   Spain established the model of colonization that other countries later attempted to imitate, a model with three major elements. First, the Crown tried to maintain tight control over the colonies, imposing a hierarchical government that allowed little autonomy to American jurisdictions. That control included, for example, carefully vetting prospective emigrants and limiting their number, and insisting that the colonies import all their manufactured goods from Spain. In order to encourage social stability, those settlers were then required to live in towns under the authorities' watchful eyes. Roman Catholic priests attempted to ensure the colonists' conformity with orthodox religious views.

Second, men constituted most of the first colonists. Although some Spanish women later immigrated to America, the men took primarily Indian—and, later, African—women as their wives or concubines, a development more often than not encouraged by colonial administrators. They thereby began creating the racially mixed population that characterizes much of Latin America to the present day.

Third, the colonies' wealth was based on the exploitation of both the native population and slaves imported from Africa. The Mesoamerican peoples were accustomed to autocratic rule. Spaniards simply took over the role once assumed by native leaders, who had exacted labor and tribute from their subjects. Cortés established the *encomienda system*, which granted Indian villages to individual conquistadors as a reward for their services, thus legalizing slavery in all but name.

In 1542, after an outcry from sympathetic Spaniards, a new code of laws reformed the system, forbidding the conquerors from enslaving Indians while still allowing them to collect money and goods from tributary villages. In response to the restrictions and to the declining Indian population, the *encomenderos*, familiar with slavery in Spain, began to import Africans in order to increase the labor force under their direct control. They employed Indians and Africans primarily in gold and silver mines, on sugar plantations, and on huge horse, cattle, and sheep ranches. African slavery was far more common in the Greater Antilles (the major Caribbean islands) than on the mainland.

Many demoralized residents of Mesoamerica accepted the Christian religion brought to New Spain by friars of the Franciscan and Dominican orders. The friars devoted their energies to persuading Mesoamerican people to move into towns and to build Roman Catholic churches. Spaniards leveled existing cities, constructing cathedrals and monasteries on sites once occupied by Aztec, Incan, and Mayan temples. In such towns, Indians were exposed to European customs and religious rituals designed to assimilate Catholic and pagan beliefs. Friars deliberately juxtaposed the cult of the Virgin Mary with that of the corn goddess, and the Indians adeptly melded aspects of their traditional world-view with Christianity, in a process called syncretism. Thousands of Indians residing in Spanish territory embraced Catholicism, at least partly because it was the religion of their new rulers and they were accustomed to obedience.

Gold, Silver, and Spain's Decline   The New World's gold and silver, initially a boon, ultimately brought about the decline of Spain as a major power. China, a huge country with silver coinage, insatiably demanded Spanish silver, gobbling up an estimated half of the total output of New World mines while paying twice the price current in Europe. Especially after the Spanish began in the 1570s to dispatch silver-laden galleons annually from Acapulco (on Mexico's west coast) to trade at their new settlement at Manila, in the Philippines, Spaniards acquired easy access to luxury Chinese goods, such as silk and Asian spices.

The influx of unprecedented wealth led to rapid inflation, which (among other adverse effects) caused Spanish products to be overpriced in international markets and imported goods to become cheaper in Spain. The once-profitable Spanish textile-manufacturing industry collapsed, as did scores of other businesses. The seemingly endless income from American colonies emboldened successive Spanish monarchs to spend lavishly on wars against the Dutch and the English. Several times in the late sixteenth and early seventeenth centuries the monarchs repudiated the state debt, wreaking havoc on the nation's finances. When the South American gold and silver mines started to give out in the mid-seventeenth century, Spain's economy crumbled and the nation lost its international importance.

THE COLUMBIAN EXCHANGE

A broad mutual transfer of diseases, plants, and animals (called the Columbian Exchange by historian Alfred Crosby) resulted directly from the European voyages of the fifteenth and sixteenth centuries and from Spanish colonization. The Eastern and Western Hemispheres had evolved separately for thousands of years, developing widely different forms of life. Many large mammals, such as cattle and horses, were native to the connected continents of Europe, Asia, and Africa, but the Americas contained no domesticated beasts larger than dogs and llamas. The vegetable crops of the Americas—particularly maize, beans, squash, cassava, and potatoes—were more nutritious and produced higher yields than those of Europe and Africa, such as wheat, millet, and rye. In time, native peoples learned to raise and consume European livestock, and Europeans and Africans became accustomed to planting and eating American crops. The diets of all three peoples were consequently vastly enriched. Partly as a result, the world's population doubled over the next three hundred years. About three-fifths of all crops cultivated in the world today were first grown in the Americas.

Smallpox and Other Diseases

Diseases carried from Europe and Africa, though, had a devastating impact on the Americas. Indians fell victim to microbes that had long infested the other continents and had repeatedly killed hundreds of thousands but had also often left survivors with some measure of immunity. The statistics are staggering. When Columbus landed on Hispaniola in 1492, approximately half a million people resided there. Fifty years later, that island had fewer than two thousand native inhabitants. Within thirty years of the first landfall at Guanahaní, not one Taíno survived in the Bahamas.

Although measles, typhus, influenza, malaria, and other illnesses severely afflicted the native peoples, as at Tenochtitlán the greatest killer was smallpox, spread primarily by direct human contact. Overall, historians estimate that the long-term effects of the alien microorganisms could have reduced the precontact American population by as much as 90 percent. The epidemics recurred at twenty- to thirty-year intervals, frequently appearing either in tandem or in quick succession, so that weakened survivors of one would be felled by a second or third. Large numbers of deaths also disrupted societies already undergoing severe strains caused by colonization, thus rendering native peoples more vulnerable to droughts, crop failures, or other challenging circumstances.

Even far to the north, where smaller American populations encountered only a few Europeans, disease also ravaged the countryside. A great epidemic, probably viral hepatitis, swept through the villages along the coast north of Cape Cod from 1616 to 1618. Again the mortality rate may have been as high as 90 percent. An English traveler several years later commented that the people had "died on heapes, as they lay in their houses," and that bones and skulls covered the ruins of villages. Because of this dramatic depopulation of the area, just a few years later English colonists were able to establish settlements virtually unopposed.

The Americans, though, seem to have taken a revenge of sorts. They probably gave the Europeans syphilis, a virulent venereal disease. The first recorded European case of the new ailment occurred in Barcelona, Spain, in 1493, shortly after Columbus's return from the Caribbean. Although less likely than smallpox to cause immediate death, syphilis was dangerous and debilitating. Carried by soldiers, sailors, and prostitutes, it spread quickly through Europe and Asia, reaching as far as China by 1505.

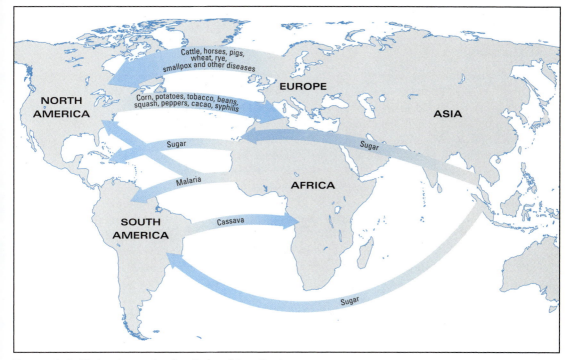

FIGURE 1.1 Major Items in the Columbian Exchange

As European adventurers traversed the world in the fifteenth and sixteenth centuries, they initiated the "Columbian Exchange" of plants, animals, and diseases. These events changed the lives of the peoples of the world forever, bringing new foods and new pestilence to both sides of the Atlantic.

Sugar, Horses, and Tobacco The exchange of three commodities had significant impacts on Europe and the Americas. Sugar, which was first domesticated in the East Indies, was being grown on the islands of the Mediterranean Atlantic by 1450. The ravenous European demand for sugar—which, after initially being regarded as a medicine, became a desirable luxury foodstuff—led Columbus to take Canary Island sugar canes to Hispaniola on his 1493 voyage. By the 1520s, plantations in the Greater Antilles worked by African slaves regularly shipped cargoes of sugar to Spain. Half a century later, the Portuguese colony in Brazil (founded 1532) was producing sugar for the European market on an even larger scale, and after 1640 (see pages 40–41), sugar cultivation became the crucial component of English and French colonization in the Caribbean.

Horses—which, like sugar, were brought to America by Columbus in 1493—fell into the hands of North American Indians during the seventeenth century. Through trade and theft, horses spread among the peoples of the Great Plains, reaching most areas by 1750. Lakotas, Comanches, and Crows, among others, came to use horses for transportation and hunting, calculated their wealth in number of horses owned, and

Maize

Maize, to Mesoamericans, was a gift from Quetzalcoatl, the plumed serpent god. Cherokees told of an old woman whose blood produced the prized stalks after her grandson buried her body in a cleared, sunny field. For the Abenakis, the crop began when a beautiful maiden ordered a youth to drag her by the hair through a burned-over field. The long hair of the Cherokee grandmother and the Abenaki maiden turned into silk, the flower on the stalks that Europeans called Indian corn. Both tales' symbolic association of corn and women intriguingly supports archaeologists' recent suggestion that—in eastern North America at least—female plant breeders were responsible for substantial improvements in the productivity of maize.

Sacred to all the Indian peoples who grew it, maize was a cereal crop, a main part of their diet. They dried the kernels, ground into meal, maize was cooked as a mush or shaped into baked flat cakes, the forerunners of modern tortillas. Indians also heated the dried kernels until they popped open, just as is done today. Although the European invaders of North and South America initially disdained maize, they soon learned that it could be cultivated in a wide variety of conditions—from sea level to twelve thousand feet, from regions with abundant rainfall to dry lands with as little as twelve inches of rain a year. Corn was also highly productive, yielding almost twice as many calories per acre as wheat. So Europeans, too, came to rely on corn, growing it not only in their American settlements but also in their homelands.

Maize cultivation spread to Asia and Africa. Today China is second only to the United States in total corn production, and corn is more widely grown in Africa than any other crop. Still, the United States produces 45 percent of the world's corn-almost half of it in the three states of Illinois, Iowa, and Nebraska-and corn is the nation's single largest crop. More than half of American corn is consumed by livestock. Much of the rest is processed into syrup, which sweetens carbonated beverages and candies, or into ethanol, a gasoline additive that reduces both pollution and dependence on fossil fuels. Corn is an ingredient in light beer and toothpaste. It is used in the manufacture of tires, wallpaper, cat litter, and aspirin. Remarkably, of the ten thousand products in a modern American grocery store, about one-fourth rely to some extent on corn.

Today this crop bequeathed to the world by ancient American plant breeders provides one-fifth of all the calories consumed by the earth's peoples. The gift of Quetzalcoatl has linked the globe.

The earliest known European drawing of maize, the American plant that was to have such an extraordinary impact on the entire world. (Typ 565.42.409F [B] Department of Printing and Graphic Arts, Houghton Library, Harvard College Library)

waged war primarily on horseback. Women no longer had to carry the band's belongings on their backs. Some groups that previously had cultivated crops abandoned agriculture. Because of the acquisition of horses, a mode of subsistence that had been based on hunting several different animals, in combination with gathering and agriculture, became one focused almost wholly on hunting buffalo.

In America, Europeans encountered tobacco, which at first they believed to have beneficial medicinal effects. Smoking and chewing the "Indian weed" became a fad in Europe after it was planted in Turkey in the sixteenth century. Despite the efforts of such skeptics as King James I of England, who in 1604 pronounced smoking "loathsome to the eye, hatefull to the Nose, harmfull to the brain, [and] dangerous to the Lungs," tobacco's popularity climbed. Its addictive nicotine and its connection to lung cancer were discovered only in the twentieth century.

The European and African invasion of the Americas therefore had a significant biological component, for the invaders carried plants and animals with them. Some creatures, such as livestock, they brought deliberately. Others, including rats (which infested their ships), weeds, and diseases, arrived unexpectedly. And the same process occurred in reverse. When the Europeans returned home, they deliberately took back such crops as maize, potatoes, and tobacco, along with that unanticipated stowaway, syphilis.

EUROPEANS IN NORTH AMERICA

Europeans were initially more interested in exploiting North America's natural resources than in the difficult task of establishing colonies there. John Cabot had reported that fish were extraordinarily plentiful near Newfoundland, so Europeans rushed to take advantage of abundant codfish, which were in great demand in their homelands as an inexpensive source of protein. The French, Spanish, and Portuguese dispatched vessels regularly to Newfoundland's waters throughout the sixteenth century. In the early 1570s, after Spain opened its markets to English shipping, the English (who previously had fished near Iceland for home consumption only) eagerly joined the Newfoundland fishery, thereafter selling salt cod to the Spanish in exchange for valuable Asian goods. The English soon became dominant in the region, which by the end of the century was the focal point of a European commerce more valuable than that with the Gulf of Mexico.

Trade Among Indians and Europeans   Fishermen quickly realized that they could increase their profits by exchanging cloth and metal goods, such as pots and knives, for native trappers' beaver pelts, used to make fashionable hats in Europe. Initially, Europeans traded from ships sailing along the coast, but later they set up outposts on the mainland to centralize and control the traffic in furs. Such outposts were inhabited chiefly by male adventurers, whose major aim was to send as many pelts as possible home to Europe.

The Europeans' demand for furs, especially beaver, was matched by the Indians' desire for European goods that could make their lives easier and establish their superiority over their neighbors. Some bands began to concentrate so completely on trapping for the European market that they abandoned their traditional economies. The Abenakis of Maine, for example, became partially dependent on food supplied by their neighbors to the south, the Massachusett tribe, because they devoted most of their energies to catching beaver to sell to French traders. The Massachusetts, in turn, intensified their production of foodstuffs, which they traded to the Abenakis in exchange for the European metal tools that they preferred to their own handmade stone implements. The intensive trade in pelts also had serious ecological consequences. In some regions beavers were wiped out. The disappearance of their dams led to soil erosion, which increased when European settlers cleared forests for farmland in later decades.

Contest Between Spain and England   English merchants and political leaders watched enviously as Spain was enriched by its valuable American possessions. In the mid-sixteenth century, English "sea dogs" like John Hawkins and Sir Francis Drake began to raid Spanish treasure fleets sailing home from the Caribbean. Their actions caused friction between the two countries and helped foment a war that in 1588 culminated in the defeat of a huge invasion force—the Spanish Armada—off the English coast. As part of the contest with Spain, English leaders started to think about planting colonies in the Western Hemisphere, thereby gaining better access to valuable trade goods while simultaneously preventing their enemy from dominating the Americas.

The first English colonial planners saw Spain's possessions as a model and a challenge. They hoped to reproduce Spanish successes by dispatching to America men who would exploit the native peoples for their own and their nation's benefit. In the mid-1570s, a group that included Sir Walter Raleigh began to promote a scheme to establish outposts that could trade with the Indians and provide bases for attacks on New Spain. Approving the idea, Queen Elizabeth I authorized Raleigh to colonize North America.

Roanoke   After two preliminary expeditions, in 1587 Sir Walter Raleigh sent 117 colonists to the territory he named Virginia, after Elizabeth, the "Virgin Queen." They established a settlement on Roanoke Island, in what is now North Carolina, but in 1590 a resupply ship—delayed in leaving England because of the Spanish Armada—could not find them. The colonists had vanished, leaving only the word *Croatoan* (the name of a nearby island) carved on a tree. Recent tree-ring studies have shown that the North Carolina coast experienced a severe drought between 1587 and 1589, which would have created a subsistence crisis for the settlers and could well have led them to abandon the Roanoke site.

Thus England's first attempt to plant a permanent settlement on the North American coast failed, as had similar efforts by Portugal on Cape Breton Island (early 1520s) and France in northern Florida (mid-1560s). All three enterprises collapsed because of the hostility of neighboring peoples and colonists' inability to be self-sustaining in foodstuffs. Spanish soldiers wiped out the French colony in 1565, and neither the Portuguese nor the English were able to maintain friendly relations with local Indians.

Harriot's *Briefe and True Report*   The explanation for such failings becomes clear in Thomas Harriot's *A Briefe and True Report of the New Found Land of Virginia*, published in 1588 to publicize Raleigh's colony. Harriot, a noted scientist who sailed with the second of the preliminary voyages to Roanoke, described the animals, plants, and people of the region for an English

A watercolor by John White, an artist with Raleigh's second preliminary expedition (and who later was governor of the ill-fated 1587 colony). He identified his subjects as the wife and daughter of the chief of Pomeioc, a village near Roanoke. Note the woman's elaborate tattoos and the fact that the daughter carries an Elizabethan doll, obviously given to her by one of the Englishmen. (©Trustees of the British Museum)

readership. His account revealed that, although the explorers depended on nearby villagers for most of their food, they needlessly antagonized their neighbors by killing some of them for what Harriot himself admitted were unjustifiable reasons.

The scientist advised later colonizers to deal with the native peoples of America more humanely than his comrades had. But the content of his book suggested why that advice would rarely be followed. *A Briefe and True Report* examined the possibilities for economic development in America. Harriot stressed three points: the availability of commodities familiar to Europeans, such as grapes, iron, copper, and fur-bearing animals; the potential profitability of exotic American products, such as maize, cassava, and tobacco; and the relative ease of manipulating the native population to the Europeans' advantage. Should the Americans attempt to resist the English by force, Harriot asserted, the latter's advantages of disciplined soldiers and superior weaponry would quickly deliver victory.

Harriot's *Briefe and True Report* depicted for his English readers a bountiful land full of opportunities for quick profit. The people residing there would, he thought, "in a short time be brought to civilitie" through conversion to Christianity, admiration for

European superiority, or conquest—if they did not die from disease, the ravages of which he witnessed. Thomas Harriot understood the key elements of the story, but his prediction was far off the mark. European dominance of North America would be difficult to achieve. Indeed, it never was fully achieved, in the sense Harriot and his compatriots intended.

SUMMARY

The process of initial contact among Europeans, Africans, and Americans that ended with Thomas Harriot near the close of the sixteenth century began approximately 250 years earlier when Portuguese sailors first set out to explore the Mediterranean Atlantic and the West African coast. Those seamen established commercial ties that brought African slaves first to Iberia and then to the islands the Europeans conquered and settled. The Mediterranean Atlantic and its island sugar plantations nurtured the mariners who, like Christopher Columbus, ventured into previously unknown waters—those who sailed to India and Brazil as well as to the Caribbean and the North American coast. When Columbus first reached the Americas, he thought he had found Asia, his intended destination. Later explorers knew better but, except for the Spanish, regarded the Americas primarily as a barrier that prevented them from reaching their long-sought goal of an oceanic route to the riches of China and the Moluccas. Ordinary European fishermen were the first to realize that the northern coasts had valuable products to offer: fish and furs, both much in demand in their homelands.

The Aztecs had predicted that their Fifth Sun would end in earthquakes and hunger. Hunger they surely experienced after Cortés's invasion, and even if there were no earthquakes, their great temples tumbled to the ground nevertheless, as the Spaniards used their stones (and Indian laborers) to construct cathedrals honoring their God and his Son, Jesus, rather than Huitzilopochtli. The conquerors employed, first, American and, later, enslaved African workers to till the fields, mine the precious metals, and herd the livestock that earned immense profits for themselves and their mother country.

The initial impact of Europeans on the Americas proved devastating. Flourishing civilizations were markedly altered in just a few short decades. Europeans' diseases killed millions of the Western Hemisphere's inhabitants; and their livestock, along with a wide range of other imported animals and plants, irrevocably modified the American environment. Europe, too, was changed: American foodstuffs like corn and potatoes improved nutrition throughout the continent, and American gold and silver first enriched, then ruined, the Spanish economy.

By the end of the sixteenth century, fewer people resided in North America than had lived there before Columbus's arrival, even taking into account the arrival of many Europeans and Africans. And the people who did live there—Indian, African, and European—resided in a world that was indeed new—a world engaged in the unprecedented process of combining foods, religions, economies, ways of life, and political systems that had developed separately for millennia. Understandably, conflict and dissension permeated that process.

2

Europeans Colonize North America 1600–1650

SPANISH, FRENCH, AND DUTCH NORTH AMERICA

Spaniards established the first permanent European settlement within the boundaries of the modern United States, but others had initially attempted that feat. Twice in the 1560s Huguenots (French Protestants), who were seeking to escape persecution, planted colonies on the south Atlantic coast. A passing ship rescued the starving survivors of the first, located in present-day South Carolina. The second, near modern Jacksonville, Florida, was destroyed in 1565 by a Spanish expedition under the command of Pedro Menéndez de Avilés. To ensure Spanish domination of the strategically important region (located near sea-lanes used by Spanish treasure ships bound for Europe), Menéndez set up a small fortified outpost, which he named St. Augustine—now the oldest continuously inhabited European settlement in the United States.

The local Guale and Timucua nations initially allied themselves with the powerful newcomers and welcomed Franciscan friars into their villages. The relationship did not remain peaceful for long, though, for the natives resisted the imposition of Spanish authority. Still, the Franciscans offered the Indians spiritual solace for the diseases and troubles besetting them after the Europeans' invasion, and eventually they gained numerous converts at missions that stretched westward across Florida and northward into the islands along the Atlantic coast.

New Mexico More than thirty years passed after the founding of St. Augustine before conquistadors ventured anew into the present-day United States. In 1598, drawn northward by rumors of rich cities, Juan de Oñate, a Mexican-born adventurer, led a group of about five hundred soldiers and settlers to New Mexico. At first, the Pueblo peoples greeted the newcomers cordially. But when the Spaniards began to use torture, murder, and rape to extort food and clothing from the villagers, the residents of Acoma killed several soldiers, among them Oñate's nephew, Juan de Zaldívar. The invaders responded ferociously, killing more than eight hundred people and capturing the remainder. All the captives above the age of twelve were ordered enslaved for twenty years, and men older than twenty-five had one foot amputated. Not surprisingly, the other Pueblo villages surrendered.

Yet Oñate's bloody victory proved illusory, for New Mexico held little wealth. It also was too far from the Pacific coast to assist in protecting Spanish sea-lanes, which had been one of Oñate's aims (he, like others, initially believed the continent to be much narrower than it actually is). Many of the Spaniards returned to Mexico, but horses remained, transforming the lives of the indigenous inhabitants. Officials considered abandoning the isolated colony, which lay 800 miles north of the nearest Spanish settlement. Still, for defensive purposes the authorities decided to maintain a small military outpost and a few Christian missions in the area, with the capital at Santa Fe (founded in 1610). As in regions to the south, Spanish leaders were granted *encomiendas* guaranteeing them control over the labor of Pueblo villagers. But in the absence of mines or fertile agricultural lands, such grants yielded small profit.

Quebec and Montreal On the Atlantic coast, the French turned their attention northward, to the area that Jacques Cartier had explored in the 1530s. Several times they tried to establish permanent bases along the Canadian coast but failed until 1605, when they founded Port Royal. Then in 1608 Samuel de Champlain set up a trading post at an interior site that the local Iroquois had called Stadacona when Cartier spent the winter there seventy-five years earlier. Champlain renamed it Quebec. He had chosen well: Quebec was the most defensible spot in the entire St. Lawrence River valley, a stronghold that controlled access to the heartland of the continent. In 1642 the French established a second post, Montreal, at the falls of the St. Lawrence (and thus at the end of navigation by oceangoing vessels), a place the Indians called Hochelaga.

Before the founding of these settlements, fishermen served as the major transporters of North American beaver pelts to France, but the new posts quickly took over control of the lucrative trade in furs (see Table 2.1). Only a few Europeans resided in New France; most were men, some of whom married Indian women. The colony's leaders gave land grants along the river to wealthy seigneurs (nobles), who then imported tenants to work their farms. A small number of Frenchmen brought their wives and took up agriculture; even so, more than twenty-five years after Quebec's founding, it had just sixty-four resident families, along with traders and soldiers. With respect to territory occupied and farmed, northern New France never grew much beyond the confines of the river valley between Quebec and Montreal. Thus it differed significantly from New Spain, characterized by scattered cities and direct supervision of Indian laborers.

CHRONOLOGY

1533 • Henry VIII divorces Catherine of Aragón

• English Reformation begins

1558 • Elizabeth I becomes queen

1565 • Founding of St. Augustine (Florida), oldest permanent European settlement in present-day United States

1598 • Oñate conquers Pueblos in New Mexico for Spain

1603 • James I becomes king

1607 • Jamestown founded, first permanent English settlement in North America

1608 • Quebec founded by the French

1610 • Founding of Santa Fe, New Mexico

1611 • First Virginia tobacco crop

1614 • Fort Orange (Albany) founded by the Dutch

1619 • Virginia House of Burgesses established, first representative assembly in the English colonies

1620 • Plymouth colony founded, first permanent English settlement in New England

1622 • Powhatan Confederacy attacks Virginia

1624 • Dutch settle on Manhattan Island (New Amsterdam)

• English colonize St. Kitts, first island in Lesser Antilles to be settled by Europeans

• James I revokes Virginia Company's charter

1625 • Charles I becomes king

1630 • Massachusetts Bay colony founded

1634 • Maryland founded

1636 • Williams expelled from Massachusetts Bay, founds Providence, Rhode Island

• Connecticut founded

1637 • Pequot War in New England

1638 • Hutchinson expelled from Massachusetts Bay, goes to Rhode Island

c. 1640 • Sugar cultivation begins on Barbados

1642 • Montreal founded by the French

1646 • Treaty ends hostilities between Virginia and Powhatan Confederacy

Jesuit Missions in New France   Missionaries of the Society of Jesus (Jesuits), a Roman Catholic order dedicated to converting nonbelievers to Christianity, also came to New France. First arriving in Quebec in 1625, the Jesuits, whom the Indians called Black Robes, tried to persuade indigenous peoples to live near French settlements and to adopt European agricultural methods. When that

TABLE 2.1 **The Founding of Permanent European Colonies in North America, 1565–1640**

Colony	Founder(s)	Date	Basis of Economy
Florida	Pedro Menéndez de Avilés	1565	Farming
New Mexico	Juan de Oñate	1598	Livestock
Virginia	Virginia Co.	1607	Tobacco
New France	France	1608	Fur trading
New Netherland	Dutch West India Co.	1614	Fur trading
Plymouth	Separatists	1620	Farming, fishing
Maine	Sir Ferdinando Gorges	1622	Fishing
St. Kitts, Barbados, et al.	European immigrants	1624	Sugar
Massachusetts Bay	Massachusetts Bay Company	1630	Farming, fishing, fur trading
Maryland	Cecilius Calvert	1634	Tobacco
Rhode Island	Roger Williams	1636	Farming
Connecticut	Thomas Hooker	1636	Farming, fur trading
New Haven	Massachusetts migrants	1638	Farming
New Hampshire	Massachusetts migrants	1638	Farming, fishing

effort failed, the Jesuits concluded that they could introduce Catholicism to their new charges without insisting that they fundamentally alter their traditional ways of life. Accordingly, the Black Robes learned Indian languages and traveled to remote regions of the interior, where they lived in twos and threes among hundreds of potential converts.

Using a variety of strategies, Jesuits sought to gain the confidence of influential men and to undermine the authority of village shamans, the traditional religious leaders. Trained in rhetoric, they won admirers with their eloquence. Immune to smallpox (for all had survived the disease already), they explained epidemics among the Indians as God's punishment for sin, their arguments aided by the ineffectiveness of the shamans' traditional remedies against the new pestilence. Drawing on European science, Jesuits predicted solar and lunar eclipses. Perhaps most important, they amazed the villagers by communicating with each other over long distances through marks on paper. The Indians' desire to learn how to harness the extraordinary power of literacy was one of the critical factors making them receptive to the missionaries' spiritual message.

Although the process took many years, the Jesuits slowly gained thousands of converts, some of whom moved to reserves set aside for Christian Indians. Catholicism offered women in particular the inspiring role model of the Virgin Mary, personified in Montreal and Quebec by communities of nuns who taught Indian women and children, and ministered to their needs. Many male and female converts followed Catholic teachings with fervor and piety, altering traditional native customs of allowing premarital sexual relationships and easy divorce, because Catholic doctrine prohibited both. Yet they resisted the Jesuits' attempts to have them adopt strict European child-rearing methods, instead retaining their more relaxed practices. Jesuits, unlike Franciscans in New Mexico, recognized that such aspects of native culture could be compatible with Christian

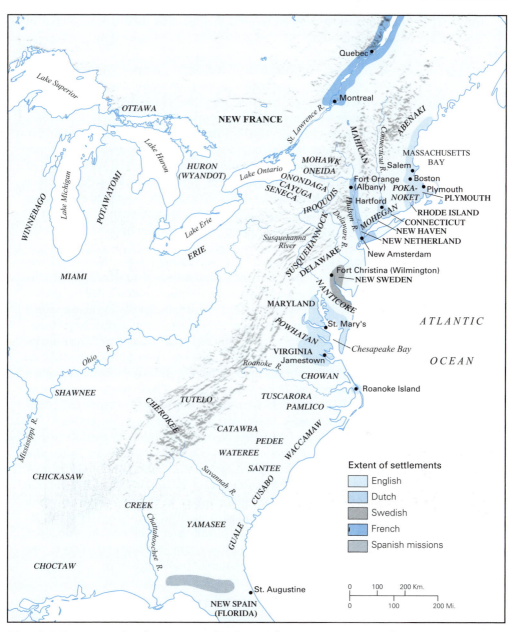

Lake Superior

OTTAWA

Quebec

Montreal

NEW FRANCE

St. Lawrence R.

ABENAKI

Lake Huron

Lake Michigan

POTAWATOMI

HURON
(WYANDOT)

Lake Ontario

MOHAWK
ONEIDA
ONONDAGA
CAYUGA
SENECA
IROQUOIS

MAHICAN

Connecticut R.

MASSACHUSETTS
BAY

Salem

Fort Orange
(Albany)   POKA-   Plymouth
Hartford   NOKET   PLYMOUTH

Boston

WINNEBAGO

Lake Erie

ERIE

Susquehanna
River

SUSQUEHANNOCK

Delaware R.

Hudson R.

MOHEGAN

RHODE ISLAND
CONNECTICUT
NEW HAVEN
NEW NETHERLAND

New Amsterdam

MIAMI

DELAWARE

NANTICOKE

Fort Christina (Wilmington)
NEW SWEDEN

MARYLAND

POWHATAN

St. Mary's

ATLANTIC

Ohio R.

VIRGINIA

Roanoke R.   Jamestown

Chesapeake Bay

OCEAN

CHOWAN

Mississippi R.

SHAWNEE

CHEROKEE

TUTELO

TUSCARORA
PAMLICO

Roanoke Island

CATAWBA
PEDEE
WATEREE

WACCAMAW

CHICKASAW

Savannah R.

SANTEE

CUSABO

Extent of settlements

	English
	Dutch
	Swedish
	French
	Spanish missions

CREEK

Chattahoochee R.

YAMASEE

GUALE

CHOCTAW

St. Augustine

NEW SPAIN
(FLORIDA)

0   100   200 Km.

0   100   200 Mi.

Map 2.1 European Settlements and Indian Tribes in Eastern North America, 1650

The few European settlements established in the East before 1650 were widely scattered, hugging the shores of the Atlantic Ocean and the banks of its major rivers. By contrast, America's native inhabitants controlled the vast interior expanse of the continent, and Spaniards had begun to move into the West.

beliefs. Their efforts to attract converts were further aided by their lack of interest in labor tribute or land acquisition.

New Netherland   Jesuit missionaries faced little competition from other Europeans for native peoples' souls, but French fur traders had to confront a direct challenge. In 1614, only five years after Henry Hudson explored the river that now bears his name, his sponsor, the Dutch West India Company, established an outpost (Fort Orange) on that river at the site of present-day Albany, New York. Like the French, the Dutch sought beaver pelts, and their presence so close to Quebec threatened French domination of the region. The Netherlands, at the time the world's dominant commercial power, aimed primarily at trade rather than at colonization. Thus New Netherland, like New France, remained small, confined largely to a river valley that offered easy access to its settlements. The colony's southern anchor was New Amsterdam, founded in 1624 on Manhattan Island, at the mouth of the Hudson River.

As the Dutch West India Company's colony in North America, New Netherland was the small outpost of a vast commercial empire that extended to Africa, Brazil, the Caribbean, and modern-day Indonesia. Autocratic directors-general ruled the colony for the company; with no elected assembly, settlers felt little loyalty to their nominal leaders. Few migrants arrived. Even an offer in 1629 of large land grants, or patroonships, to people who would bring fifty settlers to the province failed to attract takers. (Only one such tract—Rensselaerswyck, near Albany—was ever fully developed.) As late as the mid-1660s, New Netherland had only about five thousand inhabitants. Some were Swedes and Finns who resided in the former colony of New Sweden (founded in 1638 on the Delaware River), which had been taken over by the Dutch in 1655. New Sweden's chief legacy to North American settlement was log cabin construction.

The Indian allies of New France and New Netherland clashed in part because of fur-trade rivalries. In the 1640s the Iroquois, who traded chiefly with the Dutch and lived in modern upstate New York, went to war against the Hurons, who traded primarily with the French and lived in present-day Ontario. The Iroquois wanted to become the major supplier of pelts to Europeans and to ensure the security of their hunting territories. They achieved both goals by using guns supplied by the Dutch to virtually exterminate the Hurons, whose population had already been decimated by a smallpox epidemic. The Iroquois thus established themselves as a major force in the region, one that in the future Europeans could ignore only at their peril.

THE CARIBBEAN

In the Caribbean, France, the Netherlands, and England collided repeatedly in the first half of the seventeenth century. The Spanish concentrated their colonization efforts on the Greater Antilles—Cuba, Hispaniola, Jamaica, and Puerto Rico. They ignored many smaller islands, partly because of resistance by their Carib inhabitants, partly because the mainland offered greater wealth for less effort. But the tiny islands attracted other European powers: they could provide bases from which to attack Spanish vessels loaded with American gold and silver, and they could serve as sources of valuable tropical products such as dyes and fruits.

Wampum

When Europeans first came to North America, they quickly learned that native peoples highly valued small cylindrical beads made from whelk and quahog shells, known collectively as wampum. The white and purple beads had been strung on fibers for centuries to make necklaces and ornamental belts, but with the Europeans' arrival, wampum changed its character, becoming a currency widely employed by both groups.

The transformation of wampum occurred not only because the Indians prized it and would trade deerskins and beaver pelts to acquire the beads, but also because Dutch and English settlers lacked an equally handy medium of exchange. These settlers had limited access to currency from their homelands, yet they needed to do business with each other and with their native neighbors. Wampum filled a key need, especially in the first decades of settlement.

Whelk (white) and quahog (purple) shells were found primarily along the shores of Long Island Sound. Narragansetts, Montauks, Niantics, and other local peoples had long gathered the shells during the summers; women then fashioned the beads during the long northeastern winters. The shells were hard and brittle, so shaping them into hollow beads was a time-consuming task involving considerable skill. But Europeans' metal tools, including fine drills, allowed a rapid increase in the quantity and quality of wampum. Some villages gave up their hunter-gatherer modes of subsistence and settled permanently in shell-rich areas where they focused almost exclusively on the manufacture of wampum. What

had been a seasonal task for women became their year-round work.

Wampum played a key role in the early economy of both New Netherland and New England. Dutch settlers in Manhattan traded such manufactured goods as guns and kettles, axes, or knives with the wampum makers, then transported wampum up the Hudson River to Fort Orange, where they used it to purchase furs and skins from the Iroquois. In 1627 Isaac de Rasière, a Dutch trader, introduced wampum to the English colonists at Plymouth when he offered it in exchange for corn. Ten years later, the

Before Europeans arrived in North America, wampum—requiring great skill to make—served primarily ceremonial purposes for native peoples, as in the "Four Huron Nations" wampum belt presented to Samuel de Champlain in 1611 to signify the alliance of France and the Hurons. But several decades later, after Dutch and English colonists came to rely on it as a medium of exchange and European tools made it easier to manufacture, wampum became far more utilitarian in design and appearance. (Below: American Museum of Natural History, photographed by Craig Chesek; Right: Musée de L'Homme)

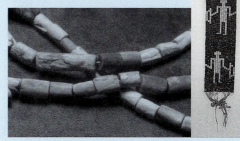

(Continued)

Wampum

Massachusetts Bay colony made wampum legal tender for the payment of debts under 12 pennies, at a rate of six white beads or three purple beads (which were rarer) to 1 penny. Wampum beads could be traded in loose handfuls but more often were strung on thin cords in set amounts worth English equivalents ranging from 1 penny to 5 shillings (60 pennies) in white beads, or 2 pennies to 10 shillings (120 pennies) in purple beads. People trading larger sums measured in wampum always feared being shortchanged. In 1660 one resident of New Netherland agreed to accept payment of a substantial debt in wampum only if his wife *personally* counted all the beads.

Wampum—originally with purely ornamental significance for its Indian makers—became an initial, indispensable link in the commerce between Europe and North America.

Warfare and Hurricanes

England was the first northern European nation to establish a permanent foothold in the smaller Caribbean islands (the Lesser Antilles), settling on St. Christopher (St. Kitts) in 1624, then later on other islands, such as Barbados (1627) and Providence (1630). France was able to colonize Guadeloupe and Martinique only by defeating the Caribs, whereas the Dutch more easily gained control of tiny St. Eustatius (strategically located near St. Kitts). In addition to indigenous inhabitants, Europeans had to worry about conflicts with Spaniards and with one another. Like Providence Island, many colonies changed hands during the seventeenth century. For example, the English drove the Spanish out of Jamaica in 1655, and the French soon thereafter took over half of Hispaniola, creating the colony of St. Domingue (modern Haiti).

Another danger, too, confronted the new settlers: the great windstorms called by the Taíno people *hurakán*, or, in English, hurricanes. Just nine months after the establishment of the first English outpost on St Christopher, wrote one colonist, "came a Hericano and blew it away." Two years later, a second storm again devastated the infant colony, leaving the settlers "very miserable," without housing or adequate provisions. Almost every year in the late summer months one or two islands suffered significant damage from hurricanes. Survivors expressed awe at the destructive force of the storms, which repeatedly forced them to rebuild and replant. To withstand the winds, they designed one- or two-story brick and stone houses with low roofs and heavy wooden shutters over the windows.

Sugar Cultivation

Why did Europeans try to gain and retain control of such imperiled volcanic islands? The primary answer is sugar. Europeans loved sugar, which provided a sweet taste and a quick energy boost, and greatly enriched those who grew and processed it for international markets. Entering Europe in substantial quantities at approximately the same time as coffee and tea—the stimulating, addictive, and bitter Asian drinks improved by sweetening—sugar quickly became a crucial element of the European diet.

English residents of Barbados, after first experimenting with tobacco, cotton, and indigo, discovered in the early 1640s that the island's soil and climate were ideal for cultivating sugar cane. At the time, the world's supply of sugar came primarily from the Madeiras, the Canaries, São Tomé, and especially Brazil, where numerous farmers, each with a few servants or slaves, grew much of the crop. Sugar cane needed to be processed within two days of being harvested, or the juice would dry, so Brazilian producers quickly took their cane to central mills, where it was crushed, boiled down, and finally refined into brown and white sugars.

Barbadians, several of whom visited northeastern Brazil while it was briefly ruled by the Dutch in the 1630s and 1640s, initially copied both the Brazilians' machinery and their small-scale methods of production, which used an existing work force of servants and slaves. But—funded by wealthy English merchants and their own profits from raising tobacco and cotton—the more substantial planters expanded their enterprises dramatically by the mid-1650s. They increased the size of their landholdings, built their own sugar mills, and purchased growing numbers of laborers.

As other Caribbean planters embraced sugar-cane cultivation, Barbadians' profit margins were reduced. Even so, sugar remained the most valuable American commodity for more than one hundred years. In the eighteenth century, sugar grown by large gangs of slaves in British Jamaica and French St. Domingue dominated the world market. Yet, in the long run, the future economic importance of the Europeans' American colonies lay on the mainland rather than in the Caribbean.

ENGLISH INTEREST IN COLONIZATION

The failure of Raleigh's Roanoke colony ended English efforts to settle in North America for nearly two decades. When the English decided in 1606 to try once more, they again planned colonies that imitated the Spanish model. Yet, greater success came when they abandoned that model and founded settlements very different from those of other European powers. Unlike Spain, France, or the Netherlands, England eventually sent large numbers of men and women to set up agriculturally based colonies on the mainland. Two major developments prompted approximately 200,000 ordinary English men and women to move to North America in the seventeenth century and led their government to encourage their emigration.

Social and Economic Change

The first was the onset of dramatic social and economic change. In the 150-year period after 1530, largely as a result of the introduction of nutritious American crops, England's population doubled. All those additional people needed food, clothing, and other goods. The competition for goods led to inflation, coupled with a fall in real wages as the number of workers increased. In these new economic and demographic circumstances, some English people—especially those with sizable landholdings that could produce food and clothing fibers for the growing population—substantially improved their lot. Others, particularly landless laborers and those with small amounts of land, fell into unremitting poverty. When landowners raised rents, took control of lands that peasants had long been allowed to use in common (enclosure), or decided to combine small holdings into large units, they forced tenants off the land. Consequently, geographical as well as social mobility increased, and the population of the cities swelled. London, for example, more than tripled in size by 1650, when 375,000 residents lived in its crowded buildings.

Wealthy English people reacted with alarm to what they saw as the disappearance of traditional ways of life. Steady streams of the landless and homeless filled the streets and highways. Obsessed with the problem of maintaining order, officials came to believe that England was overcrowded. They concluded that colonies established in North America could siphon off England's "surplus population," thus easing social strains at home. For similar reasons, many English people decided that they could improve their circumstances by migrating from a small, land-scarce, apparently over-populated island to a large, land-rich, apparently empty continent and its nearby islands. Among those attracted by prospects for emigration were such younger sons of gentlemen as William Rudyerd, who were excluded from inheriting land by wealthy families' practice of primogeniture, which reserved all real estate for the eldest son. Such economic considerations were rendered even more significant in light of the second development: a major change in English religious practice.

English Reformation   The sixteenth century witnessed a religious transformation that eventually led large numbers of English dissenters to leave their homeland. In 1533 Henry VIII, wanting a male heir and infatuated with Anne Boleyn, sought to annul his marriage to his Spanish-born queen, Catherine of Aragón, despite nearly twenty years of marriage and the birth of a daughter. When the pope refused to approve the annulment, Henry left the Roman Catholic Church. He founded the Church of England and—with Parliament's concurrence—proclaimed himself its head. In general, English people welcomed the schism, for many had little respect for the English Catholic Church. At first the reformed Church of England differed little from Catholicism in its practices, but under Henry's daughter Elizabeth I (child of his later marriage to Anne Boleyn), new currents of religious belief, which had originated on the European continent early in the sixteenth century, dramatically affected the English church.

These currents were the Protestant Reformation, led by Martin Luther, a German monk, and John Calvin, a French cleric and lawyer. Challenging the Catholic doctrine that priests were intermediaries between laypeople and God, Luther and Calvin insisted that people could interpret the Bible for themselves. That notion stimulated the spread of literacy: to understand and interpret the Bible, people had to learn how to read. Both Luther and Calvin rejected Catholic rituals, denying the need for an elaborate church hierarchy. They also asserted that the key to salvation was faith in God, rather than—as Catholic teaching had it—a combination of faith and good works. Calvin went further than Luther, stressing God's omnipotence and emphasizing the need for people to submit totally to God's will.

Puritans and Separatists   Elizabeth I tolerated diverse forms of Christianity as long as her subjects acknowledged her authority as head of the Church of England. During her long reign (1558–1603), Calvin's ideas gained influence within the English church, and some Catholics continued to practice their faith in private. By the late sixteenth century, many English Calvinists—those who came to be called Puritans, because they wanted to purify the church, or Separatists, because they wanted to leave it entirely—believed that the English Reformation had not gone far enough. Henry had simplified the church hierarchy; they wanted to abolish it altogether. Henry had subordinated the church to the interests of the state; they wanted a church free from political interference. And the Church of England, like the Catholic Church, continued to include all English people in its membership. Puritans and Separatists preferred a more restricted definition; they wanted to confine church membership to persons they believed to be "saved"—those God had selected for salvation before birth.

Paradoxically, though, a key article of their faith insisted that people could not know for certain if they were "saved" because mere mortals could not comprehend or affect their predestination to heaven or hell. Thus pious Puritans and Separatists daily confronted serious dilemmas: If the saved (or "elect") could not be identified with certainty, how could proper churches be constituted? If one was predestined and could not alter one's fate, why should one attend church or do good works? Puritans and Separatists dealt with the first dilemma by admitting that their judgments as to eligibility for church membership only approximated God's unknowable decisions. And they resolved the second by reasoning that God gave the elect the ability to accept salvation and to lead a good life. Therefore, even though one could not earn a place in heaven by piety and good works, such practices could indicate one's place in the ranks of the saved.

Stuart Monarchs   Elizabeth I's Stuart successors, her cousin James I (1603–1625) and his son Charles I (1625–1649), exhibited less tolerance for Puritans and Separatists. As Scots, they also had little respect for the traditions of representative government that had developed in England under the Tudors and their predecessors (see Table 2.2). The wealthy landowners who sat in Parliament had grown accustomed to having considerable influence on government policies, especially taxation. But James I, taking a position later endorsed by his son, publicly declared his belief in the divine right of kings. The Stuarts insisted that a monarch's power came directly from God and that his subjects had a duty to obey him. They likened the king's absolute authority to a father's authority over his children.

Both James I and Charles I believed that their authority included the power to enforce religious conformity. Because Puritans and Separatists—and the remaining English Catholics—challenged many of the most important precepts of the English church, the Stuart monarchs authorized the removal of dissenting clergymen from their pulpits. In the 1620s and 1630s, some English Puritans, Separatists, and Catholics decided to move to America, where they hoped to put their religious beliefs into practice unhindered by the Stuarts or the church hierarchy. Some fled hurriedly to avoid arrest and imprisonment.

TABLE 2.2 Tudor and Stuart Monarchs of England, 1509–1649

Monarch	Reign	Relation to Predecessor
Henry VIII	1509–1547	Son
Edward VI	1547–1553	Son
Mary I	1553–1558	Half-sister
Elizabeth I	1558–1603	Half-sister
James I	1603–1625	Cousin
Charles I	1625–1649	Son

THE FOUNDING OF VIRGINIA

The initial impulse that led to England's first permanent colony in the Western Hemisphere was, however, economic. A group of merchants and wealthy gentry in 1606 obtained a royal charter for the Virginia Company, organized as a joint-stock company, a forerunner of the modern corporation. Such enterprises, created for trading voyages, pooled the resources of many small investors through stock sales and spread out the risks. Investors usually received quick returns, but colonies required significant capital and commonly suffered from a chronic shortfall in financing. The lack of immediate returns made matters worse, generating tension between stockholders and colonists. Although at the outset investors in the Virginia Company anticipated great profits, the joint-stock company, then as later, proved to be a poor vehicle for establishing colonies, and neither settlement established by the Virginia Company—one in Maine that collapsed within a year and Jamestown—ever earned much.

Jamestown and Tsenacomoco In 1607 the company dispatched 104 men and boys to a region near Chesapeake Bay called Tsenacomoco by its native inhabitants. There in May they established the palisaded settlement called Jamestown on a swampy peninsula in a river they also named for their monarch. They quickly constructed small houses and a Church of England chapel. Ill equipped for survival in the unfamiliar environment, the colonists fell victim to dissension and disease as they attempted to maintain traditional English social and political hierarchies. Familiar with Spanish experience, the gentlemen and soldiers at Jamestown expected to rely on local Indians for food and tribute, yet the residents of Tsenacomoco refused to cooperate. Moreover, through sheer bad luck the settlers arrived in the midst of a severe drought (now known to be the worst in the region for 1,700 years), which persisted until 1612. The lack of rainfall not only made it difficult to cultivate crops but also polluted their drinking water.

The weroance (chief) of Tsenacomoco, Powhatan, had inherited rule over six Algonquian villages and later gained control of some twenty-five others. In late 1607 negotiations with Captain John Smith, one of the colony's leaders, the weroance tentatively agreed to an alliance with the Englishmen. In exchange for foodstuffs, Powhatan hoped to acquire guns, hatchets, and swords, which would give him a technological advantage over the enemies of his people. Each side in the alliance wanted to subordinate the other, but neither succeeded.

The fragile relationship soon foundered on mutual mistrust. The wereoance relocated his primary village in early 1609 to a place the newcomers could not access easily. Without Powhatan's assistance, the settlement experienced a "starving time" (winter 1609–1610), when many died and at least one colonist resorted to cannibalism. In spring 1610 the survivors packed up to leave on a newly arrived ship but en route out of the James River encountered a new governor, more settlers, and added supplies, so they returned to Jamestown. Sporadic skirmishes ensued as the standoff with the Powhatans continued. To gain the upper hand, the settlers in 1613 kidnapped Powhatan's daughter, Pocahontas, and held her hostage. In captivity, she agreed to convert to Christianity and to marry a colonist, John Rolfe. He had fallen in love with her, but she probably married him for diplomatic reasons; their union initiated a period of peace between the English and her people. Funded by the Virginia Company, she and Rolfe sailed to England to promote interest in the colony. She died at Gravesend in 1616, probably of dysentery, leaving an infant son who returned to Virginia as a young adult.

Although their royal charter nominally laid claim to a much wider territory, the Jamestown settlers saw their "Virginia" as essentially corresponding to Tsenacomoco. Powhatan's dominion was bounded on the north by the Potomac, on the south by the Great Dismal Swamp, and on the west by the fall line—the beginning of the upland Piedmont. Beyond those boundaries lay the Powhatans' enemies and (especially in the west) lands the Powhatans feared to enter. English people relied on the Powhatans as guides and interpreters, traveling along rivers and precontact paths in order to trade with the Powhatans' partners. For more than half a century, settlement in "Virginia" was confined to Tsenacomoco.

Algonquian and English Cultural Differences

In Tsenacomoco and elsewhere on the North American coast, English settlers and local Algonquians focused on their cultural differences, not their similarities, although both groups held deep religious beliefs, subsisted primarily through agriculture, accepted social and political hierarchy, and observed well-defined gender roles. From the outset English men regarded Indian men as lazy because they did not cultivate crops and spent much of their time hunting (a sport, not work, in English eyes). Indian men thought English men effeminate because they did the "woman's work" of cultivation. In the same vein, the English believed that Algonquian women were oppressed because they did heavy field labor.

The nature of Algonquian and English hierarchies differed. Among Algonquians like the Powhatans, political power and social status did not necessarily pass directly through the male line, instead commonly flowing through sisters' sons. By contrast, English gentlemen inherited their position from their father. English political and military leaders tended to rule autocratically, whereas Algonquian leaders (even Powhatan) had limited authority over their people. Accustomed to the European concept of powerful kings, the English overestimated the ability of chiefs to make treaties that would bind their people.

Furthermore, Algonquians and English had different notions of property ownership. Most Algonquian villages held their land communally. It could not be bought or sold absolutely, although certain rights to use the land (for example, for hunting or fishing) could be transferred. Once, most English villagers, too, had used land in common, but because of enclosures in the previous century they had become accustomed to individual farms and to buying and selling land. The English also refused to accept the validity of Indians' claims to traditional hunting territories, insisting that only land intensively cultivated could be regarded as owned or occupied. As one colonist put it, "salvadge peoples" who "rambled" over a region without farming it could claim no "title or propertye" in the land. Ownership of such "unclaimed" property, the English believed, lay with the English monarchy, in whose name John Cabot had laid claim to North America in 1497.

Above all, the English settlers believed unwaveringly in the superiority of their civilization. Although in the early years of colonization they often anticipated living peacefully alongside indigenous peoples, they always assumed that they would dictate the terms of such coexistence. Like Thomas Harriot at Roanoke, they expected native peoples to adopt English customs and to convert to Christianity. They showed little respect for the Indians when they believed English interests were at stake, as was demonstrated by developments in Virginia once the settlers had finally found the salable commodity they sought.

Tobacco Cultivation

That commodity was tobacco, the American crop previously introduced to Europe by the Spanish and subsequently cultivated in Turkey. In 1611 John Rolfe planted seeds of a variety from the Spanish Caribbean, which was superior to the strain grown by Virginia Indians. Nine years later, Virginians exported 40,000 pounds of cured leaves, and by the late 1620s shipments had jumped dramatically to 1.5 million pounds. The great tobacco boom had begun, fueled by high prices and substantial profits for planters as they responded to escalating demand from Europe and Africa. The price later fell almost as sharply as it had risen, fluctuating wildly from year to year in response to increasing supply and international competition. Nevertheless, tobacco made Virginia prosper.

The spread of tobacco cultivation immeasurably altered life for everyone. Successful tobacco cultivation required abundant land, because the crop quickly drained soil of nutrients. Farmers soon learned that a field could produce only about three satisfactory crops before it had to lie fallow for several years to regain its fertility. Thus the once-small English settlements began to expand rapidly: eager applicants asked the Virginia Company for large land grants on both sides of the James River and its tributary streams. Lulled into a false sense of security by years of peace, Virginians established farms at some distance from one another along the riverbanks—a settlement pattern convenient for tobacco cultivation but dangerous for defense.

Indian Assaults

Opechancanough, Powhatan's brother and successor, watched the English colonists' expansion and witnessed their attempts to convert natives to Christianity. Recognizing the danger, the war leader launched coordinated attacks all along the James River on March 22, 1622. By the end of the day, 347 colonists (about one-quarter of the total) lay dead, and only a timely warning from two Christian converts saved Jamestown itself from destruction.

Virginia reeled from the blow but did not collapse. Reinforced by new shipments of men and arms from England, the settlers repeatedly attacked Opechancanough's villages. A peace treaty was signed in 1632, but in April 1644 the elderly Opechancanough assaulted the invaders one last time, though he must have known he could not prevail. In 1646 survivors of the Powhatan Confederacy formally subordinated themselves to England. Although they continued to live in the region, their efforts to resist the spread of European settlement ended.

End of Virginia Company

The 1622 assault that failed to destroy the colony did succeed in killing its parent. The Virginia Company never made any profits from the enterprise, for internal corruption and the heavy cost of supporting the settlers offset all its earnings. But before its demise the company developed two policies that set key precedents. First, to attract settlers, the company in 1617 established the "headright" system. Every new arrival paying his or her own way was promised a land grant of 50 acres; those who financed the passage of others received similar headrights for each person. To ordinary English farmers, many of whom owned little or no land, the headright system offered a powerful incentive to move to Virginia. To wealthy gentry, it promised even more: the possibility of establishing vast agricultural enterprises worked by large numbers of laborers. Two years later, the company introduced

A comparison of the portrait of Sir Walter Raleigh and his son (left), with that of an Algonquian Indian drawn by John White, from Raleigh's Roanoke expedition (right), shows a dramatic difference in standard dress styles that, for many, must have symbolized the apparent cultural gap between Europeans and Americans. Yet the fact that both men (and the young boy) were portrayed in similar stances, with "arms akimbo," demonstrated that all were high-status individuals. In Europe, only aristocrats were represented in such a domineering pose. (Left: National Portrait Gallery, London; Right: Trustees of the British Museum)

a second reform, authorizing the landowning men of the major Virginia settlements to elect representatives to an assembly called the House of Burgesses. English landholders had long been accustomed to electing members of Parliament and controlling their own local governments; therefore, they expected the same privilege in the nation's colonies.

When James I revoked the charter in 1624, transforming Virginia into a royal colony, he continued the company's headright policy. Because he distrusted legislative bodies, though, James abolished the assembly. But Virginians protested so vigorously that by 1629 the House of Burgesses was functioning once again. Only two decades after the first permanent English settlement was planted in North America, the colonists successfully insisted on governing themselves at the local level. Thus the political structure of England's American possessions came to differ from those of the Spanish, Dutch, and French colonies, all of which were ruled autocratically.

LIFE IN THE CHESAPEAKE

By the 1630s tobacco was firmly established as the staple crop and chief source of revenue in Virginia. It quickly became just as important in the second English colony planted on Chesapeake Bay: Maryland, given by Charles I to George Calvert, first Lord Baltimore, as a personal possession (proprietorship), which was settled in 1634. (Because Virginia and Maryland both border Chesapeake Bay they are often referred to collectively as "the Chesapeake.") Members of the Calvert family intended the colony to serve as a haven for their persecuted fellow Catholics. Cecilius Calvert, second Lord Baltimore, became the first colonizer to offer freedom of religion to all Christian settlers; he understood that protecting the Protestant majority could also ensure Catholics' rights. Maryland's Act of Religious Toleration codified his policy in 1649.

In everything but religion the two Chesapeake colonies resembled each other. In Maryland as in Virginia, tobacco planters spread out along the riverbanks, establishing isolated farms instead of towns. The region's deep, wide rivers offered dependable water transportation in an age of few and inadequate roads. Each farm or group of farms had its own wharf, where oceangoing vessels could take on or discharge cargo. Consequently, Virginia and Maryland had few towns, for their residents did not need commercial centers in order to buy and sell goods.

Demand for Laborers   The planting, cultivation, harvesting, and curing of tobacco were repetitious, time-consuming, and labor-intensive tasks. Clearing land for new fields, necessary every few years, also demanded heavy labor. Above all else, then, successful Chesapeake farms required workers. But where and how could they be obtained? Nearby Indians, their numbers reduced by war and disease, could not supply such needs. Nor were enslaved Africans available: traders could more easily and profitably sell slaves to Caribbean sugar planters. Only a few people of African descent, some of them free, initially trickled into the Chesapeake. By 1650 about three hundred blacks lived in Virginia—a tiny fraction of the population.

Chesapeake tobacco farmers thus looked primarily to England to supply their labor needs. Because of the headright system (which Maryland also adopted in 1640), a tobacco farmer anywhere in the Chesapeake could simultaneously obtain both land and labor by importing workers from England. Good management would make the process self-perpetuating: a farmer could use his profits to pay for the passage of more workers and thereby gain title to more land. Success could even bring movement into the ranks of the planter gentry that began to develop in the region.

Because men did the agricultural work in European societies, colonists assumed that field laborers should be men. Such male laborers, along with a few women, immigrated to America as indentured servants—that is, in return for their passage they contracted to work for periods ranging from four to seven years. Indentured servants accounted for 75 to 85 percent of the approximately 130,000 English immigrants to Virginia and Maryland during the seventeenth century. The rest tended to be young couples with one or two children.

Males between the ages of fifteen and twenty-four composed roughly three-quarters of the servants; only one immigrant in five or six was female. Most of these young men came from farming or laboring families, and many originated in regions of England experiencing severe social disruption. Some had already moved several times within

England before relocating to America. Often they came from the middling ranks of society—what their contemporaries called the "common sort." Their youth indicated that most probably had not yet established themselves in their homeland.

Conditions of Servitude For such people the Chesapeake appeared to offer good prospects. Servants who fulfilled the terms of their indenture earned "freedom dues" consisting of clothes, tools, livestock, casks of corn and tobacco, and sometimes even land. From a distance at least, America seemed to offer chances for advancement unavailable in England. Yet immigrants' lives were difficult. Servants typically worked six days a week, ten to fourteen hours a day, in a climate much warmer than England's. Their masters could discipline or sell them, and they faced severe penalties for running away. Even so, the laws did give them some protection. For example, their masters were supposed to supply them with sufficient food, clothing, and shelter, and they were not to be beaten excessively. Cruelly treated servants could turn to the courts for assistance, sometimes winning verdicts directing that they be transferred to more humane masters or released from their indenture.

Servants and their owners alike contended with epidemic disease. Immigrants first had to survive the process the colonists called "seasoning," a bout with disease (probably malaria) that usually occurred during their first Chesapeake summer. They then often endured recurrences of malaria, along with dysentery, typhoid fever, and other illnesses. Consequently, about 40 percent of male servants did not survive long enough to become freedmen. Even young men of twenty-two who successfully weathered their seasoning could expect to live only another twenty years.

For those who survived, though, the opportunities for advancement were real. Until the last decades of the seventeenth century, former servants often became independent farmers ("freeholders"), thereafter living a modest but comfortable existence. Some even assumed positions of political prominence, such as justice of the peace or militia officer. But in the 1670s tobacco prices entered a fifty-year period of stagnation and decline. Simultaneously, good land grew increasingly scarce and expensive. In 1681 Maryland dropped its legal requirement that servants receive land as part of their freedom dues, forcing large numbers of freed servants to live for years as wage laborers or tenant farmers. By 1700 the Chesapeake was no longer the land of opportunity it once had been.

Standard of Living Life in the early Chesapeake was hard for everyone, regardless of sex or status. Farmers (and sometimes their wives) toiled in the fields alongside servants, laboriously clearing land, then planting and harvesting tobacco and corn. Because hogs could forage for themselves in the forests and needed little tending, Chesapeake households subsisted mainly on pork and corn, a filling diet but not sufficiently nutritious. Families supplemented this monotonous fare by eating fish, shellfish, and wildfowl, in addition to vegetables such as lettuce and peas, which they grew in small gardens. The near impossibility of preserving food for safe winter consumption magnified the health problems caused by epidemic disease. Salting, drying, and smoking, the only methods the colonists knew, did not always prevent spoilage.

Few households had many material possessions other than farm implements, bedding, and basic cooking and eating utensils. Chairs, tables, candles, and knives and forks were luxury items. Most people rose and went to bed with the sun, sat on crude benches or storage chests, and held plates or bowls in their hands while eating meat and vegetable stews with spoons. The ramshackle houses commonly had just one or two rooms. Colonists devoted their income to improving their farms, buying livestock, and purchasing more laborers instead of improving their standard of living. Rather than making such items as clothing and tools, tobacco-growing families imported necessary manufactured goods from England.

Chesapeake Families

The predominance of males, the incidence of servitude, and the high mortality rates combined to produce unusual patterns of family life. Female servants normally could not marry during their term of indenture because masters did not want pregnancies to deprive them of workers. Many male ex-servants could not marry at all because of the scarcity of women; such men lived alone, in pairs, or as the third member of a household containing a married couple. In contrast, nearly every adult free woman in the Chesapeake married, and widows usually remarried within a few months of a husband's death. Yet because of high infant mortality and because almost all marriages were delayed by servitude or broken by death, Chesapeake women commonly reared only one to three healthy children, in contrast to English women, who normally had at least five.

Thus Chesapeake families were few, small, and short-lived. Youthful immigrants came to America as individuals free of familial control; they commonly died while their children were still young. In one Virginia county, for example, more than three-quarters of the children had lost at least one parent by the time they either married or reached age twenty-one. Those children were put to work as soon as possible on the farms of parents, stepparents, or guardians. Their schooling, if any, was haphazard; whether Chesapeake-born children learned to read or write depended largely on whether their parents were literate and took the time to teach them.

Chesapeake Politics

Throughout the seventeenth century, immigrants composed a majority of the Chesapeake population, with important implications for regional political patterns. Most of the members of Virginia's House of Burgesses and Maryland's House of Delegates (established in 1635) were immigrants; they also dominated the governor's council, which simultaneously served as each colony's highest court, part of the legislature, and executive adviser to the governor. A cohesive, native-born ruling elite emerged only in the early eighteenth century.

Representative institutions based on the consent of the governed usually function as a major source of political stability. In the seventeenth-century Chesapeake, most property-owning white males could vote, and such freeholders chose as their legislators (burgesses) the local elites who seemed to be the natural leaders of their respective areas. But because most such men were immigrants lacking strong ties to one another or to the colonies, the assemblies' existence did not create political stability. Unusual demographic patterns thus contributed to the region's contentious politics.

THE FOUNDING OF NEW ENGLAND

The economic motives that prompted English people to move to the Chesapeake and the Caribbean colonies also drew men and women to New England, the region known as North Virginia before Captain John Smith renamed it in 1616 after exploring its

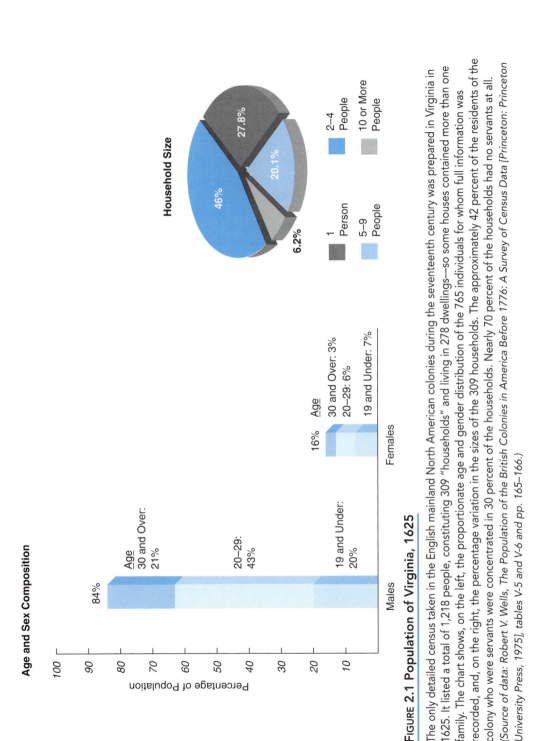

Age and Sex Composition

Percentage of Population

Males

Age
30 and Over:
21%

20–29:
43%

19 and Under:
20%

84%

Females

16% Age

30 and Over: 3%

20–29: 6%

19 and Under: 7%

Household Size

46%

27.8%

20.1%

6.2%

1
Person

2–4
People

5–9
People

10 or More
People

FIGURE 2.1 **Population of Virginia, 1625**

The only detailed census taken in the English mainland North American colonies during the seventeenth century was prepared in Virginia in 1625. It listed a total of 1,218 people, constituting 309 "households" and living in 278 dwellings—so some houses contained more than one family. The chart shows, on the left, the proportionate age and gender distribution of the 765 individuals for whom full information was recorded, and, on the right, the percentage variation in the sizes of the 309 households. The approximately 42 percent of the residents of the colony who were servants were concentrated in 30 percent of the households. Nearly 70 percent of the households had no servants at all. (*Source of data: Robert V. Wells, The Population of the British Colonies in America Before 1776: A Survey of Census Data [Princeton: Princeton University Press, 1975], tables V-5 and V-6 and pp. 165–166.*)

coast. But because Puritans organized the New England colonies and also because of environmental factors, the northern settlements turned out very differently from their counterparts to the south. The differences became apparent even as the would-be colonists left England.

Contrasting Regional Demographic Patterns

Hoping to exert control over a migration that appeared disorderly (and which included dissenters seeking to flee the authority of the Church of England), royal bureaucrats in late 1634 ordered port officials in London to collect information on all travelers departing for the colonies. The resulting records for the year 1635 are a treasure trove for historians. They document the departure of 53 vessels in that year alone—20 to Virginia, 17 to New England, 8 to Barbados, 5 to St. Kitts, 2 to Bermuda, and 1 to Providence Island. On those ships sailed almost five thousand people, with two thousand departing for Virginia, about twelve hundred for New England, and the rest for island destinations. Nearly three-fifths of all the passengers were between fifteen and twenty-four years old, reflecting the predominance of young male servants among migrants to America.

But among those bound for New England, such youths constituted less than one-third of the total; nearly 40 percent were older, and another third were younger. Whereas women made up just 14 percent of those going to Virginia, they composed almost 40 percent of the passengers to New England. Such composite figures show that New England migrants often traveled in family groups. They also brought more goods and livestock with them and tended to travel with other people from the same region. For example, aboard one vessel, more than half came from York; on another, nearly half came from Buckinghamshire. In short, people migrated to New England together with their close associates. Their lives in North America must have been more comfortable and less lonely than those of their southern counterparts.

Contrasting Regional Religious Patterns

Many of the people who colonized New England were inspired to migrate by religion, which elsewhere motivated chiefly the Catholics who moved to Maryland. Puritan congregations quickly became key institutions in colonial New England, whereas neither the Church of England nor Catholicism had much impact on the settlers or the early development of the Chesapeake colonies. Catholic and Anglican bishops in England paid little attention to their coreligionists in America, and Chesapeake congregations languished in the absence of sufficient numbers of properly ordained clergymen. (For example, in 1665 an observer noted that only ten of the fifty Virginia parishes had resident clerics.) Not until the 1690s did the Church of England begin to take firmer root in Virginia; by then it had also replaced Catholicism as the established church in Maryland.

By contrast, religion constantly affected the lives of pious Puritans, who regularly reassessed the state of their souls. Many devoted themselves to self-examination and Bible study, and families prayed together each day under the guidance of the husband and father. Yet because even the most pious could never be certain that they were numbered among the elect, anxiety about their spiritual state troubled devout Puritans. That anxiety lent a special intensity to their religious beliefs and to their concern with proper behavior—their own and that of others.

Separatists

Separatists who thought the Church of England too corrupt to be salvaged became the first religious dissenters to move to New England. In 1609 a Separatist congregation relocated to Leiden, in the Netherlands, where they found the freedom of worship denied them in Stuart England. But eventually the Netherlands worried them, for the nation that tolerated them also tolerated religions and behaviors they abhorred. Hoping to isolate themselves and their children from the corrupting influence of worldly temptations, these people, who came to be known as Pilgrims, received permission from the Virginia Company to colonize the northern part of its territory.

In September 1620 more than one hundred people, only thirty of them Separatists, set sail from England on the old and crowded *Mayflower*. Like a few English families that had settled permanently along the coast of Newfoundland during the previous decade, the Pilgrims expected to support their colony through profits from codfishery. In December they landed in America, but farther north than they had intended. Still, given the lateness of the season, they decided to stay where they were. They moved into the empty dwellings of an Indian village whose inhabitants had died in the epidemic of 1616–1618, at a fine harbor, named Plymouth by John Smith in 1616.

Pilgrims and Pokanokets

Even before they landed, the Pilgrims had to surmount their first challenge—from the "strangers," or nonSeparatists, who sailed with them to America. Because they landed outside the jurisdiction of the Virginia Company, some of the strangers questioned the authority of the colony's leaders. In response, the Mayflower Compact, signed in November 1620 on shipboard, established a "Civil Body Politic" as a temporary substitute for a charter. The male settlers elected a governor and initially made all decisions for the colony at town meetings. Later, after more towns had been founded and the population increased, Plymouth, like Virginia and Maryland, created an assembly to which the landowning male settlers elected representatives.

Like the Jamestown settlers before them, the residents of Plymouth were poorly prepared to subsist in the new environment. Only half of the *Mayflower*'s passengers lived to see the spring. That the others survived owed much to the Pokanokets (a branch of the Wampanoags), who controlled the area in which they had settled. Pokanoket villages had suffered terrible losses in the recent epidemic, so to protect themselves from the powerful Narragansetts of the southern New England coast (who had been spared the ravages of the disease), the Pokanokets allied themselves with the newcomers. In the spring of 1621, their leader, Massasoit, agreed to a treaty, and during the colony's first difficult years the Pokanokets supplied the settlers with essential foodstuffs. The colonists also relied on Squanto, an Indian who, like Malinche, served as a conduit between native peoples and Europeans. Captured by fishermen in the early 1610s and taken to Europe, Squanto had learned to speak English. Upon returning to North America, he discovered that his village had been wiped out by the epidemic. Squanto became the settlers' interpreter and a major source of information about the environment.

Massachusetts Bay Company

Before the 1620s ended, another group of Puritans (Congregationalists, who hoped to reform the Church of England from within) launched the colonial enterprise that would come to dominate New England and would absorb Plymouth in 1691. Charles I, who became king in 1625, was more hostile to Puritans than his father had been. Under his leadership, the Church of England attempted to suppress Puritan practices, driving clergymen from their pulpits and forcing congregations to worship secretly. Some Congregationalist merchants, concerned about their long-term prospects in England, sent out a body of colonists to Cape Ann (north of Cape Cod) in 1628. The following year the merchants obtained a royal charter, constituting themselves as the Massachusetts Bay Company.

The new joint-stock company quickly attracted the attention of Puritans of the "middling sort" who were becoming increasingly convinced that they no longer would be able to practice their religion freely in their homeland. They remained committed to the goal of reforming the Church of England but concluded that they should pursue that aim in America. In a dramatic move, the Congregationalist merchants decided to transfer the Massachusetts Bay Company's headquarters to New England. The settlers would then be answerable to no one in the mother country and would be able to handle their affairs, secular and religious, as they pleased. Like the Plymouth settlers, they expected to profit from the codfishery; they also planned to export timber products.

Governor John Winthrop

The most important recruit to the new venture was John Winthrop, a member of the lesser English gentry. In October 1629, the Massachusetts Bay Company elected Winthrop as its governor. (Until his death twenty years later, he served the colony continuously in one leadership post or another.) Winthrop organized the initial segment of the great Puritan migration to America. In 1630 over one thousand English men and women moved to Massachusetts—most of them to Boston. By 1643 nearly twenty thousand more had followed.

On board the *Arbella,* en route to New England in 1630, John Winthrop preached a sermon, "A Model of Christian Charity," laying out his expectations for the new colony. Above all, he stressed the communal nature of the endeavor on which he and his fellow settlers had embarked. God, he explained, "hath so disposed of the condition of mankind as in all times some must be rich, some poor, some high and eminent in power and dignity, others mean and in subjection." But differences in status did not imply differences in worth. On the contrary, God had planned the world so that "every man might have need of other, and from hence they might be all knit more nearly together in the bond of brotherly affection." In America, Winthrop asserted, "we shall be as a city upon a hill, the eyes of all people are upon us." If the Puritans failed to carry out their "special commission" from God, "the Lord will surely break out in wrath against us."

Winthrop's was a transcendent vision. He foresaw in Puritan America a true commonwealth, a community in which each person put the good of the whole ahead of his or her private concerns. Although, as in seventeenth century England, that society would be characterized by social inequality and clear hierarchies of status and power, Winthrop hoped that its members would live according to the precepts of Christian love. Of course, such an ideal was beyond human reach. Early New England and its Caribbean counterpart, Providence Island, had their share of bitter quarrels and unchristian behavior. Remarkably, though, in New England the ideal persisted well into the third and fourth generations of the immigrants' descendants.

Covenant Ideal

The Puritans expressed their communal ideal chiefly in the doctrine of the covenant. They believed God had made a covenant—that is, an agreement or contract—with them when they were chosen for the special mission to America. In turn they covenanted with one another, promising

Some scholars now believe that this 1638 painting by the Dutch artist Adam Willaerts depicts the Plymouth colony about fifteen years after its founding. The shape of the harbor, the wooden gate, and the houses straggling up the hill all coincide with contemporary accounts of the settlement. No one believes that Willaerts himself visited Plymouth, but people returning from the colony to the Netherlands, where the Pilgrims had lived for years before emigrating, could well have described Plymouth to him. (© Courtesy of Leiden American Pilgrim Museum, The Netherlands)

to work together toward their goals. The founders of churches, towns, and even colonies in Anglo-America often drafted formal documents setting forth the principles on which their institutions would be based. The Pilgrims' Mayflower Compact was a covenant; so, too, was the Fundamental Orders of Connecticut (1639), which laid down the basic law for the settlements established along the Connecticut River valley in 1636 and thereafter.

The leaders of Massachusetts Bay likewise transformed their original joint-stock company charter into the basis for a covenanted community based on mutual consent. Under pressure from landowning male settlers, they gradually changed the General Court—officially the company's small governing body—into a colonial legislature. They also granted the status of freeman, or voting member of the company, to all property-owning adult male church members. Like the Virginians who won the reestablishment of the House of Burgesses after the king had abolished it, the male residents of Massachusetts insisted that their reluctant leaders allow them a greater voice in their government. Less than two decades after the first large group of Puritans arrived in Massachusetts Bay, the colony had a functioning system of self-government composed of a governor and a two-house legislature. The General Court also established a judicial system modeled on England's, although the laws they adopted differed from those of their homeland.

New England Towns

The colony's method of distributing land helped to further the communal ideal. Unlike Virginia and Maryland, where individual applicants acquired headrights and sited their farms separately, in Massachusetts groups of men—often from the same English village—applied together to the General Court for grants of land on which to establish towns (novel governance units that did not exist in England). The men receiving such a grant determined how the land would be distributed. Understandably, the grantees copied the villages whence they had come. First they laid out lots for houses and a church. Then they gave each family parcels of land scattered around the town center: a pasture here, a woodlot there, an arable field elsewhere. They reserved the best and largest plots for the most distinguished among them, including the minister. People who had low status in England received smaller and less desirable allotments. Still, every man and even a few single women obtained land, thus sharply differentiating these villages from their English counterparts. When migrants began to move beyond the territorial limits of the Massachusetts Bay colony into Connecticut (1636), New Haven (1638), and New Hampshire (1638), the same pattern of land grants and town formation persisted. (Only Maine, with coastal regions thinly populated by fishermen and their families, deviated from the standard practice.)

Town centers developed quickly, evolving in three distinctly different ways. Some, chiefly isolated agricultural settlements in the interior, tried to sustain Winthrop's vision of harmonious community life based on diversified family farms. A second group, the coastal towns like Boston and Salem, became bustling seaports, serving as focal points for trade and places of entry for thousands of new immigrants. The third category, commercialized agricultural towns, grew up in the Connecticut River valley, where easy water transportation made it possible for farmers to sell surplus goods readily. In Springfield, Massachusetts, for example, the merchant-entrepreneur William Pynchon and his son John began as fur traders and ended as large landowners with thousands of acres. Even in New England, then, the entrepreneurial spirit characteristic of the Chesapeake found expression. Yet the plans to profit from timber and fish exports did not materialize quickly or easily; the new settlements lacked the infrastructure necessary to support such enterprises.

Pequot War and Its Aftermath

Migration into the Connecticut valley ended the Puritans' relative freedom from clashes with nearby Indians. The first English people in the valley moved there from Massachusetts Bay under the direction of their minister, Thomas Hooker. Although their new settlements were remote from other English towns, the wide river promised ready access to the ocean. The site had just one problem: it fell within the territory controlled by the powerful Pequots.

The Pequots' dominance stemmed from their role as primary intermediaries in the trade between New England Algonquians and the Dutch in New Netherland. The arrival of English settlers signaled the end of the Pequots' power over such regional trading networks, for previously subordinate bands could now trade directly with Europeans. Clashes between Pequots and English colonists began even before the establishment of settlements in the Connecticut valley, but their founding tipped the balance toward war. The Pequots tried unsuccessfully to enlist other Indians in resisting English expansion. After two English traders were killed (not by Pequots), the English raided a Pequot village. In return, the Pequots attacked the new town of Wethersfield in April 1637, killing nine and capturing two. To retaliate, a Massachusetts Bay expedition the following month attacked and burned the main Pequot town on the Mystic River. The Englishmen and their Narragansett allies slaughtered at least four hundred Pequots, mostly women and children, capturing and enslaving most of the survivors.

For the next four decades, New England Indians accommodated themselves to the European invasion. They traded with the newcomers and sometimes worked for them, but for the most part they resisted acculturation or incorporation into English society. Native Americans persisted in using traditional farming methods, which did not employ plows or fences, and women rather than men continued to be the chief cultivators. When Indian men learned "European" trades in order to survive, they chose those—like broom making, basket weaving, and shingle splitting—that most nearly accorded with their customary occupations and ensured both independence and income. The one European practice they adopted was keeping livestock, for domesticated animals provided excellent sources of meat once earlier hunting territories had been turned into English farms and wild game had consequently disappeared.

Missionary Activities

Although the official seal of the Massachusetts Bay colony showed an Indian crying, "Come over and help us," most colonists showed little interest in converting the Algonquians to Christianity. Only a few Massachusetts clerics, most notably John Eliot and Thomas Mayhew, seriously undertook missionary work. Eliot insisted that converts reside in towns, farm the land in English fashion, assume English names, wear European-style clothing and shoes, cut their hair, and stop observing a wide range of their own customs. Because Eliot demanded a cultural transformation from his adherents—on the theory that Indians could not be properly Christianized unless they were also "civilized"—he understandably met with little success. At the peak of Eliot's efforts, only eleven hundred Indians (out of many thousands) lived in the fourteen "Praying Towns" he established, and just 10 percent of those town residents had been formally baptized.

Eliot's failure to win many converts contrasted sharply with the successful missions in New France. Puritan services lacked Catholicism's beautiful ceremonies and special appeal for women, and the Calvinist Puritans could not offer pious believers assurances of a heavenly afterlife. Yet, on the island of Martha's Vineyard, Thomas Mayhew showed that it was possible to convert substantial numbers of Indians to Calvinist Christianity. He allowed Wampanoag Christians there to lead traditional lives, and he trained men of their own community to minister to them.

What attracted Indians to such religious ideas? Conversion often alienated new Christians (both Catholic and Puritan) from their relatives and traditions—a likely outcome that must have caused many potential converts to hesitate. But surely many hoped to use the Europeans' religion as a means of coping with the dramatic changes the intruders had wrought. The combination of disease, alcohol, new trading patterns, and loss of territory disrupted customary ways of life to an unprecedented extent. Shamans had little success in restoring traditional ways. Many Indians must have concluded that the Europeans' own ideas could provide the key to survival in the new circumstances.

John Winthrop's description of a great smallpox epidemic that swept through southern New England in the early 1630s reveals the relationship among smallpox, conversion to Christianity, and English land claims. "A great mortality among the Indians," he noted in his diary in 1633. "Divers of them, in their sickness, confessed that the Englishmen's God was a good God; and that if they recovered, they would serve him." But most did not recover: in January 1634 an English scout reported that smallpox had spread "as far as any Indian plantation was known to the west." By July, Winthrop observed that most of the Indians within a 300-mile radius of Boston had died of the disease. Therefore, he declared with satisfaction, "the Lord hath cleared our title to what we possess."

LIFE IN NEW ENGLAND

New England's colonizers adopted modes of life that differed from those of both their Algonquian neighbors and their Chesapeake counterparts. Algonquian bands usually moved four or five times each year to take full advantage of their environment. In spring, women planted the fields, but once crops were established, the crops did not need regular attention for several months. Villages then divided into small groups, women gathering wild foods and men hunting and fishing. The villagers returned to their fields for harvest, then separated again for fall hunting. Finally, the people wintered together in a sheltered spot before returning to the fields to start the cycle anew the following spring. Women probably determined the timing of these moves, because their activities (gathering wild foods, including shellfish along the shore, and cultivating plants) used the nearby environment more intensively than did men's.

Unlike the mobile Algonquians, English people lived year-round in the same location. And, unlike residents of the Chesapeake, New Englanders constructed sturdy dwellings intended to last. (Some survive to this day.) Household furnishings resembled those of Chesapeake residents, but New Englanders' diets were somewhat more varied. They replowed the same fields, believing it was less arduous to employ manure as fertilizer than to clear new fields every few years. Furthermore, they fenced their croplands to prevent them from being overrun by the cattle, sheep, and hogs that were their chief sources of meat. Animal crowding more than human crowding caused New Englanders to spread out across the countryside; all their livestock constantly needed more pasturage.

New England Families

Because Puritans commonly moved to America in family groups, the age range in early New England was wide; and because many more women migrated to New England than to the tobacco colonies, the population could immediately begin to reproduce itself. Lacking such tropical diseases as malaria, New England was also healthier than the Chesapeake and even the mother country, once settlements had survived the difficult first few years. Adult male migrants to the Chesapeake lost about a decade from their English life expectancy of fifty to fifty-five years; their Massachusetts counterparts gained five or more years.

Consequently, whereas Chesapeake population patterns gave rise to families that were few in number, small in size, and transitory, the demographic characteristics of New England made families there numerous, large, and long-lived. In New England most men married; immigrant women married young (at age twenty, on the average); and marriages lasted longer and produced more children, who were more likely to live to maturity. If seventeenth-century Chesapeake women could expect to rear one to three healthy children, New England women could anticipate raising five to seven.

The nature of the population had other major implications for family life. The presence of many children combined with Puritans' stress on the importance of reading the Bible led to widespread concern for the education of youth. That people lived in towns meant that small schools could be established; girls and boys were taught basic reading by their parents or a school "dame," and boys could then proceed to learn writing and eventually arithmetic and Latin. Further, New England in effect created grandparents, because in England people rarely lived long enough to know their children's children. And whereas early Chesapeake parents commonly died before their children married, New England parents exercised a good deal of control over their adult offspring. Young men could not marry without acreage to cultivate, and because of the communal land-grant system, they had to depend on their fathers for that land. Daughters, too, needed a dowry of household goods supplied by their parents. Parents relied on their children's labor and often seemed reluctant to see them marry and start their own households. These needs sometimes led to conflict between the generations. On the whole, though, children seem to have obeyed their parents' wishes, for they had few alternatives.

Impact of Religion　　Puritans controlled the governments of Massachusetts Bay, Plymouth, Connecticut, and the other early northern colonies. Congregationalism was the only officially recognized religion; except in Rhode Island, founded by dissenters from Massachusetts, members of other sects had no freedom of worship. Some non-Puritans voted in town meetings, but in Massachusetts Bay and New Haven, church membership was a prerequisite for voting in colony elections. All the early colonies taxed residents to build meetinghouses and pay ministers' salaries, but only in New England were provisions of criminal codes based on the Old Testament. Massachusetts's first bodies of law (1641 and 1648) incorporated regulations drawn from scriptures; New Haven, Plymouth, New Hampshire, and Connecticut later copied those codes. All colonists were required to attend religious services, whether or not they were church members, and people who expressed contempt for ministers or their preaching could be punished with fines or whippings.

The Puritan colonies attempted to enforce strict codes of moral conduct. Colonists there could be tried for drunkenness, card playing, dancing, or even idleness—although the frequent prosecutions for such offenses suggest that New Englanders often disobeyed the laws and thoroughly enjoyed such activities. Couples who had sex during their engagement (as revealed by the birth of a baby less than nine months after their wedding) were fined and publicly humiliated. Men, and a handful of women, who engaged in behaviors that today would be called homosexual were seen as especially sinful and reprehensible, and some were executed.

In New England, church and state were thus intertwined to a greater extent than in the Chesapeake, where few such prosecutions occurred. Puritans objected to secular interference in religious affairs but at the same time expected the church to influence the conduct of politics and the affairs of society. They also believed that the state was obliged to support and protect the one true church—theirs. As a result, although they came to America seeking freedom to worship as they pleased, they saw no contradiction in refusing to grant that freedom to others.

Roger Williams　　Roger Williams, a Separatist who migrated to Massachusetts Bay in 1631, quickly ran afoul of that Puritan orthodoxy. He told his fellow settlers that the king of England had no right to grant them land already occupied by Indians, that church and state should be kept entirely separate, and that

Puritans should not impose their religious beliefs on others. Because Puritan leaders placed a heavy emphasis on achieving consensus in both religion and politics, they could not long tolerate significant dissent. In October 1635, the Massachusetts General Court tried Williams for challenging the validity of the colony's charter and for maintaining that New England Congregationalists had not separated themselves, their churches, or their polity sufficiently from England's corrupt institutions and practices.

Convicted and banished, Williams journeyed in early 1636 to the head of Narragansett Bay, where he founded the town of Providence on land he obtained from the Narragansetts and Wampanoags. Because Williams believed that government should not interfere with religion in any way, Providence and other towns in what became Rhode Island adopted a policy of tolerating all religions, including Judaism. Along with Maryland, the tiny colony founded by Williams thus presaged the religious freedom that eventually became one of the hallmarks of the United States.

Anne Hutchinson

A dissenter who presented a more sustained challenge to Massachusetts' leaders was Mistress Anne Hutchinson. (The title *Mistress* revealed her high status.) A skilled medical practitioner popular with the women of Boston, she greatly admired John Cotton, a minister who stressed the covenant of grace, or God's free gift of salvation to unworthy human beings. By contrast, most Massachusetts clerics emphasized the need for Puritans to engage in good works, study, and reflection in preparation for receiving God's grace. (In its most extreme form, such a doctrine could verge on the covenant of works, or the idea that people could earn their salvation.) After spreading her ideas for months in the context of gatherings at childbirths—when no men were present—Mistress Hutchinson began holding women's meetings in her home to discuss Cotton's sermons. She emphasized the covenant of grace more than did Cotton himself, and she even asserted that the elect could be assured of salvation and communicate directly with God. Such ideas had an immense appeal for Puritans. Anne Hutchinson offered them certainty of salvation instead of a state of constant anxiety. Her approach also lessened the importance of the institutional church and its ministers.

Thus Hutchinson's ideas posed a dangerous threat to Puritan orthodoxy. So in November 1637, officials charged her with having maligned the colony's ministers by accusing them of preaching the covenant of works. For two days she defended herself cleverly, matching scriptural references and wits with John Winthrop himself. But then Anne Hutchinson triumphantly and boldly declared that God had spoken to her directly, explaining that he would curse the Puritans' descendants for generations if they harmed her. That assertion assured her banishment, for what member of the court could acknowledge the legitimacy of such a revelation? After she had also been excommunicated from the church, she and her family, along with some faithful followers, were exiled to Rhode Island in 1638. Several years later, after she moved to New Netherland, she and most of her children were killed by Indians.

The authorities in Massachusetts perceived Anne Hutchinson as doubly dangerous to the existing order: she threatened not only religious orthodoxy but also traditional gender roles. Puritans believed in the equality before God of all souls, including those of women, but they considered actual women (as distinct from their spiritual selves) inferior to men. Christians had long followed Saint Paul's dictum that women should keep silent in church and submit to their husbands. Mistress Hutchinson did neither. The magistrates' comments during her trial reveal that they were almost as outraged by her "masculine" behavior as by her religious beliefs. Winthrop charged her with having set wife against husband, because so many of her followers were women. A minister at her church trial told her bluntly, "You have stepped out of your place, you have rather been a Husband than a Wife and a preacher than a Hearer; and a Magistrate than a Subject."

The New England authorities' reaction to Anne Hutchinson reveals the depth of their adherence to European gender-role concepts. To them, an orderly society required the submission of wives to husbands as well as the obedience of subjects to rulers and ordinary folk to gentry. English people intended to change many aspects of their lives by colonizing North America, but not the gendered division of labor, the assumption of male superiority, or the maintenance of social hierarchies.

SUMMARY

By the middle of the seventeenth century, Europeans had come to North America and the Caribbean to stay, a fact that signaled major changes for the peoples of both hemispheres. These newcomers had indelibly altered not only their own lives but also those of native peoples. Europeans killed Indians with their weapons and diseases, and had varying success in converting them to Christianity. Contacts with indigenous peoples taught Europeans to eat new foods, speak new languages, and recognize—however reluctantly—the persistence of other cultural patterns. The prosperity and even survival of many of the European colonies depended heavily on the cultivation of American crops (maize and tobacco) and an Asian crop (sugar), thus attesting to the importance of post-Columbian ecological exchange.

Political rivalries once confined to Europe spread around the globe, as England, Spain, Portugal, France, and the Netherlands vied for control of the peoples and resources of Asia, Africa, and the Americas. In America, Spaniards reaped the benefits of their gold and silver mines, while French people earned their primary profits from the fur trade (in Canada) and cultivating sugar (in the Caribbean). Sugar also enriched the Portuguese. The Dutch concentrated on commerce—trading in furs and sugar as well as carrying human cargoes of enslaved Africans to South America and the Caribbean.

Although the English colonies, too, at first sought to rely on trade, they quickly took another form altogether when so many English people of the "middling sort" decided to migrate to North America. To a greater extent than their European counterparts, the English transferred the society and politics of their homeland to a new environment. Their sheer numbers, coupled with their need for vast quantities of land on which to grow their crops and raise their livestock, inevitably brought them into conflict with their Indian neighbors. New England and the Chesapeake differed in the sex ratio and age range of their immigrant populations, the nature of their developing economies, their settlement patterns, and the impact of religious beliefs. Yet they resembled each other in the internal and external conflicts their expansion engendered. In years to come, both regions would become embroiled in increasingly fierce rivalries besetting the European powers. Those rivalries would continue to affect Americans of all races until after the mid-eighteenth century, when France and England fought the greatest war yet known, and the Anglo-American colonies won their independence.

North America in the Atlantic World 1650–1720

THE GROWTH OF ANGLO-AMERICAN SETTLEMENTS

Between 1642 and 1646 civil war between supporters of King Charles I and the Puritan-dominated Parliament engulfed the colonists' English homeland. Parliament triumphed, leading to the execution of the king in 1649 and interim rule by the parliamentary army's leader, Oliver Cromwell, during the so-called Commonwealth period. But after Cromwell's death, Parliament decided to restore the monarchy if Charles I's son and heir agreed to restrictions on his authority. Charles II did so, and the Stuarts were returned to the throne in 1660 (see Table 3.1). The new king subsequently rewarded nobles and others who had supported him during the Civil War with huge tracts of land on the North American mainland. The colonies thereby established made up six of the thirteen polities that eventually would form the American nation: New York, New Jersey, Pennsylvania (including Delaware), and North and South Carolina. Collectively, these became known as the Restoration colonies because they were created by the restored Stuart monarchy. All were proprietorships; in each of them one man or several men held title to the soil and controlled the government.

CHRONOLOGY

1642–46 • English Civil War

1649 • Charles I executed

1651 • First Navigation Act passed to regulate colonial trade

1660 • Stuarts (Charles II) restored to throne

1663 • Carolina chartered

1664 • English conquer New Netherland
 • New York founded
 • New Jersey established

1670s • Marquette, Jolliet, and La Salle explore the Great Lakes and Mississippi valley for France

1675–76 • Bacon's Rebellion disrupts Virginia government; Jamestown destroyed

1675–78 • King Philip's War devastates New England

1680–1700 • Pueblo revolt temporarily drives Spaniards from New Mexico

1681 • Pennsylvania chartered

1685 • James II becomes king

1686–88 • Dominion of New England established, superseding all charters of colonies from Maine to New Jersey

1688–89 • James II deposed in Glorious Revolution
 • William and Mary ascend throne

1689 • Glorious Revolution in America; Massachusetts, New York, and Maryland overthrow colonial governors

1688–99 • King William's War fought on northern New England frontier

1691 • New Massachusetts charter issued

1692 • Witchcraft crisis in Salem; nineteen people hanged

1696 • Board of Trade and Plantations established to coordinate English colonial administration
 • Vice-admiralty courts established in America

1701 • Iroquois adopt neutrality policy toward France and England

1702–13 • Queen Anne's War fought by French and English

1711–13 • Tuscarora War (North Carolina) leads to capture or migration of most Tuscaroras

1715 • Yamasee War nearly destroys South Carolina

1718 • New Orleans founded in French Louisiana

New York   Charles's younger brother James, the duke of York, benefited quickly. In 1664 Charles II gave James the region between the Connecticut and Delaware Rivers, including the Hudson valley and Long Island. That the Dutch had settled there mattered little; the English and the Dutch were at the time engaged in sporadic warfare, and the English were also attacking other Dutch colonies.

TABLE 3.1 Restored Stuart Monarchs of England, 1660–1714

Monarch	Reign	Relation to Predecessor
Charles II	1660–1685	Son
James II	1685–1688	Brother
Mary	1688–1694	Daughter
William	1688–1702	Son-in-law
Anne	1702–1714	Sister, Sister-in-law

TABLE 3.2 The Founding of English Colonies in North America, 1664–1681

Colony	Founder(s)	Date	Basis of Economy
New York (formerly New Netherland)	James, duke of York	1664	Farming, fur trading
New Jersey	Sir George Carteret, John Lord Berkeley	1664	Farming
North Carolina	Carolina proprietors	1665	Tobacco, forest products
South Carolina	Carolina proprietors	1670	Rice, indigo
Pennsylvania (incl. Delaware)	William Penn	1681	Farming

In August James's warships anchored off Manhattan Island, demanding New Netherland's surrender. The colony complied without resistance. Although in 1672 the Netherlands briefly retook the colony, the Dutch permanently ceded it in 1674.

Thus James acquired a heterogeneous possession, which he renamed New York (see Table 3.2). In 1664 a significant minority of English people (mostly Puritan New Englanders on Long Island) already lived there, along with the Dutch and sizable numbers of Indians, Africans, Germans, Scandinavians, and a smattering of other European peoples. The Dutch West India Company had imported slaves into the colony, intending some for resale in the Chesapeake. Many, though, remained in New Netherland as laborers; at the time of the English conquest, almost one-fifth of Manhattan's approximately fifteen hundred free and enslaved inhabitants were of African descent. Slaves then made up a higher proportion of New York's urban population than of the Chesapeake's rural people.

Recognizing the population's diversity, James's representatives moved cautiously in their efforts to establish English authority. The Duke's Laws, a legal code proclaimed in 1665, applied solely to the English settlements on Long Island, only later being extended to the rest of the colony. James's policies initially maintained Dutch forms of local government, confirmed Dutch land titles, and allowed Dutch residents to maintain customary legal practices. Each town was permitted to decide which church (Dutch Reformed, Congregational, or Church of England) to support with its tax revenues. Much to the dismay of English residents, the Duke's Laws made no provision for a representative assembly. Like other Stuarts, James distrusted legislative bodies, and not

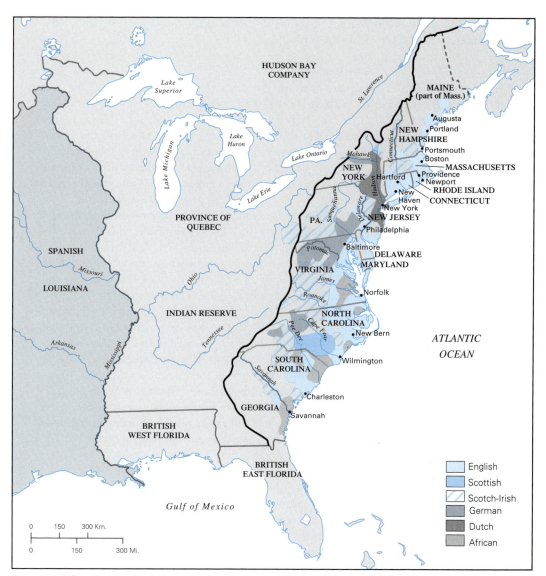

MAP 3.1 The Anglo-American Colonies in the Early Eighteenth Century

By the early eighteenth century, the English colonies nominally dominated the Atlantic coastline of North America. But the colonies' formal boundary lines are deceiving because the western reaches of each colony were still largely unfamiliar to Europeans and because much of the land was still inhabited by Native Americans.

until 1683 did he agree to the colonists' requests for an elected legislature. Before then, an autocratic governor ruled New York.

The English takeover thus had little immediate effect on the colony. Its population grew slowly, barely reaching eighteen thousand by the time of the first English census in 1698. Until the second decade of the eighteenth century, New York City remained a commercial backwater within the orbit of Boston.

New Jersey   The English conquest brought so little change to New York primarily because the duke of York in 1664 regranted the land between the Hudson and Delaware Rivers—East and West Jersey—to his friends Sir George Carteret and John Lord Berkeley. That grant left the duke's own colony hemmed in between Connecticut to the east and the Jerseys to the west and south, depriving it of much fertile land and hindering its economic growth. He also failed to promote migration. Meanwhile, the Jersey proprietors acted rapidly to attract settlers, promising generous land grants, limited freedom of religion, and—without authorization from the Crown—a representative assembly. In response, large numbers of Puritan New Englanders migrated southward to the Jerseys, along with some Barbadians and Dutch New Yorkers. New Jersey grew quickly; in 1726, at the time of its first census as a united colony, it had 32,500 inhabitants, only 8,000 fewer than New York.

Within twenty years, Berkeley and Carteret sold their interests in the Jerseys to separate groups of investors. The purchasers of all of Carteret's share (West Jersey) and portions of Berkeley's (East Jersey) were members of the Society of Friends, also called Quakers. That new, small sect rejected earthly and religious hierarchies. Quakers believed that anyone could be saved by directly receiving God's "inner light" and that all people were equal in God's sight. With no formally trained clergy, Quakers allowed anyone, male or female, to speak in meetings or become a "public Friend" and travel to spread God's word. Quakers proselytized throughout the Atlantic world in the 1650s, recruiting followers in all of England's colonies from a base in Barbados. Yet the authorities did not welcome the message of radical egalitarianism, and Quakers encountered persecution everywhere. Mary Dyer—who had followed Anne Hutchinson into exile—became a Quaker, returned to Boston as a missionary, and was hanged in 1660 (along with several men) for preaching Quaker doctrines.

Pennsylvania   The Quakers obtained their own colony in 1681, when Charles II granted the region between Maryland and New York to his close friend William Penn, a prominent member of the sect. Penn was then thirty-seven years old; he held the colony as a personal proprietorship, one that earned profits for his descendants until the American Revolution. Even so, Penn, like the Roman Catholic Calverts of Maryland before him, saw his province not merely as a source of revenue but also as a haven for persecuted coreligionists. Penn offered land to all comers on liberal terms, promised toleration of all religions (although only Christians were given the vote), guaranteed English liberties, such as the right to bail and trial by jury, and pledged to establish a representative assembly. He also publicized the ready availability of land in Pennsylvania through widely distributed promotional tracts printed in German, French, and Dutch.

Penn's activities and the Quakers' attraction to his lands gave rise to a migration whose magnitude equaled the Puritan exodus to New England in the 1630s. By mid-1683, more than three thousand people—among them Welsh, Irish, Dutch, and Germans—had already moved to Pennsylvania, and within five years the population reached twelve thousand. (By contrast, it had taken Virginia more than thirty years to achieve a comparable population.) Philadelphia, carefully sited on the easily navigable Delaware River and planned to be the major city in the province, drew merchants and artisans from throughout the English-speaking world. From mainland and Caribbean colonies alike came Quakers seeking religious freedom; they brought with them years of experience on American soil and well-established trading connections. Pennsylvania's plentiful and fertile lands soon enabled its residents to begin exporting surplus flour and other foodstuffs to the West Indies. Practically overnight Philadelphia acquired more than two thousand citizens and started to challenge Boston's commercial dominance.

A pacifist with egalitarian principles, Penn attempted to treat native peoples fairly. He learned to speak the language of the Delawares (or Lenapes), from whom he purchased tracts of land to sell to European settlers. Penn also established strict regulations for trade and forbade the sale of alcohol to Indians. His policies attracted native peoples who moved to Pennsylvania near the end of the seventeenth century to escape repeated clashes with English colonists in Maryland, Virginia, and North Carolina. Most important were the Tuscaroras, whose experiences are described later in this chapter. Likewise, Shawnees and Miamis chose to move eastward from the Ohio valley. By a supreme irony, however, the same toleration that attracted Native Americans also brought non-Quaker Europeans who showed little respect for Indian claims to the soil. In effect, Penn's policy was so successful that it caused its own downfall. The Scots-Irish, Germans, and Swiss who settled in Pennsylvania in the first half of the eighteenth century clashed repeatedly over land with Indians who had also recently migrated to the colony.

Carolina

The southernmost proprietary colony, granted by Charles II in 1663, encompassed a huge tract stretching from the southern boundary of Virginia to Spanish Florida. The area had great strategic importance: a successful English settlement there would prevent Spaniards from pushing farther north. The fertile, semitropical land also held forth the promise of producing such exotic and valuable commodities as figs, olives, wines, and silk. The proprietors named their new province Carolina in honor of Charles, whose Latin name was Carolus. The "Fundamental Constitutions of Carolina," which they asked the political philosopher John Locke to draft for them, set forth an elaborate plan for a colony governed by a hierarchy of landholding aristocrats and characterized by a carefully structured distribution of political and economic power.

But Carolina failed to follow the course the proprietors had laid out. Instead, it quickly developed two distinct population centers, which in 1729 split into separate colonies under direct royal rule. Virginia planters settled the Albemarle region that became North Carolina. They established a society much like their own, with an economy based on cultivating tobacco and exporting such forest products as pitch, tar, and timber. Because North Carolina lacked a satisfactory harbor, its planters relied on Virginia's ports and merchants to conduct their trade. The other population center, which eventually formed the core of South Carolina, developed at Charles Town, founded in 1670 near the juncture of the Ashley and Cooper Rivers. Many of its early residents migrated from overcrowded Barbados. These sugar planters expected to reestablish plantation agriculture and hoped to escape hurricanes. They were disappointed in both respects: they soon learned that sugar would not grow successfully in Carolina, and they experienced a "wonderfully horrid and destructive" hurricane in 1686.

The settlers began to raise corn and herds of cattle, which they sold to Caribbean planters hungry for foodstuffs. Like other colonists before them, they also depended on trade with nearby Indians to supply commodities they could sell elsewhere. In Carolina, those items were deerskins (almost as valuable as beaver pelts in Europe) and Indian slaves, which were shipped to the Caribbean and the northern colonies. Nearby Indian nations hunted deer with increasing intensity and readily sold captured enemies to the English settlers. During the first decade of the eighteenth century, South Carolina exported an average of 54,000 skins annually, and overseas shipments later peaked at 160,000 a year. Before 1715, Carolinians additionally exported an estimated 30,000 to 50,000 Indian slaves.

Chesapeake

The English Civil War retarded the development of the earlier English settlements. In the Chesapeake, struggles between supporters of the king and Parliament caused military clashes in Maryland and political upheavals in Virginia. But once the war ended and immigration resumed, the colonies expanded once again. Some settlers, especially those on Virginia's eastern shore and along that colony's southern border, raised grain, livestock, and flax, which they sold to English and Dutch merchants. Tobacco growers began importing increasing numbers of English indentured servants to work on their farms, which had by then begun to develop into plantations. Freed from concerns about Indian attack by the final defeat of the Powhatan Confederacy in 1646, they—especially recent immigrants—eagerly sought to enlarge their landholdings.

Although they still depended primarily on English laborers, Chesapeake tobacco planters also started to acquire small numbers of slaves. Almost all came from a population that historian Ira Berlin has termed "Atlantic creoles"—that is, people (perhaps of mixed race) who came from other European settlements in the Atlantic world, primarily from Iberian outposts. Not all the Atlantic creoles who came to the Chesapeake were bondspeople; some were free or indentured. With their arrival, the Chesapeake became what Berlin calls a "society with slaves," or one in which slavery does not dominate the economy but is one of a number of coexisting labor systems.

New England

In New England, migration essentially ceased after the Civil War began in 1642. While Puritans were first challenging the king and then governing England as a commonwealth, they had little incentive to leave their homeland, and few migrated after the Restoration. Yet the Puritan colonies' population continued to grow dramatically because of natural increase. By the 1670s, New England's population had more than tripled to reach approximately seventy thousand. Such a rapid expansion placed great pressure on available land. Colonial settlement spread far into the interior of Massachusetts and Connecticut, and many members of the third and fourth generations migrated—north to New Hampshire or Maine, south to New York or New Jersey, west beyond the Connecticut River—to find sufficient farmland for themselves and their children. Others abandoned agriculture and learned such skills as blacksmithing or carpentry to support themselves in the growing towns.

The people who remained behind in the small, yet densely populated older New England communities experienced a new phenomenon after approximately 1650: witchcraft accusations and trials. Other regions largely escaped such incidents, even though most seventeenth-century people believed that witches existed. These allies of the Devil were thought to harness invisible spirits for good or evil purposes. For example, a witch might engage in fortunetelling, prepare healing potions or charms, or harm others by causing the death of a child or valuable animals. Yet only New England witnessed many trials of accused witches (about one hundred in all before 1690). Most, though not all, of the accused were middle-aged women who had angered their neighbors. Historians have accordingly concluded that the dynamics of daily interactions in the close-knit communities, where the same families lived nearby for decades, fostered longstanding quarrels that led some colonists to believe that others had diabolically caused certain misfortunes. Even so, only a few of the accused were convicted, and fewer still were executed, because judges and juries remained skeptical of such charges.

Colonial Political Structures   That New England courts halted questionable prosecutions suggests the maturity of colonial institutions. By the last quarter of the seventeenth century, almost all the Anglo-American colonies had well-established political and judicial structures. In New England, property-holding men or the legislature elected the governors; in other regions, the king or the proprietor appointed such leaders. A council, either elected or appointed, advised the governor on matters of policy and served as the upper house of the legislature. Each colony had a judiciary with local justices of the peace, county courts, and, usually, an appeals court composed of the councilors.

Local political institutions also developed. In New England, elected selectmen initially governed the towns, but by the end of the seventeenth century, town meetings—held at least annually and attended by most free adult male residents—handled matters of local concern. In the Chesapeake colonies and both of the Carolinas, appointed magistrates ran local governments. At first the same was true in Pennsylvania, but by the early eighteenth century, elected county officials began to take over some government functions. And in New York, local elections were the rule even before the establishment of the colonial assembly in 1683.

A DECADE OF IMPERIAL CRISES: THE 1670S

As the Restoration colonies were extending the range of English settlement, the first English colonies and French and Spanish settlements in North America faced crises caused primarily by their changing relationships with America's indigenous peoples. Between 1670 and 1680, New France, New Mexico, New England, and Virginia experienced bitter conflicts as their interests collided with those of America's original inhabitants. All the early colonies changed irrevocably as a result.

New France and the Iroquois   In the mid-1670s Louis de Buade de Frontenac, the governor-general of Canada, decided to expand New France's reach into the south and west, hoping to establish a trade route to Mexico and to gain direct control of the valuable fur trade on which the prosperity of the colony rested. Accordingly, he encouraged the explorations of Father Jacques Marquette, Louis Jolliet, and René-Robert Cavelier de La Salle in the Great Lakes and Mississippi valley regions. His goal, however, brought him into conflict with the powerful Iroquois

Contemporary engraving of John Verelst's 1710 portrait of the Mohawk chief known to Hendrick to Europeans (his Indian name was rendered as "Dyionoagon" or "Tee Yee Neen Ho Ga Row"). Hendrick and three other Iroquois leaders visited London in 1710, symbolically cementing the Covenant Chain negotiated in 1677. His primarily European dress and the wampum belt in his hand accentuate his identity as a cross-cultural diplomatic emissary.   (John Carter Brown Library at Brown University)

Confederacy, composed of five Indian nations—the Mohawks, Oneidas, Onondagas, Cayugas, and Senecas. (In 1722 the Tuscaroras became the sixth.)

Under the terms of a unique defensive alliance forged early in the sixteenth century, a representative council made decisions of war and peace for the entire Iroquois Confederacy, although each nation still retained some autonomy and could not be forced to comply with a council directive against its will. Before the arrival of Europeans, the Iroquois waged wars primarily to acquire captives to replenish their population. Contact with foreign traders brought ravaging disease as early as 1633, intensifying the need for captives. Simultaneously, the Europeans' presence created an economic motive for warfare: the desire to dominate the fur trade and to gain unimpeded access to European goods. The war with the Hurons in the 1640s initiated a series of conflicts with other Indians known as the Beaver Wars, in which the Iroquois fought to achieve control of the lucrative peltry trade. Iroquois warriors did not themselves trap beaver; instead, they raided other villages in search of caches of pelts or attacked Indians from the interior as they carried furs to European outposts. Then the Iroquois traded that booty for European-made blankets, knives, guns, alcohol, and other desirable items.

In the mid-1670s, as Iroquois dominance grew, the French intervened, for an Iroquois triumph would have destroyed France's plans to trade directly with western Indians. Over the next twenty years the French launched repeated attacks on Iroquois villages. The English offered little assistance other than weapons to their trading partners, even though in 1677 New Yorkers and the Iroquois established a formal alliance known as the Covenant Chain. Its people and resources depleted by constant warfare, the confederacy in 1701 finally negotiated a neutrality treaty with France and other

MAP 3.2 Louisiana, c. 1720

By 1720 French forts and settlements dotted the Mississippi River and its tributaries in the interior of North America. Two isolated Spanish outposts were situated near the Gulf of Mexico. *(Source: Adapted from* France in America, *by William J. Eccles. Copyright © 1972 by William J. Eccles. Reprinted by permission of HarperCollins Publishers, Inc. The New American Nation Series.)*

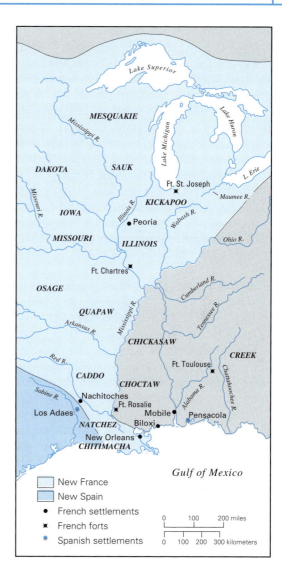

Indians. For the next half-century the Iroquois nations maintained their power through trade and skillful diplomacy rather than warfare, forming or abandoning alliances with Indian or European nations to best achieve their goals.

French Expansion   The wars against the Iroquois initiated in the 1670s were crucial components of French Canada's plan to penetrate the heartland of North America. Unlike Spaniards, French adventurers did not attempt to subjugate the Indians they encountered. Nor, at first, did they even formally claim large territories for France. Still, when France decided to strengthen its presence near the Gulf of Mexico by founding New Orleans in 1718—to counter both westward thrusts of the English colonies and eastward moves of the Spanish—the Mississippi posts became the glue of empire. *Coureurs de bois* (literally, "forest runners") used the rivers and lakes of the American interior to travel regularly between Quebec and Louisiana, carrying French goods to outposts such as Michilimackinac (at the junction of Lakes Michigan and Huron), Kaskaskia (in present-day Illinois), and Fort Rosalie (Natchez), on the lower Mississippi River.

At such sites lived a small military garrison and a priest, surrounded by powerful nations such as the Choctaws, Chickasaws, and Osages. Indians gained easy access to valuable trade goods by tolerating the minimal European presence, and France's primarily political and economic aims did not include systematic missionary work. The largest French settlements in the region, known collectively as *le pays de Illinois* ("the Illinois country"), never totaled much above three thousand in population. Located along the Mississippi south of modern St. Louis and north of Fort Chartres, the settlements produced wheat for export to New Orleans. In all the French outposts, the shortage of European women led to interracial unions between French men and Indian women, and to the creation of mixed-race people known as *metis*.

Pueblo Peoples and Spaniards In New Mexico, too, events of the 1670s led to a crisis with long-term consequences. Over the years under Spanish domination, the Pueblo peoples had added Christianity to their religious beliefs while still retaining traditional rituals, engaging in syncretic practices as had Mesoamericans. But as decades passed, Franciscans adopted increasingly brutal and violent tactics in order to erase all traces of the native religion. Priests and secular colonists who held *encomiendas* also placed heavy labor demands on the population. In 1680 the Pueblos revolted under the leadership of Popé, a respected shaman, successfully driving the Spaniards out of New Mexico. Even though Spain managed to restore its authority by 1700, imperial officials had learned their lesson. Afterward, Spanish governors stressed cooperation with native peoples, no longer attempting to violate their cultural integrity or to enslave them, though still relying on their labor. The Pueblo revolt constituted the most successful and longest-sustained Indian resistance movement in colonial North America.

When Spaniards expanded their territorial claims to the east and north, they followed the same strategy they had adopted in New Mexico, establishing their presence through military outposts (presidios) and Franciscan missions. The army maintained order among the subject Indians—to protect them from attack and ensure the availability of their labor—and guarded the boundaries of New Spain from possible incursions, especially by the French. The friars concentrated on conversions and allowed religious syncretism. By the late eighteenth century, Spain claimed a vast territory that stretched from California (first colonized in 1769 to prevent Russian sea-otter trappers from taking over the region) through Texas (settled after 1700) to the Gulf Coast. Throughout that region, the Spanish presence consisted of a mixture of missions and presidios dotting the countryside, sometimes at considerable distances from one another.

In the more densely settled English colonies, hostilities developed in the decade of the 1670s, not over religion (as in New Mexico) or trade (as in New France), but rather over land. Put simply, the rapidly expanding Anglo-American population wanted more of it. In both New England and Virginia—though for different reasons—settlers began to encroach on territories that until then had remained in the hands of Native Americans.

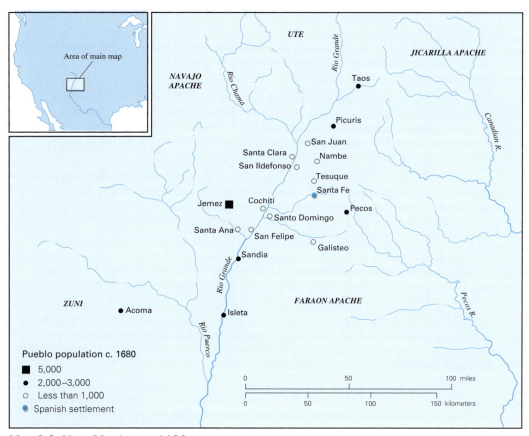

MAP 3.3 New Mexico, c. 1680

In 1680, the lone Spanish settlement at Santa Fe was surrounded and vastly outnumbered by the many Pueblo villages nearby. *(Source: Adapted from* Apache, Navaho, and Spaniard, *by Jack D. Forbes. Copyright © 1960 by the University of Oklahoma Press. Reprinted by permission of the University of Oklahoma Press.)*

King Philip's War   By the early 1670s the growing settlements in southern New England surrounded Wampanoag ancestral lands on Narragansett Bay. The local chief, Metacom, or King Philip, was troubled by the loss of territory and concerned about the impact of European culture and Christianity on his people. Philip led his warriors in attacks on nearby communities in June 1675. Other Algonquian peoples, among them Nipmucks and Narragansetts, soon joined King Philip's forces. In the fall, the Indian nations jointly attacked settlements in the northern Connecticut River valley, and the war spread to Maine, too, when the Abenakis entered the conflict. In early 1676 the Indian allies devastated villages like Lancaster, where they captured Mary Rowlandson and others, and even attacked Plymouth and Providence; later that year, Abenaki assaults forced the abandonment of most settlements in Maine. Altogether, the alliance wholly or partially destroyed twenty-seven of ninety-two towns and attacked forty others, pushing the line of English settlement back toward the east and south.

The tide turned in the south in the summer of 1676. The Indian coalition ran short of food and ammunition, and colonists began to use Christian Indians as guides and scouts. On June 12, the Mohawks—ancient Iroquois enemies of New England Algonquians—devastated a major Wampanoag encampment while most of the warriors were away attacking an English town. After King Philip was killed that August, the southern alliance crumbled. Fighting, though, continued on the Maine frontier for another two years. There the English colonists never defeated the Abenakis; both sides, their resources depleted, simply agreed to end the conflict in 1678.

In addition to the Wampanoags, Nipmucks, Narragansetts, and Abenakis who were captured and sold into slavery, still more died of starvation and disease. New Englanders had broken the power of the southern coastal tribes. Thereafter the southern Indians lived in small clusters, subordinated to the colonists and often working as servants or sailors. Only on the island of Martha's Vineyard did Christian Wampanoags preserve their cultural identity intact.

But the settlers paid a terrible price for their victory in King Philip's War: an estimated one-tenth of the able-bodied adult male population was killed or wounded. Proportional to population, it was the most costly conflict in American history. New Englanders did not fully rebuild abandoned interior towns for another three decades, and not until the American Revolution did the region's per capita income again reach pre-1675 levels.

Bacon's Rebellion   Not coincidentally, conflict simultaneously wracked Virginia. In the early 1670s, ex-servants unable to acquire land avidly eyed the territory reserved by treaty for Virginia's Indians. Governor William Berkeley, the leader of an entrenched coterie of large landowners, resisted starting a war to further the aims of settlers who were challenging his authority. Dissatisfied colonists then rallied behind the leadership of a recent immigrant, the gentleman Nathaniel Bacon, who like other new arrivals had found that all the desirable land in settled areas had already been claimed. Using as a pretext the July 1675 killing of an indentured servant by some Doeg Indians, settlers attacked not only the Doegs but also the Susquehannocks, a more powerful nation. In retaliation, Susquehannock bands raided outlying farms early in 1676.

Berkeley and Bacon soon clashed. The governor outlawed Bacon and his men; the rebels held Berkeley hostage until they won authorization to attack the Indians. As the chaotic summer of 1676 wore on, Bacon alternately pursued Indians and battled the governor. In September Bacon's forces attacked Jamestown itself, burning the capital to the ground. But when Bacon died of dysentery the following month, the rebellion began to collapse. Even so, the rebels had made their point, and a new treaty signed in 1677 opened much of the disputed territory to settlement. The end of Bacon's Rebellion thus pushed most of Virginia's Indians farther west, beyond the Appalachians.

THE ATLANTIC TRADING SYSTEM

In the 1670s and 1680s, the prosperity of the Chesapeake rested on tobacco, and successful tobacco cultivation depended, as it always had, on an ample labor supply. But fewer and fewer English men and women proved willing to indenture themselves for long terms of service in Maryland and Virginia. Population pressures had eased in England, and the founding of the Restoration colonies meant that migrants could choose other American destinations. Furthermore, fluctuating tobacco prices in Europe and the growing scarcity of land made the Chesapeake less appealing to potential settlers. That posed a problem for wealthy Chesapeake tobacco growers. Where could they obtain the workers they needed? They found the answer in the Caribbean sugar islands, where Dutch, French, English, and Spanish planters were accustomed to purchasing African slaves.

Why African Slavery?

Slavery had been practiced in Europe and Islamic lands for centuries. European Christians—both Catholics and Protestants—believed that enslaving heathen peoples, especially those of exotic origin, was justifiable in religious terms. Muslims, too, thought that infidels could be enslaved, and they imported tens of thousands of black African bondspeople into North Africa and the Middle East. Some Christians argued, piously, that holding heathens in bondage would lead to their conversion. Others believed that any heathen taken prisoner in wartime could be enslaved. Consequently, when Portuguese mariners reached the sub-Saharan coast and encountered African societies holding slaves, they purchased bondspeople along with gold and other items. Starting in the 1440s, Portugal imported large numbers of slaves into the Iberian Peninsula; by 1500, enslaved Africans composed about one-tenth of the population of Lisbon and Seville, the chief cities of Portugal and Spain. In 1555 a few of them were taken to England, where—when others followed—residents of London and Bristol in particular became accustomed to seeing black slaves on the streets.

Iberians exported African slavery to their American possessions, New Spain and Brazil. Because the Catholic Church prevented the formal enslavement of Indians in those domains and free laborers saw no reason to work voluntarily in mines or on sugar plantations when they could earn better wages under easier conditions elsewhere, African bondspeople (who had no choice) became mainstays of the Caribbean and Brazilian economies. European planters on all the sugar islands began purchasing slaves—often from the Iberians—soon after they settled in the Caribbean. Accordingly, the first African slaves in the Americas were imported from Angola, Portugal's major early trading partner, and the Portuguese word *Negro* came into use as a common descriptor.

English people had few moral qualms about enslaving other humans. Slavery, after all, was sanctioned in the Bible, and it was widely practiced by their contemporaries. Few at the time questioned the decision to hold Africans and their descendants—or captive Indians from New England or Carolina—in perpetual bondage. Yet their convoluted early attempts to define slave status nevertheless indicate that seventeenth-century English colonists initially lacked clear conceptual categories defining both "race" and "slave." For example, the 1670 Virginia law that first tried to define which people were enslaveable notably failed to employ the racial terminology that would later become commonplace. Instead, awkwardly seeking to single out imported Africans, it declared that "all servants not being christians imported into this colony by shipping shalbe slaves for their lives." Such nonracial phrasing reveals that Anglo-American settlers had not yet fully developed the meaning of *race* and *slave*, and that they did so in tandem over time, through their experience with the institution of slavery itself.

Atlantic Slave Trade The planters of the North American mainland could not have obtained the enslaved workers they wanted had it not been for the rapid development of an Atlantic trading system, the linchpin of which was the traffic in enslaved human beings. Although this elaborate Atlantic economic system has been called the triangular trade, people and products did not move across the ocean in easily diagrammed patterns. Instead, their movements created a complicated web of exchange that inextricably tied the peoples of the Atlantic world together.

The oceanic slave trade was entirely new, though enslavement was not. The expanding network of commerce between Europe and its colonies was fueled by the sale and transport of slaves, the exchange of commodities produced by slave labor, and the need to feed and clothe so many bound laborers. The European economy, previously oriented toward the Mediterranean and Asia, shifted its emphasis to the Atlantic. By the late seventeenth century, commerce in slaves and the products of slave labor constituted the basis of the European economic system. The irony of Columbus's discoveries thus became complete: seeking the wealth of Asia, Columbus instead found the lands that— along with Africa—ultimately replaced Asia as the source of European prosperity.

The various elements of the trade had different relationships to one another and to the wider web of exchange. Chesapeake tobacco and Caribbean and Brazilian sugar were in great demand in Europe, so planters shipped their products directly to their home countries. The profits paid for both the African laborers who grew their crops and European manufactured goods. The African coastal rulers who ran the entrepôts where European slavers acquired their human cargoes received their payment in European manufactures and East Indian textiles; they had little need for most American products. Europeans purchased slaves from Africa for resale in their colonies and acquired sugar and tobacco from America, in exchange dispatching their manufactures everywhere.

European nations fought bitterly to control the lucrative trade. The Portuguese, who at first dominated the trade, were supplanted by the Dutch in the 1630s. In the Anglo-Dutch wars, the Dutch lost out to the English, who controlled the trade through the Royal African Company, a joint-stock company chartered by Charles II in 1672. Holding a monopoly on all English trade with sub-Saharan Africa, the company built and maintained seventeen forts and trading posts, dispatched to West Africa hundreds of ships carrying English manufactured goods, and transported about 100,000 slaves to England's Caribbean colonies. It paid regular dividends averaging 10 percent yearly, and some of its agents made fortunes. Yet even before the company's monopoly expired in 1712, many individual English and North American traders had illegally entered the market for slaves. By the early eighteenth century, such independent traders carried most of the Africans imported into the colonies, earning huge profits from successful voyages.

West Africa and the Slave Trade Most of the enslaved people carried to North America originated in West Africa. Some came from the Rice and Grain Coasts, especially the former, but even more had resided in the Gold and Slave Coasts and the Bight of Biafra (modern Nigeria) and Angola. Certain coastal rulers—for instance, the Adja kings of the Slave Coast—served as intermediaries, allowing the establishment of permanent slave-trading posts in their territories and

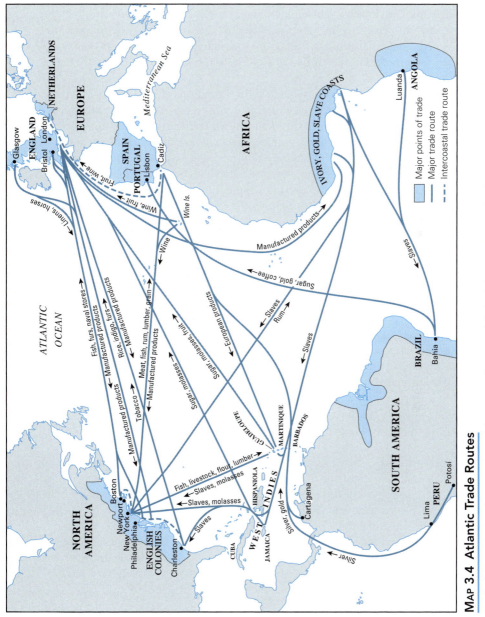

MAP 3.4 Atlantic Trade Routes

By the late seventeenth century, an elaborate trade network linked the countries and colonies bordering the Atlantic Ocean. The most valuable commodities exchanged were enslaved people and the products of slave labor.

supplying resident Europeans with slaves to fill ships that stopped regularly at coastal forts. Such rulers controlled Europeans' access to slaves and simultaneously controlled inland peoples' access to desirable trade goods, such as textiles, iron bars, alcohol, tobacco, guns, and cowry shells from the Maldive Islands (in the Indian Ocean), which were widely used as currency. Through Ouidah, Dahomey's major slave-trading port, passed at least 10 percent of all slaves exported to the Americas, and Ouidah's merchants earned substantial annual profits from the trade. Portugal, England, and France established forts there; Europeans had to pay fees to Ouidah's rulers before they could begin to acquire cargoes.

The slave trade had varying consequences for the nations of West Africa. The trade's centralizing tendencies helped to create such powerful eighteenth-century kingdoms as Dahomey and Asante (formed from the Akan States). Traffic in slaves destroyed smaller polities and disrupted traditional economic patterns, as goods once sent north toward the Mediterranean were redirected to the Atlantic and as local manufactures declined in the face of European competition. Agricultural production intensified, especially in rice-growing areas, because of the need to supply hundreds of slave ships with foodstuffs for transatlantic voyages. Because prisoners of war constituted the bulk of the exported slaves, the most active traders were also the most successful in battle. Some nations even initiated conflicts specifically to acquire valuable captives. For example, the state of Benin sold captive enemies to the Portuguese in the late fifteenth century; did not do so at the height of its power in the sixteenth and seventeenth centuries; and renewed the sale of prisoners in the eighteenth century when its waning power led to conflicts with neighboring states.

The trade therefore affected African regions unevenly. Rulers in parts of Upper Guinea, especially modern Gambia and Senegal, largely resisted involvement with the trade; the few slave vessels that departed from that area were much more likely than others to experience onboard rebellions. Despite planters' preference for male slaves, women predominated in cargoes originating in the Bight of Biafra. In such regions as the Gold Coast, the trade had a significant impact on the sex ratio of the remaining population. There a relative shortage of men increased work demands on women, encouraged polygyny, and opened new opportunities to women and their children.

New England and the Caribbean

New England had the most complex relationship to the trading system. The region produced only one item England wanted: tall trees to serve as masts for sailing vessels. To buy English manufactures, New Englanders therefore needed profits earned elsewhere, especially in the Caribbean. Those islands lacked precisely the items that New England could produce in abundance: cheap food (primarily corn and salt fish) to feed the burgeoning slave population and wood for barrels to hold sugar and molasses. By the late 1640s, decades before the Chesapeake economy became dependent on *production* by slaves, New England's already rested on *consumption* by slaves and their owners. The sale of foodstuffs and wood products to Caribbean sugar planters provided New England farmers and merchants with a major source of income. After the founding of Pennsylvania, New York, and New Jersey, those colonies, too, participated in the lucrative West Indian trade.

Shopkeepers in the interior of New England and the middle colonies bartered with local farmers for grains, livestock, and barrel staves, then traded those items to merchants located in port towns. Such merchants dispatched ships to the Caribbean, where they sailed from island to island, exchanging their cargoes for molasses, sugar, fruit, dyestuffs, and slaves. The system's sole constant was uncertainty, due to the weather, rapid shifts in supply and demand in the small island markets, and the delicate system of credit on which the entire structure depended. Once they had a full load, the ships returned to Boston, Newport, New York, or Philadelphia to dispose of their cargoes (often including a few slaves). Americans began to distill molasses into rum, a crucial aspect of the only part of the trade that could accurately be termed triangular. Rhode Islanders took rum to Africa and traded it for slaves, whom they carried to Caribbean islands to exchange for more molasses to produce still more rum.

Slaving Voyages   Tying the system together was the voyage (commonly called the middle passage) that brought Africans to the Americas, where they cultivated the profitable crops and—in the Caribbean—consumed foods produced in North America. That voyage, always traumatic, could be fatal for the people who composed a ship's cargo. An average of 10 to 20 percent of the newly enslaved died en route; on long or disease-ridden voyages, mortality rates could be much higher. In addition, another 20 percent or so of slaves died either before the ships left Africa or shortly after their arrival in the Americas. Europeans involved in the trade also died at high rates, chiefly through exposure to such diseases as yellow fever and malaria, which were endemic to Africa. To try to minimize such deaths, slaving vessels preferred to arrive on the African coast during the dry season, between November and May. But even so, one in every four or five European slave-ship sailors died on voyages, and just 10 percent of the men sent to run the Royal African Company's forts in Lower Guinea lived to return home to England.

Sailors signed on to slaving voyages reluctantly; indeed, many had to be coerced or tricked, because conditions on shipboard were difficult for the crew as well as the human cargo. Slave merchants were notoriously greedy and captains notoriously brutal—to sailors as well as to the slaves in the hold. Some crew members were themselves slaves or freedmen. Unfortunately, the sailors, often the subject of abuse, in turn frequently abused the bondspeople in their charge. Yet at the same time, through intimate contact with the enslaved, they learned the value of freedom, and sailors became well known throughout the Atlantic world for their fierce attachment to personal independence.

SLAVERY IN NORTH AMERICA AND THE CARIBBEAN

Barbados, America's first "slave society" (an economy wholly dependent on enslavement, as opposed to a "society with slaves"), spawned many others. As the island's population expanded and large planters consolidated their landholdings, about 40 percent of the early English residents dispersed to other colonies. The migrants carried their laws, commercial contacts, and slaveholding practices with them; the Barbados slave code of 1661, for example, served as the model for later codes in Jamaica, Antigua, Virginia, and South Carolina. Moreover, a large proportion of the first Africans imported into North America came via Barbados. In addition to the many Barbadians who settled in Carolina, others moved to the southern regions of Virginia (where they specialized in selling foodstuffs and livestock to their former island home), New Jersey, and New England, where they already had slave-trading partners.

African Enslavement in the Chesapeake

Newly arrived Africans in the Chesapeake tended to be assigned to outlying parts of plantations (called quarters), at least until they learned some English and the routines of American tobacco cultivation. By then, the crop that originated in the Americas was being grown in various locations in West Africa, so Chesapeake planters, who in the late seventeenth century were still experimenting with curing and processing techniques, could well have drawn on their slaves' expertise. Such Africans—the vast majority of them men—lived in quarters composed of ten to fifteen workers housed together in one or two buildings and supervised by an Anglo-American overseer. Each man was expected to cultivate about two acres of tobacco a year. Their lives must have been filled with toil and loneliness, for few spoke the same language, and all were expected to work for their owners six days a week. On Sundays, planters allowed them a day off. Many used that time to cultivate their own gardens or to hunt or fish to supplement their meager diet. Only rarely could they form families, because of the scarcity of women among newly imported Africans.

Slaves usually cost about two and a half times as much as indentured servants, but they repaid the greater investment with a lifetime of service, assuming they survived—which large numbers, weakened by the voyage and sickened by exposure to new diseases, did not. Many planters could not afford to purchase such expensive workers. Those with enough money could acquire slaves, accumulate greater wealth, and establish large plantations worked by tens, if not hundreds, of bondspeople, whereas the less affluent could not even buy indentured servants, whose price rose because of scarcity. As time passed, Anglo-American society in the Chesapeake thus became increasingly more stratified— that is, the gap between rich and poor planters steadily widened. The introduction of large numbers of Africans into the Chesapeake accordingly had a significant impact on the shape of Anglo-American society, in addition to reshaping the population as a whole.

So many Africans were imported into Virginia and Maryland so rapidly that, as early as 1690, those colonies contained more slaves than English indentured servants. By 1710 people of African descent composed one-fifth of the region's population. Even so, and despite sizable continuing imports, a decade later American-born slaves already outnumbered their African-born counterparts in the Chesapeake, and the native-born proportion of the slave population continued to increase thereafter.

African Enslavement in South Carolina

Africans who had lived in the Caribbean came with their masters to South Carolina from Barbados in 1670, composing one-quarter to one-third of the early population. The Barbadian slaveowners quickly discovered that African-born slaves had a variety of skills well suited to the semitropical environment of South Carolina. African-style dugout canoes became the chief means of transportation in the colony, which was crossed by rivers and included large islands just offshore. Fishing nets copied from African models proved more efficient than those of English origin. Baskets that enslaved laborers wove and gourds that they hollowed out came into general use as containers for food and drink. Africans' skill at killing crocodiles equipped

In 1726, William Smith, an employee of the Royal African Company, sketched this musician playing a traditional marimba-like instrument called a balafo. Later in the eighteenth century Virginians described slaves playing the same instrument, thus showing that African music came to North America with the enslaved multitudes. (Joseph Regenstein Library)

them to handle alligators. And, finally, Africans adapted their traditional techniques of cattle herding for use in America. Because meat and hides numbered among the colony's chief exports in its earliest years, Africans contributed significantly to South Carolina's prosperity.

Not until after 1700 did South Carolinians begin to import slaves directly from Africa. Nevertheless, by 1710 African-born slaves already outnumbered those born in the Americas, and they constituted a majority of the enslaved population in South Carolina until about midcentury. By then, too, bondspeople composed a majority of the colony's residents. The similarity of the South Carolinian and West African environments, coupled with the substantial African-born population, ensured the survival of more aspects of West African culture than elsewhere on the North American mainland. Only in South Carolina did enslaved parents continue to give their children African names; only there did a dialect develop that combined English words with African terms. (Known as Gullah, it has survived to the present day in isolated areas.) African skills remained useful, so techniques lost in other regions when the migrant generation died were instead passed down to the migrants' children. And in South Carolina African women became the primary petty traders, dominating the markets of Charles Town as they did those of Guinea.

Rice and Indigo

The importation of large numbers of Africans coincided with the successful introduction of rice in South Carolina. English people knew nothing about the techniques of growing and processing rice, but people from Africa's Rice Coast had spent their lives working with the crop. Although the evidence is circumstantial, the Africans' expertise almost certainly assisted their English masters in cultivating rice profitably. Productive rice-growing techniques known in West Africa, especially cultivation in inland swamps and tidal rivers, both of which involved substantial water-control projects, were widely adopted. South Carolinians preferred to purchase slaves from the Rice Coast, and, unlike Chesapeake and Caribbean planters, they preferred women as well. Those preferences are most likely explained by women's crucial role in cultivating and processing rice in West Africa, where they were responsible for sowing and weeding the crop, as well as for pounding harvested rice with a mortar and pestle to remove the hulls and bran, then winnowing to separate the grains from the chaff. Because English grindstones damaged rice kernels (not until the late eighteenth century were new processes developed), South Carolinians continued to utilize the West African system of pounding rice by hand; planters assigned men as well as women to that task.

Every field worker on rice plantations, which were far larger than Chesapeake tobacco quarters, was expected to cultivate three to four acres of rice a year. Most of those field workers were female, because many enslaved men were assigned to jobs like blacksmithing or carpentry, which were not given to women. To cut expenses, planters also expected slaves to grow part of their own food. A universally adopted "task" system of predefined work assignments provided that, after bondspeople had finished their set tasks for the day, they could then rest or work in their own garden plots or on other projects. Experienced slaves could often complete their tasks by early afternoon; after that, as on Sundays, their masters had no legitimate claim on their time. One scholar has suggested that the unique task system, which gave bondspeople more freedom than gang labor, and which was in place in South Carolina by the early eighteenth century, resulted from negotiations between slaves familiar with rice cultivation and masters who desperately needed their expertise.

Developers of South Carolina's second cash crop also used the task system and drew on slaves' specialized skills. Indigo, the only source of blue dye for the growing English textile industry, was much prized. Eliza Lucas, a young woman managing her father's plantations, began to experiment with indigo cultivation during the early 1740s. Drawing on the knowledge of slaves and overseers from the Caribbean, she developed the planting and processing techniques later adopted throughout the colony. Indigo grew on high ground, and rice was planted in low-lying regions; rice and indigo also had different growing seasons. Thus the two crops complemented each other. South Carolina indigo never matched the quality of that from the Caribbean, but indigo plantations flourished because the crop was so valuable that Parliament offered Carolinians a bounty on every pound exported to Great Britain.

Indian Enslavement in North and South Carolina Among the people held in slavery in both Carolinas were Indian captives who had been retained rather than exported. In 1708 enslaved Indians composed as much as 14 percent of the South Carolina population. The widespread and lucrative traffic in Indian slaves significantly affected South Carolina's relationship with its indigenous neighbors. Native Americans knew they could always find a ready market for captive enemies in Charles Town, so they took that means of ridding themselves of real or potential rivals. Yet native groups soon learned that Carolinians could not be trusted. As settlers and traders shifted their priorities, first one set of former allies, then another, found themselves the enslaved rather than the enslavers.

The trade in Indian slaves began when the Westos (originally known as the Eries), migrated south from the Great Lakes region in the mid-1650s, fleeing their Iroquois enemies after the Beaver Wars. Expert in the use of European firearms, the Westos began raiding Spain's lightly defended Florida missions and selling the resulting Indian captives to Virginians. With the establishment of Carolina, the proprietors took for themselves a monopoly of trade with the Westos, which infuriated local settlers shut out of the profitable commerce in slaves and deerskins. The planters secretly financed attacks on the Westos, essentially wiping them out by 1682. Southeastern Indians reacted to such slave raids—continued by other native peoples after the defeat of the Westos—by trying to protect themselves either through subordination to the English or Spanish, or by coalescing into new, larger political units, such as those known later as Creeks, Chickasaws, or Cherokees.

At first the Carolinians themselves did not engage directly in conflicts with neighboring Indians. But in 1711 the Tuscaroras, an Iroquoian people, attacked a Swiss-German settlement at New Bern, North Carolina, which had expropriated their lands. South Carolinians and their Indian allies then combined to defeat the Tuscaroras in a bloody war. Afterward, more than a thousand Tuscaroras were enslaved, and the remainder drifted northward, where they joined the Iroquois Confederacy but were not allotted a seat on the council, instead being represented by the Oneidas.

Four years later, the Yamasees, who had helped to overcome the Tuscaroras, turned on their onetime English allies. In what seems to have been long-planned retaliation for multiple abuses by traders as well as threats to their own lands, the Yamasees enlisted the Creeks and other Muskogean peoples in coordinated attacks on outlying English settlements. In the spring and summer of 1715, English and African refugees by the hundreds streamed into Charles Town. The Yamasee-Creek offensive was eventually thwarted when reinforcements arrived from the north, colonists hastily armed their African slaves, and Cherokees joined the fight against the Creeks. After the war, Carolinian involvement in the Indian slave trade ceased, because all their native neighbors moved away for self-protection: Creeks migrated west, Yamasees went south, and other groups moved north. The abuses of the Carolina slave trade thus in effect caused its own destruction. And in the war's aftermath the native peoples of the Carolinas were able to regroup and rebuild their strength, for they were no longer subjected to slavers' raids.

Slaves in Spanish and French North America   Few Indians or Africans were enslaved in any of Spain's North American territories, which had no plantations or cash crops. In 1693, as slavery took deeper root in South Carolina, Florida officials offered freedom to fugitives who would convert to Catholicism. Hundreds of South Carolina runaways took advantage of the offer, although not all won their liberty. Many settled in a town founded for them near St. Augustine, Gracia Real de Santa Teresa de Mose, headed by a former slave, Francisco Menéndez.

In early Louisiana, too, slaves—some Indians, some Atlantic creoles—at first composed only a tiny proportion of the residents. But a growing European population demanded that the French government supply them with slaves, and in 1719 officials finally acquiesced, dispatching more than six thousand Africans, mostly from Senegal, over the next decade. The residents failed to develop a successful plantation economy, although they experimented with both tobacco and indigo. They did succeed in angering the Natchez Indians, whose lands they had usurped. In 1729 the Natchez, assisted by newly arrived slaves, attacked northern reaches of the colony, killing more than 10 percent of its European people. The French struck back, slaughtering the Natchez and their enslaved allies, but throughout much of the century Louisiana remained a society with slaves rather than a slave society.

Enslavement in the North

Atlantic creoles from the Caribbean and native peoples from the Carolinas and Florida, along with local Indians sentenced to slavery for crime or debt, constituted the bondspeople in the northern mainland colonies. The intricate involvement of northerners in the web of commerce surrounding the slave trade ensured that many people of African descent lived in America north of Virginia, and that "Spanish Indians" became an identifiable component of the New England population. Some bondspeople resided in urban areas, especially New York, which in 1700 had a larger black population than any other mainland city. Women tended to work as domestic servants, men as unskilled laborers on the docks. At the end of the seventeenth century, three-quarters of wealthy Philadelphia households included one or two slaves.

Yet even in the North most bondspeople worked in the countryside, the majority at agricultural tasks. Dutch farmers in the Hudson Valley and northern New Jersey were especially likely to rely on enslaved Africans, as were the owners of large landholdings in the Narragansett region of Rhode Island. Some bondsmen toiled in new rural enterprises, such as ironworks, working alongside hired laborers and indentured servants at forges and foundries. Although relatively few northern colonists owned slaves, those who did relied extensively on their labor. Therefore, even though slavery overall did not make a substantial contribution to the northern economy, certain individual slaveholders benefited greatly from the institution and had good reason to want to preserve it.

Slave Resistance

As slavery became an integral part of the North American and Caribbean landscapes, so too did slaves' resistance to their masters. Most commonly that resistance took the form of malingering or running away, but occasionally bondspeople planned rebellions. Seven times before 1713 the English Caribbean experienced major revolts involving at least fifty slaves and causing the deaths of both whites and blacks. Twice, in 1675 and 1692, Barbados authorities thwarted plots shortly before they were to be implemented, afterward executing more than sixty convicted conspirators.

The first slave revolt in the mainland colonies took place in New York in 1712, at a time when enslaved people constituted about 15 percent of the population. The rebels, primarily recent arrivals from the Akan States of the Gold Coast, set a fire and then ambushed those who tried to put it out, killing eight and wounding another twelve. Some rebels committed suicide to avoid capture; of those caught and tried, eighteen were executed. Their decapitated bodies were left to rot outdoors as a warning to others.

IMPERIAL REORGANIZATION AND THE WITCHCRAFT CRISIS

English officials seeking new sources of revenue decided to tap into the profits of the expanding Atlantic trading system in slaves and the products of slave labor. Chesapeake tobacco and Caribbean sugar had obvious value, but other colonial products also had considerable potential. Parliament and the Stuart monarchs accordingly drafted laws designed to harness the proceeds of the trade for the primary benefit of the mother country.

Mercantilism and Navigation Acts   Like other European nations, England based its commercial policy on a series of assumptions about the operations of the world's economic system, collectively called mercantilism. The theory viewed the economic world as a collection of national states, whose governments competed for shares of a finite amount of wealth. What one nation gained, another nation lost. Each nation sought to become as economically self-sufficient as possible while maintaining a favorable balance of trade with other countries by exporting more than it imported. Colonies played an important role, supplying the mother country with valuable raw materials to be consumed at home or sent abroad and serving as a market for the mother country's manufactured goods.

Parliament's Navigation Acts—passed between 1651 and 1673—established three main principles that accorded with mercantilist theory. First, only English or colonial merchants and ships could legally trade in the colonies. Second, certain valuable American products could be sold only in the mother country or in other English colonies. At first, these "enumerated" goods included wool, sugar, tobacco, indigo, ginger, and dyes; later acts added rice, naval stores (masts, spars, pitch, tar, and turpentine), copper, and furs to the list. Third, all foreign goods destined for sale in the colonies had to be shipped through England, paying English import duties. Some years later, new laws established a fourth principle: the colonies could not export items (such as wool clothing, hats, or iron) that competed with English products.

These laws adversely affected some colonies, like those in the Chesapeake, because planters there could not seek foreign markets for their staple crops. The statutes initially helped the sugar producers of the English Caribbean by driving Brazilian sugar out of the home market, but later prevented those English planters from selling their sugar elsewhere. In some places, the impact was minimal or even positive. Builders and owners of ships benefited from the monopoly on American trade given to English and colonial merchants; the laws stimulated the creation of a lucrative colonial shipbuilding industry, especially in New England. And the northern and middle colonies produced many unenumerated goods—for example, fish, flour, meat and livestock, and barrel staves. Such products could be traded directly to the French, Spanish, or Dutch Caribbean islands as long as they were carried in English or American ships.

The English authorities soon learned, though, that writing mercantilist legislation was far easier than enforcing it. The many harbors of the American coast provided ready havens for smugglers, and colonial officials often looked the other way when illegally imported goods were offered for sale. In ports like St. Eustatius in the Dutch West Indies, American merchants could easily dispose of enumerated goods and

Exotic Beverages

The seventeenth century colonists developed a taste not only for tea (from China) but also for coffee (from Arabia), chocolate (from Mesoamerica), and rum (distilled from sugar, which also sweetened the bitter taste of the other three). The American and European demand for these once exotic beverages helped reshape the world economy after the mid-seventeenth century. Indeed, one historian has estimated that approximately two-thirds of the people who migrated across the Atlantic before 1776 were involved in one way or another, primarily as slaves, in the production of tobacco, calico, and these four drinks for the world market. The exotic beverages had a profound impact, too, on custom and culture, as they moved swiftly from luxury to necessity.

Each beverage had its own pattern of consumption. Chocolate, brought to Spain from Mexico and enjoyed there for a century before spreading more widely throughout Europe, became the preferred drink of aristocrats, consumed hot at intimate gatherings in palaces and mansions. Coffee, by contrast, became the preeminent morning beverage of English and colonial businessmen, who praised its caffeine for keeping drinkers sober and focused. Coffee was served in new public coffeehouses, patronized only by men, where politics and business were the topics of conversation. The first coffeehouse opened in London in the late 1660s; Boston had several by the 1690s. By the mid-eighteenth century, though, tea had supplanted coffee as the preferred hot, caffeinated beverage in England and America. It was consumed in the

afternoon in private homes at tea tables presided over by women. Tea embodied genteel status and polite conversation. In contrast, rum was the drink of the masses. This inexpensive, potent distilled spirit, made possible by new technology and the increasing production of sugar, was enthusiastically imbibed by free working people everywhere in the Atlantic world.

The American colonies played a vital role in the production, distribution,

The frontispiece of Peter Muguet, *Tractatus De Poto Caphe, Chinesium The et de Chocolata*, 1685. Muguet's treatise visually linked the three hot, exotic beverages recently introduced to Europeans. The drinks are being consumed by representatives of the cultures in which they originated: a turbaned Turk (with coffeepot in the foreground), a Chinese man (with teapot on the table), and an Indian drinking from a hollowed, handled gourd (with a chocolate pot and ladle on the floor in front of him). (Library of Congress)

Exotic Beverages

and consumption of each of these beverages. Chocolate, most obviously, originated in America, and cacao plantations in the South American tropics multiplied in size and number to meet the rising demand. Coffee and tea (particularly the latter) were as avidly consumed in the colonies as in England. And rum involved Americans in every phase of its production and consumption. The sugar grown on French and English Caribbean plantations was transported to the mainland in barrels and ships made from North American wood. There the syrup was turned into rum at 140 distilleries. The Americans themselves drank a substantial share of the distilleries' output—an estimated four gallons per person annually—but exported much of it to Africa. There the rum purchased more slaves to produce more sugar to make still more rum, and the cycle began again.

Thus new tastes and customs connected to four different beverages linked the colonies to the rest of the world and altered their economic and social development.

purchase foreign items on which duty had not been paid. Because American juries had already demonstrated a tendency to favor local smugglers over customs officers (a colonial customs service was instituted in 1671), Parliament in 1696 established several American vice-admiralty courts, which operated without juries and adjudicated violations of the Navigation Acts.

Colonial Autonomy Challenged The Navigation Acts imposed regulations on Americans' international trade, but by the early 1680s mainland governments and their residents had become accustomed to a considerable degree of local governmental autonomy. The tradition of local rule was especially firmly established in New England, where Massachusetts, Plymouth, Connecticut, and Rhode Island operated essentially as independent entities, subject neither to the direct authority of the king nor to a proprietor. Whereas Virginia was a royal colony and New Hampshire (1679) and New York (1685) gained that status, all other mainland settlements were proprietorships, over which the nation exercised little control. Everywhere in the English colonies, free adult men who owned more than a minimum amount of property expected to have an influential voice in their governments, especially in decisions concerning taxation.

After James II became king in 1685, such expectations clashed with those of the monarch. The new king and his successors sought to bring order to the apparently chaotic state of colonial administration by tightening the reins of government and by reducing the colonies' political autonomy. Most significantly, colonial administrators targeted Puritan New England. Reports from America convinced English officials that New England was a hotbed of smuggling. Moreover, Puritans refused to allow freedom of religion to non-Congregationalists and insisted on maintaining laws incompatible with English practice. New England thus seemed an appropriate place to exert English authority with greater vigor. The charters of all the colonies from New Jersey to Maine were revoked, and a Dominion of New England was established in 1686. Sir Edmund Andros, the governor, had immense power: Parliament dissolved all the assemblies, and Andros needed only the consent of an appointed council to make laws and levy taxes.

<table>
<tr><td>

**Glorious
Revolution
in America**

</td><td>

New Englanders endured Andros's autocratic rule for more than two years. Then they learned that James II's hold on power was crumbling. James had angered his subjects by levy-

</td></tr>
</table>

ing taxes without parliamentary approval and by announcing his conversion to Catholicism. In April 1689, Boston's leaders jailed Andros and his associates. The following month they received definite news of the bloodless coup known as the Glorious Revolution, in which James was replaced on the throne in late 1688 by his daughter Mary and her husband, the Dutch prince William of Orange. When Parliament offered the throne to the Protestants William and Mary, the Glorious Revolution affirmed the supremacy of both Parliament and Protestantism.

In other colonies, too, the Glorious Revolution emboldened people for revolt. In Maryland the Protestant Association overturned the government of the Catholic proprietor, and in New York a militia officer of German origin, Jacob Leisler, assumed control of the government. Bostonians, Marylanders, and New Yorkers alike allied themselves with the supporters of William and Mary. They saw themselves as carrying out the colonial phase of the English revolt against Stuart absolutism.

But, like James II, William and Mary believed that England should exercise tighter control over its unruly American possessions. Consequently, only the Maryland rebellion received royal sanction, primarily because of its anti-Catholic thrust. In New York, Leisler was hanged for treason, and Massachusetts (incorporating the formerly independent jurisdiction of Plymouth) became a royal colony with an appointed governor. The province retained its town meeting system of local government and continued to elect its council, but the new 1691 charter eliminated the traditional religious test for voting and office holding. A parish of the Church of England appeared in the heart of Boston. The "city upon a hill," as John Winthrop had envisioned it, had ended.

King William's War   A war with the French and their Algonquian allies compounded New England's difficulties. King Louis XIV of France allied himself with the deposed James II, and England declared war on France in 1689. (In Europe, this conflict was known as the War of the League of Augsburg, but the colonists called it King William's War.) Even before war broke out in Europe, Anglo-Americans and Abenakis clashed over the English settlements in Maine that had been reoccupied after the 1678 truce and were once again expanding. Attacks wholly or partially destroyed a number of towns, including Schenectady, New York, and such Maine communities as Falmouth (now Portland), Salmon Falls (now Berwick), and York. Expeditions organized by the colonies against Montreal and Quebec in 1690 failed miserably, and throughout the rest of the conflict New England found itself on the defensive. Even the Peace of Ryswick (1697), which formally ended the war in Europe, failed to bring much respite from warfare to the northern frontiers. Maine could not be resettled for several decades because of the continuing conflict.

The 1692 Witchcraft Crisis

During the hostilities, New Englanders understandably feared a repetition of the devastation of King Philip's War. For eight months in 1692, witchcraft accusations spread like wildfire through the rural communities of Essex County, Massachusetts—precisely the area most threatened by the Indian attacks in southern Maine and New Hampshire. Earlier incidents in which personal disputes occasionally led to isolated witchcraft charges bore little relationship to the witch fears that convulsed the region in 1692 while the war raged just to the north. Before the crisis ended, 14 women and 5 men were hanged, 1 man was pressed to death with heavy stones, 54 people confessed to being witches, and more than 140 people were jailed, some for many months.

The crisis began in late February when several children and young women in Salem Village (an outlying precinct of the bustling port of Salem) formally charged some older female neighbors with having tortured them in spectral form. Soon other accusers and confessors chimed in, some of them female domestic servants who had been orphaned in the Maine war. One had lost her grandparents in King Philip's War and other relatives in King William's War. These young women, perhaps the most powerless people in a region apparently powerless to affect its fate, offered their fellow New Englanders a compelling explanation for the seemingly endless chain of troubles afflicting them: their province was under direct assault not only by the Indians and their French allies but also by the Devil and his allied witches.

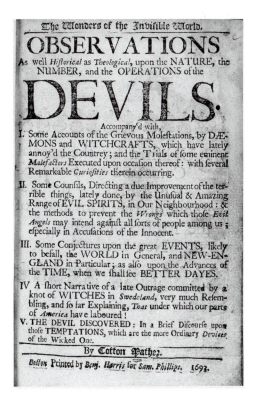

The Reverend Cotton Mather of Boston, twenty-nine years old in 1692 at the time of the Salem witchcraft crisis, rushed this book—The Wonders of the Invisible World—into print shortly after the trials ended. He tried to explain to his fellow New Englanders the "Grievous Molestations by Daemons and Witchcrafts which have lately annoy'd the Countrey" by providing both brief trial narratives and examples of similar recent occurrences elsewhere, most notably in Mohra, Sweden. (Massachusetts Historical Society)

The so-called afflicted girls accused not just the older women commonly suspected of such offenses but also prominent men from the Maine frontier who had traded with or failed to defeat the Indians. The leader of the witch conspiracy, accusers and confessors alike declared, was the Reverend George Burroughs, a Harvard graduate who had ministered in both Maine and Salem Village and was suspected of bewitching the soldiers sent to combat the Abenakis. The colony's magistrates, who were also its political and military leaders, were all too willing to believe such accusations, because, if the Devil had caused New England's current troubles, they personally bore no responsibility for the terrible losses on the frontier.

In October, the worst phase of the crisis ended when the governor dissolved the special court established to try the suspects. He and several prominent clergymen began to regard the descriptions of spectral torturers as "the Devil's testimony"—and everyone knew the Devil could not be trusted. Most critics of the trials did not think the afflicted were faking, nor did they conclude that witches did not exist or that confessions were false. Rather, they questioned whether the guilt of the accused could be legally established by the evidence presented in court. Accordingly, during the final trials (ending in May 1693) in regular courts, almost all the defendants were acquitted, and the governor quickly reprieved the few found guilty.

New Imperial Measures   In 1696 England took a major step in colonial administration by creating the fifteen-member Board of Trade and Plantations, which thereafter served as the chief organ of government concerned with the American colonies. The board gathered information, reviewed Crown appointments in America, scrutinized legislation passed by colonial assemblies, supervised trade policies, and advised successive ministries on colonial issues. Still, the Board of Trade did not have any direct powers of enforcement. It also shared jurisdiction over American affairs not only with the customs service and the navy but also with a member of the ministry. Although this reform improved the quality of colonial administration, supervision of the American provinces remained decentralized and haphazard.

That surely made it easier for Massachusetts and the rest of the English colonies in America to accommodate themselves to the new imperial order. Most colonists resented alien officials who arrived in America determined to implement the policies of king and Parliament, but they adjusted to their demands and to the trade restrictions imposed by the Navigation Acts. They fought another of Europe's wars—the War of the Spanish Succession, called Queen Anne's War in the colonies—from 1702 to 1713, without enduring the stresses of the first, despite the heavy economic burdens the conflict imposed. Colonists who allied themselves with the royal government received patronage in the form of offices and land grants, and composed "court parties" that supported English officials. Others, who were either less fortunate in their friends or more principled in defense of colonial autonomy, made up the opposition, or "country" interest. By the end of the first quarter of the eighteenth century, most men in both groups had been born in America. They were members of elite families whose wealth derived in the South from staple-crop production and in the North from commerce.

SUMMARY

The seventy years from 1650 to 1720 established the basic economic and political patterns that were to structure subsequent changes in mainland colonial society. In 1650 just two isolated centers of English population, New England and the Chesapeake, existed along the seaboard, along with the tiny Dutch colony of New Netherland. In 1720 nearly the entire East Coast of North America was in English hands, and Indian control east of the Appalachian Mountains had largely been broken by the outcomes of King Philip's War, Bacon's Rebellion, the Yamasee and Tuscarora wars, and Queen Anne's War. To the west of the mountains, though, Iroquois power reigned supreme. What had been an immigrant population was now mostly American-born, except for the many African-born people in South Carolina and the Chesapeake; economies originally based on trade in fur and skins had become far more complex and more closely linked with the mother country; and a wide variety of political structures had been reshaped into a more uniform pattern. Yet at the same time the adoption of large-scale slavery in the Chesapeake and the Carolinas differentiated their societies from those of the colonies to the north. The production of tobacco, rice, and indigo for international markets distinguished the southern regional economies. They had become true slave societies, heavily reliant on a system of perpetual servitude, not societies with slaves, in which a few bondspeople mingled with indentured servants and free wage laborers.

Even the economies of the northern colonies, though, rested on profits derived from the Atlantic trading system, the key element of which was traffic in enslaved humans, primarily Africans but also including Indians. New England sold corn, salt fish, and wood products to the West Indies, where slaves consumed the foodstuffs and whence planters shipped sugar and molasses in barrels made from staves crafted by northern farmers. Pennsylvania and New York, too, found in the Caribbean islands a ready market for their livestock, grains, and wheat flour. The rapid growth of enslavement drove all the English colonial economies in these years.

Meanwhile, from a small outpost in Santa Fe, New Mexico, and missions in Florida, the Spanish had expanded their influence throughout the Gulf Coast region and, by just after midcentury, as far north as California. The French had moved from a few settlements along the St. Lawrence to dominate the length of the Mississippi River and the entire Great Lakes region. Both groups of colonists lived near Indian nations and depended on the indigenous people's labor and goodwill. The Spanish could not fully control their Indian allies, and the French did not even try. The extensive Spanish and French presence to the south and west of the English settlements meant that future conflicts among the European powers in North America were nearly inevitable.

By 1720, the essential elements of the imperial administrative structure that would govern the English colonies until 1775 had been put firmly in place. The regional economic systems originating in the late seventeenth and early eighteenth centuries also continued to dominate North American life for another century—until after independence had been won. And Anglo-Americans had developed the commitment to autonomous local government that later would lead them into conflict with Parliament and the king.

4

American Society Transformed

1720–1770

POPULATION GROWTH AND ETHNIC DIVERSITY

Dramatic population growth characterized the British mainland colonies in the eighteenth century. Only about 250,000 European-Americans and African Americans resided in the colonies in 1700. Thirty years later, that number had more than doubled, and by 1775 it had become 2.5 million. Such rapid expansion appears even more remarkable when it is compared with the modest changes that occurred in French and Spanish North America. At the end of the eighteenth century, Texas had only about 2,500 Spanish residents and California even fewer; the largest Spanish colony, New Mexico, included just 20,000 or so. The total European population of the mainland French colonies expanded from approximately 15,000 in 1700 to about 70,000 in the 1760s, but only along the St. Lawrence River between Quebec and Montreal and in New Orleans were there significant concentrations of French settlers.

Although migration accounted for a considerable share of the growth in Anglo America, most of the gain resulted from natural increase. Once the difficult early decades of settlement had passed and the sex ratio evened out in the South (after 1700), the American population doubled approximately every twenty-five years. Such a rate of growth, unparalleled in human history until very recent times, had a variety of causes, chief among them women's youthful age at the onset of childbearing (early twenties for European-Americans, late teens for African Americans). Because married women

CHRONOLOGY

1690 • Locke's *Essay Concerning Human Understanding* published, a key example of Enlightenment thought

1721–22 • Smallpox epidemic in Boston leads to first widespread adoption of inoculation in America

1732 • Founding of Georgia

1733 • John Peter Zenger is tried for and acquitted of "seditious libel" in New York

1739 • Stono Rebellion (South Carolina) leads to increased white fears of slave revolts

• George Whitefield arrives in America; Great Awakening broadens

1739–48 • King George's War disrupts American economy

1740s • Black population of the Chesapeake begins to grow by natural increase, contributing to rise of large plantations

1741 • New York City "conspiracy" reflects whites' continuing fears of slave revolts

1747 • Princeton University founded, joining Harvard, Yale, and other earlier institutions of higher learning

1751 • Franklin's *Experiments and Observations on Electricity* published, important American contribution to the Enlightenment science

1760s • Baptist congregations take root in Virginia

1760–75 • Peak of eighteenth-century European and African migration to English colonies

1765–66 • Hudson River land riots pit tenants and squatters against large landlords

1767–69 • Regulator movement (South Carolina) tries to establish order in backcountry

1771 • North Carolina Regulators defeated by eastern militia at Battle of Alamance

became pregnant every two or three years, women normally bore five to ten children. Because the colonies, especially those north of Virginia, were relatively healthful places to live, a large proportion of children who survived infancy reached maturity and began families of their own. Consequently, about half of the American population was under sixteen years old in 1775. (By contrast, only about one-quarter of the American population was under sixteen in 2005.)

Involuntary Migrants from Africa   More Africans than Europeans came to the Americas, the overwhelming majority of them as slaves. Most went to Brazil or the Caribbean: of at least 11 million enslaved people brought to the Americas during the existence of slavery, only about 260,000 were imported by 1775 into the region that became the United States. The height of the trade occurred in the eighteenth century, when about half of all slaves were carried across the Atlantic, primarily in British or Portuguese vessels. Rice, indigo,

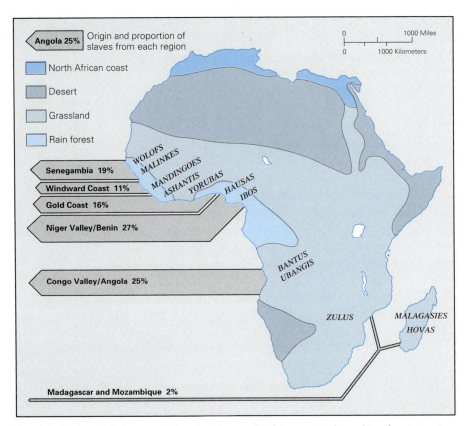

MAP **4.1 Major Origins and Destinations of Africans Enslaved in the Americas**

As this schematic map shows, enslaved Africans were drawn from many regions of western Africa (with some coming from the interior of the continent) and were shipped to areas throughout the Americas. *(Source: Joe W. Trotter, African-American Experience, 1st ed. Used by permission of Houghton Mifflin Company.)*

tobacco, and sugar plantations expanded rapidly, thus steadily increasing the demand for bondspeople. Furthermore, in the slaveholding societies of South America and the Caribbean, a surplus of males over females and appallingly high mortality rates meant that only a large, continuing influx of slaves could maintain the work force at constant levels. On the mainland, only South Carolina, where rice cultivation was difficult and unhealthful (chiefly because malaria-carrying mosquitoes bred in the rice swamps), similarly required an inflow of Africans to sustain as well as expand its labor force.

The involuntary migrants came from many different ethnic groups and regions of Africa. More than 40 percent embarked from West Central Africa (modern Congo and Angola), nearly 20 percent from the Bight of Benin (modern Togo, Benin, and southwestern Nigeria), about 13 percent from the Bight of Biafra (today's Cameroon, Gabon, and southeastern Nigeria), and approximately 9 percent from the Gold Coast (modern Ghana and neighboring countries). Smaller proportions came from East Africa and the Windward and Rice Coasts (modern Senegal, Gambia, and Sierra Leone).

Standard slave-trading practice, in which a vessel loaded an entire cargo at one port and likewise sold them in one place, meant that people from the same area (enemies as well as allies) tended to be taken to the Americas together. That tendency was heightened by planter partiality for slaves of particular ethnic groups. Virginians, for example, purchased primarily Igbos from the Bight of Biafra, whereas South Carolinians and Georgians selected Senegambians and people from West Central Africa. Louisiana planters first chose slaves from the Bight of Benin but later bought many from West Central Africa. Rice planters' desire to purchase Senegambians, who had cultivated rice in their homeland, is easily explained, but historians disagree about the reasons for the other preferences.

Thousands, possibly tens of thousands, of these enslaved Africans were Muslims. Some were literate in Arabic, and several came from aristocratic families. The discovery of noble birth could lead to slaves' being freed to return home. Job Ben Solomon, for example, arrived in Maryland in 1732. Himself a slave trader from Senegal, he had been captured by raiders while selling bondspeople in Gambia. A letter he wrote in Arabic so impressed his owners that he was liberated the next year. Abd al-Rahman, brought to Louisiana in 1788, was less fortunate. Known to his master as "Prince" because of his aristocratic origins, he was not freed until 1829, through the assistance of a European he had befriended in West Africa.

Despite the approximately 260,000 slaves brought to the mainland, American-born people of African descent came to dominate the enslaved population numerically because of high levels of natural increase, especially after 1740. Although about 40 percent of the Africans were male, women and children together composed a majority of slave imports; the girls and women were valued for their reproductive as well as productive capacities. A planter who owned adult female slaves could watch the size of his labor force expand steadily—through the births of their children, designated as slaves in all the colonies—without making additional major purchases of workers. The slaveholder Thomas Jefferson later pointed up the connections when he observed, "I consider a woman who brings a child every two years more profitable than the best man of the farm. What she produces is an addition to the capital, while his labors disappear in mere consumption."

In the Chesapeake, the number of bondspeople grew rapidly because the imports were added to an enslaved population that had begun to sustain itself through natural increase. The work routines involved in cultivating tobacco, coupled with a roughly equal sex ratio, reduced slave mortality and increased fertility. Even in unhealthful South Carolina, where substantial imports continued, American-born slaves outnumbered the African-born as early as 1750.

Newcomers from Europe   In addition to the new Africans, about 500,000 Europeans moved to British North America during the eighteenth century, most of them after 1730. Late in the seventeenth century, English officials decided to recruit German and French Protestants to prevent further large-scale emigration from England itself. Influenced by mercantilist thought, they had come to regard a large, industrious population at home as an asset rather than a liability. Thus they ordered the deportation to the colonies of such "undesirables" as vagabonds and Jacobite rebels (supporters of the deposed Stuart monarchs) but otherwise discouraged emigration. They offered foreign Protestants free lands and religious toleration, even financing the passage of some groups (for example, Germans sent to New York in the 1710s). After 1740 they relaxed citizenship (naturalization) requirements, insisting on only the payment of a small fee, seven years' residence, evidence of adherence to Protestant beliefs, and an oath of allegiance to the king. Such policies created an ethnic diversity in North America found only in Britain's possessions.

The patterns evident in Alexander McAllister's experience applied to better-off European migrants. Early arrivals wrote home, urging others to come; those contacts created chains of migration from particular regions. The most successful migrants came well prepared, having learned from their American correspondents that land and resources were abundant, especially in the inland areas known as the backcountry, but that they would need capital to take full advantage of the new opportunities. People who arrived penniless did less well; approximately 40 percent of the newcomers fell into that category, for they immigrated as bound laborers of some sort.

Worst off of all were the 50,000 or so migrants who came as criminals convicted of such offenses as theft and murder, and sentenced to transportation for two to fourteen years instead of execution. Many unskilled and perhaps one-third female, they were dispatched most often to Maryland, where they were employed in the tobacco fields, or as ironworkers or household servants. Little is known about the ultimate fate of most, but some who committed further crimes in the colonies became notorious on both sides of the Atlantic, thanks to newspaper accounts of their exploits.

Scots-Irish, Scots, and Germans   One of the largest groups of immigrants—over 150,000—came from Ireland or Scotland, largely in family units. About 70,000 Scots-Irish descendants of Presbyterian Scots who had settled in the north of Ireland during the seventeenth century joined some 35,000 people who, like Alexander McAllister, came directly to America from Scotland (see Table 4.1). Another 45,000, both Protestants and Catholics, migrated from southern Ireland (often as individuals). High rents, poor harvests, and religious discrimination (in Ireland) combined to push people from lands their families had long occupied. Many of the Irish migrants had supported themselves in Ireland by weaving linen cloth, but linen prices declined significantly in the late 1710s. Because the flax used for weaving was imported from Pennsylvania and flaxseed was exported to the same place, vessels with plenty of room for passengers regularly sailed from Ireland to Pennsylvania. By the 1720s, the migration route was well established, fueled by positive reports of prospects for advancement in North America.

Such immigrants usually landed in Philadelphia or New Castle, Delaware. They moved into the backcountry of western Pennsylvania along the Susquehanna River, where the colonial government created a county named Donegal for them. Later migrants moved farther west and south, to the backcountry of Maryland, Virginia, and the Carolinas. Frequently unable to afford any acreage, they lived illegally on land belonging to Indians, land speculators, or colonial governments. In the frontier setting, they gained a reputation for lawlessness, hard drinking, and ferocious fighting, both among themselves and with neighboring Indians.

Migrants from Germany and German-speaking areas of Switzerland numbered about 85,000, most of them emigrating from the Rhineland between 1730 and 1755. They, too, usually came in family groups and landed in Philadelphia. Because about half

TABLE 4.1 Who Moved to America from England and Scotland in the Early 1770s, and Why?

	English Emigrants	Scottish Emigrants	Free American Population
Destination			
13 British colonies	81.1%	92.7%	—
Canada	12.1	4.2	—
West Indies	6.8	3.1	—
Age Distribution			
Under 21	26.8	45.3	56.8%
21–25	37.1	19.9	9.7
26–44	33.3	29.5	20.4
45 and over	2.7	5.3	13.1
Sex Distribution			
Male	83.8	59.9	—
Female	16.2	40.1	—
Unknown	4.2	13.5	—
Traveling Alone or with Families			
In families	20.0	48.0	—
Alone	80.0	52.0	—
Known Occupation or Status			
Gentry	2.5	1.2	—
Merchandising	5.2	5.2	—
Agriculture	17.8	24.0	—
Artisanry	54.2	37.7	—
Laborer	20.3	31.9	—
Why They Left			
Positive reasons (e.g., desire to better one's position)	90.0	36.0	—
Negative reasons (e.g., poverty, unemployment)	10.0	64.0	—

Note: Between December 1773 and March 1776, the British government questioned individuals and families leaving ports in Scotland and England for the American colonies to learn who they were, where they were going, and why they were leaving. This table summarizes just a few of the findings of the official inquiries, which revealed a number of significant differences between the Scottish and English emigrants.

Source of data Bernard Bailyn, *Voyagers to the West* (New York: Knopf, 1986), Tables 4.1, 5.2, 5.4, 5.7, 5.23, and 6.1.

In December 1729, probably in New York's Hudson Valley, an unknown artist portrayed J. M. Stolle, son of a Palatine immigrant who came to North America from Germany in 1709. The young man's fancy clothing and the column and balustrade in the background suggest that the artist wanted to convey an image of the family's economic success, though whether that image was accurate is unknown. (National Gallery of Art, Washington, D.C. Gift of Edgar William and Bernice Chrysler Garbisch)

of the migrants were youths when they arrived, late in the century they and their descendants accounted for one-third of Pennsylvania's residents. More important, they—like other ethnic groups—tended to settle together, so they composed up to half of the population of some counties. Many Germans moved west and then south into the backcountry of Maryland and Virginia. Others landed in Charles Town and settled in the southern interior. The Germans belonged to a wide variety of Protestant sects—primarily Lutheran, German Reformed, and Moravian—and therefore added to the already substantial religious diversity of Pennsylvania. So many Germans had arrived by 1751 that Benjamin Franklin, for one, feared they would "Germanize" Pennsylvania. They "will never adopt our Language or Customs," he predicted inaccurately.

The most concentrated period of immigration to the colonies fell between 1760 and 1775. Tough economic times in Germany and the British Isles led many to decide to seek a better life in America; simultaneously, the slave trade burgeoned. In those fifteen years alone, more than 220,000 free and enslaved people arrived—nearly 10 percent of the entire population of British North America in 1775. Late-arriving free immigrants had little choice but to remain in the cities or move to the edges of settlement; land elsewhere was fully occupied. In the peripheries they became the tenants of, or bought property from, land speculators who had purchased giant tracts in the (usually vain) hope of making a fortune.

MAP 4.2 Non-English Ethnic Groups in the British Colonies, c. 1775

Non-African immigrants arriving in the years after 1720 were pushed to the peripheries of settlement, as is shown by these maps. Scottish, Scots-Irish, French, and German newcomers had to move to the frontiers. The Dutch remained where they had originally settled in the seventeenth century. Africans were concentrated in coastal plantation regions.

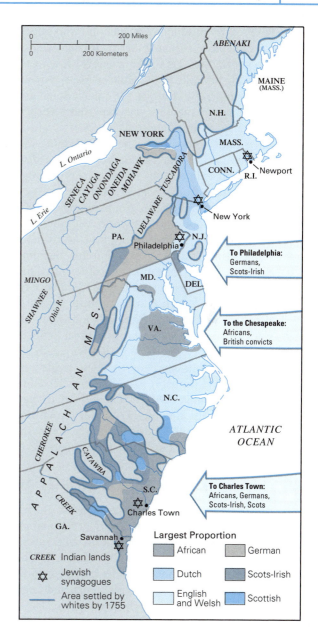

To Philadelphia:
Germans,
Scots-Irish

To the Chesapeake:
Africans,
British convicts

To Charles Town:
Africans, Germans,
Scots-Irish, Scots

Largest Proportion

African	German
Dutch	Scots-Irish
English and Welsh	Scottish

CREEK Indian lands

✡ Jewish synagogues

— Area settled by whites by 1755

Maintaining Ethnic and Religious Identities	Because of these migration patterns and the concentration of slaveholding in the South, half of the colonial population south of New England had non-English origins by 1775. Whether the migrants assimilated readily into Anglo-American culture

depended on patterns of settlement, the size of the group, and the strength of the migrants' ties to their common culture. For example, in the late seventeenth century, the French Protestants (Huguenots) who migrated to Charles Town or New York City were unable to sustain either their language or their religious practices for more than two generations. Yet the Huguenots who created the rural communities of New Paltz and New Rochelle in the Hudson Valley remained recognizably French and Calvinist for a century. By contrast, the equally small group of colonial Jews maintained a distinct identity regardless of where they settled. Most were Sephardic, descended from persecuted Spanish and Portuguese Jews who had first fled to the Netherlands or its American colonies, then later migrated into English territory. In places like New York and Newport, Rhode Island, they established synagogues and worked actively to preserve their religion (for instance, by observing dietary laws and by trying to prevent their children from marrying Christians).

Members of the larger groups of migrants (Germans, Irish, and Scots) found it easier to sustain European ways. Some ethnic groups dominated certain localities. Near Frederick, Maryland, a visitor would have heard more German than English; in Anson and Cumberland Counties, North Carolina, the same visitor might have thought she was in Scotland. Where migrants from different countries settled in the same region, ethnic antagonisms often surfaced. One German clergyman in Pennsylvania, for example, claimed that Scots-Irish migrants were "lazy, dissipated and poor" and that "it is very seldom that German and English blood is happily united in wedlock." Anglo-American elites fostered such antagonisms in order to fracture opposition and maintain their political and economic power, and they frequently subverted the colonies' generous naturalization laws, thus depriving even long-resident immigrants of a voice in government.

The elites probably would have preferred to ignore the English colonies' growing racial and ethnic diversity, but ultimately they could not do so. When they moved toward revolution in the 1770s, they recognized that they needed the support of non-English Americans. Quite deliberately, they began to speak of "the rights of man," rather than "English liberties," when they sought recruits for their cause.

ECONOMIC GROWTH AND DEVELOPMENT

The dramatic increase in the population of Anglo America caused colonial economies to grow, despite the vagaries of international markets. A comparison with French and Spanish America reveals significant differences. The population and economy of New Spain's northern Borderlands stagnated. The isolated settlements produced few items for export (notably, hides obtained from nearby Indians); residents more often exchanged goods illegally with French and English colonies than with Spanish Mexico or the Caribbean. French Canada exported large quantities of furs and fish, but the government's monopoly of trade ensured that most of the profits ended up in the home country instead of the colony. The Louisiana colony required substantial government subsidies to survive, despite its active internal trade and some agricultural exports. Of France's American possessions, only the Caribbean islands flourished economically.

Population and Economic Growth   In British North America, by contrast, each year the rising population generated ever-greater demands for goods and services, leading to the development of small-scale colonial manufacturing and a complex network of internal trade. Roads, bridges, mills, and stores were built to serve the many new settlements. A lively coastal trade developed; by the late

1760s, more than half of the vessels leaving Boston harbor sailed to other mainland colonies. Such ships not only collected goods for export and distributed imports but also sold items made in America. The colonies thus began to move away from their earlier pattern of dependence on European manufactured goods. For the first time, the American population generated sufficient demand to encourage manufacturing enterprises.

Iron making became the largest indigenous industry. Located primarily in New Jersey, Pennsylvania, and the Chesapeake, ironworks required large investments and the coordination of substantial workforces—usually indentured servants, convicts, and slaves—who dug the ore; chopped and hauled trees, then fired them under controlled conditions to make charcoal; and finally used that charcoal to smelt and refine the ore into iron bars for domestic and foreign consumption. The work was dirty, dangerous, and difficult; convicts and servants often tried to run away, but it offered enslaved men new avenues to learn valuable skills and accumulate property, because supervisors compensated them for "overwork" (doing more than their assigned tasks). By 1775 Anglo America's iron production surpassed England's.

Foreign trade nevertheless constituted the major energizing, yet destabilizing, influence on the colonial economy. Colonial prosperity still depended heavily on overseas demand for American products like tobacco, rice, indigo, fish, and timber products. The sale of such items earned the colonists the credit they needed to purchase English and European imports. If demand for American exports slowed, the colonists' income dropped, as did their ability to buy imported goods. Merchants were particularly vulnerable to economic downswings, and bankruptcies were common.

Wealth and Poverty

Despite fluctuations, the American economy slowly grew during the eighteenth century. That growth, which resulted partly from higher earnings from exports, in turn produced better standards of living for all property-owning Americans. Early in the century, as the price of British manufactures fell in relation to Americans' incomes, households began to acquire amenities such as chairs and earthenware dishes. Diet also improved as trading networks brought access to more varied foodstuffs. After 1750, luxury items like silver plate could be found in the homes of the wealthy, and the "middling sort" started to purchase imported English ceramics and teapots. Even the poorest property owners had more and better household goods. The differences lay not so much in *what* items people owned, but rather in the quality and quantity of those possessions.

Yet the benefits of economic growth were unevenly distributed: wealthy Americans improved their position relative to other colonists. The native-born elite families who dominated American political, economic, and social life by 1750 had begun the century with sufficient capital to take advantage of the changes caused by population growth. They were the urban merchants who exported raw materials and imported luxury goods, the large landowners who rented small farms to immigrant tenants, the slave traders who supplied wealthy planters with their bondspeople, and the owners of rum distilleries. The rise of this group of moneyed families helped to make the social and economic structure of mid-eighteenth-century America more stratified than before.

New arrivals did not have the opportunities for advancement that had greeted their predecessors. Even so, few free settlers in rural areas (where about 95 percent of the colonists lived) appear to have been truly poor; at least two-thirds of rural householders owned their own land by 1750. But in the cities, families of urban laborers lived on the edge of destitution, and everywhere landless workers were available for hire. By the 1760s, applicants for assistance overwhelmed public urban poor-relief systems, and some cities began to build workhouses or almshouses to shelter the growing number of poor people. Among them were recent immigrants, the elderly and infirm, and widows, especially those with small children.

Within this overall picture, different regional patterns can be identified. New England; the middle colonies (Pennsylvania, New York, and New Jersey); the Chesapeake (including North Carolina); and the Lower South (South Carolina and Georgia) each had its own economic rhythm derived from the nature of its export trade.

New England and King George's War   In New England, three elements combined to influence economic development: the nature of the landscape, New England's leadership in shipping, and the impact of imperial wars. New England's farms produced little to sell elsewhere, other than livestock and timber; the region also had the lowest average wealth per freeholder in the colonies. But New England had many wealthy merchants who earned substantial sums from trade with the Caribbean in items such as salt fish and molasses.

Boston, by the 1730s a major shipbuilding center, soon felt the impact when warfare between European powers resumed in 1739. British vessels clashed with Spanish ships in the Caribbean, sparking a conflict that became known in America as King George's War (Europeans called it the War of the Austrian Succession). The war initially energized Boston's economy, for ships—and sailors—were in great demand to serve as privateers. Merchants profited from contracts to supply military expeditions. But then New Englanders suffered major losses in Caribbean battles and forays against Canada. In 1745 a New England expedition captured the French fortress of Louisbourg (in modern Nova Scotia), which guarded the sea-lanes leading to New France. The expensive victory, though, led to heavy taxation of Massachusetts residents, and after the war unprecedented numbers of widows and children crowded Boston's relief rolls. The shipbuilding boom ended when the war did, the economy stagnated, and taxes remained high. Britain even returned Louisbourg to France in the Treaty of Aix-la-Chapelle (1748).

Middle Colonies and Chesapeake   King George's War and its aftermath affected the middle colonies and the Chesapeake more positively because prosperous landlords and farmers could readily profit from the wartime demand for grain and flour, especially from the Caribbean. In these colonies the soil was more fertile and growing seasons longer. An average Pennsylvania farm family consumed only 40 percent of what it produced, selling the rest. New York and New Jersey both had many tenant farmers who leased acreage, often paying their rent by sharing crops with their landlords. After the war, when a series of poor harvests in Europe caused flour prices to rise rapidly, Philadelphia and New York, which could draw on extensive grain- and livestock-producing areas, took the lead in the foodstuffs trade.

Increased European demand for grain had a significant impact on the Chesapeake as well. After 1745, when the price of grain began rising faster than that of tobacco, some planters began to convert tobacco fields to wheat and corn. By such diversification, they could avoid dependence on one product for their income. Tobacco remained the largest single export from the mainland colonies, yet the beginnings of conversion to grain cultivation caused a significant change in Chesapeake settlement patterns by encouraging the development of port towns (like Baltimore), where merchants and shipbuilders established businesses to handle the new trade.

Carolina and Georgia The Lower South, too, depended on staple crops and an enslaved labor force but had a distinctive pattern of economic growth. After Parliament in 1730 removed rice from the list of enumerated products, South Carolinians began to trade directly with continental Europe, especially the German states. Rice prices climbed steeply, doubling by the late 1730s. But dependence on European sales had drawbacks, as planters discovered when the outbreak of King George's War disrupted trade with the continent. Rice prices plummeted, and South Carolina entered a decade-long depression. Prosperity returned by the 1760s because of rapidly rising European demand for South Carolina's exports. But throughout the century the colony's rice and indigo crops—and sugar cane in the Caribbean islands—were periodically devastated by hurricanes. After such disasters, some overextended planters went bankrupt. Even so, the Lower South experienced more rapid economic growth than did the other colonial regions. Partly as a result, it had the highest average wealth per freeholder in mainland Anglo America by the time of the American Revolution.

Closely linked to South Carolina geographically, demographically, and economically was the newest settlement on the mainland: Georgia, chartered in 1732 as a haven for English debtors who were released from prison to relocate to the colony. Its founder, James Oglethorpe, envisioned Georgia as a garrison province peopled by sturdy farmers who would defend the southern flank of English settlement against Spanish Florida. Accordingly, its charter prohibited slavery to ensure that all adult men in the colony could be its protectors. But Carolina rice planters won the removal of the restriction in 1751. Thereafter, they essentially invaded Georgia, which—despite remaining politically independent and becoming a royal colony in 1752—developed into a rice-planting slave society resembling South Carolina.

King George's War initially helped New England and hurt the Lower South, but in the long run those effects were reversed. In the Chesapeake and the middle colonies, the war ushered in a long period of prosperity. Such variations highlight the British mainland colonies' disparate experiences within the empire. Despite increasing coastal trade, the colonies' economic fortunes depended not on their neighbors in North America but rather on the shifting markets of Europe and the Caribbean. Had it not been for an unprecedented crisis in the British imperial system (discussed in Chapter 5), it is hard to see how they could have been persuaded to join in a common endeavor. Even with that impetus, they found unity difficult to maintain.

COLONIAL CULTURES

By 1750, the population of Britain's American possessions was not only denser and more diverse than it had been a half-century earlier but also marked by new extremes of wealth and poverty, especially visible in the growing cities. Native-born colonial elites sought to distinguish themselves from ordinary folk in a variety of ways as they consolidated their hold on the local economy and political power.

Genteel Culture One historian has termed these processes "the refinement of America." Colonists who acquired wealth through trade, agriculture, or manufacturing spent their money ostentatiously, dressing fashionably, traveling in horse-drawn carriages driven by uniformed servants, and entertaining one another at lavish parties. Most notably, they built large houses containing rooms designed for such forms of socializing as dancing, cardplaying, or drinking tea. Sufficiently well-off to enjoy "leisure" time (a first for North America), they attended concerts and the theater, gambled at horse races, and played billiards and other games. They also cultivated polite manners, adopting stylized forms of address and paying attention to "proper" ways of behaving. Although the effects of accumulated wealth were most pronounced in Anglo America, elite families in New Mexico, Louisiana, and Quebec as well set themselves off from the "lesser sort." Together these wealthy families deliberately constructed a genteel culture quite different from that of ordinary colonists.

Men from such families prided themselves not only on their possessions and on their positions in the colonial political, social, and economic hierarchy, but also on their level of education and their intellectual connections to Europe. Many had been tutored by private teachers hired by their families; some even attended college in Europe or America. (Harvard, the first colonial college, founded in 1636, was joined by William and Mary in 1693, Yale in 1701, and later by several others—including Princeton in 1747.) In the seventeenth century, only aspiring clergymen attended college, studying a curriculum based on ancient languages and theology. But by the mid-eighteenth century, colleges broadened their curricula to include mathematics, the natural sciences, law, and medicine. Accordingly, a minuscule number of young men from elite or upwardly mobile families enrolled in college to study for careers other than the ministry. American women were mostly excluded from advanced education, with the exception of some who joined nunneries in Canada or Louisiana and could engage in sustained study within convent walls.

The Enlightenment The intellectual current known as the Enlightenment deeply affected the learned clergymen who headed colonial colleges and their students. Around 1650, some European thinkers began to analyze nature in order to determine the laws governing the universe. They employed experimentation and abstract reasoning to discover general principles behind phenomena like the motions of planets and stars, the behavior of falling objects, and the characteristics of light and sound. Above all, Enlightenment philosophers emphasized acquiring knowledge through reason, taking particular delight in challenging previously unquestioned assumptions. John Locke's *Essay Concerning Human Understanding* (1690), for example, disputed the notion that human beings are born already imprinted with innate ideas. All knowledge, Locke asserted, derives from one's observations of the external world. Belief in witchcraft and astrology, among other similar phenomena, thus came under attack.

The Enlightenment had an enormous impact on educated, well-to-do people in Europe and America. It supplied them with a common vocabulary and a unified view of the world, one that insisted that the enlightened eighteenth century was better, and wiser, than all previous ages. It joined them in a common endeavor, the effort to make sense of God's orderly creation. Thus American naturalists like John and William Bartram supplied European scientists with information about New World plants and animals for newly formulated universal classification systems. So, too, Americans interested in astronomy took part in an international effort to learn about the solar system by studying a rare occurrence, the transit of Venus across the face of the sun in 1769. A prime example of America's participation in the Enlightenment was Benjamin Franklin, who retired from a successful printing business in 1748 when he was just forty-two, thereafter devoting himself to scientific experimentation and public service. His *Experiments and Observations on Electricity* (1751) established the terminology and basic theory of electricity still used today.

Enlightenment rationalism affected politics as well as science. Locke's *Two Treatises of Government* (1691) and other works by French and Scottish philosophers challenged previous concepts of a divinely sanctioned, hierarchical political order originating in the power of fathers over families. Men created governments and so could alter them, Locke declared. A ruler who broke the social contract and failed to protect people's rights could legitimately be ousted from power by peaceful—or even violent—means. Government should aim at the good of the people, Enlightenment theorists proclaimed. A proper political order could prevent the rise of tyrants; God's natural laws governed even the power of monarchs.

Oral Cultures

The world in which such ideas were discussed was that of the few, not the many. Most residents of North America were illiterate. Even those who could read—a small proportion in French or Spanish America, about two-thirds of Anglo-Americans—often could not write. Books were scarce until the 1750s, and colonial newspapers did not begin publication until the 1720s or become commonly available for another three decades. Parents, older siblings, or local widows who needed extra income usually taught youngsters to read; several years later, the more fortunate boys (and genteel girls after the 1750s) might learn to write in private schools. Few Americans other than some Church of England missionaries in the South tried to instruct enslaved children. And only the most zealous Indian converts learned Europeans' literacy skills.

Thus the cultures of colonial North America were primarily oral, communal, and—at least through the first half of the eighteenth century—intensely local. Face-to-face conversation served as the major means of communication. Information tended to travel slowly and within relatively confined regions. Different locales developed divergent cultural traditions, and racial and ethnic variations heightened those differences. Public rituals served as the chief means through which the colonists forged their cultural identities.

Religious and Civic Rituals

Attendance at church was perhaps the most important such ritual. In Congregational (Puritan) churches, church leaders assigned seating to reflect standing in the community. In early New England, men and women sat on opposite sides of a central aisle, arranged in ranks according to age, wealth, and whether or not they had formally become church members. By the mid-eighteenth century, wealthy men and their wives sat in privately owned pews; their children, servants, slaves, and the less fortunate still sat in sex-segregated

Smallpox Inoculation

Smallpox, the world's greatest killer of human beings, repeatedly ravaged the population of North America, colonists and Indians alike. Thus, when the vessel *Seahorse* arrived in Boston from the Caribbean in April 1721 with smallpox-infected people on board, New Englanders feared the worst. The authorities ordered the ship and its passengers quarantined, but it was too late: smallpox escaped into the city, and by June several dozen people had caught the dread disease.

Yet there was perhaps some hope. The Reverend Cotton Mather, a member of London's Royal Society (an organization promoting Enlightenment approaches to science), had read in its journal several years earlier two accounts by physicians—one in Constantinople and one in Smyrna—of a medical technique previously unknown to Europeans but widely employed in North Africa and the Middle East. Called inoculation, it involved taking pus from the pustules (or poxes) of an infected person and inserting it into a small cut on the arm of a healthy individual. With luck, that person would experience a mild case of smallpox, thereafter gaining lifetime immunity from the disease. Mather's interest in inoculation was further piqued by his slave Onesimus, a North African who had been inoculated as a youth and who described the procedure in detail to his master.

With the disease coursing through the city, Mather circulated a manuscript among the local medical community, promoting inoculation as a solution to the current epidemic. But nearly all the city's doctors ridiculed his ideas, challenging his sources—and especially denigrating his reliance on information from Onesimus. Mather won only one major convert, Zabdiel Boylston, a physician and apothecary. The two men inoculated their own children and about two hundred others, despite bitter opposition, which included an attempt to bomb Mather's house. Yet after the epidemic ended, Bostonians could clearly see the results: of those inoculated, just 3 percent had died; among the thousands who took the disease "in the natural way," mortality was 15 percent. Even Mather's most vocal opponents were convinced, thereafter supporting inoculation as a

An Historical

ACCOUNT

OF THE

SMALL-POX

INOCULATED

IN

NEW ENGLAND,

Upon all Sorts of Persons, *Whites, Blacks,* and of all Ages and Constitutions.

With some Account of the Nature of the Infection in the NATURAL and INOCULATED Way, and their different Effects on HUMAN BODIES.

With some short DIRECTIONS to the UNEXPERIENCED in this Method of Practice.

Humbly dedicated to her Royal Highness the Princess of WALES, by *Zabdiel Boylston*, Physician.

LONDON:
Printed for S. CHANDLER, *at the* Cross-Keys *in the* Poultry.
M. DCC. XXVI.

Several years after he and Cotton Mather combated a Boston smallpox epidemic by employing inoculation, Zabdiel Boylston published this pamphlet in London to spread the news of their success. The dedication to the Princess of Wales was designed to indicate the royal family's support of the procedure. *(Private Collection)*

Smallpox Inoculation

remedy for the disease. Mather wrote reports for the Royal Society, and following their publication even Britain's royal family was inoculated.

Thus, through transatlantic links forged by the Enlightenment and enslavement, American colonists learned how to combat the deadliest disease of all. Today, thanks to a successful campaign by the World Health Organization, smallpox has been wholly eradicated.

---

fashion at the rear, sides, or balcony of the church. In eighteenth-century Virginia, seating in Church of England parishes also conformed to the local status hierarchy. Planter families purchased their own pews, and in some parishes landed gentlemen customarily strode into church as a group just before the service, deliberately drawing attention to their exalted position. In Quebec City, formal processions of men into the parish church celebrated Catholic feast days; each participant's rank determined his place in the procession. By contrast, Quaker meetinghouses in Pennsylvania and elsewhere used an egalitarian but sex-segregated seating system. The varying rituals surrounding people's entrance into and seating in colonial churches thus symbolized their place in society and the values of the local community.

Communal culture also centered on the civic sphere. In New England, governments proclaimed official days of thanksgiving (for good harvests, military victories, and so forth) and days of fasting and prayer (when the colony was experiencing such difficulties as droughts or epidemics). Everyone was expected to participate in the public rituals held in churches on such occasions. Because all able-bodied men between the ages of sixteen and sixty were required to serve in local militias—the only military forces in the colonies—monthly musters also brought the community together.

In the Chesapeake, important rituals occurred on court and election days. When the county court met, men came to file lawsuits, appear as witnesses, or serve as jurors. Attendance at court functioned as a method of civic education; from watching the proceedings men learned what behavior their neighbors expected of them. Elections served the same purpose, for property-holding men voted in public. An election official, often flanked by the candidates for office, would call each man forward to declare his preference. The voter would then be thanked politely by the gentleman for whom he had cast his oral ballot. Traditionally, the candidates afterward treated their supporters to rum at nearby taverns.

Everywhere in colonial North America, the public punishment of criminals served not just to humiliate the offender but also to remind the community of proper behavioral standards. Public hangings and whippings, along with orders to sit in the stocks, expressed the community's outrage about crimes and restored harmony to its ranks. Judges often assigned penalties that shamed miscreants in especially appropriate ways. In San Antonio, Texas, for example, one cattle thief was sentenced to be led through the town's streets "with the entrails hanging from his neck"; and when a

New Mexico man assaulted his father-in-law, he was directed not merely to pay medical expenses but also to kneel before him and beg his forgiveness publicly. New Englanders reprieved after being convicted of capital offenses did not thereby escape public humiliation: frequently they were ordered to wear a noose around their neck for years, as a constant reminder to themselves, their families, and their neighbors of their heinous violation of community norms.

Rituals of Consumption

By 1770 Anglo-American households on average allocated one-quarter of their spending to purchasing consumer goods, which fostered new rituals centered on consumption. Such purchases established novel links among the various residents of North America, creating what historians have termed "an empire of goods." First came the acquisition of desirable items. In the seventeenth century, settlers acquired necessities by bartering with neighbors or ordering products from a home-country merchant. By the middle of the eighteenth century, specialized shops selling nonessentials had proliferated in cities like Philadelphia and New Orleans. In 1770 Boston alone had more than five hundred stores, which offered consumers a vast selection of millinery, sewing supplies, tobacco, gloves, tableware, and the like. Even small towns had one or two retail establishments. Colonists would set aside time to "go shopping," a novel and pleasurable leisure activity. The purchase of an object—for example, a ceramic bowl, a mirror, or a length of beautiful fabric—initiated the consumption rituals.

Consumers would deploy their purchases in an appropriate manner: hanging the mirror prominently on a wall, displaying the bowl on a table or sideboard, turning the fabric into a special piece of clothing. Colonists took pleasure in owning lovely objects, but they also proudly displayed their acquisitions (and thus their wealth and good taste) publicly to kin and neighbors. A rich man might even hire a artist to paint his family using the objects and wearing the clothing, thereby creating a pictorial record that also would be displayed for admiration.

Tea and Madeira

Tea drinking, a consumption ritual dominated and controlled by women, played an especially important role in Anglo America. Households with aspirations to genteel status sought to acquire the items necessary for the proper consumption of tea: not just pots and cups but also strainers, sugar tongs, bowls, and even special tables. Tea provided a focal point for socializing and, because of its cost, served as a crucial marker of status. Wealthy women regularly entertained their male and female friends at afternoon tea parties. A hot and mildly stimulating drink, tea also appeared healthful. Thus even poor households consumed tea, although they could not afford the fancy equipment used by their better-off neighbors. Some Mohawk Indians adopted the custom, much to the surprise of a traveler from Sweden, who observed them drinking tea in the late 1740s.

Another drink with connotations of gentility was Madeira wine, imported from the Portuguese islands by merchants with extensive transatlantic familial connections. By 1770 Madeira had become the favored drink of the elite, expensive to purchase and consume properly. Opening the bottle, letting it breathe, decanting and serving it with appropriate glassware were all accomplished with elaborate ceremony. Colonial consumers in different regions had varying tastes, to which producers and merchants responded; mainlanders tended to like their Madeira liberally laced with brandy, whereas residents of the Caribbean preferred sweeter and darker wines without added spirits. From the 1750s on, urban dwellers could buy such wines at specialized stores. And much of what they drank must have been smuggled, because more wines were advertised for sale than were recorded in customs records.

Rituals on the "Middle Ground"   Other sorts of rituals allowed the disparate cultures of colonial North America to interact with one another. Particularly important rituals developed on what the historian Richard White has termed the "middle ground"—that is, the psychological and geographical space in which Indians and Europeans encountered each other. Most of those cultural encounters occurred in the context of trade or warfare.

When Europeans sought to trade with Indians, they encountered an indigenous system of exchange that stressed gift giving rather than formalized buying and selling. Successful bargaining required French and English traders to present Indians with gifts (cloth, rum, gunpowder, and other items) before negotiating with them for pelts and skins. Eventually, those gifts would be reciprocated, and formal trading could then take place. To the detriment of Indian societies, rum became a crucial component of these intercultural trading rituals. Traders concluded that drunken Indians would sell their furs more cheaply, and some Indians refused to hunt or trade unless they first received rum. Alcohol abuse hastened the deterioration of villages already devastated by disease and dislocation.

Intercultural rituals also developed to deal with murders. Indians and Europeans both believed that murders required a compensatory act but differed over what that act should be. Europeans sought primarily to identify and punish the murderer. To Indians, such "eye for an eye" revenge was just one of many possible responses to murder. Compensation could also be accomplished by capturing another Indian or a colonist who could take the dead person's place, or by "covering the dead"—that is, by providing the family of the deceased with compensatory goods, a crucial strategy for maintaining peace on the frontiers. Eventually, the French and the Algonquians evolved an elaborate ritual for handling frontier murders which encompassed elements of both societies' traditions: murders were investigated and murderers identified, but by mutual agreement deaths were usually "covered" by trade goods rather than by blood revenge.

COLONIAL FAMILIES

Families (rather than individuals) constituted the basic units of colonial society; never-married adults were extremely rare. People living together as families, commonly under the direction of a marital pair, everywhere constituted the chief mechanisms for both production and consumption. Yet family forms and structures varied widely in the mainland colonies, and not all were headed by couples.

Indian and Mixed-Race Families   As Europeans consolidated their hold on North America, Indians had to adapt to novel circumstances. Bands reduced in numbers by disease and warfare recombined into new units; for example, the Catawbas emerged in the 1730s in the western Carolinas from the coalescence of several earlier peoples, including Yamasees and Guales. Likewise, European secular and religious authorities reshaped Indian family forms. Whereas many Indian societies had permitted easy divorce, European missionaries frowned on such practices; and societies that had allowed polygynous marriages (including New England Algonquians) redefined such relationships, designating one wife as "legitimate" and others as "concubines."

Continued high mortality rates created Indian societies in which extended kin took on new importance, for when parents died, other relatives—even occasionally nonkin—assumed child-rearing responsibilities. Furthermore, once Europeans established dominance in any region, Indians there could no longer pursue traditional modes of subsistence. That led to unusual family structures as well as to a variety of economic strategies. In New England, for instance, Algonquian husbands and wives often could not live together, for adults supported themselves by working separately (perhaps wives as domestic servants, husbands as sailors). Some native women married African American men, unions encouraged by sexual imbalances in both populations. And in New Mexico, detribalized Navajos, Pueblos, and Apaches employed as servants by Spanish settlers clustered in the small towns of the Borderlands. Known collectively as *genizaros,* they lost contact with Indian cultures, instead living on the fringes of Latino society.

Wherever the population contained relatively few European women, sexual liaisons (both inside and outside marriage) occurred between European men and Indian women. The resulting mixed-race population of *mestizos* and *métis* worked as a familial

In eighteenth-century Spain, the existence of mixed-race North American families aroused great curiosity, creating a market for so-called casta *paintings, which illustrated different sorts of multiracial households. In 1763 the Mexican artist Miguel Cabrera depicted a Spanish father and an Indian mother, who have produced a mestiza daughter. Real families resembling this idealized picture would have been seen in New Mexico.   (Private Collection)*

"middle ground" to ease other cultural interactions. In New France and the Anglo-American backcountry, such families frequently resided in Indian villages and were enmeshed in trading networks. Often, children of these unions became prominent leaders of Native American societies. For example, Peter Chartier, son of a Shawnee mother and a French father, led a pro-French Shawnee band in western Pennsylvania in the 1740s. By contrast, in the Spanish Borderlands the offspring of Europeans and *genizaros* were treated as degraded individuals. Largely denied the privilege of legal marriage, they bore generations of "illegitimate" children of various racial mixtures, giving rise in Latino society to a wide range of labels describing degrees of skin color with a precision unknown in English or French America.

European American Families

Eighteenth-century Anglo-Americans used the word *family* to mean all the people who occupied one household (including any resident servants or slaves). The many European migrants to North America had more stable family lives than did Indian and *mestizo* peoples. European men or their widows headed households considerably larger than American families today. In 1790 the average home in the United States contained 5.7 free people; few such households included extended kin, such as grandparents. Family members—bound by ties of blood or servitude—worked together to produce goods for consumption or sale. The head of the household represented it to the outside world, voting in elections, managing the finances, and holding legal authority over the rest of the family—his wife, his children, and his servants or slaves.

In English, French, and Spanish America alike, the vast majority of European families supported themselves through agriculture, by cultivating crops and raising livestock. The scale and nature of the work varied: the production of indigo in Louisiana or tobacco in the Chesapeake required different sorts of labor from subsistence farming in New England or cattle ranching in New Mexico and Texas. Still, just as in the European, African, and Indian societies discussed in Chapter 1, household tasks were allocated by sex. The master, his sons, and his male servants or slaves performed one set of chores; the mistress, her daughters, and her female servants or slaves, a different set.

The mistress took responsibility for what Anglo-Americans called "indoor affairs." She and her female helpers prepared food, cleaned the house, did laundry, and often made clothing. Preparing food involved planting and cultivating a garden, harvesting and preserving vegetables, salting and smoking meat, drying apples and pressing cider, milking cows and making butter and cheese, not to mention cooking and baking. The head of the household and his male helpers, responsible for "outdoor affairs," also had heavy workloads. They planted and cultivated the fields, built fences, chopped wood for the fireplace, harvested and marketed crops, cared for livestock, and butchered cattle and hogs to provide the household with meat. So extensive was the work involved in maintaining a farm household that a married couple could not do it alone. If they had no children to help them, they turned to servants or slaves.

African American Families

Most African American families lived as components of European American households—sometimes on plantations that masters perceived as one large family. More than 95 percent of colonial African Americans were held in perpetual bondage. Although many lived on farms with only one or two other slaves, others had the experience of living and working in a largely black setting. In South Carolina, a majority of the population was of African origin; in Georgia, about half; and in the Chesapeake, 40 percent. Portions of the Carolina low country were nearly 90 percent African American by 1790.

The setting in which African Americans lived determined the shape of their families, yet wherever possible slaves established strong family structures in which youngsters carried relatives' names or—in South Carolina—followed African naming patterns. In the North, the scarcity of other blacks often made it difficult for bondspeople to form stable households. In the Chesapeake, men and women who regarded themselves as married (slaves could not legally wed) frequently lived on different quarters or even on different plantations. Children generally resided with their mother, seeing their father only on Sundays. Simultaneously, the natural increase of the population created wide American-born kinship networks among Chesapeake slaves. On large Carolina and Georgia rice plantations, enslaved couples not only usually lived together with their children but also accumulated property through working for themselves after they had completed their daily "tasks." Some Georgia slaves sold their surplus produce at the market in Savannah, thereby earning money to buy nice clothing or such luxuries as tobacco or jewelry, but rarely enough to purchase their freedom.

| Forms of Resistance | Because all the British colonies legally permitted slavery, bondspeople had few options for escaping servitude other than fleeing to Florida, where the Spanish offered protection. Some recently |

arrived Africans stole boats to try to return home or ran off in groups to frontier regions, to join the Indians or establish independent communities. Among American-born slaves, family ties strongly affected such decisions. South Carolina planters soon learned, as one wrote, that slaves "love their families dearly and none runs away from the other," so many owners sought to keep families together for practical reasons. In the Chesapeake, where family members often lived separately, affectionate ties could cause slaves to run away, especially if a family member had been sold or moved to a distant quarter.

Although colonial slaves rarely rebelled collectively, they often resisted enslavement in other ways. Bondspeople uniformly rejected attempts by their owners to commandeer their labor on Sundays without compensation. Extended-kin groups protested excessive punishment of relatives and sought to live near one another. The links that developed among African American families who had lived on the same plantation for several generations served as insurance against the uncertainties of existence under slavery. If parents and children were separated by sale, other relatives could help with child rearing. Among African Americans, just as among Indians, the extended family thus served a more important function than it did among European-Americans.

Most slave families managed to carve out a small measure of autonomy, especially in their working and spiritual lives, and particularly in the Lower South. Enslaved Muslims often clung to their Islamic faith, a pattern especially evident in Louisiana and Georgia. Some African Americans preserved traditional beliefs, and others converted to Christianity (often retaining some African elements), finding comfort in the assurances of their new religion that all people would be free and equal in heaven. Slaves in South Carolina and Georgia jealously guarded their customary ability to control their own time after completing their "tasks." Even on Chesapeake tobacco plantations, slaves planted their own gardens, trapped, or fished to supplement the minimal diet their masters supplied. Late in the century, some Chesapeake planters with a surplus of laborers began to hire slaves out to others, often allowing the workers to keep a small part of their earnings. Such accumulated property could buy desired goods or serve as a legacy for children.

City Life

Just as African-Americans and European-Americans resided together on plantations, so too they lived side by side in urban neighborhoods. (In 1760s Philadelphia, one-fifth of the work force was enslaved, and by 1775 blacks composed nearly 15 percent of the population of New York City.) Such cities were nothing but medium-sized towns by today's standards. In 1750 the largest, Boston and Philadelphia, had just seventeen thousand and thirteen thousand inhabitants, respectively. Life in the cities nonetheless differed considerably from that on northern farms, southern plantations, or southwestern ranches. City dwellers everywhere purchased food and wood in the markets. Urban residents lived by the clock rather than the sun, and men's jobs frequently took them away from their household. City people also had much more contact with the world beyond their own homes than did their rural counterparts.

By the 1750s, most major cities had at least one weekly newspaper, and some had two or three. Anglo-American newspapers printed the latest "advices from London" (usually two to three months old) and news from other colonies, as well as local reports. Newspapers were available (and often read aloud) at taverns and coffeehouses, so people who could not afford them, even illiterates, could learn the news. Contact with the outside world, however, had its drawbacks. Sailors sometimes brought deadly diseases into port. Boston, New York, Philadelphia, and New Orleans endured terrible epidemics of smallpox and yellow fever, which Europeans and Africans in the countryside largely escaped.

POLITICS: STABILITY AND CRISIS IN BRITISH AMERICA

Early in the eighteenth century, Anglo-American political life exhibited a new stability. Despite substantial migration from overseas, most residents of the mainland had been born in America. Men from genteel families dominated the political structures in each province, for voters (free male property holders) tended to defer to their well-educated "betters" on election days.

Colonial Assemblies

Throughout the Anglo-American colonies, political leaders sought to increase the powers of elected assemblies relative to the powers of the governors and other appointed officials. Assemblies began to claim privileges associated with the British House of Commons, such as the rights to initiate all tax legislation and to control the militia. The assemblies also developed effective ways of influencing British appointees, especially by threatening to withhold their salaries. In some colonies (Virginia and South Carolina, for example), elite members of the assemblies usually presented a united front to royal officials, but in others (such as New York), they fought among themselves long and bitterly. To win hotly contested elections, New York's genteel leaders began to appeal to "the people," competing openly for votes. Yet in 1733 the New York government imprisoned a newspaper editor, John Peter Zenger, who had too vigorously criticized its actions. Defending Zenger against the charge of "seditious libel," his lawyer argued that the truth could not be defamatory, thus helping to establish a free-press principle now found in American law.

Much of the business of colonial assemblies would today be termed administrative; only on rare occasions did they formulate new policies or pass significant laws. Assemblymen saw themselves as acting defensively to prevent encroachments on the colonists' liberties—for example, by preventing governors from imposing oppressive taxes. By midcentury, they were comparing the structure of their governments to Britain's balanced polity, reputedly a combination of monarchy, aristocracy, and democracy of the sort admired since the days of ancient Greece and Rome. Drawing rough analogies, political leaders equated their governors with the monarch, their councils with the aristocracy, and their assemblies with the House of Commons. All three were believed essential to good government, but Anglo-Americans did not regard them with the same degree of approval. They viewed governors and appointed councils as representatives of Britain who posed potential threats to customary colonial ways of life. Many colonists saw the assemblies, however, as the people's protectors. And in turn the assemblies regarded themselves as representatives of the people.

Yet such beliefs should not be equated with modern practice. The assemblies, many controlled by dominant families whose members were reelected year after year, rarely responded to the concerns of their poorer constituents. Although settlements continually expanded, assemblies failed to reapportion themselves, which led to serious grievances among backcountry dwellers, especially those from non-English ethnic groups. The colonial ideal of the assembly as the representative defender of liberty must therefore be distinguished from the colonial reality: the most dearly defended and ably represented were wealthy male colonists, particularly the assembly members themselves.

At midcentury, the political structures that had stabilized in a period of relative calm confronted a series of crises. None affected all the mainland colonies, but no colony escaped wholly untouched. The crises of various descriptions—ethnic, racial, economic, regional—exposed internal tensions building in the pluralistic American society, foreshadowing the greater disorder of the revolutionary era. Most important, they demonstrated that the political accommodations arrived at in the aftermath of the Glorious Revolution were no longer adequate to govern Britain's American empire. Once again, changes appeared necessary, and imminent.

Slave Rebellions in South Carolina and New York   One of the first crises occurred in South Carolina. Early on Sunday, September 9, 1739, about twenty enslaved men, most likely Catholics from Kongo, gathered near the Stono River south of Charles Town. September fell in the midst of the rice harvest (and thus at a time of great pressure for male Africans, less accustomed than women to rice cultivation), and September 8 was, to Catholics, the birthday of the Virgin Mary, venerated in Kongo with special fervor. Seizing guns and ammunition, the slaves killed storekeepers and nearby planter families. Then, joined by other local bondsmen, they headed toward Florida in hopes of finding refuge there. By midday, however, the alarm had been sounded among slaveowners in the district. That afternoon a troop of militia attacked the fugitives, who then numbered about a hundred, killing some and dispersing the rest. More than a week later, most of the remaining conspirators were captured. The colony quickly executed the survivors, but for over two years rumors about escaped renegades haunted the colony.

The Stono Rebellion shocked slaveholding Carolinians as well as residents of other colonies. Throughout British America, laws governing the behavior of African Americans were stiffened. The most striking response came in New York City, the site of the first mainland slave revolt in 1712. There the news from the South, coupled with fears of Spain generated by the outbreak of King George's War, set off a reign of terror in the summer of 1741. Colonial authorities suspected a biracial gang of thieves and arsonists of conspiring to foment a slave uprising under the guidance of a white schoolteacher thought to be a priest in the pay of Spain. By summer's end, thirty-one blacks and four whites had been executed for participating in the alleged plot. The Stono Rebellion and the New York "conspiracy" not only exposed and confirmed Anglo-Americans' deepest fears about the dangers of slaveholding but also revealed the assemblies' inability to prevent serious internal disorder. Events of the next two decades confirmed that pattern.

Rioters and
Regulators

By midcentury most of the fertile land east of the Appalachians had been purchased or occupied. Consequently, conflicts over land titles and conditions of landholding grew in number and

frequency. In 1746, for example, some New Jersey farmers clashed violently with agents of the East Jersey proprietors. The proprietors claimed the farmers' land as theirs and demanded annual payments, called quit-rents, for the use of the property. Similar violence occurred in the 1760s in the region that later became Vermont. There, farmers holding land grants issued by New Hampshire battled with speculators claiming title to the area through grants from New York authorities.

The most serious land riots took place along the Hudson River in 1765–1766. Late in the seventeenth century, the governor of New York had granted huge tracts in the lower Hudson Valley to prominent families. The proprietors in turn divided these estates into small farms, which they rented chiefly to poor Dutch and German migrants who regarded tenancy as a step on the road to independent freeholder status. By the 1750s some proprietors had earned large sums annually from quit-rents and other fees.

After 1740, though, increasing migration from New England and Europe brought conflict to the great New York estates. Newcomers resisted the tenancy system. Many squatted on vacant portions of the manors, rejecting all attempts at eviction. In the mid-1760s the Philipse family sued farmers who had lived on Philipse land for two decades. New York courts upheld the Philipse claim, ordering squatters to make way for tenants with valid leases. Instead of complying, a diverse group of farmers rebelled, terrorizing proprietors and loyal tenants, freeing their friends from jail, and on one occasion battling a county sheriff and his posse. The rebellion lasted nearly a year, ending only when British troops finally captured its leaders.

Violent conflicts of a different sort soon erupted in the Carolinas as well. The Regulator movements of the late 1760s (South Carolina) and early 1770s (North Carolina) pitted backcountry farmers against wealthy eastern planters who controlled the colonial governments. In South Carolina, Scots-Irish settlers protested their lack of an adequate voice in colonial political affairs. For months they policed the countryside in vigilante bands known as Regulators, complaining of lax and biased law enforcement. North Carolina Regulators, who objected primarily to heavy taxation, fought and lost a battle with eastern militiamen at Alamance in 1771. Regional, ethnic, and economic tensions thus combined to create these disturbances, which ultimately arose from frontier people's dissatisfaction with the Carolina governments.

A CRISIS IN RELIGION

The most widespread crisis, though, was religious. From the mid-1730s through the 1760s, waves of religious revivalism—today known collectively as the First Great Awakening—swept over various colonies, primarily New England (1735–1745) and Virginia (1750s–1760s). Orthodox Calvinists sought to combat Enlightenment rationalism, which denied innate human depravity. Simultaneously, the economic and political uncertainty accompanying King George's War made colonists receptive to evangelists' spiritual messages. Moreover, many recent immigrants and residents of the backcountry had no prior religious affiliation, thus presenting evangelists with many potential converts.

The Great Awakening began in New England, where descendants of the Puritan founding generation still composed the membership of Congregational churches. Whether in full or "halfway" communion—the latter, a category established in 1662 to ensure that people who had not experienced saving faith would still be subject to church discipline—such members were predominantly female. From the beginnings of the Awakening, though, men and women responded with equal fervor. In the mid-1730s, the Reverend Jonathan Edwards, a noted preacher and theologian, noticed a remarkable reaction among the youthful members of his church in Northampton, Massachusetts, to a message based squarely on Calvinist principles. Individuals could attain salvation, Edwards contended, only through recognition of their own depraved nature and the need to surrender completely to God's will. Such surrender brought to Congregationalists of both sexes an intensely emotional release from sin, coming to be seen as a single identifiable moment of conversion.

George Whitefield The effects of such conversions remained isolated until 1739, when George Whitefield, a Church of England clergyman already celebrated for leading revivals in England, arrived in America. For fifteen months he toured the British colonies, preaching to large audiences from Georgia to New England and concentrating his efforts in the major cities: Boston, New York, Philadelphia, Charles Town, and Savannah. A gripping orator, Whitefield in effect generated the Great Awakening. The historian Harry Stout has termed him "the first modern celebrity" because of his skillful self-promotion and clever manipulation of both his listeners and the newspapers. Everywhere he traveled, his fame preceded him. Readers snapped up books by and about him, the first colonial bestsellers. Thousands of free and enslaved folk turned out to listen—and to experience conversion. Whitefield's journey, the first such ever undertaken, created new interconnections among the previously distinct colonies.

Regular clerics initially welcomed Whitefield and the American-born itinerant evangelist preachers who quickly imitated him. Soon, however, many clergymen began to realize that, although "revived" religion filled their churches, it ran counter to their own approach to doctrine and matters of faith. They disliked the emotional style of the revivalists, whose itinerancy also disrupted normal patterns of church attendance because it took churchgoers away from the services they usually attended. Particularly troublesome to the orthodox were the dozens of female exhorters who took to streets and pulpits, proclaiming their right (even duty) to expound God's word.

Impact of the Awakening   Opposition to the Awakening heightened rapidly, causing congregations to splinter. "Old Lights"—traditional clerics and their followers—engaged in bitter disputes with the "New Light" evangelicals. Already characterized by numerous sects, American Protestantism fragmented even further as the major denominations split into Old Light and New Light factions and as new evangelical sects—Methodists and Baptists—gained adherents. After 1771 Methodists sent "circuit riders" (preachers on horseback) to the far reaches of settlement, where they achieved widespread success in converting frontier dwellers. Paradoxically, the angry fights and the rapid rise in the number of distinct denominations eventually led to an American willingness to tolerate religious diversity. No single sect could make an unequivocal claim to orthodoxy, so they had to coexist if they were to exist at all.

Most significantly, the Awakening challenged traditional modes of thought, for the revivalists' message directly contested the colonial tradition of deference. Itinerant preachers, only a few of whom were ordained clergymen, claimed they understood the will of God better than did elite college-educated clerics. Moreover, they and their followers divided the world into two groups—the saved and the damned—without respect to gender, age, or status, the previously dominant social categories. The revivalists' emphasis on emotion rather than learning undermined the validity of received wisdom, and New Lights questioned not only religious but also social and political orthodoxy. For example, New Lights began to defend the rights of groups and individuals to dissent from a community consensus, thereby challenging one of the fundamental tenets of colonial political life. The egalitarian themes of the Awakening simultaneously attracted ordinary folk and repelled the elite.

Virginia Baptists   Nowhere was this trend more evident than in Virginia, where tax money supported the established Church of England, and the plantation gentry and their ostentatious lifestyle dominated society. By the 1760s Baptists had gained a secure foothold in Virginia; inevitably, their beliefs and behavior clashed with the way most genteel families lived. They rejected as sinful the horseracing, gambling, and dancing that occupied much of the gentry's leisure time. They dressed plainly, in contrast to the gentry's fashionable opulence. They addressed one another as "Brother" and "Sister" regardless of social status, and they elected the leaders of their congregations—more than ninety of them by 1776. Their monthly "great meetings," which attracted hundreds of people, introduced new public rituals that rivaled the weekly Anglican services.

Strikingly, almost all the Virginia Baptist congregations included both free and enslaved members. At the founding of the Dan River Baptist Church in 1760, for example, eleven of seventy-four members were African Americans, and some congregations had African American majorities. Church rules applied equally to all members; interracial sexual relationships, divorce, and adultery were forbidden to all. In addition, congregations forbade masters' breaking up slave couples through sale. Biracial committees investigated complaints about church members' misbehavior. Churches excommunicated slaves for stealing from their masters, but they also excommunicated masters for physically abusing their slaves. One such slaveowner so dismissed in 1772 experienced a true conversion. Penalized for "burning" one of his slaves, Charles Cook apologized to the congregation and became a preacher in a largely African American church.

By injecting an egalitarian strain into Anglo-American life at midcentury, the Great Awakening had important social and political consequences, calling into question habitual modes of behavior in the secular as well as the religious realm.

SUMMARY

Over the half-century before 1770, British North America was transformed. In part, that change occurred because of the many newcomers from Germany, Scotland, Ireland, and Africa, who brought their languages, customs, and religions with them. The European immigrants settled throughout the English colonies but were concentrated in the growing cities and in the backcountry. By contrast, enslaved migrants from Africa lived and worked primarily within 100 miles of the Atlantic coast. In many areas of the colonial South, 50 to 90 percent of the population was of African origin.

The economic life of Europe's North American colonies proceeded simultaneously on two levels. On the farms, plantations, and ranches on which most colonists resided, the daily, weekly, monthly, and yearly rounds of chores for men, women, and children alike dominated people's lives while providing the goods consumed by households and sold in markets. Simultaneously, an intricate international trade network affected the economies of the British, French, and Spanish colonies. The bitter wars fought by European nations during the eighteenth century inevitably involved the colonists by creating new opportunities for overseas sales or by disrupting their traditional markets. The volatile colonial economy fluctuated for reasons beyond Americans' control. Those fortunate few who—through skill, control of essential resources, or luck—reaped the profits of international commerce made up the wealthy class of merchants and landowners who dominated colonial political, intellectual, and social life. At the other end of the economic scale, poor colonists, especially city dwellers, struggled to make ends meet.

A century and a half after European peoples first settled in North America, the colonies mixed diverse European, American, and African traditions into a novel cultural blend that owed much to Europe but just as much, if not more, to North America itself. Europeans who interacted regularly with peoples of African and American origin—and with Europeans who came from nations other than their own—had to develop new methods of accommodating intercultural differences in addition to creating ties within their own potentially fragmenting communities. Yet at the same time the dominant colonists continued to identify themselves as French, Spanish, or British rather than as Americans. That did not change in Canada, Louisiana, or the Spanish Borderlands, but in the 1760s some Anglo-Americans began to realize that their interests did not necessarily coincide with those of Great Britain or its monarch. For the first time, they offered a direct challenge to British authority.

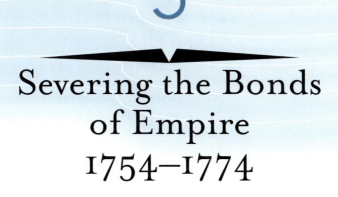

5

Severing the Bonds of Empire
1754–1774

RENEWED WARFARE AMONG EUROPEANS AND INDIANS

In the mid-eighteenth century, the British colonies along the Atlantic seaboard were surrounded by hostile, or potentially hostile, neighbors: Indians everywhere, the Spanish in Florida and along the coast of the Gulf of Mexico, the French along the great inland system of rivers and lakes that stretched from the St. Lawrence to the Mississippi. The Spanish outposts posed little direct threat, for Spain's days as a major power had passed. The French were another matter. Their long chain of forts and settlements dominated the North American interior, facilitating trading partnerships and alliances with the Indians. In none of the three Anglo-French wars fought between 1689 and 1748 was Britain able to shake France's hold on the American frontier. Under the Peace of Utrecht, which ended Queen Anne's War in 1713, the English won control of such peripheral northern areas as Newfoundland, Hudson's Bay, and Acadia (Nova Scotia). But Britain made no territorial gains in King George's War.

Iroquois Neutrality During both Queen Anne's War and King George's War, the Iroquois Confederacy maintained the policy of neutrality that it first developed in 1701. While British and French forces vied for nominal control of the North American continent, the confederacy skillfully manipulated the Europeans,

115

refusing to commit warriors fully to either side despite being showered with gifts by both. The Iroquois continued a long-standing conflict with Cherokees and Catawbas in the South, thus giving their young warriors combat experience and allowing the replacement of population losses by acquiring new captives. They also cultivated peaceful relationships with Pennsylvania and Virginia, in part to obtain the colonists' imprimatur for their domination of the Shawnees and Delawares. And they forged friendly ties with Algonquians of the Great Lakes region, thereby thwarting potential assaults from those allies of the French and simultaneously making themselves indispensable go-betweens for commerce and communication between the Atlantic coast and the West. Thus the Iroquois consolidated their control over the entire American interior north of Virginia and south of the Great Lakes.

But even the Iroquois could not prevent the region inhabited by the Shawnees and Delawares (now western Pennsylvania and Virginia, and eastern Ohio) from providing the spark that set off a major war. In a significant reversal of previous patterns, that conflict spread from America to Europe, decisively resolving the contest for North America.

Trouble began in the 1740s, when at two treaty conferences Iroquois negotiators, claiming to speak for the Delawares and Shawnees, ceded large tracts of land to Pennsylvania officials. Squatters (mainly Scots-Irish and Germans, but also some

TABLE 5.1 The Colonial Wars, 1689–1763

American Name	European Name	Dates	Participants	American Sites	Dispute
King William's War	War of the League of Augsburg	1689–97	England, Holland versus France, Spain	New England, New York, Canada	French power
Queen Anne's War	War of Spanish Succession	1702–13	England, Holland, Austria versus France, Spain	Florida, New England	Throne of Spain
King George's War	War of Austrian Succession	1739–48	England, Holland, Austria versus France, Spain, Prussia	West Indies, New England, Canada	Throne of Austria
French and Indian War	Seven Years War	1756–63	England versus France, Spain	Ohio country, Canada	Possession of Ohio country

CHRONOLOGY

1754 • Albany Congress meets to try to forge colonial unity
 • Fighting breaks out with Washington's defeat at Fort Necessity
1756 • Britain declares war on France; Seven Years War officially begins
1759 • British forces take Quebec
1760 • American phase of war ends with fall of Montreal to British troops
 • George III becomes king
1763 • Treaty of Paris ends Seven Years War
 • Pontiac's allies attack British forts in West
 • Proclamation of 1763 attempts to close land west of Appalachians to English settlement
1764 • Sugar Act lays new duties on molasses, tightens customs regulations
 • Currency Act outlaws paper money issued by the colonies
1765 • Stamp Act requires stamps on all printed materials in colonies
 • Sons of Liberty formed
1766 • Stamp Act repealed
 • Declaratory Act insists that Parliament can tax the colonies
1767 • Townshend Acts lay duties on trade within the empire, send new officials to America
1768 • Fort Stanwix treaty opens Kentucky to Anglo-American settlement
1768–70 • Townshend duties resisted; boycotts and public demonstrations divide merchants and urban artisans
1770 • Lord North becomes prime minister
 • Townshend duties repealed, except for tea tax
 • Boston Massacre kills five colonial rioters
1772 • Boston Committee of Correspondence formed
1773 • Tea Act aids East India Company
 • Boston Tea Party protests the Tea Act
1774 • Coercive Acts punish Boston and Massachusetts as a whole
 • Quebec Act reforms government of Quebec
 • First Continental Congress called

Anglo-Americans) had already moved into parts of the region and had negotiated individual agreements with the Delawares for rights to settle there; some even paid rent to native "landlords." All resided on isolated farms in Delaware territory and coexisted peacefully with their native neighbors. But the agreements reached by agents of the Penn family and the Iroquois ignored both the local Indians and the squatters, all of whom were told to move. Disgruntled Delawares and Shawnees migrated west, where they joined other displaced eastern Indians and nursed their grievances.

The region to which they moved, claimed by both Virginia and Pennsylvania, was coveted by wealthy Virginians, who, organized as the Ohio Company, received a huge land grant in 1749. As a first step, the company's agents established trading posts in the west, with the goal of controlling the crucial area where the Allegheny and Monongahela Rivers join to form the Ohio. But that "Ohio country" was also vital to the French. Because the Ohio River offered direct access by water to French posts on the Mississippi, a permanent British presence in the Ohio country would challenge France's prominence along the western rivers. Thus, in the early 1750s, Pennsylvania fur traders, Ohio Company representatives, the French military, squatters, Iroquois, Delawares, and Shawnees all jostled for position in the region. A 1752 raid by the French and their native allies on a trading outpost sited at modern Cleveland rid the region of Pennsylvanians, but the Virginians posed a more serious challenge. Accordingly, in 1753 the French pushed southward from Lake Erie, building fortified outposts at strategic points.

Albany Congress   In response to the French threat, delegates from seven northern and middle colonies gathered in Albany, New York, in June 1754. With the backing of London officials, they sought two goals: to persuade the Iroquois to abandon their traditional neutrality and to coordinate the defenses of the colonies. They succeeded in neither. The Iroquois listened politely to the colonists' arguments but saw no reason to change a policy that had served them well for half a century. And although the Albany Congress delegates adopted a Plan of Union (which would have established an elected intercolonial legislature with the power to tax), their provincial governments uniformly rejected the plan—primarily because those governments feared a loss of autonomy.

While the Albany Congress delegates deliberated, the war for which they sought to prepare was already beginning. Governor Robert Dinwiddie of Virginia sent a small militia troop to build a palisade at the forks of the Ohio, then later dispatched reinforcements. When a substantial French force arrived at the forks, the first contingent of Virginia militia surrendered, peacefully abandoning the strategic site. The French then began to construct the larger and more elaborate Fort Duquesne. Upon learning of the confrontation, the inexperienced young officer who commanded the Virginia reinforcements pressed onward instead of awaiting further instructions. He attacked a French detachment and then allowed himself to be trapped in his crudely built Fort Necessity at Great Meadows, Pennsylvania. After a day-long battle (on July 3, 1754), during which more than one-third of his men were killed or wounded, twenty-two-year-old George Washington surrendered. He and his men were allowed to return to Virginia.

Seven Years War   Washington's blunder helped ignite a war that eventually would encompass nearly the entire world. In July 1755, a few miles south of Fort Duquesne, a combined force of French and Indians attacked British and colonial troops readying a renewed assault on the fort. In the devastating defeat, General Edward Braddock was killed, and his surviving soldiers were demoralized. The Pennsylvania frontier then bore the brunt of repeated attacks by Delawares for two more years. Settlers felt betrayed because the Indians attacking them—their former neighbors—had once been (an observer noted) "allmost dayly familiars at their houses eat drank cursed and swore together were even intimate play mates."

MAP 5.1 European Settlements and Indians, 1754

By 1754 Europeans had expanded the limits of the English colonies to the eastern slopes of the Appalachian Mountains. Few independent Indian nations still existed in the East, but beyond the mountains they controlled the countryside. Only a few widely scattered English and French forts maintained the Europeans' presence there.

The First Worldwide War

Today we call two twentieth-century conflicts world wars, but the first worldwide war predated them by more than a century. The contest that historians term the "Great War for the Empire" began in spring 1754 in southwestern Pennsylvania, over a seemingly local quarrel—whether Britain or France would build a fort at the forks of the Ohio. That it eventually involved combatants around the world attests not only to the growing importance of European nations' overseas empires but also to the increasing centrality of North America to their struggles for dominance.

Previous wars among Europeans had taken place mostly in Europe, though overseas colonies occasionally got involved. But the contest at the forks of the Ohio helped to reinvigorate a conflict between Austria and Prussia that sent European nations scrambling for allies. Eventually England, Hanover, and Prussia lined up against France, Austria, and Russia, joined by Sweden, Saxony, and, later, Spain. The war in Europe would last seven years. In 1763 these nations signed a peace treaty that returned the continent to the prewar status quo, but elsewhere, in the rest of the world, Britain had decisively vanquished both France and Spain.

"Elsewhere" included a mind-boggling list of battles. In the Caribbean, Britain seized the French islands of Guadeloupe and Martinique, and took Havana from Spain. In North America, the British recaptured the French fortress of Louisbourg and at last conquered Quebec. In Africa, Britain overwhelmed France's slave-trading posts in Senegambia. In India, British forces won control of Bengal by defeating both a local ruler and French soldiers stationed there. Three years later, the British beat a French army at Pondicherry; four months after France lost Canada, its influence in India was also extinguished. At the very end of the war, a British expedition took Manila in the

In 1771 the artist Dominic Serres, the Elder, depicted British naval vessels attacking the French fortress at Chandernagore in India in 1757 (at left in background). Cannon fire from the warships was critical to the British victory, one of the keys to the conquest of India during the Seven Years War.
(National Maritime Museum, London)

The First Worldwide War

Philippines from Spain. The commander did not know that his nation had declared war on Britain, so the assault caught him unawares.

Thus the war that started in the American backcountry revealed the steadily growing links between North America and the rest of the world. And the aftermath exposed an unexpected additional link. Both winners and losers had to pay for this first worldwide war. Financial struggles in Britain and France, though separate, ultimately produced similar outcomes: revolutions abroad (for Britain, in America) and at home (for France).

After news of the debacle reached London, Britain declared war on France in 1756, thus formally beginning the Seven Years War. Even before then, Britain, poised for renewed conflict with old enemies, took a fateful step. Britons and New Englanders feared that France would try to retake Nova Scotia, where most of the population was descended from seventeenth-century French settlers who had intermarried with local Mikmaqs. Afraid that in the event of an attack the approximately twelve thousand French Nova Scotians would abandon the policy of neutrality they had followed since the early years of the century, British commanders in 1755 forced about seven thousand of them from their homeland—the first large-scale modern deportation, now called ethnic cleansing. Ships crammed with Acadians sailed to each of the mainland colonies, where the exiles encountered hostility and discrimination as they were dispersed into widely scattered communities. Many families were separated, some forever. After 1763 the survivors relocated: some returned to Canada, others traveled to France or its Caribbean islands, and many eventually settled in Louisiana, where they became known as Cajuns (derived from *Acadian*).

For three years, one disaster followed another. British officers tried without much success to coerce the colonies into supplying men and materiel to the army. Then, led by William Pitt, the civilian official placed in charge of the war effort in 1757, Britain finally pursued a successful military strategy. Pitt agreed to reimburse the colonies for their wartime expenditures and placed recruitment in local hands, thereby gaining greater American support for the war. Large numbers of colonial militiamen served alongside equally large numbers of red-coated regulars sent to North America from Britain; the two groups nevertheless had an antagonistic relationship, lacking mutual respect.

In July 1758, British forces recaptured the fortress at Louisbourg, winning control of the entrance to the St. Lawrence River and cutting the major French supply route. In the fall, the Delawares and Shawnees accepted British peace overtures, and the French abandoned Fort Duquesne. Then, in a stunning attack in September 1759, General James Wolfe's regulars defeated the French on the Plains of Abraham and took Quebec. Sensing a British victory, the Iroquois abandoned their traditional neutrality, hoping to gain a postwar advantage by allying themselves with Britain. A year later, the British captured Montreal, the last French stronghold on the continent, and the American phase of the war ended.

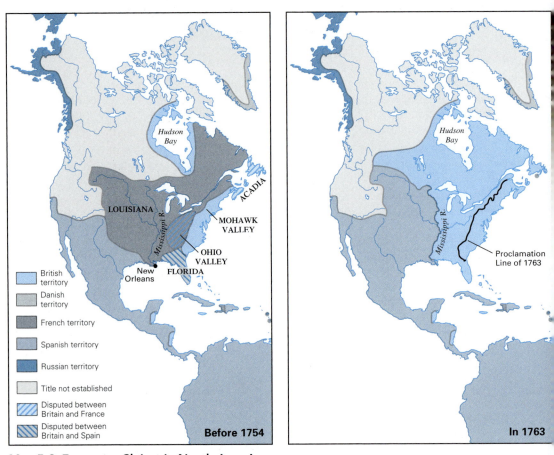

MAP 5.2 European Claims in North America

The dramatic results of the British victory in the Seven Years (French and Indian) War are vividly demonstrated in these maps, which depict the abandonment of French claims to the mainland after the Treaty of Paris in 1763.

In the Treaty of Paris (1763), France ceded its major North American holdings to Britain. Spain, an ally of France toward the end of the war, gave Florida to the victors. France, meanwhile, ceded Louisiana west of the Mississippi to Spain, in partial compensation for its ally's losses elsewhere. The British thus gained control of the continent's fur trade. No longer would the English seacoast colonies have to worry about the threat to their existence posed by France's extensive North American territories.

The overwhelming British triumph stimulated some Americans to think expansively. Men like Benjamin Franklin, who had long touted the colonies' wealth and potential, predicted a glorious new future for British North America—a future that included not just geographical expansion but also economic development and population growth. Such men were to lead the resistance to British measures in the years after 1763. They uniformly opposed any laws that would retard America's growth and persistently supported steps to increase Americans' control over their own destiny. Many of them also speculated in western lands.

1763: A TURNING POINT

The great victory over France had an irreversible impact on North America, felt first by the indigenous peoples of the interior. With France excluded from the continent altogether and Spanish territory now confined to west of the Mississippi, the diplomatic strategy of playing Europeans off against one another, which the Indians had long adopted, became obsolete. The consequences were immediate and devastating.

Even before the Treaty of Paris, southern Indians had to adjust to new circumstances. After Britain gained the upper hand in the American war in 1758, Creeks and Cherokees lost their ability to force concessions by threatening to turn instead to France or Spain. In desperation, and in retaliation for British atrocities, Cherokees attacked the Carolina and Virginia frontiers in 1760. Though initially victorious, the Indians were defeated the following year by a force of British regulars and colonial militia. Late in 1761 the two sides concluded a treaty under which the Cherokees allowed the construction of British forts in their territories and opened a large tract to European settlement.

Neolin and Pontiac The fate of the Cherokees in the South portended events in the Ohio country. There, the Ottawas, Chippewas, and Potawatomis reacted angrily when Great Britain, no longer facing French competition, raised the price of trade goods and ended traditional gift-giving practices. Settlers rapidly moved into the Monongahela and Susquehanna valleys. A shaman named Neolin (also known as the Delaware Prophet) urged Indians to oppose the incursion on their lands and European influence on their culture. For the first time since King Philip in 1675, an influential native leader called for the unity of all tribes in the face of an Anglo-American threat. Contending that Indian peoples were destroying themselves by dependence on European goods (especially alcohol), Neolin advocated resistance, both peaceful and armed. If all Indians west of the mountains united to reject the invaders, Neolin declared, the Master of Life would replenish the depleted deer herds and once again look kindly upon his people. Yet, ironically, Neolin's call for a return to native traditions itself revealed European origins; his reference to a single Master of Life showed the influence on his thinking of a syncretic Christianity.

Pontiac, war chief of an Ottawa village near Detroit, became the leader of a movement based on Neolin's precepts. In spring 1763, Pontiac forged an unprecedented alliance among Hurons, Chippewas, Potawatomis, Delawares, Shawnees, and Mingoes (Pennsylvania Iroquois). Pontiac then besieged Fort Detroit while war parties attacked other British outposts in the Great Lakes. Detroit withstood the siege, but by late June all the other forts west of Niagara and north of Fort Pitt (formerly Fort Duquesne) had fallen to the alliance. Indians then raided the Virginia and Pennsylvania frontiers throughout the summer, slaying at least two thousand settlers. Still, they could not take Niagara, Fort Pitt, or Detroit. In early August, colonial militiamen soundly defeated a combined Indian force at Bushy Run, Pennsylvania. Conflict ceased when Pontiac broke off the siege of Detroit in late October. A treaty ending the war was finally negotiated three years later.

The warfare on the Pennsylvania frontier in 1755–1757 and 1763 ended what had once been a uniquely peaceful relationship between European settlers and Indians in that province. For nearly eighty years the residents of "Penn's Woods" had avoided

Benjamin West, the first well-known American artist, engraved this picture of a prisoner exchange at the end of Pontiac's Uprising, with Colonel Henry Bouquet supervising the return of settlers abducted during the war. In the foreground, a child resists leaving the Indian parents he had grown to love. Many colonists were fascinated by the phenomenon West depicted—the reluctance of captives to abandon their adoptive Indian families. (Ohio Historical Society)

major conflicts with each other. But first the Indian attacks and then the settlers' response—especially the massacre of several families of defenseless Conestoga Indians in December 1763 by fifty Scots-Irish men known as the Paxton Boys—revealed that violence in the region would subsequently become endemic.

Proclamation of 1763

Pontiac's war demonstrated that the huge territory Britain had acquired from France would be difficult to govern. London officials had no experience managing such a vast area, particularly one inhabited by restive peoples: the remaining French settlers along the St. Lawrence and the many Indian communities. In October the ministry issued the Proclamation of 1763, which designated the headwaters of rivers flowing into the Atlantic from the Appalachians as the temporary western boundary for colonial settlement. Its promulgators expected the proclamation to prevent clashes by forbidding colonists to move onto Indian lands until land cessions had been negotiated. But it infuriated two distinct groups of colonists: those who had already squatted west of the line (among them many Scots-Irish immigrants) and land speculation companies from Pennsylvania and Virginia.

In the years after 1763, the latter groups (which included such men as George Washington, Thomas Jefferson, Patrick Henry, and Benjamin Franklin) lobbied vigorously to have their claims validated by colonial governments and London administrators. At a treaty conference at Fort Stanwix, New York, in 1768, they negotiated with Iroquois representatives to push the boundary line farther west and south, opening Kentucky to their speculations. The Iroquois, still claiming to speak for the Delawares and the Shawnees—who used Kentucky as their hunting grounds—agreed to the deal, which brought them valuable trade goods and did not affect their own territories. Yet even though the Virginia land companies eventually gained the support of the House of Burgesses for their claims, they never made any headway where it really mattered—in London—because administrators there realized that significant western expansion would require the expenditure of funds they did not have.

George III

The hard-won victory in the Seven Years War had cost Britain millions of pounds and created an immense war debt. The problem of paying it, and of finding the money to defend the newly acquired territories, bedeviled King George III, who in 1760 succeeded his grandfather, George II. The twenty-two-year-old monarch, an intelligent, passionate man with a mediocre education, was unfortunately an erratic judge of character. During the crucial years between 1763 and 1770, when the rift with the colonies grew ever wider and a series of political crises beset England, the king replaced ministries with bewildering rapidity. Although determined to assert the power of the monarchy, George III was immature and unsure of himself. He stubbornly regarded adherence to the status quo as the hallmark of patriotism.

The man he selected as prime minister in 1763, George Grenville, believed that the American colonies could be more tightly administered. Grenville confronted a financial crisis: England's burden of indebtedness had nearly doubled since 1754, from £73 million to £137 million. Annual expenditures before the war had amounted to no more than £8 million; now the yearly interest on the debt alone came to £5 million. Grenville's ministry had to find new sources of funds, and the British people themselves were already heavily taxed. Because the colonists had benefited greatly from wartime expenditures, Grenville concluded that Anglo-Americans should be asked to pay a larger share of the cost of running the empire.

Theories of Representation

Grenville did not question Great Britain's right to levy taxes on the colonies. Like all his countrymen, he believed that government's legitimacy derived ultimately from the consent of the people, but he defined consent differently than the colonists. Americans had come to believe that they could be represented only by men who lived nearby and for whom they or their property-holding neighbors actually voted; otherwise, they could not count on legislators to represent their interests properly. Grenville and his English contemporaries, however, believed that Parliament—king, lords, and commons acting together—by definition represented all British subjects, wherever they resided (even overseas) and whether or not they could vote.

Parliament saw itself as collectively representing the entire nation; the particular constituency that chose a member of the House of Commons had no special claim on that member's vote, nor did the member have to live near his constituents. According to this theory, called virtual representation, all Britons—including colonists—were represented in Parliament. Thus their consent to acts of Parliament could be presumed. In the colonies, by contrast, members of the lower houses of the assemblies were viewed as specifically representing the regions that had elected them. Before Grenville proposed to tax the colonists, the two notions coexisted because no conflict exposed the central contradiction. But events of the 1760s revealed the incompatibility of the two definitions of representation.

Real Whigs

The same events threw into sharp relief Americans' attitudes toward political power. The colonists had become accustomed to a central government that wielded limited authority over them, affecting their daily lives very little. Consequently, they believed that a good government was one that largely left them alone, a view in keeping with the theories of a group of British writers known as the Real Whigs. Drawing on a tradition of dissenting thought that reached back to John Locke and even to the English Civil War, the Real Whigs stressed the dangers inherent in a powerful government, particularly one headed by a monarch. Some of them even favored republicanism, which proposed to eliminate monarchs altogether and rest political power more directly on the people. Real Whigs warned the people to guard constantly against government's attempts to encroach on their liberty and seize their property. Political power was always to be feared, wrote John Trenchard and Thomas Gordon in their essay series *Cato's Letters* (originally published in London in 1720–1723 and reprinted many times thereafter in the colonies). The people had to exercise perpetual vigilance to prevent rulers' attempts to corrupt and oppress them.

Britain's efforts to tighten the reins of government and to raise revenues from the colonies in the 1760s and early 1770s convinced many Americans that the Real Whigs' reasoning applied to their circumstances, especially because of the link between liberty and property rights. Excessive and unjust taxation, they believed, could destroy their freedoms. They eventually interpreted British measures in light of the Real Whigs' warnings and saw oppressive designs behind the actions of Grenville and his successors. Historians disagree over the extent to which those perceptions were correct, but by 1775 a large number of colonists believed they were. In the mid-1760s, however, colonial leaders did not immediately accuse Grenville of conspiring to oppress them. Rather, they questioned the wisdom of the laws he proposed.

Sugar and Currency Acts

Parliament passed the first such measures, the Sugar and Currency Acts, in 1764. The Sugar Act (also known as the Revenue Act) revised existing customs regulations and laid new duties on some foreign imports into the colonies. Its key provisions, strongly advocated in London by influential Caribbean planters, aimed at discouraging American rum distillers from smuggling French West Indian molasses, thereby improving the market for British sugar. It also established a vice-admiralty court at Halifax, Nova Scotia, to adjudicate violations of the law, along with other maritime offenses. Although the Sugar Act appeared to resemble the Navigation Acts, which the colonies had long accepted as legitimate, it broke with tradition in being explicitly designed to raise revenue, not to channel American trade through Britain. The Currency Act effectively outlawed most colonial issues of paper money, because British merchants had long complained that Americans were paying their debts in inflated local currencies. Americans could accumulate little sterling because they imported more than they exported; colonists complained that the act deprived them of a useful medium of exchange.

The Sugar and Currency Acts were imposed on an economy already in the midst of depression. A business boom accompanied the Seven Years War, but the brief spell of prosperity ended abruptly in 1760 when the war shifted overseas. Atlantic trade routes were disrupted; urban merchants found few buyers for imported goods; and the loss of the military's demand for foodstuffs hurt American farmers. The bottom dropped out of the European tobacco market, threatening the livelihood of Chesapeake planters. Sailors were thrown out of work, and artisans had few customers. In such circumstances, the prospect of increased import duties and inadequate supplies of currency aroused merchants' hostility.

Individual American essayists and incensed colonial governments protested the new policies. But, lacking any precedent for a united campaign against acts of Parliament, Americans in 1764 took only hesitant and uncoordinated steps. Eight colonial legislatures sent separate petitions to Parliament requesting the Sugar Act's repeal. They argued that its commercial restrictions would hurt Britain as well as the colonies and that they had not consented to its passage. The protests had no effect. The law remained in force, and Grenville proceeded with another revenue plan.

THE STAMP ACT CRISIS

The Stamp Act (1765), Grenville's most important proposal, was modeled on a law that had been in effect in Britain for almost a century. It touched nearly every colonist by requiring tax stamps on most printed materials, but it placed the heaviest burden on merchants and other members of the colonial elite, who used printed matter more frequently than did ordinary folk. Anyone who purchased a newspaper or pamphlet, made a will, transferred land, bought dice or playing cards, applied for a liquor license, accepted a government appointment, or borrowed money would have to pay the tax, which was doubled for foreign-language newspapers. Never before had a revenue measure of such scope been proposed for the colonies. The act also required that tax stamps be purchased with scarce sterling coin. Violators would be tried by vice-admiralty courts, in which judges alone rendered decisions, leading Americans to fear the loss of their right to trial by a jury of their peers. Finally, such a law would break decisively with the colonial tradition of self-imposed taxation.

James Otis's Rights of the British Colonies   The most important colonial pamphlet protesting the Sugar Act and the proposed Stamp Act was *The Rights of the British Colonies Asserted and Proved,* by James Otis Jr., a brilliant young Massachusetts attorney. Otis starkly exposed the dilemma that confounded the colonists for the next decade. How could they justify their opposition to certain acts of Parliament without questioning Parliament's authority over them? On the one hand, Otis asserted, Americans were "entitled to all the natural, essential, inherent, and inseparable rights" of Britons, including the right not to be taxed without their consent. "No man or body of men, not excepting the parliament . . . can take [those rights] away," he declared. On the other hand, Otis admitted that, under the British system established after the Glorious Revolution, "the power of parliament is uncontrollable but by themselves, and we must obey. . . . Let the parliament lay what burthens they please on us, we must, it is our duty to submit and patiently bear them, till they will be pleased to relieve us."

Otis's first contention, drawing on colonial notions of representation, implied that Parliament could not constitutionally tax the colonies, because Americans were not represented in its ranks. Yet his second point both acknowledged political reality and accepted the prevailing theory of British government: that Parliament was the sole, supreme authority in the empire. Even unconstitutional laws enacted by Parliament had to be obeyed until Parliament decided to repeal them.

According to orthodox British political theory, there could be no middle ground between absolute submission to Parliament and a frontal challenge to its authority. Otis tried to find such a middle ground by proposing colonial representation in Parliament, but his idea was never taken seriously on either side of the Atlantic. The British believed that colonists were already virtually represented in Parliament, and Anglo-Americans quickly realized that a handful of colonial delegates to London would be outvoted. Otis published his pamphlet before the Stamp Act was passed. When Americans first learned of the act's adoption in the spring of 1765, they reacted indecisively. Few colonists—even appointed government officials—publicly favored the law. But colonial petitions had already failed to prevent its adoption, and further lobbying appeared futile. Perhaps Otis was correct: the only course open to Americans was to pay the stamp tax, reluctantly but loyally. Acting on that assumption, colonial agents in London sought the appointment of their American friends as stamp distributors so that the law would at least be enforced equitably.

Patrick Henry and the Virginia Stamp Act Resolves   Not all the colonists resigned themselves to paying the new tax. A twenty-nine-year-old lawyer serving his first term in the Virginia House of Burgesses was appalled by his fellow legislators' unwillingness to oppose the Stamp Act. Patrick Henry later recalled that he was "young, inexperienced, unacquainted with the forms of the house and the members that composed it"—but he decided to act. "Alone, unadvised, and unassisted, on a blank leaf of an old law book," he wrote the Virginia Stamp Act Resolves.

Little in Henry's earlier life foreshadowed his success in the political arena that he entered so dramatically. The son of a prosperous Scots immigrant to western Virginia, Henry had little formal education. After marrying at eighteen, he failed at both farming and storekeeping before turning to the law as a means of supporting his wife and their six children. Henry lacked legal training, but his oratorical skills made him an effective advocate, first for his clients and later for his political beliefs. A prominent Virginia lawyer observed, "He is by far the most powerful speaker I ever heard. Every word he says not only engages, but commands the attention."

Patrick Henry introduced his seven proposals near the end of the legislative session, when many burgesses had already departed for home. Henry's fiery speech led the Speaker of the House to accuse him of treason. (Henry denied the charge, contrary to the nineteenth-century myth that he exclaimed, "If this be treason, make the most of it!") The few burgesses remaining in Williamsburg adopted five of Henry's resolutions by a bare majority. Although they repealed the most radical of the five the next day, their action had far-reaching effects. Some colonial newspapers printed Henry's seven original resolutions as if they had been uniformly passed by the House, even though one was rescinded and two others were never debated or voted on at all.

The four propositions adopted by the burgesses repeated Otis's arguments, asserting that colonists had never forfeited the rights of British subjects, among which was consent to taxation. The other three resolutions went much further. The repealed resolution claimed for the burgesses "the only exclusive right" to tax Virginians, and the final two (those never considered) asserted that Virginians need not obey tax laws passed by other legislative bodies (namely, Parliament), terming any opponent of that opinion "an Enemy to this his Majesty's Colony."

Continuing Loyalty to Britain The burgesses' decision to accept only the first four of Henry's resolutions anticipated the position most Americans would adopt throughout the following decade. Though willing to contend for their rights, the colonists did not seek independence. The Maryland lawyer Daniel Dulany, whose *Considerations on the Propriety of Imposing Taxes on the British Colonies* was the most widely read pamphlet of 1765, expressed the consensus: "The colonies are dependent upon Great Britain, and the supreme authority vested in the king, lords, and commons, may justly be exercised to secure, or preserve their dependence." But, warned Dulany, a superior did not have the right "to seize the property of his inferior when he pleases"; there was a crucial distinction between a condition of "dependence and inferiority" and one of "absolute vassalage and slavery."

Over the next ten years, America's political leaders searched for a formula that would enable them to control their internal affairs, especially taxation, but remain under British rule. The chief difficulty lay in British officials' inability to compromise on the issue of parliamentary power. The notion that Parliament could exercise absolute authority over all colonial possessions inhered in the British theory of government. Even the harshest British critics of the ministries of the 1760s and 1770s questioned only the wisdom of specific policies, not the principles on which they rested. In effect, the Americans wanted British leaders to revise their fundamental understanding of the workings of their government. That was simply too much to expect.

The ultimate effectiveness of Americans' opposition to the Stamp Act rested on more than ideological arguments over parliamentary power. The decisive and inventive actions of some colonists during the late summer and fall of 1765 gave the resistance its primary force.

Anti–Stamp Act Demonstrations In August, the Loyal Nine, a Boston social club of printers, distillers, and other artisans, organized a demonstration against the Stamp Act. Hoping to show that people of all ranks opposed the act, they approached the leaders of the city's rival laborers' associations, based in Boston's North End and South End neighborhoods. The two gangs, composed of unskilled workers and poor tradesmen, often battled each other, but the Loyal Nine convinced them to lay aside their differences to participate in the demonstration. All colonists, not just affluent ones, would have to pay the stamp taxes.

Early on August 14, the demonstrators hung an effigy of Andrew Oliver, the province's stamp distributor, from a tree on Boston Common. That night a large crowd led by a group of about fifty well-dressed tradesmen paraded the effigy around the city. The crowd tore down a small building they thought was intended as the stamp office, making a bonfire near Oliver's house with wood from the structure. Beheading the effigy, they added it to the flames. Demonstrators broke most of Oliver's windows and threw stones at officials who tried to disperse them. In the midst of the melee, the North End and South End leaders drank a toast to their successful union. The Loyal Nine achieved success when Oliver publicly promised not to fulfill the duties of his office. One Bostonian jubilantly wrote to a relative, "I believe people never was more Universally pleased not so much one could I hear say he was sorry, but a smile sat on almost every ones countinance."

But another crowd action twelve days later, aimed this time at Oliver's brother-in-law, Lieutenant Governor Thomas Hutchinson, drew no praise from Boston's respectable citizens. On the night of August 26, a mob reportedly led by the South End leader Ebenezer MacIntosh attacked the homes of several customs officers. The crowd then completely destroyed Hutchinson's elaborately furnished townhouse in one of Boston's most fashionable districts. The lieutenant governor reported that by the next morning "one of the best finished houses in the Province had nothing remaining but the bare walls and floors." His trees and garden were ruined, his valuable library was lost, and the mob "emptied the house of every thing whatsoever except a part of the kitchen furniture." But Hutchinson took some comfort in the fact that "the encouragers of the first mob never intended matters should go this length and the people in general express the utmost detestation of this unparalleled outrage."

Americans' Divergent Interests   The differences between the two Boston mobs of August 1765 exposed divisions that would continue to characterize subsequent colonial protests. Few colonists sided with Britain during the 1760s, but various colonial groups had divergent goals. The skilled craftsmen who composed the Loyal Nine and merchants, lawyers, and other members of the educated elite preferred orderly demonstrations confined to political issues. For the city's laborers, by contrast, economic grievances may have been paramount. Certainly, their "hellish Fury" as they wrecked Hutchinson's house suggests resentment against his ostentatious display of wealth.

Colonists, like Britons, had a long tradition of crowd action in which disfranchised people took to the streets to redress deeply felt local grievances. But the Stamp Act controversy for the first time drew ordinary urban folk into transatlantic politics, including recent non-English-speaking immigrants targeted by the double taxation of foreign-language newspapers. Matters that previously had been of concern only to the gentry or to members of colonial legislatures were now discussed on every street corner and in every tavern. Benjamin Franklin's daughter observed as much when she informed her father, then serving as a colonial agent in London, that "nothing else is talked of, the Dutch [Germans] talk of the stompt act the Negroes of the tamp, in short every body has something to say."

The entry of unskilled workers, slaves, and women into the realm of imperial politics both threatened and aided the elite men who wanted to mount effective opposition to British measures. On the one hand, crowd action could have a stunning impact. Anti-Stamp Act demonstrations occurred in cities and towns stretching from Halifax in the north to the Caribbean island of Antigua in the south. They were so successful that, by November 1, when the law was scheduled to take effect, not one stamp distributor was willing to carry out his duties. Thus the act could not be enforced. On the other hand, wealthy men recognized that mobs composed of the formerly powerless—whose goals were not always identical to theirs (as the Boston experience showed)—could endanger their own dominance of the society. What would happen, they wondered, if the "hellish Fury" of the crowd turned against them?

Sons of Liberty

They therefore attempted to channel resistance into acceptable forms by creating an intercolonial association, the Sons of Liberty. New Yorkers organized the first such group in early November, and branches spread rapidly through the coastal cities. Composed of merchants, lawyers, and prosperous tradesmen, the Sons of Liberty by early 1766 linked protest leaders from Charleston, South Carolina, to Portsmouth, New Hampshire. Not surprisingly, in light of the central role of taverns as settings for the exchange of news and opinions, a considerable number of members were tavern owners.

The Sons of Liberty could influence events but not control them. In Charleston (formerly Charles Town) in October 1765, an informally organized crowd shouting, "Liberty Liberty and stamp'd paper" forced the resignation of the South Carolina stamp distributor. The victory celebration a few days later—the largest demonstration the city had ever known—featured a British flag with the word "Liberty" emblazoned on it. But the new Charleston chapter of the Sons of Liberty was horrified when in January 1766 local slaves paraded through the streets similarly crying, "Liberty!" Freedom from slavery was not the sort of liberty elite slaveowners had in mind.

In Philadelphia, too, resistance leaders were dismayed when an angry mob threatened to attack Benjamin Franklin's house. The city's laborers believed Franklin to be partly responsible for the Stamp Act because he had obtained the post of stamp distributor for a close friend. But Philadelphia's artisans—the backbone of the opposition movement there and elsewhere—were fiercely loyal to Franklin, one of their own who had made good. They gathered to protect his home and family from the crowd. The house was saved, but the resulting split between Philadelphia's better-off tradesmen and common laborers prevented the establishment of an alliance as successful as Boston's.

Opposition and Repeal

During the fall and winter of 1765–1766, opponents of the Stamp Act pursued several different strategies. Colonial legislatures petitioned Parliament to repeal the hated law, and courts closed because they could not obtain the stamps now required for all legal documents. In October, nine colonies sent delegates to a general congress, the first since the 1754 Albany Congress. The Stamp Act Congress met in New York to draft a statement of protest that stressed the law's adverse economic effects rather than its perceived violations of Americans' rights. At the same time, the Sons of Liberty held mass meetings, attempting to rally public support for the resistance movement. Finally, American merchants organized nonimportation associations to pressure British exporters. By the 1760s, one-quarter of all British exports went to the colonies, and American merchants reasoned that London merchants whose sales suffered severely would lobby for repeal. Because times were bad and American merchants were finding few customers for imported goods anyway, a general moratorium on future purchases would also help to reduce their bloated inventories.

In March 1766, Parliament repealed the Stamp Act. The nonimportation agreements had had the anticipated effect, creating allies for the colonies among wealthy

London merchants. But boycotts, formal protests, and crowd actions were less important in winning repeal than was the appointment of a new prime minister, chosen by George III for reasons unrelated to colonial politics. Lord Rockingham, who replaced Grenville in the summer of 1765, had opposed the Stamp Act, not because he believed Parliament lacked power to tax the colonies, but because he thought the law unwise and divisive. Thus, although Rockingham proposed repeal, he linked it to passage of a Declaratory Act, which asserted Parliament's authority to tax and legislate for Britain's American possessions "in all cases whatsoever."

News of the repeal arrived in Newport, Rhode Island, in May, and the Sons of Liberty quickly dispatched messengers to carry the welcome tidings throughout the colonies. They organized celebrations commemorating the glorious event, all of which stressed the Americans' unwavering loyalty to Britain. Their goal achieved, the Sons of Liberty dissolved. Few colonists saw the ominous implications of the Declaratory Act.

RESISTANCE TO THE TOWNSHEND ACTS

The colonists had accomplished their immediate aim, but the long-term prospects were unclear. In the summer of 1766, another change in the ministry in London revealed how fragile their victory had been. The new prime minister, William Pitt, had fostered cooperation between the colonies and Britain during the Seven Years War. But Pitt fell ill, and another man, Charles Townshend, became the dominant force in the ministry. An ally of Grenville and a supporter of colonial taxation, Townshend decided to renew the attempt to obtain additional funds from Britain's American possessions (see Table 5.2).

The duties Townshend proposed in 1767 were to be levied on trade goods like paper, glass, and tea; thus they seemed to extend the existing Navigation Acts. But the Townshend duties differed from previous customs levies in two ways. First, they applied to items imported into the colonies from Britain, not to those from foreign countries. Accordingly, they violated mercantilist theory. Second, the revenues would be used to

TABLE 5.2 British Ministries and Their American Policies

Head of Ministry	Major Acts
George Grenville	Sugar Act (1764) Currency Act (1764) Stamp Act (1765)
Lord Rockingham	Stamp Act repealed (1766) Declaratory Act (1766)
William Pitt/ Charles Townshend	Townshend Acts (1767)
Lord North	Townshend duties (except for the tea tax) repealed (1770) Tea Act (1773) Coercive Acts (1774) Quebec Act (1774)

pay some royal officials in the colonies. Assemblies, in short, would no longer be able to threaten to withhold salaries in order to win those officials' cooperation. Additionally, Townshend's scheme established an American Board of Customs Commissioners and vice-admiralty courts at Boston, Philadelphia, and Charleston. Both moves angered merchants, whose profits would be threatened by more vigorous enforcement of the Navigation Acts.

John Dickinson's Farmer's Letters In 1765, months passed before the colonists protested the Stamp Act. The passage of the Townshend Acts, however, drew a quick response. One series of essays in particular, *Letters from a Farmer in Pennsylvania,* by the prominent lawyer John Dickinson, expressed a broad consensus. Eventually all but four colonial newspapers printed Dickinson's essays; in pamphlet form they went through seven American editions. Dickinson contended that Parliament could regulate colonial trade but could not exercise that power to raise revenue. By distinguishing between trade regulation and unacceptable commercial taxation, Dickinson avoided the sticky issue of consent and how it affected colonial subordination to Parliament. But his argument created a different, and equally knotty, problem. In effect it obligated the colonies to assess Parliament's motives in passing any law pertaining to trade before deciding whether to obey it. That was unworkable in the long run.

The Massachusetts assembly responded to the Townshend Acts by drafting a letter to circulate among the other colonial legislatures, calling for unity and suggesting a joint petition of protest. Not the letter itself but the ministry's reaction to it united the colonies. When Lord Hillsborough, recently named to the new post of secretary of state for America, learned of the circular letter, he ordered Governor Francis Bernard of Massachusetts to insist that the assembly recall it. He also directed other governors to prevent their assemblies from discussing the letter. Hillsborough's order gave colonial assemblies an incentive to join forces to oppose this new threat to their prerogatives. In late 1768, the Massachusetts legislature met, debated, and resoundingly rejected recall by a vote of 92 to 17. Bernard immediately dissolved the assembly, and other governors followed suit when their legislatures debated the circular letter.

Rituals of Resistance The number of votes cast against recalling the circular letter—92—assumed ritual significance for the supporters of resistance. The number 45 already had symbolic meaning because John Wilkes, a radical Londoner sympathetic to the American cause, had been jailed for libel for publishing an essay entitled *The North Briton,* No. 45. In Boston, the silversmith Paul Revere made a punchbowl weighing 45 ounces that held 45 gills (half-cups) and was engraved with the names of opposition legislators; James Otis, John Adams, and others publicly drank 45 toasts from it. In Charleston the city's tradesmen decorated a tree with 45 lights and set off 45 rockets. Carrying 45 candles, they adjourned to a tavern where 45 tables were set with 45 bowls of wine, 45 bowls of punch, and 92 glasses.

Such public rituals served important unifying and educational functions. Just as the pamphlets by Otis, Dulany, Dickinson, and others acquainted literate colonists with the issues raised by British actions, so public rituals taught illiterate Americans about the reasons for resistance and familiarized them with the terms of the argument. When

Boston's revived Sons of Liberty invited hundreds of city residents to dine with them each August 14 to commemorate the first Stamp Act demonstration, and the Charleston Sons of Liberty held their meetings in public, crowds gathered to watch and listen. Likewise, the public singing of songs supporting the American cause helped to spread the word. The participants in such events openly expressed their commitment to the cause of resistance and encouraged others to join them.

The Sons of Liberty and other American leaders made a deliberate effort to involve ordinary folk in the campaign against the Townshend duties. Most important, they urged colonists of all ranks and both sexes to sign agreements not to purchase or consume British products. The new consumerism that previously had linked colonists economically now linked them politically as well, supplying them with a ready method of displaying their allegiance. As "A Tradesman" wrote in a Philadelphia paper in 1770, it was essential "for the Good of the Whole, to strengthen the Hands of the Patriotic Majority, by agreeing not to purchase British Goods."

Daughters of Liberty

As the primary purchasers of textiles and household goods, women played a central role in the nonconsumption movement. More than three hundred Boston matrons publicly promised not to buy or drink tea, "Sickness excepted." As Janet Schaw later noted, the women of Wilmington, North Carolina, burned their tea after walking through town in a solemn procession. Women throughout the colonies exchanged recipes for tea substitutes or drank coffee instead. The best known of the protests, the so-called Edenton Ladies Tea Party, actually had little to do with tea. It was a meeting of prominent North Carolina women who pledged formally to work for the public good and to support resistance to British measures.

Women also encouraged home manufacturing. In many towns, young women calling themselves Daughters of Liberty met to spin in public squares to try to persuade other women to make homespun and to encourage colonists to wear homespun clothing, thereby ending the colonies' dependence on British cloth. These symbolic displays of patriotism—publicized by newspapers and broadsides—served the same purpose as the male rituals involving the numbers 45 and 92. When young ladies from well-to-do families sat outdoors at spinning wheels all day, eating only American food, drinking local herbal tea, and listening to patriotic sermons, they served as political instructors. Many women took great satisfaction in their newfound role. When a satirist hinted that women discussed only "such triffling subjects as Dress, Scandal and Detraction" during their spinning bees, three Boston women replied angrily, "Inferior in abusive sarcasm, in personal invective, in low wit, we glory to be, but inferior in veracity, sincerity, love of virtue, of liberty and of our country, we would not willingly be to any."

Divided Opinion over Boycotts

But the colonists were by no means united in support of nonimportation and nonconsumption. If the Stamp Act protests had occasionally (as in Boston and Philadelphia) revealed a division between artisans and merchants on the one side and common laborers on the other, resistance to the Townshend Acts exposed new splits in American ranks. The most significant—which arose from a change in economic circumstances—divided urban artisans and merchants, allies in 1765.

The Stamp Act boycotts had helped to revive a depressed economy by creating a demand for local products and reducing merchants' inventories. But in 1768 and 1769, merchants were enjoying boom times and had no financial incentive to support a boycott. Consequently, merchants signed the agreements reluctantly and sometimes secretly violated them. In contrast, artisans supported nonimportation enthusiastically, recognizing that the absence of British goods would create a ready market for their own manufactures. Thus tradesmen formed the core of the crowds that coerced both importers and their customers by picketing stores, publicizing offenders' names, and sometimes destroying property.

Such tactics were effective: colonial imports from England dropped dramatically in 1769, especially in New York, New England, and Pennsylvania. But the tactics also aroused heated opposition, dividing opinion in another way. Some Americans who supported resistance to British measures began to question the use of violence to force others to join the boycott. In addition, the threat to private property inherent in the campaign frightened wealthier and more conservative men and women. Political activism by ordinary colonists challenged the ruling elite's domination, just as its members had feared in 1765.

Disclosures that leading merchants had violated the nonimportation agreement caused dissension in the ranks of the boycotters, so Americans were relieved when news arrived in April 1770 that the Townshend duties had been repealed, with the exception of the tea tax. A new prime minister, Lord North, persuaded Parliament that duties on trade within the empire were ill-advised. Although some colonial leaders argued that nonimportation should continue until the tea tax was repealed, merchants quickly resumed importing. The other Townshend Acts remained in force, but repealing the duties made the provisions for paying officials' salaries and tightening customs enforcement appear less objectionable.

CONFRONTATIONS IN BOSTON

Initially the new ministry did nothing to antagonize the colonists. Yet on the very day Lord North proposed repeal of the Townshend duties, a confrontation between civilians and soldiers in Boston led to five Americans' deaths. The origins of the event that patriots called the Boston Massacre lay in repeated clashes between customs officers and the people of Massachusetts. The decision to base the American Board of Customs Commissioners in Boston ultimately caused the confrontation.

Mobs targeted the customs commissioners from the day they arrived in November 1767. In June 1768 their seizure of the patriot leader John Hancock's sloop *Liberty* on suspicion of smuggling caused a riot in which prominent customs officers' property was destroyed. The riot in turn helped to convince the ministry that troops were needed to maintain order in the unruly port. The assignment of two regiments of regulars to their city confirmed Bostonians' worst fears; the redcoats constantly reminded city dwellers of the oppressive potential of British power. Guards on Boston Neck, the entrance to the city, checked all travelers and their goods. Redcoat patrols roamed the city day and night, questioning and sometimes harassing passersby. Military parades on Boston Common were accompanied by martial music and often the public whipping of deserters and other violators of army rules. Parents began to fear for the safety of their daughters, who were subjected to soldiers' coarse sexual insults. But the greatest potential for violence lay in the uneasy relationship between the soldiers and Boston laborers. Many redcoats sought employment in their off-duty hours, competing for unskilled jobs with the city's workingmen. Members of the two groups brawled repeatedly in taverns and on the streets.

Boston Massacre Early on the evening of March 5, 1770, a crowd of laborers began throwing hard-packed snowballs at soldiers guarding the Customs House. Goaded beyond endurance, the sentries acted against express orders and fired on the crowd, killing four and wounding eight, one of whom died a few days later. Reportedly the first to die was Crispus Attucks, a sailor of mixed Nipmuck and African origins. Resistance leaders idealized Attucks and the other dead rioters as martyrs for the cause of liberty, holding a solemn funeral and later commemorating March 5 annually with patriotic orations. Paul Revere's engraving of the massacre was part of the propaganda campaign.

Leading patriots wanted to ensure that the soldiers did not become martyrs as well. Despite the political benefits the patriots derived from the massacre, they probably did not approve the crowd action that provoked it. Ever since the destruction of Hutchinson's house in August 1765, men allied with the Sons of Liberty had supported orderly demonstrations and expressed distaste at such uncontrolled riots as the one that provoked the Boston Massacre. Thus, when the soldiers were tried for the killings in November, John Adams and Josiah Quincy Jr., both unwavering patriots, acted as their defense attorneys. Almost all the accused were acquitted, and the two men convicted were released after being branded on the thumb. Undoubtedly the favorable outcome of the trials persuaded London officials not to retaliate against the city.

A British Plot? For more than two years after the Boston Massacre and the repeal of the Townshend duties, a superficial calm descended on the colonies. In June 1772, Rhode Islanders angry with overzealous customs enforcement by the British naval schooner *Gaspée* attacked and burned it as it lay aground at low tide in Narragansett Bay near Providence, but because a subsequent investigation failed to identify the perpetrators, no adverse consequences followed for the colonists. The most outspoken newspapers, such as the *Boston Gazette,* the *Pennsylvania Journal,* and the *South Carolina Gazette,* published essays drawing on Real Whig ideology and accusing Great Britain of deliberately scheming to oppress the colonies. After the Stamp Act's repeal, the protest leaders had praised Parliament; following repeal of the Townshend duties, they warned of impending tyranny. What had seemed to be an isolated mistake, a single ill-chosen stamp tax, now appeared to be part of a plot against American liberties. Essayists pointed to Parliament's persecution of the British radical John Wilkes, the stationing of troops in Boston, and the growing number of vice-admiralty courts as evidence of plans to enslave the colonists. Indeed, patriot writers played repeatedly on the word *enslavement.* Most free colonists had direct knowledge of slavery (either as slaveholders themselves or as neighbors of slaveowners), and the threat of enslavement by Britain must have hit them with peculiar force.

Still, no one yet advocated independence from the mother country. Although some colonists were becoming increasingly convinced that they should seek freedom from parliamentary authority, they continued to acknowledge their British identity and allegiance to George III. They began, therefore, to envision a system that would enable them to be ruled by their own elected legislatures while remaining subordinate to the king. But any such scheme violated Britons' conception of the nature of their government, which posited that Parliament wielded sole, undivided sovereignty over the empire. Furthermore, in the British mind, Parliament encompassed the king as well as lords and commons, so separating the monarch from the legislature was impossible.

Then, in the fall of 1772, the North ministry began to implement the Townshend Act that provided for governors and judges to be paid from customs revenues. In early November, voters at a Boston town meeting established a Committee of Correspondence to publicize the decision by exchanging letters with other Massachusetts towns. Heading the committee was Samuel Adams, who had proposed its formation.

Samuel Adams and Committees of Correspondence Fifty-one in 1772, Samuel Adams was about a decade older than the other leaders of American resistance, including his distant cousin John. He had been a Boston tax collector, a member and clerk of the Massachusetts assembly, an ally of the Loyal Nine, and one of the Sons of Liberty. Unswerving in his devotion to the American cause, Adams drew a sharp contrast between a corrupt, vice-ridden Britain and the colonies, peopled by simple, liberty-loving folk. An experienced political organizer, Adams continually stressed the necessity of prudent collective action in speeches in the Boston town meeting. His Committee of Correspondence thus undertook the task of creating an informed consensus among the residents of Massachusetts.

Such committees, which were eventually established throughout the colonies, represented the next logical step in the organization of American resistance. Until 1772, the protest movement was confined largely to the seacoast and primarily to major cities and towns. Adams realized that the time had come to widen the movement's geographic scope, to attempt to involve more colonists in the struggle. Accordingly, the Boston town meeting directed the Committee of Correspondence "to state the Rights of the Colonists and of this Province in particular"; to list "the Infringements and Violations thereof that have been, or from time to time may be made"; and to send copies to the other towns in the province. In return, Boston requested "a free communication of their Sentiments on this Subject."

The statement of colonial rights prepared by the Bostonians declared that Americans had absolute rights to life, liberty, and property. The idea that "a British house of commons, should have a right, at pleasure, to give and grant the property of the colonists" was "irreconcileable" with "the first principles of natural law and Justice . . . and of the British Constitution in particular." The list of grievances complained of taxation without representation, the presence of unnecessary troops and customs officers on American soil, the use of imperial revenues to pay colonial officials, the expanded jurisdiction of vice-admiralty courts, and even the nature of the instructions given to American governors by their superiors in London.

The entire document, which was printed as a pamphlet for distribution to the towns, exhibited none of the hesitation that had characterized colonial claims against Parliament in the 1760s. No longer were resistance leaders—at least in Boston—preoccupied with defining the precise limits of parliamentary authority. No longer did they mention

Shortly after the Boston Massacre, Paul Revere printed this illustration of the confrontation near the customs house on March 5, 1770. Offering visual support for the patriots' version of events, it showed the British soldiers firing on an unresisting crowd (instead of the aggressive mob described at the soldiers' trial) and—even worse—a gun firing from the building itself, which has been labeled "Butchers Hall." (Courtesy of the John Carter Brown Library at Brown University)

the necessity of obedience to Parliament. They were committed to a course that placed American rights first, loyalty to Great Britain a distant second.

The response of the Massachusetts towns to the committee's pamphlet must have caused Samuel Adams to rejoice. Some towns disagreed with Boston's assessment of the state of affairs, but most aligned themselves with the city. From Braintree came the assertion that "all civil officers are or ought to be Servants to the people and dependent upon them for their official Support, and every instance to the Contrary from the Governor downwards tends to crush and destroy civil liberty." The town of Holden declared that "the People of New England have never given the People of Britain any Right of Jurisdiction over us." The citizens of Petersham commented that resistance to tyranny was "the first and highest social Duty of this people." And Pownallborough warned, "Allegiance is a relative Term and like Kingdoms and commonwealths is local and has its bounds." Beliefs like these made the next crisis in Anglo-American affairs the last.

Tea and Turmoil

The tea tax was the only Townshend duty still in effect by 1773. In the years after 1770, some Americans continued to boycott English tea, while others resumed drinking it either openly or in secret. As was explained in Chapter 4, tea figured prominently in both the colonists' diet and their social lives, so observing the boycott required them not only to forgo a favorite beverage but also to alter habitual forms of socializing. Tea thus retained an explosively symbolic character even though the boycott began to disintegrate after 1770.

Reactions to the Tea Act In May 1773, Parliament passed an act designed to save the East India Company from bankruptcy. The company, which held a monopoly on British trade with the East Indies, was critically important to the British economy and to the financial well-being of many prominent British politicians who had invested in its stock. According to the Tea Act, legal tea would henceforth be sold in America only by the East India Company's designated agents, which would enable the company to avoid intermediaries in both Britain and the colonies, and to price its tea competitively with that offered by smugglers. The net result would be cheaper tea for American consumers. Resistance leaders, however, interpreted the new measure as a pernicious device to make them admit Parliament's right to tax them, for the less expensive tea would still be taxed under the Townshend law. Others saw the Tea Act as the first step in the establishment of an East India Company monopoly on all colonial trade. Residents of the four cities designated to receive the first shipments of tea accordingly prepared to respond to what they perceived as a new threat to their freedom.

In New York City, tea ships never arrived. In Philadelphia, Pennsylvania's governor persuaded the captain to sail back to Britain. In Charleston, the tea was unloaded and stored; some was destroyed, the rest sold in 1776 by the new state government. The only confrontation occurred in Boston, where both sides—the town meeting, including participants from nearby towns, and Governor Thomas Hutchinson, two of whose sons were tea agents—rejected compromise.

The first of three tea ships, the *Dartmouth,* entered Boston harbor on November 28. The customs laws required cargo to be landed and the appropriate duty paid by its owners within twenty days of a ship's arrival; otherwise, the cargo had to be seized by customs officers and sold at auction. After a series of mass meetings, Bostonians voted to post guards on the wharf to prevent the tea from being unloaded. Hutchinson refused to permit the vessels to leave the harbor.

On December 16, one day before the cargo would have been confiscated, more than five thousand people (nearly a third of the city's population) crowded into Old South Church. The meeting, chaired by Samuel Adams, made a final attempt to convince Hutchinson to send the tea back to England. But the governor remained adamant. In the early evening Adams reportedly announced "that he could think of nothing further to be done—that they had now done all they could for the Salvation of their Country." Cries then rang out from the back of the crowd: "Boston harbor a tea-pot tonight! The Mohawks are come!" Small groups pushed their way out of the meeting. Within a few minutes, about sixty men crudely disguised as Indians assembled at the wharf, boarded the three ships, and dumped the cargo into the harbor. By 9 P.M. their work was done: 342 chests of tea worth approximately £10,000 floated in splinters on the water.

Among the "Indians" were many representatives of Boston's artisans, including the silversmith Paul Revere. Five masons, eleven carpenters and builders, three leather-workers, a blacksmith, two barbers, a coachmaker, a shoemaker, and twelve apprentices have been identified as participants. That their ranks also included four farmers from outside Boston, ten merchants, two doctors, a teacher, and a bookseller illustrated the widespread support for the resistance movement. The next day John Adams exulted in his diary that the Tea Party was "so bold, so daring, so firm, intrepid and inflexible" that "I cant but consider it as an Epocha in history."

Coercive and Quebec Acts The North administration reacted with considerably less enthusiasm when it learned of the Tea Party. In March 1774, Parliament adopted the first of four laws that became known as the Coercive, or Intolerable, Acts. It ordered the port of Boston closed until the tea was paid for, prohibiting all but coastal trade in food and firewood. Later in the spring, Parliament passed three other punitive measures. The Massachusetts Government Act altered the province's charter, substituting an appointed council for the elected one, increasing the governor's powers, and forbidding most town meetings. The Justice Act provided that a person accused of committing murder in the course of suppressing a riot or enforcing the laws could be tried outside the colony where the incident had occurred. Finally, the Quartering Act allowed military officers to commandeer privately owned buildings to house their troops. Thus the Coercive Acts punished not only Boston but also Massachusetts as a whole, alerting other colonies to the possibility that their residents, too, could be subject to retaliation if they opposed British authority.

After passing the last of the Coercive Acts, Parliament turned its attention to much-needed reforms in the government of Quebec. The Quebec Act thereby became linked with the Coercive Acts in the minds of the patriots. Intended to ease strains that had arisen since the British conquest of the formerly French colony, the Quebec Act granted greater religious freedom to Catholics—alarming Protestant colonists, who equated Roman Catholicism with religious and political despotism. It also reinstated French civil law, which had been replaced by British procedures in 1763, and it established an appointed council (rather than an elected legislature) as the governing body of the colony. Finally, in an attempt to provide northern Indians with some protection against Anglo-American settlement, the act annexed to Quebec the area west of the Appalachians, east of the Mississippi River, and north of the Ohio River. That region, still with few European inhabitants, was thus removed from the jurisdiction of the sea-coast colonies. The wealthy colonists who hoped to develop the Ohio country to attract additional settlers now faced the prospect of dealing with officials in Quebec.

Members of Parliament who voted for the punitive legislation believed that at long last they had solved the problem posed by the troublesome Americans. But resistance leaders showed little inclination to bow to Parliament's authority. In their eyes, the Coercive Acts and the Quebec Act proved what they had feared since 1768: that Britain had embarked on a deliberate plan to oppress them. If the port of Boston could be closed, why not the ports of Philadelphia or New York? If the royal charter of Massachusetts could be changed, why not the charter of South Carolina? If certain people could be transferred to distant colonies for trial, why not any violator of any law? If troops could be forcibly quartered in private houses, did that not portend the occupation of all America? If the Catholic Church could receive favored status in Quebec, why not everywhere? It seemed as though the full dimensions of the plot against American rights and liberties had at last been revealed.

The Boston Committee of Correspondence urged all colonies to join an immediate boycott of British goods. But other provinces hesitated to take such a drastic step. Rhode Island, Virginia, and Pennsylvania each suggested that another intercolonial congress be convened to consider an appropriate response, and in mid-June 1774 Massachusetts acquiesced. Few people wanted to take hasty action; even the most ardent patriots remained loyal Britons and hoped for reconciliation. Despite their objections to British policy, they continued to see themselves as part of the empire. Americans were approaching the brink of confrontation, but they had not committed themselves to an irrevocable break. So the colonies agreed to send delegates to Philadelphia in September to attend a Continental Congress.

SUMMARY

Just twenty years earlier, at the outbreak of the Seven Years War in the wilderness of western Pennsylvania, no one could have predicted that the future would bring such swift and dramatic change to Britain's mainland colonies. Yet that conflict simultaneously removed France from North America and created a huge debt that Britain had to find means to pay, developments with major implications for the imperial relationship.

In the years after the war ended in 1763, momentous changes occurred in the ways colonists thought about themselves and their allegiances. The number of colonists who defined themselves as political actors increased substantially. Once linked unquestioningly to Great Britain, they began to develop a sense of their own identity as Americans, including a recognition of the cultural and social gulf that separated them from Britons. They started to realize that their concept of the political process differed from that held by people in the mother country. Most important, they held a different definition of what constituted representation and appropriate consent to government actions. They also came to understand that their economic interests did not necessarily coincide with those of Great Britain. Colonial political leaders reached such conclusions only after a long train of events, some of them violent, had altered their understanding of their relationship with the mother country. Parliamentary acts such as the Stamp Act and the Townshend Acts elicited colonial responses—both ideological and practical—that produced further responses from Britain. Tensions escalated until they climaxed when Bostonians destroyed the East India Company's tea. From that point on, there would be no turning back.

In the late summer of 1774, Americans were committed to resistance but not to independence. Even so, they had started to sever the bonds of empire. During the next decade, they would forge the bonds of a new American nationality to replace those rejected Anglo-American ties.

6

A Revolution, Indeed
1774–1783

GOVERNMENT BY CONGRESS AND COMMITTEE

When the fifty-five delegates to the First Continental Congress convened in Philadelphia in September 1774, they knew that any measures they adopted were likely to enjoy widespread support. That summer, well-publicized open meetings held throughout the colonies had endorsed the idea of another nonimportation pact. Participants in such meetings promised (in the words of the freeholders of Johnston County, North Carolina) to "strictly adhere to, and abide by, such Regulations and Restrictions as the Members of the said General Congress shall agree to." Most of the congressional delegates were selected by extralegal provincial conventions whose members were chosen at local gatherings, because governors had forbidden regular assemblies to conduct formal elections. Thus the very act of designating delegates to attend the Congress involved Americans in open defiance of British authority.

First Continental Congress   The colonies' leading political figures—most of them lawyers, merchants, and planters representing every colony but Georgia—attended the Philadelphia Congress. The Massachusetts delegation included both Samuel Adams, the experienced organizer of Boston resistance, and his younger cousin John, an ambitious lawyer. Among others, New York sent

CHRONOLOGY

1774 • First Continental Congress meets in Philadelphia, adopts Declaration of Rights and Grievances

• Continental Association implements economic boycott of Britain; committees of observation established to oversee boycott

1774–75 • Provincial conventions replace collapsing colonial governments

1775 • Battles of Lexington and Concord; first shots of war fired

• Second Continental Congress begins

• Washington named commander-in-chief

• Dunmore's proclamation offers freedom to patriots slaves who join British forces

1776 • Paine publishes *Common Sense,* advocating independence

• British evacuate Boston

• Declaration of Independence adopted

• New York City falls to British

1777 • British take Philadelphia

• Burgoyne surrenders at Saratoga

1778 • French alliance brings vital assistance to America

• British evacuate Philadelphia

1779 • Sullivan expedition destroys Iroquois villages

1780 • British take Charleston

1781 • Cornwallis surrenders at Yorktown

1782 • Peace negotiations begin

1783 • Treaty of Paris signed, granting independence to the United States

John Jay, a talented young attorney. From Pennsylvania came the conservative Joseph Galloway and his long-time rival, John Dickinson. Virginia elected Richard Henry Lee and Patrick Henry, both noted for their patriotic zeal, as well as George Washington. Most of these men had never met, but in the weeks, months, and years that followed they became the chief architects of the new nation.

The congressmen faced three tasks when they convened at Carpenters' Hall on September 5. The first two were explicit: defining American grievances and developing a plan for resistance. The third—articulating their constitutional relationship with Great Britain—was less clear-cut and proved troublesome. The most radical congressmen, like Lee of Virginia, argued that colonists owed allegiance only to George III and that Parliament had no legitimate authority over the colonies. The conservatives— Joseph Galloway and his allies—proposed a formal plan of union that would have required Parliament and a new American legislature to consent jointly to all laws pertaining to the colonies. After heated debate, delegates narrowly rejected Galloway's proposal, but they were not prepared to embrace the radicals' position either.

Finally, they accepted wording proposed by John Adams. The crucial clauses in the Congress's Declaration of Rights and Grievances declared that Americans would obey Parliament, but only voluntarily, and that they would resist all taxes in disguise, like the Townshend duties. Remarkably, such a position—which only a few years before would have been regarded as radical—represented a compromise in the fall of 1774. The Americans had come a long way since their first hesitant protests against the Sugar Act ten years earlier.

Continental Association   With the constitutional issue resolved, the delegates readily agreed on the laws they wanted repealed (notably the Coercive Acts) and decided to implement an economic boycott while petitioning the king for relief. They adopted the Continental Association, which called for nonimportation of British goods (effective December 1, 1774), nonconsumption of British products (effective March 1, 1775), and nonexportation of American goods to Britain and the British West Indies (effective September 10, 1775).

The provisions of the Association—far more comprehensive than any previous economic measure adopted by the colonies—were carefully designed to appeal to different groups and regions. For example, the inclusive language of the nonimportation agreement banned commerce in slaves as well as manufactures, which accorded with a long-standing desire of the Virginia gentry to halt, or at least to slow, the arrival of enslaved Africans on their shores. (Leading Virginians believed that continuing slave importations had discouraged the immigration to their colony of free Europeans with useful skills.) Delaying nonconsumption until three months after implementing nonimportation allowed northern urban merchants time to sell items they had acquired legally before December 1. And both the novel tactic of nonexportation and its postponement for nearly a year served other interests. In 1773 small farmers in Virginia had already vowed to stop exporting tobacco, to raise prices in a then-glutted market. The next year, they enthusiastically welcomed an Association that accomplished the same end while permitting them to profit from higher prices for their 1774 crop, which needed to be dried and cured before shipment. Postponing the nonexportation agreement also benefited the northern exporters of wood products and foodstuffs to the Caribbean, giving them a final season of sales before the embargo began.

Committees of Observation   To enforce the Continental Association, Congress recommended the election of committees of observation and inspection in every American locality. By specifying that committee members be chosen by all men qualified to vote for members of the lower houses of assembly, Congress guaranteed the committees a broad popular base. The seven to eight thousand committeemen—some experienced officeholders, some new to politics—became the local leaders of American resistance.

Such committees were officially charged only with overseeing implementation of the boycott, but in the course of the next six months they became de facto governments. They examined merchants' records, publishing the names of those who continued to import British goods. They promoted home manufactures, encouraging Americans to adopt simple modes of dress and behavior to symbolize their commitment to liberty and virtuous conduct. Because expensive leisure-time activities were believed to reflect vice and corruption, Congress (as Janet Schaw learned) urged Americans to forgo dancing, gambling, horseracing, cardplaying, cockfighting, and other forms of "extravagance and dissipation." Some committees extracted apologies from people caught gambling, drinking to excess, or racing. Thus private activities acquired public significance.

The committees gradually extended their authority over many aspects of American life. They attempted to identify opponents of American resistance, developing elaborate spy networks, circulating copies of the Continental Association for signatures, and investigating reports of questionable remarks and activities. Suspected dissenters were urged to support the colonial cause publicly; if they refused, the committees had them watched, restricted their movements, or tried to force them to leave the area. People engaging in casual political exchanges with friends one day could find themselves charged with "treasonable conversation" the next. One Massachusetts man, for example, was called before his local committee for maligning the Congress as "a Pack or Parcell of Fools" that was "as tyrannical as Lord North and ought to be opposed & resisted." When he refused to recant, the committee put him under surveillance.

Provincial Conventions

While the committees of observation were expanding their power during the winter and early spring of 1775, the regular colonial governments were collapsing. Only a few legislatures

continued to meet without encountering challenges to their authority. In most colonies, popularly elected provincial conventions took over the task of running the government, sometimes entirely replacing the legislatures and at other times holding concurrent sessions. In late 1774 and early 1775, these conventions approved the Continental Association, elected delegates to the Second Continental Congress (scheduled for May), organized militia units, and gathered arms and ammunition. Unable to stem the tide of resistance, the British-appointed governors and councils watched helplessly as their authority crumbled.

Royal officials suffered humiliation after humiliation. Courts were prevented from meeting; taxes were paid to the conventions' agents rather than to provincial tax collectors; sheriffs' powers were challenged; and militiamen would muster only when committees ordered. In short, during the six months preceding the battles at Lexington and Concord, independence was being won at the local level, but without formal acknowledgment and for the most part without bloodshed. Not many Americans fully realized what was happening. The vast majority still proclaimed their loyalty to Great Britain, denying that they sought to leave the empire.

CONTEST IN THE BACKCOUNTRY

While the committees of observation were consolidating their authority in the East, some colonists were heading west. Ignoring the Proclamation of 1763, pronouncements by colonial governors, and the threat of Indian attacks alike, land-hungry folk—many of them recent immigrants from Ireland and soldiers who demobilized in North America after the Seven Years War—swarmed onto lands along the Ohio River and its tributaries after the mid-1760s. Sometimes they purchased property from opportunists with grants of dubious origin; often, they simply surveyed and claimed land, squatting on it in hopes that their titles would eventually be honored. Britain's 1771 decision to abandon (and raze) Fort Pitt removed the final restraints on settlement in the region, for the withdrawal rendered the Proclamation of 1763 unenforceable. By late 1775, thousands of new homesteads dotted the landscape of the backcountry from western Pennsylvania south through Virginia and eastern Kentucky into western North Carolina.

Distrust and Warfare

Few of the backcountry folk viewed the region's native peoples positively. (Rare exceptions were the Moravian missionaries who settled with their Indian converts in three small frontier communities in the upper Ohio valley.) The frontier dwellers had little interest in the small-scale trade that had once helped to sustain an uneasy peace in the region; they wanted only land on which to grow crops and pasture their livestock.

In 1774 Virginia, headed by a new governor, Lord Dunmore, moved vigorously to assert its title to the rapidly developing backcountry. During the spring and early summer, tensions mounted as Virginians surveyed land in Kentucky on the south side of the Ohio River—territory claimed by the Shawnees, who rejected the Fort Stanwix treaty of 1768. "Lord Dunmore's war" consisted of one large-scale confrontation between Virginia militia and some Shawnee warriors. Neither side won a clear-cut victory, but in the immediate aftermath thousands of settlers—including Daniel Boone and his associates—flooded across the mountains.

When the Revolutionary War began just as large numbers of people were migrating into Kentucky, the loyalties of Indians and settlers in the backcountry remained, like Boone's, fluid and uncertain. They were hostile to each other, but which side should either take in the imperial struggle? The answer might well depend on which could better serve their interests. Understanding that, the Continental Congress moved to reoccupy the site of Fort Pitt and to establish other garrisons in the Ohio country. Relying on such protection, as many as twenty thousand settlers poured into Kentucky and western Pennsylvania by 1780. Yet frontier affiliations were not clear: the growing town of Pittsburgh, for example, harbored many active loyalists.

The native peoples' grievances against the European American newcomers predisposed many toward an alliance with Great Britain. Yet some chiefs urged caution: after all, the British abandonment of Fort Pitt (and them) suggested that Britain lacked the will and ability to protect them in the future. Furthermore, Britain hesitated to make full, immediate use of its potential native allies. Officials on the scene understood that neither the Indians' style of fighting nor their war aims necessarily coincided with British goals and methods. Accordingly, they at first sought from Indians only a promise of neutrality.

Recognizing their poor standing with native peoples, patriots also sought Indians' neutrality. In 1775 the Second Continental Congress sent a general message to Indian communities, describing the war as "a family quarrel between us and Old England" and requesting that they "not join on either side" because "you Indians are not concerned in it." The Iroquois responded with a pledge of neutrality. But a group of Cherokees led by Chief Dragging Canoe decided to take advantage of the "family quarrel" to regain some land. In summer 1776, they attacked settlements in western Virginia and the Carolinas. After a militia campaign destroyed many Cherokee towns, along with crops and supplies, Dragging Canoe and his die-hard followers fled to the West, establishing new villages. Other Cherokees agreed to a treaty that ceded still more of their land.

Frontier Hostilities

Bands of Shawnees and Cherokees continued to attack settlements in the backcountry throughout the war, but dissent in their own ranks crippled their efforts. The British victory over France in 1763 had destroyed the Indian nations' most effective means of maintaining their independence: playing European powers off against one another. Successful strategies were difficult to envision under these new circumstances, and Indian leaders no longer concurred on a unified course of action. Communities split asunder as older and younger men, or civil and war leaders, disagreed vehemently over what policy to adopt. Only a few communities (among them the Stockbridge Indians of New England and the Oneidas in New York) unwaveringly supported the American revolt; most other native villages either tried to remain neutral or sporadically aligned themselves with the British. And the settlers fought back: in 1778 and early 1779 a frontier militia force under George Rogers Clark captured British posts in modern Illinois (Kaskaskia) and Indiana (Vincennes). Still, the revolutionaries could never mount an effective attack against the redcoats' major stronghold at Detroit.

Warfare between settlers and Indians persisted in the backcountry long after fighting between patriot and redcoat armies had ceased. Indeed, the Revolutionary War itself constituted a brief chapter in the ongoing struggle for control of the region west of the Appalachians, which began in 1763 and continued into the next century.

CHOOSING SIDES

In 1765 protests against the Stamp Act had won the support of most colonists in the Caribbean and Nova Scotia as well as in the future United States. Demonstrations occurred in Halifax (the major Nova Scotian port, founded 1748) as well as in Boston, New York, and Charleston. Although provisions of the 1764 Sugar Act benefited Britain's Caribbean possessions, the Stamp Act levied higher duties on them than on the mainland colonies; the residents of St. Christopher and Nevis in particular joined mainlanders in demonstrating against the law (see Map 5.3). When the act went into effect, though, islanders loyally paid the stamp duties until repeal. And eventually a significant number of colonists in North America and the West Indies began to question both the aims and the tactics of the resistance movement. Doubts arose with particular urgency in Nova Scotia and the Caribbean.

Nova Scotia and The Caribbean Both the northern mainland and the southern island colonies depended heavily on Great Britain militarily and economically. Despite the overwhelming British victory in the Seven Years War, they believed themselves vulnerable to French counterattack and eagerly sought regular troops and naval vessels stationed within their borders. Additionally, sugar planters—on some islands outnumbered by their bondspeople twenty-five to one—feared the potential for slave revolts in the absence of British troops. Neither region had a large population of European descent, nor were local political structures very strong. Fewer people lived in Halifax in 1775 than in the late 1750s, and the sugar islands had only a few resident planters to provide leadership, because successful men headed to England to buy great manors, leaving supervision of their property to hired managers.

Both Nova Scotians and West Indians had major economic reasons for ultimately choosing to support the mother country. In the mid-1770s the northerners finally broke into the Caribbean market with their cargoes of dried and salted fish. They also began to reduce New England's domination of the northern coastal trade, and once the shooting started they benefited greatly from Britain's retaliatory measures against the rebels' commerce. British sugar producers relied for their profits primarily on their monopoly of trade within the empire, for more efficient French planters were able to sell their sugar for one-third less. Further, the West Indian planters' effective lobbyists in London won the islands' exclusion from some provisions of the Townshend Acts. Accordingly, they could well have concluded that their interests could be adequately protected within the empire. Neither islanders nor Nova Scotians had reason to believe that they would be better off independent.

Patriots

Many residents of the thirteen colonies—especially members of the groups that dominated colonial society numerically or politically—reached different conclusions, choosing to support resistance, then independence. Active revolutionaries accounted for about two-fifths of the European American population. Among them were small and middling farmers, members of dominant Protestant sects (both Old and New Lights), Chesapeake gentry, merchants dealing mainly in American commodities, city artisans, elected officeholders, and people of English descent. Wives usually adopted their husbands' political beliefs, but not always. Although all these patriots supported the Revolution, they pursued divergent goals within the broader coalition, as they had in the 1760s. Some sought limited political reform; others, extensive political change; and still others, social and economic reforms. (The ways their concerns interacted are discussed in Chapter 7.)

Some colonists, though, found that they could not in good conscience endorse independence. Like their more radical counterparts, most objected to parliamentary policies, but they preferred the remedy of imperial constitutional reform. The events of the crucial year between the passage of the Coercive Acts and the outbreak of fighting in Massachusetts crystallized their thinking. Their objections to violent protest, their desire to uphold legally constituted government, and their fears of anarchy combined to make them sensitive to the dangers of resistance.

Loyalists

About one-fifth of the European American population remained loyal to Great Britain, firmly rejecting independence. Most loyalists had long opposed the men who became patriot leaders, though for varying reasons. British-appointed government officials; Anglican clergy everywhere and lay Anglicans in the North, where their denomination was in the minority; tenant farmers, particularly those whose landlords sided with the patriots; members of persecuted religious sects; many of the backcountry southerners who had rebelled against eastern rule in the late 1760s and early 1770s; and non-English ethnic minorities, especially Scots—all these groups feared the power wielded by those who controlled the colonial assemblies and who had shown little concern for their welfare in the past. Joined by merchants whose trade depended on imperial connections and by former officers and enlisted men from the British army who had settled in America after 1763, they formed a loyalist core that remained true to a self-conception that revolutionaries proved willing to abandon.

During the war, loyalists congregated in cities held by the British army. When those posts were evacuated at war's end, loyalists scattered to different parts of the British Empire—Britain, the Bahamas, and especially Canada. In the provinces of Nova Scotia, New Brunswick, and Ontario they re-created their lives as colonists, laying the foundations of British Canada. All told, perhaps as many as seventy thousand Americans preferred exile to life in a nation independent of British rule.

Neutrals

Between the patriots and the loyalists, there remained in the middle perhaps two-fifths of the European American population. Some who tried to avoid taking sides were sincere pacifists, such as Quakers. Others opportunistically shifted their allegiance to whatever side currently happened to be winning. Still others simply wanted to be left alone; they cared little about politics and usually obeyed whoever was in power. Such colonists also resisted British and Americans alike when the demands on them seemed too heavy—when taxes became too high or when calls for militia service came too often. Their attitude might best be summed up as "a plague on both your houses." Such people made up an especially large proportion of the population in the backcountry (including Boone's Kentucky), where Scots-Irish settlers had little love for either the patriot gentry or the English authorities.

To patriots, apathy or neutrality was as heinous as loyalism: those who were not for them were surely against them. By the winter of 1775–1776, the Second Continental Congress was recommending that all "disaffected" persons be disarmed and arrested. State legislatures passed laws prescribing severe penalties for suspected loyalists or neutrals. Many began to require all voters (or, in some cases, all free adult men) to take oaths of allegiance; the penalty for refusal was usually banishment to England or extra taxes. After 1777 many states confiscated the property of banished persons, using the proceeds for the war effort.

The patriots' policies helped to ensure that their scattered and persecuted opponents could not band together to threaten the revolutionary cause. But loyalists and neutrals were not the patriots' only worry, for revolutionaries could not assume that their slaves would support them.

Slaves

In New England, with few resident bondspeople, revolutionary fervor was widespread, and free African Americans enlisted in local patriot militias. The middle colonies, where slaves constituted a small but substantial proportion of the population, were more divided but still largely revolutionary. In Virginia and Maryland, where free people constituted a slender majority, the potential for slave revolts raised occasional but not disabling fears. By contrast, South Carolina and Georgia, where slaves composed more than half of the population, were noticeably less enthusiastic about resistance to Britain. Georgia sent no delegates to the First Continental Congress and reminded its representatives at the second one to consider its circumstances, "with our blacks and tories [loyalists] within us," when voting on the question of independence. On the mainland as well as in the Caribbean islands, therefore, colonists feared the potential enemy in their midst.

Bondspeople themselves faced a dilemma during the Revolution. Above all, their goal was *personal* independence. But how best could they escape from slavery? Should they fight with or against their masters? African Americans made different decisions, but to most slaves, supporting the British appeared more promising. In late 1774 and early 1775, groups of slaves began to offer to assist the British army in return for freedom. The most serious incident occurred in 1775 in Charleston, where Thomas Jeremiah, a free black harbor pilot, was brutally executed after being convicted of attempting to foment a slave revolt.

New Nations

The American Revolution not only created the United States but led directly to the formation of three other nations: English-dominated Canada, Sierra Leone, and Australia.

In northern North America before the Revolution, only Nova Scotia had a sizable number of English-speaking settlers. Those people, largely New Englanders, had been recruited after 1758 to repopulate the region forcibly taken from the exiled Acadians. During and after the Revolution, however, many loyalist families, especially those from the northern and middle colonies, moved to the region that is now Canada, which remained under British rule. The provinces of New Brunswick and Upper Canada (later Ontario) were established to accommodate them, and some exiles

Thomas Rowlandson, an English artist, sketched the boatloads of male and female convicts as they were being ferried to the ships that would take them to their new lives in the prison colony of Australia. Note the gibbet on the shore with two hanging bodies—symbolizing the fate these people were escaping.
(National Library of Australia)

settled in Quebec as well. In just a few years, the loyalist refugees transformed the sparsely populated former French colony, laying the foundation of the modern bilingual (but majority English-speaking) Canadian nation.

Sierra Leone, too, was founded by colonial exiles—African Americans who had fled to the British army during the war, many of whom ended up in London. Seeing the refugees' poverty, a group of charitable merchants—calling themselves the Committee for Relief of the Black Poor—developed a plan to resettle the African Americans elsewhere. After the refugees refused to be sent to the Bahamas, fearing that in the Caribbean they would be reenslaved, they concurred in a scheme to return them to the land of their ancestors. In early 1787, vessels carrying about four hundred settlers reached Sierra Leone in West Africa, where representatives of the Black Poor Committee acquired land from local rulers. The first years of the new colony were difficult, and many of the newcomers died of disease and deprivation. But in 1792 they were joined by several thousand other loyalist African Americans who had originally moved to Nova Scotia. The influx ensured the colony's survival; it remained a part of the British Empire until achieving its independence in 1961.

While the Sierra Leone migrants were preparing to sail from London in late 1786, the first prison ships were simultaneously being readied for Australia. At the Paris peace negotiations in 1782, American diplomats adamantly rejected British suggestions that the United States continue to serve as a dumping ground for convicts, as had been true throughout the eighteenth

New Nations

century. Britain thus needed another destination for the convicts sentenced in its courts to transportation for crimes such as theft, assault, and man-slaughter. It decided to send them halfway round the world, to the continent Captain James Cook had explored and claimed in 1770. Britain continued to dispatch convicts to some parts of Australia until 1868, but long before then voluntary migrants had also begun to arrive. The modern nation was created from a federation of separate colonial governments on January 1, 1901.

Thus the founding event in the history of the United States links the nation to the formation of its northern neighbor and to new nations in West Africa and the Asian Pacific.

The slaveowners' worst fears were realized in November 1775, when Virginia's royal governor, Lord Dunmore, offered to free any slaves and indentured servants who would leave their patriot masters to join the British forces. Dunmore hoped to use African Americans in his fight against the revolutionaries and to disrupt the economy by depriving planters of their labor force. About one thousand African Americans initially rallied to the British standard; although many of them perished in a smallpox epidemic, three hundred survived to reach occupied New York City under British protection. Because other commanders later renewed Dunmore's proclamation, tens of thousands of runaway slaves eventually joined the British, and at the end of the war at least nine thousand left with the redcoats.

Although slaves did not pose a serious threat to the revolutionary cause in its early years, the patriots turned rumors of slave uprisings to their own advantage. In South Carolina, resistance leaders argued that unity under the Continental Association would protect masters from their slaves at a time when royal government was unable to muster adequate defense forces. Undoubtedly many wavering Carolinians were drawn into the revolutionary camp by fear that an overt division among the colony's free people would encourage rebellion by the bondspeople.

Patriots could never completely ignore the threats posed by loyalists, neutrals, slaves, and Indians as well, but only rarely did fear of these groups seriously hamper the revolutionary movement. Occasionally backcountry militiamen refused to turn out for duty on the seacoast because they feared Indians would attack at home in their absence. Sometimes southern troops refused to serve in the North because they (and their political leaders) were unwilling to leave their regions unprotected against a slave insurrection. But the practical impossibility of a large-scale slave revolt, coupled with dissension in Indian communities and the patriots' successful campaign to disarm and neutralize loyalists, ensured that the revolutionaries would by and large remain firmly in control of the countryside as they fought for independence.

WAR AND INDEPENDENCE

On January 27, 1775, Lord Dartmouth, secretary of state for America, addressed a fateful letter to General Thomas Gage in Boston, urging him to take a decisive step. Opposition could not be "very formidable," Dartmouth wrote, and even if it were, "it will surely be better that the Conflict should be brought on, upon such ground, than in a riper state of Rebellion."

Battles of Lexington and Concord

After Gage received Dartmouth's letter on April 14, he sent an expedition to confiscate colonial military supplies stockpiled at Concord. Bostonians dispatched two messengers, William Dawes and Paul Revere (later joined by Dr. Samuel Prescott), to rouse the countryside. So, when the British vanguard of several hundred men approached Lexington at dawn on April 19, they found a ragtag group of seventy militiamen—about half of the adult male population of the town—mustered on the common. Realizing they could not halt the redcoats' advance, the Americans' commander ordered his men to withdraw. But as they began to disperse, a shot rang out; the British soldiers then fired several volleys. When they stopped, eight Americans lay dead, and another ten had been wounded. The British moved on to Concord, 5 miles away.

There the contingents of militia were larger, Concord residents having been joined by groups of men from nearby towns. An exchange of gunfire at the North Bridge spilled the first British blood of the Revolution: three men were killed and nine wounded. Thousands of militiamen then fired from houses and from behind trees and bushes at the British forces as they retreated to Boston. By the end of the day, the redcoats had suffered 272 casualties, including 70 deaths. Only the arrival of reinforcements and the American militia's lack of coordination prevented much heavier British losses. The patriots suffered just 93 casualties.

First Year of War

By the evening of April 20, thousands of American militiamen had gathered around Boston, summoned by local committees that spread the alarm across the countryside. Many did not stay long (they went home for spring planting), but those who remained, along with newer recruits, were organized into formal units. Officers under the command of General Artemas Ward of the Massachusetts militia ordered that latrines be dug, the water supply protected, supplies purchased, military discipline enforced, regular drills held, and defensive fortifications constructed.

For nearly a year the two armies sat and stared at each other across those siege lines. The redcoats attacked their besiegers only once, on June 17, when they drove the Americans from trenches atop Breed's Hill in Charlestown. In that misnamed Battle of Bunker Hill, the British incurred their greatest losses of the entire war: over 800 wounded and 228 killed. The Americans, though forced to abandon their position, lost less than half that number.

During the same eleven-month period, patriots captured Fort Ticonderoga, a British fort on Lake Champlain, acquiring much-needed cannon. Trying to bring Canada into the war on the American side, they also mounted a northern campaign that ended in disaster at Quebec in early 1776 after their troops were ravaged by smallpox. But the chief significance of the war's first year lay in the long lull in fighting between the main armies at Boston. The delay gave both sides a chance to regroup, organize, and plan their strategies.

British Strategy   Lord North and his new American secretary, Lord George Germain, made three central assumptions about the war they faced. First, they concluded that patriot forces could not withstand the assaults of trained British regulars. They and their generals were convinced that the 1776 campaign would be the first and last of the war. Accordingly, they dispatched to America the largest force Great Britain had ever assembled anywhere: 370 transport ships carrying 32,000 troops and tons of supplies, accompanied by 73 naval vessels and 13,000 sailors. Such an extraordinary effort, they thought, would ensure a quick victory. Among the troops were thousands of German mercenaries (many from the state of Hesse); eighteenth-century armies were often composed of such professional soldiers who hired out to the highest bidder.

Second, British officials and army officers treated this war as comparable to conflicts in Europe. They adopted a conventional strategy of capturing major American cities and defeating the rebel army decisively without suffering serious casualties themselves. Third, they assumed that a clear-cut military victory would achieve their goal of retaining the colonies' allegiance.

All three assumptions proved false. North and Germain vastly underestimated Americans' commitment to armed resistance. Battlefield defeats did not lead patriots to abandon their political aims and sue for peace. London officials also failed to recognize the significance of the American population's dispersal over an area 1,500 miles long and more than 100 miles wide. Although Britain would control each of the largest American ports at some time during the war, less than 5 percent of the population lived in those cities. Furthermore, the coast offered so many excellent harbors that essential commerce was easily rerouted. In other words, the loss of cities did little to damage the American cause, while British generals repeatedly squandered their resources to capture such ports.

Most of all, London officials did not initially understand that military triumph would not necessarily lead to political victory. Securing the colonies permanently would require hundreds of thousands of Americans to return to their original allegiance. After 1778 the ministry adopted a strategy designed to achieve that goal through the expanded use of loyalist forces and the restoration of civilian authority in occupied areas. But the new policy came too late. Britain's leaders never fully realized that they were fighting, not a conventional European war, but rather an entirely new kind of conflict: the first modern war of national liberation.

Second Continental At least Great Britain had a bureaucracy ready to supervise the
Congress   war effort. The Americans had only the Second Continental Congress, originally intended simply to consider the ministry's response to the Continental Association. Instead, the delegates who convened in Philadelphia on May 10, 1775, had to assume the mantle of intercolonial government. "Such a vast Multitude of objects, civil, political, commercial and military, press and crowd upon us so fast, that we know not what to do first," John Adams wrote a close

friend early in the session. Yet as the summer passed, Congress slowly organized the colonies for war. It authorized the printing of money with which to purchase necessary goods, established a committee to supervise relations with foreign countries, and took steps to strengthen the militia. Most important, it created the Continental Army and appointed its generals.

Until Congress met, the Massachusetts provincial congress had supervised Ward and the militiamen encamped at Boston. But that army, composed of men from all over New England, constituted a heavy drain on limited local resources. Consequently, Massachusetts asked the Continental Congress to assume the task of directing the army. As a first step, Congress had to choose a commander-in-chief, and many delegates recognized the importance of naming someone who was not a New Englander. John Adams later recalled that in mid-June he proposed the appointment of a Virginian "whose Skill and Experience as an Officer, whose independent fortune, great Talents and excellent universal Character, would command the Approbation of all America": George Washington. The Congress unanimously concurred.

George Washington

Neither fiery radical nor reflective political thinker, Washington had not participated prominently in the pre-revolutionary agitation. Devoted to the American cause, he was dignified, conservative, and respectable—a man of unimpeachable integrity. The younger son of a Virginia planter, Washington did not expect to inherit substantial property and planned to work as a surveyor. But the early death of his older brother and his marriage to the wealthy widow Martha Custis made George Washington one of the largest slaveholders in Virginia. Though an aristocrat, he was unswervingly committed to representative government. After his mistakes at the beginning of the Seven Years War, he had repaired his reputation by rallying the troops and maintaining a calm demeanor under fire during Braddock's defeat in 1755.

Washington also had remarkable stamina. In over eight years of war, he never had a serious illness and took only one brief leave of absence. Moreover, he both looked and acted like a leader. More than six feet tall in an era when most men were five inches shorter, he displayed a stately and commanding presence. Other patriots praised his judgment, steadiness, and discretion, and even a loyalist admitted that Washington could "atone for many demerits by the extraordinary coolness and caution which distinguish his character."

British Evacuate Boston

Washington needed all the coolness and caution he could muster when he took command of the army outside Boston in July 1775. The new general continued Ward's efforts to organize and sustain those troops. By March 1776, when the arrival of cannon from Ticonderoga finally enabled him to put direct pressure on the redcoats in the city, the army was prepared to act. Yet an assault on Boston proved unnecessary. Sir William Howe, the new commander, had been considering an evacuation; he wanted to transfer his men to New York City. The patriots' cannon decided the matter. On March 17, the British and more than a thousand of their loyalist allies abandoned Boston forever.

That spring of 1776, as the British fleet left Boston for the temporary haven of Halifax, the colonies were moving inexorably toward independence. Although they had been at war for months, American leaders denied seeking a break with Great Britain until a pamphlet published in January 1776 advocated such a step.

Common Sense   Thomas Paine's *Common Sense* exploded on the American scene, quickly selling tens of thousands of copies. The author, a radical English printer who had lived in America only since 1774, called stridently for independence. Paine also challenged many common American assumptions about government and the colonies' relationship to Britain. Rejecting the notion that only a balance of monarchy, aristocracy, and democracy could preserve freedom, he advocated the establishment of a republic, a government by the people with no king or nobility. Instead of acknowledging the benefits of links to the mother country, Paine insisted that Britain had exploited the colonies unmercifully. And for the frequently heard assertion that an independent America would be weak and divided he substituted an unlimited confidence in America's strength once freed from European control.

He expressed these striking sentiments in equally striking prose. Scorning the rational style of most other pamphleteers, Paine adopted an enraged tone, describing the king as a "royal brute," a "wretch" unconcerned for the colonists' welfare. His pamphlet reflected the oral culture of ordinary folk. Couched in everyday language, its primary source of authority was the Bible, the only book familiar to most Americans. No wonder the pamphlet had a wider distribution than any other political publication of its day.

It is unclear how many people were converted to the cause of independence by reading *Common Sense.* But by late spring, independence had become inevitable. On May 10, the Second Continental Congress formally recommended that individual colonies form new governments, replacing their colonial charters with state constitutions. Perceiving the trend, the few loyalists still connected with Congress severed their ties to that body.

Then on June 7 came confirmation of the movement toward independence. Richard Henry Lee of Virginia, seconded by John Adams of Massachusetts, introduced the crucial resolution: "that these United Colonies are, and of right ought to be, free and independent States, that they are absolved of all allegiance to the British Crown, and that all political connection between them and the State of Great Britain is, and ought to be, totally dissolved." Congress debated but did not immediately adopt Lee's resolution. Instead, it postponed a vote until early July, to allow time for consultation and public reaction. In the meantime, a five-man committee—including Thomas Jefferson, John Adams, and Benjamin Franklin—was directed to draft a declaration of independence.

The committee assigned primary responsibility for writing the declaration to Jefferson, who was well known for his eloquent style. Years later John Adams recalled that Jefferson had modestly protested his selection, suggesting that Adams prepare the initial draft. The Massachusetts revolutionary recorded his frank response: "You can write ten times better than I can."

Jefferson and the Declaration of Independence   Thirty-four-year-old Thomas Jefferson, a Virginia lawyer, had been educated at the College of William and Mary and in the law offices of a prominent attorney. A member of the House of Burgesses, he had read widely in history and political theory. That broad knowledge was evident not only in the declaration but also in his draft of the Virginia state constitution, completed just a few days before his appointment to the committee. Jefferson, an intensely private man, loved his home and family deeply. This early stage of his political career was marked by his beloved wife Martha's repeated difficulties in childbearing. While he wrote and debated in Philadelphia, she suffered a miscarriage at their home, Monticello. Not until after her death in 1782, from complications following the birth of their sixth (but only third surviving) child in ten years of marriage, did Jefferson fully commit himself to public service.

The draft of the declaration was laid before Congress on June 28, 1776. The delegates officially voted for independence four days later, then debated the wording of the declaration for two more days, adopting it with some changes on July 4. Since Americans had long ago ceased to see themselves as legitimate subjects of Parliament, the Declaration of Independence concentrated on George III (see the appendix), who provided an identifiable villain. The document accused the king of attempting to destroy representative government in the colonies and of oppressing Americans through the unjustified use of excessive force.

The declaration's chief long-term importance, however, did not lie in its lengthy catalogue of grievances against George III (including, in a section deleted by Congress, Jefferson's charge that the British monarchy had forced slavery on America). It lay instead in the ringing statements of principle that have served ever since as the ideal to which Americans aspire: "We hold these truths to be self-evident: That all men are created equal; that they are endowed by their Creator with certain unalienable rights; that among these are life, liberty and the pursuit of happiness; that, to secure these rights, governments are instituted among men, deriving their just powers from the consent of the governed; that whenever any form of government becomes destructive of these ends, it is the right of the people to alter or to abolish it, and to institute new government." These phrases have echoed down through American history like no others.

The delegates in Philadelphia who voted to accept the Declaration of Independence could not predict the consequences of their audacious act. When they adopted the declaration, they were committing treason. Therefore, when they concluded with the assertion that they "mutually pledge[d] to each other our lives, our fortunes, and our sacred honor," they spoke no less than the truth. The real struggle still lay before them, and few had Thomas Paine's boundless confidence in success.

THE STRUGGLE IN THE NORTH

In late June 1776, the first ships carrying Sir William Howe's troops from Halifax appeared off the coast of New York. On July 2, the day Congress voted for independence, redcoats landed on Staten Island. Washington marched his army of seventeen thousand south from Boston to defend Manhattan. Because Howe waited until more troops arrived from England before attacking, Americans could prepare to defend the city.

New York and New Jersey   But Washington and his men, still inexperienced in fighting and maneuvering, made major mistakes, losing battles at Brooklyn Heights and on Manhattan Island. The city fell to the British, who captured nearly three thousand American soldiers. (Those men spent most of the rest of the war on British prison ships anchored in New York harbor, where many died of smallpox and other diseases.) Washington slowly retreated across New

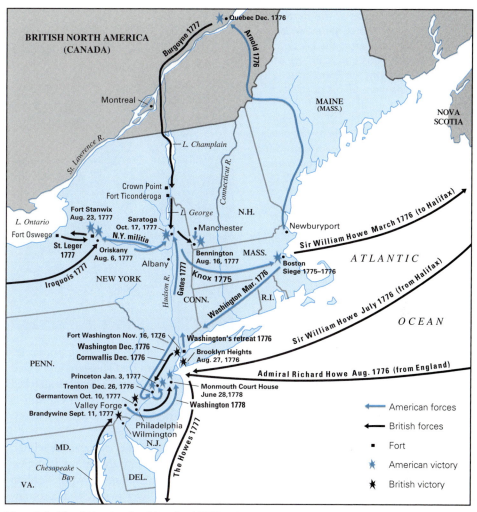

MAP 6.1 The War in the North, 1775–1777

The early phase of the Revolutionary War was dominated by British troop movements in the Boston area, the redcoats' evacuation to Nova Scotia in the spring of 1776, and the subsequent British invasion of New York and New Jersey.

Jersey into Pennsylvania, and British forces took control of most of New Jersey. Occupying troops met little opposition; the revolutionary cause appeared to be in disarray. "These are the times that try men's souls," wrote Thomas Paine in his pamphlet *The Crisis.* "The summer soldier and the sunshine patriot will, in this crisis, shrink from the service of his country; . . . yet we have this consolation with us, that the harder the conflict, the more glorious the triumph."

The British then forfeited their advantage as redcoats stationed in New Jersey went on a rampage of rape and plunder. Washington determined to strike back. Moving quickly, he crossed the Delaware River at night to attack a Hessian encampment at Trenton early

George Washington at the Battle of Princeton, 1779, by Charles Willson Peale. Two years after the battle, Peale created this heroic image of the Continental Army's commander, intended (as were all his portraits of revolutionary leaders) to instill patriotic sentiments and pride in its viewers. (Courtesy of the Pennsylvania Academy of Fine Arts, Philadelphia. Gift of Maria McKean Allen and Phoebe Warren)

on the morning of December 26, while the Germans were still recuperating from celebrating Christmas. The patriots captured more than nine hundred Hessians and killed another thirty; only three Americans were wounded. A few days later, Washington attacked again at Princeton. Having gained command of the field and buoyed American spirits with the two swift victories, Washington set up winter quarters at Morristown, New Jersey.

Campaign of 1777   British strategy for 1777, sketched in London over the winter, aimed to cut New England off from the other colonies. General John Burgoyne, a subordinate of Howe and one of the planners, would lead an invading force of redcoats and Indians down the Hudson River from Canada to rendezvous near Albany with a similar force that would move east along the Mohawk River valley. The combined forces would then presumably link up with Howe's troops in New York City. But in New York Howe simultaneously prepared his own plan to capture Philadelphia. Consequently, in 1777 the British armies in America would operate independently; the result would be disaster.

Howe took Philadelphia, but he did so in inexplicable fashion, delaying for months before beginning the campaign, then taking six weeks to transport his troops by sea instead of marching them overland. Incredibly, at the end of the lengthy voyage, he ended up only 40 miles closer to Philadelphia than when he started. By the time Howe advanced on Philadelphia, Washington had had time to prepare its defenses. Twice, at Brandywine Creek and again at Germantown, the two armies clashed near the patriot capital. Although the British won both engagements, the Americans handled themselves well. The redcoats captured Philadelphia in late September, but to little effect. The campaign season was nearly over; the revolutionary army had gained confidence in itself and its leaders; and, far to the north, Burgoyne was going down to defeat.

Burgoyne and his men had set out from Montreal in mid-June, traveling first by boat on Lake Champlain, then later marching slowly overland toward the Hudson, forced as they went to clear giant trees felled across their path by patriot militiamen. An easy triumph at Fort Ticonderoga in July was followed in August by two setbacks—the redcoats and Indians marching east along the Mohawk River turned back after a battle at Oriskany, New York; and in a clash near Bennington, Vermont, American militiamen nearly wiped out eight hundred of Burgoyne's German mercenaries. The general's dawdling had given American troops time to prepare for his arrival. After several skirmishes with an American army commanded by General Horatio Gates, Burgoyne was surrounded near Saratoga, New York. On October 17, 1777, he surrendered his entire force of more than six thousand men.

Iroquois Confederacy Splinters

The August 1777 battle at Oriskany divided the Iroquois Confederacy. Although the Six Nations had formally pledged to remain neutral in the war, two influential Mohawk leaders, the siblings Mary and Joseph Brant, believed that the Iroquois should ally themselves with the British to protect their territory from land-hungry colonists. The Brants won over the Senecas, Cayugas, and Mohawks, all of whom contributed warriors to the 1777 expedition. But the Oneidas—who had been converted to Christianity by Protestant missionaries—preferred the American side and brought the Tuscaroras with them. The Onondagas split into three factions, one on each side and one supporting neutrality. At Oriskany, some Oneidas and Tuscaroras joined

Joseph Brant, the Iroquois leader who helped to persuade the Mohawks, Senecas, and Cayugas to support the British in the latter stages of the Revolution, as painted by Charles Willson Peale in 1797. (Independence National Historic Park Collection)

patriot militiamen in fighting their Iroquois brethren, shattering a three-hundred-year-old league of friendship.

The collapse of Iroquois unity and the confederacy's abandonment of neutrality had significant consequences. In 1778 Iroquois warriors allied with the British raided frontier villages in Pennsylvania and New York. To retaliate, the Americans the following summer dispatched an expedition under General John Sullivan to burn Iroquois crops, orchards, and settlements. The resulting devastation led many bands to seek food and shelter north of the Great Lakes during the winter of 1779–1780. A large number of Iroquois people never returned to New York but settled permanently in Canada.

Burgoyne's surrender at Saratoga brought joy to patriots, discouragement to loyalists and Britons. In exile in London, Thomas Hutchinson wrote of "universal dejection" among loyalists there. "Everybody in a gloom," he commented, "most of us expect to lay our bones here." The disaster prompted Lord North to authorize a peace commission to offer the Americans what they had requested in 1774—in effect, a return to the imperial system of 1763. That proposal came far too late: the patriots rejected the overture, and the peace commission sailed back to England empty-handed in mid-1778.

Most important, the American victory at Saratoga drew France formally into the conflict. Ever since 1763, the French had sought to avenge their defeat in the Seven Years War, and the American Revolution gave them that opportunity. Even before Benjamin Franklin arrived in Paris in late 1776, France covertly supplied the revolutionaries with military necessities. Indeed, 90 percent of the gunpowder used by the Americans during the war's first two years came from France, transported via the French Caribbean island of Martinique.

Franco-American Alliance of 1778   Benjamin Franklin worked tirelessly to strengthen ties between the two nations. He adopted a plain style of dress that made him conspicuous amid the luxury of the court of King Louis XVI. Presenting himself as a representative of American simplicity, Franklin played on the French image of Americans as virtuous farmers. His efforts culminated in 1778 when the countries signed two treaties. In the Treaty of Amity and Commerce, France recognized American independence, establishing trade ties with the new nation. In the Treaty of Alliance, France and the United States promised—assuming that France would declare war on Britain, which it soon did—that neither would negotiate peace with the enemy without consulting the other. France also formally abandoned any claim to Canada and to North American territory east of the Mississippi River. In the years that followed, the most visible symbol of Franco-American cooperation was the Marquis de Lafayette, a young nobleman who volunteered for service with George Washington in 1777 and fought with American forces until the conflict ended.

The French alliance had two major benefits for the patriot cause. First, France began to aid the Americans openly, sending troops and naval vessels in addition to arms, ammunition, clothing, and blankets. Second, Britain could no longer focus solely on the American mainland, for it had to fight France in the Caribbean and elsewhere. Spain's entry into the war in 1779 as an ally of France (but not of the United States) magnified Britain's problems, for the Revolution then became a global war. The French aided the Americans throughout the conflict, but in its last years that assistance proved vital.

LIFE IN THE ARMY AND ON THE HOME FRONT

Only in the first months of the war was the revolutionaries' army manned primarily by the semi-mythical "citizen-soldier," the militiaman who exchanged his plow for a gun to defend his homeland. After a few months or at most a year, the early arrivals went home. They reenlisted only briefly and only if the contending armies neared their farms and towns. In such militia units, elected officers and the soldiers who chose them reflected existing social hierarchies in their regions of origin, yet also retained a freedom and flexibility absent from the Continental Army, composed of men in formally organized statewide units led by appointed officers.

Continental Army   Continental soldiers, unlike militiamen, were primarily young, single, or propertyless men who enlisted for long periods or for the war's duration, in part to earn monetary bonuses or allotments of land after the war. They responded to calls for "manly resistance" to Britain, seeing in military service an opportunity to protect homes and families, assert their masculine identity, and claim postwar citizenship and property-owning rights. As the fighting dragged on, the bonuses grew larger and more enticing. To meet their quotas, towns and states eagerly recruited everyone they could. Regiments from the middle states contained an especially large proportion of recent immigrants; about 45 percent of Pennsylvania soldiers were of Irish origin, and about 13 percent were German, some serving in German-speaking regiments.

Dunmore's proclamation led Congress in January 1776 to modify an earlier policy that had prohibited the enlistment of African Americans in the regular American army,

Barzillai Lew, a free African American born in Groton, Massachusetts, in 1743, served in the Seven Years War before enlisting with patriot troops in the American Revolution. An accomplished fifer, Lew fought at the Battle of Bunker Hill. Like other freemen in the north, he cast his lot with the revolutionaries, in contrast to southern bondspeople, who tended to favor the British. (Courtesy of Mae Theresa Bonitto)

and recruiters in northern states turned increasingly to slaves, who were often promised freedom after the war. Enslaved substitutes for their masters constituted about 10 percent of eastern Connecticut enlistees, for example, along with another 5 percent identified as free blacks, who earned enlistment bounties. Southern states initially resisted the trend, but later all except Georgia and South Carolina also enlisted black soldiers. Approximately five thousand African Americans eventually served in the Continental Army. They commonly served in racially integrated units but were assigned tasks that others shunned, such as burying the dead, foraging for food, and driving wagons. Overall, at any given time they composed about 10 percent of the regular army, although they seldom served in militia units.

Also attached to the American forces were a number of women, the wives and widows of poor soldiers, who came to the army with their menfolk because they were too impoverished to survive alone. Such camp followers—estimated to be about 3 percent of the total number of troops—worked as cooks, nurses, and launderers in return for rations and low wages. The women, along with civilian commissaries and militiamen who floated in and out of camp at irregular intervals, made up an unwieldy assemblage that officers found difficult to manage, especially because none of them could be subjected to the same military discipline as regular soldiers. Yet the army's shapelessness also reflected its greatest strength: an almost unlimited reservoir of manpower and womanpower.

Officer Corps

The officers of the Continental Army developed an intense sense of pride and commitment to the revolutionary cause. The hardships they endured, the battles they fought, the difficulties they overcame all helped to forge an esprit de corps that outlasted the war. The realities of warfare were often dirty, messy, and corrupt, but the officers drew strength from a developing image of themselves as professionals who sacrificed personal gain for the good of the entire nation. When Benedict Arnold, an officer who fought heroically for the patriot cause early in the war, defected to the British, they made his name a metaphor for villainy. "How black, how despised, loved by none, and hated by all," wrote one officer.

The officers' wives, too, prided themselves on their and their husbands' service to the nation. Unlike poor women, they did not travel with the army but instead came for extended visits while the troops were in camp (usually during the winters). Martha Washington and other officers' wives, for example, lived at Valley Forge in the winter of 1777–1778. They brought with them food, clothing, and household furnishings to make their stay more comfortable, and they entertained each other and their menfolk at teas, dinners, and dances. Socializing and discussing current events created friendships later renewed in civilian life when some of their husbands became the new nation's leaders.

Hardship and Disease

Life in the American army was difficult for everyone, although ordinary soldiers endured more hardships than their officers. Wages were small, and often the army could not meet the payroll. Rations (a daily standard allotment of bread, meat, vegetables, milk, and beer) did not always appear, and men had to forage for their own food. Clothing and shoes the army supplied were often of poor quality; soldiers had to make do or find their own. While in camp, soldiers occasionally hired themselves out as laborers to nearby farmers to augment their meager rations or earnings. When conditions deteriorated, troops threatened mutiny (though only a few carried out that threat) or, more often, simply deserted. Punishments for desertion or other offenses such as theft and assault were harsh; convicted soldiers were sentenced to hundreds of lashes, whereas officers were publicly humiliated, deprived of their commission, and discharged in disgrace.

Endemic disease in the camps—especially dysentery, various fevers, and, early in the war, smallpox—made matters worse, sometimes discouraging recruiting. Most native-born colonists had neither been exposed to smallpox nor inoculated against the disease, so soldiers and civilians were vulnerable when smallpox spread through the northern countryside after the early months of 1774. The disease ravaged residents of Boston during the British occupation, the troops attacking Quebec in 1775–1776, and the African Americans who fled to join Lord Dunmore (1775) or Lord Cornwallis (1781). Because most British soldiers had already survived smallpox (which was endemic in Europe), it did not pose a significant threat to redcoat troops.

Washington recognized that smallpox could potentially decimate the revolutionaries' ranks, especially after it helped cause the failure of the 1775 Quebec expedition. Thus, in Morristown in early 1777, he ordered that entire regular army and all new recruits be inoculated, although some would die from the risky procedure and survivors would be incapacitated for weeks. Those dramatic measures, coupled with the increasing numbers of foreign-born (and mostly immune) men who enlisted, helped to protect Continental soldiers later in the war, contributing significantly to the eventual American victory.

Home Front

Men who enlisted in the army or served in Congress were away from home for long periods of time. In their absence their womenfolk, who previously had handled only the "indoor affairs" of the household, shouldered the responsibility for "outdoor affairs" as well. As the wife of a Connecticut soldier later recalled, her husband "was out more or less during the remainder of the war [after 1777], so much so as to be unable to do anything on our farm. What was done, was done by myself." Similarly, John and Abigail Adams took great pride in Abigail's developing skills as a "farmeress." Like other female contemporaries, Abigail Adams stopped calling the farm "yours" in letters to her husband and began referring to it as "ours"—a revealing change of pronoun. Most women did not work in the fields themselves, but they supervised field workers and managed their families' resources.

Wartime disruptions affected the lives of all Americans. Even far from the battlefields, people suffered from shortages of necessities like salt, soap, and flour. Small luxuries like new clothing or even ribbons or gloves were essentially unavailable. Severe inflation added to the country's woes, eroding the value of any income. For those who lived near the armies' camps or lines of march, difficulties were compounded. Soldiers of both sides plundered farms and houses, looking for food or salable items; they burned fence rails in their fires and took horses and oxen to transport their wagons. Moreover, they carried smallpox and other diseases with them wherever they went. In such circumstances and in the absence of their husbands, women had to make the momentous decision whether to deliberately risk their children's lives by inoculating them with smallpox or to take the chance of the youngsters' contracting the disease "in the natural way," with its even greater risk of death. Many, including Abigail Adams, chose the former course of action and were relieved when their children survived.

VICTORY IN THE SOUTH

In early 1778, in the wake of the Saratoga disaster, Lord George Germain and British military leaders reassessed their strategy. The loyalist exiles in London persuaded them to shift the field of battle southward, contending that loyal southerners would welcome the redcoat army as liberators. Once the South had been pacified and returned to friendly civilian control, it could then serve as a base for once again attacking the middle and northern states.

South Carolina and the Caribbean Sir Henry Clinton, who replaced Sir William Howe, oversaw the regrouping of British forces in America. He ordered the evacuation of Philadelphia in June 1778 and sent a convoy that successfully captured the French Caribbean island of St. Lucia, which thereafter served as a key base for Britain. He also dispatched a small expedition to Georgia at the end of the year. When Savannah and then Augusta fell easily into British hands, Clinton became convinced that a southern strategy would succeed. In late 1779 he sailed down the coast from New York to besiege Charleston, the most important city in the South. Although afflicted by smallpox, the Americans trapped in the city held out for months. Still, on May 12, 1780, General Benjamin Lincoln was forced to surrender the entire southern army—5,500 men—to the invaders. In the following weeks, the redcoats spread through South Carolina, establishing garrisons at key points in the interior. Hundreds of South Carolinians renounced allegiance to the United States, proclaiming their renewed loyalty to the Crown. Clinton organized loyalist regiments, and the process of pacification began.

Yet the triumph was less complete than it appeared. The success of the southern campaign depended on control of the seas, for the British armies were so widely dispersed and travel by land was so difficult that only through British naval vessels could the armies coordinate their efforts. For the moment, the Royal Navy safely dominated the American coastline, but French naval power posed a threat to the entire southern enterprise. American privateers infested Caribbean waters, seizing valuable cargoes bound to and from the British islands. Furthermore, after late 1778 France picked off those islands one by one, including Grenada—second only to Jamaica in sugar production—and, in 1781, St. Christopher as well. Even though in early 1781 the British captured and plundered St. Eustatius (the Dutch island that after French entry into the war served as the main conduit for the movement of military supplies from Europe to America), the victory did them little good. Indeed, it might well have cost them the war, for Admiral Sir George Rodney, occupied with securing the victory (and his personal profits from the plunder), failed to pursue the French fleet under Admiral François de Grasse when it subsequently sailed from the Caribbean to Virginia, where it played a major role in the battle at Yorktown.

Then, too, the redcoats never managed to establish full control of the areas they seized in South Carolina or Georgia. Patriot bands operated freely, and loyalists could

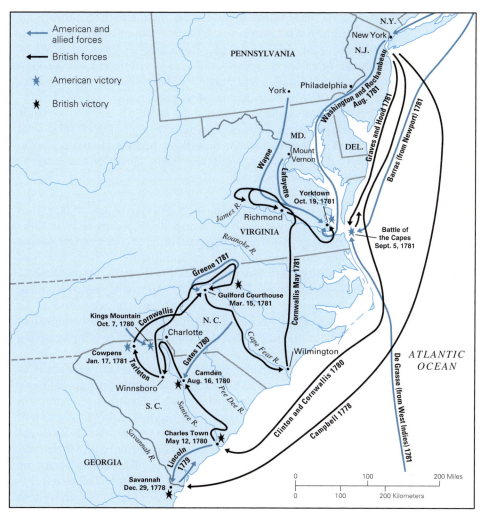

MAP 6.2 **The War in the South**

The southern war—after the British invasion of Georgia in late 1778—was characterized by a series of British thrusts into the interior, leading to battles with American defenders in both North and South Carolina. Finally, after promising beginnings, Cornwallis's foray into Virginia ended with disaster at Yorktown in October 1781.

not be adequately protected. The fall of Charleston failed to dishearten the patriots; instead, it spurred them to greater exertions. As one Marylander declared confidently, "The Fate of America is not to be decided by the Loss of a Town or Two." Patriot women in four states formed the Ladies Association, which collected money to purchase shirts for needy soldiers. Recruiting efforts were stepped up.

Nevertheless, the war in South Carolina went badly for the patriots throughout most of 1780. At Camden in August, forces under Lord Cornwallis, the new British commander in the South, crushingly defeated a reorganized southern army led by Horatio Gates. Thousands of enslaved African Americans joined the redcoats, seeking the freedom promised by Lord Dunmore and later by Sir Henry Clinton. Running away from their patriot masters individually and as families, they seriously disrupted planting and harvesting in the Carolinas and Georgia in 1780 and 1781. Tens of thousands of slaves were lost to their owners as a result of the war. Not all of them joined the British or won their freedom if they did, but their flight had exactly the effect the British sought. Many served the redcoats as scouts and guides, or as laborers in camps or occupied cities like New York.

Greene and the Southern Campaign

After the Camden defeat, Washington (who had to remain in the North to contain the British army occupying New York) appointed General Nathanael Greene to command the southern campaign. Appalled by conditions in South Carolina, Greene told a friend that "the word difficulty when applied to the state of things here . . . is almost without meaning, it falls so far short" of reality. His troops needed clothing, blankets, and food, but "a great part of this country is already laid waste and in the utmost danger of becoming a desert." Incessant guerrilla warfare had, he commented, "so corrupted the principles of the people that they think of nothing but plundering one another."

In such dire circumstances, Greene had to move cautiously. He adopted a conciliatory policy toward the many Americans who had switched sides, an advantageous move in a region in which people could well have altered their allegiance up to seven times in less than two years. He also ordered his troops to treat captives fairly and not to loot loyalist property. Recognizing that the patriots needed to convince a war-weary populace that they could bring stability to the region, he helped the shattered provincial congresses of Georgia and South Carolina to reestablish civilian authority in the interior—a goal the British were never able to accomplish. Because he had so few regulars (only sixteen hundred when he took command), Greene had to rely on western volunteers and could not afford to have frontier militia companies occupied in defending their homes from Indian attack. He accordingly pursued diplomacy aimed at keeping the Indians out of the war. Although royal officials cooperating with the redcoat invaders initially won some Indian allies, Greene's careful maneuvers eventually proved successful. By war's end, only the Creeks remained allied with Great Britain.

Even before Greene took command of the southern army in December 1780, the tide had begun to turn. In October, at King's Mountain, a force from the backcountry defeated a large party of redcoats and loyalists. Then in January 1781 Greene's trusted aide Daniel Morgan brilliantly routed the British regiment Tarleton's Legion at Cowpens. Greene himself confronted the main body of British troops under Lord Cornwallis at Guilford Court House, North Carolina, in March. Although Cornwallis controlled the field at the end of the day, most of his army had been destroyed. He had to retreat to Wilmington, on the coast, to receive supplies and fresh troops from New York by sea. Meanwhile, Greene returned to South Carolina, where, in a series of swift strikes, he forced the redcoats to abandon their interior posts and retire to Charleston.

Surrender at Yorktown

Cornwallis headed north into Virginia, where he joined forces with a detachment of redcoats commanded by the American traitor Benedict Arnold. Instead of acting decisively with his new army of 7,200 men, Cornwallis withdrew to the peninsula between the York and James Rivers, where he fortified Yorktown and awaited supplies and reinforcements. Seizing the opportunity, Washington quickly moved more than 7,000 French and American troops south from New York City. When De Grasse's fleet arrived from the Caribbean just in time to defeat the Royal Navy vessels sent to relieve Cornwallis, the British general was trapped. On October 19, 1781, Cornwallis surrendered.

When news of the defeat reached London, Lord North's ministry fell. Parliament voted to cease offensive operations in America, authorizing peace negotiations. Washington returned with the main army to the environs of New York, where his underpaid—and, they thought, underappreciated—officers grew restive. In March 1783 they threatened to mutiny unless Congress guaranteed them adequate compensation for their services. Washington, warned in advance of the so-called Newburgh Conspiracy, met the challenge brilliantly. Summoning his officers, he defused the crisis with a well-reasoned but emotional speech drawing on their patriotism. How could they, he asked, "open the flood Gates of Civil discord, and deluge our rising Empire in Blood"? When at one point he fumbled for glasses, remarking in passing that "I have grown gray in your service and now find myself growing blind," eyewitnesses reported that many of the rebellious officers began to cry. At the end of the year, he stood before Congress and formally resigned his commission as commander-in-chief. Through such actions at the end of the conflict, Washington established an enduring precedent: civilian control of the American military.

The war had been won, but at terrible cost. More than 25,000 American men died in the war, only about one-quarter of them from wounds suffered in battle. The rest were declared missing in action or died of disease or as prisoners of war. In the South, years of guerrilla warfare and the loss of thousands of runaway slaves shattered the economy. Indebtedness soared, and local governments were crippled for lack of funds, as few people could afford to pay their taxes. In the 1780s in Charles County, Maryland, for example, men commonly refused to serve in elective or appointive office because their personal estates would become liable for any taxes or fines they were unable to collect. Many of the county's formerly wealthy planters descended into insolvency, and in the 1790s a traveler observed that the countryside "wears a most dreary aspect," remarking on the "old dilapidated mansions" that had once housed well-to-do slaveowners.

Treaty of Paris

Yet Charles County residents and Americans in general "all rejoiced" when they learned of the signing of the preliminary peace treaty at Paris in November 1782. The American diplomats—Benjamin Franklin, John Jay, and John Adams—ignored their instructions from Congress to be guided by France and instead negotiated directly with Great Britain. Their instincts were sound: the French government was more an enemy to Britain than a friend to the United States. In fact, French ministers worked secretly behind the scenes to try to prevent the establishment of a strong, unified government in America. Spain's desire to lay claim to the region between the Appalachian Mountains and the Mississippi River further complicated the negotiations. But the American delegates proved adept at power politics, achieving their main goal: independence as a united nation. Weary of war, the new British ministry, headed by Lord Shelburne (formerly an outspoken critic of Lord North's American policies), made numerous concessions—so many, in fact, that Parliament ousted the ministry shortly after peace terms were approved.

The treaty, signed formally on September 3, 1783, granted unconditional independence to a nation named "the United States of America." Generous boundaries delineated that new nation: to the north, approximately the present-day boundary with Canada; to the south, the 31st parallel (about the modern northern border of Florida); to the west, the Mississippi River. Florida, which Britain had acquired in 1763, reverted to Spain. The Americans also gained unlimited fishing rights off Newfoundland. In ceding so much land to the United States, Great Britain ignored the territorial rights of its Indian allies, sacrificing their interests to the demands of European politics. British diplomats also poorly served loyalists and British merchants. The treaty's ambiguously worded clauses pertaining to the payment of prewar debts and the postwar treatment of loyalists caused trouble for years to come, proving impossible to enforce.

SUMMARY

The long war finally over, the victorious Americans could look back on their achievement with satisfaction and awe. Having unified the disparate mainland colonies, they had claimed their place in the family of nations and forged a successful alliance with France. With an inexperienced army composed of militia and regulars, they had defeated the professional soldiers of the greatest military power in the world. They accomplished their goal more through persistence and commitment than through brilliance on the battlefield, a persistence that involved wives and families on the home front as well as soldiers. They had won only a few actual victories—most notably, at Trenton, Saratoga, and Yorktown—but their army always survived defeats to fight again, even after the devastating losses at Manhattan and Charleston. Ultimately, the Americans simply wore their enemy down.

In winning the war, the Americans reshaped the physical and mental landscapes in which they lived. They abandoned the British identity once so important to them, excluding from their new nation their loyalist neighbors who were unwilling to make a break with the mother country. They established republican governments at state and national levels. In the families of Continental Army soldiers in particular they began the process of creating new national loyalties. They also laid claim to most of the territory east of the Mississippi River and south of the Great Lakes, thereby greatly expanding the land potentially open to their settlements and threatening the traditional Indian dominance of the continent's interior.

In achieving independence, Americans surmounted formidable challenges. But in the future they faced perhaps an even greater one: ensuring the survival of their republican polity in a world dominated by the bitter rivalries among Britain, France, and Spain.

7

Forging a National Republic 1776–1789

CREATING A VIRTUOUS REPUBLIC

When the colonies declared independence, John Dickinson recalled many years later, "there was no question concerning forms of Government, no enquiry whether a Republic or a limited Monarchy was best.... We knew that the people of this country must unite themselves under some form of Government and that this could be no other than the republican form"—in short, self-government by the people. But how should that goal be implemented?

Varieties of Republicanism   Three different definitions of republicanism emerged in the new United States. Ancient history and political theory informed the first, held chiefly by members of the educated elite (such as the Adamses of Massachusetts). The histories of popular governments in Greece and Rome suggested that republics could succeed only if they were small in size and homogeneous in population. Unless a republic's citizens were willing to sacrifice their own private interests for the good of the whole, the government would collapse. A truly virtuous man, classical republican theory insisted, had to forgo personal profit and work solely for the best interests of the nation. In return for sacrifices, though, a republic offered its citizens equality of opportunity. Under such a government, rank would be based on merit rather than on inherited wealth and status. Society would be governed by members of a "natural aristocracy," men whose talent had elevated them from what might have been humble beginnings to positions of power and privilege. Rank would not be abolished but instead would be founded on merit.

A second definition, advanced by other members of the elite but also by some skilled craftsmen, drew more on economic theory than on political thought. Instead of perceiving the nation as an organic whole composed of people nobly sacrificing for the common good, this version of republicanism followed the Scottish theorist Adam Smith in emphasizing individuals' pursuit of rational self-interest. The huge profits some men reaped from patriotism by selling supplies to the army underscored such an approach. The nation could only benefit from aggressive economic expansion, argued men such as Alexander Hamilton. When republican men sought to improve their own economic and social circumstances, the entire nation would benefit. Republican virtue would be achieved through the pursuit of private interests, rather than through subordination to communal ideals. Such thinking decisively abandoned the old notion of the Puritan covenant, which the first definition perpetuated in its emphasis on consensus, though not in its stress on an aristocracy of talent rather than birth.

The third notion of republicanism was less influential but more egalitarian than the other two, both of which contained considerable potential for inequality. Many of its illiterate or barely literate proponents could write little to promote their beliefs. Men who advanced the third version of republicanism, the most prominent of whom was Thomas Paine, called for widening men's participation in the political process. They also wanted government to respond directly to the needs of ordinary folk, rejecting any notion that the "lesser sort" should automatically defer to their "betters." They were, indeed, democrats in more or less the modern sense. For them, the untutored wisdom of the people embodied republican virtue.

Despite the differences, the three strands of republicanism shared many of the same assumptions. All three contrasted the industrious virtue of America with the corruption of Britain and Europe. In the first version, that virtue manifested itself in frugality and self-sacrifice; in the second, it would prevent self-interest from becoming vice; in the third, it was the justification for including propertyless free men in the ranks of voters. "Virtue, Virtue alone . . . is the basis of a republic," asserted Dr. Benjamin Rush of Philadelphia, an ardent patriot, in 1778. His fellow Americans concurred, even if they defined virtue differently. Most agreed that a virtuous country would be composed of hard-working citizens who would dress simply and live plainly, elect wise leaders to public office, and forgo the conspicuous consumption of luxury goods.

Virtue and the Arts As citizens of the United States set out to construct their republic, they believed they were embarking on an unprecedented enterprise. With great pride in their new nation, they expected to replace the vices of monarchical Europe—immorality, selfishness, and lack of public spirit—with the sober virtues of republican America. They sought to embody republican principles not only in their governments but also in their society and culture, expecting painting, literature, drama, and architecture to convey messages of nationalism and virtue to the public.

Americans faced a crucial contradiction at the outset of their efforts. To some republicans, fine arts were manifestations of vice. Their presence in a virtuous society,

CHRONOLOGY

1776 • Second Continental Congress directs states to draft constitutions

• Abigail Adams advises her husband to "Remember the Ladies"

1777 • Articles of Confederation sent to states for ratification

• Vermont becomes first jurisdiction to abolish slavery

1781 • Articles of Confederation ratified

1783 • Treaty of Paris signed, formalizing American independence

1784 • Diplomats sign treaty with Iroquois at Fort Stanwix, but Iroquois repudiate it two years later

1785 • Land Ordinance of 1785 provides for surveying and sale of national lands in Northwest Territory

1785–86 • United States negotiates treaties at Hopewell, South Carolina, with Choctaws, Chickasaws, and Cherokees

1786 • Annapolis Convention meets, discusses reforming government

1786–87 • Shays's Rebellion in western Massachusetts raises questions about future of the republic

1787 • Royall Tyler's *The Contrast*, first successful American play, performed

• Northwest Ordinance organizes territory north of Ohio River and east of Mississippi River

• Constitutional Convention drafts new form of government

1788 • Hamilton, Jay, and Madison write *The Federalist* to urge ratification of the Constitution by New York

• Constitution ratified

1789 • William Hill Brown publishes *The Power of Sympathy*, first American novel

• Massachusetts orders towns to support public schools

1800 • Weems publishes his *Life of Washington*

many contended, signaled the existence of luxury and corruption. Why did a frugal farmer need a painting or a novel? Why should anyone spend hard-earned wages to see a play in a lavishly decorated theater? The first American artists, playwrights, and authors confronted an impossible dilemma. They wanted to produce works embodying virtue, but many viewed those very works as corrupting, regardless of their content.

Still, authors and artists tried. William Hill Brown's *The Power of Sympathy* (1789), the first novel written in the United States, related a lurid tale of seduction as a warning to young women. In Royall Tyler's *The Contrast* (1787), the first successful American play, the virtuous conduct of Colonel Manly was contrasted (hence the title) with the reprehensible behavior of the fop Billy Dimple. The most popular book of the era, Mason Locke Weems's *Life of Washington*, published in 1800 shortly after George Washington's death, was intended by its author to "hold up his great Virtues . . . to the imitation of Our Youth." Weems could hardly be accused of subtlety. The famous tale

Novels

The citizens of the United States, fiercely patriotic and proud of achieving political independence from Great Britain, also sought intellectual and cultural independence. In novels, poems, paintings, plays, and histories they explored aspects of their new national identity. Ironically, though, the standards against which they measured themselves and the models they followed were European, primarily British.

That was especially true of the most widely read form of literature in the new United States: the novel. Susanna Haswell Rowson's *Charlotte: A Tale of Truth,* the most popular early "American" novel, was actually composed in England, where the novel originated as a literary form. In the mid-eighteenth century, Samuel Richardson had composed the first works of fiction that today are called novels, the very name revealing their "newness," or novelty. Written in epistolary style (that is, through letters drafted by the various characters) Richardson's novels—*Pamela* (1740), *Clarissa* (1748), and *Sir Charles Grandison* (1753)—all revolved around the courtship and sexual relationships of young adults. The same

themes permeated *Charlotte* and Richardson's other American imitators, and for good reason. Changing social mores in the late eighteenth century largely freed English and American young people from parental supervision of their marital decisions. While giving them greater individual choice, that freedom also rendered girls particularly vulnerable to new dangers of deception and seduction by unscrupulous suitors. And these same young women, as a group, were the most avid readers of novels, especially as expanded women's education increased female literacy rates.

William Hill Brown's *Power of Sympathy* (1789) and Hannah Foster's *Coquette* (1797), fictional versions of true "seduction and abandonment" tales, had avid readerships, but neither matched the sales of *Charlotte,* which despite its subtitle, *A Tale of Truth,* had no known factual basis. Rowson, born in England but raised in Massachusetts as the daughter of a customs officer in the British service, lived with her family in England during the Revolution but permanently returned to the United States in 1793. Her popular

This "Eighth American Edition" (such statements on the title pages of early novels can rarely be trusted because some printings were pirated) of Susanna Rowson's *Charlotte Temple* included a "portrait" of its entirely fictional heroine. That engraving thus reinforced the subtitle, *A Tale of Truth.* (AC7.R7997.79lc 1809 Houghton Library, Harvard University)

Novels

novel, first published in London in 1791, was reprinted in Philadelphia three years later and eventually went through more than 160 editions. *Charlotte* (later titled *Charlotte Temple*) narrates the story of a naive young woman who elopes, pregnant and unmarried, with her seducer, only to be deserted when a beautiful, rich, and virtuous rival appears on the scene. After giving birth to her baby, Charlotte dies in her father's arms, with her last breath directing him to care for the child. "Oh my dear girls," Rowson cautions her readers, "pray for fortitude to resist the impulses of inclination, when it runs counter to the precepts of religion and virtue."

Generations of young American women sobbed over Charlotte's fate, visiting Trinity churchyard in lower Manhattan, where a real-life counterpart of the fictional heroine was reputed to be buried. Their tears and women's preference on both sides of the Atlantic for such sentimental novels linked the young readers and their nation to the former mother country from which they were nominally so eager to separate.

---

he invented—six-year-old George bravely admitting cutting down his father's favorite cherry tree—ended with George's father exclaiming, "Run to my arms, you dearest boy. . . . Such an act of heroism in my son, is worth more than a thousand trees, though blossomed with silver, and their fruit of purest gold."

Painting and architecture, too, were expected to exemplify high moral standards. Two of the most prominent artists of the period, Gilbert Stuart and Charles Willson Peale, painted innumerable portraits of upstanding republican citizens. John Trumbull's vast canvases depicted such milestones of American history as the Battle of Bunker Hill and Cornwallis's surrender at Yorktown. Such portraits and historical scenes were intended to instill patriotic sentiments in their viewers. Architects likewise hoped to convey in their buildings a sense of the young republic's ideals. When the Virginia government asked Thomas Jefferson, then minister to France, for advice on the design of the state capitol in Richmond, Jefferson unhesitatingly recommended copying a Roman building, the Maison Carrée at Nîmes. "It is very simple," he explained, "but it is noble beyond expression." Jefferson set forth ideals that would guide American architecture for a generation to come: simplicity of line, harmonious proportions, a feeling of grandeur.

Despite the artists' efforts (or, some would have said, because of them), some Americans began to detect signs of luxury and corruption by the mid-1780s. The resumption of European trade after the war brought a return to up-to-date imported fashions for both men and women. Elite families again attended balls and concerts. Parties no longer seemed complete without gambling and cardplaying. Social clubs for young people multiplied; Samuel Adams worried in print about the opportunities for corruption lurking behind plans for tea drinking and genteel conversation among Boston youths. Especially alarming to fervent republicans was the establishment in

1783 of the Society of the Cincinnati, a hereditary association for Revolutionary War officers and their firstborn male descendants. Although the organizers hoped to advance the notion of the citizen-soldier, opponents feared that the group would become the nucleus of a native-born aristocracy. All these developments directly challenged the United States' self-image as a virtuous republic.

Educational Reform

Americans' deep-seated concern for the future of the infant republic focused their attention on children, the "rising generation." Education had previously been seen as a private means to personal advancement, the concern of individual families. Now schooling would serve a public purpose. If young people were to resist the temptations of vice and become useful citizens prepared for self-government, they would need a good education. In fact, the very survival of the nation depended on it. The 1780s and 1790s thus witnessed two major changes in educational practice.

First, some northern states began to use tax money to support public elementary schools. In 1789 Massachusetts became one of the first states to require towns to offer their citizens free public elementary education. Second, schooling for girls was improved. Recognizing the importance of the rising generation led Americans to conclude that mothers would have to be properly educated if they were to instruct their children adequately. Therefore, Massachusetts insisted that town elementary schools teach girls as well as boys. Throughout the United States, private academies were founded to give teenage girls from well-to-do families an opportunity for advanced schooling. No one yet proposed opening colleges to women, but a few fortunate girls could study history, geography, rhetoric, and mathematics. The academies also trained female students in fancy needlework—the only artistic endeavor considered appropriate for genteel women.

Judith Sargent Stevens (later Murray), by John Singleton Copley, c. 1770–1772. The eventual author of tracts advocating improvements in women's education sat for this portrait two decades earlier, during her first marriage. Her clear-eyed gaze suggests both her intelligence and her seriousness of purpose. (Terra Museum of American Art, Chicago, IL / Art Resource, NY)

Judith Sargent Murray

Judith Sargent Murray of Gloucester, Massachusetts, became the chief theorist of early women's education in the early republic. Murray argued in several essays that women and men had equal intellectual capacities, although women's inadequate education might make them seem less intelligent. "We can only reason from what we know," she declared, "and if an opportunity of acquiring knowledge hath been denied us, the inferiority of our sex cannot fairly be deduced from thence." Therefore, concluded Murray, boys and girls should be offered equivalent schooling. She further contended that girls should be taught to support themselves by their own efforts: "Independence should be placed within their grasp."

Murray's direct challenge to the traditional colonial belief that, as one man put it, girls "knew quite enough if they could make a shirt and a pudding" was part of a general rethinking of women's position that occurred as a result of the Revolution. Both men and women realized that female patriots had made vitally important contributions to the American independence movement. Consequently, Americans began to develop new ideas about the roles women should play in a republican society.

Women and the Republic

The best-known expression of those new ideas appeared in a letter Abigail Adams addressed to her husband in March 1776. "In the new Code of Laws which I suppose it will be necessary for you to make I desire you would Remember the Ladies," she wrote. "Remember all Men would be tyrants if they could. . . . If perticuliar care and attention is not paid to the Laidies [sic] we are determined to foment a Rebelion, and will not hold ourselves bound by any Laws in which we have no voice, or Representation." With these words, Abigail Adams took a step that would be duplicated by other disfranchised Americans. She deliberately applied the ideology developed to combat parliamentary supremacy to purposes revolutionary leaders had never intended. They assumed that wives had no interests different from those of their husbands. Yet Abigail Adams argued that, because men were "Naturally Tyrannical," the United States should reform colonial marriage laws, which subordinated wives to their husbands, giving men control of family property and denying wives the right to independent legal action.

Abigail Adams did not ask for woman suffrage, but others claimed that right. The drafters of the New Jersey state constitution in 1776 defined voters carelessly as "all free inhabitants" who met certain property qualifications. They thereby unintentionally gave the vote to property-holding white spinsters and widows, as well as to free black landowners. Qualified women and African Americans regularly voted in New Jersey's local and congressional elections until 1807, when they were disfranchised by the state legislature, which falsely charged them with widespread vote fraud. Yet the fact that women voted at all was evidence of their altered perception of their place in the political life of the country.

Such dramatic episodes were unusual. After the war, European-Americans still viewed women in traditional terms, affirming that women's primary function was to be good wives, mothers, and mistresses of households. They perceived significant differences between male and female character, which eventually enabled a resolution of the conflict between the two most influential strands of republican thought and led to new roles for some women. Because wives could not own property or participate directly in economic life, women came to be seen as the embodiment of self-sacrificing, disinterested republicanism. Through new female-run charitable associations founded after the war, better-off women assumed public responsibilities, in particular through caring for poor widows and orphaned children. Thus men were freed from the naggings of conscience as they pursued their economic self-interest (that other republican virtue), secure in the knowledge that their wives and daughters were fulfilling the family's obligation to the common good. The ideal republican man, therefore, was an individualist, seeking advancement for himself and his family. The ideal republican woman, by contrast, always put the well-being of others ahead of her own.

Together, European American men and women established the context for the creation of a virtuous republic. But nearly 20 percent of the American population was of African descent. How did approximately 700,000 African Americans fit into the developing national plan?

THE FIRST EMANCIPATION AND THE GROWTH OF RACISM

Revolutionary ideology exposed one of the primary contradictions in American society. Both European-Americans and African Americans saw the irony in slaveholders' claims that they sought to prevent Britain from "enslaving" them. Many revolutionary leaders voiced the theme. In 1773 Dr. Benjamin Rush called slavery "a vice which degrades human nature," warning ominously that "the plant of liberty is of so tender a nature that it cannot thrive long in the neighborhood of slavery." Common folk also pointed out the contradiction. When Josiah Atkins, a Connecticut soldier, saw Washington's plantation, he observed in his journal: "Alas! That persons who pretend to stand for the rights of mankind for the liberties of society, can delight in oppression, & that even of the worst kind!"

African Americans did not need revolutionary ideology to tell them that slavery was wrong, but they quickly took advantage of that ideology. In 1779 a group of slaves from Portsmouth, New Hampshire, asked the state legislature "from what authority [our masters] assume to dispose of our lives, freedom and property," pleading "that the name of slave may not more be heard in a land gloriously contending for the sweets of freedom." The same year, several bondsmen in Fairfield, Connecticut, petitioned the legislature for their freedom, characterizing slavery as a "dreadful Evil" and "flagrant Injustice." How could men who were "nobly contending in the Cause of Liberty," they asked, continue "this detestable Practice"?

Emancipation and Manumission   Both legislatures responded negatively, but the postwar years witnessed the gradual abolition of slavery in the North, a process that has become known as "the first emancipation." Vermont, still an independent jurisdiction, banned slavery in its 1777 constitution. Responding to lawsuits filed by enslaved men and women, Massachusetts courts decided in 1783 that the state constitution prohibited slavery. Other states north of Maryland adopted gradual emancipation laws between 1780 (Pennsylvania) and 1804 (New Jersey). New Hampshire did not formally abolish slavery, but only eight slaves were reported on the 1800 census and none in 1810. Although no southern state adopted general emancipation laws, the legislatures of Virginia (1782), Delaware (1787), and Maryland (1790 and 1796) altered laws that earlier had restricted slaveowners' ability to free their bondspeople. Yet South Carolina and Georgia never considered adopting such acts, and

A sailor of African descent posed proudly for this portrait around 1790. Unfortunately, neither the name of the sailor nor the name of the artist is known today. (Private collection, photograph courtesy of Hirschl & Adler Galleries, New York)

North Carolina insisted that all manumissions (emancipations of individual slaves) be approved by county courts.

Revolutionary ideology thus had limited impact on the well-entrenched economic interests of large slaveholders. Only in the northern states—societies with slaves, not slave societies—could state legislatures vote to abolish slavery. Even there, legislators' concern for the property rights of owners of human chattel—the Revolution, after all, was fought for *property* as well as for life and liberty—led them to favor gradual emancipation over immediate abolition. For example, New York's law freed children born into slavery after July 4, 1799, but only after they had reached their mid-twenties (by then having through their labor more than paid back the cost of their upbringing). The laws failed to emancipate the existing slave population, thereby leaving the owners' current human property largely intact. For decades, then, African Americans in the North lived in an intermediate stage between slavery and freedom. Although the emancipation laws forbade the sale of slaves to jurisdictions in which the institution remained legal, slaveowners regularly circumvented such provisions. The 1840 census recorded the presence of slaves in several northern states; not until later that decade did Rhode Island and Connecticut, for instance, abolish all vestiges of slavery.

Growth of Free Black Population

Despite the slow progress of abolition, the number of free people of African descent in the United States grew dramatically in the first years after the Revolution. Before the war they had been few in number; in 1755, for example, only 4 percent of African Americans in Maryland were free. Most slaves emancipated before the war were mulattos, born of unions between bondswomen and their masters, who then manumitted the children. But wartime disruptions radically augmented the freed population. Wartime escapees from plantations, slaves who had served in the American army, and still others who had been emancipated by their owners or by state laws were now free. By 1790 nearly 60,000 free people of color lived in the United States; ten years later they numbered more than 108,000, nearly 11 percent of the total African American population.

In the Chesapeake, manumissions were speeded by economic changes, such as declining soil fertility and the shift from tobacco to grain production, as well as by the rising influence of antislavery Baptists and Methodists. One prominent Baptist convert, the immensely wealthy planter Robert Carter, manumitted all of his bondspeople after he became convinced that slaveowning was sinful. Because grain cultivation was less labor-intensive than tobacco growing, planters began to complain about "excess" slaves. They occasionally solved that problem by freeing some of their less productive or more favored bondspeople. The enslaved also seized the opportunity to negotiate agreements with their owners allowing them to live and work independently until they could purchase themselves with their accumulated earnings. The free black population of Virginia more than doubled between 1790 and 1810, and by the latter year nearly one-quarter of Maryland's African American population was no longer in legal bondage.

Freedpeople's Lives

In the 1780s and thereafter, freedpeople from rural areas often made their way to northern port cities, such as Boston and Philadelphia. Women outnumbered men among the migrants by a margin of three to two, for they had better employment opportunities in the cities, especially in domestic service. Some freedmen also worked in domestic service, but larger numbers were employed as unskilled laborers and sailors. A few of the women and a sizable proportion of men (nearly one-third of those in Philadelphia in 1795) were skilled workers or retailers. These people chose new names for themselves, exchanging the surnames of former masters for names like Newman or Brown, and as soon as possible they established independent two-parent families instead of continuing to live in their employers' households. They also began to occupy distinct neighborhoods, probably as a result of discrimination.

Emancipation did not bring equality. Even whites who recognized African Americans' right to freedom were unwilling to accept them as equals. Laws discriminated against freedpeople as they had against slaves. Several states—among them Delaware, Maryland, and South Carolina—quickly adopted laws denying property-owning black men the vote. South Carolina forbade free blacks from testifying against whites in court. New Englanders used indenture contracts to control freed youths, who were also often denied education in public schools. Freedmen found it difficult to purchase property and find good jobs. And though in many areas African Americans were accepted as members—even ministers—of evangelical churches, they were rarely allowed an equal voice in church affairs.

Gradually, freedpeople developed their own institutions, often based in their own neighborhoods. In Charleston, mulattos formed the Brown Fellowship Society, which provided insurance coverage for its members, financed a school, and helped to support orphans. In 1794 former slaves in Philadelphia and Baltimore, led by the Reverend Richard Allen, founded societies that eventually formed the African Methodist Episcopal

(AME) denomination. AME churches later sponsored schools and, along with African Baptist, African Episcopal, and African Presbyterian churches, became cultural centers of the free black community. Freedpeople quickly learned that, to survive and prosper, they had to rely on collective effort rather than on the goodwill of their white compatriots.

Development of Racist Theory Their endeavors were all the more important because the postrevolutionary years witnessed the development of formal racist theory in the United States. European-Americans had long regarded their slaves as inferior, but the most influential writers attributed that inferiority to environmental factors. They argued that African slaves' seemingly debased character derived from their enslavement, rather than enslavement's being the consequence of inherited inferiority. In the Revolution's aftermath, though, slaveowners needed to defend holding other human beings in bondage against the proposition that "all men are created equal." Consequently, they began to argue that people of African descent were less than fully human and that the principles of republican equality applied only to European-Americans. In other words, to avoid having to confront the contradiction

MAP 7.1 African American Population, 1790: Proportion of Total Population

The first census clearly indicated that the African American population was heavily concentrated in just a few areas of the United States, most notably in coastal regions of South Carolina, Georgia, and Virginia. Although there were growing numbers of blacks in the backcountry—presumably taken there by migrating slaveowners—most parts of the North and East, with the exception of the immediate vicinity of New York City, had few African American residents. (Source: From Lester J. Cappon et al., eds., *Atlas of Early American History: The Revolutionary Era, 1760–1790.* Copyright © 1976 by Princeton University Press. Reprinted by permission of Princeton University Press.)

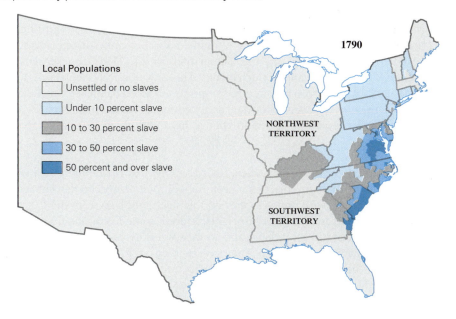

1790

Local Populations

Unsettled or no slaves
Under 10 percent slave
10 to 30 percent slave
30 to 50 percent slave
50 percent and over slave

NORTHWEST TERRITORY

SOUTHWEST TERRITORY

between their practice and the egalitarian implications of revolutionary theory, they redefined the theory so that it would not apply to African Americans.

Simultaneously, the very notion of "race" appeared in coherent form applied to groups defined by skin color as "whites," "reds," and "blacks." The rise of egalitarian thinking among European-Americans both downplayed status distinctions within their own group and differentiated all "whites" from people of color—Indians and African Americans. (That differentiation soon manifested itself in new miscegenation laws adopted in both northern and southern states to forbid intermarriage between whites and blacks or Indians.) Indians from disparate nations, especially in the southeastern United States, had decades earlier begun to refer to themselves as "red." Meanwhile, experience as slaves on American soil forged the identity "African" or "black" from the various ethnic and national affiliations of people who had survived the transatlantic crossing. Strikingly, among the first to term themselves "Africans" were oceanic sailors—men whose wide-ranging contacts with Europeans caused them to construct a unified (and separate) identity for themselves. Thus in the revolutionary era "whiteness," "redness," and "blackness"—along with the superiority of the first, the inferiority of the latter two—developed in tandem as contrasting terms.

Such racism had several intertwined elements. First came the assertion that, as Thomas Jefferson insisted in 1781, blacks were "inferior to the whites in the endowments both of body and mind." (He was less certain about the inferiority of Indians.) There followed the belief that blacks were congenitally lazy and disorderly. Even though owners had often argued, conversely, that slaves were "natural" workers, no one seemed to notice the inherent contradiction. Third was the notion that all blacks were sexually promiscuous and that African American men lusted after European American women. The specter of interracial sexual intercourse involving black men and white women haunted early American racist thought. Significantly, the more common reverse circumstance—the sexual exploitation of enslaved women by their masters—aroused little comment or concern.

African Americans did not allow these developing racist notions to go unchallenged. Benjamin Banneker, a free black mathematical genius, directly disputed Thomas Jefferson's belief in Africans' intellectual inferiority. In 1791 Banneker sent Jefferson a copy of his latest almanac (which included his astronomical calculations) as an example of blacks' mental powers. Jefferson's response admitted Banneker's intelligence but indicated that he regarded Banneker as exceptional; Jefferson insisted that he needed more evidence before he would change his mind about people of African descent generally.

A White Men's Republic

At its birth, then, its leaders defined the republic as a white male enterprise. Even though men of African descent served with honor in the Continental Army, laws from the 1770s on linked "whiteness" and male citizenship rights. Indeed, some historians have argued that the subjugation of blacks, Indians, and women was a necessary precondition for theoretical equality among white men. They have pointed out that identifying common racial antagonists helped to create white solidarity and to lessen the threat to gentry power posed by the enfranchisement of poorer men. Moreover, excluding women from the political realm reserved all power for men, specifically those of the "better sort." That was perhaps one reason why after the Revolution the division of American society between slave and free was transformed into a division between blacks—some of whom were free—and whites. The white male wielders of power ensured their continued dominance in part by substituting race for enslavement as the primary determinant of African Americans' status.

DESIGNING REPUBLICAN GOVERNMENTS

In May 1776, even before adoption of the Declaration of Independence, the Second Continental Congress directed states to devise new republican governments to replace the popularly elected provincial conventions and committees that had met since colonial governments collapsed in 1774 and 1775. Thus American men initially concentrated on drafting state constitutions and devoted little attention to their national government—an oversight they later had to remedy.

State Constitutions   At the state level, political leaders immediately faced the problem of defining a "constitution." Americans wanted to create tangible documents specifying the fundamental structures of government, but at first legislators could not decide how to accomplish that goal. States eventually concluded that regular legislative bodies should not draft their constitutions. Following the lead established by Vermont in 1777 and Massachusetts in 1780, they began to elect conventions for the sole purpose of drafting constitutions. Thus states sought direct authorization from the people—the theoretical sovereigns in a republic—before establishing new governments. After preparing new constitutions, delegates submitted them to voters for ratification.

The framers of state constitutions concerned themselves primarily with outlining the distribution of and limitations on government power—both crucial to the survival of republics. If authority was not confined within reasonable limits, the states might become tyrannical, as Britain had. Americans' experience with British rule permeated every provision of their new constitutions. States experimented with different solutions to the problems the framers perceived, and the early constitutions varied considerably in specifics while remaining broadly comparable in outline.

Under their colonial charters, Americans had learned to fear the power of the governor—usually the appointed agent of the king or proprietor—and to see the legislature as their defender. Accordingly, the first state constitutions typically provided for the governor to be elected annually (commonly by the legislature), limited the number of terms he could serve, and gave him little independent authority. Simultaneously, the constitutions expanded the legislature's powers. Every state except Pennsylvania and Vermont retained a two-house structure, with members of the upper house having longer terms and required to meet higher property-holding standards than members of the lower house. But they also redrew electoral districts to more accurately reflect population patterns, and they increased the number of members in both houses. Finally, most states lowered property qualifications for voting. As a result, the legislatures came to include some members who before the war would not have been eligible to vote. Thus the revolutionary era witnessed the first deliberate attempt to broaden the base of American government, a process that has continued to the present day.

**Limiting State
Governments**

But the state constitutions' authors knew that governments designed to be responsive to the people would not necessarily provide sufficient protection if tyrants were elected to office. They consequently included explicit limitations on government authority in the documents they composed, attempting to protect what they regarded as the inalienable rights of individual citizens. Seven constitutions contained formal bills of rights, and others had similar clauses. Most guaranteed citizens freedom of the press, rights to fair trials and to consent to taxation, and protection against general search warrants. An independent judiciary was charged with upholding such rights. Most states also guaranteed freedom of religion, but with restrictions. For example, seven states required that all officeholders be Christians, and some continued to support churches with tax money. (Not until 1833 did Massachusetts become the last state to remove all vestiges of a religious establishment.)

In general, the constitution makers put greater emphasis on preventing state governments from becoming tyrannical than on making them effective wielders of political authority. Their approach to shaping governments was understandable, given the American experience with Great Britain. But establishing such weak political units, especially in wartime, practically ensured that the constitutions would need revision. Soon some states began to rewrite constitutions they had drafted in 1776 and 1777.

**Revising State
Constitutions**

Invariably, the revised versions increased the powers of the governor and reduced the scope of the legislature's authority. By the mid-1780s, some American political leaders had concluded that the best way to limit government power was to balance legislative, executive, and judicial powers, a design called checks and balances. The national Constitution that they drafted in 1787 also embodied that principle.

Yet the constitutional theories that Americans applied at the state level did not immediately influence their conception of national government. Because American officials initially focused on organizing the military struggle against Britain, the powers and structure of the Continental Congress evolved by default. Not until late 1777 did Congress send the Articles of Confederation—the document outlining a national government—to the states for ratification, and those Articles simply wrote into law the unplanned arrangements of the Continental Congress.

**Articles of
Confederation**

The chief organ of national government was a unicameral (one-house) legislature in which each state had one vote. Its powers included conducting foreign relations, mediating interstate disputes, controlling maritime affairs, regulating Indian trade, and valuing state and national coinage. The Articles did not give the national government the ability to raise revenue effectively or to enforce a uniform commercial policy. The United States of America was described as "a firm league of friendship" in which each state "retains its sovereignty, freedom and independence, and every Power, Jurisdiction and right, which is not by this confederation expressly delegated to the United States, in Congress assembled."

The Articles required unanimous consent of state legislatures for ratification or amendment, and a clause concerning western lands proved troublesome. The draft accepted by Congress allowed states to retain all land claims derived from their original

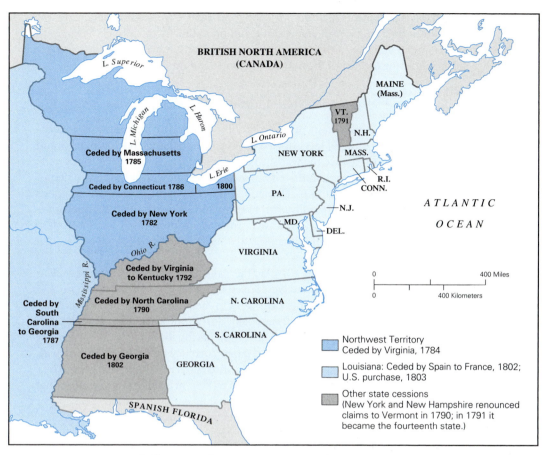

MAP 7.2 Western Land Claims and Cessions, 1782–1802

After the United States achieved independence, states competed with one another for control of valuable lands to which they had possible claims under their original charters. That competition led to a series of compromises among the states or between individual states and the new nation, indicated on this map.

charters. But states with definite western boundaries in their charters (such as Maryland and New Jersey) wanted other states to cede to the national government their landholdings west of the Appalachian Mountains. Otherwise, they feared, states with large claims could expand and overpower their smaller neighbors. Maryland refused to accept the Articles until 1781, when Virginia finally promised to surrender its western holdings to national jurisdiction. Other states followed suit, establishing the principle that unorganized lands would be held by the nation as a whole.

The capacity of a single state to delay ratification for three years portended the fate of American government under the Articles of Confederation. The unicameral legislature, whether it was called the Second Continental Congress (until 1781) or the Confederation Congress (thereafter), was too inefficient and unwieldy to govern effectively. The Articles' authors had not given adequate thought to the distribution of power within the national government or to the relationship between the Confederation and the states. The Congress they created was simultaneously a legislative body and a collective executive (there was no judiciary), but it had no independent income and no authority to compel the states to accept its rulings. Under the Articles, national government lurched from crisis to crisis. (See the appendix for the text of the Articles of Confederation.)

TRIALS OF THE CONFEDERATION

Finance posed the most persistent problem faced by both state and national governments. Because legislators at all levels levied taxes only reluctantly, both Congress and the states at first tried to finance the war simply by printing currency. Even though the money was backed only by good faith, it circulated freely and without excessive depreciation during 1775 and most of 1776. Demand for military supplies and civilian goods was high, stimulating trade (especially with France) and local production. Indeed, the amount of money issued in those years was probably no more than what a healthy economy required as a medium of exchange.

Financial Affairs But in late 1776, as the American army suffered reverses in New York and New Jersey, prices began to rise, and inflation set in. The currency's value rested on Americans' faith in their government, a faith that was sorely tested in the years that followed, especially during the dark days of British triumphs in the South (1779 and 1780). State governments fought inflation by controlling wages and prices and requiring acceptance of paper currency on an equal footing with specie (coins). States also borrowed funds, established lotteries, and levied taxes. Their efforts were futile. So, too, was Congress's attempt to stop printing currency altogether and to rely solely on money contributed by the states. By early 1780 it took forty paper dollars to purchase one silver dollar. Soon Continental currency was worthless.

In 1781, faced with total collapse of the monetary system, Congress undertook ambitious reforms. After establishing a department of finance under the wealthy Philadelphia merchant Robert Morris, it asked the states to amend the Articles of Confederation to allow a national duty of 5 percent on imported goods. Morris put national finances on a solid footing, but the customs duty was never adopted. First Rhode Island and then New York refused to agree to the tax. The states' resistance reflected fear of a too-powerful central government. As one worried citizen wrote in 1783, "If permanent Funds are given to Congress, the aristocratical Influence, which predominates in more than a major part of the United States, will fully establish an arbitrary Government."

Foreign Affairs Because the Articles denied Congress the power to establish a national commercial policy, the realm of foreign trade also exposed the new government's weaknesses. Immediately after the war, Britain, France, and Spain restricted American trade with their colonies. Americans, who had hoped independence would bring about trade with all nations, were outraged but could do little to change matters. Members of Congress watched helplessly as British manufactured goods flooded the United States while American produce could no longer be sold in the British West Indies, once its prime market. Although Americans reopened commerce with other European countries and started a profitable trade with China in 1784, neither substituted for access to closer and larger markets.

Congress furthermore had difficulty dealing with the Spanish presence on the nation's southern and western borders. Determined to prevent the republic's expansion, Spain in 1784 closed the Mississippi River to American navigation, thereby depriving the growing settlements west of the Appalachians of access to the Gulf of Mexico. Congress, through its Department of Foreign Affairs, opened negotiations with Spain in 1785, but even John Jay, one of the nation's most experienced diplomats, could not win the necessary concessions. The talks collapsed the following year after Congress divided sharply: southerners and westerners insisted on navigation rights on the Mississippi, whereas northerners were willing to abandon that claim in order to win commercial concessions in the West Indies. The impasse made some congressmen question the possibility of a national consensus on foreign affairs.

Peace Treaty Provisions

Provisions of the 1783 Treaty of Paris, too, caused serious problems. Article Four, which promised payment of prewar debts (most of them owed by Americans to British merchants), and Article Five, which recommended that states allow loyalists to recover their confiscated property, aroused considerable opposition. States passed laws denying

A British cartoon ironically reflected Americans' hopes for post-war trade, hopes that were dashed after 1783. The Indian woman symbolizing America sits on a pile of tobacco bales, with rice and indigo casks bound for Europe nearby. The artist was satirizing the failed 1778 British peace commission and Britons' willingness to make concessions to the rebellious colonies, but his image captured Americans' belief in the importance of their produce. (Chicago Historical Society)

British subjects the right to sue for recovery of debts or property in American courts, and town meetings decried the loyalists' return. As residents of Norwalk, Connecticut, put it, few Americans wanted to permit the "Tory Villains" to return "while filial Tears are fresh upon our Cheeks and our Murdered Brethren scarcely cold in their Graves." State governments also had reason to oppose enforcement of the treaty. Sales of loyalists' land, houses, and other possessions had helped finance the war. Because many purchasers were prominent patriots, states hesitated to raise questions about the legitimacy of their property titles.

The refusal of state and local governments to comply with Articles Four and Five gave Britain an excuse to maintain military posts on the Great Lakes long after its troops were supposed to have withdrawn. Furthermore, Congress's inability to convince states to implement the treaty disclosed its lack of power, even in an area—foreign affairs—in which it had authority under the Articles. Concerned nationalists argued publicly that failure to enforce the treaty, however unpopular, challenged the republic's credibility. "Will foreign nations be willing to undertake anything with us or for us," asked Alexander Hamilton, "when they find that the nature of our governments will allow no dependence to be placed on our engagements?"

ORDER AND DISORDER IN THE WEST

Congressmen also confronted knotty problems when they considered the status of land beyond the Appalachians. Although British and American diplomats did not discuss tribal claims, the United States assumed that the Treaty of Paris cleared its title to all land east of the Mississippi except the area still held by Spain. Still, recognizing that land cessions should be obtained from the most powerful tribes, Congress initiated negotiations with both northern and southern Indians.

Indian Relations   At Fort Stanwix, New York, in 1784, American diplomats negotiated a treaty with chiefs who claimed to represent the Iroquois; and at Hopewell, South Carolina, in late 1785 and early 1786, they did the same with emissaries from the Choctaw, Chickasaw, and Cherokee nations. In 1786 the Iroquois formally repudiated the Fort Stanwix treaty, denying that the men who attended the negotiations had been authorized to speak for the Six Nations. The confederacy threatened new attacks on frontier settlements, but everyone knew the threat was empty; the flawed treaty stood by default. At intervals until the end of the decade, New York purchased large tracts of land from individual Iroquois nations. By 1790 the once-dominant confederacy was confined to a few scattered reservations. In the South, too, the United States took the treaties as confirmation of its sovereignty, authorizing settlers to move onto the territories in question. European-Americans poured over the southern Appalachians, provoking the Creeks—who had not agreed to the Hopewell treaties—to defend their territory by declaring war. Only in 1790 did they come to terms with the United States.

Western nations, such as the Shawnees, Chippewas, Ottawas, and Potawatomis, had already started to reject Iroquois hegemony as early as the 1750s. After the collapse of Iroquois power, they formed their own confederacy and demanded direct

MAP 7.3 Cession of Tribal Lands to the United States, 1775–1790

The land claims of the United States meant little as long as Indian nations still controlled vast territories within the new country's formal boundaries. A series of treaties in the 1780s and 1790s opened some lands to white settlement. (Source: From Lester J. Cappon et al., eds., *Atlas of Early American History: The Revolutionary Era, 1760–1790.* Copyright © 1976 by Princeton University Press. Reprinted by permission of Princeton University Press.)

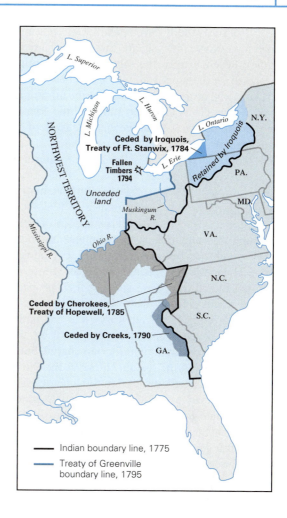

negotiations with the United States. They intended to present a united front so as to avoid the piecemeal surrender of land by individual bands and villages. But they faced a difficult task. In the postwar world, Indian nations could no longer pursue the diplomatic strategy that had worked so well for so long: playing off European and American powers against one another. France was gone; Spanish territory lay far to the west and south; and British power was confined to Canada, north of the Great Lakes. Only the United States remained.

Ordinance of 1785   At first the national government ignored the western confederacy. Shortly after state land cessions were completed, Congress began to organize the Northwest Territory, bounded by the Mississippi River, the Great Lakes, and the Ohio River (see Map 7.2). Ordinances passed in 1784, 1785, and 1787 outlined the process through which the land could be sold to settlers and formal governments organized.

To ensure orderly development, Congress in 1785 directed that the land be surveyed into townships 6 miles square, each divided into thirty-six sections of 640 acres (1 square mile). Revenue from the sale of the sixteenth section of each township was to be reserved for the support of public schools—the first instance of federal aid to education in American history. One dollar was the minimum price per acre; the minimum sale was one section. Thus Congress showed little concern for the small farmer: the resulting minimum outlay, $640, lay beyond the reach of ordinary Americans, except those veterans who received part of their army pay in land warrants. Proceeds from western land sales constituted the first independent revenues available to the national government.

Northwest Ordinance

The most important of the three land policies—the Northwest Ordinance of 1787—contained a bill of rights guaranteeing settlers freedom of religion and the right to a jury trial, forbidding cruel and unusual punishments, and nominally prohibiting slavery. Eventually, that prohibition became an important symbol for antislavery northerners, but at the time it had little effect. Some residents of the territory already held slaves, and Congress did not intend to deprive them of their property. Moreover, the ordinance also contained a provision allowing slaveowners to "lawfully reclaim" runaway bondspeople who took refuge in the territory—the first national fugitive slave law. The ordinance prevented slavery from taking deep root by discouraging slaveholders from moving into the territory with their human chattel, but not until 1848 was enslavement abolished throughout the region, known as the Old Northwest. And by omission Congress implied that slavery was legal in the territories south of the Ohio River.

The ordinance of 1787 also specified the process by which territorial residents could organize state governments and seek admission to the Union "on an equal footing with the original States." Early in the nation's history, therefore, Congress laid down a policy of admitting new states on the same basis as the old and assuring residents of the territories the same rights held by citizens of the original states. Having suffered under the rule of a colonial power, congressmen understood the importance of preparing the new nation's first "colony" for eventual self-government. Nineteenth- and twentieth-century Americans were to be less generous in their attitudes toward residents of later territories, many of whom were non-European or non-Protestant. But the nation never fully lost sight of the egalitarian principles of the Northwest Ordinance.

In a sense, though, in 1787 the ordinance was purely theoretical. Miamis, Shawnees, and Delawares in the region refused to acknowledge American sovereignty. They opposed settlement violently, attacking unwary pioneers who ventured too far north of the Ohio River. In 1788 the Ohio Company, to which Congress had sold a large tract of land at reduced rates, established the town of Marietta at the juncture of the Ohio and Muskingum Rivers. But Indians prevented the company from extending settlement very far into the interior.

The problems the United States encountered in ensuring safe settlement of the Northwest Territory revealed the basic weakness of the Confederation government. Not until after the Articles of Confederation were replaced with a new constitution could the United States muster sufficient force to implement the Northwest Ordinance. Thus, although the ordinance is often viewed as one of the few lasting accomplishments of the Confederation Congress, it must be seen within a context of political impotence.

FROM CRISIS TO THE CONSTITUTION

Americans involved in finance, overseas trade, and foreign affairs became acutely aware of the inadequacies of the Articles of Confederation. Congress could not levy taxes, nor could it impose its will on the states to establish a uniform commercial policy or ensure the enforcement of treaties. Partly as a result, the American economy slid into a depression less than a year after war's end. Exporters of staple crops (especially tobacco and rice) and importers of manufactured goods suffered from the postwar restrictions that European powers imposed on American commerce. Although recovery began by 1786, the war's effects proved impossible to erase, particularly in the Lower South. Some estimates suggest that between 1775 and 1790 America's per capita gross national product declined by nearly 50 percent.

Economic Change and Commercial Reform   The war wrought permanent change in the American economy. The near-total cessation of foreign commerce in nonmilitary items during the war stimulated domestic manufacturing. Consequently, despite the influx of European goods after 1783, the postwar period witnessed the stirrings of American industrial development. For example, the first American textile mill began production in Pawtucket, Rhode Island, in 1793. Because of continuing population growth, the domestic market assumed greater relative importance in the overall economy. Moreover, foreign trade patterns shifted from Europe and toward the West Indies, continuing a trend that had begun before the war. Foodstuffs shipped to the French and Dutch Caribbean islands became America's largest single export, replacing tobacco (and thus accelerating the Chesapeake's conversion from tobacco to grain production). South Carolina resumed importing slaves on a large scale, as planters sought to replace workers lost to wartime disruptions. Yet without British subsidies American indigo could not compete with that produced in the Caribbean, and even rice planters struggled to find new markets.

Recognizing the Confederation Congress's inability to deal with commercial matters, representatives of Virginia and Maryland met at Mt. Vernon (George Washington's plantation) in March 1785 to negotiate an agreement about trade on the Potomac River, which divided the two states for much of its length. The successful meeting led to an invitation to other states to discuss trade policy generally at a convention in Annapolis, Maryland. Although nine states named representatives to the meeting in September 1786, only five delegations attended. Those present realized that so few people could not have any significant impact on the political system. They issued a call for another convention, to be held in Philadelphia nine months later, "to devise such further provisions as shall . . . appear necessary to render the constitution of the federal government adequate to the exigencies of the Union."

Shays's Rebellion   The other states did not respond immediately. But then an armed rebellion in Massachusetts did what a polite invitation could not: convince doubters that reform was needed. Men from several western counties, many of them veterans from leading families, violently opposed high taxes levied by the eastern-dominated legislature to pay off war debts. Such obligations consisted largely of securities issued during the war to soldiers in lieu of pay and to others in return for supplies and loans. But during the hard times immediately following the war, many veterans and creditors were forced to sell the securities at heavy discounts to a relative handful of speculators. The state legislature nevertheless levied taxes to pay off the securities (plus interest) at full price in specie before the end of the decade. Men with little prospect of obtaining specie without selling their land responded furiously when the state moved to collect the new taxes.

Daniel Shays, a former officer in the Continental Army, assumed nominal leadership of the disgruntled westerners. On January 25, 1787, he led about fifteen hundred troops in an assault on the federal armory at Springfield, attempting to capture the military stores housed there. The militiamen mustered to defend the armory fired on their former comrades-in-arms, who withdrew after suffering twenty-four casualties. Some (including Shays) fled the state, never to return; two were hanged; and most escaped punishment by paying small fines and taking oaths of allegiance to Massachusetts. The state legislature, for its part, soon dramatically reduced the burden on landowners by enacting new import duties and by easing tax collections.

Even so, the words of the Shaysites reverberated around the new nation. Terming Massachusetts "tyrannical" and styling themselves "Regulators" (like backcountry Carolinians in the 1760s), they had insisted that "whenever any encroachments are made either upon the liberties or properties of the people, if redress cannot be had without, it is virtue in them to disturb government." Thus they linked their rebellion to the earlier independence struggle.

Constitutional Convention

Such explosive assertions convinced many political leaders that the nation's problems extended far beyond trade policy. To some, the rebellion confirmed the need for a much stronger federal government. After most of the states had already appointed delegates, the Confederation Congress belatedly endorsed the proposed convention, "for the sole and express purpose of revising the Articles of Confederation." In mid-May 1787, fifty-five men, representing all the states but Rhode Island, assembled in Philadelphia to begin deliberations.

The vast majority of delegates to the Constitutional Convention were substantial men of property. They all favored reform; otherwise, they would not have come to Philadelphia. Most wanted to give the national government new authority over taxation and foreign commerce. Yet simultaneously they sought to advance their states' interests. Many had been state legislators, and some had helped to draft state constitutions. Their understanding of the success or failure of those constitutions influenced their Philadelphia deliberations. Their ranks included merchants, planters, physicians, generals, governors, and especially lawyers—twenty-three had studied the law. Most had been born in America; many came from families that had arrived a century earlier. Most were Congregationalists, Presbyterians, or Anglicans. In an era when only a tiny handful of men had advanced education, more than half had attended college. A few had been educated in Britain, but most had graduated from American institutions: Princeton, with ten, counted the most alumni participants. The youngest delegate was twenty-six, the oldest—Benjamin Franklin—eighty-one. Like George Washington, whom they elected their presiding officer, most were in their vigorous middle years. A dozen men did the bulk of the convention's work. Of those, James Madison of Virginia most fully deserves the title "Father of the Constitution."

**Madison and
the Constitution**

The frail, shy James Madison was thirty-six years old in 1787. A Princeton graduate raised in western Virginia, he served on the local Committee of Safety and was elected successively to the provincial convention, the state's lower and upper houses, and the Continental Congress (1780–1783). Although Madison returned to Virginia to serve in the state legislature in 1784, he remained in touch with national politics, partly through continuing correspondence with his close friend Thomas Jefferson. A promoter of the Annapolis Convention, he strongly supported its call for further reform.

Madison stood out among the delegates for his systematic preparation for the Philadelphia meeting. Through Jefferson in Paris he bought more than two hundred books on history and government, carefully analyzing their accounts of past confederacies and republics. A month before the Constitutional Convention began, he summed up the results of his research in a lengthy paper entitled "Vices of the Political System of the United States." After listing the flaws he perceived in the current structure of the government (among them "encroachments by the states on the federal authority" and lack of unity "in matters where common interest requires it"), Madison revealed the conclusion that would guide his actions over the next few months. What the government most needed, he declared, was "such a modification of the sovereignty as will render it sufficiently neutral between the different interests and factions, to controul one part of the society from invading the rights of another, and at the same time sufficiently controuled itself, from setting up an interest adverse to that of the whole Society."

Madison thus believed that government had to be constructed in such a way that it could not become tyrannical or fall wholly under the influence of a particular faction. He regarded the large size of a potential national republic as an advantage in that respect. Rejecting the common assertion that republics had to be small to survive, Madison asserted that a large, diverse republic should be preferred. Because the nation would include many different factions, no one of them would be able to control the government. Political stability would result from compromises among the contending parties.

**Virginia and
New Jersey Plans**

The so-called Virginia Plan, introduced on May 29 by Edmund Randolph, embodied Madison's conception of national government. The plan provided for a two-house legislature, the lower house elected directly by the people and the upper house selected by the lower; representation in both houses proportional to property or population; an executive elected by Congress; a national judiciary; and congressional veto over state laws. The Virginia Plan gave Congress the broad power to legislate "in all cases to which the separate states are incompetent." Had it been adopted intact, it would have created a government in which national authority reigned unchallenged and state power was greatly diminished. Proportional representation in both houses (however reckoned) would also have given large states a dominant voice in the national government.

The convention included many delegates who recognized the need for change but believed the Virginia Plan went too far in the direction of national consolidation. After two weeks of debate on Randolph's proposal, disaffected delegates—particularly those from small states—united under the leadership of William Paterson of New Jersey. On June 15 Paterson presented an alternative scheme, the New Jersey Plan, calling for strengthening the Articles rather than completely overhauling the government. Paterson proposed retaining a unicameral Congress in which each state had an equal vote, but giving Congress new powers of taxation and trade regulation. Earlier Paterson had made his position clear in debate. Asserting that the Articles were "the proper basis of all the proceedings of the convention," he contended that the delegates' proper task was "to mark the orbits of the states with due precision and provide for the use of coercion" by the national government. Although the convention initially rejected Paterson's position, he and his allies won a number of victories in the months that followed.

Debates over Congress　　The delegates began their work by discussing the structure and functions of Congress. They readily agreed that the new national government should have a two-house (bicameral) legislature. Further, in accordance with Americans' long-standing opposition to virtual representation, they concurred that "the people" (however that term was defined) should be directly represented in at least one house of Congress. But they discovered that they differed widely in their answers to three key questions: Should representation in both houses of Congress be proportional to population? How was representation in either or both houses to be apportioned among the states? And, finally, how were the members of the two houses to be elected?

The last issue proved the easiest to resolve. To quote John Dickinson, the delegates thought it "essential" that members of the lower branch of Congress be elected directly by the people and "expedient" that members of the upper house be chosen by state legislatures. Because legislatures had selected delegates to the Confederation Congress, they would expect a similar privilege in the new government. If the convention had not agreed to allow state legislatures to elect senators, the Constitution would have run into significant opposition among state political leaders. The plan also had the virtue of placing the election of one house of Congress one step removed from the "lesser sort," whose judgment the wealthy convention delegates did not wholly trust.

The possibility of representation proportional to population in the Senate caused considerably greater disagreement. The delegates accepted without much debate the principle of proportional representation in the House of Representatives. But small states, through their spokesman Luther Martin of Maryland, argued for equal representation in the Senate. Such a scheme, they rightly supposed, would give them relatively more power at the national level. Large states, on the other hand, supported a proportional plan, for they would then be allotted more votes in the upper house. For weeks the convention deadlocked, neither side able to obtain a majority. A committee appointed to work out a compromise recommended equal representation in the Senate, coupled with a proviso that all appropriation bills originate in the lower house. But not until the convention accepted a suggestion that a state's two senators vote as individuals rather than as a unit was a breakdown averted.

Slavery and the Constitution　　The remaining critical question divided the nation along sectional lines rather than by size of state: how was representation in the lower house to be apportioned among states? Delegates concurred that a census should be conducted every ten years to determine the nation's actual population, and they agreed that Indians who paid no taxes should be excluded for purposes of representation. Delegates from states with large numbers of slaves wanted African and European inhabitants to be counted equally; delegates from states with few slaves wanted only free people counted. Slavery thus became inextricably linked to the foundation of the new government. Delegates resolved the dispute by using a formula developed by the Confederation Congress in 1783 to allocate financial assessments among states: three-fifths of slaves would be included in population totals. (The formula reflected delegates' judgment that slaves were less efficient producers of wealth than free people, not that they were 60 percent human and 40 percent property.) The three-fifths compromise on representation won unanimous approval. Only two delegates, Gouverneur Morris of New York and George Mason of Virginia, later spoke out against the institution of slavery.

Although the words *slave* and *slavery* do not appear in the Constitution (the framers used such euphemisms as "other persons"), the document contained both direct and indirect protections for slavery. The three-fifths clause, for example, assured white southern male voters not only congressional representation out of proportion to their numbers but also a disproportionate influence on the selection of the president, because the number of each state's votes in the electoral college (see below) was determined by the size of its congressional delegation. In return for southerners' agreement that commercial regulations could be adopted by a simple majority vote in Congress (rather than two-thirds), New Englanders agreed that Congress could not end the importation of slaves for at least twenty years. Further, the fugitive slave clause required all states to return runaways to their masters. By guaranteeing that the national government would aid any states threatened with "domestic violence," the Constitution promised aid in putting down future slave revolts, as well as incidents like Shays's Rebellion.

Congressional and Presidential Powers

Once delegates agreed on the knotty, conjoined problems of slavery and representation, they readily achieved consensus on the other issues confronting them. All concurred that the national government needed the authority to tax and to regulate foreign and interstate commerce. But instead of giving Congress the nearly unlimited scope proposed in the Virginia Plan, delegates enumerated congressional powers and then provided for flexibility by granting it all authority "necessary and proper" to carry out those powers. Discarding the congressional veto contained in the Virginia Plan, the convention implied but did not explicitly authorize a national judicial veto of state laws. The Constitution plus national laws and treaties would constitute "the supreme law of the land; and the judges in every state shall be bound thereby," Article VI declared ambiguously. As another means of circumscribing state powers, delegates drafted a long list of actions forbidden to states. And—contrary to many state constitutions—they provided that religious tests could never be required of U.S. officeholders.

The convention placed primary responsibility for conducting foreign affairs in the hands of a new official, the president, who was also designated commander-in-chief of the armed forces. That decision raised the question, left unspecified in the Constitution's text, of whether the president (or Congress, for that matter) acquired special powers in times of war. With the consent of the Senate, the president could appoint judges and other federal officers. To select the president, delegates established an elaborate mechanism, the electoral college, whose members would be chosen in each state by legislatures or qualified voters. If a majority of electors failed to unite behind one candidate, the House of Representatives (voting as states, not as individuals) would choose the president. Delegates also agreed that the chief executive would serve for four years but be eligible for reelection, rejecting proposals that he serve one longer term.

The final document still showed signs of its origins in the Virginia Plan, but compromises created a system of government less powerful at the national level than Madison and Randolph had envisioned. The key to the Constitution was the distribution of political authority—that is, separation of powers among executive, legislative, and judicial branches of the national government, and division of powers between states and nation (called *federalism*). Two-thirds of Congress and three-fourths of the states, for example, had to concur on amendments. The branches balanced one another, their powers deliberately entwined to prevent each from acting independently. The president could veto congressional legislation, but that veto could be overridden by two-thirds majorities in both houses, and his treaties and major appointments required the Senate's consent. Congress could impeach the president and federal judges, but courts appeared to have the final say on interpreting the Constitution. These checks and balances would make it difficult for the government to become tyrannical. At the same time, though, the elaborate system would sometimes prevent the government from acting quickly and decisively. Furthermore, the Constitution drew such a vague line between state and national powers that the United States fought a civil war in the next century over that very issue.

The convention held its last session on September 17, 1787. Of the forty-two delegates present (others had returned home weeks earlier), only three refused to sign the Constitution, two of them in part because of the lack of a bill of rights. Benjamin Franklin had written a speech calling for unity; because his weak voice could not be heard, another delegate read it for him. "I confess that there are several parts of this constitution which I do not at present approve," Franklin admitted. Yet he urged its acceptance "because I expect no better, and because I am not sure, that it is not the best." Only then was the Constitution made public. The convention's proceedings had been entirely secret—and remained so until the delegates' private notes were published in the nineteenth century. (See the appendix for the full text of the Constitution.)

OPPOSITION AND RATIFICATION

Later the same month, the Confederation Congress submitted the Constitution to the states. The ratification clause provided for the new system to take effect once it was approved by special conventions in at least nine states, with delegates being elected by qualified voters. Thus the national Constitution, unlike the Articles of Confederation, would rest directly on popular authority (and the presumably hostile state legislatures would be circumvented).

As states began to elect delegates to the special conventions, discussion of the proposed government grew more heated. Newspaper essays and pamphlets vigorously defended or attacked the Philadelphia convention's decisions. The extent of the debate was unprecedented. Every newspaper in the country printed the full text of the Constitution, and most supported its adoption. It quickly became apparent, though, that disputes within the Constitutional Convention had been mild compared to divisions of opinion within the populace as a whole. Although most citizens concurred that the national government should have more power over taxation and foreign and interstate commerce, some believed that the proposed government held the potential for tyranny. As happened in Carlisle, Pennsylvania, the vigorous debate between the two sides frequently spilled out into the streets.

Federalists and Antifederalists

Those supporting the proposed Constitution called themselves Federalists. They built on the notions of classical republicanism, holding forth a vision of a virtuous, collectivist, self-sacrificing republic vigorously led by a manly aristocracy of talent. Claiming that the nation did not need to fear centralized authority when good men drawn from the elite were in charge, they argued that the carefully structured government would preclude the possibility of tyranny. A republic could be large, they declared, if the government's design prevented any one group from controlling it. The separation of powers among legislative, executive, and judicial branches, and the division of powers between states and nation, would accomplish that goal. Thus people did not need to be protected in a formal way from the powers of the new government. Instead, their liberties would be guarded by "distinguished worthies"—men of the "better sort" whose only goal (said George Washington) was "to merit the approbation of good and virtuous men."

The Federalists termed those who opposed the Constitution Antifederalists, thus casting them in a negative light. Antifederalists, while recognizing the need for a national source of revenue, feared a too-powerful central government. They saw the states as the chief protectors of individual rights; consequently, weakening the states could bring the onset of arbitrary power. Antifederalist arguments against the Constitution often consisted of lists of potential abuses of government authority.

Heirs of the Real Whig ideology of the late 1760s and early 1770s, Antifederalists stressed the need for constant popular vigilance to avert oppression. Indeed, some of the Antifederalists had originally promulgated those ideas—Samuel Adams, Patrick Henry, and Richard Henry Lee led the opposition to the Constitution. Such older Americans, whose political opinions had been shaped prior to the centralizing, nationalistic Revolution, peopled the Antifederalist ranks. Joining them were small farmers preoccupied with guarding their property against excessive taxation, backcountry Baptists and Presbyterians, and ambitious, upwardly mobile men who would benefit from an economic and political system less tightly controlled than that the Constitution envisioned. Federalists denigrated such men as disorderly, licentious, and even "unmanly" and "boyish" because they would not follow the elites' lead in supporting the Constitution.

Bill of Rights

As public debate continued, Antifederalists focused on the Constitution's lack of a bill of rights. Even if the new system weakened the states, critics believed, people could still be protected from tyranny by specific guarantees of rights. The Constitution did contain some prohibitions on congressional power. For example, the writ of habeas corpus, which prevented arbitrary imprisonment, could not be suspended except in "cases of rebellion or invasion." But Antifederalists found such constitutional provisions to be few and inadequate. Nor were they reassured by Federalist assertions that the new government could not violate people's rights because it had only limited powers. Opponents wanted the national governing document to incorporate a bill of rights, as had most state constitutions.

Letters of a Federal Farmer, perhaps the most widely read Antifederalist pamphlet, listed the rights that should be protected: freedom of the press and religion, trial by jury, and guarantees against unreasonable searches. From Paris, Thomas Jefferson added his voice to the chorus. Replying to Madison's letter conveying a copy of the Constitution, Jefferson declared, "I like much the general idea" but not "the omission of a bill of rights. . . . A bill of rights is what the people are entitled to against every government on earth, general or particular, and what no just government should refuse, or rest on inference."

Ratification As state conventions considered ratification, delegates tended to put state and local interests first. Thus many were persuaded when Federalists argued that the establishment of a national government with the power to tax foreign commerce would lessen the financial burdens that had prompted Shays's Rebellion and localized protests in other states. Yet the lack of a bill of rights loomed ever larger as a flaw in the proposed government. Four of the first five states to ratify did so unanimously, but serious disagreements then surfaced. Massachusetts, in which Antifederalist forces had been bolstered by a backlash against the state government's heavy-handed treatment of the Shays rebels, ratified by a majority of only 19 votes out of 355 cast and recommended amendments identifying rights. In June 1788, when New Hampshire ratified, the requirement of nine states was satisfied. But New York and Virginia had not yet voted, and everyone realized the new Constitution could not succeed unless those key states accepted it.

Despite a valiant effort by the Antifederalist Patrick Henry, pro-Constitution forces won by 10 votes in the Virginia convention, which likewise recommended the addition of specifications of rights. In New York, James Madison, John Jay, and Alexander Hamilton, writing collectively as "Publius," published *The Federalist,* a series of eighty-five political essays explaining the theory behind the Constitution and masterfully answering its critics. Their reasoned arguments, coupled with Federalists' promise to add a bill of rights to the Constitution, helped win the battle. On July 26, 1788, New York ratified the Constitution by the slim margin of 3 votes. Although the last states—North Carolina and Rhode Island—did not join the Union until November 1789 and May 1790, respectively, the new government was a reality.

Celebrating Ratification Americans in many cities celebrated ratification (somewhat prematurely) with a series of parades on July 4, 1788, ritualistically linking the acceptance of the Constitution to the formal adoption of the Declaration of Independence. The carefully planned processions dramatized the history and symbolized the unity of the new nation, seeking to counteract memories of the dissent that had so recently engulfed such towns as Carlisle, Pennsylvania. Like pre-Revolution protest meetings, the parades served as political lessons for literate and illiterate Americans alike. The processions aimed to educate men and women about the significance of the new Constitution and to instruct them about political leaders' hopes for industry and frugality on the part of a virtuous American public.

Symbols expressing those goals filled the Philadelphia parade, planned by the artist Charles Willson Peale. About five thousand people participated in the procession, which featured floats portraying such themes as "The Grand Federal Edifice" and stretched for a mile and a half. Marchers representing the first pioneers and Revolutionary War troops paraded with groups of farmers and artisans dramatizing their work. More than forty groups of tradesmen, including barbers, hatters, printers, cloth manufacturers, and clockmakers, sponsored floats. Lawyers, doctors, clergymen of all denominations, and congressmen followed the artisans. A final group of marchers symbolized the nation's future: students from the University of Pennsylvania and other city schools bore a flag labeled "The Rising Generation."

SUMMARY

During the 1770s and 1780s the nation took shape as a political union. It began to develop an economy independent of the British Empire and attempted to chart its own course in the world in order to protect the national interest, defend the country's borders, and promote beneficial trade. Some Americans prescribed guidelines for the cultural and intellectual life they thought appropriate for a republic, outlining artistic and educational goals for a properly virtuous people. An integral part of the formation of the Union was the systematic formulation of American racist thought. Emphasizing race (rather than status as slave or free) as a determinant of African Americans' standing in the nation allowed men who now termed themselves "white" to define republicanism to exclude most men but themselves and to ensure that they would dominate the country for the foreseeable future. White women, viewed primarily as household dependents, had a limited role to play in the republic, as mothers of the next generation and as selfless contributors to the nation's welfare.

The experience of fighting a war and struggling for survival as an independent nation altered the political context of American life in the 1780s. In 1775 most Americans believed that "that government which governs best governs least," but by the late 1780s many had changed their minds. They were the drafters and supporters of the Constitution, who concluded from the republic's vicissitudes under the Articles of Confederation that a more powerful central government was needed. During ratification debates they contended that their proposals were just as "republican" in conception as (if not more so than) the Articles.

Both sides concurred in a general adherence to republican principles, but they emphasized different views of republicanism. Federalists advanced a position based on the principles of classical republicanism, stressing the community over the individual. Antifederalists, fearing that elected leaders would not subordinate personal gain to the good of the whole, wanted a weak central government, formal protection of individual rights, and a loosely regulated economy. The Federalists won their point when the Constitution was adopted, however narrowly. The process of consolidating the states into a national whole was thereby formalized. The 1790s, the first decade of government under the Constitution, would witness hesitant steps toward the creation of a true nation, the United States of America.

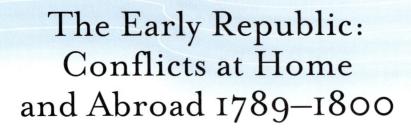

The Early Republic: Conflicts at Home and Abroad 1789–1800

BUILDING A WORKABLE GOVERNMENT

At first, consensus appeared possible, as the nationalistic spirit expressed in the processions celebrating ratification of the Constitution carried over to the first session of Congress. Only a few Antifederalists ran for office in the congressional elections held late in 1788, and even fewer were elected. Thus the First Congress consisted chiefly of men who supported a strong national government. The drafters of the Constitution had deliberately left many key issues undecided, so the nationalists' domination of Congress meant that their views on those points quickly prevailed.

First Congress   Congress faced four immediate tasks when it convened in April 1789: raising revenue to support the new government, responding to states' calls for a bill of rights, setting up executive departments, and organizing the federal judiciary. The last task was especially important. The Constitution established a Supreme Court but left it to Congress to decide whether to have other federal courts.

James Madison, representing Virginia in the House of Representatives, soon became as influential in Congress as he had been at the Constitutional Convention. A few months

CHRONOLOGY

1789 • Washington inaugurated as first president
- Judiciary Act of 1789 organizes federal court system
- French Revolution begins

1790 • Hamilton's *Report on Public Credit* proposes assumption of state debts

1791 • First ten amendments (Bill of Rights) ratified
- First national bank chartered

1793 • France declares war on Britain, Spain, and the Netherlands
- Washington's neutrality proclamation keeps the United States out of war
- Democratic-Republican societies founded, the first grassroots political organizations

1794 • Wayne defeats Miami Confederacy at Fallen Timbers
- Whiskey Rebellion in western Pennsylvania protests taxation

1795 • Jay Treaty with England resolves issues remaining from the Revolution
- Pinckney's Treaty with Spain establishes southern boundary of the United States
- Treaty of Greenville with Miami Confederacy opens Ohio to settlement

1796 • First contested presidential election: Adams elected president, Jefferson vice president

1798 • XYZ affair arouses American opinion against France
- Sedition Act penalizes dissent
- Virginia and Kentucky Resolutions protest suppression of dissent

1798–99 • Quasi-War with France
- Fries's Rebellion in Pennsylvania protests taxation

1800 • Franco-American Convention ends Quasi-War
- Gabriel's Rebellion threatens Virginia slaveowners

1801 • Thomas Jefferson elected president by the House of Representatives after stalemate in electoral college

into the first session, he persuaded Congress to adopt the Revenue Act of 1789, imposing a 5 percent tariff on certain imports. Thus the First Congress quickly achieved what the Confederation Congress never had: an effective national tax law. The new government would have problems in its first years, but lack of revenue would not be one of them.

Bill of Rights   Madison also took the lead with respect to constitutional amendments. During and after the convention, he had opposed additional limitations on the national government. He believed it unnecessary to guarantee people's rights explicitly when the government had limited powers. But Madison recognized that Congress should respond to amendments proposed in state ratifying conventions. Accordingly, he introduced nineteen amendments, based on those presented in the states. The states formally ratified ten, which officially became part of the Constitution on December 15, 1791 (see the appendix for the Constitution and all amendments, including the Twenty-seventh, which was one of Madison's nineteen). Their adoption defused Antifederalist opposition and rallied support for the new government.

The First Amendment prohibited Congress from passing any law restricting the right to freedom of religion, speech, press, peaceable assembly, or petition. The next two amendments arose directly from the former colonists' fear of standing armies. The Second Amendment guaranteed the right "to keep and bear arms," because of the need for a "well-regulated Militia." Thus the constitutional right to bear arms was based on the expectation that most able-bodied men would serve the nation as citizen-soldiers, and there would be little need for a permanent army. The Third Amendment limited the conditions under which troops could be quartered in private homes. The next five pertained to judicial procedures. The Fourth Amendment prohibited "unreasonable searches and seizures"; the Fifth and Sixth established the rights of accused persons; the Seventh specified the conditions for jury trials in civil (as opposed to criminal) cases; and the Eighth forbade "cruel and unusual punishments." The Ninth and Tenth Amendments reserved to the people and the states other unspecified rights and powers. In short, the amendments' authors insisted that, in listing some rights, they did not mean to preclude the exercise of others.

Executive and Judiciary

While debating proposed amendments, Congress also considered the organization of the executive branch. It readily agreed to continue the three administrative departments established under the Articles of Confederation: War, Foreign Affairs (renamed State), and Treasury. Congress instituted two lesser posts: the attorney general—the nation's official lawyer—and the postmaster general. Controversy arose over whether the president alone could dismiss officials whom he had originally appointed with the Senate's consent. After some debate, the House and Senate agreed that he had such authority. That established the important principle that the heads of executive departments are accountable solely to the president.

The most far-reaching law that the First Congress adopted, the Judiciary Act of 1789, defined the jurisdiction of the federal judiciary and established a six-member Supreme Court, thirteen district courts, and three circuit courts of appeal. Its most important provision, Section 25, allowed appeals from state to federal courts when cases raised certain types of constitutional questions. The act presumed that Article VI of the Constitution, which stated that federal statutes and treaties were to be considered "the supreme Law of the Land," implied the right of appeal from state to federal courts, yet the Constitution did not explicitly permit such actions. In the nineteenth century, judges and legislators committed to states' rights would challenge the constitutionality of Section 25.

During its first decade, the Supreme Court handled few cases of any importance, and several members resigned. (John Jay, the first chief justice, served only six years.) But in a significant 1796 decision, *Ware v. Hylton,* the Court for the first time declared a state law unconstitutional. That same year it also reviewed the constitutionality of an act of Congress, upholding its validity in the case of *Hylton v. U.S.* The most important case of the decade, *Chisholm v. Georgia* (1793), established that states could be sued in federal courts by citizens of other states. Five years later, the Eleventh Amendment to the Constitution overturned that decision, which was unpopular with state governments.

Debate over
Slavery

Despite the constitutional provisions forbidding Congress from prohibiting the importation of slaves for twenty years, in early 1790 three groups of Quakers submitted petitions to Congress favoring abolition and calling for an end to slave importations. In the ensuing debates, the nation's first political leaders directly addressed the questions they had suppressed in euphemisms in the Constitution. Southerners vigorously asserted that Congress should not only reject the petitions, but also not even discuss them. Had southern states thought that the federal government would consider interfering with the institution of slavery, such congressmen argued, they would never have ratified the Constitution. The legislators developed a positive defense of slavery that forecast most of the arguments offered on the subject during the next seven decades. They insisted that slavery was integral to the Union and that abolition would cause more problems than it solved, primarily by confronting the nation with the question of how to deal with a sizable population of freed people.

Some northern congressmen—and, in his last published essay, Benjamin Franklin—contested the southerners' position, but a consensus soon emerged to quash such discussions in the future. Congress accepted a committee report denying it the power either to halt slave importations before 1808 or to emancipate slaves at any time, that authority "remaining with the several States alone." The precedent that Congress could not abolish slavery held until the Civil War.

DOMESTIC POLICY UNDER WASHINGTON AND HAMILTON

George Washington did not seek the presidency. In 1783 he returned to Mount Vernon eager for the peaceful life of a Virginia planter. But his fellow countrymen never regarded Washington as just another private citizen. Unanimously elected to preside at the Constitutional Convention, he did not participate in debates but consistently voted for a strong national government. After the adoption of the new governmental structure, Americans concurred that only George Washington had sufficient stature to serve as the republic's first president, an office designed largely with him in mind. The unanimous vote of the electoral college merely formalized that consensus.

Reluctant to return to public life, George Washington nevertheless knew he could not ignore his country's call. Awaiting the summons to New York City, the nation's capital, he wrote to an old friend, "My movements to the chair of Government will be accompanied by feelings not unlike those of a culprit who is going to the place of his execution. . . . I am sensible, that I am embarking the voice of my Countrymen and a good name of my own, on this voyage, but what returns will be made for them, Heaven alone can foretell." Symbolically he donned a suit of homespun for the inaugural ceremony.

Washington's
First Steps

Washington acted cautiously during his first months in office in 1789, knowing that whatever he did would set precedents for the future. When the title by which he should be addressed aroused controversy (Vice President John Adams favored "His Highness, the President of the United States of America, and Protector of their Liberties"), Washington said nothing. The accepted title soon became a plain "Mr. President." By using the heads of the executive departments collectively as his chief advisers, he created the cabinet. As the Constitution required, he sent Congress an annual State of the Union message. Washington also concluded that he should exercise his veto power over congressional legislation sparingly—only, indeed, if he became convinced a bill was unconstitutional.

Early in his term, Washington undertook elaborately organized journeys to all the states. At each stop, he was ritually welcomed by uniformed militia units, young women strewing flowers in his path, local leaders, groups of Revolutionary War veterans, and respectable citizens who presented him with formal addresses reaffirming their loyalty to the United States. The president thus personally came to embody national unity, simultaneously drawing ordinary folk into the sphere of national politics.

Washington's first major task as president was to choose the heads of the executive departments. For the War Department he selected an old comrade-in-arms, Henry Knox of Massachusetts, who had been his reliable general of artillery during much of the Revolution. His choice for the State Department was his fellow Virginian Thomas Jefferson, who had just returned to the United States from his post as minister to France. And for the crucial position of secretary of the treasury, the president chose the brilliant, intensely ambitious Alexander Hamilton.

Alexander Hamilton

The illegitimate son of a Scottish aristocrat and a woman whose husband had divorced her for adultery and desertion, Hamilton was born in the British West Indies in 1757. His early years were spent in poverty; after his mother's death when he was eleven, he worked as a clerk for a mercantile firm. In 1773 Hamilton enrolled at King's College (later Columbia University) in New York City. Only eighteen months later, in late 1774, the precocious seventeen-year-old contributed a pamphlet to the prerevolutionary publication wars. Devoted to the patriot cause, Hamilton volunteered for service in the American army, where he came to Washington's attention. In 1777 Washington appointed the young man as one of his aides, and the two developed great mutual affection.

The general's patronage helped the poor youth of dubious background to marry well. At twenty-three he wed Elizabeth Schuyler, daughter of a wealthy New York family. After the war, Hamilton practiced law in New York City and served as a delegate to the Annapolis Convention and later the Constitutional Convention. Although he exerted little influence at either gathering, his contributions to *The Federalist* in 1788 revealed him as one of the chief political thinkers in the republic.

In his dual role as treasury secretary and presidential adviser, Hamilton exhibited two traits distinguishing him from most of his contemporaries. First, his primary loyalty lay with the nation. Caribbean-born, Hamilton had no natal ties to any state; he neither sympathized with nor fully understood demands for local autonomy. His fiscal policies always aimed at consolidating national power. Hamilton never feared the exercise of centralized executive authority, as did older compatriots who had clashed repeatedly with colonial governors, and he openly favored maintaining close political and economic ties with Britain.

Second, Hamilton regarded his fellow humans with unvarnished cynicism. Perhaps because of his difficult early life and his own overriding ambition, Hamilton believed people to be motivated primarily by self-interest—particularly economic self-interest. He placed no reliance on people's capacity for virtuous, self-sacrificing behavior. This outlook set him apart from those Americans who foresaw a rosy future in which public-spirited citizens would pursue the common good rather than their own private advantage. Although other Americans (for instance, James Madison) also stressed the role of private interests in a republic, Hamilton went further in his emphasis on self-interest as the major motivator of human behavior. Those beliefs significantly influenced the way he tackled the monumental task before him: straightening out the new nation's tangled finances.

National and State Debts

Congress ordered the new secretary of the treasury to assess the public debt and to submit recommendations for supporting the government's credit. Hamilton found that the country's remaining war debts fell into three categories: those owed by the nation to foreign governments and investors, mostly to France (about $11 million); those owed by the national government to merchants, former soldiers, holders of revolutionary bonds, and the like (about $27 million); and, finally, similar debts owed by state governments (roughly $25 million). With respect to the national debt, few disagreed: Americans recognized that, if their new government was to succeed, it would have to repay at full face value those financial obligations the nation had incurred while winning independence.

The state debts were another matter. Some states—notably, Virginia, Maryland, North Carolina, and Georgia—had already paid off most of their war debts by levying taxes and handing out land grants in lieu of monetary payments. They would oppose the national government's assumption of responsibility for other states' debts because their citizens would be taxed to pay such obligations. Massachusetts, Connecticut, and South Carolina, by contrast, still had sizable unpaid debts and would welcome a system of national assumption. The possible assumption of state debts also had political implications. Consolidating the debt in the hands of the national government would help to concentrate economic and political power at the national level. A contrary policy would reserve greater independence of action for the states.

Hamilton's Financial Plan

Hamilton's first *Report on Public Credit,* sent to Congress in January 1790, stimulated lively debate. The treasury secretary proposed that Congress assume outstanding state debts, combine them with national obligations, and issue new securities covering both principal and accumulated unpaid interest. Hamilton thereby hoped to ensure that holders of the public debt—many of them wealthy merchants and speculators—had a significant financial stake in the new government's survival. The opposition coalesced around James Madison, who opposed the assumption of state debts for two reasons. First, his state of Virginia had already paid off most of its obligations, and second, he wanted to avoid rewarding wealthy speculators who had purchased state and national debt certificates at a small fraction of their face value from needy veterans and farmers.

Prompted in part by Madison, the House initially rejected the assumption of state debts. The Senate, however, adopted Hamilton's plan largely intact. A series of compromises followed, in which the assumption bill became linked to the other major controversial issue of that congressional session: the location of the permanent national capital. Several related political deals were struck. A southern site on the Potomac River (favored by Washington and close to Mount Vernon) was selected for the capital, and the first part of Hamilton's financial program became law in August 1790.

First Bank of the United States   Four months later, Hamilton submitted to Congress a second report on public credit, recommending the chartering of a national bank modeled on the Bank of England. This proposal, too, aroused much opposition, primarily after Congress had already voted to establish the bank.

The Bank of the United States, to be chartered for twenty years, was to be capitalized at $10 million. Just $2 million would come from public funds, while private investors supplied the rest. The bank would act as collecting and disbursing agent for the Treasury, and its notes would circulate as the nation's currency. Most political leaders recognized that such an institution would be beneficial, especially because it would solve the problem of America's perpetual shortage of an acceptable medium of exchange. But another issue loomed large: did the Constitution give Congress the power to establish such a bank?

Interpreting the Constitution   James Madison answered that question with a resounding no. He pointed out that Constitutional Convention delegates had specifically rejected a clause authorizing Congress to issue corporate charters. Consequently, he argued, that power could not be inferred from other parts of the Constitution. Madison's contention disturbed President Washington, who decided to request other opinions before signing the bill into law. Edmund Randolph, the attorney general, and Thomas Jefferson, the secretary of state, agreed with Madison that the bank was unconstitutional. Jefferson referred to Article I, Section 8, of the Constitution, which gave Congress the power "to make all Laws which shall be necessary and proper for carrying into Execution the foregoing Powers." The key word, Jefferson argued, was *necessary:* Congress could do what was needed, but without specific constitutional authorization could not do what was merely desirable. Thus Jefferson formulated the strict-constructionist interpretation of the Constitution.

Washington asked Hamilton to reply to the negative assessments of his proposal. Hamilton's *Defense of the Constitutionality of the Bank,* presented to the president in February 1791, brilliantly expounded a broad-constructionist view of the Constitution. Hamilton argued forcefully that Congress could choose any means not specifically prohibited by the Constitution to achieve a constitutional end. He reasoned thus: if the end was constitutional and the means was not *un*constitutional, then the means was constitutional.

Washington concurred, and the bill became law. The bank proved successful, as did the scheme for funding the national debt and assuming the states' debts. The new nation's securities became desirable investments for its own citizens and for wealthy foreigners, especially those in the Netherlands, who rushed to purchase American debt certificates. The influx of new capital, coupled with the high prices that American grain now commanded in European markets, eased farmers' debt burdens and contributed to a new prosperity. But two other aspects of Alexander Hamilton's wide-ranging financial scheme did not fare so well.

Report on Manufactures

In December 1791, Hamilton presented to Congress his *Report on Manufactures,* the third and last of his prescriptions for the American economy. It outlined an ambitious plan for encouraging and protecting the United States' infant industries, such as shoemaking and textile manufacturing. Hamilton argued that the nation could never be truly independent as long as it relied heavily on Europe for manufactured goods. He urged Congress to promote the immigration of technicians and laborers, and to support industrial development through a limited use of protective tariffs. Many of Hamilton's ideas were implemented in later decades, but few congressmen in 1791 could see much merit in his proposals. They firmly believed that America's future lay in agriculture and the carrying trade, and that the mainstay of the republic was the yeoman farmer. Congress therefore rejected the report.

That same year Congress accepted another feature of Hamilton's financial program, levying an excise tax on whiskey distilled within the United States. Although proceeds from the Revenue Act of 1789 covered the interest on the national debt, the decision to fund state debts meant that the national government required additional income. A tax on whiskey affected relatively few westerners—the farmers who grew corn and the small and large distillers who turned that corn into whiskey—and might also reduce the consumption of whiskey. (Eighteenth-century Americans, notorious for their heavy drinking, consumed about twice as much alcohol per capita as today's rate.) Moreover, Hamilton knew that those western farmers and distillers were Jefferson's supporters, and he saw the benefits of taxing them rather than the merchants who favored his own policies.

Whiskey Rebellion

News of the tax set off protests in frontier areas of Pennsylvania, where residents were dissatisfied with the army's defense of their region from threats of Indian attack. To their minds, the same government that protected them inadequately was now proposing to tax them disproportionately. Unrest continued for two years on the frontiers of Pennsylvania, Maryland, and Virginia. Large groups of men drafted petitions protesting the tax, deliberately imitated crowd actions of the 1760s, and occasionally harassed tax collectors.

President Washington responded with restraint until violence erupted in July 1794, when western Pennsylvania farmers resisted two excisemen trying to collect the tax. About seven thousand rebels convened on August 1 to plot the destruction of Pittsburgh but decided not to face the heavy guns of the fort guarding the town. Washington then took decisive action to prevent a crisis reminiscent of Shays's Rebellion. On August 7, he called on the insurgents to disperse and summoned nearly thirteen thousand militia from Pennsylvania and neighboring states. By the time federal forces marched westward in October and November (led at times by Washington himself), the disturbances had ceased. The troops met no resistance and arrested only twenty suspects. Two, neither of them prominent leaders of the rioters, were convicted of treason, but—continuing his policy of restraint—Washington pardoned both. The leaderless and unorganized rebellion ended with little bloodshed.

The importance of the Whiskey Rebellion lay not in military victory over the rebels—for there was none—but in the forceful message it conveyed to the American people. The national government, Washington had demonstrated, would not allow violent resistance to its laws. In the republic, change would be effected peacefully, by legal means. People dissatisfied with the law should try to amend or repeal it, not take extralegal action as they had during the colonial era.

THE FRENCH REVOLUTION AND THE DEVELOPMENT OF PARTISAN POLITICS

By 1794 some Americans were already beginning to seek change systematically through electoral politics, even though traditional political theory regarded organized opposition—especially in a republic—as illegitimate. In a monarchy, formal opposition groups, commonly called factions, were to be expected. In a government of the people, by contrast, sustained factional disagreement was taken as a sign of corruption and subversion. Such negative judgments, though widely held, still did not halt the growth of partisan sentiment.

Republicans and Federalists   Jefferson and Madison became convinced as early as 1792 that Hamilton's policies of favoring wealthy commercial interests at the expense of agriculture aimed at imposing a corrupt, aristocratic government on the United States. Characterizing themselves as the true heirs of the Revolution, they charged that Hamilton was plotting to subvert republican

A Federalist political cartoon from the 1790s shows "Mad Tom" Paine "in a rage," trying to destroy the federal government as carefully constructed (in classical style) by President Washington and Vice President Adams. That Paine is being aided by the Devil underscores the hostility to partisanship common in the era. (The Huntington Library & Art Collections, San Marino, California)

principles. To dramatize their point, Jefferson, Madison, and their followers in Congress began calling themselves Republicans. Hamilton in turn accused Jefferson and Madison of the same crime: attempting to destroy the republic. Hamilton and his supporters began calling themselves Federalists, to legitimize their claims and link themselves with the Constitution. Each group accused the other of being an illicit faction working to sabotage the republican principles of the Revolution. Newspapers aligned with the two sides fanned the flames of partisanship, publishing virulent attacks on their political opponents.

At first, President Washington tried to remain aloof from the political dispute that divided Hamilton and Jefferson, his chief advisers. The growing controversy did help persuade him to promote political unity by seeking office again in 1792. But in 1793 and thereafter, developments in foreign affairs magnified the disagreements, for France (America's wartime ally) and Great Britain (America's most important trading partner) resumed the periodic hostilities that had originated a century earlier.

French Revolution

In 1789 Americans had welcomed the news of the French Revolution. The French people's success in limiting, and then overthrowing, an oppressive monarchy seemed to vindicate the United States' own revolution. Americans saw themselves as the vanguard of an inevitable historical trend that would reshape the world in a republican mold. But by the early 1790s the reports from France were disquieting. Outbreaks of violence continued, and political leaders succeeded each other with bewildering rapidity. Executions mounted; the king himself was beheaded in early 1793. Although many Americans, including Jefferson and Madison, retained sympathy for the revolution, others—among them Alexander Hamilton—began to cite France as a prime example of the perversion of republicanism.

Debates within the United States intensified when the newly republican France became enmeshed in conflict with other European nations. Both because French leaders feared that neighboring monarchies would intervene to crush the revolution and because they sought to spread the republican gospel throughout the continent, they declared war first on Austria and then, in 1793, on Britain, Spain, and Holland. That confronted the Americans with a dilemma. The 1778 Treaty of Alliance with France bound them to that nation "forever," and a mutual commitment to republicanism created ideological bonds. Yet the United States was connected to Great Britain as well. In addition to their shared history and language, America and Britain had again become important economic partners. Americans still purchased most of their manufactured goods from Great Britain. Indeed, because the revenues of the United States depended heavily on import tariffs, the nation's economic health in effect required uninterrupted trade with the former mother country.

Edmond Genêt

The political and diplomatic climate grew even more complicated in April 1793, when Edmond Genêt, a representative of the French government, arrived in Charleston, South Carolina. As Genêt made his way north to New York City, he recruited Americans for expeditions against British and Spanish colonies in the Western Hemisphere, freely distributing privateering commissions. Genêt's arrival raised troubling questions for President Washington. Should he receive Genêt, thus officially recognizing the French revolutionary government? Should he acknowledge an obligation to aid France under the terms of the 1778 Treaty of Alliance? Or should he proclaim American neutrality?

Washington resolved his dilemma by receiving Genêt but also issuing a proclamation informing the world that the United States would adopt "a conduct friendly and impartial toward the belligerent powers." Federalist newspapers vociferously defended the proclamation, and partisan leaders organized rallies to praise the president's action. Republicans who favored assisting France reluctantly accepted the neutrality policy, which had overwhelming popular support.

Genêt's faction fell from power in Paris, and he subsequently sought political asylum in the United States. But his disappearance from the diplomatic scene did not diminish the impact of the French Revolution in America. The domestic divisions Genêt helped to widen were perpetuated by clubs called Democratic societies, formed by Americans sympathetic to the French Revolution and worried about the policies of the Washington administration. Such societies reflected a growing grassroots concern about the same developments that troubled Jefferson and Madison.

Democratic Societies More than forty Democratic societies organized between 1793 and 1800. Their members saw themselves as heirs of the Sons of Liberty, seeking the same goal as their predecessors: protection of people's liberties against encroachments by corrupt and self-serving rulers. To that end, they publicly protested government fiscal and foreign policy, and repeatedly proclaimed their belief in "the equal rights of man," particularly the rights to free speech, free press, and assembly. Like the Sons of Liberty, the Democratic societies comprised chiefly artisans and craftsmen, although professionals, farmers, and merchants also joined. Although locally based, they communicated effectively through a network of newspapers and allied themselves nationally with congressional Republicans.

The rapid spread of such citizens' groups, outspokenly critical of the administration, disturbed Hamilton and Washington. Federalist writers charged that the organizations were dangerously subversive, because elected officials, not "self-created societies," should formulate public policy. The groups' "real design," a newspaper asserted, was "to involve the country in war, to assume the reins of government and tyrannize over the people." The counterattack climaxed in the fall of 1794, when Washington accused the societies of fomenting the Whiskey Rebellion. Republican leaders and newspaper editors responded by defending the societies but condemning the insurgents.

In retrospect, Washington and Hamilton's reaction to the Democratic societies seems disproportionately hostile. But factional disputes were believed to endanger the survival of republics. As the first organized political dissenters in the United States, the Democratic societies alarmed administration officials, who had not yet accepted the idea that one component of a free government was an organized loyal opposition.

PARTISAN POLITICS AND RELATIONS WITH GREAT BRITAIN

In 1794 George Washington dispatched Chief Justice John Jay to London to negotiate several unresolved questions in Anglo-American relations. The British had recently seized some American merchant ships trading in the French West Indies. The United

States wanted to establish the countervailing principle of freedom of the seas and to assert its right, as a neutral nation, to trade freely with both combatants. Further, Great Britain still held posts in the American Northwest, thus violating the 1783 peace treaty. Settlers there believed that the British were responsible for renewed warfare with neighboring Indians, and they wanted that threat removed. The Americans also hoped for a commercial treaty and sought compensation for the slaves who left with the British army at the end of the war.

Jay Treaty Debate　The negotiations in London proved difficult, because Jay had little to offer in exchange for the concessions he sought. Britain did agree to evacuate the western forts and ease restrictions on American trade to England and the West Indies. (Some limitations were retained, however, violating the Americans' desire for open commerce.) The treaty established two arbitration commission—one to deal with prewar debts Americans owed to British creditors and the other to hear claims for captured American merchant ships—but Britain adamantly refused slaveowners compensation for their lost bondspeople. Under the circumstances, Jay had probably done the best he could. Nevertheless, most Americans, including the president, at first expressed dissatisfaction with at least some clauses of the treaty.

The Senate debated the Jay Treaty in secret. Not until after ratification in late June 1795 (by 20 to 10, the exact two-thirds the Constitution required) did members of the public learn its provisions. Immediate protests followed, in the form of both newspaper essays and popular gatherings that adopted resolutions asking Washington to reject the treaty. Especially vehement opposition arose in the South, as planters criticized the lack of compensation for runaway slaves and objected to the commission on prewar debts, which might make them pay off obligations to British merchants dating back to the 1760s. But Federalists countered with meetings and publications of their own, contending that, upon careful examination, the Jay Treaty would prove preferable to the alternative—no treaty at all. The president, displeased by the Republicans' organized vocal opposition and convinced by pro-treaty arguments, signed the pact in mid-August. Just one opportunity remained to prevent it from going into effect: Congress had to appropriate funds to carry out the treaty, and, according to the Constitution, appropriation bills had to originate in the House of Representatives.

Washington delayed submitting the treaty to the House until March 1796, futilely hoping that by then the opposition would have dissipated. During the debate, Republicans argued loudly against approving the appropriations, and they won a vote asking Washington to submit to the House all documents pertinent to the negotiations. In successfully resisting the request, Washington established a power still used today—executive privilege, in which the president may withhold information from Congress if he deems it necessary.

The treaty's opponents initially commanded a congressional majority, but pressure for appropriating the necessary funds built as time passed, fostered by an especially vigorous Federalist campaign of publications and petitions targeting middle-state congressmen whose districts would benefit from approval. Constituent petitions contended that failure to fund the treaty would lead to war with Britain, thus endangering Pennsylvania frontier settlements and New York and New Jersey commercial interests alike. Further, Federalists successfully linked the Jay Treaty with another, more popular pact. In 1795 Thomas Pinckney of South Carolina had negotiated a treaty with Spain giving the United States navigation privileges on the Mississippi River and the right to land and store goods at New Orleans tax free, thus boosting the nation's economy. The overwhelming support for Pinckney's Treaty (the Senate ratified it unanimously) helped to overcome opposition to the Jay Treaty. In late April, the House appropriated the money by the narrow margin of 51 to 48. The vote divided along partisan and regional lines: all but 2 southerners opposed the treaty; all but 3 congressional Federalists supported it; and a majority of middle-state representatives also voted yes.

Despite the Federalists' success in the treaty dispute, their campaign to sway public opinion had ironically violated their fundamental philosophy of government. They believed that ordinary people should defer to the judgment of elected leaders, yet in this instance, in order to persuade the House to follow the president's lead, they had actively engaged in grassroots politicking. The Federalists had won the battle, but in the long run they lost the war, for Republicans ultimately proved far more effective in appealing to the citizenry at large.

Bases of Partisanship

To describe the growing partisanship in Congress and the nation is easier than to explain such divisions in the electorate. The terms used by Jefferson and Madison (the people versus aristocrats) or by Hamilton and Washington (true patriots versus subversive rabble) do not adequately explain the growing divisions. Simple economic differences between agrarian and commercial interests do not provide the answer either, as more than 90 percent of Americans still lived in rural areas. Moreover, Jefferson's vision of a prosperous agrarian America rested on commercial farming, not rural self-sufficiency. Nor did the divisions in the 1790s simply repeat the Federalist–Antifederalist debate of 1787–1788. Even though most Antifederalists became Republicans, the party's leaders, Madison and Jefferson, had supported the Constitution.

Yet certain distinctions can be made. Republicans, especially prominent in the southern and middle states, tended to be self-assured, confident, and optimistic about both politics and the economy. Southern planters, in control of their region and dominating a class of enslaved laborers, foresaw a prosperous future based partly on continued westward expansion, a movement they expected to dominate. Republicans employed democratic rhetoric to win the allegiance of small farmers south of New England. Members of non-English ethnic groups—especially Irish, Scots, and Germans—found Republicans' words attractive. Artisans also joined the coalition; they saw themselves as the urban equivalent of small farmers, cherishing their independence from domineering bosses. Republicans of all descriptions emphasized developing America's own resources, worrying less than Federalists did about the nation's place in the world. Republicans also remained sympathetic to France in international affairs.

By contrast, Federalists, concentrated among the commercial interests of New England, came mostly from English stock. Insecure, they stressed the need for order, hierarchy, and obedience to political authority. Wealthy New England merchants aligned themselves with the Federalists, but so, too, did the region's farmers who, prevented from expanding agricultural production because of New England's poor soil, gravitated toward the more conservative party. Federalists, like Republicans, assumed that southern and middle-state interests would dominate western lands, so they had little incentive to work actively to develop that potentially rich territory. In Federalist eyes, potential enemies—both internal and external—perpetually threatened the nation, which required a continuing alliance with Great Britain for its own protection. Given the dangers posed to the nation by European warfare, Federalists' vision of international affairs may have been accurate, but it was also unappealing. Because the Federalist view held out little hope of a better future to the voters of any region, it is not surprising that the Republicans prevailed in the end.

Washington's Farewell Address

After the treaty debate, wearied by the criticism to which he had been subjected, George Washington decided to retire. (Presidents had not yet been limited to two terms, as they have been since the adoption of the Twenty-second Amendment in 1951.) In September Washington published his Farewell Address, most of which had been written by Hamilton. In it Washington outlined two principles that guided American foreign policy at least until the late 1940s: to maintain commercial but not political ties to other nations and to enter no permanent alliances. He also drew sharp distinctions between the United States and Europe, stressing America's uniqueness—its exceptionalism—and the need for independent action in foreign affairs, today called unilateralism.

Washington lamented the existence of factional divisions among his countrymen. Some historians have interpreted his call for an end to partisan strife as the statement of a man who could see beyond political affiliations to the good of the whole. But in the context of the impending presidential election, the Farewell Address appears rather as an attack on the legitimacy of the Republican opposition. Washington advocated unity behind the Federalist banner, which he viewed as the only proper political stance. The Federalists (like the Republicans) continued to see themselves as the sole guardians of the truth and the only true heirs of the Revolution. Both sides perceived their opponents as misguided, unpatriotic troublemakers who sought to undermine revolutionary ideals.

Election of 1796

The two organized groups actively contending for office made the presidential election of 1796 the first serious contest for the position. To succeed Washington, the Federalists in Congress put forward Vice President John Adams, with the diplomat Thomas Pinckney as his running mate. Congressional Republicans chose Thomas Jefferson as their presidential candidate; the lawyer, Revolutionary War veteran, and active Republican politician Aaron Burr of New York agreed to run for vice president.

That the election was contested does not mean that the people decided its outcome. In most states, legislatures appointed electors, some even before Federalists and Republicans designated their nominees. Moreover, the method of voting in the electoral college did not take into account the possibility of party slates. The Constitution's drafters had not foreseen the development of competing national political organizations, so the Constitution provided no way to express support for one person for president and another for vice president. The electors simply voted for two people. The man with the highest total became president; the second highest, vice president.

This procedure proved to be the Federalists' undoing. Adams won the presidency with 71 votes, but a number of Federalist electors (especially those from New England) failed to cast ballots for Pinckney. Thomas Jefferson won 68 votes, 9 more than Pinckney, to become vice president. The incoming administration was thus politically divided. During the next four years the new president and vice president, once allies and close friends, became bitter enemies.

JOHN ADAMS AND POLITICAL DISSENT

John Adams took over the presidency peculiarly blind to the partisan developments of the previous four years. As president he never abandoned an outdated notion discarded by George Washington as early as 1794: that the president should be above politics, an independent and dignified figure who did not seek petty factional advantage. Thus Adams kept Washington's cabinet intact, despite its key members' allegiance to his chief Federalist rival, Alexander Hamilton. Adams often adopted a passive posture, letting others (usually Hamilton) take the lead when the president should have acted decisively. As a result, his administration gained a reputation for inconsistency. But Adams's detachment from Hamilton's maneuverings did enable him to weather the greatest international crisis the republic had yet faced: the Quasi-War with France.

XYZ Affair The Jay Treaty improved America's relationship with Great Britain, but it provoked the French government to retaliate by ordering its ships to seize American vessels carrying British goods. In response, Congress increased military spending, authorizing the building of ships and the stockpiling of weapons and ammunition. President Adams also sent three commissioners to Paris to negotiate a settlement. For months, the American commissioners sought talks with Talleyrand, the French foreign minister, but Talleyrand's agents demanded a bribe of $250,000 before negotiations could begin. The Americans retorted, "No, no; not a sixpence" and reported the incident in dispatches that the president received in early March 1798. Adams informed Congress of the impasse and recommended further increases in defense appropriations.

Convinced that Adams had deliberately sabotaged the negotiations, congressional Republicans insisted that the dispatches be turned over to Congress. Adams complied, aware that releasing the reports would work to his advantage. He withheld only the names of the French agents, referring to them as X, Y, and Z. The revelation that the Americans had been treated with contempt stimulated a wave of anti-French sentiment in the United States. A journalist's version of the commissioners' reply, "Millions for defense, but not a cent for tribute," became the national slogan. Cries for war filled the air. Congress formally abrogated the Treaty of Alliance and authorized American ships to seize French vessels.

Quasi-War with France Thus began an undeclared war with France fought in Caribbean waters between warships of the U.S. Navy and French privateers. Although Americans initially suffered heavy losses of merchant shipping, by early 1799 the U.S. Navy had established its superiority in the West Indies. Its ships captured eight French privateers and naval vessels, easing the threat to America's vital Caribbean trade.

The Republicans, who opposed war and continued to sympathize with France, could do little to stem the tide of anti-French feelings. Because Agent Y had boasted of the existence of a "French party in America," Federalists flatly accused Republicans (including the eccentric envoy George Logan) of traitorous designs. A New York newspaper declared that anyone who remained "lukewarm" after reading the XYZ dispatches was a "criminal—and the man who does not warmly reprobate the conduct of the French must have a soul black enough to be fit for treason Strategems and spoils." John Adams wavered between calling the Republicans traitors and acknowledging their right to oppose administration measures. His wife was less tolerant. "Those whom the French boast of as their Partizans," Abigail Adams declared, should be "adjudged traitors to their country." If Jefferson had been president, she added, "we should all have been sold to the French."

Alien and Sedition Acts

Federalists saw this climate of opinion as an opportunity to deal a death blow to their Republican opponents. Now that the country seemed to see the truth of what they had been saying ever since the Whiskey Rebellion in 1794—that Republicans were subversive foreign agents—Federalists sought to codify that belief into law. In 1798 the Federalist-controlled Congress adopted a set of four laws known as the Alien and Sedition Acts, intended to suppress dissent and to prevent further growth of the Republican faction.

Three of the acts targeted recently arrived immigrants, whom Federalists accurately suspected of being Republican in their sympathies. The Naturalization Act lengthened the residency period required for citizenship and ordered all resident aliens to register with the federal government. The two Alien Acts, though not immediately implemented, provided for the detention of enemy aliens in time of war and gave the president authority to deport any alien he deemed dangerous to the nation's security.

In 1798, in hopes of appealing to the American market, a potter in Liverpool, England, created this pitcher with President John Adams's portrait on one side and an eagle on the other, surrounded by 16 rings representing the states. (Left and Right: National Museum of American History, Smithsonian Institution, Washington, D.C.)

The fourth statute, the Sedition Act, sought to control both citizens and aliens. It outlawed conspiracies to prevent the enforcement of federal laws, setting the maximum punishment for such offenses at five years in prison and a $5,000 fine. The act also tried to control speech. Writing, printing, or uttering "false, scandalous and malicious" statements against the government or the president "with intent to defame . . . or to bring them or either of them, into contempt or disrepute" became a crime punishable by as much as two years' imprisonment and a fine of $2,000. Today, any such law punishing speech alone would be unconstitutional. But in the eighteenth century, when organized political opposition was by definition suspect, many Americans supported the Sedition Act's restrictions on free speech.

The Sedition Act led to fifteen indictments and ten convictions, including one congressman, Matthew Lyons of Vermont, and several outspoken Republican newspaper editors who failed to mute their criticism of the administration. One was James Callender, a Scots immigrant and scandalmonger, who relentlessly attacked Federalists while being subsidized by Thomas Jefferson. Callender's exposé forced Alexander Hamilton to admit to an extramarital affair. After turning his attention to President Adams, Callender was convicted, fined, and jailed for nine months, but he continued to produce pro-Jeffersonian writings from the Richmond prison.

Virginia and Kentucky Resolutions

Faced with prosecutions of their political allies, Jefferson and Madison sought an effective means of combating the acts. Petitioning the Federalist-controlled Congress to repeal the laws would clearly fail. Furthermore, Federalist judges refused to allow accused individuals to question the Sedition Act's constitutionality. Accordingly, the Republican leaders turned to the only other forum available for protest: state legislatures. Carefully concealing their own role—the vice president and congressman wanted to avoid being indicted for sedition—Jefferson and Madison drafted different sets of resolutions that were introduced into the Kentucky and Virginia legislatures, respectively, in the fall of 1798. Because a compact among the states had created the Constitution, the resolutions contended, people speaking through their states had a legitimate right to judge the constitutionality of actions taken by the federal government. Both pronounced the Alien and Sedition Acts unconstitutional, and thus (declared Kentucky) "void and of no force," advancing the doctrine later known as nullification.

Although no other state endorsed them, the Virginia and Kentucky Resolutions nevertheless had considerable influence. First, they constituted superb political propaganda, rallying Republican opinion throughout the country. They placed the opposition party squarely in the revolutionary tradition of resistance to tyrannical authority. Second, the theory of union that they proposed inspired the Hartford Convention of 1814 and southern states' rights advocates in the 1830s and thereafter. Jefferson and Madison had identified a key constitutional issue: How far could states go in opposing the national government? How could a conflict between the two be resolved? These questions would not be definitively answered until the Civil War.

Convention of 1800 Just as the Sedition Act was being implemented and northern state legislatures were rejecting the Virginia and Kentucky Resolutions, Federalists split over the course of action the United States should take toward France. Hamilton and his supporters called for a declaration legitimizing the undeclared naval war. Adams, though, received a number of private signals—among them George Logan's report—that the French government regretted its treatment of the American commissioners.

Acting on such assurances, Adams dispatched the envoy William Vans Murray to Paris to negotiate with Napoleon Bonaparte, France's new leader, who was consolidating his hold on the country and eager to end messy foreign conflicts. The United States sought two goals: compensation for ships the French had seized since 1793 and abrogation of the treaty of 1778. The Convention of 1800, which ended the Quasi-War, provided for the latter but not the former. Still, it freed the United States from its only permanent alliance, thus allowing it to follow the independent diplomatic course George Washington had urged in his Farewell Address.

THE WEST IN THE NEW NATION

By the end of the eighteenth century, the nation had added three states (Vermont, Kentucky, and Tennessee) to the original thirteen and more than 1 million people to the nearly 4 million counted by the 1790 census. It also nominally controlled all the land east of the Mississippi River and north of Spanish Florida, divided by the Ohio River. Control of the land north of the Ohio was achieved only after considerable bloodshed, for initially the land was dominated by a powerful western confederacy of eight Indian nations led by the Miamis.

War in the Northwest Territory
General Arthur St. Clair, first governor of the Northwest Territory, futilely tried to open more land to settlement through failed treaty negotiations with the western confederacy in early 1789. Subsequently, Little Turtle, the confederacy's able war chief, defeated forces led by General Josiah Harmar (1790) and by St. Clair himself (1791) in major battles near the present border between Indiana and Ohio. More than six hundred of St. Clair's men died, and scores more were wounded, in the United States' worst defeat in the entire history of the American frontier.

In 1793 the Miami Confederacy declared that peace could be achieved only if the United States recognized the Ohio River as its northwestern boundary. But the national government refused to relinquish its claims in the region. A reorganized and newly invigorated army under the command of General Anthony Wayne, a Revolutionary War hero, attacked and defeated the confederacy in August 1794 at the Battle of Fallen Timbers (near present-day Toledo, Ohio). Peace negotiations then began.

In August 1795, Wayne reached agreement with the Miami Confederacy. The Treaty of Greenville gave each side a portion of what it wanted. The United States gained the right to settle much of what was to become Ohio, the indigenous peoples retaining only the northwest corner of the region. Indians, though, received the acknowledgment they had long sought: American recognition of their rights to the soil. At Greenville, the United States formally accepted the principle of Indian sovereignty, by virtue of residence, over all lands the native peoples had not ceded. Never again would the U.S. government claim that it had acquired Indian territory solely through negotiation with a European or North American country.

South of the Ohio, Pinckney's Treaty with Spain that same year established the 31st parallel as the boundary between the United States and Florida. Nevertheless, Spanish influence in the Old Southwest continued to raise questions about the loyalty of American settlers in the region, much of it still unceded and occupied by Creeks, Cherokees, and other Indian nations. A Southwest Ordinance (1790) attempted to organize the territory; by permitting slavery, it made the region attractive to slaveholders.

"Civilizing" the Indians

Increasingly, even Indian peoples who lived independent of federal authority came within the orbit of U.S. influence. The nation's stated goal was to "civilize" them. "Instead of exterminating a part of the human race," Henry Knox, Washington's secretary of war, contended in 1789, the government should "impart our knowledge of cultivation and the arts to the aboriginals of the country." The first step in such a project, Knox suggested, should be to introduce to Indian peoples "a love for exclusive property"; to that end, he proposed that the government give livestock to individual Indians. Four years later, the Indian Trade and Intercourse Act of 1793 codified Knox's plan, promising that the federal government would supply Indians with animals and agricultural implements, and also provide appropriate instructors.

The well-intentioned plan reflected federal officials' blindness to the realities of native peoples' lives. Not only did it incorrectly posit that the Indians' traditional commitment to communal notions of landowning could easily be overcome, it also ignored the centuries-long agricultural experience of eastern Indian peoples. The policymakers focused only on Indian men: because they hunted, male Indians were "savages" who had to be "civilized" by being taught to farm. That in these societies women traditionally did the farming was irrelevant because, in the eyes of the officials, Indian women—like those of European descent—should properly confine themselves to child rearing, household chores, and home manufacturing.

Iroquois and Cherokees

Indian nations at first responded cautiously to the "civilizing" plan. The Iroquois Confederacy had been devastated by the war; its people in the 1790s lived in what one historian has called "slums in the wilderness." Restricted to small reservations increasingly surrounded by Anglo-American farmlands, men could no longer hunt and often spent their days in idle carousing. Quaker missionaries started a demonstration farm among the Senecas, intending to teach men to plow, but they quickly learned that women showed greater interest in their message. The same was true among the Cherokees of Georgia, where Indian agents found that women eagerly sought to learn both new farming methods and textile-manufacturing skills. As their southern hunting territories were reduced, Cherokee men did begin to raise cattle and hogs, but they startled the reformers by treating livestock like wild game, allowing the animals to run free in the woods and simply shooting them when needed, in the same way they had once killed deer. Men also started to plow the fields, although Cherokee women continued to bear primary responsibility for cultivation and harvest.

Iroquois men became more receptive to the Quakers' lessons after the spring of 1799, when a Seneca named Handsome Lake experienced a remarkable series of visions. Like other prophets stretching back to Neolin in the 1760s, Handsome Lake preached that Indian peoples should renounce alcohol, gambling, and other destructive European customs. Even though he directed his followers to reorient men's and women's work assignments as the Quakers advocated, Handsome Lake aimed above all to preserve Iroquois culture by doing so. He recognized that, because men could no longer obtain meat through hunting, only by adopting a sexual division of labor that had originated in Europe could the Iroquois retain an autonomous existence.

"REVOLUTIONS" AT THE END OF THE CENTURY

Three events in the last two years of the eighteenth century can be deemed real or potential revolutions: Fries's Rebellion, Gabriel's Rebellion, and the election of Thomas Jefferson. Although they differed significantly, all these events mirrored the tensions and uncertainties of the young republic. The Fries rebels resisted national authority to tax. Gabriel and his followers directly challenged the slave system that was crucial to the Chesapeake economy. And the venomous, hard-fought presidential election of 1800 exposed a structural flaw in the Constitution that would have to be corrected by amendment.

Fries's Rebellion   The tax resistance movement known by the name of one of its prominent leaders, the militia captain and Revolutionary War veteran John Fries, arose in Pennsylvania's Lehigh Valley in 1798–1799, among German American farmers. To finance the Quasi-War, Congress had enacted taxes on land, houses, and legal documents. German Americans, imbued with revolutionary ideals (at least two-fifths of them were veterans, like Fries), saw in the taxes a threat to their liberties and livelihoods, as well as an echo of the hated Stamp Act of 1765. Asserting a right of resistance to unconstitutional laws, they raised liberty poles, signed petitions to Congress, and nonviolently prevented assessors from evaluating their homes. They voiced repeated threats but harmed no one.

Even so, a federal judge in Philadelphia ordered the arrest of 20 resisters. In response, in March 1799 Fries led a troop of 120 militiamen to Bethlehem, where they surrounded the tavern that temporarily housed the prisoners. Lengthy negotiations failed to win their release, but eventually, fearing a violent confrontation, a federal marshal let the men go. President Adams described the militiamen's actions as "treason, being overt acts of levying war against the United States." Fries and many of his neighbors were arrested and tried; he and 2 others were convicted of treason; 32 more, of violating the Sedition Act. Although Fries and the other "traitors" were sentenced to hang, Adams pardoned them (and all the others) just two days before their scheduled execution, having concluded that they were rioters rather than traitors. Despite clemency from a Federalist president, the region's residents became, and remained, Republican partisans.

Gabriel's Rebellion   Like their white compatriots in the Lehigh Valley and elsewhere, African Americans both slave and free became familiar with concepts of liberty and equality during the Revolution. They, too, witnessed the benefits of fighting collectively for freedom, rather than resisting individually or running away—a message reinforced by the dramatic news of the successful slave revolt in St. Domingue in 1793. Gabriel, an enslaved Virginia blacksmith who planned the second end-of-the-century revolution, drew on both Haitian and American experiences as well as his religious beliefs.

For months, often accompanied by his preacher brother, Martin, Gabriel visited Sunday services at black Baptist and Methodist congregations, where bondspeople gathered free of the watchful eyes of their owners. Gabriel first recruited to his cause other skilled African

Americans who like himself lived in semi-freedom under minimal supervision. Next he enlisted rural slaves. The rebels planned to attack Richmond on the night of August 30, 1800; set fire to the city; seize the state capitol; and capture the governor, James Monroe. At that point, Gabriel believed, other slaves and perhaps poor whites would join in.

The plan showed considerable political sophistication, but heavy rain forced a postponement. Several planters then learned of the plot from informers and spread the alarm. Gabriel avoided arrest for weeks, but militia troops quickly apprehended and interrogated most of the other leaders of the rebellion. Twenty-six rebels, including Gabriel himself, were hanged. Ironically, only those slaves who betrayed their fellows won freedom as a result of the rebellion.

At his trial, one of Gabriel's followers made explicit the links that so frightened Chesapeake slaveholders. He told his judges that, like George Washington, "I have adventured my life in endeavouring to obtain the liberty of my countrymen, and am a willing sacrifice in their cause." Southern state legislatures responded to such claims by increasing the severity of the laws regulating slavery. Before long, all talk of emancipation ceased in the South, and slavery became even more firmly entrenched as an economic institution and way of life.

Election of 1800

The third end-of-the-century revolution was a Republican "takeover—the election of Thomas Jefferson as president and a Congress dominated by Republicans—and the culmination of a decade of increasing partisanship. Prior to November 1800, Federalists and Republicans not only campaigned for congressional seats but also maneuvered furiously to control the outcome in the electoral college. Each side feared victory by the other, and both wanted to avoid reproducing the divided results of 1796. Republicans again nominated Thomas Jefferson and Aaron Burr; Federalists named John Adams, with Charles Cotesworth Pinckney of South Carolina as vice president. When the votes were counted, Jefferson and Burr had tied with 73 (no Republican elector wanted to chance omitting Burr's name from his ballot), while Adams had 64 and Pinckney 63. Under Article II, Section 1, of the Constitution, the election had to be decided in the existing House of Representatives; the newly elected Jeffersonians would not take office until the president did.

Balloting continued for six days and thirty-five ballots, with Federalists uniformly supporting Burr, whereas Republicans held firm for Jefferson. Finally, James Bayard, a Federalist and the sole congressman from Delaware, concluded (perhaps correctly) that "we must risk the Constitution and a civil war or take Mr. Jefferson." He brokered a deal that gave the Virginian the presidency on the thirty-sixth ballot. A crucial consequence of the election was the adoption of the Twelfth Amendment, which provided that electors would henceforth cast separate ballots for president and vice president.

The defeated Federalists turned to strengthening their hold on the judiciary while they could. President Adams named his secretary of state, John Marshall, chief justice; Marshall would serve for thirty-four years, leaving a lasting imprint on constitutional interpretation. Adams spent his last hours in office on March 3, 1801, appointing so-called midnight justices to new positions created in the hastily adopted Judiciary Act of 1801, which also reduced the number of Supreme Court justices from six to five. The fiercely partisan Federalists thus hoped to prevent Jefferson from exerting immediate influence on the judicial branch, despite Republican control of the presidency and Congress.

Haitian Refugees

Although many European-Americans initially welcomed the news of the French Revolution in 1789, few expressed similar sentiments about the slave rebellion that broke out soon thereafter in the French colony of St. Domingue (later Haiti), which shared the island of Hispaniola with Spanish Santo Domingo. The large number of refugees who soon flowed into the new United States from that nearby revolt brought with them consequences deemed undesirable by most political leaders. Less than a decade after winning independence, the new nation confronted its first immigration crisis.

Among the approximately 600,000 residents of St. Domingue in the early 1790s were about 100,000 free people, almost all of them slaveowners; half were whites, the rest mulattos. When in the wake of the French Revolution those free mulattos split the slaveholding population by seeking greater social and political equality, the slaves seized the opportunity to revolt. By 1793 they had triumphed under the leadership of a former slave, Toussaint L'Ouverture, and in 1804 they finally ousted the French, thereafter establishing the republic of Haiti. Thousands of whites and mulattos, accompanied by as many slaves as they could readily transport, sought asylum in the United States during those turbulent years.

Although willing to offer shelter to refugees from the violence, American political leaders nonetheless feared the consequences of their arrival. Southern plantation owners shuddered at the thought that slaves so familiar with ideas of freedom and equality would mingle with their own bondspeople. Many were uncomfortable with the immigration of numerous free people of color, even though the immigrants were part of the slaveholding class. Most of the southern states adopted laws forbidding the entry of Haitian slaves and free mulattos, but the laws were difficult if not impossible to enforce, as was a later congressional act to the same effect. So, more than 15,000 refugees—white, black, and of mixed-race origins—flooded into the United States and Spanish Louisiana. Many ended up in Virginia (which did not pass an

A free woman of color in Louisiana early in the nineteenth century, possibly one of the refugees from Haiti. Esteban Rodriguez Miró, named governor of Spanish Louisiana in 1782, ordered all slave and free black women to wear head wraps rather than hats—which were reserved for whites—but this woman and many others subverted his order by nominally complying, but nevertheless creating elaborate headdresses. (Louisiana State Museum)

(Continued)

219

Haitian Refugees

exclusion law) or the cities of Charleston, Savannah, and New Orleans.

There they had a considerable impact on the existing population. In both New Orleans and Charleston, the influx of mulattos gave rise to a heightened color consciousness that placed light-skinned people at the top of a hierarchy of people of color. Not coincidentally, the Charleston Brown Fellowship Society, composed exclusively of free mulattos, was founded in 1793. After the United States purchased Louisiana in 1803, the number of free people of color in the territory almost doubled in three years, largely because of a final surge of immigration from the new Haitian republic. And in Virginia, stories of the successful revolt helped to inspire local slaves in 1800 when they planned the action that has become known as Gabriel's Rebellion.

The Haitian refugees thus linked both European-Americans and African Americans to current events in the West Indies, indelibly affecting both groups of people.

SUMMARY

As the nineteenth century began, inhabitants of the United States faced changed lives in the new republic. Indian peoples east of the Mississippi River found that they had to surrender some aspects of their traditional culture to preserve others. Some African Americans struggled unsuccessfully to free themselves from the inhuman bonds of slavery, then subsequently confronted more constraints than ever because of increasingly restrictive laws.

European-Americans, too, adjusted to changed circumstances. The first eleven years of government under the Constitution established many enduring precedents for congressional, presidential, and judicial action—among them establishment of the cabinet, interpretations of key clauses of the Constitution, and stirrings of judicial review of state and federal legislation. Building on successful negotiations with Spain (Pinckney's Treaty), Britain (the Jay Treaty), and France (the Convention of 1800), the United States developed its diplomatic independence, striving to avoid entanglement with European countries and their continental wars.

Yet especially after 1793 internal political consensus proved elusive. The 1790s spawned vigorous debates over foreign and domestic policy, and saw the beginnings of a system of organized factionalism and grassroots politicking, if not yet formal parties. The Whiskey and Fries Rebellions showed that regional conflicts persisted even under the new government. The waging of an undeclared war against France proved extremely contentious, splitting one faction and energizing another. In 1801, after more than a decade of struggle, the Jeffersonian view of the future of agrarian, decentralized republicanism prevailed over Alexander Hamilton's vision of a powerful centralized economy and a strong national government.

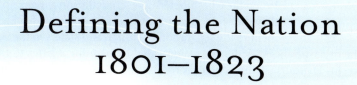

9

Defining the Nation
1801–1823

POLITICAL VISIONS

In his inaugural address, Jefferson reached out to his opponents. Standing in the Senate chamber, the only completed part of the Capitol, he appealed to the electorate not as party members but as citizens with common beliefs: "We are all republicans, we are all federalists." Nearly a thousand people strained to hear his vision of a restored republicanism. "A wise and frugal government, which shall restrain men from injuring one another, which shall leave them free to regulate their pursuits of industry and improvement, and shall not take from the mouth of labor the bread it had earned. This is the sum of good government," he concluded.

But outgoing president John Adams was not there to hear Jefferson's call for unity. He had left Washington before dawn to avoid the Republican takeover. He and Jefferson had once been close friends but had grown to dislike each other intensely. Despite the spirit of Jefferson's inaugural address, the Democratic-Republicans—as the Republicans of the 1790s now called themselves, after the Democratic societies of the 1790s—and the Federalists remained bitter opponents. These parties held different visions of how society and government should be organized. The Federalists advocated a strong national government with centralized authority to promote economic development. The Democratic-Republicans, by contrast, sought to restrain the national government, believing that limited government would foster Republican virtue. The Jeffersonians believed that virtue derived from agricultural endeavors. Nearly two decades later, Jefferson would refer to his election as "the revolution of 1800," which was "as real a revolution in the principles of our government as that of 1776 was in its form."

Separation of Church and State

When the Cheshire farmers sent Jefferson a mammoth cheese, they did so in large part to express gratitude for his commitment to the separation of church and state. On the very day he received the overripe cheese, Jefferson reciprocated by penning a letter to the Baptist association in Danbury, Connecticut, proclaiming that the Constitution's First Amendment supported a "wall of separation between church and state." Jefferson's letter articulated a core component of his vision of limited government. The president declared that "religion is a matter which lies solely between Man & his God." It lay beyond the purview of the government. New England Baptists hailed Jefferson as a hero, but New England Federalists felt their worst fears had been confirmed. During the election of 1800, Federalists had waged a venomous campaign against Jefferson, incorrectly labeling him an atheist. Their rhetoric proved so effective that, after Jefferson's election, some New England women hid their Bibles in their gardens and wells to foil Democratic-Republicans allegedly bent on confiscating them. Jefferson's letter to the Danbury Baptists seemingly vindicated such hysteria.

Jefferson came to office during a period of religious revivalism, particularly among Methodists and Baptists, whose democratic preaching—all humans, they said, were equal in God's eyes—fed into a growing democratic political culture. Emboldened by a combination of secular and religious ideologies about human equality, society's non-elites articulated their own political visions in the early republic. They did not simply take stands in debates defined by their social and political betters. They worked, too, to reshape the debates. When the Cheshire Baptists sent their cheese to President Jefferson, for example, they pointedly informed the Virginia planter that it had been made "without a single slave to assist."

This portrait of President Thomas Jefferson was painted by Rembrandt Peale in 1805. Charles Willson Peale (Rembrandt's father) and his five sons helped establish the reputation of American art in the new nation. Rembrandt Peale achieved fame for his presidential portraits; here he has captured Jefferson in a noble pose without the usual symbols of office or power, befitting the Republican age. (© Collection of the New-York Historical Society)

CHRONOLOGY

1801 • Marshall becomes chief justice
 • Jefferson inaugurated as president
1801–05 • United States defeats Barbary pirates
1803 • *Marbury v. Madison*
 • Louisiana Purchase
1804 • Jefferson reelected president, Clinton vice president
1804–06 • Lewis and Clark explore Louisiana Territory
1805 • Tenskwatawa emerges as Shawnee leader
1807 • *Chesapeake* affair
 • Embargo Act halts legal foreign trade
1808 • Congress bans importation of slaves
 • Madison elected president, Clinton vice president
1808–13 • Tenskwatawa and Tecumseh organize Indian resistance
1811 • Work begins on the National Road
1812 • Madison reelected president, Gerry vice president
1812–15 • War of 1812 with Great Britain
1813 • Tecumsehs death weakens pan-Indian resistance
 • Boston Manufacturing Company starts textile mill in Waltham, Massachusetts
1814 • Treaty of Ghent ends War of 1812
1814–15 • Hartford Convention
1815 • Battle of New Orleans
 • Steamboat travels upriver on Mississippi
1817–1825 • Erie Canal constructed
1819 • *McCulloch v. Maryland*
 • Adams-Onis Treaty
1819–early 1820s • First major depression
1820–1821 • Missouri Compromise
1823 • Monroe Doctrine

Political Mobilization The revolution of 1800, which gave the Democratic-Republicans majorities in both houses of Congress in addition to the presidency, resulted from an electorate that was limited largely, but not exclusively, to property-holding men. The Constitution left the regulation of voting to the individual states. In no state but New Jersey could women vote even if they met property qualifications, and in New Jersey that right was granted inadvertently and later revoked in 1807. In 1800 free black men who met property qualifications had the right to vote in all states but Delaware, Georgia, South Carolina, and Virginia, but local custom often kept them from exercising that right. Yet partisan politics nonetheless captured nearly all Americans' imaginations, and politicians actively courted nonvoters as well as voters. Most political mobilization took place locally, where partisans rallied popular support for candidates and their ideologies on militia training grounds, in taverns and churches, at court gatherings, and during holiday celebrations. Voters and nonvoters alike expressed their views by marching in parades, signing petitions, singing songs, and debating politically charged sermons. Perhaps most important, they devoured a growing print culture that included pamphlets, broadsides (posters), almanacs, and—especially—newspapers.

The Partisan Press

Newspapers provided a forum for a sustained political conversation. Read aloud in taverns, artisans' workshops, and homes, newspapers helped give national importance to local events. Without newspaper publicity, Cheshire's mammoth cheese would have been little more than a massive hunk of curdled milk. With it, a cheese became worthy of presidential response. In 1800 the nation had 260 newspapers; by 1810 it had 396, virtually all of which were unabashedly partisan.

The parties adopted official organs. Shortly after his election, Jefferson persuaded the *National Intelligencer* to move from Philadelphia to the new capital of Washington, where it became the voice of the Democratic-Republicans. In 1801 Alexander Hamilton launched the *New York Evening Post* as the Federalist vehicle. It boosted Federalists while frequently calling Jefferson a liar and depicting him as the head of a slave harem. The party organs—published six or seven times a week, year in and year out—helped ensure that the growing American obsession with partisan politics was not limited to electoral campaigns.

Limited Government

Jefferson needed public servants as well as supporters. To bring into his administration men who shared his vision of individual liberty, an agrarian republic, and limited government, Jefferson refused to recognize appointments that Adams had made in the last days of his presidency and dismissed Federalist customs collectors from ports. He awarded vacant treasury and judicial offices to Republicans. Federalists accused Jefferson of "hunting the Federalists like wild beasts" and abandoning the peaceful overtures of his inaugural address.

Even a government filled with Democratic-Republicans should be limited, Jeffersonians believed, so the president, his cabinet, and Congress worked to make the government leaner. If Alexander Hamilton had viewed the national debt as the engine of economic growth, Jefferson saw it as the source of government corruption. Secretary of the Treasury Albert Gallatin cut the army budget in half and reduced the 1802 navy budget by two-thirds. He then moved to reduce the national debt from $83 million to $57 million, as part of a plan to retire it altogether by 1817. Jefferson's austerity led him to close two of the nation's five diplomatic missions abroad, at The Hague and in Berlin. Jeffersonians attacked taxes as well as spending: the Democratic Republican–controlled Congress oversaw the repeal of all internal taxes, including the despised whiskey tax of 1791.

In addition to frugality, ideas of liberty distinguished Democratic-Republicans from Federalists. The Alien and Sedition Acts of 1798 had helped unite the Republicans in opposition. Jefferson now declined to use the acts against his opponents and pardoned those who had been convicted under the provisions. Congress let the Sedition Act expire in 1801 and the Alien Act in 1802. Congress also repealed the Naturalization Act of 1798, which had required fourteen years of residency for citizenship. The 1802 act that replaced it, while stipulating the registration of aliens, required of would-be citizens only five years of residency, loyalty to the Constitution, and the forsaking of foreign allegiances and titles. The new act would remain the basis of naturalized American citizenship into the twentieth century.

Judicial Politics   To many Democratic-Republicans, the judiciary represented a centralizing and undemocratic force, especially as judges were appointed rather than elected and served for life. Partisan Democratic-Republicans thus targeted opposition judges. At Jefferson's prompting, the House impeached (indicted) and the Senate convicted Federal District Judge John Pickering of New Hampshire. Allegedly deranged and alcoholic, Pickering made an easy mark. On the same day in 1803 that Pickering was ousted from office, the House impeached Supreme Court Justice Samuel Chase for judicial misconduct. A staunch Federalist, Chase had pushed for prosecutions under the Sedition Act, had actively campaigned for Adams in 1800, and had repeatedly denounced Jefferson's administration from the bench. But in the Senate the Democratic-Republicans failed to muster the two-thirds majority necessary for conviction. The failure to remove Chase preserved the Court's independence and established the precedent that criminal actions, not political disagreements, justified impeachment.

The Marshall Court   Although Jefferson appointed three new Supreme Court justices during his two administrations, the Court nonetheless remained a Federalist stronghold under the leadership of his distant cousin John Marshall. Marshall adopted some outward trappings of Republicanism—opting for a plain black gown over the more colorful academic robes of his fellow justices—but he adhered steadfastly to Federalist ideology. Even after the Democratic-Republicans achieved a majority of Court seats in 1811, Marshall remained extremely influential during his tenure as chief justice (1801–1835). Under the Marshall Court, the Supreme Court consistently upheld federal supremacy over the states while protecting the interests of commerce and capital.

Marshall made the Court an equal branch of the government in practice as well as theory. Previously regarded lightly, judicial service became a coveted honor for ambitious and talented men. Marshall, moreover, strengthened the Court by having it speak with a more unified voice; rather than issuing a host of individual concurring judgments, the justices now issued joint majority opinions. Marshall himself became the voice of the majority: from 1801 through 1805 he wrote twenty-four of the Court's twenty-six decisions; through 1810 he wrote 85 percent of the opinions, including every important one.

Judicial Review   One of the most important involved Adams's midnight appointments. In his last hours in office, Adams had named Federalist William Marbury a justice of the peace in the District of Columbia. But Jefferson's secretary of state, James Madison, declined to certify the appointment, so that the new president could appoint a Democratic-Republican instead. Marbury sued, requesting a writ of mandamus (a court order forcing the president to appoint him). *Marbury v. Madison* presented a political dilemma. If the Supreme Court ruled in Marbury's favor, the president probably would not comply with the writ, and the Court had no way to force him to do so. Yet, if the Federalist-dominated bench refused to issue the writ, it would hand the Democratic-Republicans a victory.

Marshall brilliantly recast the issue to avoid both pitfalls. Writing for the Court, he ruled that Marbury had a right to his appointment but that the Supreme Court could not compel Madison to honor the appointment because the Constitution did not grant the Court power to issue a writ of mandamus. In the absence of any specific mention in the Constitution, Marshall ruled, the section of the Judiciary Act of 1789 that authorized the Court to issue writs was unconstitutional. Thus the Supreme Court denied itself the power to issue writs of mandamus but established its far greater power to judge the constitutionality of laws passed by Congress. In doing so, Marshall fashioned the theory of judicial review. Because the Constitution was "the supreme law of the land," Marshall wrote, any federal or state act contrary to the Constitution must be null and void. The Supreme Court, whose duty it was to uphold the law, would decide whether a legislative act contradicted the Constitution. "It is emphatically the province and duty of the judicial department," Marshall ruled, "to say what the law is." This power of the Supreme Court to determine the constitutionality of legislation and presidential acts permanently enhanced the independence of the judiciary and breathed life into the Constitution. "Marshall found the Constitution paper and made it power," President James A. Garfield later observed.

Election of 1804

In the first election after the Twelfth Amendment's ratification, Jefferson took no chances: he dropped Burr as his running mate and, in keeping with the already established convention of having a North-South balance on the ticket, chose George Clinton of New York. Their ticket swamped their opponents—South Carolinian Charles Cotesworth Pinckney and New Yorker Rufus King—in the electoral college by 162 votes to 14, carrying fifteen of the seventeen states.

That 1804 election escalated the long-standing animosity between Burr and Hamilton, who supported Burr's rival in the New York gubernatorial election. When Hamilton called Burr a liar, Burr challenged Hamilton to a duel. Believing his honor was at stake, Hamilton accepted the challenge even though his son Philip had died in 1801 from dueling wounds. Because New York had outlawed dueling, the encounter took place across the Hudson River in New Jersey. Hamilton decided not to fire and paid for the decision with his life. In New York and New Jersey, prosecutors indicted Burr for murder.

Facing arrest if he returned to either state and with his political career in ruins, Burr fled to the West, where he and Brigadier General James Wilkinson schemed to create a new empire by using military force to acquire what is now Texas and by persuading already existing western territories to leave the United States and join the new empire. The plan fizzled when Wilkinson, fearful of the negative repercussions for himself, revealed the plot to Jefferson. The president personally assisted the prosecution in Burr's 1807 trial for treason, which was overseen by Jefferson's political rival Chief Justice Marshall. (At the time, Supreme Court justices presided over circuit courts.) Prompted by Marshall to interpret treason in a very narrow sense, the jury acquitted Burr, who fled to Europe.

NATIONAL EXPANSION WESTWARD

Little excited the popular imagination more than the West and its seeming abundance of unoccupied land. By 1800 hundreds of thousands of white Americans had settled in the rich Ohio River and Mississippi River valleys, intruding on Indian lands. In the Northwest they raised foodstuffs, primarily wheat, and in the Southwest they cultivated cotton. At the time of the American Revolution, cotton production was profitable only for the Sea Island planters in South Carolina and Georgia, who grew the long-staple variety. Short-staple cotton, which grew readily in the interior and in all kinds of soil, was unmarketable because its sticky seeds could be removed only by hand. After a young New England inventor named Eli Whitney designed a cotton gin (short for "engine") in 1793, allowing one person to remove the same number of seeds that previously required fifty people working by hand, the cultivation of short-staple cotton spread rapidly westward into the fertile lands of Louisiana, Mississippi, Alabama, Arkansas, and Tennessee. By exponentially increasing the efficiency with which cotton fiber could be extracted from raw cotton, the cotton gin greatly increased the demand for slaves, who seeded, tended, and harvested cotton fields.

Whatever crops they marketed, American settlers depended on free access to the Mississippi River and its Gulf port, New Orleans. "The Mississippi," wrote Secretary of State James Madison, "is to them [western settlers] everything. It is the Hudson, the Delaware, the Potomac and all navigable rivers of the Atlantic States formed into one stream." Whoever controlled the port of New Orleans had a hand on the throat of the American economy.

New Orleans

Spain, which had acquired France's territory west of the Mississippi in the settlement of the Seven Years War (1763), secretly transferred it back to France in 1800 and 1801. American officials learned of the transfer only in 1802, when Napoleon seemed poised to rebuild a French empire in the New World. "Every eye in the United States is now focused on the affairs of Louisiana," Jefferson wrote to Robert R. Livingston, the American minister in Paris. American concerns intensified when Spanish officials, on the eve of ceding control to the French, violated Pinckney's treaty by denying Americans the privilege of storing their products (or exercising their "right of deposit") at New Orleans prior to transshipment to foreign markets. Western farmers and eastern merchants, who traded through New Orleans, thought a devious Napoleon had closed the port; they talked war.

To relieve the pressure for war and win western farmers' support, Jefferson urged Congress to authorize the call-up of eighty thousand militiamen but at the same time sent Virginia Governor James Monroe to join Robert Livingston in France with instructions to buy the port of New Orleans and as much of the Mississippi valley as possible. Arriving in Paris in April 1803, Monroe learned with astonishment that France had already offered to sell all 827,000 square miles of Louisiana to the United States for a mere $15 million. With St. Domingue torn from French control by revolution and slave revolt, Napoleon gave up dreams of a New World empire and no longer needed Louisiana as its breadbasket. His more urgent need was for money to wage war against Britain. On April 30, Monroe and Livingston signed a treaty buying the vast territory whose exact borders and land remained uncharted.

Louisiana Purchase

The Louisiana Purchase appealed to Americans with divergent ideas about how best to achieve national greatness and personal prosperity. The purchase ensured that the United States would control the Mississippi's mouth, giving peace of mind to western settlers who relied on the river to market their goods. It also inspired the commercial visions of those who imagined the United States as the nexus of international trade networks reaching between Europe and Asia. Louisiana promised to fulfill the dreams of easterners seeking cheap, fertile lands. Its vast expanse meant, too, that land could be set aside for Indians displaced by the incursion of white settlers and their black slaves, soothing the consciences of those white Americans who preferred to "civilize" rather than to exterminate the continent's first settlers. The purchase had its critics, though: some doubted its constitutionality (even Jefferson agonized over it); others worried that it belied the Democratic-Republicans' commitment to debt reduction; and some New England Federalists complained that it undermined their commercial interests and threatened the sustainability of the republic itself by spreading the population beyond the bounds of where it could be properly controlled. Overall, though, the Louisiana Purchase was the most popular achievement of Jefferson's presidency.

Louisiana was not, however, the "vast wilderness" that some Federalists lamented and most Republicans coveted. When the United States acquired the territory, hundreds of thousands of people who had not been party to the agreement became American subjects. These included Native Americans from scores of nations who made their homes within the enormous territory, as well as people of European and African descent—or, often, a mixture of the two—who congregated primarily along the Gulf Coast. Around New Orleans, Louisiana's colonial heritage was reflected in its people: creoles of French and Spanish descent, slaves of African descent, free people of color, and Acadians, or Cajuns (descendants of French settlers in eastern Canada), as well as some Germans and English. The 1810 census, the first taken after the purchase, reported that 97,000 non-Indians lived in the Louisiana Purchase area, of whom the great majority (77,000) lived in what is now the state of Louisiana. Not all these new Americans welcomed their new national identity. Although Jefferson imagined the West as an "empire of liberty," free blacks and slaves soon discovered that they lost some rights accorded them under French and Spanish law.

Lewis and Clark Expedition

Jefferson had a long-standing interest in the trans-Mississippi West, envisioning it as punctuated with volcanoes and mountains of pure salt, where llamas and mammoths roamed and Welshmen settled. He felt an urgent need to explore it, fearing that, if Americans did not claim it as their own, the British, who still controlled the northern reaches of the continent (in present-day Canada) and parts of the Pacific Northwest, surely would. He lost no time in launching a military-style mission that would chart the region's commercial possibilities—its water passages to the Pacific as well as its trading opportunities with Indians—while cataloguing its geography, flora, and fauna.

The expedition, headed by Meriwether Lewis and William Clark, began in May 1804 and lasted for more than two years; it traveled up the Missouri River, across the Rockies, and then down the Columbia to the Pacific Ocean—and back. Along the way, the expedition's members "discovered" (as they saw it) dozens of previously unknown

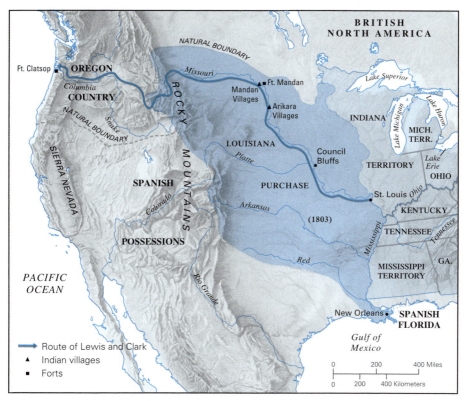

MAP 9.1 **Louisiana Purchase**

The Louisiana Purchase (1803) doubled the area of the United States and opened the trans-Mississippi West for American settlement.

Indian tribes, many of whom had long before discovered Europeans. Lewis and Clark found the Mandans and Hidatsas already well supplied with European trade goods, such as knives, corduroy trousers, and rings. Although the Corps of Discovery, as the expedition came to be called, expected to find Indians and prepared for possible conflict, its goal was peaceable: to foster trade relations, win political allies, and take advantage of Indians' knowledge of the landscape. Accordingly, Lewis and Clark brought with them twenty-one bags of gifts for Native American leaders, both to establish goodwill and to stimulate interest in trading for American manufactured goods. Most of the corps' interactions with native peoples were cordial, but when Indians failed to be impressed by Lewis and Clark's gifts, tensions arose. After an encounter with the Lakota (or Sioux), Lewis denounced them as "the vilest miscreants of the savage race."

Although military in style, the Corps of Discovery proved unusually democratic in seating enlisted men on courts-martial and allowing Clark's black slave York as well as the expedition's female guide and translator Sacagawea to vote on where to locate winter quarters in 1805. But, unlike the expedition's other members, neither York nor Sacagawea drew wages, and when York later demanded his freedom for his services, Clark repaid him with—in Clark's own words—"a severe trouncing."

Lewis and Clark failed to discover a Northwest Passage to the Pacific, and the route they mapped across the Rockies proved more perilous than practical. But their federally sponsored expedition helped set the stage for additional government-sponsored exploration, capturing the imagination of white Americans seeking land for farming and profit.

In seeking land, white Americans mostly ignored the presence of Native Americans. Although Jefferson had more sympathy for Indians than did many of his contemporaries—he took interest in their cultures and believed Indians to be intellectually equal to whites—he nonetheless lobbied, unsuccessfully, for a constitutional amendment that would transport them west of the Mississippi into the newly acquired Louisiana Territory. He became personally involved in efforts to pressure the Chickasaws to sell their land, and in the event that legal methods for removing Indians should fail, he advocated trickery. Traders, he suggested, might run the "good and influential individuals" into debt, which they would have to repay "by a cessation of lands."

Divisions Among Indian Peoples   Some Indian nations decided to deal with white intruders by adopting white customs as a means of survival and often agreeing to sell their lands and move west. These "accommodationists" (or "progressives") were opposed by "traditionalists," who urged adherence to native ways and refused to relinquish their lands. Distinctions between accommodationists and traditionalists were not always so clear-cut, however, as the Seneca Handsome Lake had demonstrated just a few years before.

In the early 1800s, two Shawnee brothers, Tenskwatawa–(1775–1837) and Tecumseh (1768–1813), led a traditionalist revolt against American encroachment by fostering a pan-Indian federation that centered in the Old Northwest and reached into parts of the South. During the two brothers' own lifetimes, the Shawnees had lost most of their Ohio land; by the 1800s they occupied only scattered sites in Ohio and in the Michigan and Louisiana territories. Despondent, Lalawethika—as Tenskwatawa had been called as a youth—had turned to a combination of European remedies (particularly whiskey) and Native American ones, becoming a shaman in 1804. But when European diseases ravaged his village, he despaired.

Tenskwatawa and Tecumseh   Lalawethika emerged from his own battle with illness in 1805 as a new man, renamed Tenskwatawa ("the Open Door")—by whites—"the Prophet." Claiming to have died and been resurrected, he traveled widely in the Ohio River valley as a religious leader, attacking the decline of moral values among Native Americans, warning against whiskey, condemning intertribal battles, and stressing harmony and respect for elders. He urged Indians to return to the old ways and to abandon white ways: to hunt with bows and arrows, not guns; to stop wearing hats; and to give up bread for corn and beans. Tenskwatawa was building a religious movement that offered hope to the Shawnees, Potawatomis, and other displaced western Indians.

By 1808 Tenskwatawa and his older brother Tecumseh talked less about spiritual renewal and more about resisting American aggression. They invited Indians from all nations to settle in pan-Indian towns in Indiana, first at Greenville (1806–1808) and then at Prophetstown (1808–1812), near modern-day Lafayette. The new towns challenged the treaty-making process by denying the claims of Indians who had been guaranteed the same land as part of the Treaty of Greenville of 1795 in exchange for enormous cessions. Younger Indians, in particular, flocked to Tecumseh, the more politically oriented of the two brothers.

Convinced that only an Indian federation could stop the advance of white settlement, Tecumseh sought to unify northern and southern Indians by preaching Indian resistance across a wide swath of territory, ranging from Canada to Georgia. Among southern Indians, only one faction of the Creek nation welcomed him, but his efforts to spread his message southward nonetheless alarmed white settlers and government officials. In November 1811, while Tecumseh was in the South, Indiana governor William Henry Harrison moved against Tenskwatawa and his followers. During the battle of Tippecanoe, the army burned their town; as they fled, the Indians exacted revenge on white settlers. "What other course is left for us to pursue," asked Harrison, "but to make a war of extirpation upon them." With the stakes raised, Tecumseh entered a formal alliance with the British, who maintained forts in southern Ontario. This alliance, along with issues over American neutral rights on the high seas, were already propelling the United States toward war with Britain.

THE NATION IN THE ORBIT OF EUROPE

A decade earlier, in 1801, when Jefferson had sought to set a new course for the nation, he tried to put tensions with France to rest. "Peace, commerce, and honest friendship with all nations, entangling alliances with none," he had proclaimed in his first inaugural address. Yet the economy of the early republic relied heavily on both fishing and the carrying trade, in which the American merchant marine transported commodities between nations. Merchants in Boston, Salem, and Philadelphia traded with China, sending cloth and metal to swap for furs with Chinook Indians on the Oregon coast, and then sailing to China to trade for porcelain, tea, and silk. The slave trade lured American ships to Africa. America's commercial interests were clearly focused on the seas, and not long after Jefferson's first inaugural address, the United States was at war with Tripoli—a state along the Barbary Coast of North Africa—over a principle that would long be a cornerstone of American foreign policy: freedom of the seas. In other words, outside of national territorial waters, the high seas should be open for free transit of all vessels.

First Barbary War   In 1801 the bashaw (pasha) of Tripoli declared war on the United States for its refusal to pay tribute for safe passage of its ships, sailors, and passengers through the Mediterranean. Jefferson deployed a naval squadron to protect American ships. After two years of stalemate, Jefferson declared a blockade of Tripoli, but when the American frigate *Philadelphia* ran aground in the harbor, its three hundred officers and sailors were imprisoned. Jefferson refused to ransom them, and a small American force accompanied by Arab, Greek, and African mercenaries marched from Egypt to the "shores of Tripoli" (memorialized to this day in the Marine Corps anthem) to seize the port of Derne. A treaty ended the war in 1805, but the United States continued to pay tribute to the three other Barbary states—Algiers, Morocco, and Tunis—until 1815. In the intervening years, the United States became embroiled in European conflicts.

At first Jefferson managed to distance the nation from the turmoil in Europe in the wake of the French Revolution. After the Senate ratified the Jay Treaty in 1795, the United States and Great Britain appeared to reconcile their differences. Britain withdrew from its western forts on American soil (while still retaining those in Canada and the Pacific Northwest) and interfered less in American trade with France. Then, in May 1803, two weeks after Napoleon sold Louisiana to the United States, France was at war against Britain and, later, Britain's continental allies, Prussia, Austria, and Russia. The Napoleonic wars again trapped the United States between belligerents on the high seas. But at first the United States—as the world's largest neutral shipping carrier—actually benefited from the conflict, and American merchants gained control of most of the West Indian trade. After 1805, however, when Britain defeated the French and Spanish fleets at Trafalgar, Britain's Royal Navy tightened its control of the oceans. Two months later, Napoleon crushed the Russian and Austrian armies at Austerlitz. Stalemated, France and Britain launched a commercial war, blockading each other's trade. As a trading partner of both countries, the United States paid a high price.

Threats to American Sovereignty

One British tactic in particular threatened American sovereignty. To replenish their supply of sailors, British vessels stopped American ships and impressed (forcibly recruited) British deserters, British-born naturalized American seamen, and other sailors suspected of being British. Perhaps six to eight thousand Americans were seized in this way between 1803 and 1812. Moreover, alleged deserters—many of them American citizens—faced British courts-martial. Americans saw impressment as a direct assault on their nation's independence. The principle of "once a British subject, always a British subject" mocked U.S. citizenship and sovereignty. Americans also resented the British interfering with their West Indian trade as well as their searching and seizing American vessels within U.S. territorial waters.

In April 1806 Congress responded with the Non-Importation Act, barring British manufactured goods from entering American ports. Because the act exempted most cloth and metal articles, it had little impact on British trade; instead, it warned the British what to expect if they continued to violate American neutral rights. In November Jefferson suspended the act temporarily while William Pinkney, a Baltimore lawyer, joined James Monroe in London to negotiate a settlement. But the treaty they carried home violated Jefferson's instructions—it did not so much as mention impressment—and the president never submitted it to the Senate for ratification.

Anglo-American relations steadily deteriorated, coming to a head in June 1807 when the USS *Chesapeake,* sailing out of Norfolk for the Mediterranean, was stopped by the British frigate *Leopard,* whose officers demanded to search the ship for British deserters. Refused, the *Leopard* opened fire, killing three Americans and wounding eighteen others, including the captain. The British then seized four deserters, three of whom held American citizenship; one of them was hanged. The *Chesapeake* affair outraged Americans while also exposing American military weakness.

The Embargo of 1807

Had the United States been better prepared militarily, public indignation over the incident might have resulted in a declaration of war. Instead, Jefferson opted for what he called "peaceable coercion." In July, the president closed American waters to British warships and soon thereafter increased military and naval expenditures. In December 1807, Jefferson again put economic pressure on Great Britain by invoking the Non-Importation Act, followed eight days later by a new restriction, the Embargo Act. Jefferson and his congressional supporters saw the embargo, which forbade all exports from the United States to any country, as a short-term measure to avoid war by pressuring Britain and France to respect American rights and by preventing confrontation between American merchant vessels and European warships.

The embargo's biggest economic impact, however, fell on the United States. Exports declined by 80 percent in 1808, squeezing New England shippers and their workers as economic depression set in. Manufacturers, by contrast, received a boost, as the domestic market became theirs exclusively, and merchants began to shift their capital from shipping to manufacturing. In 1807 there were twenty cotton and woolen mills in New England; by 1813 there were more than two hundred. Meanwhile, merchants who were willing to engage in smuggling profited enormously.

International Slave Trade

They had only to look at the vibrant slave trade to see how scarcity bred demand. With Jefferson's encouragement, Congress had voted in 1807 to abolish the international slave trade as of January 1, 1807—the earliest date permissible under the Constitution. South Carolina alone still allowed the legal importation of slaves, but most of the state's influential planters favored a ban on the trade, nervous (having seen what happened in St. Domingue) about adding to the black population of a state in which whites were already outnumbered. Congressional debate focused not on whether it was a good idea to abolish the trade but on what should become of any Africans imported illegally after the ban took effect. The final bill provided that smuggled slaves would be sold in accordance with the laws of the state or territory in which they arrived. It underscored, in other words, that slaves (even illegal ones) were property. Had the bill not done so, threatened one Georgia congressman, the result might have been "resistance to the authority of the Government," even civil war. Although the debate over the slave trade did not fall along strictly sectional (or regional) lines, sectional tensions never lay far beneath the surface in this era of heated partisan conflict.

In anticipation of the higher prices that their human property would fetch once the law took effect, traders temporarily withheld their slaves from the market in the months after the law's passage. During the last four months of 1807 alone, sixteen thousand African slaves arrived at Gadsden Wharf in Charleston, where they were detained by merchants eager to wait out the January 1 deadline. Although many of these slaves—hundreds, if not thousands—died in the cramped, disease-ridden holding pens before they could be sold, merchants calculated that the increased value of those who survived until the ban took effect would outweigh the losses. Not that January 1, 1808, brought an end to the international slave trade; a brisk—and profitable—illegal trade took over. As Justice Joseph Story noted in 1819, the slave trade "is still carried on with all the implacable ferocity and insatiable rapacity of former times. Avarice has grown more subtle in its evasions; and watches and seizes its prey with an appetite quickened rather than suppressed by its guilty vigils." In 1819 Congress passed a law authorizing the president to use force to intercept slave ships along the African coast, but the small American navy could not halt the illicit trade in human beings.

Election of 1808

As discussion of the international slave trade subsided, debate over the embargo heated up, especially with the approach of the 1808 presidential election. Democratic-Republicans suffered from factional dissent and dissatisfaction in seaboard states hobbled by the trade restrictions. Although nine state legislatures passed resolutions urging Jefferson to run again, the president followed George Washington's lead in declining a third term. He supported James Madison, his secretary of state, as the Democratic-Republican standard-bearer. For the first time, however, the Democratic-Republican nomination was contested. Madison won the endorsement of the party's congressional caucus, but Virginia Democratic-Republicans put forth James Monroe, who later withdrew, and some easterners supported Vice President George Clinton. Madison and Clinton headed the ticket. Charles Cotesworth Pinckney and Rufus King again ran on the Federalist ticket, but with new vigor.

The younger Federalists, led by Harrison Gray Otis and other Bostonians, made the most of the widespread disaffection with Democratic-Republican policy, especially the embargo. Pinckney received only 47 electoral votes to Madison's 122, but he carried all of New England except Vermont, won Delaware, and carried some electoral votes in two other states. Federalists also gained seats in Congress and captured the New York State legislature. Although the Federalist future looked promising, the transition from one Democratic-Republican administration to the next went smoothly.

Women and Politics

This transition was eased, in part, by the wives of elected and appointed officials in the new capital, who encouraged political and diplomatic negotiation. Such negotiations often took place in social settings, even private homes, where people with divergent interests could bridge their ideological divides through personal relationships. Women played crucial roles, fostering conversation, providing an ear or a voice for unofficial messages, and—in the case of international affairs—standing as surrogates for their nation. Elite women hosted events that muted domestic partisan rivalries, events at which Federalists and

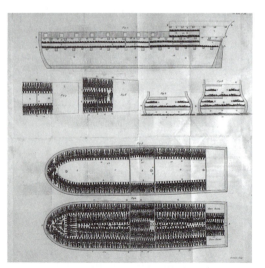

In an effort to win support for measures to end the international slave trade and slavery itself, abolitionists published drawings of the inhumanely cramped slave ships, where each person was allotted a space roughly the size of a coffin. Disease spread rapidly under such conditions, causing many slaves to die before reaching American shores. (The Huntington Library & Art Collections, San Marino, California)

Democratic-Republicans could find common ground in civility, if not always politics. Political wives' interactions among themselves served political purposes, too: when First Lady Dolley Madison visited congressmen's wives, she cultivated goodwill for her husband while collecting recipes that allowed her to serve regionally diverse cuisine at White House functions. Mrs. Madison hoped her menus would help keep simmering sectional tensions from reaching a boiling point.

But it was women's buying power that may have proved most influential in the era of the embargo. Recalling women's support of revolutionary-era boycotts, Jeffersonians appealed directly for women's support of their embargo. Sympathetic women responded by spurning imported fabric and making (or directing their slaves to make) homespun clothing for themselves and their families. Federalists, however, encouraged women to "keep commerce alive," and sympathetic women bought smuggled goods.

Failed Policies   Under the pressure of domestic opposition, the embargo eventually collapsed. In its place, the Non-Intercourse Act of 1809 reopened trade with all nations except Britain and France, and authorized the president to resume trade with those two nations once they respected American neutral rights. The new act solved only the problems created by the embargo; it did not prevent further British and French interference with American commerce. For one brief moment it appeared to work. In June 1809, President Madison reopened trade with Britain after its minister to the United States offered assurances that Britain would repeal restrictions on American trade. His Majesty's government in London, though, repudiated the minister's assurances, and Madison reverted to nonintercourse.

When the Non-Intercourse Act expired in 1810, Congress substituted a variant, Macon's Bill Number 2, which reopened trade with both Great Britain and France but provided that, when either nation stopped violating American commercial rights, the president would suspend American commerce with the other. When Napoleon accepted the offer, Madison declared nonintercourse on Great Britain in 1811. Although the French continued to seize American ships, Britain became the main focus of American hostility because its Royal Navy dominated the seas.

In spring 1812, the British admiralty ordered its ships not to stop, search, or seize American warships, and in June Britain reopened the seas to American shipping. But Britain's response came too late. Before word of the change in British policy reached American shores, Congress declared war.

Mr. Madison's War   The vote was sharply divided. The House voted 79 to 49 for war; the Senate, 19 to 13. Democratic-Republicans favored war by a vote of 98 to 23; Federalists opposed it 39 to 0. Those who favored war, including President Madison, pointed to impressment, violation of neutral trading rights, British alliances with western Indians, and affronts to American independence and honor. The British, in other words, had assaulted American sovereignty. Others saw in the war an opportunity to conquer and annex British Canada. Most militant were land-hungry southerners and westerners—the "War Hawks"—led by John C. Calhoun of South Carolina and first-term congressman and House Speaker Henry Clay of Kentucky. John Randolph of Virginia, an opponent of war, charged angrily, "Agrarian cupidity, not maritime rights, urges war!" He heard "but one word" in

Congress: "Canada! Canada! Canada!" Most representatives from the coastal states, and especially from the Northeast, feared disruption to commerce and opposed what they called "Mr. Madison's War."

The War of 1812 did not begin badly for the Federalists, who benefited from anti-war sentiment. They joined renegade Democratic-Republicans in supporting New York City mayor DeWitt Clinton for president in the election of 1812. Clinton lost to President Madison by 128 to 89 electoral votes—a respectable showing against a wartime president—and the Federalists gained some congressional seats and carried many local elections. But the South and the West—areas that favored the war—remained solidly Democratic-Republican.

THE WAR OF 1812

For lack of a better term, the war has come down to us as the War of 1812. It lasted until 1815, unfolding in a series of scuffles and skirmishes (see Map 9.2), for which the U.S. armed forces, kept lean by Jeffersonian fiscal policies, were ill prepared. Officers executed campaigns poorly, and full-scale battles were rare. Although the U.S. Navy had a corps of experienced officers, it was no match for the Royal Navy. The U.S. Army had neither an able staff nor an adequate force of enlisted men. By 1812 the U.S. Military Academy at West Point, founded in 1802, had produced only eighty-nine regular officers. Senior army officers were aged Revolutionary War veterans or political appointees.

Nor did the United States succeed at mustering sufficient forces. The government's efforts to lure recruits—with sign-up bonuses and promises of three months' pay and rights to purchase 160 acres of western land upon discharge—met with mixed success. At first, recruitment went well among westerners, who were motivated by civic spirit, desire for land, strong anti-Indian sentiment, and fears of Tecumseh's pan-Indian organization. But after word spread of delays in pay, as well as inadequate supplies and rations, recruitment dwindled. In New England, raising an army was even more difficult. Federalists discouraged enlistments, and even some New England Democratic-Republicans declined to raise volunteer companies. Others promised their men that they would serve only in defensive roles, as in Maine, where they would guard the coastline. Militias in New England and New York often refused to fight outside their own states. Desperate for soldiers, New York offered freedom to slaves who enlisted, and compensation to their owners, and the U.S. Army made the same offer to slaves in the Old Northwest and in Canada. In Philadelphia, black leaders formed a "Black Brigade" to defend the city. But in the Deep South, fear of arming slaves kept them out of the military except in New Orleans, where a free black militia dated back to Spanish control of Louisiana. The British, on the other hand, recruited slaves by promising freedom in exchange for service. In the end, British forces—made up of British regulars, their Indian allies, fugitive slaves, and Canadians, many of whom were loyalists who had fled to Canada during the American Revolution—outnumbered the Americans overall.

Invasion of Canada Despite their recruitment problems, Americans had expected to take Canada easily. Canada's population was sparse, its army small, and the Great Lakes inaccessible to the Royal Navy in the Atlantic. Americans hoped, too, that the French in Canada might welcome U.S. forces.

American strategy aimed to split Canadian forces and isolate pro-British Indians, especially Tecumseh, whom the British had promised an Indian nation in the Great Lakes region. In July 1812, U.S. general William Hull, territorial governor of Michigan, marched his troops into Upper Canada (modern Ontario), hoping to conquer Montreal. Although his forces outnumbered those of the British and their allies, Hull waged a timid campaign, retreating more than he attacked. His abandonment of Mackinac Island and Fort Dearborn and his surrender of Fort Detroit left the entire Midwest exposed to the enemy. The only bright spot was the September 1812 defense of Fort Harrison in Indiana Territory by Captain Zachary Taylor, who provided the Americans with their first land victory. By the winter of 1812–1813, the British controlled about half of the Old Northwest. The United States had no greater success on the Niagara Front, where New York borders Canada, in large part because New York militiamen refused to leave their state to join the invasion of Canada.

Naval Battles

Despite victories on the Atlantic by the USS *Constitution* (nicknamed "Old Ironsides" after its rout of the HMS *Guerrière*), the USS *Wasp,* and the USS *United States,* the American navy—which began the war with just seventeen ships—could not match the powerful Royal Navy. The Royal Navy blockaded the Chesapeake and Delaware Bays in December 1812, and by 1814 the blockade covered nearly all American ports along the Atlantic and Gulf coasts. After 1811, American trade overseas declined by nearly 90 percent, and the decline in revenue from customs duties threatened to bankrupt the federal government and prostrate New England.

The contest for control of the Great Lakes, the key to the war in the Northwest, evolved as a shipbuilding race. Under Master Commandant Oliver Hazard Perry and shipbuilder Noah Brown, the United States outbuilt the British on Lake Erie and defeated them at the bloody Battle of Put-in-Bay on September 10, 1813, gaining control of Lake Erie.

Burning Capitals

General William Henry Harrison then began what would be among the United States' most successful land campaigns. A ragged group of Kentucky militia volunteers, armed only with swords and knives, marched 20 to 30 miles a day to join Harrison's forces in Ohio. Now 4,500 strong, Harrison's forces attacked and took Detroit before crossing into Canada, where at the Battle of the Thames they defeated British, Shawnee, and Chippewa forces in October 1813. Among the fallen was Tecumseh. The Americans went on to raze the Canadian capital of York (now Toronto), looting and burning the Parliament building before withdrawing.

After defeating Napoleon in Europe in April 1814, the British launched a land counteroffensive against the United States, concentrating on the Chesapeake Bay region. In retaliation for the burning of York—and to divert American troops from Lake Champlain, where the British planned a new offensive—royal troops occupied Washington, D.C., in August and set it ablaze, leaving the presidential mansion and parts of the city burning all night. Chaos ruled. The president and cabinet fled. Dolley Madison stayed in town long enough to oversee the removal of cabinet documents and, famously, to save a Gilbert Stuart portrait of George Washington.

The British intended the attack on the capital only as a diversion. The major battle occurred in September 1814 at Baltimore, where the Americans held firm. Francis Scott Key, detained on a British ship, watched the bombardment of Fort McHenry from Baltimore harbor and the next morning wrote the verses of "The Star-Spangled Banner" (which became the national anthem in 1931). Although the British inflicted heavy damage, they achieved little militarily; their offensive on Lake Champlain proved equally unsuccessful when American ships turned back a British flotilla at Plattsburgh. The British halted their offensive; the war had reached a stalemate.

War in the Old Southwest

To the south, the war's final campaign began with an American attack on the Red Stick Creeks along the Gulf of Mexico and the British around New Orleans. The Red Sticks had responded to Tecumseh's call (his mother was a Creek) to resist U.S. expansion. Some had died in Indiana Territory, when General Harrison's troops routed Shawnee forces at Tippecanoe in 1811. In 1813 the Red Sticks attacked Fort Mims, about 40 miles from Mobile, killing hundreds of white men, women, and children who had sought protection there. Seeking revenge, General Andrew Jackson of Tennessee rallied his militiamen as well as Indian opponents of the Red Sticks (including other Creeks who favored accommodation with whites) and crushed the Red Sticks at Horseshoe Bend (in present-day Alabama) in March 1814. The victory helped clear additional land for white American settlement. In the 1814 Treaty of Fort Jackson, the Creeks ceded 23 million acres of their land, or about half of their holdings, and withdrew to the southern and western part of Mississippi Territory.

Jackson became a major general in the regular army and continued south toward the Gulf of Mexico, with his eye on New Orleans. After seizing Pensacola (in Spanish Florida) and then securing Mobile, Jackson's forces continued on to New Orleans, where for three weeks they played a game of cat-and-mouse with the British soldiers.

Americans rejoiced that the War of 1812 had reaffirmed their independence from the British monarchy. The sailor's foot here steps upon the crown while broken chains of bondage lie nearby. (Picture Research Consultants & Archives)

Finally, on January 8, 1815, the two forces met head-on. In fortified positions, Jackson's poorly trained army held its ground against two British frontal assaults. At day's end, more than two thousand British soldiers lay dead or wounded (a casualty rate of nearly one-third), while the Americans suffered only twenty-one casualties.

The Battle of New Orleans took place two weeks after the war's official conclusion: word had not yet reached the United States that British and American diplomats had signed the Treaty of Ghent on December 24, 1814. Although militarily unnecessary, the Battle of New Orleans helped catapult General Andrew Jackson to national political prominence, and a soon legendary victory over a formidable foe inspired a sense of national pride.

Treaty of Ghent

The Treaty of Ghent essentially restored the prewar status quo. It provided for an end to hostilities with the British and with Native Americans, release of prisoners, restoration of conquered territory, and arbitration of boundary disputes. But the United States received no satisfaction on impressment, blockades, or other maritime rights for neutrals, and the British demands for territorial cessions from Maine to Minnesota went unmet. The British dropped their promise to Tecumseh of an independent Indian nation.

Why did the negotiators settle for so little? Napoleon's defeat allowed the United States to discard its prewar demands, because peace in Europe made impressment and interference with American commerce moot issues. Similarly, war-weary Britain—its treasury nearly depleted—stopped pressing for military victory.

American Sovereignty Reasserted

Yet the War of 1812 had significant consequences for America's status in the world. It affirmed the independence of the American republic and ensured Canada's independence from the United States. Although conflict with Great Britain over trade and territory continued, it never again led to war. The experience strengthened America's resolve to steer clear of European politics.

The return of peace with Europe also allowed the United States to again turn its attention to the Barbary Coast, where the dey (governor) of Algiers had taken advantage of the American preoccupation with British forces to declare his own war on the United States. In the Second Barbary War, U.S. forces seized prisoners, as the bashaw of Tripoli had done in 1801, holding hundreds of Algerians captive while negotiating a treaty in the summer of 1815 that forever freed the United States from having to pay tributes for passage in the Mediterranean. The Second Barbary War helped reaffirm American sovereignty, as well as its commitment to the principle of freedom of the seas.

Domestic Consequences

The War of 1812 had profound domestic consequences, too. The Federalists' hopes of once again becoming a national party all but evaporated with the Hartford Convention. With the war stalemated and the New England economy shattered by embargo and war, delegates from New England met in Hartford, Connecticut, for three weeks in the winter of 1814–1815 to discuss revising the national compact or pulling out of the republic. Moderates prevented a resolution of secession—a resolution to withdraw from the Union—but the twenty-six convention delegates condemned the war and the embargo while endorsing changes in constitution that would weaken the South's power vis-à-vis the North and make it harder to declare war. When news arrived in upcoming weeks of, first, Jackson's victory in New Orleans and, then, the Treaty of Ghent, the Hartford Convention made the Federalists look wrong-headed, if not treasonous. Although the Federalists survived in a handful of states until the 1820s, the party faded from the national scene.

With the death of Tecumseh, midwestern Indians lost their most powerful political and military leader; with the withdrawal of the British, they lost their strongest ally. In the South, the Red Sticks had ceded vast tracts of fertile land. The war did not bring disaster to all Indians—some accommodationists, such as the Cherokees, temporarily flourished in its aftermath—but it effectively disarmed traditionalists bent on resisting American expansion. Although the Treaty of Ghent pledged the United States to end hostilities with Indians and to restore their prewar "possessions, rights, and privileges," Indians did not have the power to make the United States live up to the terms of the agreement.

For American farmers, the war opened vast tracts of formerly Indian land for the cultivation of cotton in the Old Southwest and wheat in the Old Northwest. For young industries, the war also, in the end, proved a stimulant, as Americans could no longer rely on overseas imports to fill their demands for manufactured goods, particularly textiles. The War of 1812 thus fueled the demand for raw cotton, and the newly acquired lands in the Southwest beckoned southerners who migrated there either with their slaves or with expectations of someday owning slaves.

The conclusion of the war accelerated three trends that would dominate U.S. history for upcoming decades: westward expansion, industrial takeoff, and the entrenchment of slavery. Increasingly, political elites, including Democratic-Republicans, came to believe that the federal government ought to give direction to the American economy.

THE NATIONALIST PROGRAM

In his last year as president, James Madison and the Democratic-Republicans embraced a nationalist agenda, absorbing the Federalist idea that the federal government should encourage economic growth. In his December 1815 message to Congress, Madison recommended economic development and military expansion. His agenda, which Henry Clay later called the American System, included a national bank, improved transportation, and a protective tariff—a tax on imported goods that was designed to protect American manufacturers from foreign competition. Yet Madison did not stray entirely from his Jeffersonian roots; only a constitutional amendment, he argued, could authorize the federal government to build local roads and canals.

American System   Clay and other leaders in Congress, such as Calhoun of South Carolina, thought that the American System would unify the nation as it expanded, bridging sectional divides. The tariff would stimulate New England industry. Goods produced in New England would find markets in the South and West. At the same time, the agricultural products of the South and West—cotton and foodstuffs—would feed New England mills and their workers. Manufactured goods and agricultural products would move in all directions along roads and canals—what contemporaries called internal improvements—which tariff revenues would fund. A national bank would handle the transactions.

In the last year of Madison's administration, the Democratic-Republican Congress enacted much of the nationalist program. In 1816 it chartered the Second Bank of the United States (the charter on the first bank had expired in 1811) to serve as a depository for federal funds and to issue currency, collect taxes, and pay the government's debts. The Second Bank of the United States was responsible, too, for overseeing state and local banks, making certain that their paper money had backing in specie (precious metals). Like its predecessor, the bank mixed public and private ownership; the government provided one-fifth of the bank's capital and appointed one-fifth of its directors.

Congress also passed a protective tariff to aid industries that had flourished during the War of 1812 but were now threatened by the resumption of overseas trade. The Tariff of 1816 levied taxes on imported woolens and cottons, as well as on iron, leather, hats, paper, and sugar. Foreshadowing a growing trend, though, the tariff served more to divide than to unify the nation. New England as well as the western and Middle Atlantic states stood to benefit from it and thus applauded it, whereas many in the South opposed it because it raised the price on goods they purchased while also raising the possibility that Britain would retaliate with a tariff on cotton.

Some southerners did press for internal improvements. Calhoun vocally promoted roads and canals to "bind the republic together." However, on March 3, 1817, the day before he left office, President Madison, citing constitutional scruples, stunned Congress by vetoing Calhoun's "Bonus Bill," which would have authorized federal funding for such public works.

Early Internal Improvements

Constitutional scruples aside, Federalists and Democratic-Republicans agreed on the need for internal improvements. Improved transportation was necessary for both parties' vision of the nation's route to prosperity. Federalists saw roads and canals as a way to spur the nation's commercial development; Jeffersonians, as the route to the nation's western expansion and agrarian growth. In 1806 Congress had passed (and Jefferson had signed into law) a bill authorizing federal funding for the Cumberland Road (later, the National Road) running between Cumberland, Maryland, and Wheeling, Virginia (now West Virginia). Construction on the road began in 1811, stretching the 130 miles to Wheeling in 1818. In 1820 Congress authorized a survey of the National Road to Columbus, Ohio, a project that was funded in 1825 and completed in 1833; the road would ultimately extend into Indiana.

After President Madison's veto of the Bonus Bill, though, most transportation initiatives received funding from states, private investors, or a combination of the two. In 1817 the State of New York began construction on the Erie Canal, linking the Great Lakes to the Atlantic seaboard; the project would be completed in 1825. Although modest canals were built in southern states, the South relied mostly on rivergoing steamboats that quickly dominated river trade following Robert Fulton's successful trial of a steam-powered vessel in 1807. In 1815 a steamboat made the first upriver voyage on the Mississippi; by 1817, steamboats began making the trip regularly. Canals and steamboats greatly reduced the time and costs involved in transporting western agricultural products to market, and fueled the nation's westward expansion. Unlike steamboats, though, canals expanded commercial networks into regions that did not have natural waterways. Although the Mississippi provided the great commercial highway of the Early Republic, canals would begin to reorient midwestern commerce through the North.

The Era of Good Feelings

James Monroe, Madison's successor, continued Madison's domestic program, supporting tariffs and vetoing the Cumberland Road Bill (for repairs) in 1822. Monroe was the last president to have attended the Constitutional Convention and the third Virginian elected president since 1801. A former senator and twice governor of Virginia, he had served under Madison as secretary of state and of war, and had used his close association with Jefferson and Madison to attain the presidency. In 1816 he and his running mate, Daniel Tompkins, trounced the last Federalist presidential nominee, Rufus King, garnering all the electoral votes except those of the Federalist strongholds of Massachusetts, Connecticut, and Delaware. A Boston newspaper dubbed this one-party period the "Era of Good Feelings."

Led by Federalist chief justice John Marshall, the Supreme Court became the bulwark of the nationalist point of view. In *McCulloch v. Maryland* (1819), the Court struck down a Maryland law taxing banks within the state that were not chartered by the Maryland legislature—a law aimed at hindering the Baltimore branch of the federally chartered Second Bank of the United States. The bank had refused to pay the tax and sued. At issue was state versus federal jurisdiction. Writing for a unanimous Court, Marshall asserted the supremacy of the federal government over the states. "The Constitution and the laws thereof are supreme," he declared. "They control the constitution and laws of the respective states and cannot be controlled by them." The Court also unanimously ruled that Congress had the power to charter banks under the Constitution's clause that endowed it with the authority to pass "all laws which shall be necessary and proper for carrying into execution" the enumerated powers of government. The Marshall Court thus provided a bulwark for the Federalist view that the federal government could promote interstate commerce.

Government Promotion of Market Expansion

Later Supreme Court cases validated government promotion of economic development and encouraged business enterprise and risk taking. In *Gibbons v. Ogden* (1824), the Supreme Court overturned the New York law that had given Robert Fulton and Robert Livingston (and their successor, Aaron Ogden) a monopoly on the New York–New Jersey steamboat trade. Chief Justice John Marshall ruled that the federal power to license new enterprises took precedence over New York's grant of monopoly rights and declared that Congress's power under the commerce clause of the Constitution extended to "every species of commercial intercourse," including transportation. The *Gibbons v. Ogden* ruling built on earlier Marshall Court decisions, such as those in *Dartmouth College v. Woodward* (1819), which protected the sanctity of contracts against state interference, and *Fletcher v. Peck* (1810), which voided a Georgia law that violated individuals' rights to make contracts. Within two years of *Gibbons v. Ogden,* the number of steamboats operating in New York increased from six to forty-three. A later ruling under Chief Justice Roger Taney, *Charles River Bridge v. Warren Bridge* (1837), encouraged new enterprises and technologies by favoring competition over monopoly and the public interest over implied privileges in old contracts.

Federal and state courts, in conjunction with state legislatures, also encouraged the proliferation of corporations—organizations entitled to hold property and transact business as if they were individuals. Corporation owners, called shareholders, were granted limited liability, or freedom from personal responsibility for the company's debts beyond their original investment. Limited liability encouraged investors to back new business ventures.

The federal government assisted the development of a commercial economy in other ways. The U.S. Post Office fostered the circulation of information, a critical element of the market economy. The number of post offices grew from three thousand in 1815 to fourteen thousand in 1845. To create an atmosphere conducive to economic growth and individual creativity, the government protected inventions and domestic industries. Patent laws gave inventors a seventeen-year monopoly on their inventions, and tariffs protected American industry from foreign competition.

Boundary Settlements

Monroe's secretary of state, John Quincy Adams, matched the self-confident Marshall Court in assertiveness and nationalism. Adams, the son of John and Abigail Adams, managed the nation's foreign policy from 1817 to 1825, stubbornly pushing for expansion, fishing rights for Americans in Atlantic waters, political distance from Europe, and peace. An ardent expansionist, he nonetheless believed that expansion must come through negotiations, not war, and that newly acquired territories must bar slavery.

Under Adams's leadership, the United States settled outstanding points of conflict with both Britain and Spain. In 1817 the United States and Great Britain agreed in the Rush-Bagot Treaty to limit their naval forces to one ship each on Lake Champlain and Lake Ontario, and to two ships each on the four other Great Lakes. This first disarmament treaty of modern times led to the demilitarization of the border between the United States and Canada. Adams then pushed for the Convention of 1818, which fixed the U.S.-Canadian border from Lake of the Woods in Minnesota westward to the Rockies along the 49th parallel. When they could not agree on the boundary west of the Rockies, Britain and the United States settled on joint occupation of Oregon for ten years (renewed indefinitely in 1827).

Adams's negotiations resulted in the Adams-Onís Treaty, in which the United States gained Florida, already occupied by General Andrew Jackson under pretext of suppressing Seminole raids against American settlements across the border during the First Seminole War of 1817–1818. Although the Louisiana Purchase had omitted reference to Spanish-ruled West Florida, the United States claimed the territory as far east as the Perdido River (the present-day Florida-Alabama border). During the War of 1812, the United States had seized Mobile and the remainder of West Florida, and after the war—with Spain preoccupied with its own domestic and colonial troubles—Adams had laid claim to East Florida. In 1819 Don Luís de Onís, the Spanish minister to the United States, agreed to cede Florida to the United States without payment if the United States renounced its dubious claims to northern Mexico (Texas) and assumed $5 million of claims by American citizens against Spain. The Adams-Onís (or Transcontinental) Treaty also defined the southwestern boundary of the Louisiana Purchase and set the line between Spanish Mexico and Oregon Country at the 42nd parallel.

John Quincy Adams's desire to insulate the United States and the Western Hemisphere from European conflict brought about his greatest achievement: the Monroe Doctrine. The immediate issue was the recognition of the new governments in Latin America. Between 1808 and 1822, the United Provinces of Río de la Plata (present-day northern Argentina, Paraguay, and Uruguay), Chile, Peru, Colombia, and Mexico all broke free from Spain. In 1822, shortly after the ratification of the Adams-Onís Treaty, the United States became the first nation outside Latin America to recognize the new states, including Mexico. But in Europe, reactionary regimes were in the ascendancy, and with France now occupying Spain to suppress a liberal rebellion, the United States feared that continental powers would attempt to return the new Latin American states to colonial rule. Having withdrawn from an alliance with continental nations, Britain proposed a joint declaration with the United States against European intervention in the Western Hemisphere. But Adams rejected Britain's offer as just the kind of entanglement he sought to avoid, despite clear advantages to allying with the British and their powerful navy.

Monroe Doctrine   Monroe presented to Congress in December 1823 what became known as the Monroe Doctrine. His message announced that the American continents "are henceforth not to be considered subjects for future colonization by any European power." This principle addressed American anxiety not only about Latin America but also about Russian expansion beyond Alaska and its settlements in California. Monroe demanded nonintervention by Europe in the affairs of independent New World nations, and he pledged noninterference by the United States in European affairs, including those of Europe's existing New World colonies. Although Monroe's words carried no force—European nations stayed out of New World affairs because they feared the Royal Navy, not the United States' proclamations—they proved popular at home, tapping American nationalism as well as anti-British and anti-European feelings.

SECTIONALISM EXPOSED

The embargo, the War of 1812, and the postwar spurt of internal improvements encouraged the southern and northern economies to develop in different but interrelated ways. While the South would become ever more dependent on cotton, the North saw an acceleration of industrial development, whose groundwork had been laid two decades earlier. Although Jeffersonians, committed to frugal government and an agrarian nation, did not promote industry, a small number of entrepreneurs did.

Early Industrial Development   For all of their efforts to define themselves as a separate nation, Americans relied on British technology to bring together the many steps of textile manufacturing—carding (or disentangling) fibers, spinning yarn, and weaving cloth—under one factory roof. The first American water-powered spinning mill was established in 1790 by Samuel Slater, a British immigrant who reconstructed from memory the complex machines he had used as an apprentice and then as a supervisor in a British cotton-spinning factory. But Slater's mill only carded and spun yarn; that yarn still needed to be hand-woven into cloth, work that was often done by farm women seeking to earn extra cash. In 1810 Bostonian Francis Cabot Lowell, determined to introduce water-powered mechanical weaving in the United States, visited the British textile center of Manchester, where he toured factories during the day and at night sketched from memory what he had seen. In 1813 he and his business associates, calling themselves the Boston Manufacturing Company, brought together all phases of textile manufacturing under one roof in Waltham, Massachusetts. A decade later, the Boston Manufacturing Company established what it saw as a model industrial village—named for its now-deceased founder—along the banks of the Merrimack River. At Lowell, Massachusetts, there would be boarding houses for workers, a healthy alternative to the tenements and slums of Manchester. American industrialists envisioned that America would industrialize without the poverty and degradation associated with European industrialization.

The American textile factory had been born in the midst of the War of 1812. When the British began flooding the American market with cheap textiles after the Treaty of Ghent, Lowell realized the market now needed to be protected. He lobbied hard for the inclusion of cotton textiles in the Tariff of 1816, playing a crucial role in persuading reluctant South Carolinians to support the provision.

The growth of early industry, primarily in the northern states, was inextricably linked to slavery. Much of the capital behind early industrialization came from merchants who had made their fortunes at least in part through the trade in African slaves, and two of the most prominent industries—textiles and shoes—expanded in tandem with a growing southern cotton economy. Southern cotton fed northern textile mills, and northern shoe factories sold their "Negro brogans" (work shoes) to southern planters. Even in an older form of northern industrial labor which took place in private homes—outwork—the connections to the slave South were strong: New England farm girls wove palm-leaf hats for merchants who sold them to southern planters for their slaves.

Panic of 1819

Immediately after the war, the American economy boomed. The demand for (and price of) American commodities on the international market reached new heights. Poor weather in Europe led to crop failures and thus to an increased demand for northern agricultural exports, and European textile manufacturers clamored for the South's raw cotton. The demand for American wheat and cotton touched off western land speculation. Speculators raced to buy large tracts of land at modest, government-established prices and then to resell it at a hefty profit to would-be settlers. This American expansion was built on easy credit. With easily obtained loans and paper money, farmers and speculators bought land, while manufacturers established new enterprises or enlarged existing ones.

Prosperity proved short-lived. Now recovered from war as well as weather, by the late 1810s Europeans could grow their own food, and Britain's new Corn Laws established a high tariff on imported foodstufs—further lessening demand for American agricultural exports. Cotton prices fell in England. Wars in Latin America interfered with mining and reduced the supply of precious metals, leading European nations to hoard specie; in response, American banks furiously printed paper money and expanded credit even further. Fearful of inflation, the Second Bank of the United States, which had itself issued more loans than it could back in hard currency, demanded in

Industrial Piracy

Although Americans pride themselves on inventiveness and hard work, their start in industrial development depended on importing technology, sometimes by stealth. Great Britain, which in the late eighteenth century had pioneered the invention of mechanical weaving and power looms, knew the value of its head start in the industrial revolution and prohibited the export of textile technology. But the British-born brothers Samuel and John Slater, their Scottish-born power-loom-builder William Gilmore, and Bostonians Francis Cabot Lowell and Nathan Appleton evaded British restrictions and patents to establish America's first textile factories.

As an apprentice and then a supervisor in a British cotton-spinning factory, Samuel Slater had mastered the machinery and the process. Britain forbade the export of textile technology, so Slater emigrated to the United States disguised as a farmer. In 1790 in Pawtucket, Rhode Island, he opened the first water-powered spinning mill in America on the Blackstone River, rebuilding the complex machines from memory. With his brother John and their Rhode Island partners—Moses and Obadiah Brown and William Almy—Slater later built and oversaw mills in Rhode Island and Massachusetts. In 1815 he hired a recent immigrant, William Gilmore, to build a water-powered loom like those used in Britain. Later in the 1820s, the Slaters introduced British steam-powered looms. Spinning and weaving would now be done in New England factories organized along British models.

In 1810 Francis Cabot Lowell had the same idea as the Slaters: to build modern mills with mechanical, water-powered looms. Lowell took a family vacation to Britain, and in Edinburgh, Scotland, he met fellow Bostonian Nathan Appleton. Impressed by the textile mills they had seen in Britain, they laid plans to introduce water-powered mechanical weaving into the United States. They knew they had to acquire the "improved manufactures" from Britain that had

This contemporary painting shows the Boston Manufacturing Company's 1814 textile factory at Waltham, Massachusetts. All manufacturing processes were brought together under one roof, and the company built its first factories in rural New England to tap roaring rivers as a power source. (Courtesy of Gore Place Society, Waltham, Massachusetts)

Industrial Piracy

made Manchester famous as a textile center. Lowell went to Manchester, during the day visiting and observing the factories, and meeting the factory managers. At night he returned to his hotel to sketch from memory the power looms and processes that he had seen. Back in the United States, he and others formed the Boston Associates, which created the Waltham–Lowell Mills based on Lowell's industrial piracy. Within a few years, textiles would be a major American industry, and the Boston Associates would dominate it.

Thus the modern American industrial revolution began with international links, not homegrown American inventions. Ingenuity and industrial piracy put the United States on the road to industrial advancement.

1819 that state banks repay loans in specie. State banks in turn called in the loans and mortgages they had made to individuals and companies. The falling prices of commodities meant that farmers could not pay their mortgages, and the decline of land values—from 50 to 75 percent in portions of the West—meant they could not meet their debts even by selling their farms. The nation's banking system collapsed. The 1819 financial panic reminded Americans all too starkly that they still lived within the economic orbit of Europe.

Hard times came to countryside and city alike. Foreclosures soared. Unemployment skyrocketed, even in older manufacturing areas that had focused on industries like iron making and tobacco processing. In Philadelphia it reached 75 percent. The contraction devastated workers and their families. As a Baltimore physician noted in 1819, working people felt hard times "a thousand fold more than the merchants." They could not build up savings during boom times to get them through the hard times; often they could not make it through the winter without drawing on charity for food, clothing, and firewood.

The depression sent tremors throughout American society. Americans from all regions contemplated the virtues and hazards of rapid market expansion, disagreeing most intensely on where to place the blame for its shortcomings. Westerners blamed easterners; farmers and workers blamed bankers. Even as the nation's economy began to rebound in the early 1820s, amid a flurry of internal improvement projects, no one could predict with confidence where—in what region, in what sector—the nation's economic and political fortunes would lie.

Missouri Compromise   Just as financial panic struck the nation in 1819, so, too, did political crisis. The issue was slavery's westward expansion. Although economic connections abounded between North and South, slavery had long been politically explosive. Since the drafting of the Constitution, Congress had tried to avoid the issue; the one exception had been debates over the international slave trade. In 1819, however, slavery once again burst onto the national political agenda when residents of the Missouri Territory—carved out of the

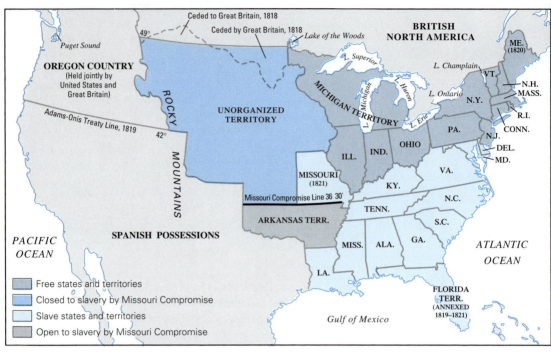

MAP 9.2 Missouri Compromise and the State of the Union, 1820

The compromise worked out by House Speaker Henry Clay established a formula that avoided debate over whether new states would allow or prohibit slavery. In the process, it divided the United States into northern and southern regions.

Louisiana Territory—petitioned Congress for admission to the Union with a constitution permitting slavery. At stake was more than the future of slavery in an individual state. Missouri's admission to the Union would give the slaveholding states a two-vote majority in the Senate, and what happened in Missouri would surely set a precedent for all the new western states created from the vast Louisiana Purchase. "This momentous question," wrote former President Jefferson, fearful for the life of the Union, "like a fire bell in the night, awakened and filled me with terror."

Following the Louisiana Purchase and especially after the end of the War of 1812, the American population had surged westward, leading five new states to join the Union: Louisiana (1812), Indiana (1816), Mississippi (1817), Illinois (1818), and Alabama (1819). Of these, Louisiana, Mississippi, and Alabama permitted slavery. Because Missouri was on the same latitude as free Illinois, Indiana, and Ohio (a state since 1803), its admission as a slave state would thrust slavery not just westward but also farther northward, as well as tilt the uneasy balance in the Senate.

For two and a half years the issue dominated Congress, with the fiery debate transcending the immediate issue of slavery in Missouri. When Representative James Tallmadge Jr. of New York proposed gradual emancipation in Missouri, some southerners accused the North of threatening to destroy the Union. "If you persist, the Union will be dissolved," Thomas W. Cobb of Georgia shouted at Tallmadge. Only "seas of blood" could extinguish the fire Tallmadge had ignited, warned Cobb. "Let it come," retorted Tallmadge. The House, which had a northern majority, passed the Tallmadge Amendment, but the Senate rejected it.

House Speaker Henry Clay—himself a western slaveholder—put forward a compromise in 1820. Maine, carved out of Massachusetts, would enter as a free state, followed by Missouri as a slave state, maintaining the balance between slave and free states—at twelve to twelve. In the rest of the Louisiana Territory north of Missouri's southern border of 36°30′, slavery would be prohibited forever.

The compromise carried but almost unraveled when Missouri submitted a constitution barring free blacks from entering the state, a provision that opponents contended would violate the federal constitutional provision that citizens of each state were "entitled to all privileges and immunities of citizens in the several States." Proponents countered that many states, North and South, already barred free blacks from entering. In 1821 Clay proposed a second compromise: Missouri would guarantee that none of its laws would discriminate against citizens of other states. (The compromise carried, but once admitted to the Union, Missouri twice adopted laws barring free blacks.) For more than three decades, the Missouri Compromise would govern congressional policy toward admitting new slave states. But the compromise masked rather than suppressed the simmering political conflict over slavery's westward expansion.

SUMMARY

The partisanship of the 1790s, though alarming to the nation's political leaders, captured Americans' imaginations, making the early republic a period of pervasive and vigorous political engagement. Troubled by vicious partisanship, President Jefferson sought both to unify the nation and to solidify Democratic-Republican control of the government. With a vision of an agrarian nation that protected individual liberty, Jeffersonians promoted a limited national government—one that stayed out of religious affairs and spent little on military forces, diplomatic missions, and economic initiatives. The rival Federalists, who exerted most of their influence through the judiciary, declared federal supremacy over the states even as the judiciary affirmed its own supremacy over other branches of the government. Federalists hoped a strengthened federal government would help promote commerce and industry.

Despite his belief in limited government, Jefferson considered the acquisition of the Louisiana Territory and the commissioning of the Corps of Discovery among his most significant presidential accomplishments. The enormous expanse of fertile lands fueled the Jeffersonian dream of an agrarian republic: Americans soon streamed into the Louisiana Territory. Even more would have done so, had it not been for the Indians (and their British allies) who stood in their way and for poorly developed transportation routes.

Jefferson's vision rested, too, on American disentanglement from foreign affairs. But with its economy so focused on international shipping, the United States soon found that its greatest threats came from abroad, not from partisan or sectional divisions. In its wars with the Barbary states, the United States sought to guard its commerce and ships on the high seas. The second war with Britain—the War of 1812—was fought for similar reasons but against a much more formidable power. Although a military stalemate, the war helped to inspire a new sense of nationalism and to launch a new era of American development.

The Treaty of Ghent reaffirmed American independence; thereafter the nation was able to settle disputes with Great Britain at the bargaining table. The war also dealt a serious blow to Indian resistance in the Midwest and Southwest. At the same time, embargoes and war accelerated the pace of American industrial growth. Because the Federalists' opposition to the war undermined their political credibility, their party all but disappeared from the national political scene by 1820. The absence of well-organized partisan conflict created what contemporaries called an Era of Good Feelings.

Although overt tension was muted in the heady postwar years, competing visions of America's route to prosperity and greatness endured. Under Chief Justice John Marshall, the Supreme Court supported the Federalist agenda, issuing rulings that stimulated commerce and industry through economic nationalism. The Democratic-Republicans looked, instead, toward the South and West, the vast and fertile Louisiana Territory. Whether they supported agrarian or industrial development, almost all Americans could agree on the need for improved transportation, though most internal improvements took place in the North.

During the first quarter of the nineteenth century, the United States vastly expanded its territorial reach, not just through the Louisiana Purchase but also with the acquisition of Florida. Fearful of European intentions to reassert their influence in the Americas and emboldened by the nation's expanding boundaries, President Monroe proclaimed that the United States would not tolerate European intervention in American affairs. But even as its expanding boundaries strengthened the United States' international presence, that same territorial expansion would threaten the nation's newfound political unity at home.

That threat became most apparent in 1819, when the postwar economic boom came to a grinding halt and when congressmen predicted dire consequences if they could not settle the dispute over whether to admit Missouri as a slave state. The compromise brokered by Henry Clay removed the issue of slavery's expansion from political center stage, but—by addressing only those territories already owned by the United States—it did not permanently settle the issue.

10

The Rise of the South
1815–1860

THE "DISTINCTIVE" SOUTH

Not until the first half of the 1800s did the region of slaveholding states from the Chesapeake and Virginia to Missouri, and from Florida across to Texas, come to be designated as the South. Today many still consider it America's most distinctive region. Historians have long examined how the Old South was like and unlike the rest of the nation. Because of its unique history, has the South, in the words of poet Allen Tate, always been "Uncle Sam's other province"? Or, as southern writer W. J. Cash said in 1940, is the South "a tree with many age rings, with its limbs and trunk bent and twisted by all the winds of the years, but with its tap root in the Old South?" Analyzing just why the South seems more religious, more conservative, or more tragic than other regions of America has been an enduring practice in American culture and politics.

Certain American values, such as materialism, individualism, and faith in progress, have been associated with the North and values such as tradition, honor, and family loyalty, with the South. The South, so the stereotype has it, was static, even "backward," and the North was dynamic in the decades leading up to the Civil War. There are many measures of just how different South was from North in the antebellum era. At the same time, there were many Souths: low-country rice and cotton regions with dense slave populations; mountainous regions of small farmers and subsistence agriculture; semitropical

251

wetlands in the Southeast; plantation culture in the Cotton Belt and especially the Mississippi valley; Texas grasslands; tobacco- and wheat-growing regions in Virginia and North Carolina; cities with bustling ports; wilderness areas with only the rare homestead of hillfolk.

South-North Similarity   The South was distinctive because of its commitment to slavery, but it also shared much in common with the rest of the nation. The geographic sizes of the South and the North were roughly the same. In 1815 white southerners shared with their fellow free citizens in the North a heritage of heroes and ideology from the era of the American Revolution and the War of 1812. With varying accents, southerners spoke the same language and worshiped the same Protestant God as northerners. Southerners lived under the same Constitution as northerners, and they shared a common mixture of nationalism and localism in their attitudes toward government. Down to the 1840s, northerners and southerners invoked with nearly equal frequency the doctrine of states' rights against federal authority. A sense of American mission and dreams inspired by the westward movement were as much a part of southern as of northern experience.

Indeed, some of the most eloquent visions of America as a land of yeomen—independent, self-sufficient farmers—expanding westward had come from a southerner, Thomas Jefferson. Jefferson believed that "virtue" rested in those who tilled the soil, that farmers made the best citizens. In 1804 Jefferson declared his "moral and physical preference of the agricultural over the manufacturing man." But as slavery and the plantation economy expanded, the South did not become a land of individual opportunity in the same manner as the North.

During the forty-five years before the Civil War, the South shared in the nation's economic booms and busts. Research has shown that, despite its enormous cruelties, slavery was a profitable labor system for planters. Southerners and northerners shared an expanding capitalist economy. As it grew, the slave-based economy of money-crop agriculture reflected the rational choices of planters. More land and more slaves generally converted into more wealth.

By the eve of the Civil War in 1860, the distribution of wealth and property in the two sections was almost identical: 50 percent of free adult males owned only 1 percent of real and personal property, and the richest 1 percent owned 27 percent of the wealth. One study comparing Texas and Wisconsin in 1850 shows that the richest 2 percent of families in each state owned 31 to 32 percent of the wealth. So, both North and South had ruling classes, even if their wealth was invested in different kinds of property. Entrepreneurs in both sections whether forging plantations out of Mississippi Delta land or shoe factories and textile mills in New England river towns, sought their fortunes in an expanding market economy. The southern "master class" was, in fact, more likely than propertied northerners to move west to make a profit.

South-North Dissimilarity   There were important differences between the North and the South. The South's climate and longer growing season gave it an unmistakably rural and agricultural destiny. Many great rivers provided rich soil and transportation routes to market. The South's people, white and black, developed an intense attachment to place, to the ways people were related to

1810–20 • 137,000 slaves are forced to move from the Upper South to Alabama, Mississippi, and other western regions

1822 • Vesey's insurrection plot is discovered in South Carolina

1830s • Vast majority of African American slaves are native-born in America

1830s–40s • Cotton trade grows into largest source of commercial wealth and America's leading export

1831 • Turner leads a violent slave rebellion in Virginia

1832 • Virginia holds the last debate in the South about the future of slavery; gradual abolition is voted down

• Publication of Dew's proslavery tract *Abolition of Negro Slavery*

1836 • Arkansas gains admission to the Union as a slave state

1839 • Mississippi's Married Women's Property Act gives married women some property rights

1845 • Florida and Texas gain admission to the Union as slave states

• Publication of Douglass's *Narrative of the Life of Frederick Douglass, an American Slave, Written by Himself*

1850 • Planters' share of agricultural wealth in the South is 90 to 95 percent

1850–60 • Of some 300,000 slaves who migrate from the Upper to the Lower South, 60 to 70 percent go by outright sale

1857 • Publication of Hinton R. Helper's *The Impending Crisis,* denouncing the slave system

• Publication of George Fitzhugh's *Southern Thought,* an aggressive defense of slavery

1860 • 405,751 mulattos in the United States, 12.5 percent of the African American population

• Three-quarters of all southern white families own no slaves

• South produces largest cotton crop ever

the land and to one another. The South developed as a biracial society of brutal inequality, where the liberty of one race depended directly on the enslavement of another. White wealth was built on highly valued black labor.

Cotton growers spread out over as large an area as possible to maximize production and income. As a result, population density in the South was low; by 1860 there were only 2.3 people per square mile in vast and largely unsettled Texas, 15.6 in Louisiana, and 18.0 in Georgia. By contrast, population density in the nonslaveholding states east of the Mississippi River was almost three times higher. The Northeast had an average of 65.4 people per square mile. Massachusetts had 153.1 people per square mile, and New York City compressed 86,400 people into each square mile. When, in the 1850s, young Frederick Law Olmsted of Connecticut, later renowned as a landscape architect, toured the South as a journalist, he traveled mostly on horseback along primitive trails.

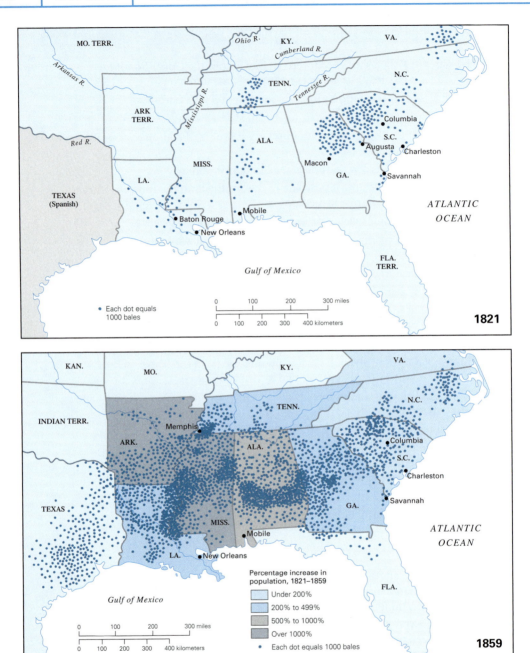

MAP 10.1 Cotton Production in the South

These two maps reveal the rapid westward expansion of cotton production and its importance to the antebellum South.

Between Columbus, Georgia, and Montgomery, Alabama, Olmsted found "a hilly wilderness, with a few dreary villages, and many isolated cotton farms." For one who would design Central Park in New York City, this was just too much ruralness.

Where people were scarce, it was difficult to finance and operate schools, churches, libraries, and even inns and restaurants. Similarly, the rural character of the South and the significance of the plantation as a self-sufficient social unit meant that the section put few resources into improving disease control and public health. Southerners were strongly committed to their churches, and some believed in the importance of universities, but all such institutions were far less developed than those in the North. Factories were rare, because planters invested most of their capital in slaves. A few southerners did invest in iron or textiles on a small scale. But the largest southern "industry" was lumbering, and the largest factories used slave labor to make cigars. More decisively, the South was slower than the North to develop a unified market economy and a regional transportation network. Despite concerted efforts, the South had only 35 percent of the nation's railroad mileage in 1860.

The Old South never developed its own banking and shipping capacity to any degree. If it had, its effort to be an international cartel might have succeeded longer. Most southern bank deposits, like those of Pierce Butler, were in the North, and southern cotton planters became ever more dependent on New York for shipping. As early as 1822, one-sixth of all southern cotton cleared for Liverpool or Le Havre from the port of New York and constituted two-fifths of all that city's exports. Many New York merchants and bankers developed deep interests in the fate of slavery and cotton prices. In a series of economic conventions held from 1837 to 1839, southern delegates debated the nature of foreign trade, dependence on northern importers and financiers, and other alleged threats to their commercial independence and security. But nothing, save

America, 1841, *lithograph and watercolor by Edward Williams Clay. An idealized portrayal of loyal and contented slaves, likely distributed by northern apologists for slavery. All is well on the plantation as well-dressed slaves dance and express their gratitude to their master and his perfect family. The text includes the old slave saying: "God bless you master! You feed and clothe us. When we are sick you nurse us, and when too old to work, you provide for us!" The master replies piously: "These poor creatures are a sacred legacy from my ancestors and while a dollar is left me, nothing shall be spared to increase their comfort and happiness."* (Library of Congress)

rhetoric, came of these conventions; it was the last time southern planters would organize to break from their Yankee middlemen and shippers.

The South lagged far behind the North in nearly any measure of industrial growth. Its urban centers were mostly ports like New Orleans and Charleston, which became crossroads of commerce and small-scale manufacturing. In the interior were small market towns dependent on agricultural trade—"urbanization without cities," as one historian has said. Slavery slowed urban growth. As a system of racial control, slavery did not work well in cities. Likewise, because of a lack of manufacturing jobs, the South did not attract immigrants as readily as did the North. By 1860 only 13 percent of the nation's foreign-born population lived in the slave states.

Like most northerners, antebellum southerners were adherents to evangelical Christianity. Americans from all regions held in common a faith in a personal God and in conversion and piety as the means to salvation. But southern evangelicalism was distinct from its northern practice. In the South, Baptists and Methodists concentrated on personal rather than social improvement. By the 1830s in the North, evangelicalism was a major wellspring of reform movements (see Chapter 9); but in states where blacks were so numerous and unfree, and where the very social structure received increasingly aggressive attacks from abolitionists, religion, as one scholar has written, preached "a hands-off policy concerning slavery." Although slaves began to convert to Christianity in the early-nineteenth-century South, many southern whites feared a reform impulse that would foster what one historian has called an "interracial communion" in their churches. Moreover, those women who may have been reform minded were prevented from developing frequent associations with other reformers because of distance and sparse population. The only reform movements that did take hold in the emerging Bible Belt of the South, such as that for temperance, focused on personal behavior, not social reform.

The slave system made it inevitable that the interests and social structures of the North and the South would diverge after 1815. Because of its inherently conservative social structure, antebellum southern law restricted the authority of the courts, reinforcing a tradition of planter control. Penitentiaries tended to house only whites, as most blacks were under the authority of personal masters. Law-breaking in the South tended to involve crimes of violence rather than crimes against property.

A Southern World-View and the Proslavery Argument

Perhaps in no way was the South more distinctive than in its embrace of a particular world-view, a system of thought and meaning held especially by the planter class, but also influencing the entire society. Like those of all people, southerners' justifications for slavery were not so different from those of any other civilization trying to defend the institutions it inherits. But at the heart of the proslavery argument was a deep and abiding racism. The persistence of modern racism in all sections of the United States is all the more reason to comprehend antebellum southerners' rationalizations for human slavery.

In the wake of the American Revolution, the Enlightenment ideas of natural rights and equality did stimulate antislavery sentiment in the Upper South, produced a brief flurry of manumissions, and led to considerable hope for gradual emancipation. In 1796 Virginian St. George Tucker argued that "slavery not only violates the laws of nature and of civil society, it also wounds the best forms of government." But confidence that the exercise of reason among gentlemen might end such a profitable system as slavery waned in the new nation. As slavery spread, southerners soon vigorously defended it. In 1816 George Bourne, a Presbyterian minister exiled from Virginia for his antislavery sermons and for expulsion of slaveholders from his church, charged that, whenever southerners were challenged on slavery, "they were fast choked, for they had a Negro stuck fast in their throats." After walking home with South Carolina statesman and proslavery advocate John C. Calhoun from an 1820 cabinet meeting, John Quincy Adams confided to his diary that too many southerners "writhe in agonies of fear at the very mention of human rights as applicable to men of color."

By the 1820s white southerners went on the offensive, actively justifying slavery as a "positive good" and not merely a "necessary evil." They used the antiquity of slavery, as well as the Bible's many references to slaveholding, to foster a historical argument for bondage. Slavery, they deemed, was the natural status of blacks. Whites were the more intellectual race, and blacks the race more inherently physical and therefore destined for labor. Whites were the creators of civilizations, blacks the appointed hewers of wood and drawers of water. Proslavery writers did not mince words. In a proslavery tract written in 1851, John Campbell confidently declared that "there is as much difference between the lowest tribe of negroes and the white Frenchman, Englishman, or American, as there is between the monkey and the negro."

Some southerners defended slavery in practical terms; they simply saw their bondsmen as economic necessities and symbols of their quest for prosperity. In 1845 James Henry Hammond of South Carolina argued that slaveholding was essentially a matter of property rights. Unwilling to "deal in abstractions" about the "right and wrong" of slavery, Hammond considered property sacred and protected by the Constitution, because slaves were legal property—end of argument. The deepest root of the proslavery argument was a hierarchical view of the social order as slavery's defenders believed God or nature had prescribed it. Southerners cherished tradition, duty, and honor, believing social change should come only in slow increments, if at all. As the Virginia legislature debated the gradual abolition of slavery in 1831–1832, in the wake of Nat Turner's rebellion, Thomas R. Dew, a slaveholder and professor of law and history at the College of William and Mary, contended that "that which is the growth of *ages* may require ages to remove." Dew's widely read work *Abolition of Negro Slavery* (1832) ushered in an outpouring of proslavery writing that would intensify over the next thirty years. Until Turner's bloody rebellion, Dew admitted, emancipation in the South had "never been seriously discussed." But as slavery expanded westward and fueled national prosperity, Dew cautioned southerners that any degree of gradual abolition threatened the whole region's "irremediable ruin." Dew declared black slavery part of the "order of nature," an indispensable part of the "deep and solid foundations of society" and the basis of the "well-ordered, well-established liberty" of white Americans. Dew's well-ordered society also included his conception of the proper division of men and women into separate spheres and functions.

Proslavery advocates held views very different from those of northern reformers on the concepts of freedom, progress, and equality. They turned natural-law doctrine to their favor, arguing that the natural state of humankind was inequality of ability and condition, not equality. A former U.S. senator in South Carolina, William Harper, charged in 1837 that Jefferson's famous dictum about equality in the Declaration of Independence was no more than a "sentimental phrase." "Is it not palpably nearer the truth to say that no man was ever born free," Harper argued, "and that no two men were ever born equal?" Proslavery writers believed that people were born to certain stations in life; they stressed dependence over autonomy and duty over rights as the human condition. As Virginia writer George Fitzhugh put it in 1854, "Men are not born entitled to equal rights. It would be far nearer the truth to say, that some were born with saddles on their backs, and others booted and spurred to ride them."

Many slaveholders believed that their ownership of people bound them to a set of paternal obligations as guardians of a familial relationship between masters and slaves. Although contradicted by countless examples of slave resistance and escape, as well as by slave sales, planters needed to believe in and exerted great energy in constructing the idea of the contented slave. The slaveholders who promoted their own freedom and pursued personal profits through the bondage of blacks had to justify themselves endlessly.

A Slave Society   Slavery and race affected everything in the Old South. Whites and blacks alike grew up, were socialized, married, reared children, worked, conceived of property, and honed their most basic habits of behavior under the influence of slavery. This was true of slaveholding and nonslaveholding whites, as well as of blacks who were slave and free. Slavery shaped the social structure of the South, fueled almost anything meaningful in its economy, and came to dominate its politics. Rudolphe Lucien Desdunes, a Louisiana sugar planter, remembered growing up in a society where "slavery was the pivot around which everything revolved."

The South was interdependent with the North, the West, and even with Europe in a growing capitalist market system. To keep the cotton trade flowing, southerners relied on northern banks, on northern steamship companies working the great western rivers, and on northern merchants. But there were elements of that system that southerners increasingly rejected during the antebellum era, especially urbanism, the wage labor system, a broadening right to vote, and any threat to their racial and class order.

In the antebellum era, as later, there were many Souths, but Americans have always been determined to define what one historian called the "Dixie difference." "The South is both American and something different," writes another historian, "at times a mirror or magnifier of national traits and at other times a counterculture." This was most acutely true in the decades before the Civil War.

Culturally, the South developed a proclivity to tell its own story. Its ruralness and its sense of tradition may have given southerners a special habit of telling tales. "Southerners . . . love a good tale," said Mississippi writer Eudora Welty. "They are born reciters, great memory retainers, diary keepers, letter exchangers, and letter savers, history tracers, and debaters, and—outstaying all the rest—great talkers." The South's story is both distinctive and national, and it begins in what we have come to call the Old South, a term only conceivable after the eviction of native peoples from the region.

SOUTHERN EXPANSION, INDIAN RESISTANCE AND REMOVAL

Americans were a restless, moving people when the trans-Appalachian frontier opened in the wake of the War of 1812. Some 5 to 10 percent of the booming population moved each year, usually westward. In the first two decades of the century, they poured into the

Ohio valley; by the 1820s, after the death of the Shawnee chief Tecumseh and the collapse of the pan-Indian federation, they were migrating into the Mississippi River valley and beyond. By 1850 two-thirds of Americans lived west of the Appalachians.

A Southern Westward Movement

As much as in any other region, this surging westward movement was a southern phenomenon. After 1820 the heart of cotton cultivation and the slave-based plantation system shifted from the coastal states to Alabama and the newly settled Mississippi valley—Tennessee, Louisiana, Arkansas, and Mississippi. Southern slaveholders forced slaves to move with them to the newer areas of the South, and yeoman farmers followed, also hoping for new wealth through cheap land and the ownership of other people.

A wave of migration was evident everywhere in the Southeast. As early as 1817, Georgian Samuel McDonald observed a "disease prevalent" in his region. "The patient," he said, first exhibited a "great love" of talking about "the new country" to the west. Then he tried to "make sale of his stock" and "lastly . . . to sell his plantation." Once attacked by this "Alabama fever," most never recovered and were carried "off to the westward." That same year, a Charleston, South Carolina, newspaper reported with alarm that migration out of that state had already reached "unprecedented proportions." Indeed, almost half of the white people born in South Carolina after 1800 left the state, most for the Southwest. And by 1833, Tyrone Power, an Irish actor riding a stagecoach from Georgia into Alabama, encountered many "camps of immigrants" and found the roads "covered" by such pilgrims.

The way to wealth for seaboard planters in the South was to go west to grow cotton for the booming world markets, by purchasing ever more land and slaves. The population of Mississippi soared from 73,000 in 1820 to 607,000 in 1850, with African American slaves in the majority. Across the Mississippi River, the population of Arkansas went from 14,000 in 1820 to 210,000 in 1850. By 1835 the American immigrant population in Texas reached 35,000, including 3,000 slaves, and outnumbering Mexicans two to one. Aggressive American settlers declared Texas's independence from Mexico in 1836, spurring further American immigration into the region. By 1845 "Texas fever" had boosted the Anglo population to 125,000. Statehood that year opened the floodgates to more immigrants from the east and to a confrontation with Mexico that would lead to war.

As the cotton kingdom grew to what southern political leaders dreamed would be national and world dominion, this westward migration, fueled at first by an optimistic nationalism, ultimately made migrant planters more sectional and more southern. In 1817 Congressman John C. Calhoun embraced national expansion as the means to "bind the Republic together," as he provided the process its unquestioned assumption: "Let us conquer space." In time, political dominance in the South migrated westward into the Cotton Belt as well. By the 1840s and 1850s, these energetic capitalist planters, ever mindful of world markets and fearful that their slave-based economy was under attack, sought to protect and expand their system. Increasingly, they saw themselves, as one historian has written, less as "landowners who happened to own slaves" than as "slaveholders who happened to own land."

Before all this expansion could take place, other, older groups of Americans already occupied much of this land. Before 1830 large swaths of upper Georgia

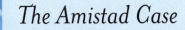
The Amistad Case

In April 1839 a Spanish slave ship, *Tecora,* sailed from Lomboko, the region of West Africa that became Sierre Leone. On board were Mende people, captured and sold by their African enemies. In June they arrived in Havana, Cuba, a Spanish colony. Two Spaniards purchased 53 of the Mende and set sail aboard *La Amistad* for their plantations elsewhere in Cuba. After three days at sea, the Africans revolted. Led by a man the Spaniards called Joseph Cinque, they killed the captain and seized control of the vessel. They ordered the two Spaniard owners to take them back to Africa, but the slave-holders sailed east by day and north by night, trying to reach the shores of the American South. Far off course, the *Amistad* was seized by the USS *Washington* in Long Island Sound and brought ashore in Connecticut.

The "Amistad Africans" were soon a celebrated moral and legal cause for abolitionists and slaveholders, as well as in U.S.-Spanish relations. The Africans were imprisoned in New Haven, and a prolonged dispute ensued around many questions: Were they slaves and murderers, and the property of their Cuban owners, or were they free people exercising their natural rights? Were they Spanish property, seized on the high seas in violation of a 1795 treaty? If a northern state could "free" captive Africans, what did it mean for enslaved African Americans in the South? Connecticut abolitionists immediately went to court, where a U.S. Circuit Court judge dismissed the charges of mutiny and murder but refused to release the Africans because their Spanish owners claimed them as property.

Meanwhile, the Mende were desperate to tell their own story. A Yale professor of ancient languages, Josiah Gibbs, visited the captives and learned their words for numbers. In New York he walked up and down the docks repeating the Mende words until an African seaman, James Covey, responded. Covey journeyed to New Haven, conversed with the jubilant Africans, and soon their harrowing tale garnered sympathy all over Yankee New England.

In a new trial, the judge ruled that the Africans were illegally enslaved and

Return to Africa of the Amistad Captives, by Hale Woodruff, depicting the repatriated Amistad Africans back on the shores of their native continent. The figures are Cinque, the missionaries, and the young black woman, Marsgue, who in later years had a son who returned to graduate from Yale University with a Ph.D. (Savery Library Archives, Talladega College, Gift of George W. Crawford, 1973 NHCH © 1973.20c)

The Amistad Case

ordered them returned to their home-land. Although slavery might be legal in Cuba, the slave trade between Africa and the Americas had been outlawed in a treaty between Spain and Great Britain. Spain's lawyers demanded the return of their "merchandise." In need of south-ern votes to win reelection, President Martin Van Buren supported the Spanish claims and advocated the Africans' return to a likely death in Cuba.

The administration appealed the case to the Supreme Court in February 1841. Arguing the abolitionists' case, former president John Quincy Adams famously pointed to a copy of the Declaration of Independence on the wall of the court chambers, invoked the natural rights to life and liberty, and chastised the Van Buren administration for its "immense array of power . . . on the side of injus-tice." In a 7-to-1 decision, the Court ruled that the Africans were "freeborn" with the right of self-defense, while remaining silent on slavery's legality in the United States.

Fund-raising and speaking tours fea-turing Cinque made the return voyage possible. On November 27, 1841, thirty-five survivors and five American mission-aries disembarked for Africa. They arrived in Sierre Leone on January 15, 1842, whereupon Cinque wrote a letter to the Amistad Committee. "I thank all 'merican people," he said, "I shall never forget 'merican people." But the inter-national meanings of the Amistad case would endure. Sarah Magru, one of the child captives on the *Amistad,* stayed in America to attend Oberlin College and later returned to work at the Mende mis-sion in Sierre Leone.

The Amistad case showed how inter-twined slavery was with freedom, and the United States with the world. It poisoned diplomatic relations between America and Spain for a generation, and stimu-lated Christian mission work in Africa.

belonged to the Cherokees, and huge regions of Alabama and Mississippi were either Creek, Choctaw, or Chickasaw land. Indians were also on the move, but in forced migrations. The indigenous cultures of the eastern and southern woodlands had to be uprooted to make way for white expansion. For the vast majority of white Americans, the Indians were in the way of their growing empire. Taking Indian land, so the rea-soning went, merely reflected the natural course of history: the "civilizers" had to dis-place the "children of the forest" in the name of progress. National leaders provided all the rhetoric and justification needed. "Nothing," said General Andrew Jackson as early as 1816, "can promote the welfare of the United States, and particularly the south-western frontier so much as bringing into market . . . the whole of this fertile country." As president in 1830, Jackson spoke with certainty about why the Indians must go. "What good man would prefer a country," he asked, "covered with forests and ranged by a few thousand savages to our extensive Republic, studded with cities, towns, and prosperous farms?"

Indian Treaty Making

In theory, under the U.S. Constitution, the federal government recognized Indian sovereignty and treated Indian peoples as foreign nations. Indeed, the United States received Indian delegations with pomp and ceremony, exchanging gifts as tokens of friendship. Agreements between Indian nations and the United States were signed, sealed, and ratified like other international treaties. In practice, however, swindle and fraud dominated the government's approach to treaty making and Indian sovereignty. The United States imposed conditions on Indian representatives, and as the country expanded, new treaties replaced old ones, shrinking Indian land holdings.

Indians could delay but rarely thwart removal. Although Indian resistance persisted against such pressure after the War of 1812, it only slowed the process. In the 1820s, native peoples in the middle West, Ohio valley, Mississippi valley, and other parts of the cotton South ceded lands totaling 200 million acres for a pittance.

Indian Accommodation

Increasingly, Indian nations east of the Mississippi sought to survive through accommodation. In the first three decades of the century, the Choctaw, Creek, and Chickasaw peoples in the lower Mississippi became suppliers and traders in the nation's expanding market economy. Under treaty provisions, Indian commerce took place through trading posts and stores that provided Indians with supplies, and purchased or bartered Indian-produced goods. The trading posts extended credit to chiefs, who increasingly fell into debt that they could pay off to the federal government only by selling their land.

By 1822 the Choctaw nation had sold 13 million acres but still carried a debt of $13,000. The Indians struggled to adjust, increasing agricultural production and hunting, working as farmhands and craftsmen, and selling produce at market stalls in Natchez and New Orleans. As the United States expanded westward, white Americans promoted their assimilation, through education and conversion to Christianity, with renewed urgency. "Put into the hand of [Indian] children the primer and the hoe," the House Committee on Indian Affairs recommended in 1818, "and they will naturally, in time, take hold of the plough; and, as their minds become enlightened and expand, the Bible will be their book, and they will grow up in habits of morality and industry." In 1819, in response to missionary lobbying, Congress appropriated $10,000 annually for "civilization of the tribes adjoining the frontier settlements." Protestant missionaries administered the "civilizing fund" and established mission schools.

Within five years, thirty-two boarding schools enrolled Indian students. They substituted English for American Indian languages and taught agriculture alongside the Christian gospel. But this emphasis on agriculture and the value of private property did not deter settlers eyeing Indian land; assimilation through education seemed too slow a process. Wherever native peoples lived, illegal settlers disrupted their lives. The federal government only halfheartedly enforced the integrity of treaties, as legitimate Indian land rights gave way to the advance of white civilization.

Over time, however, the Indians could not prevent the spread of the cotton economy that arose all around them, and they could not cede enough acreage to satisfy land-hungry whites. With loss of land came dependency. The Choctaws came to rely on white Americans not only for manufactured goods but even for food. Dependency, coupled with disease, facilitated removal of American Indian peoples to western lands. While the population of other groups increased rapidly, the Indian population fell, some nations declining by 50 percent in only three decades. The French traveler and author Alexis de Tocqueville noticed the contrast. "Not only have these wild tribes receded, but they are destroyed," Tocqueville concluded, after personally observing the tragedy of forced removal in 1831, "and as they give way or perish, an immense and increasing people fill their place. There is no instance upon record of so prodigious a growth or so rapid a destruction." As many as 100,000 eastern and southern Indian peoples were removed between 1820 and 1850; about 30,000 died in the process.

The wanderings of the Shawnees, the people of the Prophet and Tecumseh (see pages 000–000), illustrate the uprooting of Indian peoples. After giving up 17 million acres in Ohio in a 1795 treaty, the Shawnees scattered to Indiana and eastern Missouri. After the War of 1812, some Shawnees sought protection from either the British in Canada or from Mexico. Yet another group moved to the Kansas territory in 1825. By 1854 Kansas was open to white settlement, and the Shawnees had to cede seven-eighths of their land, or 1.4 million acres.

Removal had a profound impact on all Shawnees. The men lost their traditional role as providers; their methods of hunting and their knowledge of woodland animals were useless on the prairies of Kansas. As grain became the tribe's dietary staple, Shawnee women played a greater role as providers, supplemented by government aid under treaty provisions. Remarkably, the Shawnees preserved their language and culture in the face of these devastating dislocations.

Indian Removal as Federal Policy

Attention focused on southeastern tribes—Cherokees, Creeks, Choctaws, Chickasaws, and Seminoles—because much of their land had remained intact after the War of 1812, and they had aggressively resisted white encroachment. In his last annual message to Congress in late 1824, President James Monroe proposed that all Indians be moved beyond the Mississippi River. Monroe described his proposal as an "honorable" one that would protect Indians from invasion and provide them with independence for "improvement and civilization." Force would be unnecessary, he believed; Indians would willingly accept western land free from white encroachment.

Monroe's proposition targeted the Cherokees, Creeks, Choctaws, and Chickasaws, and they unanimously rejected it. Between 1789 and 1825 the four nations had negotiated thirty treaties with the United States, and they had reached their limit. Most wished to remain on what little was left of their ancestral land.

Pressure from Georgia had prompted Monroe's policy. In the 1820s, the state had accused the federal government of not fulfilling its 1802 promise to remove the Cherokees and Creeks from northwestern Georgia in return for the state's renunciation of its claim to western lands. Georgia remained unsatisfied by Monroe's removal messages and by the Creeks' recalcitrance. In 1826, under federal pressure, the Creek nation ceded all but a small strip of its Georgia acreage, but Georgians remained unmoved. Only the complete removal of the Georgia Creeks to the West could resolve the conflict between the state and the federal government.

For the Creeks the outcome was devastating. In an ultimately unsuccessful attempt to hold fast to the remainder of their traditional lands, which were in Alabama, they radically altered their political structure. In 1829, at the expense of traditional village autonomy, they centralized tribal authority and forbade any chief from ceding land. In the end, they lost not only their land but also their traditional forms of social and political organization.

In 1830, after extensive debate and a narrow vote in both houses, Congress passed the Indian Removal Act, authorizing the president to negotiate treaties of removal with all tribes living east of the Mississippi. The bill, which provided federal funds for such relocations, would likely not have passed the House without the additional representation afforded slave states due to the three-fifths clause in the Constitution.

Cherokees

Adapting to American ways seemed no more successful than resistance in forestalling removal. No people met the challenge of assimilating to American standards more thoroughly than the Cherokees, whose traditional home centered on eastern Tennessee and northern Alabama and Georgia. Between 1819 and 1829 the tribe became economically self-sufficient and politically self-governing; during this Cherokee renaissance the nearly fifteen thousand adult Cherokees came to think of themselves as a nation, not a collection of villages. In 1821 and 1822, Sequoyah, a self-educated Cherokee, devised an eighty-six-character phonetic alphabet that made possible a Cherokee-language Bible and a bilingual tribal newspaper, *Cherokee Phoenix* (1828). Between 1820 and 1823, the Cherokees created a formal government with a bicameral legislature, a court system, and a salaried bureaucracy. In 1827 they adopted a written constitution modeled after that of the United States.

Cherokee land laws, however, differed from U.S. law. The nation collectively owned all Cherokee land and forbade land sales to outsiders. Nonetheless, economic change paralleled political adaptation. Many became individual farmers and slaveholders; by 1833 they held fifteen hundred black slaves. They transformed their economy from hunting, gathering, and subsistence agriculture to commodity trade based on barter, cash, and credit.

But Cherokees' political and economic changes failed to win respect or acceptance from white southerners. In the 1820s, Georgia pressed them to sell the 7,200 square miles of land they held in the state. Congress appropriated $30,000 in 1822 to buy the Cherokee land in Georgia, but the Cherokees resisted. Impatient with their refusals to negotiate cession, Georgia annulled the Cherokees' constitution, extended the state's sovereignty over them, prohibited the Cherokee National Council from meeting except to cede land, and ordered their lands seized. Then, the discovery of gold on Cherokee land in 1829 further whetted Georgia's appetite for Cherokee territory.

Cherokee Nation v. Georgia

Backed by sympathetic whites but not by President Andrew Jackson, the Cherokees under Chief John Ross turned to the federal courts to defend their treaty with the United States. Their legal strategy reflected their growing political sophistication. In *Cherokee Nation v. Georgia* (1831), Chief Justice John Marshall ruled that under the federal Constitution an Indian tribe was neither a foreign nation nor a state and therefore had no standing in federal courts. Indians' relationship with the United States was "marked," said Marshall, "by cardinal and peculiar distinctions which exist nowhere else." They were deemed "domestic, dependent nations." Legally, they were in but not of the United States. Nonetheless, said Marshall, the Indians had an unquestionable right to their lands; they could lose title only by voluntarily giving it up.

A year later, in *Worcester v. Georgia,* Marshall defined the Cherokee position more clearly. The Indian nation was, he declared, a distinct political community in which "the laws of Georgia can have no force" and into which Georgians could not enter without permission or treaty privilege. The Cherokees cheered. *Phoenix* editor Elias Boudinot called the decision "glorious news." Jackson, however, whose reputation had been built as an Indian fighter, did his best to usurp the court's action. Newspapers widely reported that Jackson had said, "John Marshall has made his decision: now let him enforce it." Keen to open up new lands for settlement, Jackson favored expelling the Cherokees.

Georgians, too, refused to comply; they would not tolerate a sovereign Cherokee nation within their borders, and they refused to hear the pleas of Indian people to share their American dream. A Cherokee census indicated that they owned 33 grist mills, 13 sawmills, 1 powder mill, 69 blacksmith shops, 2 tanneries, 762 looms, 2,486 spinning wheels, 172 wagons, 2,923 plows, 7,683 horses, 22,531 cattle, 46,732 pigs, and 2,566 sheep. "You asked us to throw off the hunter and warrior state," declared the Cherokee leader, John Ridge, in 1832. "We did so—you asked us to form a republican government: We did so—adopting your own as a model. You asked us to cultivate the earth, and learn the mechanic arts: We did so. You asked us to learn to read: We did so. You asked us to cast away our idols, and worship your God: We did so." But neither the plow nor the Bible earned the Cherokees respect in the face of the economic, imperial, and racial quests of their fellow southerners.

Trail of Tears

The Choctaws went first; they made the forced journey from Mississippi and Alabama to the West in the winter of 1831 and 1832. Alexis de Tocqueville was visiting Memphis when they passed through: "The wounded, the sick, newborn babies, and the old men on the point of death. . . . I saw them embark to cross the great river," he wrote, "and the sight will never fade from my memory. Neither sob nor complaint rose from that silent assembly. Their afflictions were of long standing, and they felt them to be irremediable." Other tribes soon joined the forced march. The Creeks in Alabama resisted removal until 1836, when the army pushed them westward. A year later the Chickasaws followed.

Having fought removal in the courts, the Cherokees were divided. Some believed that further resistance was hopeless and accepted removal as the only chance to preserve their civilization. The leaders of this minority agreed in 1835 to exchange their southern home for western land, in the Treaty of New Echota. Most, though, wanted to stand firm. John Ross, with petitions signed by fifteen thousand Cherokees, lobbied the Senate against ratification of the treaty. He lost. But when the time for evacuation came in 1838, most Cherokees refused to move. President Martin Van Buren sent federal troops to round them up. About twenty thousand Cherokees were evicted, held in detention camps, and marched under military escort to Indian Territory in present-day Oklahoma. Nearly one-quarter of them died of disease and exhaustion on what came to be known as the Trail of Tears.

When the forced march to the West ended, the Indians had traded about 100 million acres east of the Mississippi for 32 million acres west of the river plus $68 million. Only a few scattered remnants, among them the Seminoles in Florida and the Cherokees in the southern Appalachian Mountains, remained east of the Mississippi River.

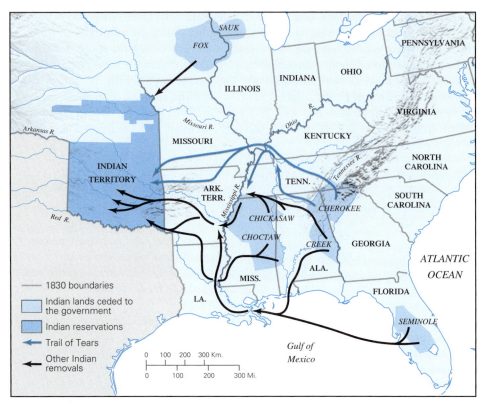

MAP **10.2 Removal of Native Americans from the South, 1820–1840**

Over a twenty-year period, the federal government and southern states forced Native Americans to exchange their traditional homes for western land. Some tribal groups remained in the South, but most settled in the alien western environment. (*© Martin Gilbert, 2002, Routledge Atlas of American History, 4th edition. Published by Routledge 2002. Reproduced by permission of Taylor & Francis Books UK*)

Forced removal had a disastrous impact on the Cherokees and other displaced Indian nations. In the West they encountered an alien environment; lacking traditional ties, few felt at peace with the land. Unable to live off the land, many became dependent on government payments for survival. Removal also brought new internal conflicts. The Cherokees in particular struggled over their tribal government. In 1839 followers of John Ross assassinated the leaders of the protreaty faction. Violence continued sporadically until a new treaty in 1846 imposed a temporary truce. In time the Cherokees managed to reestablish their political institutions and a governing body in Tahlequah, in northeastern Oklahoma.

Seminole Wars   In Florida a small band of Seminoles continued to resist. Some Seminole leaders agreed in the 1832 Treaty of Payne's Landing to relocate to the West within three years, but others opposed the treaty, and some probably did not know it existed. A minority under Osceola, a charismatic leader, refused to

The Trail of Tears, *by twentieth-century Pawnee artist Brummet Echohawk. About twenty thousand Cherokees were evicted in 1838–1839, and about one-quarter of them died on the forced march to present-day Oklahoma.* (Thomas Gilcrease Institute of American History and Art)

vacate their homes and fought the protreaty group. When federal troops were sent to impose removal in 1835, Osceola waged a fierce guerrilla war against them.

The Florida Indians were a varied group that included many Creeks and mixed Indian–African Americans (ex-slaves or descendants of runaway slaves). The U.S. Army, however, considered them all Seminoles, subject to removal. General Thomas Jesup believed that the runaway slave population was the key to the war. "This, you may be assured, is a Negro, not an Indian war," he wrote a friend in 1836, "and if it be not speedily put down, the South will feel the effects of it on their slave population before the end of the next season."

Osceola was captured under a white flag of truce and died in an army prison in 1838, but the Seminoles fought on under Chief Coacoochee (Wild Cat) and other leaders. In 1842 the United States abandoned the removal effort. Most of Osceola's followers agreed to move west to Indian Territory after another war in 1858, but some Seminoles remained in the Florida Everglades, proud of having resisted conquest.

LIMITS OF MOBILITY IN A HIERARCHICAL SOCIETY

As Indians increasingly were forced westward, their lands were now open to restless and mobile white settlers. A large majority of white southern families (three-quarters in 1860) owned no slaves. Some lived in towns and ran stores or businesses, but most were yeoman farmers who owned their own land and grew their own food. The social distance between poorer whites and the planter class could be great, although the line between slaveholder and nonslaveholder was fluid. Still greater was the distance between whites and blacks with free status. White yeomen, landless whites, and free blacks occupied the broad base of the social pyramid in the Old South.

Yeoman Farmers   Many of the white farmers who pioneered the southern wilderness, moving into undeveloped regions or Indian land after removal, owned no slaves. After the War of 1812 they moved in successive waves down the southern Appalachians into the Gulf lands or through the Cumberland Gap into Kentucky and Tennessee. In large sections of the South, especially inland from the coast and away from large rivers, small, self-sufficient farms were the norm. Lured by stories of good land, many men repeatedly uprooted their wives and children. So many shared the excitement over new lands that one North Carolinian wrote in alarm, "The Alabama Fever rages here with great violence. . . . I am apprehensive if it continues to spread as it has done, it will almost depopulate the country."

These farmers were individualistic and hard working. Unlike their northern counterparts, their lives were not transformed by improvements in transportation. They could be independent thinkers as well, but their status as a numerical majority did not mean that they set the political or economic direction of the slave society. Self-reliant and often isolated, absorbed in the work of their farms, they operated both apart from and within the slave-based staple-crop economy.

On the southern frontier, men cleared fields, built log cabins, and established farms, while their wives labored in the household economy and patiently re-created the social ties—to relatives, neighbors, fellow churchgoers—that enriched everyone's experience. Women seldom shared the men's excitement about moving. They dreaded the isolation and loneliness of the frontier. "We have been [moving] all our lives," lamented one woman. "As soon as ever we git comfortably settled, it is time to be off to something new."

Some yeomen acquired large tracts of level land, purchased slaves, and became planters. They forged part of the new wealth of the cotton boom states of Mississippi and Louisiana, where mobility into the slaveowning class was possible. Others clung to familiar mountainous areas or sought self-sufficiency as farmers because, as one frontiersman put it, they disliked "seeing the nose of my neighbor sticking out between the trees." As one historian has written, though they owned no slaves, yeomen were jealous of their independence, and "the household grounded their own claims to masterhood." Whatever the size of their property, they wanted control over their economic and domestic lives.

Yeoman Folk Culture   The yeomen enjoyed a folk culture based on family, church, and local region. Their speech patterns and inflections recalled their Scots-Irish and Irish backgrounds. They flocked to religious revivals called camp meetings, and in between they got together for house-raisings, logrollings, quilting bees, corn-shuckings, and hunting for both food and sport. Such occasions combined work with fun and fellowship, offering food and liquor in abundance.

A demanding round of work and family responsibilities shaped women's lives in the home. They worked in the fields to an extent that astonished travelers like Frederick Law Olmsted and British writer Frances Trollope, who believed yeomen had rendered their wives "slaves of the soil." Throughout the year, the care and preparation of food consumed much of women's time. Household tasks continued during frequent pregnancies and childcare. Primary nursing and medical care also fell to mothers, who often relied on folk wisdom. Women, too, wanted to be masters of their household, the only space and power over which they could claim domain, although it came at the price of their health.

Yeomen's Livelihoods   Among the men, many aspired to wealth, eager to join the scramble for slaves and cotton profits. North Carolinian John F. Flintoff kept a diary of his struggle for success. At age eighteen in 1841, Flintoff went to Mississippi to seek his fortune. Like other aspiring yeomen, he worked as an overseer of slaves but often found it impossible to please his employers. At one point he gave up and returned to North Carolina, where he married and lived for a while in his parents' house. But Flintoff was "impatient to get along in the world," so he tried Louisiana next and then Mississippi again.

Flintoff's health suffered in the Gulf region and, routinely, "first rate employment" alternated with "very low wages." Moreover, as a young man working on isolated plantations, Flintoff often felt lonely. Even a revival meeting in 1844 proved "an extremely cold time" with "little warm feeling." His uncle and other employers found fault with his work, and in 1846 Flintoff concluded in despair that "managing negroes and large farms is soul destroying."

But a desire to succeed kept him going. At twenty-six, even before he owned any land, Flintoff bought his first slave, "a negro boy 7 years old." Soon he had purchased two more children, the cheapest slaves available. Conscious of his status as a slaveowner, Flintoff resented the low wages he was paid. In 1853, with nine young slaves and a growing family, Flintoff faced "the most unhappy time of my life." Fired by his uncle, he returned to North Carolina, sold some of his slaves, and purchased 124 acres with help from his in-laws. By 1860 he owned animal stock and several slaves and was paying off his debts. As the Civil War approached, he looked forward to freeing his wife from labor and possibly sending his sons to college. Although Flintoff demonstrated that a farmer could move in and out of the slaveholding class, he never achieved the cotton planter status (owning roughly twenty or more slaves) that he desired.

Probably more typical of the southern yeoman was Ferdinand L. Steel, who as a young man moved from North Carolina to Tennessee to work as a river boatman but eventually took up farming in Mississippi. Steel rose every day at 5 a.m. and worked until sundown. He and his family raised corn and wheat, though cotton was his cash product: he sold five or six bales (about two thousand pounds) a year to obtain money for sugar, coffee, salt, calico, gunpowder, and a few other store-bought goods.

Thus Steel entered the market economy—the broader commercial exchange of goods—as a small farmer, but with mixed results. He picked his own cotton and complained that it was brutal work and not profitable. He felt like a serf in cotton's kingdom. When cotton prices fell, a small grower like Steel could be driven into debt and lose his farm.

Steel's life in Mississippi in the 1840s retained much of the flavor of the frontier and survived on a household economy. He made all the family's shoes; his wife and sister sewed dresses, shirts, and "pantaloons." The Steel women also rendered their own soap and spun and wove cotton into cloth; the men hunted game. Steel doctored his illnesses with boneset tea and other herbs. As the nation fell deeper into crisis over the future of free or slave labor, this independent southern farmer never came close to owning a slave.

The focus of Steel's life was family and religion. Family members prayed together daily, and he studied Scripture for an hour after lunch. "My Faith increases, & I enjoy much of that peace which the world cannot give," he wrote in 1841. Seeking to prepare himself for Judgment Day, Steel borrowed histories, Latin and Greek grammars, and religious books from his church. Eventually he became a traveling Methodist minister. "My life is one of toil," he reflected, "but blessed be God that it is as well with me as it is."

Landless Whites   Toil with even less security was the lot of two other groups of free southerners: landless whites and free blacks. A sizable minority of white southern workers—from 25 to 40 percent, depending on the state—were hired hands who owned no land and worked for others in the countryside and towns. Their property consisted of a few household items and some animals—usually pigs—that could feed themselves on the open range. The landless included some immigrants, especially Irish, who did heavy and dangerous work, such as building railroads and digging ditches.

In the countryside, white farm laborers struggled to purchase land in the face of low wages or, if they rented, unpredictable market prices for their crops. By scrimping, saving, and finding odd jobs, some managed to climb into the ranks of yeomen. When James and Nancy Bennitt of North Carolina succeeded in their ten-year struggle to buy land, they decided to avoid the unstable market in cotton; thereafter they raised extra corn and wheat as sources of cash. People like the Bennitts were both participants in and victims of an economy dominated by cotton producers who relied on slave labor.

Herdsmen with pigs and other livestock had a desperate struggle to succeed. By 1860, as the South anticipated war to preserve its society, between 300,000 and 400,000 white people in the four states of Virginia, North and South Carolina, and Georgia—approximately one-fifth of the total white population—lived in genuine poverty. Their lives were harsh. An early antebellum traveler in central South Carolina described the white folk he encountered in the countryside: they "looked yellow, poor, and sickly. Some of them lived the most miserably I ever saw any poor people live." Land and slaves determined wealth in the Old South, and many whites possessed neither.

Yeomen's Demands and White Class Relations   Class tensions emerged in the western, nonslaveholding parts of the seaboard states by the 1830s. There, yeoman farmers resented their underrepresentation in state legislatures and the corruption in local government. After vigorous debate, the reformers won many battles. Voters in the more recently settled states of the Old Southwest adopted white manhood suffrage and other electoral reforms, including popular election of governors, legislative apportionment based on white population only, and locally chosen county government. Slaveowners with new wealth, however, knew that a more open government structure could permit troubling class conflicts and were determined to hold the ultimate reins of power.

Given such tensions, it was perhaps remarkable that slaveholders and nonslaveholders did not experience more overt conflict. Historians have offered several explanations. One of the most important factors was race. The South's racial ideology stressed the superiority of all whites to blacks. Thus slavery became the basis of equality among whites, and white privilege inflated the status of poor whites and gave them a common interest with the rich. At the same time, the dream of upward mobility blunted some class conflict. The Old South was to some extent a fluid society in which some people rose in status by acquiring land or slaves and those who did not wished that they could.

Most important, before the Civil War most yeomen were able to pursue their independent lifestyle largely unhindered by slaveholding planters. They worked their farms, avoided debt, and marked progress for their families in rural habitats of their own making. Likewise, slaveholders pursued their goals quite independently of yeomen. Planters farmed for the market but also for themselves. Suppression of dissent also played an increasing role. After 1830 white southerners who criticized the slave system out of moral conviction or class resentment were intimidated, attacked, legally prosecuted, or rendered politically powerless in a society held together in part by white racial solidarity.

Still, there were signs that the relative lack of conflict between slaveholders and non-slaveholders was coming to an end in the late antebellum period. As cotton lands filled up, nonslaveholders faced narrower economic prospects; meanwhile, wealthy planters enjoyed expanding profits. The risks of entering cotton production were becoming too great and the cost of slaves too high for many yeomen to rise in society. From 1830 to 1860 the percentage of white southern families holding slaves declined steadily from 36 to 25 percent. Although slaveowners were a distinct minority in the white population, planters' share of the South's agricultural wealth remained at between 90 and 95 percent.

Anticipating possible secession and the prospect of a war to defend slavery, slave-owners expressed growing fear about the loyalty of nonslaveholders during the late ante-bellum years. But for the moment slaveowners stood secure. In the 1850s they occupied from 50 to 85 percent of the seats in state legislatures and a similarly high percentage of the South's congressional seats. And planters' interests controlled all the other major social institutions, such as churches and colleges.

Free Blacks

The nearly quarter-million free blacks in the South in 1860 also yearned for mobility. But their condition was generally worse than the yeoman's and often little better than the slave's. The free blacks of the Upper South were usually descendants of men and women manumitted by their own-ers in the 1780s and 1790s. A remarkable number of slaveholders in Virginia and the Chesapeake region had freed their slaves because of religious principles and revolu-tionary ideals in the wake of American independence (see Chapter 7). Many free blacks also became free as runaways, especially by the 1830s, disappearing into the southern population; a few made their way northward.

White southerners were increasingly desperate to restrict this growing free black presence in their midst. "It seems the number of free Negroes," complained a Virginia slaveholder, "always exceeds the number of Negroes freed." Some free blacks worked in towns or cities, but most lived in rural areas and struggled to survive. They usually did not own land and had to labor in someone else's fields, often beside slaves. By law, free blacks could not own a gun, buy liquor, violate curfew, assemble except in church, tes-tify in court, or (throughout the South after 1835) vote. Despite these obstacles, a minority bought land, and others found jobs as skilled craftsmen, especially in cities.

A few free blacks prospered and bought slaves. In 1830 there were 3,775 free black slaveholders in the South; 80 percent lived in the four states of Louisiana, South Carolina, Virginia, and Maryland, and approximately half of the total lived in the two cities of New Orleans and Charleston. Most of them purchased their own wives and children, whom they nevertheless could not free, because laws required newly emancipated blacks to leave their state. In order to free family members whom they had purchased, hundreds of black slaveholders petitioned for exemption from the antimanumission laws passed in most southern states. At the same time, a few mulattos in New Orleans were active slave traders in its booming market. The complex world of southern free blacks received new attention through Edward P. Jones's *The Known World*, a hugely successful novel published in 2003 about a Virginia family that rises from slavery to slaveownership. Although rare in the United States, the greed and the tragic quest for power that lay at the root of slavery could cross any racial or ethnic barrier.

Free Black Communities   In the Cotton Belt and Gulf regions, a large proportion of free blacks were mulattos, the privileged offspring of wealthy white planters. Not all planters freed their mixed-race offspring, but those who did often recognized the moral obligation of giving their children a good education and financial backing. In a few cities like New Orleans, Charleston, and Mobile, extensive interracial sex, as well as migrations from the Caribbean, had produced a mulatto population that was recognized as a distinct class.

In many southern cities by the 1840s, free black communities formed, especially around an expanding number of churches. By the late 1850s, Baltimore had fifteen churches, Louisville nine, and Nashville and St. Louis four each—most of them African Methodist Episcopal. Class and race distinctions were important to southern free blacks, but outside a few cities, which developed fraternal orders of skilled craftsmen and fellowships of light-skinned people, most mulattos experienced hardship. In the United States, "one drop" of black "blood" (any observable racial mixture to white people's eyes) made them black, and potentially enslaveable.

THE PLANTERS' WORLD

At the top of the southern social pyramid were slaveholding planters. As a group they lived well, but most lived in comfortable farmhouses, not on the opulent scale that legend suggests. The grand plantation mansions, with fabulous gardens and long rows of outlying slave quarters, are an enduring symbol of the Old South. But a few statistics tell the fuller story: in 1850, 50 percent of southern slaveholders had fewer than five slaves; 72 percent had fewer than ten; 88 percent had fewer than twenty. Thus the average slaveholder was not a wealthy aristocrat but an aspiring farmer.

The Newly Rich   Louisiana cotton planter Bennet Barrow, a newly rich planter of the 1840s, was preoccupied with moneymaking. He worried constantly over his cotton crop, filling his diary with weather reports and gloomy predictions of his yields. Yet Barrow also strove to appear above such worries. He hunted frequently and had a passion for racing horses and raising hounds. He could report the loss of a slave without feeling, but emotion broke through his laconic manner when illness afflicted his sporting animals. "Never was a person more unlucky than I am," he mourned. "My favorite pup never lives." His strongest feelings surfaced when his horse Jos Bell—equal to "the best Horse in the South"—"broke down running a mile . . . ruined for Ever." The same day, the distraught Barrow gave his human property a "general Whipping." In 1841 diary entries he worried about a rumored slave insurrection. He gave a "severe whipping" to several of his slaves when they disobediently killed a hog. And when a slave named Ginney Jerry "sherked" his cotton-picking duties and was rumored "about to run off," Barrow whipped him one day and the next, recorded matter-of-factly: "took my gun found him in the Bayou behind the Quarter, shot him in his thigh—etc. raining all around."

The richest planters used their wealth to model genteel sophistication. Extended visits, parties, and balls to which women wore the latest fashions provided opportunities for friendship, courtship, and display. Such parties were held during the Christmas holidays, but also on such occasions as molasses stewing, a bachelors' ball, a horserace, or the crowning of the May queen. These entertainments were especially important as diversions for plantation women, and at the same time they sustained a rigidly gendered society. Young women relished social events to break the monotony of their domestic lives. In 1826 a Virginia girl was ecstatic about the "week . . . I was in Town. . . . There were five beaux and as many belles in the house constantly," she declared, and all she and her companions did was "eat, visit, romp, and sleep."

Most of the planters in the cotton-boom states of Alabama and Mississippi were newly rich by the 1840s. As one historian put it, "a number of men mounted from log cabin to plantation mansion on a stairway of cotton bales, accumulating slaves as they climbed." And many did not live like rich men. They put their new wealth into cotton acreage and slaves even as they sought refinement and high social status.

William Faulkner immortalized the new wealthy planter in a fictional character, Thomas Sutpen, in his novel *Absalom, Absalom!* (1936). After a huge win at riverboat gambling , Sutpen arrives in a Mississippi county in the 1830s, buys a huge plantation which he calls Sutpen's Hundred, and with his troop of slaves converts it into a wealthy enterprise. Sutpen marries a local woman, and although he is always viewed as a mysterious outsider by earlier residents of the county, he becomes a pillar of the slaveholding class, eventually an officer in the Confederate Army. But Sutpen is a self-made man of indomitable will and slave-based wealth. Although his ambition is ultimately his undoing, one of the earliest lessons he learns about success in the South is that "you got to have land and niggers and a fine house."

The cotton boom in the Mississippi valley created one-generation aristocrats. A nonfictional case in point is Greenwood Leflore, a Chocktaw chieftain who owned a plantation in Mississippi with four hundred slaves. After selling his cotton on the world market, he spent $10,000 in France to furnish a single room of his mansion with hand-woven carpets, furniture upholstered with gold leaf, tables and cabinets ornamented with tortoise-shell inlay, a variety of mirrors and paintings, and a clock and candelabra of brass and ebony.

Social Status and Planters' Values   Slave ownership was the main determinant of wealth in the South, and slave labor was the primary means of cultivating cotton and other cash crops on a large scale. Slaves were a commodity and an investment, much like gold; people bought them on speculation, hoping for a steady rise in their market value. Across the South, variations in wealth from county to county corresponded very closely to variations in slaveholding. Wealth in slaves also translated into political power: a solid majority of political officeholders were slaveholders, and the most powerful were usually large-scale planters.

Slavery's influence spread throughout the social system, until even the values and mores of nonslaveholders bore its imprint. The availability of slave labor tended to devalue free labor: where strenuous work under supervision was reserved for an enslaved race, few free people relished it. When Alexis de Tocqueville crossed from Ohio into Kentucky in his travels of 1831, he observed "the effect that slavery produces on society. On the right bank of the Ohio [River] everything is activity, industry; labor is honoured; there are no slaves. Pass to the left bank and the scene changes so suddenly that you think yourself on the other side of the world; the enterprising spirit is gone. There, work is not only painful; it is shameful." Tocqueville's own class impulses found a home in the South, however. There he found a "veritable aristocracy which . . . combines many prejudices with high sentiments and instincts."

The values of the aristocrat—lineage, privilege, pride, honor, and refinement of person and manner—commanded respect throughout the South. Many of those qualities were in short supply, however, in the recently settled portions of the cotton kingdom, where frontier values of courage and self-reliance ruled during the 1820s and 1830s. By the 1850s, a settled aristocratic group of planters did rule, however, in much of the Mississippi valley. In this geographically mobile society, independence and codes of honor motivated both planter and frontier farmer alike.

Instead of gradually disappearing, as it did in the North, the Code Duello, which required men to defend their honor through violence, lasted much longer in the South. In North Carolina in 1851, wealthy planter Samuel Fleming sought to settle disputes with lawyer William Waightstill Avery by "cowhiding" him on a public street. According to the code, Avery had two choices: to redeem his honor violently or to brand himself a coward through inaction. Three weeks later, he shot Fleming dead at point-blank range during a session of the Burke County Superior Court. A jury took only ten minutes to find Avery not guilty, and the spectators gave him a standing ovation.

In their pride, aristocratic planters expected not only to wield power but also to receive deference from poorer whites. But the sternly independent yeoman class resented infringements of their rights, and many belonged to evangelical faiths that exalted values of simplicity and condemned the planters' love of wealth. Yeomen sometimes challenged the political pretensions of planters. Much of the planters' power and their claims to leadership, after all, were built on their assumption of a monopoly on world cotton and on a foundation of black slave labor.

King Cotton in a Global Economy

Planters always had their eyes on the international growth of the cotton markets. Cash crops such as cotton were for export; the planters' fate depended on world trade, especially with Europe. The American South so dominated the world's supply of cotton that southern planters gained enormous confidence that the cotton boom was permanent and that the industrializing nations of England and France in particular would always bow to King Cotton.

American cotton production doubled in yield each decade after 1800 and provided three-fourths of the world's supply by the 1840s. Southern staple crops were fully three-fifths of all American exports by 1850, and one of every seven workers in England depended on American cotton for his job. Indeed, cotton production made slaves the single most valuable financial asset in the United States—greater in dollar value than all of America's banks, railroads, and manufacturing combined. In 1860 dollars, the slaves' total value as property came to an estimated $3.5 billion. In early-twenty-first-century dollars, that would be approximately $70 billion.

"Cotton is King," the *Southern Cultivator* declared in 1859, "and wields an astonishing influence over the world's commerce." Until 1840 the cotton trade furnished much of the export capital to finance northern economic growth. After that date, however, the northern economy expanded without dependence on cotton profits. Nevertheless, southern planters and politicians continued to boast of King Cotton's supremacy. "Our cotton is the most wonderful talisman in the world," announced a planter in 1853. "By its power we are transmuting whatever we choose into whatever we want." "No power on earth dares . . . to make war on cotton," James Hammond lectured the U.S. Senate in 1858; "Cotton is king." Although the South produced 4.5 million bales in 1861, its greatest cotton crop ever, such world dominance was about to collapse. Thereafter, cotton was more a shackle to the South than a king.

Paternalism

Slaveholding men often embraced a paternalistic ideology that justified their dominance over both black slaves and white women. Instead of stressing the profitable aspects of commercial agriculture, they stressed their obligations, viewing themselves as custodians of the welfare of society in general, and of the black families they owned in particular. The paternalistic planter saw himself not as an oppressor but as the benevolent guardian of an inferior race.

Paul Carrington Cameron, who was North Carolina's largest slaveholder, exemplifies this mentality. After a period of sickness among his one thousand North Carolina slaves (he had hundreds more in Alabama and Mississippi), Cameron wrote, "I fear the Negroes have suffered much from the want of proper attention and kindness under this late distemper no love of lucre shall ever induce me to be cruel." On another occasion he described to his sister the sense of responsibility he felt: "Do you remember a cold & frosty morning, during [our mother's] illness, when she said to me 'Paul my son the people ought to be shod' this is ever in my ears, whenever I see any ones shoes in bad order; and in my ears it will be, so long as I am master."

It was comforting to rich planters to see themselves in this way, and slaves—accommodating to the realities of power—encouraged their masters to think that their benevolence was appreciated. Paternalism also served as a defense against abolitionist criticism. Still, paternalism was often a matter of self-delusion, a means of avoiding some harsh dimensions of slave treatment. In reality, paternalism grew as a give-and-take relationship between masters and slaves, each extracting from the other what they desired—owners took labor from the bondsmen, while slaves obligated masters to provide them a measure of autonomy and living space. As one historian has argued, paternalism "grew out of the necessity to discipline and morally justify a system of exploitation, . . . a fragile bridge across the intolerable contradictions inherent" in a slave society dependent on "the willing reproduction and productivity of its victims."

Even Paul Cameron's benevolence vanished with changed circumstances. After the Civil War, he bristled at African Americans' efforts to be free and made sweeping economic decisions without regard for their welfare. Writing on Christmas Day 1865, Cameron showed little Christian charity (but a healthy profit motive) when he declared, "I am convinced that the people who gets rid of the free negro first will be the first to advance in improved agriculture. Have made no effort to retain any of mine." With that he turned off his land nearly a thousand black people, rented his fields to several white farmers, and invested in industry.

Relations between men and women in the planter class were similarly defined by paternalism. The upper-class southern woman was raised and educated to be a wife, mother, and subordinate companion to men. South Carolina's Mary Boykin Chesnut wrote of her husband, "He is master of the house. To hear is to obey. . . . All the comfort of my life depends upon his being in a good humor." In a social system based on the coercion of an entire race, women found it very difficult to challenge society's rules on sexual or racial relations.

Planters' daughters usually attended one of the South's rapidly multiplying boarding schools. There they formed friendships with other girls and received an education. Typically, the young woman could entertain suitors whom her parents approved. But very soon she had to choose a husband and commit herself for life to a man whom she generally had known for only a brief time. Young women were often alienated and emotionally unfulfilled. They had to follow the wishes of their family, especially their father. "It was for me best that I yielded to the wishes of papa," wrote a young North Carolinian in 1823. "I wonder when my best will cease to be painful and when I shall begin to enjoy life instead of enduring it."

Upon marriage, a planter-class woman ceded to her husband most of her legal rights, becoming part of his family. Most of the year she was isolated on a large plantation, where she had to oversee the cooking and preserving of food, manage the house, supervise care of the children, and attend sick slaves. All these realities were more rigid and confining on the frontier, where isolation was even greater. Women sought refuge in their extended family and associations with other women. In 1821 a Georgia woman wrote to her brother of the distress of a cousin's wife: "They are living . . . in the frontiers of the state and [a] perfectly uncivilized place. Cousin W. gets a good practice [the husband] but she is almost crazy to get to Alabama where one of her sisters is living." Men on plantations could occasionally escape into the public realm—to town, business, or politics. Women could retreat from rural plantation culture only into kinship.

Marriage and Family Among Planters

It is not surprising that a perceptive young white woman sometimes approached marriage with anxiety. Women could hardly help viewing their wedding day, as one put it in 1832, as "the day to fix my fate." Lucy Breckinridge, a wealthy Virginia girl of twenty, lamented the autonomy she surrendered at the altar. In her diary she recorded this unvarnished observation on marriage: "If [husbands] care for their wives at all it is only as a sort of servant, a being made to attend to their comforts and to keep the children out of the way. A woman's life after she is married, unless there is an immense amount of love, is nothing but suffering and hard work."

Lucy loved young children but knew that childbearing often involved grief, poor health, and death. In 1840 the birth rate for white southern women in their childbearing years was almost 30 percent higher than the national average. The average southern white woman could expect to bear eight children in 1800; by 1860 the figure had decreased to only six, with one or more miscarriages likely. Complications of childbirth were a major cause of death, occurring twice as often in the hot, humid South as in the Northeast.

Sexual relations between planters and slaves were another source of problems that white women had to endure but were not supposed to notice. "Violations of the moral law . . . made mulattos as common as blackberries," protested a woman in Georgia, but wives had to play "the ostrich game." "A magnate who runs a hideous black harem," wrote Mrs. Chesnut, ". . . poses as the model of all human virtues to these poor women whom God and the laws have given him."

Southern men tolerated little discussion by women of the slavery issue. In the 1840s and 1850s, as abolitionist attacks on slavery increased, southern men published a barrage of articles stressing that women should restrict their concerns to the home. The *Southern Quarterly Review* declared, "The proper place for a woman is at home. One of her highest privileges, to be politically merged in the existence of her husband."

But some southern women were beginning to seek a larger role. A study of women in Petersburg, Virginia, a large tobacco-manufacturing town, revealed behavior that valued financial autonomy. Over several decades before 1860, the proportion of women who never married, or did not remarry after the death of a spouse, grew to exceed 33 percent. Likewise, the number of women who worked for wages, controlled their own property, and ran dressmaking businesses increased. In managing property, these and other women benefited from legal changes enacted to protect families from the husband's indebtedness during business panics and recessions. These reforms gave married women some property rights.

Planters forged a society around their domestic lives and local mores. But they did so through the energies and lives of generations of enslaved African Americans who helped them extract great wealth from southern soil.

SLAVE LIFE AND LABOR

For African Americans, slavery was a burden that destroyed some people and forced others to develop modes of survival. Slaves knew a life of poverty, coercion, toil, and resentment. They provided the physical strength, and much of the know-how, to build an agricultural empire. But their daily lives embodied the nation's most basic contradiction: in the world's model republic, they were on the wrong side of a brutally unequal power relationship.

Slaves' Everyday Conditions   Southern slaves enjoyed few material comforts beyond the bare necessities. Although they generally had enough to eat, their diet was monotonous and nonnutritious. Clothing, too, was plain, coarse, and inexpensive. Few slaves received more than one or two changes of clothing for hot and cold seasons, and one blanket each winter. Children of both sexes ran naked in hot weather and wore long cotton shirts in winter. Many slaves had to go without shoes until December, even as far north as Virginia. The bare feet of slaves were often symbolic of their status and one reason why, after freedom, many black parents were so concerned with providing their children with shoes. These conditions were generally better in cities, where slaves frequently lived in the same dwelling as their owners and were hired out to employers on a regular basis, enabling them to accumulate their own money.

Some of the richer plantations provided substantial houses, but the average slave lived in a crude, one-room cabin. The gravest drawback of slave cabins was not lack of comfort but unhealthfulness. Each dwelling housed one or two entire families. Crowding and lack of sanitation fostered the spread of infection and such contagious diseases as typhoid fever, malaria, and dysentery. White plantation doctors were hired to care for sick slaves on a regular basis, but some "slave doctors" attained a degree of power in the quarters and with masters by practicing health care and healing through herbalism and spiritualism.

Slave Work Routines

Hard work was the central fact of slaves' existence. The long hours and large work gangs that characterized Gulf Coast cotton districts operated almost like factories in the field. Overseers rang the morning bell before dawn, and black people of varying ages, tools in hand, walked toward the fields. Slaves who cultivated tobacco in the Upper South worked long hours picking the sticky, sometimes noxious, leaves under harsh discipline. And, as one woman recalled when interviewed in the 1930s, "it was way after sundown fore they could stop that field work. Then they had to hustle to finish their night work [such as watering livestock or cleaning cotton] in time for supper, or go to bed without it."

Working "from sun to sun" became a norm in much of the South. As one planter put it, slaves were the best labor because "you could command them and make them do what was right." Profit took precedence over paternalism. Slave women did heavy field-work, often as much as the men and even during pregnancy. Old people were kept busy caring for young children, doing light chores, or carding, ginning, and spinning cotton. The black abolitionist orator Frances Ellen Watkins captured the grinding economic reality of slavery in an 1857 speech, charging that slaveholders had "found out a fearful alchemy by which . . . blood can be transformed into gold. Instead of listening to the cry of agony, they listen to the ring of dollars and stoop down to pick up the coin."

By the 1830s slaveowners found that labor could be similarly motivated by the clock. Incentives had to be part of the labor regime and the master-slave relationship as well. Planters in the South Carolina and Georgia low country used a task system whereby slaves were assigned measured amounts of work to be performed in a given amount of time. So much cotton on a daily basis was to be picked from a designated field, so many rows hoed or plowed in a particular slave's specified section. When their tasks were finished, slaves' time was their own for working garden plots, tending hogs, even hiring out their own extra labor. From this experience and personal space, many slaves developed their own sense of property ownership. When the task system worked best, slaves and masters alike embraced it, fostering a degree of reciprocal trust.

Slave children were the future of the system and widely valued as potential labor. Of the 1860 population of 4 million slaves, fully half were under the age of sixteen. "A child raised every two years," wrote Thomas Jefferson, "is of more profit than the crop of the best laboring man." And in 1858 a slaveowner writing in an agricultural magazine calculated that a slave girl he purchased in 1827 for $400 had borne three sons now worth $3,000 as his working field hands. Slave children gathered kindling, carried water to the fields, swept the yard, lifted cut sugar-cane stalks into carts, stacked wheat, chased birds away from sprouting rice plants, and labored at many levels of cotton and tobacco production. "Work," wrote one historian, "can be rightly called the thief who stole the childhood of youthful bond servants."

As slave children matured, they faced many psychological traumas. They faced a feeling of powerlessness as they became aware that their parents ultimately could not protect them. They had to muster strategies to fight internalizing what whites assumed was their inferiority. Thomas Jones, who grew up in North Carolina, remembered that his greatest struggle with the sense of "suffering and shame" as he "was made to feel . . . degraded." Many former slaves resented foremost their denial of education. "There is one sin that slavery committed against me which I will never forgive," recollected the minister James Pennington. "It robbed me of my education." And for girls reaching maturity, the potential trauma of sexual abuse loomed over their lives.

Violence and Intimidation Against Slaves   Slaves could not demand much autonomy, of course, because the owner enjoyed a monopoly on force and violence. Whites throughout the South believed that slaves "can't be governed except with the whip." One South Carolinian frankly explained to a northern journalist that he whipped his slaves regularly, "say once a fortnight; . . . the fear of the lash kept them in good order." Evidence suggests that whippings were less frequent on small farms than on large plantations. But beatings symbolized authority to the master and tyranny to the slaves, who made them a benchmark for evaluating a master. In the words of former slaves, a good owner was one who did not "whip too much," whereas a bad owner "whipped till he's bloodied you and blistered you."

As these reports suggest, terrible abuses could and did occur. The master wielded virtually absolute authority on his plantation, and courts did not recognize the word of chattel. Slaveholders rarely had to answer to the law or to the state. Pregnant women were whipped, and there were burnings, mutilation, torture, and murder. Yet physical cruelty may have been less prevalent in the United States than in other slaveholding parts of the New World. Especially in some of the sugar islands of the Caribbean, treatment was so poor and death rates so high that the heavily male slave population shrank in size. In the United States, by contrast, the slave population experienced a steady natural increase, as births exceeded deaths and each generation grew larger.

The worst evil of American slavery was not its physical cruelty but the nature of slavery itself: coercion, belonging to another person, virtually no hope for mobility or change. Recalling their time in bondage, some former slaves emphasized the physical abuse, or the "bullwhip days," as one woman described her past. But memories of physical punishment focused on the tyranny of whipping as much as the pain. Delia Garlic made the essential point: "It's bad to belong to folks that own you soul an' body. I could tell you 'bout it all day, but even then you couldn't guess the awfulness of it." Thomas Lewis put it this way: "There was no such thing as being good to slaves. Many people were better than others, but a slave belonged to his master and there was no way to get out of it." To be a slave was to be the object of another person's will and material gain, to be owned, as the saying went, "from the cradle to the grave."

Most American slaves retained their mental independence and self-respect despite their bondage. Contrary to popular belief at the time, they were not loyal partners in their own oppression. They had to be subservient and speak honeyed words to their masters, but they talked and behaved quite differently among themselves. In *Narrative of the Life of Frederick Douglass, an American Slave, Written by Himself* (1845), Douglass wrote that most slaves, when asked about "their condition and the character of their masters, almost universally say they are contented, and that their masters are kind." Slaves did this, said Douglass, because they were governed by the maxim that "a still tongue makes a wise head," especially in the presence of unfamiliar people. Because they were "part of the human family," slaves often quarreled over who had the best master. But at the end of the day, Douglass remarked, when one had a bad master, he sought a better master; and when he had a better one, he wanted to "be his own master."

Slave-Master Relationships   Some former slaves remembered warm feelings between masters and slaves, but the prevailing attitudes were distrust and antagonism. Slaves saw through acts of kindness. One woman said her mistress was "a mighty good somebody to belong to" but only " 'cause she was raisin' us to work for her." A man recalled that his owners took good care of their slaves, "and Grandma Maria say, 'Why shouldn't they—it was their money.' " Slaves also resented being used as beasts of burden. One man observed that his master "fed us reg'lar on good, 'stantial food, just like you'd tend to your horse, if you had a real good one."

Slaves were alert to the thousand daily signs of their degraded status. One man recalled the general rule that slaves ate cornbread and owners ate biscuits. If blacks did get biscuits, "the flour that we made the biscuits out of was the third-grade sorts." A former slave recalled, "Us catch lots of 'possums," but "the white folks at [ate] 'em." If the owner took his slaves' garden produce to town and sold it for them, the slaves often suspected him of pocketing part of the profits.

Suspicion often grew into hatred. When a yellow fever epidemic struck in 1852, many slaves saw it as God's retribution. An elderly ex-slave named Minnie Fulkes cherished the conviction that God was going to punish white people for their cruelty to blacks. She described the whippings that her mother had to endure, and then she exclaimed, "Lord, Lord, I hate white people and the flood waters goin' to drown some more." On the plantation, of course, slaves had to keep such thoughts to themselves. Often they expressed one feeling to whites, another within their own household. In their daily lives slaves created many ways to survive and to sustain their humanity in this world of repression.

SLAVE CULTURE AND RESISTANCE

A people is always "more than the sum of its brutalization," wrote African American novelist Ralph Ellison in 1967. What people create in the face of hard luck and oppression is what provides hope. The resource that enabled slaves to maintain such defiance was their culture: a body of beliefs, values, and practices born of their past and maintained in the present. As best they could, they built a community knitted together by stories, music, a religious world-view, leadership, the smells of their cooking, the sounds of their own voices, and the tapping of their feet. "The values expressed in folklore," wrote African American poet Sterling Brown, provided a "wellspring to which slaves . . . could return in times of doubt to be refreshed." That they endured and found loyalty and strength among themselves is a tribute to their courage and to the triumph of the human spirit.

African Cultural Survival   Slave culture changed significantly after 1808, when Congress banned further importation of slaves and the generations born in Africa died out. For a few years South Carolina reopened the international slave trade, but by the 1830s, the vast majority of slaves in the South were native-born Americans. Many blacks, in fact, can trace their American ancestry back further than most white Americans.

Yet African influences remained strong, despite lack of firsthand memory, especially in appearance and forms of expression. Some slave men plaited their hair into rows and fancy designs; slave women often wore their hair "in string"—tied in small bunches secured by a string or piece of cloth. A few men and many women wrapped their heads in kerchiefs of the styles and colors of West Africa. Some could remember the names of African ancestors passed on to them by family lore. In burial practices, slaves used jars and other glass objects to decorate graves, following similar African traditions.

Music, religion, and folktales were parts of daily life for most slaves. Borrowing partly from their African background, as well as forging new American folkways, they developed what scholars have called a sacred world-view, which affected all aspects of work, leisure, and self-understanding. Slaves made musical instruments with carved motifs that resembled African stringed instruments. Their drumming and dancing followed African patterns that made whites marvel. One visitor to Georgia in the 1860s described a ritual dance of African origin: "A ring of singers is formed. . . . They then utter a kind of melodious chant, which gradually increases in strength, and in noise, until it fairly shakes the house, and it can be heard for a long distance." This observer of the "ring shout" also noted the agility of the dancers and the African call-and-response pattern in their chanting.

Many slaves continued to believe in spirit possession. Whites, too, believed in ghosts and charms, but the slaves' belief resembled the African concept of the living dead—the idea that deceased relatives visit the earth for many years until the process of dying is complete. Slaves also practiced conjuration and quasi-magical root medicine. By the 1850s the most notable conjurers and root doctors were reputed to live in South Carolina, Georgia, Louisiana, and other isolated coastal areas with high slave populations.

These cultural survivals provided slaves with a sense of their separate past. Such practices and beliefs were not static "Africanisms" or mere "retentions." They were cultural adaptations, living traditions re-formed in the Americas in response to new experience. African American slaves in the Old South were a people forged by two centuries of cultural mixture in the Atlantic world, and the South itself was a melding of many African and European cultural forces.

As they became African Americans, slaves also developed a sense of racial identity. In the colonial period, Africans had arrived in America from many different states and kingdoms, represented in distinctive languages, body markings, and traditions. Planters had used ethnic differences to create occupational hierarchies. By the early antebellum period, however, old ethnic identities gave way as American slaves increasingly saw themselves as a single group unified by race. Africans had arrived in the New World with virtually no concept of "race"; by the antebellum era, their descendants had learned through bitter experience that race was now the defining feature of their lives. They were a transplanted and transformed people.

Slaves' Religion and Music

As African culture gave way to a maturing African American culture, more and more slaves adopted Christianity. But they fashioned Christianity into an instrument of support and resistance. Theirs was a religion of justice and deliverance, quite unlike their masters' religious propaganda directed at them as a means of control. "You ought to have heard that preachin'," said one man. "'Obey your master and mistress, don't steal chickens and eggs and meat,' but nary a word about havin' a soul to save." Slaves believed that Jesus cared about their souls and their plight. In their interpretations of biblical stories, as one historian has said, they were "literally willing themselves reborn."

For slaves, Christianity was a religion of personal and group salvation. Devout men and women worshiped every day, "in the field or by the side of the road" or in special "prayer grounds" that afforded privacy. Some slaves held fervent secret prayer meetings that lasted far into the night. Many slaves nurtured an unshakable belief that God would enter history and end their bondage. This faith—and the joy and emotional release that accompanied worship—sustained them.

Slaves also adapted Christianity to African practices. In West African belief, devotees are possessed by a god so thoroughly that the god's own personality replaces the human personality. In the late antebellum era, Christian slaves experienced possession by the Protestant "Holy Spirit." The combination of shouting, singing, and dancing that seemed to overtake black worshipers formed the heart of their religious faith. "The old meeting house caught fire," recalled an ex-slave preacher. "The spirit was there. . . . God saw our need and came to us. I used to wonder what made people shout but now I don't. There is a joy on the inside and it wells up so strong that we can't keep still. It is fire in the bones. Any time that fire touches a man, he will jump." Out in brush arbors or in meetinghouses, slaves took in the presence of God, thrust their arms to heaven, made music with their feet, and sang away their woes. Some travelers observed "bands" of "Fist and Heel Worshippers." Many postslavery black choirs could not perform properly without a good wooden floor to use as their "drum."

Rhythm and physical movement were crucial to slaves' religious experience. In black preachers' chanted sermons, which reached out to gather the sinner into a narrative of meanings and cadences along the way to conversion, an American tradition was born. The chanted sermon was both a message from Scripture and a patterned form that required audience response punctuated by "yes sirs!" and "amens!" But it was in song that the slaves left their most sublime gift to American culture.

Through the spirituals, slaves tried to impose order on the chaos of their lives. Many themes run through the lyrics of slave songs. Often referred to later as the "sorrow songs," they also anticipate imminent rebirth. Sadness could immediately give way to joy: "Did you ever stan' on a mountain, wash yo hands in a cloud?" Rebirth was at the heart as well of the famous hymn "Oh, Freedom": "Oh, Oh, Freedom / Oh, Oh, Freedom over me— / But before I'll be a slave, / I'll be buried in my grave, / And go home to my Lord, / And Be Free!"

This tension and sudden change between sorrow and joy animates many songs: "Sometimes I feel like a motherless chile . . . / Sometimes I feel like an eagle in the air, / . . . Spread my wings and fly, fly, fly!" Many songs also express a sense of intimacy and closeness with God. Some songs display an unmistakable rebelliousness, such as the enduring "He said, and if I had my way / If I had my way, if I had my way, / I'd tear this building down!" And some spirituals reached for a collective sense of hope in the black community as a whole.

> O, gracious Lord! When shall it be,
> That we poor souls shall all be free;
> Lord, break them slavery powers—
> Will you go along with me?
> Lord break them slavery powers,
> Go sound the jubilee!

This photograph of five generations of a slave family, taken in Beaufort, South Carolina, in 1862, is silent but powerful testimony to the importance that enslaved African Americans placed on their ever-threatened family ties. (Library of Congress)

In many ways, American slaves converted the Christian God to themselves. They sought an alternative world to live in—a home other than the one fate had given them on earth. In a thousand variations on the Br'er Rabbit folktales—in which the weak survive by wit and power is reversed—and in the countless refrains of their songs, they fashioned survival and resistance out of their own cultural imagination.

The Black Family in Slavery

American slaves clung tenaciously to the personal relationships that gave meaning to life. Although American law did not recognize slave families, masters permitted them; in fact, slaveowners *expected* slaves to form families and have children. As a result, even along the rapidly expanding edge of the cotton kingdom, there was a normal ratio of men to women, young to old. Studies have shown that, on some of the largest cotton plantations of South Carolina, when masters allowed their slaves increased autonomy through work on the task system, the property accumulation in livestock, tools, and garden produce thus fostered led to more stable and healthier families.

Following African kinship traditions, African Americans avoided marriage between cousins (commonplace among aristocratic slaveowners). By naming their children after relatives of past generations, African Americans emphasized their family histories. Kinship networks and broadly extended families are what held life together in many slave communities.

For slave women, sexual abuse and rape by white masters were ever-present threats to themselves and their family life. By 1860 there were 405,751 mulattos in the United States, comprising 12.5 percent of the African American population. White planters were sometimes open with their behavior toward slave women, but not in the way they talked about it. As Mary Chesnut remarked, sex between slaveholding men and their slave women was "the thing we can't name." Buying slaves for sex was all too common at the New Orleans slave market. In what was called the "fancy trade" (a "fancy" was a young, attractive slave girl or woman), females were often sold for prices as much as 300 percent higher than the average. At such auctions for young women, slaveholders exhibited some of the ugliest values at the heart of the slave system—patriarchal dominance demonstrated by paying $3,000 to $5,000 for female "companions."

Slave women had to negotiate this confused world of desire, threat, and shame. Harriet Jacobs, who spent much of her youth and early adult years dodging her owner's relentless sexual pursuit, described this circumstance as "the war of my life." In recollecting her desperate effort to protect her children and help them find a way north to freedom, Jacobs asked a haunting question that many slave women carried with them to their graves: "Why does the slave ever love? Why allow the tendrils of the heart to twine around objects which may at any moment be wrenched away by the hand of violence?"

The Domestic Slave Trade

Separation by violence from those they loved, sexual appropriation, and sale were what slave families most feared and hated. Many struggled for years to keep their children together and, after emancipation, to reestablish contact with loved ones lost by forced migration and sale. Between 1820 and 1860, an estimated 2 million slaves were moved into the region extending from western Georgia to eastern Texas. When the Union Army registered thousands of black marriages in Mississippi and Louisiana in 1864 and 1865, fully 25 percent of the men over forty reported that they had been forcibly separated from a previous wife. Thousands of black families were disrupted every year to serve the needs of the expanding cotton economy. The Butler auction of 1859, described in the chapter-opening vignette, was only one in a gruesome series.

Many antebellum white southerners made their living from the slave trade. In South Carolina alone by the 1850s, there were over one hundred slave-trading firms selling an annual average of approximately 6,500 slaves to southwestern states. Although southerners often denied it, vast numbers of slaves moved west by outright sale and not by migrating with their owners. A typical trader's advertisement read, "NEGROES WANTED. I am paying the highest cash prices for young and likely NEGROES, those having good front teeth and being otherwise sound." One estimate from 1858 indicated that slave sales in Richmond, Virginia, netted $4 million that year alone. A market guide to slave sales that same year in Richmond listed average prices for "likely ploughboys," ages twelve to fourteen, at $850 to $1,050; "extra number 1 fieldgirls" at $1,300 to $1,350; and "extra number 1 men" at $1,500.

Slave traders were practical, roving businessmen. They were sometimes considered degraded by white planters, but many slaveowners did business with them. Market forces, as the Butler auction indicates, drove this commerce in humanity. At slave "pens" in cities like New Orleans, traders promoted "a large and commodious showroom . . . prepared to accommodate over 200 Negroes for sale." Traders did their utmost to make their slaves appear young, healthy, and happy, cutting gray whiskers off men, using paddles as discipline so as not to scar their merchandise, and forcing people to dance and sing as buyers arrived for an auction. When transported to the southwestern markets, slaves were often chained together in "coffles," which made journeys of 500 miles or more on foot.

The complacent mixture of racism and business among traders is evident in their own language. "I refused a girl 20 year[s] old at 700 yesterday," one trader wrote to another in 1853. "If you think best to take her at 700 I can still get her. She is very badly whipped but good teeth." Some sales were transacted at owners' requests, often for tragically inhumane reasons. "Bought a cook yesterday that was to go out of state," wrote a trader; "she just made the people mad that was all." Some traders demonstrated how deeply slavery and racism were intertwined. "I have bought the boy Isaac for 1100," wrote a trader in 1854 to his partner. "I think him very prime. . . . He is a . . . house servant . . . first rate cook . . . and splendid carriage driver. He is also a fine painter and varnisher and . . . says he can make a fine panel door. . . . Also he performs well on the violin. . . . He is a genius and its strange to say I think he is smarter than I am."

Strategies of Resistance   Slaves brought to their efforts at resistance the same common sense and determination that characterized their struggle to secure their family lives. The scales weighed heavily against overt revolution, and they knew it. But they seized opportunities to alter their work conditions. They sometimes slacked off when they were not being watched. Thus owners complained that slaves "never would lay out their strength freely."

Daily discontent and desperation were also manifest in sabotage of equipment; in wanton carelessness about work; in theft of food, livestock, or crops; or in getting drunk on stolen liquor. Some slaves who were hired out might show their anger by hoarding their earnings. Or they might just fall into recalcitrance. "I have a boy in my employ called Jim Archer," complained a Vicksburg, Mississippi, slaveholder in 1843. "Jim does not want to be under anyones control and says . . . he wants to go home this summer." A woman named Ellen, hired as a cook in Tennessee in 1856, quietly put mercury poison into a roasted apple for her unsuspecting mistress. And some slave women resisted as best they could by trying to control their own pregnancy, either by avoiding it or by seeking it as a way to improve their physical conditions.

Many male, and some female, slaves acted out their defiance by violently attacking overseers or even their owners. Southern court records and newspapers contain accounts of these resistant slaves who gave the lie to the image of the docile bondsman. The price they paid was high. Such lonely rebels were customarily secured and flogged, sold away, or hanged.

Many individual slaves attempted to run away to the North, and some received assistance from the loose network known as the Underground Railroad (see page 378). But it was more common for slaves to run off temporarily to hide in the woods. Approximately 80 percent of runaways were male; women simply could not flee as readily because of their responsibility for children. Fear, disgruntlement over treatment, or family separation might motivate slaves to risk all in flight. Only a minority of those who tried such escapes ever made it to freedom in the North or Canada, but these fugitives made slavery a very insecure institution by the 1850s.

But American slavery also produced some fearless revolutionaries. Gabriel's Rebellion involved as many as a thousand slaves when it was discovered in 1800, just before it would have exploded in Richmond, Virginia (see pages 215–216). According to controversial court testimony, a similar conspiracy existed in Charleston in 1822, led by a free black named Denmark Vesey. Born a slave in the Caribbean, Vesey won a lottery of $1,500 in 1799, bought his own freedom, and became a religious leader in the black community. According to one long-argued interpretation, Vesey was a heroic revolutionary determined to free his people or die trying. But, in a recent challenge, historian Michael Johnson points out that the court testimony is the only reliable source on the alleged insurrection. Might the testimony reveal less of reality than of white South Carolina's fears of slave rebellion? The court, says Johnson, built its case on rumors and intimidated witnesses, and "conjured into being" an insurrection that was not about to occur in reality. Whatever the facts, when the arrests and trials were over, thirty-seven "conspirators" were executed, and more than three dozen others were banished from the state.

Nat Turner's Insurrection

The most famous rebel of all, Nat Turner, struck for freedom in Southampton County, Virginia, in 1831. The son of an African woman who passionately hated her enslavement, Nat Turner was a precocious child who learned to read when he was very young. Encouraged by his first owner to study the Bible, he enjoyed certain privileges but also endured hard work and changes of masters. His father successfully escaped to freedom.

Young Nat eventually became a preacher with a reputation for eloquence and mysticism. After nurturing his plan for several years, Turner led a band of rebels from farm to farm in the predawn darkness of August 22, 1831. The group severed limbs and crushed skulls with axes or killed their victims with guns. Before alarmed planters stopped them, Nat Turner and his followers had in forty-eight hours slaughtered sixty whites of both sexes and all ages. The rebellion was soon put down, and in retaliation whites killed slaves at random all over the region, including in adjoining states. Turner was eventually caught and then hanged. As many as two hundred African Americans, including innocent victims of marauding whites, lost their lives as a result of the rebellion.

Nat Turner remains one of the most haunting symbols in America's unresolved history with racial slavery and discrimination. While in jail awaiting execution, Turner was interviewed by a Virginia lawyer and slaveholder, Thomas R. Gray. Their intriguing creation, *The Confessions of Nat Turner,* became a bestseller within a month of Turner's hanging. Turner told of his early childhood, his religious visions, his zeal to be free; Gray called the rebel a "gloomy fanatic," but in a manner that made him fascinating and produced one of the most remarkable documents in the annals of American slavery. In the wake of Turner's insurrection, many states passed stiffened legal codes against black education and religious practice.

Most importantly, in 1832 the state of Virginia, shocked to its core, held a full-scale legislative and public debate over gradual emancipation as a means of ridding itself of slavery and of blacks. The plan debated would not have freed any slaves until 1858, and it provided that eventually all blacks would be colonized outside Virginia. But when the House of Delegates voted, gradual abolition lost, 73 to 58. In the end, Virginia opted to do nothing except reinforce its own moral and economic defenses of slavery. It was the last time white southerners would debate any kind of emancipation until war forced their hand.

SUMMARY

During the four decades before the Civil War, the South grew in land, wealth, and power along with the rest of the country. Although the southern states were deeply enmeshed in the nation's heritage and political economy, they also developed as a distinctive region, ideologically and economically, because of slavery. Far more than the North, the antebellum South was a biracial society; whites grew up directly influenced by black folkways and culture; and blacks, the vast majority of whom were slaves, became predominantly native-born Americans and the cobuilders with whites of a rural, agricultural society. From the Old South until modern times, white and black southerners have always shared a tragic mutual history.

With the sustained cotton boom, as well as state and federal policies of Indian Removal, the South grew into a huge slave society. The coercive influence of slavery affected virtually every element of southern life and politics, and increasingly produced a leadership determined to preserve a conservative, hierarchical social and racial order. Despite the white supremacy that united them, the democratic values of yeomen often clashed with the profit motives of aristocratic planters. The benevolent self-image and paternalistic ideology of slaveholders ultimately had to stand the test of the slaves' own judgments. African American slaves responded by fashioning over time a rich, expressive folk culture and a religion of personal and group deliverance. Their experiences could be profoundly different from one region and kind of labor to another. Some blacks were crushed by bondage; many others transcended it in an epic of survival and resistance.

By 1850, through their own wits and on the backs of African labor, white southerners had aggressively built one of the last profitable, expanding slave societies on earth. North of them and deeply intertwined with them in the same nation, economy, constitutional system, and history, a different kind of society had grown even faster—driven by industrialism and free labor. The clash of these two deeply connected, yet mutually fearful and divided societies would soon explode in political storms over the nation's future.

11

The Modernizing North
1815–1860

OR IS IT THE NORTH THAT WAS DISTINCTIVE?

Historian James McPherson has proposed a new twist to the old question of southern distinctiveness: perhaps it was the *North*—New England, the Middle Atlantic, and the Old Northwest—that diverged from the norm. At the republic's birth, the two regions had much in common, with some similarities persisting for decades: slavery, ethnic homogeneity, an overwhelming proportion of the population engaged in agricultural pursuits, a small urban population. As late as the War of 1812, the regions were more similar than dissimilar. But all that started to change with postwar economic development. Although often couched in nationalist terms, such development was undertaken mostly by state and local governments as well as private entrepreneurs, and it took place much more extensively and rapidly in the North. As the North embraced economic progress, it—rather than the South—diverged from the international norm. The North, writes McPherson, "hurtled forward toward a future that many Southerners found distasteful if not frightening."

While the South expanded as a slave society, the North changed rapidly and profoundly. It transformed, as one historian has put it, from a society with markets to a market society. In the colonial era, settlers lived in a society with markets, one in which they engaged in long-distance trade—selling their surpluses to merchants, who in turn

CHRONOLOGY

1825 • Erie Canal completed

1830 • Railroad era begins

1830s–50s • Urban riots commonplace

1834 • Women workers strike at Lowell textile mills

1835 • Arkansas passes first women's property law

1836 • Second Bank of the United States closes

1837 • Panic of 1837 begins economic downturn

1839–43 • Economic depression

1842 • *Commonwealth v. Hunt* declares strikes lawful

1844 • Federal government grant sponsors first telegraph line

• Lowell Female Reform Association formed

sent raw materials to Europe, using the proceeds to purchase finished goods for resale—but in which most settlers remained self-sufficient. During and after the War of 1812, the North became more solidly a market society, one in which participation in long-distance commerce fundamentally altered people's aspirations and activities. With trade with Europe largely cut off during the war, entrepreneurs invested in domestic factories, setting off a series of changes in the organization of daily life. More men, women, and children began working for others in exchange for wages—rather than for themselves on a family farm—making the domestic demand for foodstuffs soar. The result was a transformation of agriculture itself. Farming became commercialized, with individual farmers abandoning self-sufficiency and specializing instead in crops that would yield cash on the market. With the cash that farmers earned when things went well, they now bought goods that they had once made for themselves, such as cloth, candles, and soap, as well as some luxuries. Unlike the typical southern yeoman, they were not self-reliant, and isolation was rare. In the North, market expansion altered, sometimes dramatically, virtually every aspect of life. Some historians see these rapid and pervasive changes as a market revolution.

Preindustrial Farms At the beginning of the nineteenth century, few yeoman farmers, North or South, were entirely independent. Most practiced what is called mixed agriculture: they raised a variety of crops and livestock. Their goal was to procure what they called a "competence": everyday comforts and economic opportunities for their children. When they produced more than they needed, they traded the surplus with neighbors or sold it to local storekeepers. Such transactions often took place without money; farmers might trade eggs for shoes, or they might labor in their neighbor's fields in exchange for bales of hay. Even farmers like James and Mary Ann Archbald, whose main goals were to secure their own independence and seek opportunities for their children, engaged in long-distance market exchange. They did not simply trade their farm goods with neighbors but rather sold them for cash to merchants, who then sent the goods on their way to people whom the Archbalds would never meet, living perhaps hundreds of miles away. The Archbalds practiced mixed agriculture—they grew rye, corn, barley, peas, oats, and potatoes in addition to raising livestock—while also producing cloth to sell. But for Mary Ann Archbald, the main reason to earn cash was not to accumulate wealth but to pay off the family's land debt. Families like the Archbalds indulged in the occasional luxury—for Mary Ann Archbald, that meant buying books—but security mattered more than profit.

The main source of farm labor was family members, though some yeoman farmers, North and South, also relied on slaves or indentured servants. Work generally divided along gender lines. Men and boys worked in the fields, herded livestock, chopped firewood, fished, and hunted. Women and girls tended gardens, milked cows, spun and wove, processed and preserved food, prepared meals, washed clothes, and looked after infants and toddlers.

In their quest for independence, farmers cooperated with one another. They lent each other farm tools, harvested each other's fields, bartered goods, and raised their neighbors' barns and husked their corn. Little cash exchanged hands, in large part because money was in short supply. Still, New England farmers often kept elaborate account books in which they recorded what they owed and were owed (without assigning monetary value), whereas most farmers in the South rejected such formalities and simply made mental notes of debts. In both regions, years might pass without debts being repaid, and when they were, they were not always repaid directly. A farmer who owed a neighbor two days' labor might bring the local storekeeper his eggs, to be credited to the neighbor's account.

Many farmers engaged simultaneously in this local economy and in long-distance trade. In the local economy—where they exchanged goods with people whom they knew—a system of "just price" prevailed, in which neighbors calculated value in terms of how much labor was involved in producing a good or providing a service. When the same farmers engaged in long-distance trade—when they sold their goods to merchants who resold it to other merchants before the goods eventually traveled as far away as coastal cities or even Europe—they set prices based on what the market would bear. In the long-distance market, credit and debt were reckoned in monetary value.

Preindustrial Artisans

Farmers who lived near towns or villages often purchased crafted goods from local cobblers, saddlers, black- smiths, gunsmiths, silversmiths, and tailors. Most artisans, though, lived in the nation's seaports, where master craftsmen (independent businessmen who owned their own shops and tools) oversaw workshops that employed apprentices and journeymen. Although the vast majority of craftsmen, North and South, were white, free blacks were well represented in some cities' urban trades, such as tailoring and carpentry in Charleston, South Carolina. Teenage apprentices lived with their masters, who taught them a craft, lodged and fed them, and offered parental oversight in exchange for labor. The master's wife, assisted by her daughters, cooked, cleaned, and sewed for her husband's workers. The relationship between a master craftsmen and his workers was often familial in nature, if not always harmonious. When the term of their apprenticeship expired, apprentices became journeymen who earned wages, usually with an eye toward saving money to open their own shops. The workplace had little division of labor or specialization. A tailor measured, designed, and sewed an entire suit; a cobbler did the same with shoes.

Although separating flax fibers from their woody base could be arduous work, flax-scutching bees—much like corn-husking bees—brought together neighbors for frivolity as well as work. (National Gallery of Art, Washington, D.C. Gift of Edgar William and Bernice Chrysler Garbisch)

Men, women, and children worked long days on farms and in workshops, but the pace of work was generally uneven and unregimented. During busy periods, they worked dawn to dusk; the pace of work slowed after the harvest or after a large order had been completed. Market and court days were as much about exchanging gossip and offering toasts as exchanging goods and watching justice unfold. Husking bees and barn raisings brought people together to shuck corn and raise buildings, but also to eat, drink, dance, and flirt. Busy periods did not stop artisans from punctuating the day with grog breaks or from taking turns reading the newspaper aloud; they might even close their shops entirely to attend a political meeting. Nor did each workday adhere to a rigid schedule; journeymen craftsmen often staggered in late on Monday mornings, if they showed up at all, after a long night of carousing on their day off. Although the master craftsman remained the boss, his workers exerted a good deal of influence over the workplace.

Early Industrialization

By the War of 1812, these preindustrial habits had already changed, more noticeably in some places than in others. Early industry in the United States reorganized daily work routines and market relationships. Women and children had long made the clothing, hats, soap, candles, and other goods on which their families relied for their daily existence. In the late eighteenth and early nineteenth centuries, a "putting-out" system—similar to one that existed in parts of western Europe—began to develop in the Northeast, particularly in Massachusetts, New Jersey, and Pennsylvania. Women and children continued to produce goods as they always had but now did so in much greater quantities and for the consumption of people beyond their own families and communities. A merchant supplied them with raw materials, paid them a wage (usually a price for each piece they produced), and sold their wares in distant markets, pocketing the profit for himself. "Outwork," as it is sometimes called, appealed to women eager to earn cash, whether to secure some economic independence or to save money for additional land on which their children could set up their own farms. Particularly in New England—where population density, small farms, and tired soil conspired to constrict farming opportunities and thus to create a surplus labor pool—the putting-out system provided opportunities to earn money with which to buy cheaper, more fertile western lands without requiring that family members seek employment away from home.

The earliest factories grew up in tandem with the putting-out system. When Samuel Slater helped set up the first American water-powered spinning mill in Rhode Island in 1790—using children to card and spin raw cotton into thread—he sent the spun thread to nearby farm families who wove it into cloth before sending it back to Slater, from whom they received a wage. Early shoe factories relied on a similar system: factory workers cut cowhide into uppers and bottoms that were sent to rural homes. There, women sewed the uppers while men lasted (or shaped) and pegged the bottoms, a process that also sometimes took place in small workshops. The change was subtle but significant: although the work remained familiar, women now operated their looms for wages and produced cloth for the market, not primarily for their families, while male cobblers made shoes for feet that would never walk into their shops or homes.

THE TRANSPORTATION REVOLUTION

In order to market goods at substantial distances from where they were produced, internal improvements were needed. Before the War of 1812, natural waterways provided the most readily available and cheapest transportation routes for people and goods, but their limitations were readily apparent. Boatmen poled bateaux (cargo boats) down shallow rivers or floated flatboats down deep ones. Cargo generally moved in one direction only—downstream—and most boats were broken up for lumber once they reached their destination. On portions of a few rivers, including the Mississippi and the Hudson, sailing ships could tack their way upstream under the right wind conditions, but upstream commerce was very limited.

Roads

Overland transport was limited, too. Although some roads had been built during the colonial and revolutionary eras, they often became obstructed by fallen trees, soaked by mud, or clouded in dust. To reduce mud and dust, some turnpike companies built "corduroy" roads, whose tightly lined-up logs resembled the ribbed cotton fabric. But passengers complained of nausea from being continually jolted, and merchants remained wary of transporting fragile wares by wagon. Land transportation was slow and expensive, demanding a good deal of human and animal power. In 1800, according to a report commissioned by the federal government, it cost as much to ship a ton of goods 30 miles into the country's interior as to ship the same goods from New York to England. The lack of cheap, quick transportation impeded the westward expansion of the population as well as industrial growth. Fed up with the frigid winters in upstate New York, the Archbald family considered moving to Ohio in 1810 but decided against it because, as Mary Ann Archbald explained, "it is at a great distance from markets."

After the American Revolution, some northern states chartered private stock companies to build turnpikes (toll roads). These roads expanded commercial possibilities in southern New England and the Middle Atlantic, but during the War of 1812 the nation's lack of a road system in its more northerly and southerly reaches impeded the movement of troops and supplies, prompting renewed interest—in the name of defense—in building roads. Aside from the National Road, the financing fell on the states and private investors, and generally the enthusiasm for building turnpikes greatly outpaced the money and manpower expended. The new turnpike companies that emerged did sometimes adopt improvements, such as laying hard surfaces made of crushed stone and gravel, but many of the newly built roads suffered from the old problems. With natural water routes unpredictable and roads predictably bad, an urgent need arose not just for more, but also for better transportation.

Steamboats

The first major innovation was the steamboat. In 1807 Robert Fulton's *Clermont* traveled between New York and Albany on the Hudson River in thirty-two hours, demonstrating the feasibility of using steam engines to power boats. After the Supreme Court's 1814 ruling against steamboat monopolies in *Gibbons v. Ogden* (1824), steamboat companies flourished on eastern rivers and, to a lesser extent, on the Great Lakes. These boats carried more passengers than freight, transporting settlers to the Midwest, where they would grow grain and raise pigs that fed northeastern factory workers. Along western rivers like the Mississippi and the Ohio, steamboats played a more direct commercial role, carrying midwestern timber and grain, and southern cotton, to New Orleans, where they were transferred to ocean-going vessels destined for northern and international ports. In the 1850s, steamboats began plying rivers as far west as California and Washington Territory. Steamboats were privately owned and operated but became subject to federal regulations after frequent and deadly accidents in which boilers exploded, fires ignited, and boats collided.

To travel between Ohio and New Orleans by flatboat in 1815 took several months; in 1840 the same trip by steamboat took just ten days. But the steamboat did not supplant the flatboat. Rather, the number of flatboats traveling downstream to New Orleans more than doubled between 1816 and 1846. Now that flatboat crews could return upstream by steamboat rather than by foot, the greatest investment in flatboat travel—time—had been greatly reduced.

Canals

In the late eighteenth and early nineteenth centuries, private companies (sometimes with state subsidies) built small canals to transport goods and produce to and from interior locations previously accessible only by difficult-to-navigate rivers or by poorly maintained roads. These projects rarely reaped the substantial profits for which investors hoped, making it difficult to court investors for other projects. In 1815 only three canals in the United States measured more than 2 miles long; the longest was 27 miles. After Madison's veto of the Bonus Bill dashed commercially minded New Yorkers' hopes for a canal connecting Lake Erie to the port of New York, Governor DeWitt Clinton pushed hard and successfully for a state-sponsored initiative. What later became known as the Erie Canal was to run 363 miles between Buffalo and Albany, and was to be 4 feet deep. Skeptics derided it as "Clinton's Big Ditch."

But the optimists prevailed. Construction began—amid much symbolism and fanfare—on July 4, 1817. The canal, its promoters emphasized, would help the nation fulfill its revolutionary promises. It would demonstrate how American ingenuity and hard work could overcome any obstacle, including imposing natural ones, such as the combined ascent and descent of 680 feet between Buffalo and Albany. By so doing, it would help unify the nation and secure its commercial independence from Europe.

Over the next eight years, nearly nine thousand laborers felled forests, shoveled and piled dirt, picked at tree roots, blasted rock, heaved and hauled boulders, rechanneled streams, and molded the canal bed. Stonemasons and carpenters built aqueducts and locks. The work was dangerous. Much of it took place in malaria- and rattlesnake-infested swamps. Where the landscape was rock-solid, gunpowder explosions blew up some workers along with the rock. Collapsing canal beds smothered yet others, while some fell to their death from aqueducts and locks.

The canal's promoters celebrated the waterway as the work of "republican free men," a tribute to the nation's republican heritage. But few of those involved in the canal's construction would have perceived their work as fulfilling Jefferson's notion of republican freedom. Although farmers and artisans provided important labor, unskilled laborers—including many immigrants and some convicts—outnumbered them. Once completed, the Erie Canal relied heavily on the labor of children. Boys led the horses who pulled the canal boats between the canal's eighty-three locks, while girls cooked and cleaned on the boats. When the canal froze shut during winter, many canal workers found themselves with neither employment nor shelter. Some tried, successfully, to get themselves imprisoned as vagrants; many of the rest experienced destitution.

After its completion in November 1825, the Erie Canal became an immediate commercial success. Horse-drawn boats, stacked high with bushels of wheat, barrels of oats, and piles of logs, streamed steadily eastward from western New York and Buffalo, where shipments from ports all around Lake Erie were transferred to canal boat. Tens of thousands of passengers—forty thousand in 1825 alone—traveled on the new waterway each year. The canal shortened the journey between Buffalo and New York City from twenty to six days and reduced freight charges by nearly 95 percent—thus securing New York City's position as the nation's preeminent port. Goods that previously had not been readily available in the nation's interior now could be had easily and cheaply. Home production of cloth, for example, fell sharply after canal boats began carrying factory-made fabric from the eastern seaboard to central New York.

Other states rushed to construct their own canals. By 1840 canals crisscrossed the Northeast and Midwest, and total canal mileage reached 3,300. Many fewer canals were dug in the South, where the region's easily navigable rivers made them less necessary. None of the new canals, North or South, enjoyed the Erie's financial success. As the high cost of construction combined with an economic contraction, investment in canals slumped in the 1830s. Several midwestern states could not repay their canal loans, leading them to bankruptcy or near-bankruptcy. By mid-century more miles were abandoned than built. The canal era had ended, though the Erie Canal (by then twice enlarged and rerouted) continued to prosper and remained in commercial operation until the late twentieth century.

Railroads

The future belonged to railroads. Trains moved faster than canal boats and could operate year-round. Unlike canals, railroads did not need to be built near natural sources of water and could therefore connect even the most remote locations to national and international markets. The "improvement" in travel and shipping made possible by the expansion of railroads, noted the editor of the *American Farmer* in 1839, is "truly astonishing." By 1860 the United States had 60,000 miles of track, most of it in the North, and railroads had dramatically reduced the cost and the time involved in shipping goods by land—and they had excited the popular imagination in the process.

The railroad era in the United States began in 1830 when Peter Cooper's locomotive, Tom Thumb, first steamed along 13 miles of Baltimore & Ohio Railroad track. In 1833 the nation's second railroad ran 136 miles from Charleston to Hamburg in South Carolina. Not until the 1850s, though, did railroads offer long-distance service at reasonable rates. Even then, the lack of a common standard for the width of track thwarted development of a national system. Pennsylvania and Ohio railroads, for example, had no fewer than seven different track widths. A journey from Philadelphia to Charleston involved eight different gauges, which meant that passengers and freight had to change trains seven times. Only at Bowling Green, Kentucky, did northern and southern railroads connect to one another. Although northerners and southerners alike raced to construct internal improvements, the nation's canals and railroads did little to unite the regions and promote nationalism, as the earliest proponents of government-sponsored internal improvements had hoped.

Government Promotion of Internal Improvements

Northern state and local governments and private investors spent substantially more on internal improvements than did southerners. Pennsylvania and New York together accounted for half of all state monies invested. Southern states did invest in railroads, but—with smaller free populations—they collected fewer taxes, leaving them with less to spend.

For capitalists seeking dividends, southern railroads often seemed a poor bet. To be both profitable for investors and affordable for shippers, trains could not ship only one way; if they took agricultural products to market, their cars had to be filled with manufactured or finished goods for the return trip. But slaves and cash-strapped farmers did not provide much of a consumer base. Although planters did buy northern ready-made clothes and shoes for their slaves, such purchases—made on an annual basis— did not constitute a regular source of incoming freight. Because the wealthiest men lived along rivers and could send their cotton to market on steamboats, they sometimes saw little need for railroads. Many continued to reinvest in land and slaves, believing them a surer bet than risky railroad ventures.

The North and South laid roughly the same amount of railroad track per person before the Civil War, but when measured in terms of overall mileage, the more populous North had a web of tracks that stretched considerably farther, forming an integrated system of local lines branching off major trunk lines. In the South, though, railroads remained local in nature. Southern travelers had to patch together trips that involved railroads, stagecoaches, and boats. Neither people nor goods moved easily across the South, unless they traveled via steamboat or flatboat along the Mississippi River system—and even then, flooded banks disrupted passage for weeks at a time.

Regional Connections

Unlike southern investments in river improvements and steamboats, which disproportionately benefited the planters whose lands bordered the region's riverbanks, the North's frenzy of canal and railroad building expanded transportation networks far into the hinterlands, proving not only more democratic but also more unifying. In 1815 nearly all the produce from the Old Northwest floated down the Mississippi to New Orleans, tying that region's fortunes to the South. By the 1850s, though, canals and railroads had strengthened the economic, cultural, and political links between the Old Northwest—particularly the more densely populated northern regions—and the Northeast.

Internal improvements hastened the population's westward migration. They eased the journey itself while also making western settlement more appealing by providing easy access to eastern markets and the comforts of home. News, visitors, and luxuries now traveled regularly to previously remote areas of the Northeast and Midwest. Delighted that the Erie Canal made fresh seafood available in central New York, hundreds of miles from the sea, Mary Archbald explained that "distance . . . is reduced to nothing here."

With Samuel F. B. Morse's invention of the telegraph in 1844, the compression of distance and time became even starker. News traveled almost instantaneously along telegraph wires. By 1852 more than 23,000 miles of lines had been strung across the nation. With time reduced to "nothing," the telegraph made possible the birth of modern business practices involving the coordination of market conditions, production, and supply across great distances. Together, internal improvements and the telegraph allowed people in previously isolated areas to proclaim themselves—as did one western New Yorker—a "citizen of the world."

Ambivalence Toward Progress

Many northerners hailed internal improvements as symbols of progress. One New York farmer likened the construction of the Erie Canal to "building castles in the air." Northerners proclaimed that, by building canals and railroads, they had completed God's design for the North American continent. On a more practical level, canals and railroads would allow them to seek better opportunities for themselves and their children in the West.

But people who welcomed such opportunities could find much to lament. Mary Ann Archbald savored her fresh seafood dinners but regretted that her sons turned to speculation. Others decried the presence of enormous numbers of Irish canal diggers and railroad track layers, whom they deemed depraved and racially inferior. Still others worried that, by promoting urban growth, transportation innovations fostered social ills.

The degradation of the natural world proved worrisome, too. When streams were rerouted, swamps drained, and forests felled, natural habitats were disturbed, even destroyed. Humans soon felt the consequences. Deprived of water power, mills no longer ran. Without forests to sustain them, wild animals—on which many rural people (Native American and European American) had relied for protein—sought homes elsewhere. Fishermen, too, found their sources of protein (and cash) dried up when natural waterways were dammed or rerouted to feed canals. If many northerners embraced progress, they also regretted its costs.

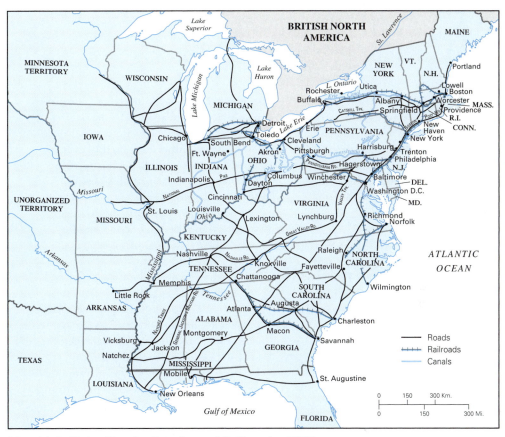

MAP 11.1 Major Roads, Canals, and Railroads, 1850

A transportation network linked the seaboard to the interior. Settlers followed those routes westward, and they sent back grain, grain products, and cotton to the port cities.

FACTORIES AND INDUSTRIALIZATION

By dramatically lowering transportation costs, internal improvements made possible the Northeast's rapid manufacturing and commercial expansion. After canals and railroads opened up the trans-Appalachian West for wide-scale settlement, western farmers supplied raw materials and foodstuffs for northeastern factories and their workers. They also created a larger domestic market for goods manufactured in the Northeast. With most of their time devoted to cultivating their lands, western settlers preferred to buy rather than make cloth, shoes, and other goods. They needed northeastern iron, too—for farm implements (plows, pitchforks, scythes), for nails (to build houses and other buildings, particularly in the Midwest's rapidly burgeoning cities), and for railroad tracks.

One of the oldest industries in North America, iron production was centered in the Middle Atlantic states, especially Pennsylvania, but stretched as far south as Richmond and as far north as Albany. Iron forges, which tended to be small enterprises, flourished

The United States as a Developing Nation

In the early nineteenth century, the United States was a "developing nation," as its economy slowly shifted from dependence on agriculture and raw materials to producing manufactured goods. In order to develop, the United States imported capital to finance international trade, internal improvements, and early factories.

American political and economic leaders in the early nineteenth century talked as if they were masters of their own fate. In many ways, however, the United States remained economically dependent on Great Britain. The political independence that the United States won in the Revolutionary War and affirmed in the War of 1812 was not matched in the economic sphere.

Following the War of 1812, Americans depended on Britain for capital investment: 90 percent of all U.S. foreign capital came from Britain, and around 60 percent of all British capital exports flowed to the United States. Americans used British capital to develop, first, the canals, then the railroads that facilitated American industrial development. For instance, from 1817 to 1825 the British invested $7 million in New York State bonds to finance the Erie Canal. Altogether, European investors provided 80 percent of the money to build the Erie.

The United States imported more goods than it exported. In other words, Americans consumed more than they produced. Imported capital balanced the trade deficit. As in most developing countries, exports were concentrated in agricultural commodities; 50 percent of the value of all exports was in cotton. And British credit financed cotton sales.

Workers near the entrance of the Erie Canal into the Hudson River prepare to ship agricultural products from western New York and the Midwest to the international port of New York.
(© Collection of the New-York Historical Society)

The United States as a Developing Nation

U.S. dependency on international capital was highlighted when imported capital was interrupted, as in the Panics of 1819 and 1837. Although these financial crises began in the United States, the hard times were exacerbated in both cases when British investors and creditors squeezed Americans. Economic crises in England led investors to pull out capital from the United States while merchants demanded that Americans pay what they owed to British creditors. Money became tight, and the economy declined.

Thus both economic development and hard times revealed the significance of international capital links to the United States, a developing nation.

wherever ore deposits lay and sources of fuel abounded. During the 1840s, ironworks, which previously heated their furnaces with charcoal, turned increasingly to coal and then steam. But production methods in iron making changed little, with smaller firms remaining more efficient than larger ones. Although the industry expanded, daily work stayed largely the same.

Factory Work   But in many other industries, daily life changed dramatically. Much early industrialization involved processing raw materials—milling flour, turning hogs into packaged meat, sawing lumber—and the pork-packing industry illustrates strikingly how specialization turned skilled craftsmen into laborers. Traditionally, each butcher cut up an entire pig. Under the new industrial organization, each worker was assigned a particular task—such as cutting off the right front leg or scooping out the entrails—as the pig made it way down a "disassembly line."

The impersonal nature and formal rules of factory work contrasted sharply with the informal atmosphere of artisan shops and farm households. The bell, the steam whistle, or the clock governed the flow of work. In large factories, laborers never saw owners, working instead under paid supervisors, nor did they see the final product of their labor. Factory workers lost their sense of autonomy as impersonal market forces seemed to dominate their lives. Their jobs were insecure, as competition—particularly from European immigrants, who arrived in enormous numbers starting in the 1840s—frequently led to layoffs and replacement by cheaper, less-skilled workers or children. Perhaps most demoralizing, opportunities for advancement in the new system were virtually nil.

Machinery made mass production possible in some industries. Although at first Americans imported machines or copied British designs, they soon built their own. The American System of manufacturing, as the British called it, used precision machinery to produce interchangeable parts that did not require individual adjustment to fit. Eli Whitney, the cotton gin's inventor, promoted the idea of interchangeable parts in 1798, when he contracted with the federal government to make ten thousand rifles in twenty-eight months. In the 1820s the United States Ordnance Department contracted with private firms to introduce machine-made interchangeable parts for firearms. The American System quickly spread beyond the arsenals, producing the machine-tool industry—the manufacture of machines for the purpose of mass production. With the time and skill involved in manufacturing greatly reduced, the new system permitted mass production at low costs: Waltham watches, Yale locks, and other goods became inexpensive but high-quality household items.

Textile Mills   In no industry was mechanization more dramatic than in textiles, whose production was centered in New England, near sources of water to power the spinning machines and looms. After 1815 the rudimentary cotton mills of New England developed into modern factories in which machines mass-produced goods. Cotton cloth production rose from 4 million yards in 1817 to 323 million in 1840. Mechanization did not make workers obsolete; rather, more workers were needed to monitor the machines. In the mid-1840s, the cotton mills employed approximately eighty thousand "operatives," more than half of them women. Mill owners employed a resident manager to run the mills, thus separating ownership from management. Workers received wages, and the cloth they produced was sold throughout the United States.

Unable to find enough laborers in the vicinity of their mills, managers recruited New England farm daughters, whom they paid wages and housed in dormitories and boarding houses in what became known as the Waltham or Lowell plan of industrialization. People who made their living off the land often harbored suspicions of those who did not—particularly in the young United States, where an agrarian lifestyle was often associated with virtue itself—so some rural parents hesitated to send their daughters to textile mills. To ease such concerns, mill owners offered paternalistic oversight to the mill girls; they enforced curfews, prohibited alcohol, and required church attendance. Despite its restrictions, the system in Waltham offered farm girls opportunities to socialize with women of the same age and to gain a sense of independence that came from living away from home and earning wages. Workers wrote literary pieces for the owner-subsidized *Lowell Offering* and attended educational lectures in the evenings.

Most women imagined their factory stints as temporary, and the conditions of the work itself—the deafening roar of the power looms, the long hours, the regimentation—made few change their minds. They nonetheless welcomed the social and cultural opportunities as well as the wages, which they used to help their families buy land or send a brother to college, to save for their own dowries or education, or to spend on personal items, such as fashionable clothing. The average girl arrived at sixteen and stayed only five years, usually leaving to get married—often to men they met in town rather than to farm boys at home. When they left the mills, other younger women took their places.

Although the Waltham plan drew international attention for its novelty, more common was the Rhode Island (or Fall River) plan employed by Samuel Slater, among others. Mills hired entire families, whom they lodged in company boarding houses. Men often worked farm plots around the factories while their wives and children worked in the mills, though as the system developed, men were more likely to work in the factories full-time, directly supervising the labor of their wives and children in small, family-based work units.

This young mill girl at Waltham or Lowell, probably in the late 1840s, posed for an early daguerreotype. Her swollen and rough hands contrast with her youth, neat dress, and carefully tied, beribboned hair. Her hands suggest that she worked, as did most twelve- and thirteen-year-olds, as a warper, straightening the strands of cotton or wool as they entered the looms. (Courtesy of Jack Naylor)

Labor Protests   Life in the textile mills got harder over time, especially during the depression of 1837 to 1843, when demand for cloth declined and most mills ran only part-time. To increase productivity, managers sped up the machines and required each worker to operate more machines. Between 1836 and 1850 the number of spindles and looms in Lowell increased 150 and 140 percent, respectively, whereas the number of workers increased by only 50 percent. In the race for profits, owners lengthened hours, cut wages, tightened discipline, and packed the boarding houses.

Workers organized, accusing their bosses of treating them like wage slaves. In 1834, in reaction to a 25 percent wage cut, they unsuccessfully "turned out" (struck) against the Lowell mills. Two years later, when boarding house fees increased, they turned out again. As conditions continued to worsen and as strikes continued to fail, workers resisted in new ways. In 1844 Massachusetts mill women formed the Lowell Female Reform Association and joined forces with other workers to press, without success, for state legislation mandating a ten-hour day—as opposed to the fourteen-hour days that some workers endured.

Women aired their complaints in worker-run newspapers: in 1842, the *Factory Girl* appeared in New Hampshire, the *Wampanoag and Operatives' Journal* in Massachusetts. Two years later, mill workers founded the *Factory Girl's Garland* and the *Voice of Industry,* nicknamed "the factory girl's voice." Even the *Lowell Offering,* the owner-sponsored paper that was the pride of mill workers and managers alike, became embroiled in controversy when workers charged that its editors had suppressed articles criticizing working conditions.

The women's organizational efforts were weakened by worker turnover. Few militant native-born mill workers stayed on to fight the managers and owners, and gradually, fewer New England daughters entered the mills. In the 1850s, Irish immigrant women replaced them. Technological improvements in the looms and other machinery had made the work less skilled and more routine. The mills could thus pay lower wages and draw from a reservoir of unskilled labor.

Male workers, too, protested the changes wrought by the market economy and factories. But, unlike women, they could vote. Labor political parties first formed in Pennsylvania, New York, and Massachusetts in the 1820s, and then spread elsewhere; they advocated free public education and an end to imprisonment for debt, and opposed banks and monopolies. Some advocated for free homesteads, a reminder that most early industrial workers still aspired to land ownership.

Labor Unions Organized labor's greatest achievement came through the courts, with protection from conspiracy laws. When journeyman shoemakers organized during the first decade of the century, their employers accused them of criminal conspiracy. The cordwainers' (shoemakers') cases between 1806 and 1815 left labor organizations in an uncertain position. Although the courts acknowledged the journeymen's right to organize, judges viewed strikes as illegal until a Massachusetts case, *Commonwealth v. Hunt* (1842), ruled that Boston journeyman bootmakers could strike "in such manner as best to subserve their own interests."

The first unions arose among urban journeymen in printing, woodworking, shoemaking, and tailoring. They tended to be local; the strongest resembled medieval guilds, in that members sought protection against competition from inferior workmen by regulating apprenticeships and establishing minimum wages. Umbrella organizations composed of individual craft unions, like the National Trade Union (1834), arose in several cities in the 1820s and 1830s. But the movement fell apart amid wage reductions and unemployment in the hard times of 1839–1843.

Workers found permanent labor organizations difficult to sustain. Skilled craftsmen looked down on unskilled and semiskilled workers. Moreover, workers divided along ethnic, religious, racial, and gender lines.

CONSUMPTION AND COMMERCIALIZATION

By producing inexpensive cloth, the New England mills spawned the ready-made clothing industry. Before the 1820s, women sewed most clothing at home, and some people purchased used clothing. Tailors and seamstresses made wealthy men's and women's clothing to order. By the 1820s and 1830s, much clothing was mass-produced for sale in retail clothing stores. The process often involved little more than the reorganization of work; instead of a tailor's performing every task in the process of making an article of clothing—from measuring to finishing work—the process was now divided. Measuring was replaced by standard sizes, and efficiency was created by a division of labor. One worker cut patterns all day, another sewed hems, another affixed buttons, still another attached collars. The invention of the sewing machine in 1846 sped the process along, especially after it became widely available in the 1850s.

Many farm families continued to make their own clothing, but when they could afford to do so, they often bought their clothes, creating more time for raising both crops and children.

The Garment Industry

Market expansion created a demand for mass-produced clothing. Rural girls who left farms for factories no longer had time to sew clothes. Young immigrant men—often separated by thousands of miles from mothers and sisters—had to buy the crudely made, loose-fitting clothing. But the biggest market for ready-made clothes, at least initially, was in the cotton South. With the success of the textile industry driving up the demand and price for raw cotton, planters in the cotton kingdom bought ready-made shoes and clothes for slaves, in whose hands they would rather place a hoe than a needle and thread. Doing so made good economic sense.

Retailers often bought goods wholesale, though many manufactured shirts and trousers in their own factories. Lewis and Hanford of New York City boasted of cutting more than 100,000 garments in the winter of 1848–1849. The New York firm did business mostly in the South and owned its own retail outlet in New Orleans. Paul Tulane, a New Orleans competitor, owned a New York factory that made goods for his Louisiana store. In the Midwest, Cincinnati became the center of the new men's clothing industry. But although southerners and westerners became involved in the clothing trade, its center remained in New York.

Specialization of Commerce

Commerce expanded with manufacturing. Commercial specialization transformed some traders in big cities, especially New York, into virtual merchant princes. After the Erie Canal opened, New York City became a stop on every major trade route from Europe, southern ports, and the West. New York traders were the intermediaries for southern cotton and western grain. Merchants in other cities played a similar role. Traders in turn sometimes invested their profits in factories, further stimulating urban manufacturing. Some cities specialized: Rochester became a milling center ("The Flour City"), and Cincinnati ("Porkopolis") became the first meatpacking center.

Merchants who engaged in complex commercial transactions required large office staffs, mostly all male. At the bottom of the hierarchy were messenger boys, often preteens, who delivered documents. Above them were copyists, on high stools, who hand-copied documents. Clerks processed documents and shipping papers, and did translations. Above them were the bookkeeper and the confidential chief clerk. Those seeking employment in such an office, called a countinghouse, often took a course from a writing master to acquire a "good hand." All hoped to rise someday to the status of partner, although their chances of doing so grew increasingly slim.

The specialization of commerce came more quickly to cities than to small towns, where merchants continued to exchange some goods with local farm women—trading flour or pots and pans for eggs and other produce. Local craftsmen continued to sell their own finished goods, such as shoes and clothing. In some rural areas, particularly newly settled ones, peddlers acted as general merchants. But as transportation improved and towns grew, small-town merchants also began to specialize.

Commercial Farming

Even amid the boom in manufacturing and commerce, agriculture remained the backbone of the nation's economy, North and South. But the expansion of southern cotton production in the Southwest did little to bring about economic change in other parts of the South; instead, profitable farmers reinvested their capital in the slave economy, and poorer farmers continued to farm much as they had before. In the North, by contrast, the transportation revolution and market expansion transformed formerly semisubsistence farms into commercial enterprises. Many families stopped practicing mixed agriculture and began to specialize in cash crops. Although most northerners continued to farm on the eve of the Civil War, their daily lives and relationships often looked very different from those of their parents and grandparents.

By the 1820s, eastern farmers had cultivated nearly all the land available to them, and small farms and their uneven terrains did not lend themselves to the new labor-saving farm implements introduced in the 1830s, such as mechanical sowers, reapers, and threshers. As a result, many northern farmers either moved west or gave up farming for jobs in merchants' houses and factories. Those farmers who remained, however, proved as adaptable on the farm as were their children working at water-powered looms or in countinghouses, their efforts encouraged by state governments that energetically promoted agricultural innovation. Massachusetts in 1817 and New York in 1819 began to subsidize agricultural prizes and county fairs. To spread innovation, New York published the winners' essays about how they grew their prize crops.

In 1820 about one-third of all northern produce was intended for the market, but by 1850 the amount surpassed 50 percent. As farmers shifted toward specialization and market-oriented production, they often invested in additional land (buying the farms of neighbors who moved west), new farming equipment (such as improved iron and steel plows), and new sources of labor (hired hands). Many New England and Middle Atlantic farm families faced steep competition from midwestern farmers after the opening of the Erie Canal and began abandoning the production of wheat and corn. Instead, they raised livestock, especially cattle, and specialized in vegetable and fruit production. Much of what they produced ended up in the stomachs of the North's rapidly growing urban and manufacturing populations.

Farmers financed innovations through land sales and debts. Indeed, increasing land values, not the sale of agricultural products, promised the greatest profit. Farm families who owned their own land flourished, but it became harder to take up farming in the first place. By the 1840s it took more than ten years for a rural laborer in the Northeast to save enough money to buy a farm. The number of tenant farmers and hired hands increased, and provided labor to drive commercial expansion. Farmers who had previously relied mostly on the labor of unpaid family members and enslaved workers now leased portions of their farms or hired waged labor to help raise their livestock and crops.

Farm Women's Changing Labor

As the commercial economy expanded, rural women took on additional responsibilities that added to their already substantial farm and domestic chores. Some took in outwork. Many increased their production of eggs, dairy products, and garden produce for sale; others raised bees or silkworms.

With the New England textile mills producing more and more finished cloth, farm women and children often abandoned time-consuming spinning and weaving, bought factory-produced cloth, and dedicated the saved time to producing additional products, such as butter and cheese, for the market. Women had always made butter and cheese; now they produced it in large quantities with intentions of profiting from its sale. Some mixed-agriculture farms converted entirely to dairy production, with men taking over formerly female tasks. Canals and railroads carried cheese to eastern ports, where wholesalers sold it around the world, shipping it to California, England, and China. In 1844 Britain imported more than 5 million pounds of cheese from the United States.

Rural Communities Although agricultural journals and societies exhorted farmers to manage their farms like time-efficient businesses, not all farmers abandoned the old practices of gathering at market, general stores, taverns, and church. They did not forgo barn raisings and husking bees, but by the 1830s there were fewer young people at such events to dance and flirt. Many young women had gone to work in textile mills, and young men often worked as clerks or factory hands. Those who stayed behind were more likely to come dressed in store-bought clothing and to consume pies made with store-bought flour.

Even as they continued to swap labor and socialize with neighbors, farmers became more likely to reckon debts in dollars. They kept tighter accounts and watched national and international markets more closely. When financial panics hit, shortages of cash almost halted business activity, casting many farmers further into debt, not infrequently to the point of bankruptcy. Faced with the possibility of losing their land, farmers did what many would have considered unthinkable before: they called in debts with their neighbors, sometimes causing fissures in long-established relationships.

Cycles of Boom and Bust The expansion of the market economy led to a cycle of booms and busts. Prosperity stimulated demand for finished goods, such as clothing and furniture. Increased demand in turn led not only to higher prices and still higher production, but also, because of business optimism and expectation of higher prices, to speculation in land. Investment money was plentiful as Americans saved and foreign, mostly British, investors bought U.S. bonds and securities. Then production surpassed demand, causing prices and wages to fall; in response, land and stock values collapsed, and investment money flowed out of the United States. This boom-and-bust cycle influenced every corner of the country, but particularly the Northeast, where even the smallest localities became enmeshed in regional and national markets.

Although the 1820s and 1830s were boom times, financial panic triggered a bust cycle in 1837, the year after the Second Bank of the United States closed. Economic contraction remained severe through 1843. Internal savings and foreign investments declined sharply. Many banks could not repay their depositors, and states, facing deficits because of the decline in the economy, defaulted on their bonds. European, especially British, investors became suspicious of all U.S. loans and withdrew money from the United States.

Hard times had come. Philadelphia took on an eerie aura. "The streets seemed deserted," Sidney George Fisher observed in 1842. "The largest [merchant] houses are shut up and to rent, there is no business . . . no money, no confidence." New York countinghouses closed their doors. Former New York mayor Philip Hone later observed, "a deadly calm pervades this lately flourishing city. No goods are selling, no businesses stirring." The hungry formed bread lines in front of soup societies, and beggars crowded the sidewalks. Some workers looted. Crowds of laborers demanding their deposits gathered at closed banks. Sheriffs sold seized property at one-quarter of pre-hard-time prices. In smaller cities like Lynn, Massachusetts, shoemakers weathered the hard times by fishing and tending gardens, while laborers became scavengers, digging for clams and harvesting dandelions. Once-prosperous businessmen—some victims of the market, others of their own recklessness—lost nearly everything, prompting Congress to pass the Federal Bankruptcy Law of 1841; by the time the law was repealed two years later, 41,000 bankrupts had sought protection under its provisions.

FAMILIES IN FLUX

Anxieties about economic fluctuations reverberated beyond factories and counting-houses into northern homes. Sweeping changes in the household economy, rural as well as urban, led to new ideals of the family. In the preindustrial era, families had been primarily economic units; now they became a moral and cultural institution, though in reality few families could live up to the new ideal.

The "Ideal" Family In the North, the market economy increasingly separated the home from the workplace, leading to a new middle-class ideal in which men functioned in the public sphere, while women oversaw the private or domestic sphere. The home became, in theory, an emotional retreat from the competitive, selfish world of business, where men increasingly focused on their work, equally eager to prosper and fearful of failure in the unpredictable market economy. At the home's center was a couple that married for love rather than for economic convenience or advantage. Men provided and protected, while women nurtured and guarded the family's morality, making sure that the excesses of the capitalist world did not invade the private sphere. Childhood became focused more on education than on work, and the definition of childhood itself expanded: children were to remain at home until their late teens or early twenties. This ideal came to be known as separate-sphere ideology, or sometimes the cult of domesticity or the cult of true womanhood. Although it rigidly separated the male and female spheres, this ideology gave new standing to domestic responsibilities. In her widely read *Treatise on Domestic Economy* (1841), Catharine Beecher approached housekeeping as a science even as she trumpeted mothers' role as their family's moral guardian. Although Beecher advocated the employment of young, single women as teachers, she believed that, once married, women belonged in the home. She maintained that women's natural superiority as moral, nurturing caregivers made them especially suited for teaching (when single) and parenting (once married). Although Beecher saw the public sphere as a male domain, she insisted that the private sphere be elevated to the same status as the public.

Shrinking Families These new domestic ideals depended on smaller families in which parents, particularly mothers, could give children more attention, better education, and more financial help. With the market economy, parents could afford to have fewer children because children no longer played a vital economic role. Urban families produced fewer household goods, and commercial farmers, unlike self-sufficient ones, did not need large numbers of workers year-round, turning instead to hired laborers during peak work periods. Although smaller families resulted in part from first marriages' taking place at a later age—shortening the period of potential childbearing—they also resulted from planning, made easier when cheap rubber condoms became available in the 1850s. Some women chose, too, to end accidental pregnancies with abortion.

In 1800 American women bore seven or eight children; by 1860 the figure had dropped to five or six. This decline occurred even though many immigrants with large-family traditions were settling in the United States; thus the birth rate among native-born women declined even more sharply. Although rural families remained larger than urban ones, birth rates among both groups declined comparably.

Yet, even as birth rates fell, few northern women could fulfill the middle-class ideal of separate spheres. Most wage-earning women provided essential income for their families and could not stay home. They often saw domestic ideals as oppressive, as middle-class reformers mistook poverty for immorality, condemning working mothers for letting their children work or scavenge rather than attend school. Although most middle-class women could stay home, new standards of cleanliness and comfort weighed heavily on their time. These women's contributions to their families were generally assessed in moral terms, even though their economic contributions were significant. When they worked inside their homes, they provided, without remuneration, the labor for which wealthier women paid when they hired domestic servants to perform daily chores. Without servants, moreover, women could not devote themselves primarily to their children's upbringing, placing the ideals of the cult of domesticity beyond the reach of even many middle-class families.

Women's Paid Labor

In working-class families, women left their parental home as early as age twelve, earning wages most of their life, with only short respites for bearing and rearing children. Unmarried girls and women worked primarily as domestic servants or in factories; married and widowed women worked as laundresses, seamstresses, and cooks. Some hawked food and wares on city streets; other did piecework at home, earning wages in the putting-out system; and some became prostitutes. Few of these occupations enabled women to support themselves or a family at a comfortable level.

Middle-class Americans sought to keep women closer to home. If young girls left the home to work—in New England's textile mills, in new urban stores as clerks—it was only for a brief interval before marriage. Otherwise, teaching was the only occupation consistent with genteel notions of femininity. In 1823 the Beecher sisters, Catharine and Mary, established the Hartford Female Seminary and offered history and science in addition to the traditional women's curriculum of domestic arts and religion. A decade later, Catharine Beecher successfully campaigned for teacher-training schools for women. She argued in part for women's moral superiority and in part for their economic value; because these women would be single, she contended, they did not need to earn as much as their male counterparts, whom she presumed to be married, though not all were. Unmarried women earned about half the salary of male teachers. By 1850 schoolteaching had become a woman's profession. Many women worked for a time as teachers, usually for two to five years.

The proportion of single women in the population increased significantly in the nineteenth century. In the East, some single women would have preferred to marry but found market and geographic expansion working against them: more and more young men headed west in search of opportunity, leaving some eastern communities with a disproportionate number of young women. But other women chose to remain independent, hoping to take advantage of opportunities opened by the market economy and urban expansion. Because women's work was generally poorly paid, those who forswore marriage and a family faced serious challenges, and many single women found it difficult to support themselves without charitable or family assistance.

THE GROWTH OF CITIES

To many contemporary observers, cities came to symbolize what market expansion had wrought—for better or for worse—on northern society. No period in American history saw more rapid urbanization than the years between 1820 and 1860. The percentage of people living in urban areas (defined as a place with a population of 2,500 or more) grew from just over 7 percent in 1820 to nearly 20 percent in 1860. Most of this growth took place in the Northeast and the Midwest. Although most northerners continued to live on farms or in small villages, the population of individual cities boomed. Many of those residents were temporary—soon moving on to another city or the countryside— and many came from foreign shores.

Urban Boom   Even as new cities sprang up, existing cities saw a tremendous growth in their population (see Map 11.2). In 1820 the United States had 13 places with a population of 10,000 or more; in 1860 it had 93. New York City, already the nation's largest city in 1820, saw its population grow from 123,709 people in that year to 813,669 in 1860—a growth factor of six and a half times. Philadelphia, the nation's second-largest city in both 1820 and 1860, saw the size of its population multiply ninefold during that same forty-year period. In 1815 Rochester, New York, had a population of just 300 persons. By 1830, the Erie Canal had turned the sleepy agricultural town into a bustling manufacturing center; it was now the nation's twenty-fifth-largest city, with a population of just over 9,000. Its population continued to multiply at fantastic rates, even doubling in a single decade. By 1860 it had more than 50,000 residents.

Cities experienced geographic expansion as well as population growth. New York City, for example, had burst its boundaries by around 1830. Until then, New Yorkers could walk from one end of the city to the other in an hour. In 1825 Fourteenth Street was the city's northern boundary. By 1860, 400,000 people lived above that divide, and Forty-second Street was the city's northern limit. Gone were the cow pastures, kitchen gardens, and orchards. Public transit made city expansion possible. Horse-drawn omnibuses appeared in New York in 1827, and the Harlem Railroad, completed in 1832, ran the length of Manhattan. By the 1850s, all big cities had horse-drawn streetcars, allowing wealthier residents who could afford the fare to settle on larger plots of land on the cities' outskirts.

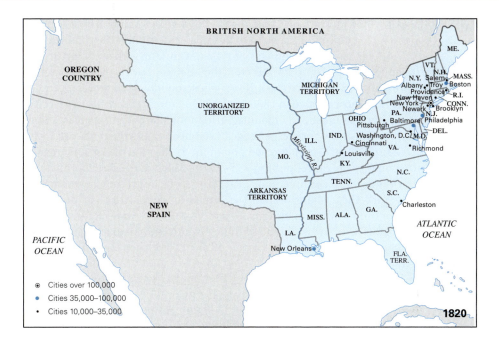

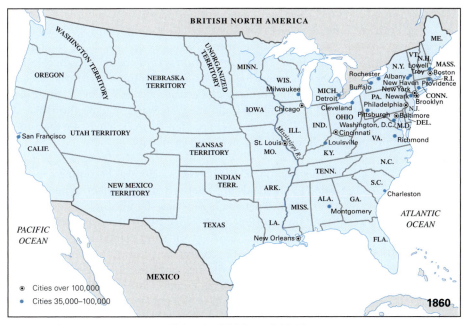

MAP 11.2 Major American Cities in 1820 and 1860

The number of Americans who lived in cities increased rapidly between 1820 and 1860, and the number of large cities grew as well. In 1820 only New York City had a population exceeding 100,000; forty years later, eight more cities had surpassed that level.

Market-Related Development Cities helped sustain the North's market revolution by serving as transportation hubs, commercial centers, and— in some cases— manufacturing sites. Some cities grew up with manufacturing. The Boston Manufacturing Company selected the site for Lowell, Massachusetts, because of its proximity to the Merrimack River, whose rapidly flowing waters could power their textile mill. Incorporated in 1826, by the 1850s it was the second-largest city in New England. Although most early manufacturing took place in rural areas, some commercial cities, such as New York, experienced what historians sometimes call metropolitan industrialization, a form that relied not on mechanization but on a reorganization of labor, similar to the earlier putting-out system. Much of the early production of ready-made clothing, for example, took place not in factories but in tenements throughout New York City, where women performed an urban form of outwork, spending hour after hour sewing on buttons for a piece of ready-made clothing, while others sewed hem after hem. In 1860, 25,000 women worked in manufacturing jobs in New York City, where they constituted a quarter of the waged labor force. Two-thirds of them worked in the garment industry.

The North urbanized more quickly than the South, but what was most striking about northern urbanization was where it took place. With only a few exceptions, southern cities were seaports, whereas the period between 1820 and 1860 saw the creation of many inland cities in the North—usually places that sprang to life with the creation of transportation lines or manufacturing establishments.

Northern cities developed elaborate systems of municipal services but lacked adequate taxing power to provide services for all. At best, they could tax property adjoining new sewers, paved streets, and water mains. New services and basic sanitation depended on residents' ability to pay. Another solution was to charter private companies to sell basic services, such as providing gas for lights. Baltimore first chartered a private gas company in 1816. By mid-century every major city was lit by a private gas supplier. Private firms lacked the capital to build adequate water systems, though, and they laid pipe only in commercial and well-to-do residential areas, bypassing the poor. The task of supplying water ultimately fell on city governments.

Extremes of Wealth Throughout the United States, wealth was becoming concentrated in the hands of a relatively small number of people. By 1860 the top 5 percent of American families owned more than half of the nation's wealth, and the top 10 percent owned nearly three-quarters. In the South, the extremes of wealth were most apparent on rural plantations, but in the North, cities provided the starkest evidence of economic inequities.

Despite the optimistic forecasts of early textile manufacturers that American industrialization need not engender the poverty and degradation associated with European industrialization, America's industrial cities soon resembled European ones. A number of factors contributed to widespread poverty: poor wages, the inability of many workers to secure full-time employment, and the increasingly widespread employment of women and children, which further drove down wage rates for everyone. Women and children, employers rationalized, did not need a living wage because they were—in the employers' way of thinking—dependent by nature, meaning that they could rely on men to support them and did not need to earn a wage that allowed self-sufficiency. In reality, though, not all women or children had men to support them, nor did men's wages always prove adequate to support a family comfortably.

New York provides a striking example of the extremes of wealth accompanying industrialization. Where workers lived, conditions were crowded, unhealthy, and dangerous. Houses built for two families often held four; tenements built for six families held twelve. Some of those families took in lodgers to pay the rent, adding to the unbearably crowded conditions that encouraged poorer New Yorkers to spend as much time as possible outdoors. But streets in poor neighborhoods were filthy. Excess sewage from outhouses drained into ditches that carried urine and fecal matter into the streets. People piled garbage into gutters or left it to accumulate in backyards or alleys. Pigs, geese, dogs, and vultures scavenged the streets, while enormous rats roamed under cities' wooden sidewalks and through large buildings. Disease thrived. Typhoid, dysentery, malaria, and tuberculosis regularly visited the poorer sections of cities. Epidemics of cholera struck in 1831, 1849, and again in 1866, claiming thousands of victims.

But within walking distance of poverty-stricken neighborhoods grew up neighborhoods that boasted lavish mansions, whose residents could escape to their country estates during the summer's brutal heat or during epidemics. Much of this wealth was inherited. For every John Jacob Astor, who became a millionaire in the western fur trade after beginning life in humble circumstances, ten others had inherited or married

This gouache, attributed to Nicholino Calyo, depicts the Haight family in their drawing room in 1848. Richard K. Haight was a wealthy New York City merchant, trading internationally, as the globe in the foreground suggests. Sarah Rogers Haight was a famous beauty and socialite, and the family's clothing, art, library, and furniture all stand in sharp contrast to the poverty, homelessness, and orphans found on the city's streets.
(Museum of the City of New York. Bequest of Elizabeth Cushing Iselin)

money. These rich New Yorkers were not idle, though; they worked at increasing their fortunes and power by investing in commerce and manufacturing.

Between the two extremes of wealth sat a distinct middle class, larger than the wealthy elite but substantially smaller than the working classes. They were businessmen, traders, and professionals, and the rapid turn toward industrialization and commercial specialization made them a much larger presence in northern cities than in southern ones. Middle-class families enjoyed new consumer items: wool carpeting, fine wallpaper, and rooms full of furniture replaced the bare floors, whitewashed walls, and relative sparseness of eighteenth-century homes. Houses were large, often having from four to six rooms. Middle-class children slept one to a bed, and by the 1840s and 1850s, middle-class families used indoor toilets that were mechanical, though not yet flushing. Middle-class families formed the backbone of urban clubs and societies, filled the family pews in church, and sent their sons to college. They were as distinct from the world of John Jacob Astor as they were from the milieu of the working class and the poor.

Immigration

Many of the urban poor were immigrants. The 5 million immigrants who came to the United States between 1830 and 1860 outnumbered the country's entire population in 1790. The vast majority were Europeans, primarily from Ireland and the German states (see Figure 11.1). During the peak period of pre-Civil War immigration (1847–1857), 3.3 million immigrants entered the United States, including 1.3 million Irish and 1.1 million Germans. By 1860, 15 percent of the white population was foreign-born, with 90 percent of immigrants living in northern states. Not all planned to stay permanently, and many, like the Irish, saw themselves as exiles from their homeland.

A combination of factors "pushed" Europeans from their homes and "pulled" them to the northern United States. In Ireland, the potato famine (1845–1850)—a period of widespread starvation caused by a diseased potato crop—drove millions from their homeland. Although economic conditions pushed most Germans as well, some were political refugees—liberals, freethinkers, Socialists, communists, and anarchists—who fled after the abortive revolutions of 1848. Europeans' awareness of the United States grew as employers, states, and shipping companies promoted opportunities across the Atlantic. Often the message was stark: work and prosper in America, where everyone could aspire to be an independent farmer, or starve in Europe. Although boosters promised immigrants a land of milk and honey, many soon became disillusioned, and hundreds of thousands returned home.

Many early immigrants lived or worked in rural areas. Like the Archbalds, a few settled immediately on farms and eventually bought land. Others, unable to afford even a modest down payment on a farm, worked as hired farm hands, canal diggers, or railroad track layers—often with the hope of buying land later. Pádraig Cúndún was among the lucky. The Irishman used his earnings as a canal laborer to buy land in western New York, proclaiming proudly in 1834 that "I have a fine farm of land now, which I own outright. No one can demand rent from me. My family and I can eat our fill of bread and meat, butter and milk any day we like throughout the year, so I think being here is better than staying in Ireland, landless and powerless, without food or clothing." By the 1840s and 1850s—when the steady stream of immigration turned into a flood— the prospects of buying land became more remote.

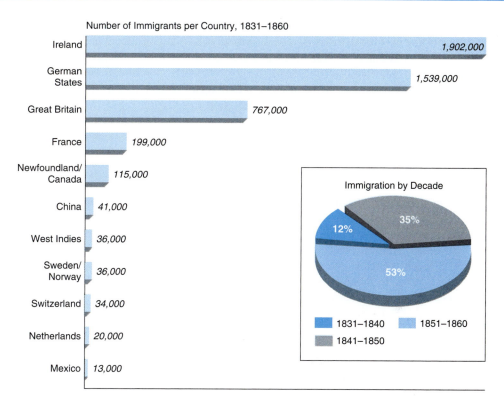

FIGURE 11.1 Major Sources of Immigration to the United States, 1831–1860

Most immigrants came from two areas: Great Britain, of which Ireland was a part, and the German states. These two areas sent more immigrants between 1830 and 1860 than the inhabitants of the United States enumerated at the first census in 1790. By 1860, 15 percent of the white population was of foreign birth.
(*Source: Data from Stephan Thernstrom, ed., Harvard Encyclopedia of American Ethnic Groups [Cambridge, Mass., and London: Harvard University Press, 1980], 1047.*)

By 1860 most immigrants settled in cities, often the port at which they arrived. The most destitute among them could not afford the canal or railroad fare to places farther inland. Others arrived with resources but fell victim to the swindlers who preyed on newly arrived immigrants. The ethnic flair of urban life induced still others to stay put. In 1855, 52 percent of New York's 623,000 inhabitants were immigrants, 28 percent from Ireland and 16 percent from the German states. Boston, another major entry port for the Irish, took on a European tone; throughout the 1850s the city was about 35 percent foreign-born, of whom more than two-thirds were Irish.

Most of the new immigrants from Ireland were young, poor, from rural districts, and Roman Catholic. Women found work as domestic servants or mill hands, while men worked in construction or transportation. Very few Germans settled in New England; most of them came with enough resources to head to the upper Mississippi and Ohio valleys, to states such as Ohio, Illinois, Wisconsin, and Missouri. Although some southern cities like Charleston and Savannah had significant numbers of Irish immigrants, the vast majority of European immigrants, many of whom arrived with aversions to slavery and to semitropical heat, settled in the Northeast or Midwest.

Ethnic Tensions   Tension—often resulting from anxieties over the era's economic changes—characterized the relationship between native-born Americans and immigrants, particularly Irish Catholics. Native-born workers blamed immigrants for scarce job opportunities and low wages. Middle-class whites blamed them for poverty and crime. As they saw it, immigrants' moral depravity—not poor wages—led to poverty.

Native-born Americans often associated the Irish with another group whom they deemed morally inferior: African Americans. White northerners often portrayed Irish immigrants as nonwhite, as African in appearance. But Irish and African Americans did not develop a sense of solidarity. Instead, some of the era's most virulent riots erupted between Irish immigrants and African Americans.

Closely related to racial stereotyping was anti-Catholicism, which became strident in the 1830s. In Boston anti-Catholic riots occurred frequently. Nearby Charlestown, Massachusetts, saw a mob burn a convent in 1834. In Philadelphia a crowd attacked priests and nuns, and vandalized churches in 1844, and in Lawrence, Massachusetts, a mob leveled the Irish neighborhood in 1854. Anti-Catholic violence was not limited to urban areas—riots between native-born and Irish workers erupted along the nation's canals and railroads—but urban riots usually attracted more newspaper attention, fueling fears that cities were violent, depraved places.

German immigrants, at least the majority who were Protestants, mostly fared better than the Irish. In part because Germans generally arrived with some resources and skills, Americans stereotyped them as hard working, self-reliant, and intelligent. But non-Protestant Germans—Catholics and Jews (whom white Americans considered a separate race) frequently encountered hostility fed by racial and religious prejudice.

Immigrants often lived in ethnic enclaves. Intolerance between Protestants and Catholics ran both ways, and Irish Catholics tended to live in their own neighborhoods, where they set up Catholic churches and schools. In larger cities, immigrants from the same German states clustered together. Immigrants set up social clubs and mutual-aid societies, such as the Hibernian Society and Sons of Erin (Irish), and B'nai B'rith (Jewish).

People of Color   African Americans also forged their own communities and culture. As late as the 1830s, significant numbers of them remained enslaved in New York and New Jersey, but the numbers of free African Americans grew steadily, and by 1860 nearly 250,000 (many of them refugees from southern slavery) lived in the urban North. Despite differences in status, occupation, wealth, education, and religion, African Americans often felt a sense of racial solidarity. African Methodist Episcopal churches and preachers helped forge communities. Chapels and social halls functioned as town halls and school buildings. Ministers were political leaders, and their halls housed political forums, conventions, and protest meetings.

But white racism impinged on every aspect of northern African Americans' lives. Streetcars, hotels, restaurants, and theaters could turn away African Americans with no legal penalty. City laws barred African Americans from entering public buildings. Even where laws were more liberal, popular attitudes among whites constrained African Americans' opportunities. In Massachusetts, for example, African Americans enjoyed more legal rights than anywhere else in the country. Yet laws protecting civil and political rights could not make whites shop at black businesses. "Colored men in business in Massachusetts receive more respect, and less patronage than in any place I know of," proclaimed a prominent African American lawyer.

African Americans were excluded from factory and clerical jobs. Women worked as house servants, cooks, washerwomen, and child nurses. Most African American men worked as construction workers, porters, longshoremen, or day laborers—all jobs subject to frequent periods of unemployment. Others found employment in the lower-paying but more stable service industry, working as servants, waiters, cooks, barbers, and janitors. Many African American men hired on as sailors and merchant seamen, as commercial sailing offered regular employment and opportunities for advancement, though not protection from racial taunts.

In the growing cities, African Americans turned service occupations into businesses, opening their own restaurants, taverns, hotels, barber shops, and employment agencies for domestic servants. Some became caterers. Others sold used clothing or were junk dealers or small-job contractors. A few became wealthy, invested in real estate, and loaned money. With professionals—ministers, teachers, physicians, dentists, lawyers, and newspaper editors—they formed a small but growing African American middle class.

In cities large and small, African Americans became targets of urban violence. Philadelphia experienced the most violence, with five major riots in the 1830s and 1840s, and major riots occurred in Providence and New York as well. White rioters clubbed and stoned African Americans, and destroyed their houses, churches, and businesses—in some cases, sending African Americans fleeing for their lives. By 1860 many hundreds had died in urban riots.

Urban Culture

Living in cramped, squalid conditions, working-class families—white and black, immigrant and native-born—spent little time indoors. In the 1840s, a working-class youth culture developed on the Bowery, one of New York's entertainment strips. The lamp-lit promenade, lined with theaters, dance halls, and cafés, became an urban midway. Older and more elite New Yorkers often feared the "Bowery boys and gals." The Bowery boys' greased hair, distinctive clothing, and swaggering gait frightened many middle-class New Yorkers, as did the Bowery girls' colorful costumes and ornate hats, which contrasted with genteel ladies' own modest veils and bonnets. Equally scandalous to an older generation were the middle-class clerks who succumbed to the city's temptations, most notably prostitution.

Gangs of garishly dressed young men and women—flaunting their sexuality, using foul language, sometimes speaking in foreign tongues, and drinking to excess—drove self-styled respectable citizenry to establish private clubs and associations. Some joined the Masonic order, which offered everything the bustling, chaotic city did not: an elaborate hierarchy, an older code of deference between ranks, harmony, and shared values. Although the Masons admitted men only, women organized their own associations, including literary clubs and benevolent societies.

Increasingly, urban recreation and sports became formal commodities to be purchased. One had to buy a ticket to go to the theater, the circus, P. T. Barnum's American Museum in New York City, the racetrack, or the ballpark. Horseracing, walking races, and, in the 1850s, baseball began to attract large urban male crowds. Starting in 1831, enthusiasts could read the all-sports newspaper, *Spirit of the Times.* A group of Wall Street office workers formed the Knickerbocker Club in 1842 and in 1845 drew up rules for the game of baseball. By 1849 news of boxing was so much in demand that a round-by-round account of a Maryland boxing match was telegraphed throughout the East.

A theater was often the second public building constructed in a town, after a church. Large cities boasted two or more theaters catering to different classes, though some plays cut across class lines; Shakespeare was performed so often and appreciated so widely that even illiterate theatergoers knew his plays well. In the 1840s, singing groups, theater troupes, and circuses traveled from city to city. Particularly popular were minstrel shows, in which white men (often Irish) in burnt-cork makeup imitated African Americans in song, dance, and patter. In the early 1830s, Thomas D. Rice of New York became famous for his role as Jim Crow, an old southern slave. In ill-fitting patched clothing and torn shoes, the blackface Rice shuffled, danced, and sang. Minstrel performers told jokes mocking economic and political elites, and evoked nostalgia for preindustrial work habits and morality, as supposedly embodied by carefree black men. At the same time, though, the antics of blackface actors encouraged a racist stereotyping of African Americans as sensual and lazy.

Cities as Symbols of Progress

Many northerners saw cities—with their mixtures of people, rapid growth, municipal improvements, and violence—as symbolizing at once progress and decay. On the one hand, cities represented economic advancement; new ones grew at the crossroads of transportation and commerce. Cities nurtured churches, schools, civil governments, and museums—all signs of civilization and culture. As canals and railroads opened the West for mass settlement, many white northerners applauded the appearance of what they called "civilization"—church steeples, public buildings—in areas that had recently been what they called "savage wilderness"; that is, territory controlled by Native Americans. One Methodist newspaper remarked in 1846 that the nation's rapid expansion westward would outpace "our means of moral and intellectual improvement." But the remedies, the editor noted, were evident: bring churches, schools, and moral reform societies to the West. "Cities, civilization, religion, mark our progress," he declared. To many nineteenth-century white Americans, cities represented the moral triumph of civilization over savagery and heathenism.

Yet some of the same Americans deplored the everyday character of the nation's largest cities, which they saw as havens of disease, poverty, crime, and vice. To many middle-class observers, disease combined with crime to represent moral decline. They considered epidemics to be divine scourges, which struck primarily those who were filthy, intemperate, and immoral. Many middle-class and wealthy people believed that epidemics resulted from the moral degradation of the urban poor. Theft and prostitution provided evidence of moral vice, and wealthy observers perceived these crimes not as by-products of poverty but as signs of individual failing. They responded by pressing for laws against vagrancy and disturbing the peace, and by pushing city officials to establish the nation's first police forces. Boston hired uniformed policemen in 1837 to supplement its part-time watchmen and constables, and New York hired its own police force in 1845.

How did northerners reconcile the vices and depravity of the city with their view of cities as symbols of progress? Middle-class reformers focused on purifying cities of

Thomas D. Rice playing "Jim Crow" in blackface at the Bowery Theater in New York City, 1833. The rowdy audience climbed onto the stage, leaving Rice little room to perform. In representing African Americans on stage, Rice and other minstrels contributed to establishing both black and white as racial categories. (© Collection of the New-York Historical Society)

their disease and vice. If disease was a divine punishment—rather than an offshoot of cramped conditions engendered by economic change—then it was within Americans' power to fix things. Middle-class reformers took to the streets and back alleys, trying to convince the urban working classes that life would improve if they gave up alcohol, worked even harder, and prayed frequently. They talked about how the northern working poor—unlike southern slaves—could improve their condition through hard work and virtuous habits. This belief in upward mobility became central to many northerners' ideas about progress.

Belief in upward mobility related to the idea of free labor, the concept that, in a competitive marketplace, those who worked hard and lived virtuous lives could improve their status. Free-labor ideology appealed especially to manufacturers and merchants eager to believe that their own success emerged from hard work and moral virtue—and eager as well to encourage their factory hands and clerks to work hard and live virtuously, to remain optimistic despite current hardships. Many laborers initially rejected free-labor ideology, seeing it as little more than a veiled attempt to tout industrial work habits, to rationalize poor wages, and to quell worker protest. But by the 1850s, when the question of slavery's westward expansion returned to the political foreground, more and more northerners would embrace free-labor ideology and come to see slavery as antithetical to the modernizing, free-labor ideology of the North. It was this way of thinking, perhaps more than anything else, that made the North distinctive.

SUMMARY

During the first half of the nineteenth century, the North became rapidly enmeshed in a commercial culture. Northern states and capitalists invested heavily in internal improvements, helping to propel the North down a new development track. Most northerners now turned either toward commercial farming or, in smaller numbers, toward industrial wage labor. Farmers gave up mixed agriculture and specialized in cash crops, while their children often went to work in factories or countinghouses.

To many northerners, the market economy symbolized progress, in which they found much to celebrate: easier access to cheap western lands, employment for surplus farm laborers, and the ready commercial availability of goods that had once been time-consuming to produce. At the same time, though, the market economy led to increased specialization, a less personal workplace, complex market relationships, more regimentation, a sharper divide between work and leisure, and a degradation of natural resources. Northerners' involvement in the market economy also tied them more directly to fluctuating national and international markets, and during economic downturns, many northern families experienced destitution.

With parents relying less directly on children's labor, northerners began producing smaller families. Even as working-class children continued to work as canal drivers and factory hands (or to scavenge urban streets), middle-class families began to create a sheltered model of childhood in which they tried to shield children from the perceived dangers of the world outside the family. Their mothers, in theory, became moral guardians of the household, keeping the home safe from the encroachment of the new economy's competitiveness and selfishness. Few women, though, had the luxury to devote themselves entirely to nurturing their children and husbands.

Immigrants and free African Americans performed much of the lowest-paying work in the expanding economy, and many native-born whites blamed them for the problems that accompanied the era's rapid economic changes. Anti-immigrant (especially anti-Catholic) and antiblack riots became commonplace. At the same time, immigrants and African Americans worked to form their own communities.

Cities came to symbolize for many Americans both the possibilities and the limits of market expansion. Urban areas were marked by extremes of wealth, and they fostered vibrant working-class cultures even as they encouraged poverty and crime. To reconcile the seeming contradictions of progress—the coexistence, for example, of abundance and destitution—middle-class northerners articulated an ideology of free labor, touting the possibility for upward mobility in a competitive marketplace. This ideology would become increasingly central to northern regional identity.

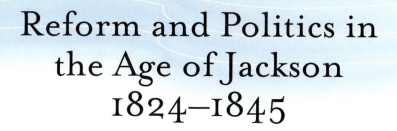

12

Reform and Politics in the Age of Jackson 1824–1845

FROM REVIVAL TO REFORM

A series of religious revivals in the late eighteenth and early nineteenth centuries—sometimes called the Second Great Awakening for their resemblance to revivals of the Great Awakening of the eighteenth century—raised people's hopes for the Second Coming of the Christian messiah and the establishment of the Kingdom of God on earth. Revivalists resolved to speed the millennium, or the thousand years of peace on earth that would accompany Christ's Second Coming, by combating sin. Some believed that the United States had a special mission in God's design and a special role in eliminating evil. If sin and evil could be eliminated, individuals and society could be perfected. Revivalists called on individuals to renounce personal sins, such as drinking, swearing, and licentiousness. They also called on individuals to combat social evils, including—most prominently—slavery, but also dueling and desecration of the Sabbath. Not until all Americans had been converted, and all social evils suppressed, would Christ make his Second Coming.

Because it was not enough for an individual to embrace God and godliness, revivalists strove for large-scale conversions. Rural women, men, and children traveled long distances to camp meetings, where they listened to fiery sermons preached day and night from hastily constructed platforms and tents in forests or open fields. In cities, women in particular attended daily church services and prayer meetings, sometimes for months on end. Converts renounced personal sin, vowed to live sanctified lives, and committed themselves to helping others see the light.

Revivals   The most famous revival was at Cane Ridge, Kentucky, in August 1801. One report estimated that 25,000 people attended, including men and women, free and enslaved, at a time when Kentucky's largest city, Lexington, had fewer than 2,000 inhabitants. The call to personal repentance and conversion invigorated Protestantism throughout the South, giving churches an evangelical base. Although laws often restricted or outlawed black churches and preachers, particularly after Nat Turner's bloody revolt in 1831, in practice black and mixed churches often flourished on the local level, with black and white evangelicals forging a united front against their profane neighbors. During the 1840s and 1850s, though, as the slavery issue increasingly worked itself into public debate, southern Presbyterian, Baptist, and Methodist churches seceded from their denominations' national conferences. For the white leaders of these secessionist churches, slavery did not impede human perfectibility but rather ensured it; the paternal guidance of benevolent masters, they reasoned, would bring Africans to Christ.

All revivalists shared a belief in individual self-improvement, but northern revivalists also emphasized communal improvement, making them missionaries for both individual salvation and social reform. Wherever they preached, northern evangelists generated new religious groups and voluntary reform societies. Preachers like Lyman Beecher, who made his base in New England before moving to Cincinnati, and Charles Finney, who traveled the canals and roads that linked the Northeast to the Midwest, argued that evil was avoidable, that Christians were not doomed by original sin, and that anyone could achieve salvation. In everyday language, Finney—a former lawyer—preached that "God has made man a moral free agent." Finney's brand of revivalism transcended sects, class, and race. At first a Presbyterian, he eventually found his home in Methodism. Revivalism had a particularly strong base among Methodists and Baptists, whose denominational structures maximized democratic participation and drew their ministers from ordinary folk.

Finney experienced his greatest successes in the area of western New York that had experienced rapid changes in transportation and industrialization—in what he called the "Burned-Over District" because of the intensity of the region's evangelical fires. Rapid change raised fears of the social evils that might accompany economic progress—the dissolution of the family, drinking, swearing, and prostitution. Many individuals worried, too, whether their status would improve or decline in an economy that cycled through booms and busts.

When northern revivalist preachers emphasized the importance of good works—that is, good deeds and piety—they helped ignite many of the era's social reform movements, which began in the Burned-Over District and spread eastward to New England and the Middle Atlantic, and westward to the upper Midwest. Evangelically inspired reform associations together constituted what historians call the "benevolent empire." Even as they advocated for distinct causes, these associations shared an overall commitment to human perfectibility, and they often turned to the same wealthy men for financial resources and advice.

CHRONOLOGY

1790s–1840s	• Second Great Awakening spreads religious fervor
1820s	• Reformers in New York and Pennsylvania establish model penitentiaries
1824	• No presidential candidate wins a majority in electoral college
1825	• House of Representatives elects Adams president
1826	• American Society for the Promotion of Temperance founded
1828	• Tariff of Abominations passed
	• Jackson elected president
1830s–40s	• Democratic-Whig competition gels in second party system
1831	• Garrison begins abolitionist newspaper *The Liberator*
	• Antimasons are first political party to hold national convention
1832	• Jackson vetoes rechartering Second Bank of the United States
	• Jackson reelected president
1832–33	• South Carolina nullifies Tariffs of 1828 and 1832, prompting nullification crisis
1836	• Specie Circular ends credit purchase of public lands
	• Van Buren elected president
1837	• *Caroline* affair sparks tension with Britain
	• Financial panic ends boom of the 1830s
1838–39	• United States and Canada mobilize militias over Maine–New Brunswick border dispute
1839–43	• Hard times spread unemployment and deflation
1840	• Whigs win presidency under Harrison
1841	• Tyler assumes presidency after Harrison's death
1848	• Woman's Rights Convention at Seneca Falls, New York, calls for female suffrage.

Moral Reform   Those resources allowed them to make good use of the era's new technologies—steam presses and railroads—to spread the evangelical word. By mass-producing pamphlets and newspapers for distribution far into the interior of the country, reformers spread their message throughout the Northeast and Midwest, strengthening the cultural connections between regions increasingly tied together economically. With canals and railroads making travel easier, reformers could attend annual conventions and contact like-minded people personally, and local reform societies could host speakers from distant places. Most reform organizations, like political parties, sponsored weekly newspapers, creating a virtual community of reformers.

While the new wealth of industrialists and merchants provided financial resources for evangelical reform, their wives and daughters did the everyday work of soliciting new members and circulating petitions. Women more than men tended to feel personally

Samuel Waldo and William Jewett's oil portrait of Charles Finney around 1834 captures Finney at his peak. The charismatic Finney mesmerized his audiences, and contemporaries credited him with converting 500,000 people. (Oberlin College Archives, Oberlin, OH)

responsible for counteracting the social evils of the expanding market economy. The cult of domesticity, which arose in tandem with industrialization and the revivals, assigned women the role of moral guardianship of their families; evangelical reformers expanded that role beyond the domestic sphere into the public realm. Women undertook to do more than provide moral guidance to their own children; they would help run reformatories for wayward youth or establish asylums for orphans. Participation in reform movements thus allowed some women to exercise their moral authority outside the household, giving them a new sense of purpose. Their influence might both improve people's lives and hasten the millennium. Women also enjoyed the friendships with other women that came from participation in benevolent societies. Although some elite women in Upper South cities also formed and joined reform societies, moral reform was primarily a northeastern and midwestern phenomenon.

For women and some men, reform represented their primary form of political involvement at a time when the vote was restricted to property-owning men. The aftermath of an 1830 exposé of prostitution in New York City illustrates how reform led to political action. Even as female reformers organized a shelter for the city's prostitutes and tried to secure respectable employment for them, they publicized the names of brothel clients in an effort to shame the men who contributed to the women's waywardness. The New York women organized themselves into the Female Moral Reform Society and soon expanded their geographic scope and activities. By 1840 the society had 555 affiliated chapters across the nation. In the next few years, it entered the political sphere by lobbying successfully for criminal sanctions in New York State against men who seduced women into prostitution. If only prostitutes could be freed from the corrupting reach of the men who preyed on them, reformers believed, so-called fallen women might be morally uplifted.

Penitentiaries and Asylums A similar belief in perfectibility led reformers to establish institutions to impose discipline on criminals and delinquents. Rather than simply punishing criminals, reformers tried to transform them into productive members of society. Their model penitentiaries aimed to rehabilitate criminals through disciplined regimens.

Other reformers sought to reform treatment of the mentally ill, who were frequently imprisoned, often alongside criminals, and put in cages or dark dungeons, chained to walls, brutalized, or held in solitary confinement. Dorothea Dix, the leader of this crusade, exemplifies the early-nineteenth-century reformer who started with a religious belief in individual self-improvement and human perfectibility, and moved into social action by advocating collective responsibility. Investigating asylums, petitioning the Massachusetts legislature, and lobbying other states and Congress, Dix moved from reform to politics and helped create a new public role for women. In response to Dix's efforts, twenty-eight of thirty-three states had built public institutions for the mentally ill by 1860.

Temperance Advocates of temperance, who pushed for either partial or full abstinence from alcoholic beverages, likewise crossed from the personal into the political sphere. Drinking was widespread in the early nineteenth century, when men like Sam Patch frequently gathered in public houses and rural inns to drink whiskey, rum, and hard cider while they gossiped, talked politics, and played cards. Contracts were sealed, celebrations commemorated, and harvests toasted with liquor. "Respectable" women did not drink in public, but many regularly tippled alcohol-based patent medicines promoted as cure-alls.

Evangelicals considered drinking sinful, and in many denominations, forsaking alcohol was part of conversion. Preachers condemned alcohol for violating the Sabbath—the only day workers had off, which some spent at the public house. Factory owners condemned alcohol for making their workers unreliable. Civic leaders connected alcohol with crime. Middle-class reformers, often women, condemned it for squandering wages, diverting men from their family responsibilities, and making them more likely to be abusive when they came home from the tavern. In the early 1840s, thousands of ordinary women formed Martha Washington societies to protect families by reforming alcoholics, raising children as teetotalers, and spreading the temperance message. Abstinence from alcohol, reformers believed, would help achieve both religious perfectibility and secular progress. They hoped to stamp out the raucous drinking culture of the likes of Sam Patch.

As the temperance movement gained momentum, its goal shifted from moderation to voluntary abstinence and finally to prohibition. By the mid-1830s, five thousand state and local temperance societies touted teetotalism, and more than a million people had taken the pledge of abstinence, including several hundred thousand children who enlisted in the Cold Water Army. Per capita consumption of alcohol fell from five gallons per year in 1800 to below two gallons in the 1840s. The American Society for the Promotion of Temperance, organized in 1826 to promote pledges of abstinence, became a pressure group for legislation that would end alcohol manufacture and sale. In 1851 Maine became the first state to ban alcohol except for medicinal purposes, and by 1855 similar laws had been enacted throughout New England and in New York, Pennsylvania, and the Midwest.

The temperance campaign had a nativist—or anti-immigrant and anti-Catholic—strain to it. The Irish and Germans, complained the *American Protestant Magazine* in

1849, "bring the grog shops like the frogs of Egypt upon us." Along the nation's canals, reformers lamented the hundreds of taverns that catered to the largely Irish work force, and in the cities, they expressed outrage at the Sunday tradition of urban German families' gathering at beer gardens to eat and drink, to dance and sing, and sometimes to play cards. Their efforts had some success, as Catholics took the pledge of abstinence and formed their own organizations, such as the St. Mary's Mutual Benevolence Total Abstinence Society in Boston.

But temperance spawned strong opposition, too. Many workers—Protestants as well as Catholics—rejected what they saw as middle-class efforts to impose middle-class values on people whose lives they did not understand, and they steadfastly defended their right to drink whatever they pleased. Workers agreed that poverty and crime were indeed problems but that poor wages, not drinking habits, were to blame. Even some who abstained from alcohol opposed prohibition, believing that drinking should be a matter of self-control, not state coercion.

Public Schools

Protestants and Catholics often came into conflict over education as well. Public education almost always included religious education, but when teachers taught Protestant beliefs and used the King James version of the Bible, Catholics established their own schools, which taught Catholic doctrines. This move led some Protestants to fear that Catholics would never be assimilated into American culture, and some charged Catholics with being exclusionists, plotting to undermine the republic and impose papal control. Yet, even as these conflicts brewed, public education touched the lives of more Americans than did any other reform movement.

The leader of this movement was Horace Mann, a Massachusetts lawyer and reformer who came from humble beginnings. He advocated free, tax-supported education to replace church schools and the private schools set up by untrained, itinerant young men. Universal education, Mann proposed, would end misery and crime, and would help Americanize immigrants. "If we do not prepare children to become good citizens," he argued, "if we do not develop their capacities, imbue their hearts with the love of truth and duty, and a reverence for all things sacred and holy, then our republic must go down to destruction."

During Mann's tenure as secretary of the Massachusetts Board of Education from 1837 to 1848, Massachusetts led the "common school" movement which established training for teachers, lengthened the school year, and raised teachers' salaries to make the profession more attractive. In keeping with the era's notions that women had special claims to morality and with the practical advantage that they could be paid less, Mann envisioned a system in which women would prepare future clerks, farmers, and workers with a practical curriculum that deemphasized classics in favor of geography, arithmetic, and science. Like so many other reform movements, educational reform rested on the notions of progress and perfectibility; given the proper guidance, individuals could educate themselves out of their circumstances, material and moral alike.

Thanks to the expansion of public education, by 1850 every state offered some publication of its own, and the vast majority of native-born white Americans were literate. Newspapers and magazines proliferated, and bookstores spread. Power printing presses and better transportation made possible wide distribution of books and periodicals. The religious press—of both traditional sects and revivalists—produced pamphlets, hymnals, Bibles, and religious newspapers. Americans also read secular publications. Newspapers and magazines—political organs, literary journals, and the voices of working groups like the mill girls at Lowell—abounded in the 1830s and after.

COMMUNITARIAN EXPERIMENTS

While moral reformers tried to perfect American society, some idealists dreamed of an entirely new social order. They established dozens of utopian communities—ideal communities that could then serve as models for broader society—based on either religious principles, a desire to resist what they saw as the excessive individualism of the market economy, or a combination of the two. Some groups, like the Shakers, had originated in eighteenth-century Europe, while others, like the Mormons, arose in the wake of the religious ferment of the Second Great Awakening. Utopian communities attempted to recapture what they perceived as the more communal nature of the past, even as they offered sometimes-radical departures from established practices of marriage and child rearing.

Utopian Communities The Shakers, the largest of the communal utopian experiments, reached their peak between 1820 and 1860, when six thousand members lived in twenty settlements in eight states. Shaker communities emphasized agriculture and handcrafts, selling their produce and manufactured goods beyond the bounds of their own community; most managed to become self-sufficient and profitable enterprises. The community's craft tradition contrasted with the new factory regime. But the Shakers were essentially a spiritual community. Founded in England in 1772 by Mother Ann Lee, they got their name from their worship service, which included shaking their entire bodies as well as singing, dancing, and shouting. Ann Lee's children had died in infancy, and she believed that their deaths were retribution for her sin of intercourse; thus she advocated celibacy. After imprisonment in England in 1773–1774, she fulfilled a vision by settling in America.

In religious practice and social relations, Shakers offered an alternative to the era's rapid changes in urban and rural life. Shakers lived communally, with men and women in separate quarters; individual families were abolished. Leadership was shared equally between men and women. Many Shaker settlements became temporary refuges for orphans, widows, runaways, abused wives, and unemployed workers during hard times. Their settlements depended on constant enlistment of new recruits, not only because the practice of celibacy meant that they could not reproduce themselves, but also because some members soon left, unsuited to either communal living or the Shakers' spiritual message.

Other influential utopian communities also sought to resist the social changes brought about by industrialism. John Humphrey Noyes, a lawyer who had been converted by Finney's revivals, established two perfectionist communities: first in Putney, Vermont, in 1835, and then—after being indicted for adultery—in Oneida, New York, in 1848. Noyes decried individualism and instead advocated communal ownership of property, communal child rearing, and "complex marriage," in which all men in the community were married to all women, but in which a woman was free to accept or reject a sexual proposition. In the Oneida Colony, exclusive sexual relationships were forbidden, and men were to practice "male continence," or intercourse without ejaculation, in order to promote relationships built on more than sexual fulfillment. All pregnancies were to be planned; couples would apply to Noyes for permission to have a child, or Noyes would assign two people to reproduce with each other. Robert Dale Owen's community in New Harmony, Indiana (1825–1828), also abolished private property and advocated communal child rearing. The Fourierists, named after French philosopher Charles Fourier, established more than two dozen communities in the Northeast and Midwest; these communities, too, resisted the individualism of market society and promoted equality between the sexes.

The most famous Fourier community was Brook Farm, in West Roxbury, Massachusetts, near Boston. Inspired by transcendentalism—the belief that the physical world is secondary to the spiritual realm, which human beings can reach not by custom and experience but only by intuition—Brook Farm's members rejected materialism. Their rural communalism combined spirituality, manual labor, intellectual life, and play. Originally founded in 1841 by the Unitarian minister George Ripley, a literary critic and friend of transcendentalist lecturer and essayist Ralph Waldo Emerson, Brook Farm attracted farmers, craftsmen, and writers, among them the novelist Nathaniel Hawthorne. Although the Unitarians were not evangelicals, their largely middle- and upper-class followers had a long-standing "devotion to progress," as one of their most influential ministers put it. The Brook Farm school drew students from outside the community, and Brook Farm residents contributed regularly to the *Dial*, the leading transcendentalist journal. In 1845 Brook Farm's hundred members organized themselves into model phalanxes (working-living units) along the model suggested by Fourier. As rigid regimentation replaced individualism, membership dropped. A year after a disastrous fire in 1846, the experiment collapsed.

American Renaissance

Though short-lived, Brook Farm played a significant role in the flowering of a national literature. During these years, Hawthorne, Emerson, and *Dial* editor Margaret Fuller joined Henry David Thoreau, Herman Melville, and others in a literary outpouring known today as the American Renaissance. In philosophical intensity and moral idealism, their work was both distinctively American and an outgrowth of the European romantic movement. Their themes were universal, their settings and characters American. Hawthorne, for instance, used Puritan New England as a backdrop, and Melville wrote of great spiritual quests as seafaring adventures.

Essayist Ralph Waldo Emerson was the prime mover of the American Renaissance and a pillar of the transcendental movement. Emerson had followed his father and grandfather into the ministry but quit his Boston Unitarian pulpit in 1831. After a two-year sojourn in Europe, he returned to lecture and write, preaching individualism and self-reliance. "We live in succession, in division, in parts, in particles," Emerson wrote. "We see the world piece by piece, as the sun, the moon, the animal, the tree; but the whole, of which these are the shining parts, is the soul." Intuitive experience of God is attainable, insisted Emerson, because "the Highest dwells" within every individual in the form of the "Over-soul." What gave Emerson's writings force was, for his times, a simple, direct prose. In his first book, *Nature* (1836), and in "The American Scholar" (1837), a Phi Beta Kappa address at Harvard, Emerson explored human nature and American culture. Widely admired, he influenced Thoreau, Fuller, Hawthorne, and other members of Brook Farm.

Mormons

No communitarian experiment had a more lasting influence than the Church of Jesus Christ of Latter-day Saints, whose members were known as the Mormons. During the religious ferment of the 1820s in western New York, Joseph Smith, a young farmer, reported that an angel called Moroni had given him divinely engraved gold plates. Smith published his revelations as the *Book of Mormon* and organized a church in 1830. The next year, the community moved west to Ohio to build a "New Jerusalem" and await the Second Coming of Jesus.

But angry mobs drove the Mormons from Ohio, and they settled in Missouri. Anti-Mormons charged that Mormonism was fraudulent, a scam by Joseph Smith. Opponents feared Mormon economic and political power. In 1838 the governor of Missouri charged Smith with fomenting insurrection and gathered evidence to indict him and other leaders for treason.

Smith and his followers resettled in Nauvoo, Illinois. The state legislature gave them a city charter that made them self-governing and authorized a local militia. But again the community met antagonism, especially after Smith introduced the practice of polygamy in 1841, allowing men to have several wives at once. The next year Smith became mayor, and this consolidation of religious and political power, as well as Nauvoo's petition to the federal government to be a self-governing territory, further antagonized opponents, who now included some former Mormons. In 1844, after Smith and his brother were charged with treason and jailed, and then murdered, the Mormons left Illinois to seek security in the western wilderness. Under the leadership of Brigham Young, they set up a cooperative community in the Great Salt Lake valley.

There, the Mormons distributed agricultural land according to family size. An extensive irrigation system, constructed by men who contributed their labor in proportion to the quantity of land they received and the amount of water they expected to use, transformed the arid valley into a rich oasis. As the colony developed, the church elders gained control of water, trade, industry, and eventually the territorial government of Utah.

ABOLITIONISM

While moral reformers tried to eliminate individual sin and utopians established model communities apart from mainstream society, evangelical abolitionists tried to eradicate what they saw as a communal sin suffusing American society: slavery. Inspired by the Second Great Awakening, their efforts built on those of an earlier generation of anti-slavery activists.

Early Abolitionism and Colonization

From the nation's earliest days—in places like Philadelphia, New York, Albany, Boston, and Nantucket—free blacks formed societies to petition legislatures, seek judicial redress, stage public marches, and, especially, publish tracts that chronicled the horrors of life in bondage. African American abolitionists wrote about slavery's devastating impact on both black and white families, advocated an immediate end to slavery, offered assistance to fugitive slaves, and promoted legal equality for free blacks. By 1830 there were fifty African American abolitionist societies in the United States. But it was the writings of one man, David Walker, that captured white Americans' attention like none other. In his *Appeal . . . to the Colored Citizens* (1829), Walker—a southern-born free African

American—advocated the violent overthrow of slavery, sending shock waves of fear throughout the white South and much of the North as well.

Violent overthrow could not have been further from the goals of the white abolitionists who, in the years after the American Revolution, had come together in places like Boston and, especially, Philadelphia, with its large population of Quakers, whose religious beliefs emphasized human equality. These early antislavery advocates pressed for slavery's gradual abolition and an end to the international slave trade. Although they aided African Americans who sought freedom through judicial decisions, their assumptions about blacks' racial inferiority made them stop short of advocating for equal rights. These early white abolitionists tended to be wealthy, socially prominent men who excluded women, African Americans, and less elite men from their societies.

Elites were more likely to support the colonization movement, which crystallized in 1816 with the organization of the American Colonization Society. Its members planned to purchase and then relocate American slaves, as well as free blacks, to Africa or the Caribbean. Among its supporters were Thomas Jefferson, James Madison, James Monroe, and Henry Clay, as well as many lesser-known men and women who came from the North and, especially, the Upper South. In 1824 the society founded Liberia, on the west coast of Africa, and began to establish a settlement for African Americans who were willing to go. The society had resettled nearly twelve thousand people in Liberia by 1860. Some colonizationists aimed to strengthen slavery by ridding the South of troublesome slaves or to purge the North of African Americans altogether. Others hoped colonization would improve African Americans' conditions. Although some African Americans supported the movement, black abolitionists generally denounced it.

In the early 1830s, a new group of more radical white abolitionists—most prominently, William Lloyd Garrison—rejected both the violent overthrow advocated by David Walker and the gradual approaches of white legal reformers and colonizationists. Instead, they demanded immediate, complete, and uncompensated emancipation. In the first issue of *The Liberator,* which he began publishing in 1831, Garrison declared, "I am in earnest—I will not equivocate—I will not excuse—I will not retreat a single inch—and *I will be heard*." Two years later, he founded the American Antislavery Society, which became the era's largest abolitionist organization.

Immediatism

Immediatists, as they came to be called, believed that slavery was an absolute sin needing urgent eradication. They were influenced by African American abolitionist societies and by evangelicals' notion that humans, not God, determined their own spiritual fate by deciding whether to choose good or evil. In that sense, all were equal before God's eyes. When all humans had chosen good over evil, the millennium would come. Slavery, however, denied enslaved men and women the ability to make such choices, the ability to act as what Finney called "moral free agents." For every day that slavery continued, then, the millennium was also delayed.

Because the millennium depended on *all* hearts having been won over to Christ, because it depended on the perfectibility of all human beings, including slaveowners, Garrison's brand of abolitionism focused on "moral suasion." He and his followers hoped to bring about emancipation, not through coercion, but rather by winning over the hearts of slaveowners as well as other white Americans who supported or tolerated slavery. Evangelical abolitionism depended, then, on large numbers of ministers and laypeople spreading the evangelical message to all corners of the nation.

The Lane Debates   In 1829 Congregationalists and Presbyterians founded the Lane Seminary in Cincinnati to train ministers who would carry the evangelical message into the West. With Lyman Beecher as president, it drew students from North and South, and encouraged "people of color" to apply. Not long after Theodore Weld, one of Charles Finney's most faithful converts, arrived at the Lane Seminary in 1833, he organized what became known as the Lane Debates, eighteen days of discussion among the school's students and faculty about the relative merits of colonization and immediatism. Immediatism won.

Led by Weld, the Lane students and faculty next founded an antislavery society, and began reaching out more fully to the growing African American population of Cincinnati, who in 1829 had been the target of a brutal attack by white people. Fearful that Weld and his students would provoke renewed disorder, white business leaders protested the creation of the antislavery society. Lane's trustees responded by banning antislavery organizations on campus and barring further debate on the topic of slavery. Beecher supported the trustees. Weld and the other "Lane Rebels" publicly broke from the seminary and the following year enrolled in a new seminary at Oberlin, a town in northern Ohio founded as a Christian perfectionist settlement. The new seminary, which was dedicated to immediatism, would become the first college to admit women and one of the first to admit African Americans. Weld turned down a faculty post at Oberlin, preferring instead to carry the abolitionist message directly into the western countryside as an agent for the American Antislavery Society.

The American Antislavery Society   By 1838, at its peak, the society had 2,000 local affiliates and a membership of over 300,000. In stark contrast to an earlier generation of white abolitionists, the immediatists welcomed men and women of all racial and class backgrounds into their organizations. Lydia Maria Child, Maria Chapman, and Lucretia Mott served on its executive committee; Child edited its official paper, the *National Anti-Slavery Standard,* from 1841 to 1843, and Chapman coedited it from 1844 until 1848. The society sponsored black and female speakers, and women undertook most of the day-to-day conversion efforts.

In rural and small-town northern and midwestern communities, women addressed mail, collected signatures, raised money, organized boycotts of textiles made from slave-grown cotton, and increased awareness of their cause. With the "great postal campaign," launched in 1835, the society's membership flooded the mails with antislavery tracts. Women went door to door collecting signatures on antislavery petitions; by 1838 more than 400,000 petitions, each with numerous signatures, had been sent to Congress. Abolitionist-minded women met in "sewing circles," where they made clothes for fugitive slaves while organizing future activities, such as antislavery fairs at which they sold goods—often items they had made themselves—and later donated the proceeds to antislavery causes, such as abolitionist publications. These fairs also increased the visibility of abolitionism itself and drew more Americans into direct contact with abolitionists and their ideas.

African American Abolitionists   Even as white abolitionist societies opened membership to African Americans and sponsored speaking tours by former slaves, African Americans continued into the 1840s and 1850s their independent efforts to end slavery and to improve the status of free African Americans. Former slaves—most famously, Frederick Douglass, Henry Bibb, Harriet Tubman, and

The International Antislavery Movement

The heart of the international antislavery movement had been in Great Britain, but in the 1830s many of Britain's local antislavery societies thought that they had accomplished their mission and disbanded. Over the previous three decades, the international slave trade had greatly diminished, and in 1833 Parliament ended slavery in the British Empire. At the same time, however, abolitionism in the United States was on the rise, and now American abolitionists extended their work across the Atlantic. They revived the international movement to end slavery where it still existed—in Spanish possessions like Cuba, in independent and colonial South America, in Africa and Asia, and in the United States.

American abolitionism in the 1830s was invigorated by the militancy of black abolitionists and by the conversion of William Lloyd Garrison to immediatism. Seeking to raise money and to put international pressure on the United States to abolish slavery, African American abolitionists in the 1840s toured Britain regularly. On the lecture circuit and in published narratives, they appealed for support. Especially effective were exslaves, who recounted their firsthand experiences of slavery and bared their scarred bodies.

Black abolitionists spoke in small towns and villages, and in Britain's industrial centers. After fugitive slave Moses Gandy toured England, he published his autobiography, the first of dozens of slave narratives published in London. The next year, 1845, Frederick Douglass began a nineteen-month tour,

giving three hundred lectures in Britain.

In 1849 black abolitionists William Wells Brown, Alexander Crummell, and J. W. C. Pennington were among the twenty American delegates at the international Paris Peace Conference. There, Brown likened war to slavery, telling the eight hundred delegates from western Europe and the United States that "it is impossible to maintain slavery without maintaining war." His scheduled brief lecture tour in Britain turned into a five-year exile because, after passage of the 1850 Fugitive Slave Law, he feared

William Wells Brown's autobiography stirred abolitionists in the United States and England. In 1849 Brown was among the American delegates to the Paris Peace Conference, then spent the next five years as an exile in Britain, fearing being sent back to slavery under the 1850 Fugitive Slave Act. He returned to the United States only after British abolitionists purchased his freedom from his former master.
(Southern Historical Collection, the Library of the University of North Carolina, Chapel Hill)

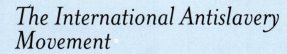

The International Antislavery Movement

being seized and sent back to slavery if he returned to the United States. In 1854 he became free when British abolitionists purchased his freedom from his former master.

Gandy, Douglass, Brown, and dozens of other former slaves helped revive abolitionism as an international issue. They energized the British and Foreign Anti-Slavery Society, founded in 1839, and hundreds of more militant local societies. By the early 1850s, national abolitionist movements succeeded in abolishing slavery in Colombia, Argentina, Venezuela, and Peru. Although the United States continued to resist internal and international pressure, its black abolitionists were instrumental not only in reviving the worldwide antislavery movement, but also, as advocates of women's rights, international peace, temperance, and other reforms, in linking Americans to reform movements around the world.

Sojourner Truth—dedicated their lives to ending slavery through their speeches, publications, and participation in a secret network known as the Underground Railroad, which spirited enslaved men, women, and children to freedom. By the thousands, less famous African Americans continued the work of the postrevolutionary generation and established their own churches, founded their own moral reform societies, published their own newspapers, created schools and orphanages for African American children, and held conventions to consider tactics for improving African Americans' status within the free states.

Although genuine friendships emerged among white and black abolitionists, many white abolitionists treated blacks as inferiors, driving some African Americans to reject white antislavery organizations and to strike out on their own. Others lacked the patience for the supposed immediatism of William Lloyd Garrison; they did not object to moral suasion, but they thought there were even more immediate solutions, such as legislation, to the problems African Americans faced in both the South and the North.

Opposition to Abolitionism

African American abolitionists nonetheless took heart in the immediatists' success at winning converts. But that very success also gave rise to a virulent, even violent, opposition. In the South, mobs blocked the distribution of antislavery tracts. The state of South Carolina intercepted and burned abolitionist literature, and in 1835 proslavery assailants killed four abolitionists in South Carolina and Louisiana, as well as forty people allegedly plotting a slave rebellion in Mississippi and Louisiana that summer.

White northerners had their own reasons for opposing abolition: they recognized cotton's vital role in the nation's economy, and they feared that emancipation would prompt an enormous influx of freed slaves into their own region. Like many southerners, they questioned the institution's morality but not its practicality: They believed blacks to be inherently inferior and incapable of acquiring the attributes—virtue and diligence—required of freedom and citizenship. Some northerners, too, objected to

Women played an activist role in reform, especially in abolitionism. A rare daguerreotype from August 1850 shows women and men, including Frederick Douglass, on the podium at an abolitionist rally in Cazenovia, New York. (Collection of J. Paul Getty Museum, Los Angeles, California)

white women's involvement in abolitionism, believing that women's proper role lay within the home.

The North saw its share of anti-abolitionist violence. In Boston, David Walker died under mysterious circumstances in 1830, after a bounty had apparently been put on his head. Among those northerners who despised abolitionists most were "gentlemen of property and standing"—a nineteenth-century term for commercial and political elites—who often had strong economic connections to the southern cotton economy and who maintained political connections to leading southerners. Northern gentlemen incited anti-abolitionist riots. In Utica, New York, in 1835 merchants and professionals broke up the state Anti-Slavery Convention, which had welcomed blacks and women. Mob violence peaked that year, with more than fifty riots aimed at abolitionists or African Americans. In 1837 in Alton, Illinois, a mob murdered abolitionist editor Elijah P. Lovejoy, and rioters sacked his printing office. The following year, rioters in Philadelphia hurled stones and insults at three thousand black and white women attending the Anti-Slavery Convention of American Women held in the brand-new Pennsylvania Hall, a building constructed to house abolitionist meetings and an abolitionist bookstore. The following day, a mob burned the building to the ground, just three days after its dedication.

Moral Suasion Versus Political Action

The violent reaction to abolitionism made some immediatists question whether moral suasion was a realistic tactic. Among them was James G. Birney, the son of a Kentucky slaveowner, who embraced immediatism but sought to end slavery by electing abolitionists who would push for a legislative end to slavery. Those who favored a more practical, political solution saw little room for women within the abolitionist movement. The end of slavery, they believed, could be brought about only in the male sphere of politics. To involve women violated the natural order of things while detracting from the ultimate goal: freedom for slaves.

Thus, when William Lloyd Garrison, an ardent supporter of women's rights, endorsed the appointment of Abby Kelly to the business committee of the American Anti-Slavery Society in 1840, he provoked an irreparable split in the abolitionist movement. Arthur Tappan and Theodore Weld led a dissident group that formed the new American and Foreign Anti-Slavery Society. That society in turn established a new political party: the Liberty Party, which nominated Birney for president in 1840 and 1844.

Although committed to immediate abolitionism, members of the Liberty Party doubted the federal government had the authority to abolish slavery where it already existed. It was up to the states, not the federal government, to determine the legality of slavery within their bounds. Where the government could act, they felt, was in the western territories, and they demanded that all new territories prohibit slavery. Some prominent black abolitionists, including Frederick Douglass, endorsed the party, whose leaders emphasized the need to combat not just southern slavery but also northern prejudice.

WOMEN'S RIGHTS

Frustrated by their treatment within the abolitionist movement, some female abolitionists took the lead in advocating women's rights. At the first World Anti-Slavery Convention in London in 1840, abolitionists Lucretia Mott and Elizabeth Cady Stanton first met, united in their dismay that female abolitionists were denied seats in the convention's main hall; eight years later, the two would help organize the first American women's rights convention. Angelina and Sarah Grimké had been born to a slaveholding family in South Carolina but later moved north and became active in the abolitionist movement. After critics attacked them for speaking to audiences that included men, they rejected claims that women should obey, not lecture, men, and the sisters took the lead in advocating for women's legal and social equality.

Religious revivalism and moral reform led other women to reexamine their positions in society. Revivals helped women to see themselves as inherently equal to men, and reform movements brought middle-class women outside the home and into the public sphere. Female reformers' lobbying had helped to effect legal change, and some women believed the next step was obvious: women should be granted full citizenship rights.

Legal Rights　　There were a great many legal obstacles to overcome. After independence, American states carried over traditional English marriage law, which gave husbands absolute control over the family. Men owned their wives' personal property, were legal guardians of their children, and owned whatever family members produced or earned. A father had the legal authority to oppose his daughter's choice of husband, though by 1800 most American women chose their own marriage partner.

Married women made modest gains in property and spousal rights from the 1830s on. Arkansas in 1835 passed the first married women's property law, and by 1860 sixteen more states had followed. In those states, women—singled, married, or divorced—could own and convey property. When a wife inherited property, it was hers, not her husband's, though money that she earned or acquired in some other way continued to belong to her husband. Women could also write wills. Such laws were particularly popular among wealthy Americans, South and North, who hoped to protect their family fortunes during periods of economic boom and bust; property in a woman's name was safe from her husband's creditors. In the 1830s, states also liberalized divorce laws, adding cruelty and desertion as grounds for divorce, but divorce remained rare.

Despite these changes, a few radical reformers argued that marriage constituted a form of bondage. Among the most outspoken critics of marriage was Lucy Stone, who finally consented to marry fellow abolitionist Henry Blackwell, but only under the condition that she not take a vow of obedience and that she keep her own name. The term "Lucy Stoner" entered common parlance as a reference to married women who did not adopt their husband's name.

Political Rights By the time Lucy Stone and Harry Blackwell married in 1855, both had become active in the organized movement to secure women's political rights. That movement had been launched in July 1848, when Elizabeth Cady Stanton, Lucretia Mott, Mary Ann McClintock, Martha Wright, and Jane Hunt—all abolitionists and, except Stanton, Quakers—organized the first Woman's Rights Convention at Seneca Falls, New York. Three hundred women and men gathered to demand social and economic equality for women, and some added political equality to the list of demands. They protested women's legal disabilities as well as their social restrictions, such as exclusion from advanced schooling and many occupations. Their Declaration of Sentiments, modeled on the Declaration of Independence, broadcast the injustices suffered by women and launched the women's rights movement. "All men and women are created equal," the declaration proclaimed. The similar premises of abolitionism and women's rights led many reformers, including former slaves like Sojourner Truth, to work simultaneously for both movements in the 1850s. Even among those who supported the movement's general aims, the question of female suffrage became divisive. Some men were supporters, notably William Lloyd Garrison and Frederick Douglass, but most men actively opposed women's right to vote. At Seneca Falls, the resolution on woman suffrage passed only after Frederick Douglass spoke passionately for it, but even then some participants refused to sign. In 1851 Elizabeth Cady Stanton joined forces with Susan B. Anthony, a temperance advocate, to become the most vocal and persistent activists for women's voting rights. Despite their best efforts, Stanton and Anthony won relatively few converts and many critics.

JACKSONIANISM AND PARTY POLITICS

No less than reformers, politicians sought to control the direction of change in the expanding nation. With changes to suffrage laws, they reframed their political visions to appeal to an increasingly broad-based electorate. Hotly contested elections helped make politics the great nineteenth-century American pastime, drawing the interest and participation of voters and nonvoters alike.

Expanding Political Participation Property restrictions for voters, which states began abandoning during the 1810s, remained in only seven of twenty-six states by 1840. Some states even allowed foreign nationals who had officially declared their intention of becoming American citizens to vote. The net effect was a sharply higher number of votes cast in presidential elections. Between 1824 and 1828 that number increased threefold, from 360,000 to over 1.1 million. In 1840, 2.4 million men cast votes. The proportion of eligible voters who cast ballots also grew, from about 27 percent in 1824 to more than 80 percent in 1840.

At the same time, the method of choosing presidential electors became more democratic. Previously, a caucus of party leaders had done so in most states, but by 1824 eighteen out of twenty-four states chose electors by popular vote, compared to just five of sixteen in 1800. As a result, politicians augmented their direct appeals to voters, and the election of 1824 saw the end of the congressional caucus, when House and Senate members of the same political party came together to select their candidate.

Election of 1824   As a result, five candidates, all of whom identified as Democratic-Republicans, came forward to run for president in 1824. The poorly attended Republican caucus chose William H. Crawford of Georgia, secretary of the treasury, as its presidential candidate. But other Democratic-Republicans boycotted the caucus as undemocratic, ending Congress's role in nominating presidential candidates. Instead, state legislatures nominated candidates, offering the expanded electorate a slate of sectional candidates. John Quincy Adams drew support from New England, while westerners backed House Speaker Henry Clay of Kentucky. Some southerners at first supported Secretary of War John C. Calhoun, who later dropped his bid for the presidency and ran for the vice presidency instead. The Tennessee legislature nominated Andrew Jackson, a military hero whose political views were unknown.

Among the four candidates who remained in the presidential race until the election, Jackson led in both electoral and popular votes, but no candidate received a majority in the electoral college. Adams finished second, and Crawford and Clay trailed far behind. Under the Constitution, the House of Representatives, voting by state delegation, one vote to a state, would select the next president from among the three leaders in electoral votes. Clay, who had the fewest votes, was dropped, but the three others courted his support, hoping he would influence his electors to vote for them. Crawford, disabled from a stroke that he suffered before the election, never received serious consideration. Clay backed Adams, who won with thirteen of the twenty-four state delegations and thus became president. Adams named Clay to the cabinet position of secretary of state, the traditional steppingstone to the presidency.

Angry Jacksonians denounced the election's outcome as a "corrupt bargain," claiming that Adams had stolen the election from their candidate by offering Clay a cabinet position in exchange for his votes. Jackson's bitterness fueled his later emphasis on the people's will. The Republican Party split. The Adams wing emerged as the National Republicans, and the Jacksonians became the Democrats; they immediately began planning for 1828.

After taking the oath of office, Adams proposed a strong nationalist policy incorporating Henry Clay's American System, a program of protective tariffs, a national bank, and internal improvements. Adams believed the federal government's active role should extend to education, science, and the arts. He proposed a national university in Washington, D.C. Brilliant as a diplomat and secretary of state, Adams fared less well as chief executive. He underestimated the lingering effects of the Panic of 1819 and the resulting staunch opposition to a national bank and a protective tariff.

Presidential candidate Andrew Jackson is portrayed on a trinket or sewing box in 1824. This is an example both of how campaigns entered popular culture and of the active role of women, excluded from voting, in politics. (Collection of David J. and Janice L. Frent)

Election of 1828

The 1828 election pitted Adams against Jackson in a rowdy campaign. Nicknamed "Old Hickory" after the toughest of American hardwood, Andrew Jackson was a rough-and-tumble, ambitious man. Born in South Carolina in 1767, he rose from humble beginnings to become a wealthy Tennessee planter and slaveholder. Jackson was the first American president from the West and the first born in a log cabin; he was at ease among both frontiersmen and planters. Having served in the Revolution as a boy, Jackson claimed a connection to the founding generation. In the Tennessee militia, General Jackson led the campaign to remove Creeks from the Alabama and Georgia frontier. He burst onto the national scene in 1815 as the hero of the Battle of New Orleans and in 1818 enhanced his glory in an expedition against Seminoles in Spanish Florida. Jackson also served as a congressman and senator from Tennessee, and as the first territorial governor of Florida (1821), before running for president in 1824.

Voters and nonvoters, too, displayed their enthusiasm for Jackson with badges, medals, and other campaign paraphernalia, which were mass-produced for the first time. The contest was also intensely personal. Jackson's supporters accused Adams of stealing the 1824 election and, when he was envoy to Russia, of having secured prostitutes for the czar. Anti-Jacksonians published reports that Jackson's wife, Rachel, had married Jackson before her divorce from her first husband was final; she was, they sneered, an adulterer and a bigamist. In 1806 Jackson, in an attempt defend Rachel's integrity, had killed a man during a duel, and the cry of "murderer!" was revived in the election.

Although Adams kept the states he had won in 1824, his opposition was now unified behind a single candidate, and Jackson swamped him, polling 56 percent of the popular vote and winning in the electoral college by 178 to 83 votes. Jacksonians believed that the will of the people had finally been served. Through a lavishly financed coalition of state parties, political leaders, and newspaper editors, a popular movement had elected the president. The Democratic Party became the first well-organized national political party in the United States, and tight party organization became the hallmark of nineteenth-century American politics.

Democrats

The Democrats represented a wide range of views but shared a fundamental commitment to the Jeffersonian concept of an agrarian society. They viewed a strong central government as the enemy of individual liberty, and they believed that government intervention in the economy benefited special-interest groups and created corporate monopolies that favored the rich. They sought to restore the independence of the individual—the artisan and the ordinary farmer—by ending federal support of banks and corporations, and by restricting the use of paper currency. Jackson and his supporters also opposed reform movements. They believed, for instance, that public schools restricted individual liberty by interfering with parental responsibility and undermined freedom of religion by replacing church schools. When it came to westward expansion, though, Jackson and his followers called for federal intervention. It was Jackson who initiated Indian removal despite the protests of northeastern reformers.

By restraining government and emphasizing individualism, Jacksonians sought to restore traditional republican virtues, such as self-discipline and self-reliance, traits supposedly undermined by economic and social change. Jackson looked to Jefferson and the founding generation as models of traditional values. "My political creed," Jackson wrote to Tennessee congressman James K. Polk in 1826, "was formed in the old republican school." Jackson rejected elitism and advocated for popular government. Time and again he declared that sovereignty resided with the people, not with the states or the courts. In this respect Jackson himself was a reformer; he sought government by majority, not elite, rule.

Like Jefferson, Jackson strengthened the executive branch of government even as he advocated limited government. In combining the roles of party leader and chief of state, he centralized power in the White House. He relied on political friends, his "Kitchen Cabinet," for advice, only rarely consulting his official cabinet. Jackson commanded enormous loyalty and rewarded his followers handsomely. Rotating officeholders, Jackson claimed, made government more responsive to the public will and allowed him to appoint loyal Democrats to office, a practice that his critics called the spoils system, in which the victor gives the spoils of victory to his supporters. Although Jackson was not the first president to do so—Jefferson had replaced many of Adams's appointees—his own outcry against corrupt bargains made him an easy target for inflammatory rhetoric. The spoils system, opponents charged, corrupted the government itself because appointments were based on loyalty, not competency.

King Andrew

Opponents mocked Jackson as "King Andrew I," charging him with abuse of power by ignoring the Supreme Court's ruling on Cherokee rights, by sidestepping his cabinet, and by removing experienced officeholders in favor of his own political cronies. They rejected his claim of restoring republican virtue and accused him of recklessly destroying the economy.

Perhaps nothing rankled Jackson's critics more than his frequent use of the veto, which he used to promote his vision of a limited government. In 1830 he vetoed the Maysville Road bill, which would have funded construction of a 60-mile turnpike from Maysville to Lexington, Kentucky. A federally subsidized internal improvement confined to one state was unconstitutional, he insisted; states bore responsibility for such projects. The veto undermined Henry Clay's American System and personally embarrassed Clay because the project was in his home district.

From George Washington to John Quincy Adams, the first six presidents had vetoed nine bills; Jackson alone vetoed twelve. Previous presidents believed that vetoes were justified only on constitutional grounds, but Jackson considered policy disagreements legitimate grounds as well. He made the veto an effective weapon for controlling Congress, because representatives and senators had to weigh the possibility of a presidential veto as they deliberated.

FEDERALISM AT ISSUE: THE NULLIFICATION AND BANK CONTROVERSIES

Soon after the Maysville Road veto, Jackson directly faced the question of state versus federal power. The slave South feared federal power and no state more so than South Carolina, where the planter class was the strongest and slavery the most concentrated. Southerners also resented protectionist tariffs, one of the foundations of Clay's American System, which in 1824 and 1828 protected manufactures by imposing import duties on manufactured cloth and iron. But in protecting northern factories, the tariff raised the costs of manufactured goods to southerners, who quickly labeled the high tariff of 1828 the Tariff of Abominations.

Nullification

South Carolina's political leaders rejected the 1828 tariff, invoking the doctrine of nullification, according to which a state had the right to overrule, or nullify, federal legislation. Nullification was based on the idea expressed in the Virginia and Kentucky Resolutions of 1798—that the states, representing the people, have a right to judge the constitutionality of federal actions. Jackson's vice president, John C. Calhoun of South Carolina, argued in his unsigned *Exposition and Protest* that, in any disagreement between the federal government and a state, a special state convention—like the conventions called to ratify the Constitution—should decide the conflict by either nullifying or affirming the federal law. Only the power of nullification, Calhoun asserted, could protect the minority against the tyranny of the majority.

As Jackson's running mate in 1828, Calhoun had avoided endorsing nullification and thus embarrassing the Democratic ticket; he also hoped to win Jackson's support as the Democratic presidential heir apparent. Thus, in early 1830, Calhoun presided silently over the Senate and its packed galleries when Senator Daniel Webster of Massachusetts and Senator Robert Y. Hayne of South Carolina debated states' rights. The debate started over a resolution to restrict western land sales but soon touched on the tariff. From there, it focused on the nature of the Union, with nullification a subtext. Hayne charged that the North was threatening to bring disunity. For two days Webster eloquently defended New England and the republic, as he kept supporters of nullification on the defensive. Although debating Hayne, he aimed his remarks at Calhoun. At the climax of the debate, Webster invoked two powerful images. One was the outcome of nullification: "states dissevered, discordant, belligerent; on a land rent with civil feuds, or drenched . . . in fraternal blood!" The other was a patriotic vision of a great nation flourishing under the motto "Liberty and Union, now and forever, one and inseparable."

Though sympathetic to states' rights and distrustful of the federal government, Jackson rejected the idea of state sovereignty. He strongly believed that sovereignty rested with the people. Believing deeply in the Union, he shared Webster's dread of nullification. Soon after the Webster-Hayne debate, the president made his position clear at a Jefferson Day dinner with the toast "Our Federal Union, it must and shall be preserved." Vice President Calhoun, when his turn came, toasted "The Federal Union— next to our liberty the most dear," revealing his adherence to states' rights. Calhoun and Jackson grew apart, and Jackson looked to Secretary of State Martin Van Buren, not Calhoun, as his successor.

Tension resumed when Congress passed a new tariff in 1832, reducing some duties but retaining high taxes on imported iron, cottons, and woolens. Although a majority of southern representatives supported the new tariff, South Carolinians refused to go along. In their eyes, the constitutional right to control their own destiny had been sacrificed to the demands of northern industrialists. They feared the act could set a precedent for congressional legislation on slavery. In November 1832 a South Carolina state convention nullified both the 1828 and the 1832 tariffs, declaring it unlawful for federal officials to collect duties in the state.

The Force Act

Privately, Jackson threatened to invade South Carolina and hang Vice President Calhoun; publicly, he took measured steps. In December Jackson issued a proclamation opposing nullification. He moved troops to federal forts in South Carolina and prepared U.S. marshals to collect the required duties. At Jackson's request, Congress passed the Force Act, authorizing the president to call up troops but also offering a way to avoid force by collecting duties before foreign ships reached Charleston's harbor. At the same time, Jackson extended an olive branch by recommending tariff reductions.

Calhoun, disturbed by South Carolina's drift toward separatism, resigned as vice president and soon won election to represent South Carolina in the U.S. Senate. There he worked with Henry Clay to draw up the compromise Tariff of 1833. Quickly passed by Congress and signed by the president, the new tariff lengthened the list of duty-free items and reduced duties over nine years. Satisfied, South Carolina's convention repealed its nullification law. In a final salvo, it also nullified Jackson's Force Act. Jackson ignored the gesture.

Nullification offered a genuine debate on the nature and principles of the republic. Each side believed it was upholding the Constitution and opposing special privilege and subversion of republican values. South Carolina's leaders opposed the tyranny of the federal government and manufacturing interests. Jackson fought the tyranny of South Carolina, whose refusal to bow to federal authority threatened to split the republic. Neither side won a clear victory, though both claimed to have done so. It took another crisis, over a central bank, to define the powers of the federal government more clearly.

Second Bank of the United States

At stake was survival of the Second Bank of the United States, whose twenty-year charter was scheduled to expire in 1836. The bank served as a depository for federal funds and provided credit for businesses. Its bank notes circulated as currency throughout the country; they could be readily exchanged for gold, and the federal government accepted them as payment in all transactions. Through its twenty-five branch offices, the Second Bank acted as a clearing-house for state banks, refusing to accept bank notes of any state bank lacking sufficient gold in reserve. Most state banks resented the central bank's police role: by presenting a state bank's notes for redemption all at once, the Second Bank could easily ruin a state bank. Moreover, with less money in reserve, state banks found themselves unable to compete on an equal footing with the Second Bank.

Many state governments also regarded the national bank as unresponsive to local needs. Westerners and urban workers remembered with bitterness the bank's conservative credit policies during the Panic of 1819. As a private, profit-making institution, its policies reflected the interest of its owners, especially its president, Nicholas Biddle, who controlled the bank completely. An eastern patrician, Biddle symbolized all that westerners found wrong with the bank. The bank became the prime issue in the presidential campaign of 1832, the first in which political parties held conventions.

Anti-Masonry

The national political convention was the innovation of the Antimason Party, which had started in upstate New York in the mid-1820s as a grassroots movement against Freemasonry, a secret male fraternity that attracted middle- and upper-class men prominent in commerce and civic affairs. Opponents of Masonry claimed the fraternity to be unrepublican; Masons colluded to bestow business and political favors on each other, and—in the incident that sparked the organized Antimasonry movement—Masons had obstructed justice in the investigation of the 1826 disappearance of a disgruntled former member who had written an exposé of the society. Evangelicals considered Masons sacrilegious, claiming that they talked of being Christians but behaved in unchristian ways. Masonry, they said, encouraged men to neglect their families for alcohol and ribald entertainment at Masonic lodges. Antimasonry soon developed into a vibrant political movement in the Northeast and parts of the Midwest. In the 1828 presidential election, the Antimasons had opposed Jackson, himself a Mason. With their confidence bolstered by strong showings in gubernatorial elections in 1830, the Antimasons held the first national political convention in Baltimore in 1831, nominating William Wirt of Maryland for president and Amos Ellmaker of Pennsylvania for vice president.

Election of 1832

Following the Antimasons' lead, the Democrats and National Republicans held their own conventions. The Democrats reaffirmed the choice of Jackson, who had already been nominated by state legislatures, for president and nominated Martin Van Buren of New York for vice president. The National Republican convention selected Clay and John Sergeant of Pennsylvania. The Independent Democrats ran John Floyd and Henry Lee of Virginia; as governor of Virginia, Floyd had supported nullification, winning him the hearts of many South Carolinians.

Jacksonians denounced the bank as a vehicle for special privilege and economic power, while the Republicans supported it as a pillar of their plan for economic nationalism. The bank's charter was valid until 1836, but as part of his campaign strategy, Clay persuaded Biddle to ask Congress to approve an early rechartering. If Jackson signed the rechartering bill, then Clay could attack the president's inconsistency on the issue. If he vetoed it, then—Clay reasoned—the voters would give the nod to Clay. The plan backfired. The president vetoed the bill and issued a pointed veto message appealing to those voters who feared that the era's rapid economic development spread its advantages undemocratically. Jackson acknowledged that prosperity could never be evenly dispersed, but he took a strong stand against special interests that tried to use the government to their own unfair advantage. "It is to be regretted," he wrote, "that the rich and powerful too often bend the acts of government to their selfish purposes." The message was powerful and successful. Jackson won 54 percent of the popular vote to Clay's 37 percent; he fared even better in the electoral college, where he captured 76 percent of electors. Although the Antimasons won just one state, Vermont, they nonetheless helped galvanize the anti-Jackson opposition.

Jackson's Second Term

After his sweeping victory and second inauguration, Jackson moved in 1833 to dismantle the Second Bank. He deposited federal funds in state-chartered banks (critics called them his "pet banks"). Without federal money, the Second Bank shriveled. When its federal charter expired in 1836, it became just another Pennsylvania-chartered private bank. Five years later it closed its doors.

As Congress allowed the Bank of the United States to die, it passed the Deposit Act of 1836 with Jackson's support. The act authorized the secretary of the treasury to designate one bank in each state and territory to provide services formerly performed by the Bank of the United States. The act provided that the federal surplus in excess of $5 million be distributed to the states as interest-free loans beginning in 1837. These loans were never repaid—a fitting Jacksonian restraint on the federal purse.

The surplus had derived from wholesale speculation in public lands: speculators borrowed money to purchase public land, used the land as collateral for credit to buy additional acreage, and repeated the cycle. Between 1834 and 1836, federal receipts from land sales rose from $5 million to $25 million. The state banks providing the loans issued bank notes. Jackson, an opponent of paper money, feared that the speculative craze threatened the stability of state banks and undermined the interests of settlers, who could not compete with speculators in bidding for the best land.

Specie Circular

In keeping with his opposition to paper currency, the president ordered Treasury Secretary Levi Woodbury to issue the Specie Circular. It provided that after August 1836 only specie—gold or silver—or Virginia scrip (paper money) would be accepted as payment for land. By ending credit sales, it significantly reduced purchases of public land and the federal budget surplus. As a result, the government suspended payments to the states.

The policy was a disaster. Although federal land sales fell sharply, speculation continued as land available for sale became scarce. The increased demand for specie squeezed banks, and many suspended the redemption of bank notes for specie. Credit contracted further as banks issued fewer notes and made fewer loans. Jackson aggravated the situation by pursuing a tight money policy. More important, the Specie Circular was similar to a bill defeated in the Senate just three months earlier, so Jackson used presidential powers to override the legislative will. Jackson's opponents thus saw King Andrew at work. In the waning days of Jackson's administration, Congress voted to repeal the circular, but the president pocket-vetoed the bill by holding it unsigned until Congress adjourned. Finally, in May 1838, a joint resolution of Congress overturned the circular. Sales of land resumed, and the speculative fervor ended.

THE WHIG CHALLENGE AND THE SECOND PARTY SYSTEM

In the 1830s, opponents of the Democrats, including remnants of the National Republican and Antimason Parties, joined together to become the Whig Party. Resentful of Jackson's domination of Congress, the Whigs borrowed the name of the eighteenth-century British party that opposed the tyranny of Hanoverian monarchs. They, too, were the loyal opposition. From 1834 through the 1840s, the Whigs and the

Democrats competed on nearly equal footing, and each drew supporters from all regions. The era's political competition—the second party system—was more intense and better organized than what scholars have labeled as the first party system of Democratic-Republicans versus Federalists.

Whigs and Reformers

Whigs favored economic expansion through an activist government. They supported corporate charters, a national bank, and paper currency; Democrats opposed all three. Whigs generally professed a strong belief in progress and perfectibility, and they favored social reforms, including public schools, prison and asylum reform, and temperance. Whigs did not object to helping special interests if doing so promoted the general welfare. The chartering of corporations, they argued, expanded economic opportunity for everyone, laborers and farmers alike. Democrats, distrustful of concentrated economic power and of moral and economic coercion, held fast to the Jeffersonian principle of limited government.

Whigs stressed a "harmony of interests" among all classes and interests. Their philosophy was one of equal opportunity. Democrats tended to see society as divided into the "haves" and the "have nots," and they embraced a motto of "equal rights." They championed "heroic artisans" like Sam Patch, whereas Whigs remained wary of the "excesses of democracy" and preferred to see society ruled from the top down. Whigs believed in free-labor ideology and thought that society's wealthy and powerful had risen by their own merits. Democrats alleged that, instead, their political opponents had benefited from special favors.

But religion and ethnicity, as much as class, influenced party affiliation. The Whigs' support for energetic government and moral reform won the favor of evangelical Protestants. Methodists and Baptists were overwhelmingly Whigs, as were the small number of free black voters. In many locales the membership rolls of reform societies overlapped those of the party. Indeed, Whigs practiced a kind of political revivalism. Their rallies resembled camp meetings; their speeches employed pulpit rhetoric; their programs embodied reformers' perfectionist beliefs.

In their appeal to evangelicals, Whigs alienated members of other faiths. The evangelicals' ideal Christian state had no room for nonevangelical Protestants, Catholics, Mormons, or religious freethinkers. Those groups opposed Sabbath laws and temperance legislation in particular, and state interference in moral and religious questions in general. In fact, they preferred to keep religion and politics separate. As a result, more than 95 percent of Irish Catholics, 90 percent of Reformed Dutch, and 80 percent of German Catholics voted Democratic.

The parties' platforms thus attracted what might seem to be an odd coalition of voters. Whigs appealed more to those who benefited from the era's rapid economic changes, whereas Democrats often remained wary of those changes and committed to agrarian expansion. The Whigs drew antislavery supporters as well as northern businessmen and workers pledged to maintaining good relations with the South. Well-settled slave owners, especially in the Upper South, often voted Whig, as did black New Englanders. Both groups favored halting slavery's westward expansion—the former, to protect their own investments from cheap western competition and the latter, to undercut slavery itself. Democrats' promises to open additional lands for settlement attracted yeoman farmers, wage earners, frontier slaveowners, and immigrants. With such broad coalitions of voters, there was room within each party for a broad spectrum of beliefs, particularly when it came to slavery.

Politicians recognized, however, the potentially divisive nature of slavery, and some went to extremes to keep it out of the national political debate. In response to the American Anti-Slavery Society's petitioning campaign, the House of Representatives in 1836 adopted what abolitionists labeled the "gag rule," which automatically tabled abolitionist petitions, effectively preventing debate on them. In a dramatic defense of the right of petition, former president John Quincy Adams, now a representative from Massachusetts, took to the floor again and again to speak against the gag rule, which was ultimately repealed in 1844.

Election of 1836

Vice President Martin Van Buren, handpicked by Jackson, headed the Democratic ticket in the 1836 presidential election. Van Buren was a career politician who had built a political machine—the Albany Regency—in New York and then left to join Jackson's cabinet in 1829, first as secretary of state and then as American minister to Great Britain.

Because the Whigs in 1836 had not yet coalesced into a national party, they entered three sectional candidates: Daniel Webster (New England), Hugh White (the South), and William Henry Harrison (the West). By splintering the vote, they hoped to throw the election into the House of Representatives. Van Buren, however, comfortably captured the electoral college even though he had only a 25,000-vote edge out of a total of 1.5 million votes cast. No vice-presidential candidate received a majority of electoral votes, and for the only time in American history, the Senate decided a vice-presidential race, selecting Democratic candidate Richard M. Johnson of Kentucky.

Van Buren and Hard Times

Van Buren took office just weeks before the American credit system collapsed. In response to the Specie Circular, New York banks stopped redeeming paper currency with gold in mid-1837. Soon all banks suspended payments in hard coin. A downward economic spiral began, curtailing bank loans and strangling business confidence. Credit contraction made things worse. After a brief recovery, hard times persisted from 1839 until 1843.

Van Buren followed Jackson's hard-money policies. He cut federal spending, causing prices to drop further, and he opposed a national bank, which would have expanded credit. The president proposed, too, a new regional treasury system for government deposits. The proposed treasury branches would accept and disperse only gold and silver coin; they would not accept paper currency or checks drawn on state banks. Van Buren's independent treasury bill became law in 1840. By increasing the demand for hard coin, it deprived banks of gold and accelerated price deflation. Whigs and Democrats faced off at the state level over these issues. Whigs favored new banks, more paper currency, and readily available corporate and bank charters. As the party of hard money, Democrats favored eliminating paper currency altogether. Increasingly the Democrats became distrustful even of state banks, and by the mid-1840s a majority favored eliminating all bank corporations.

Anglo-American Tensions

Amid hard times came a renewal of Anglo-American tensions. One of the most troublesome disputes arose from the *Caroline* affair. After the privately owned steamer *Caroline* carried supplies to aid an unsuccessful Canadian uprising against Great Britain, a group of British loyalists burned the ship, killing an American citizen in the process. Britain refused to apologize, and American newspapers called for revenge. Fearing that popular support for the Canadian rebels would ignite war, President Van Buren posted troops under General Winfield Scott at the border to discourage Americans from seeking vigilante retaliation. Tensions subsided in late 1840 when New York arrested a Canadian deemed responsible for the American's death aboard the *Caroline.* The alleged murderer was acquitted. Had the verdict gone otherwise, Lord Palmerston, the British foreign minister, might have sought war.

At almost the same time, an old border dispute between Maine and New Brunswick disrupted Anglo-American relations. Great Britain had accepted an 1831 arbitration decision fixing a new boundary, but the U.S. Senate rejected it. Thus, when Canadian lumbermen cut trees in the disputed region in the winter of 1838–1839, a posse of Maine citizens assembled to expel them. The lumbermen captured the posse, both sides mobilized their militias, and Congress authorized a call-up of fifty thousand men. General Scott was now dispatched to Aroostook, Maine, where he arranged a truce. The Webster-Ashburton Treaty (1842) settled the boundaries between Maine and New Brunswick, and along the Great Lakes, but it left unresolved the still-disputed northern boundary of Oregon, joint occupancy of which had been renewed in 1827.

William Henry Harrison and the Election of 1840

With the nation in the grip of hard times, the Whigs faced the election of 1840 with confidence. Their strategy was simple: maintain loyal supporters and win over independents by blaming hard times on the Democrats. The Whigs rallied behind a military hero, General William Henry Harrison, conqueror of the Shawnees at Tippecanoe Creek in 1811. The Democrats renominated President Van Buren, and the newly formed Liberty Party ran James Birney.

Harrison, or "Old Tippecanoe," and his running mate, John Tyler of Virginia, ran a "log cabin and hard cider" campaign—a people's crusade—against the aristocratic president in "the Palace." Although descended from a Virginia plantation family, Harrison presented himself as an ordinary farmer. Party hacks bluntly blamed hard times on the Democrats, but Harrison himself remained silent, earning himself the nickname "General Mum." The Whigs wooed voters with huge rallies, parades, songs, posters, campaign mementos, and a party newspaper, *The Log Cabin.* They reached out to voters as well as nonvoters, including women, who attended their rallies and speeches. One Virginia woman's support for the Whigs led her to publish two pamphlets backing Harrison's candidacy. In a huge turnout, 80 percent of eligible voters cast ballots. Harrison won the popular vote by a narrow margin but swept the electoral college by 234 to 60.

Immediately after taking office in 1841, President Harrison convened a special session of Congress to pass the Whig program: repeal of the independent treasury system, a new national bank, and a higher protective tariff. But the sixty-eight-year-old Harrison caught pneumonia and died within a month of his inauguration. His vice president, John Tyler, who had left the Democratic Party to protest Jackson's nullification proclamation, now found himself the first vice president whose president had died in office. The Constitution did not stipulate what should happen in such circumstances, but Tyler quickly took full possession of executive powers and set a crucial precedent that would not be codified in the Constitution until the latter part of the twentieth century with the Twenty-fifth Amendment.

President Tyler In office, Tyler became more a Democrat than a Whig. He repeatedly vetoed Clay's protective tariffs, internal improvements, and bills aimed at reviving the Bank of the United States. Two days after Tyler's second veto of a bank bill, the entire cabinet except Secretary of State Daniel Webster resigned; Webster, once done negotiating the Webster-Ashburton treaty, followed. Tyler became a president without a party, and the Whigs lost the presidency without losing an election. Disgusted Whigs referred to Tyler as "His Accidency."

Like Jackson, Tyler expanded presidential powers and emphasized westward expansion. His expansionist vision contained Whig elements, though: he had his eye on commercial markets in Hawaii and China. During his presidency, the United States negotiated its first treaties with China, and Tyler expanded the Monroe Doctrine to include Hawaii (or the Sandwich Islands). But, more than anything else, Tyler's vision for the nation's path to greatness fixed on Texas and the westward expansion of slavery.

SUMMARY

Religion and reform shaped politics from 1824 through the 1840s. Driven by a belief in human perfectibility, many evangelicals, especially women, worked tirelessly to right the wrongs of American society. By doing so, they hoped to trigger the millennium, the thousand years of peace on earth that would accompany Christ's Second Coming. Reformers battled the evils of prostitution and alcohol, and sought to reform criminals and delinquents, improve insane asylums, and establish public schools. Some rejected the possibility of reforming American society from within and instead joined experimental communities that modeled radical alternatives to the social and economic order. Abolitionists combined the reformers' and utopians' approaches; they worked to perfect American society from within but through radical means—the eradication of slavery. As women entered the public sphere as advocates of reform and, especially, abolitionism, some of them turned toward the equally radical proposition of full legal and political rights for women.

Reform remade politics, and politicians reshaped public discourse to appeal to the broadening electorate. As did reformers, President John Quincy Adams raised expectations about an expanded governmental role. The struggles between the National Republicans and the Democrats, then between the Democrats and the Whigs, stimulated even greater interest in campaigns and political issues. The Democrats, who rallied around Andrew Jackson, and Jackson's opponents, who found shelter under the Whig tent, competed almost equally for the loyalty of voters. Both parties built strong organizations that faced off in national and local elections. And both parties favored economic expansion but by different means: The Whigs advocated centralized government initiative to spur commercial growth, whereas Democrats advocated limited government and sought agricultural expansion. Jackson did not hesitate, however, to use presidential authority, and his opponents called him King Andrew. The controversies over the Second Bank of the United States and nullification exposed different interpretations of the nation's founding principles.

The late 1830s and early 1840s would be a period of uncertainty: the economy once again cycled through a period of bust; tensions with the British resurfaced; and—for the first time—a president died in office. As John Tyler, derided by his critics as "His Accidency," took office, he tenaciously articulated a vision of American greatness that depended on its westward expansion.

13

The Contested West
1815–1860

THE WEST IN THE AMERICAN IMAGINATION

For historian Frederick Jackson Turner, writing in the late nineteenth century, it was the West, not the South or the North, that was distinctive. With its abundance of free land, the western frontier—what he saw as the "meeting point between savagery and civilization"—bred American democracy, shaped the American character, and made the United States exceptional among nations. Modern historians generally eschew the notion of American exceptionalism, stressing instead the deep and complex connections between the United States and the rest of the world. But although today's scholars also reject the racialist assumptions of Turner's definition of *frontier*, some do see continued value in the term when it is understood as a meeting place of different cultures. Others see the West as fundamentally a place, not a process, though they offer conflicting definitions of what delineates it.

Defining the West   For early-nineteenth-century Americans of European descent, the West would have included anything west of the Appalachian Mountains. But it was, first and foremost, a place that represented the future—a place where they might seek economic and social betterment for themselves and their children. For many, that betterment would come through land ownership; the West seemed

CHRONOLOGY

1812 • Congress establishes General Land Office

1820 • Congress lowers price of public lands

1821 • William Becknell charts Santa Fe Trail
 • Mexico becomes independent nation

1823 • Mexico allows Stephen Austin to settle U.S. citizens in Mexico

1824 • Congressional General Survey Act empowers military to chart transportation routes
 • Jedediah Smith publicizes the South Pass to the Far West
 • Indian Office (later Bureau of Indian Affairs) established

1825–1832 • *Empresario* contracts signed for American settlement of Texas

1826 • Failed Fredonia rebellion in Texas

1830 • Indian Removal Act (see Chapter 10)

1832 • Black Hawk War

1834 • Cyrus McCormick patents mechanical reaper

1836 • Lone Star Republic founded
 • U.S. Army Corps of Topographical Engineers established

1840–1860 • 250,000 to 500,000 migrants travel overland to the Far West

1841 • Log Cabin Bill allows settlers to claim 160 acres of public land on credit

1844 • Presidential campaign features annexation of Texas

1845 • Democratic editor coins "manifest destiny"
 • Texas annexed by joint resolution of Congress (March 1) and becomes twenty-eighth state (December 29)

1846–1848 • War with Mexico (see Chapter 14)

1847 • Mormons settle in Great Salt Lake valley

1848 • Gold discovered in California

1849–50s • Farmers and prospectors stream into the Great Plains and Far West

1855 • Massacre of Indians at Ash Hollow triggers warfare between the Lakota and the United States

1857–1858 • Mormons and U.S. Army engage in armed conflict

1862 • Homestead Act allots 160 acres of free land to those who improve it

to have such an abundance of land that even the poor could hope to own a farm and achieve economic and political independence. Men who already owned land, like Pettis Perkinson, looked westward for cheaper, bigger, and more fertile landholdings. With the discovery of gold in California in 1848, the West became a place to strike it rich and then return home, where one might live in increased comfort or even opulence.

Many people arrived in the West only under the threat of force. These included enslaved men, women, and children whose owners moved them, often against their

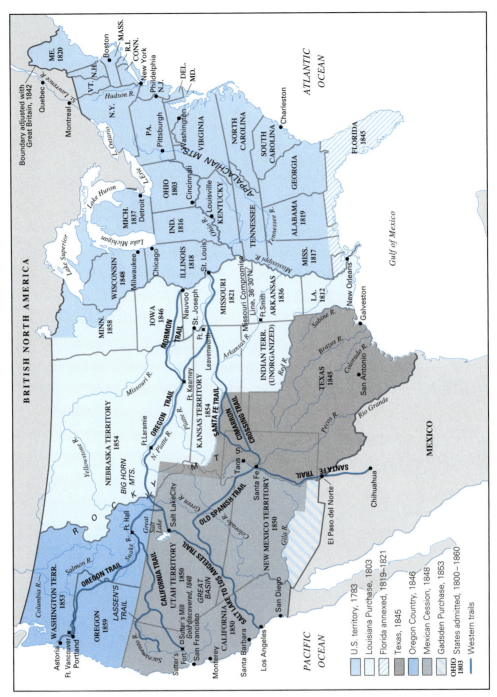

MAP 13.1 Westward Expansion, 1800–1860

Through exploration, purchase, war, and treaty, the United States became a continental nation, stretching from the Atlantic to the Pacific.

will, as well as Indians removed from their eastern homelands by the U.S. military under the provisions of the Indian Removal Act of 1830.

To others, the very notion of the West would have been baffling. Emigrants from Mexico and Central or South America traveled north to get to what European-Americans called the West. The 25,000 or so Chinese who went to California during the 1850s traveled from the East. Many Indians simply considered it home. Other Indians and French Canadians journeyed southward to the West. All these people, much like European-Americans, arrived in the western portion of the North American continent because of a combination of factors that pushed and pulled them.

Frontier Literature   For European-Americans, Daniel Boone became the archetypical frontiersman, a man whose daring individualism opened the Eden-like West for virtuous and hard-working freedom lovers from the East and Europe. Through biographies published by John Filson during Boone's lifetime and by Timothy Flint after Boone's death, Boone became a familiar figure in American and European households. The mythical Boone lived in the wilderness, became "natural" himself, and shrank from society, feeling the need to move on as soon as he saw smoke billowing from a neighboring cabin. He single-handedly overpowered bears and Indians. Even as he took on the ways of the wilderness, according to legend, Boone became the pathfinder for civilization. As a friend wrote shortly after Boone's death, he "has been the instrument of opening the road to millions of the human family from the pressure of sterility and want, to a Land flowing with milk and honey." By borrowing the language of the Bible—the land of milk and honey referred to the Promised Land, the idyllic place that God promised to the beleaguered Israelites—Boone's friend suggested that Boone was a sort of Moses leading his people to a land of abundance.

Stories about Boone mythologized the West as much as they did the man. The Indian-fighting Boone, according to Flint's bestselling biography, had wrested for civilized society "the great west—the garden of the earth." Little matter that the real Boone regretted having killed any Indians and had often struggled to support his own family. When Boone became the heroic model for James Fenimore Cooper's *Leatherstocking Tales*—set on the frontier of western New York—he came to symbolize not only American adventure but also individualism and freedom.

With the invention of the steam press in the early 1830s, western adventure stories were cheap and widely read. Davy Crockett, another real-life figure turned into mythical hero, was featured in many of them. In real life, Crockett had first fought the Creeks under Andrew Jackson but later came to champion Indian rights, rebuking the Indian removal bill. After he lost his life defending the Alamo mission during Texas's fight for independence (1836), though, Crockett often appeared in stories that portrayed the West as violent, a place where one escaped from civilized society and instead fought Indians and Mexicans. But even in this version of the western myth, the American West symbolized what white Americans saw as their nation's core value: freedom.

Western Art   Inspired in part by such literature, many easterners yearned to see the West and its native peoples, and artists hastened to accommodate them. Yet the images they produced often revealed more about white Americans' ideals than about the West itself. In these portrayals, the West was sometimes an untamed wilderness inhabited by savages (noble or otherwise), and sometimes a cultivated garden, a land of milk and honey where the Jeffersonian agrarian dream was realized.

The first Anglo-American artists to travel west were Samuel Seymour and Titian Ramsay Peale, whom the federal government hired to accompany explorer Stephen H. Long on his expedition to the Rocky Mountains in 1820. They pioneered an influential genre of art: facsimiles in government reports. Between 1840 and 1860, Congress published nearly sixty works on western exploration, featuring hundreds of lithographs and engravings of the region's plants, animals, and people. Some of these reports became bestsellers. The most popular was the twelve-volume Pacific Railway Survey (1855–1860), chronicling expeditions to explore four competing routes for a western railroad. The government distributed more than 53,000 copies of that single volume, helping easterners to visualize for themselves the continent's western reaches.

Although government reports often faithfully reproduced original paintings, they sometimes made telling alterations. When Richard Kern accompanied explorer James H. Simpson in 1849 to the Southwest, for example, he painted a Navajo man in a submissive pose. The reproduction of his painting for general distribution transformed the man's pose into a rebellious one. In other cases, the government reports transformed artists' depictions of Indian-occupied landscapes into empty terrain seemingly free for the taking.

Yet the original paintings and sketches did not necessarily offer an accurate view of the West either. Artists pictured their subjects through the lens of their own cultural assumptions, and commercial artists produced what they thought the public craved. When George Catlin traveled west in the early 1830s, he may have genuinely hoped to

In one of his most famous portraits, George Catlin painted Wi-Jun-Jon, an Assiniboine Indian, both before and after he had mingled with white men. In the "before" stance, the Indian is a dignified, peace-pipe-bearing warrior; in the "after" portrait, the "corrupted" Indian has abandoned dignity for vanity and his peace pipe for a cigar. (Smithsonian American Art Museum, Washington, DC/ Art Resource, NY)

paint what he saw as the Indians' vanishing way of life. But he also aimed to attract a paying public of easterners to his exhibitions. Traveling and painting in the immediate aftermath of the Indian Removal Act of 1830, Catlin painted the West with a moral in mind. Indians came in two varieties—those who had preserved their original, almost noble qualities, characterized by freedom and moderation, and those who, after coming in contact with whites, had become "dissolute." Indians, he implied, would benefit from removal from the corrupting influence of white Americans.

Western artwork became familiar to Americans as facsimiles appeared in magazines and books, and even on banknotes. Such images nurtured easterners' curiosities and fantasies—and sometimes their itch to move westward.

Countering the Myths

But the western reality often clashed with promoters' promises, and disappointed settlers sometimes tried to clarify matters for future migrants. From Philadelphia in the 1850s came a song parodying the familiar call of "to the West":

> At the west they told me there was wealth to be won,
> The forest to clear, was the work to be done;
> I tried it—couldn't do it—gave it up in despair,
> And just see if you'll ever again catch me there.
> The little snug farm I expected to buy,
> I quickly discovered was just all in my eye,
> I came back like a streak—you may go—but I'm bless'd
> If you'll ever again, sirs, catch me at the west.

Rebecca Burlend, an English immigrant who settled in Illinois, encountered hardships aplenty—intemperate weather, difficult working conditions, swindlers—and with her son wrote an autobiographical account, *A True Picture of Emigration* (1831), which alerted her countrymen to what awaited them in the American West. The Burlends had themselves been lured to Illinois by an Englishman's letters extolling "a land flowing with milk and honey." Burlend reckoned that he must have "gathered his honey rather from thorns than flowers." Her account did not seek to discourage emigration, but to substitute a realistic for a rosy description.

EXPANSION AND RESISTANCE IN THE OLD NORTHWEST

Americans had always been highly mobile, but never as much as they became after the War of 1812 weakened Indian resistance and set off a flurry of transportation projects. In the 1820s and 1830s, settlers streamed into the Old Northwest and the Old Southwest. They traveled by foot, horseback, wagon, canal boat, steamboat, or—often—by some combination of means. Many people, like Pettis Perkinson and his slaves, moved several times, pulling up their stakes in search of better opportunities, and when opportunities failed to materialize, some returned home.

The Northwest Territory grew at phenomenal rates in the early nineteenth century. In the first federal census of 1790, the region had a white population that numbered just a few hundred people. By 1860 nearly 7 million people called the region home. Between

MAP 13.2 Settlement in the Old Southwest and Old Northwest, 1820 and 1840

Removal of Indians and a growing transportation network opened up land to white and black settlers in the regions known as the Old Southwest and the Old Northwest, as the U.S. population grew from 9.6 million in 1820 to 17.1 million in 1840.

1810 and 1830, the population of Ohio more than quadrupled, while Indiana and Illinois grew fourteenfold and thirteenfold, respectively. Michigan's population multiplied by fifty times in the thirty years between 1820 and 1850. Migration rather than birth rates accounted for most of this growth, and once in the Old Northwest, people did not stay put. By the 1840s, more people left Ohio than moved into it. Geographic mobility, the search for more and better opportunities, and connections to the market economy came to define the region that became known as the Midwest following the acquisition of U.S. territory farther to the west. This region came to symbolize, for many northerners, the heart of American values: freedom and upward mobility, both of which could be achieved (for European immigrants and white Americans) through hard work and virtuous behavior.

Deciding Where to Move   The decision to move west—and then to move on again—was often difficult to make. Moving west meant leaving behind worn-out soil and settled areas where little land was available for purchase, but it also meant leaving behind family, friends, and communities. The trip itself promised to be arduous and expensive, as did the backbreaking labor of clearing new lands for cultivation. The West was a land of opportunity but also of uncertainty. What if the soil proved less fertile than anticipated? What if neighbors—white as well as Indian—proved unfriendly, or even worse? What if homesickness became simply unbearable?

Given all that settlers risked when moving west, they understandably tried to control as many variables as possible. Like Pettis Perkinson, people often relocated to communities where they had relatives or friends, and they often made the journey with people they knew from home. They sought out areas with climates similar to those they left behind. Massachusetts farmers headed to western New York or Ohio, Virginians and North Carolinians went to Missouri, Georgians populated Mississippi and Texas, and Europeans—mostly Germans and Irish—headed to the Old Northwest in much larger numbers than to the Old Southwest. Migrants settled in ethnic communities or sought out people of similar religious values and affiliations. As a result, the Midwest was—in the words of two of its historians—"more like an ethnic and cultural checkerboard than the proverbial melting pot."

When westward-bound Americans fixed on particular destinations, their decisions rested in no small part on the status of slavery in those places. Some white southerners, tired of the undue social and political power wielded by the planter elite, sought homes in areas free from slavery—or at least where plantations did not dominate the landscape. Many others, though, went west to increase their chances of owning slaves, or of owning more slaves. White northerners mostly hoped to distance themselves from slavery, but rarely out of sympathy for slaves themselves. Rather, they, too, had grown to detest the economic and political power exerted by elite slaveowners. The thought of planters appropriating more lands farther west concerned them, as did the thought of black laborers' working those lands. Many northerners hoped to settle in areas free from slavery—and, better yet, free from *any* black people. In the 1850s, many midwestern states passed "black laws" prohibiting African Americans, free as well as enslaved, from living within their boundaries. (In the Far West, Oregon would do the same.) Ironically, many free blacks had themselves migrated west believing that the region would be freer from prejudice than the East.

Between 1815 and 1860, few western migrants settled on the Great Plains, a region reserved for Indians and closed to white settlement until the 1850s, and relatively few easterners risked the overland journey to California and Oregon before the completion of the transcontinental railroad in 1869. Although at first the Southwest seemed to hold the edge in attracting new settlers, the Midwest—with its better-developed transportation routes, its more democratic access to economic markets, its smaller African American population, its smaller and cheaper average landholding, and its climatic similarity to New England and northern Europe—proved considerably more attractive in the decades after 1820. The Midwest's thriving transportation hubs also made good first stops for western migrants, American and foreign-born, lacking cash to purchase land. They found work unloading canal boats, planting and harvesting wheat on nearby farms, grinding wheat into flour, or sawing trees into lumber—or, more often, they cobbled together a combination of these seasonal jobs. The South offered fewer such opportunities. With the Old Northwest's population growing at a much faster rate, white southerners became increasingly worried about congressional representation and laws regarding slavery.

Indian Removal and Resistance　　In both the Midwest and the Southwest, the expansion of white settlement depended on the removal of the region's Indians. Even as the U.S. Army escorted Indians out of the Old Southwest, the federal government also arranged treaties in which northeastern Indian nations relinquished their land titles in exchange for lands west of the Mississippi River. Between 1829 and 1851, eighty-six treaties were signed between the U.S. government and northern Indian tribes.

Some northern Indians managed to evade removal, including the Miamis in Indiana, the Ottawas and Chippewas in the upper Midwest, and the Winnebagos in southern Wisconsin. In 1840, for example, chiefs of the Miamis had acceded to pressure to exchange 500,000 acres of land in Indiana for an equivalent number of acres in Indian Country. Under the terms of the treaty, their people had five years to move. When they failed to do so, federal troops arrived to escort them west. But about half of the Miami nation managed to dodge the soldiers—and many of those who did make the trek to Indian Country later returned unauthorized. In Wisconsin, some Winnebagos similarly eluded removal or returned to Wisconsin after being escorted by soldiers to points west of the Mississippi.

Black Hawk War　　The Sauks (or "Sacs") and Fox fared much less well. In a series of treaties between 1804 and 1830, their leaders exchanged their tribes' lands in northwestern Illinois and southwestern Wisconsin for lands across the Mississippi River in Iowa Territory. Black Hawk, a Sauk warrior who had sided with the British during the War of 1812, disputed the validity of the treaties and vowed his people would return to their ancestral lands. In 1832 he led a group of Sauk and Fox families to Illinois, causing panic among white settlers. The state's governor called up the militia, who were later joined in their pursuit of Black Hawk by militia units from surrounding states and territories, as well as by U.S. Army regular soldiers. Over the next several months, hundreds of Indians and dozens of whites died under often-gruesome circumstances in what is known as the Black Hawk War. As the Sauks and Fox tried to flee across the Mississippi River, they were fired on indiscriminately by American soldiers on steamboats and on land. Those men, women, and children who managed to survive the river crossing were met with gunfire on the western shore by Lakota (Sioux), their longtime enemies now allied with the Americans.

Black Hawk survived to surrender, and U.S. officials undertook to impress on him and the uprising's other leaders the futility of resistance. After being imprisoned, then sent to Washington, D.C., along a route meant to underscore the immense size and population of the United States, and then imprisoned again, the Indians were returned to their homes. The Black Hawk War marked the end of militant Indian uprisings in the Old Northwest, adding to the region's appeal to white settlers.

Selling the West   Land speculators, developers of "paper towns" (which existed on paper only), steamboat companies, and manufacturers of farming implements did their best to promote the Midwest as tranquil place of unbounded opportunity. Land proprietors emphasized the region's connections to eastern ways of life and markets. They knew that, when families uprooted themselves to relocate in the West, they did not—the mythical Daniel Boone and Davy Crockett aside—seek to escape civilization. When Michael D. Row, the proprietor of Rowsburg in northern Ohio, sought to sell town lots in 1835, he emphasized that Rowsburg was in a "thickly settled" area, stood at the crossroads of public transportation leading in every direction, and had established mills and tanning yards.

Settlement in the West generally followed rather than preceded connections to national and international markets. Eastern farmers, seeking to escape tired soil or tenancy, sought fertile lands on which to grow commercial crops. Labor-saving devices, such as Cyrus McCormick's reaper (1834) and John Deere's steel plow (1837), made the West more alluring. McCormick, a Virginia inventor, patented a horse-drawn reaper that allowed two men to harvest the same number of acres of wheat that would previously have required between four and sixteen men, depending on the type of hand-held tool they wielded. Because the reaper's efficiency achieved its greatest payoffs on the prairies, where tracts of land were larger and flatter than in the Shenandoah valley, McCormick relocated his factory to Chicago in 1847 and began a dogged campaign to sell his reaper—which at $100 was an expensive investment for the average farmer—and, along with it, the West itself. Without John Deere's steel plow, which unlike wooden and iron plows could break through tough grass and roots, and did not require constant cleaning, "breaking the plains" might not have been possible at all.

Clearing the Land   Most white Americans who went west intended to farm. After locating a suitable land claim, they immediately constructed a rudimentary cabin if one did not already exist. Time did not permit more elaborate structures, for—contrary to McCormick reaper ads—few western settlers found plowed fields awaiting them. First they had to clear the land.

For those who settled in wooded areas, the quickest and easiest way to get crops in the ground was to girdle, or to cut deep notches with an ax around a tree's base, cutting off the flow of sap. A few weeks later, the trees would lose their leaves, which farmers burned for fertilizer. As soon as enough light came through, settlers would plant corn—a durable and nutritious crop. Eventually the dead trees would fall and could be chopped for firewood and fences, leaving stumps whose removal was a backbreaking task in itself. At the rate of five to ten acres a year, depending on a family's size, the average family needed ten years to fully clear a farm, assuming they did not move on earlier. Prairie land took less time. Throughout the 1850s, though, many farmers dismissed lands free of timber as the equivalent of deserts, unfit for cultivation.

Whereas farming attracted families, lumbering and mining appealed mostly to single young men. By the 1840s, the nation's timber industry was centered around the Great Lakes. As forests became depleted in the eastern United States and Canada, northeastern lumber companies and their laborers migrated to Wisconsin, Michigan, and Minnesota. Recently arrived Scandinavians and French Canadians also worked in the booming lumber industry, which provided construction materials for growing cities and wooden ties for expanding railroads. As the Great Lakes forests thinned, lumbermen moved on once again—some to the Gulf States' pine forests, some to Canada, and some to the Far West, where Mexicans in California and British in Canada had already established flourishing lumber industries. With the rapid growth of California's cities following the Gold Rush of 1849, the demand for timber soared, drawing midwestern lumbermen farther west.

The Midwest's own cities nurtured the settlement of the surrounding countryside. Steamboats turned river settlements like Louisville and Cincinnati into rapidly growing commercial centers, while Chicago, Detroit, and Cleveland grew up on the banks of the Great Lakes. By the mid-nineteenth century, Chicago, with its railroads, stockyards, and grain elevators, was positioned to dominate the region's economy; western farmers transported their livestock and grain by rail to that city, where pigs became packed meat and grain became flour before being shipped farther east. The promise of future flour and future pigs gave rise to commodities markets. Some of the most sophisticated and speculative economic practices in the world took place in Chicago.

THE FEDERAL GOVERNMENT AND WESTWARD EXPANSION

Few white Americans considered settling in the West before the region had been explored, surveyed, secured, and "civilized," by which they meant not only the removal of native populations but also the establishment of churches, businesses, and American legal structures. Although some individuals did head west in advance of European civilization, wide-scale settlement became possible only with the sponsorship of the federal government.

The Fur Trade   No figure better represents the mythical westerner than the mountain man: the loner who wandered the mountains, trapping beaver, living off the land, casting off all semblance of civilization, and daring to go where no white person had ever trod. Fur trappers were, in fact, among the first white Americans in the trans-Appalachian West, but in reality, their lives bore only faint resemblance to the myth. Although many had little contact with American society, they interacted regularly with the West's native peoples. Fur trappers lived among Indians, became multilingual, and often married Indian women, who also became their business partners. Indian women did the arduous work of transforming an animal carcass into a finished pelt, and they also helped smooth trade relations between their husbands and their own native communities. The children of such marriages—métis or mestizos (people of mixed Indian and European heritage)—often became involved in the fur trade themselves and added to the cultural complexity of the West.

The fur trade was an international business, with many pelts from deep in the American interior finding their way to Europe and to Asia. Until the 1820s, it was dominated by British companies, but American ventures prospered in the 1820s and 1830s. The American Fur Company made John Jacob Astor the wealthiest man in the United States. While Astor lived lavishly in his mansion in New York City, his business employed hundreds of trappers and traders who lived and worked among native peoples in the Great Lakes and Pacific Northwest regions. From its base in Astoria on the Columbia

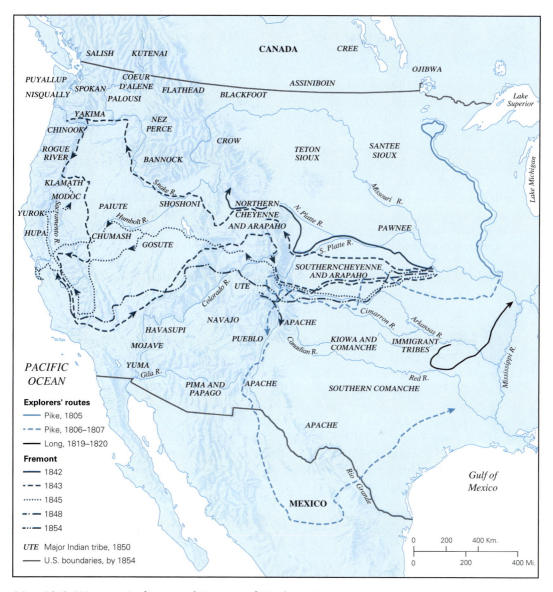

MAP 13.3 Western Indians and Routes of Exploration

Although western explorers believed they were discovering new routes and places, Indians had long lived in most of the areas through which explorers traveled.

River, just a few miles from the Pacific Ocean in present-day Oregon, the American Fur Company made millions by sending furs to China.

Even for the great majority of trappers who never made it to Astoria, the fur trade had an international dimension. Beginning in the 1820s, they came together annually for a "rendezvous"—a multiday gathering at which they traded fur for guns, tobacco,

Gold in California

When James Marshall discovered gold in Sutter's Mill, California, in January 1848, word spread quickly—and quite literally around the world. Within a year, tens of thousands of adventurers from other countries rushed to California, making it the most cosmopolitan place in North America, and perhaps the entire world.

In an era before the telegraph crossed the oceans, it is surprising how fast the news traveled. Mexicans heard of the gold strike first. Next, word spread to Chile, Peru, and throughout South America; then across the Pacific to Hawai'i, China, and Australia; and then to Europe—Ireland, France, and the German states. How did the news travel? Overland travelers brought the news south to Baja California and Sonora in Mexico. By spring 1849 some six thousand Mexicans were panning for gold around the newly established town of Sonora, California. Many of the Mexicans came north seasonally to seek gold, spreading news of California on every trip home.

Sailing ships brought news of California gold to Hawai'i. The newspaper *Honolulu Polynesian* announced it in the kingdom on June 24, 1848. "Honolulu has never before witnessed such an excitement as the gold fever has created," the *Polynesian* reported later that summer. Gold seekers and merchants sailed from Hawai'i to California, and their letters home recruited others to come. The constant traffic led to regular steamship service between Hawai'i and California as early as 1853.

A ship brought news of California gold discoveries to Valparaiso, Chile, in August 1848. More dramatically, a few weeks later, another sailing vessel landed with $2,500 in gold dust aboard. Although Chilean newspapers initially ignored the discovery, people in Chile's cities talked feverishly about gold. By November, newspapers were reporting rumors of overnight riches in California. Before year's end, two thousand Chileans had left for California, and many

This 1855 Frank Marryat drawing of a San Francisco saloon dramatizes the international nature of the California gold rush. Like theater performers, the patrons of the saloon dress their parts as Yankees, Mexicans, Asians, and South Americans.
(© Collection of the New-York Historical Society)

Gold in California

Chilean merchants opened branch stores in San Francisco.

Word of gold and California reached Australia in December 1848. Gold seekers quickly made travel arrangements, and by 1850 every ship in Sydney Harbour was destined for California. News had already reached China in mid-1848. A San Francisco merchant headed for the gold fields, Chum Ming, had written a cousin about his hopes for wealth. Four months later, the cousin arrived in San Francisco, with fellow villagers whom he had recruited. Widespread poverty and the allure of gold prompted many other Chinese to follow. By the mid-1850s, one in five gold miners was Chinese.

Californians, new and old, foreign and native-born, expressed amazement at the ethnic variety. One described it as "the most curious Babel of a place imaginable." In 1850 the new state of California had nearly 40 percent foreign-born inhabitants, the majority non-European. Through word of mouth, rumor, letters home, and newspaper reports, the discovery of gold in 1848 linked California to millions of ordinary people around the globe.

---

and beads that they could later exchange with Indians while also sharing stories and alcohol, and gambling. Modeled on similar Indian gatherings that had occurred for generations, the rendezvous brought together Americans, Indians, Mexicans, and people of mixed heritage from all over the West—from as far north as Canada and as far south as Mexico. Rendezvous took place in remote mountain locations, but they were cosmopolitan affairs.

By the 1840s, the American fur trade was in decline. Beavers had been overhunted, and fashions had shifted, with silk supplanting beaver fur as the preferred material for hats. The traders' legacy includes setting a pattern of resource extraction and depletion (and boom and bust); introducing native peoples to devastating diseases; and developing trails across the trans-Mississippi West.

Transcontinental Exploration A desire for quicker and safer routes for transporting furs and other goods to trading posts drove much early exploration. William Becknell, an enterprising merchant, helped in 1821 to chart the Santa Fe Trail running between Missouri and Santa Fe, New Mexico, where it connected to the Chihuahua Trail running southward into Mexico, allowing American and Mexican merchants to develop a vibrant exchange of American manufactured goods for furs and other items. Fur trader Jedediah Smith rediscovered in 1824 the South Pass; this 20-mile break in the Rocky Mountains in present-day Wyoming had previously been known only to Native Americans and a handful of fur trappers from the Pacific Fur Company who had passed through in 1812. The South Pass became the route followed by most people headed overland to California and Oregon. Less well-known traders, trappers, missionaries, and gold seekers, often assisted by Native

American guides, also discovered traveling routes throughout the West, and some— most famously, mountain man Kit Carson—aided government expeditions.

Lewis and Clark's Corps of Discovery was only the first of many federally sponsored expeditions to chart the trans-Mississippi West. These expeditions often had diplomatic goals, aiming to establish cordial relations with Indian groups with whom Americans might trade or enter military alliances. Some had scientific missions, charged with recording information about the region's native inhabitants, flora, and fauna. But they were always also commercial in purpose. Just as Lewis and Clark had hoped to find what proved to be an elusive Northwest Passage to the Pacific, so, too, did later explorers hope to locate land, water, and rail routes that would allow American businessmen and farmers to engage in national and international trade.

In 1805 the U.S. Army dispatched Zebulon Pike to find the source of the Mississippi and a navigable route west. Along the way, he was to collect information on natural resources and native peoples, and foster diplomatic relationships with Indian leaders whom he encountered. He was also to purchase land from Indians; before the Supreme Court ruled in *Johnson v. M'Intosh* (1823) that Indians did not own land but rather had only a "right of occupancy," government officials instructed Pike and other explorers to identify and purchase lands suitable for military garrisons.

Although Pike failed to identify the source of the Mississippi and had only limited success in cultivating relationships and purchasing land, he nonetheless gathered important information about the terrain he covered. Shortly after returning from present-day Minnesota, he set out for what are now Missouri, Nebraska, Kansas, and Colorado. After Pike and his men wandered into Spanish territory to the south, military officials held Pike captive for several months in Mexico, inadvertently giving him a tour of areas that he might not have explored on his own. After his release, Pike wrote an account of his experiences that described a potential market in southwestern cities, as well as bountiful furs and precious metals. The province of Tejas (Texas), with its fertile soil and rich grasslands, enchanted him. At the same time, Pike dismissed the other northern provinces of Mexico, whose boundaries stretched to the northern borders of present-day Nevada and Utah, as unsuitable for human habitation. Although nomadic Indians might sustain themselves there, he explained, the region was unfit for cultivation by civilized people.

Stephen Long, another army explorer, similarly declared in 1820 that the region comprising modern-day Oklahoma, Kansas, and Nebraska was "the Great American Desert," incapable of cultivation. Until the 1850s, when a transcontinental railroad was planned, this "desert" was reserved for Indian settlement, and most army-sponsored exploration focused on other parts of the West.

In 1838 Congress established the U.S. Army Corps of Topographical Engineers to systematically explore the West in advance of widespread settlement. As a second lieutenant in that corps, John C. Frémont undertook three expeditions to the region between the upper Mississippi and Missouri rivers, the Rockies, the Great Basin, Oregon, and California. He helped survey the Oregon Trail. With the assistance of his wife, Jessie Benton Frémont, Frémont published bestselling accounts of his explorations, earning him the nickname "The Pathfinder" and paving the way for a political career. The Corps of Topographical Engineers' most significant contributions came in the 1850s with its surveying of possible routes for a transcontinental railroad.

The federal government spent millions publicizing the results of its explorations, much more than it allotted for exploration itself. Westward migrants often carried two books with them: the Bible and Frémont's account of his army explorations.

A Military Presence The army did more than explore the West. It also helped ready it for settlement. With the General Survey Act of 1824, Congress empowered the military to chart transportation improvements deemed vital to the nation's military protection or commercial growth. In addition to working on federally funded projects, army engineers helped design state- and privately-sponsored roads, canals, and railroads, and its soldiers did the laborious work of clearing forests and laying roadbeds. A related bill, also in 1824, authorized the army to help improve the Ohio and Mississippi rivers, and a later amendment did the same for the Missouri.

By the 1850s, 90 percent of the U.S. military was stationed west of the Mississippi River. When Indians refused to relinquish their lands, the army escorted them westward; when they inflicted harm on whites or their property, the army waged war. The army sometimes destroyed the crops and buildings of white squatters who refused to vacate lands they had settled without legal title. But, primarily, the army presence assisted overland migration. Army forts on the periphery of Indian Country intimidated Indians, defended settlers and migrants from Indian attacks, and supplied them with information and provisions. In theory, the army was also supposed to protect Indians by driving settlers off Indian lands and enforcing laws prohibiting the sale of alcohol to Indians. Yet

Charles Koppel portrayed the Colorado Desert and Signal Mountain for the Pacific Railway Reports (1853). The desert appears vast and unlimited, and those who travel through it seem to be advancing into the unknown. (The Center for American History, The University of Texas at Austin)

the army's small size compared to the territory it regulated made it virtually impossible to enforce such policies even when officers were disposed to do so.

The Office of Indian Affairs handled the government's other interactions with Indians, including the negotiation of treaties, the management of schools, and the oversight of trade. Created in 1824 as part of the War Department, the Indian Office cooperated with the military in removing Indians from lands that stood in the way of American expansion and in protecting those citizens who staked their future in the West. In 1849 the Indian Office became part of the newly established Department of the Interior, and it soon shifted its focus from removal to civilization, through a reservation system. Whereas some Indians accepted reservations as the best protection from white incursion, others rejected them, sometimes setting off deadly intratribal disagreements.

Public Lands   The federal government controlled vast tracts of land, procured either from the states' cessions of their western claims after the Revolution or through treaties with foreign powers, including Indian nations. The General Land Office, established in 1812 as part of the Treasury Department, handled the distribution of those lands. Its earliest policies, crafted with an eye toward raising revenue, divided western lands into 640-acre tracts to be sold at public auction at a minimum price of $2 an acre. These policies favored speculators over individual, cash-poor farmers. Speculators bought up millions of acres of land. Unable to afford federal lands, many settlers became squatters, prompting Congress in 1820 to lower the price of land to $1.25 per acre and to make available tracts as small as 80 acres. Twelve years later, it began selling 40 acre tracts. Yet it also demanded that the land be bought outright, and in a cash-poor society (particularly in the aftermath of the Panic of 1819), few would-be western settlers had enough cash to purchase a farm from the government. Because speculators sold land on credit, many small-time farmers bought from them instead, but at inflated prices.

Farmers pressed for a federal policy of preemption—that is, the right to settle on land without obtaining title, to improve it, and to buy it later at the minimum price ($1.25 an acre) established by law. Although some states offered their lands through preemption, and although Congress authorized preemption of federal lands in particular instances in the 1820s and 1830s, a more general preemption law did not come until 1841 with the so-called Log Cabin Bill, and even then, it applied to surveyed land only. The right of preemption extended to unsurveyed lands with the Homestead Act of 1862, which provided that land would be provided free to any U.S. citizen (or foreigner who had declared his or her intention of becoming a citizen), provided he or she resided on it for five years and improved it. Alternatively, settlers could buy the land outright at $1.25 an acre after six months of living on it, an arrangement that allowed them to use the land as collateral for loans with which to purchase additional land, farming supplies, or machinery. By the time of the Homestead Act, though, much of the land left in the federal domain was arid, and 160 acres was not always enough for an independent farm.

THE SOUTHWESTERN BORDERLANDS

Along the southwestern border of the Louisiana Territory were vast provinces that fell under the domain not of the United States but of different national governments, first Spain and then—after 1821—the newly independent nation of Mexico. New Mexico, with its bustling commercial centers of Albuquerque and Santa Fe, remained under Mexican federal control until the United States conquered the territory during its War with Mexico. Texas, by contrast, had a much more attenuated relationship with the Mexican government; in 1824 it became an autonomous state, giving it substantially more political independence from federal authorities in Mexico City than New Mexico enjoyed. This situation would help foster Texas's struggle for national independence and then annexation to the United States, which in turn would return the divisive issue of slavery to the center of the American political agenda.

Southwestern Slavery

By the time Anglo-Americans became interested in the northern reaches of Mexico, slavery had existed in the Southwest for centuries. Yet slavery as practiced there by indigenous peoples—the Apaches, Comanches, Kiowas, Navajos, Utes, and Pueblos—and Spaniards differed from the chattel slavery of Africans and African Americans in the American South. Southwestern slavery was no less violent, but it centered on capturing women and children, who were then assimilated into their captors' communities, where they provided labor but also status. Captives also fostered economic and diplomatic exchanges with the communities from which they had been captured.

This system of "captives and cousins," as one scholar has put it, was built on racial mixing—a practice that was anathema to most white Americans. As white slaveholders from the Southeast pushed their way into Mexican territory during the 1820s and 1830s, they often justified their conquest in racial terms. Even the region's Hispanic settlers, they reasoned, had been rendered lazy and barbarous by racial intermixing and were thus destined to be supplanted, whether peaceably or otherwise.

The New Mexican Frontier

When Mexico gained independence from Spain in 1821, the population of the province of New Mexico was dominated by Hispanic peoples, who outnumbered the indigenous Pueblo peoples by three to one. There were 28,000 Hispanics, including people born in Spain and, especially, criollos, people born in New Spain to parents of Spanish descent. Whether Spanish, Indian, criollo, or mestizo, most New Mexicans engaged in irrigated agriculture. To the north of Santa Fe, they worked small plots of land, but to that settlement's south, larger farms and ranches predominated. Rancheros' wealth came from selling their wool and corn in distant markets, and from relying on laborers whom they did not need to pay: farm hands, often their own relatives, bound to the rancheros by debt. United by a threat from the province's raiding Indian tribes—the Apaches, Utes, Navajos, and sometimes the Comanches—Hispanics, Pueblos, and mestizos sometimes came together in common defense. But relations among Hispanics and the sedentary Pueblos were not always peaceful. Their numerical superiority allowed Hispanics to take over many of the Pueblos' villages and lands in the rich northern river valleys of an otherwise arid region.

The Santa Fe Trail caused a commercial explosion in New Mexico, doubling the value of imports in just two years. Whereas the Spanish had tried to keep foreigners out, the Mexican government offered enormous land grants to Anglo-American and French entrepreneurs, sometimes in partnership with the region's Hispanic residents, in the hope that they would develop the region's industry and agriculture, and strengthen commercial ties with the United States.

MAP 13.4 Mexico's Far North

What is now considered the American Southwest was made up of the northern provinces of Mexico until the United States conquered the territory during the Mexican War (1846–1848). *(From Andres Resendez,* Changing National Identities and the Frontier: Texas and New Mexico, 1800–1850, *2005, p. 19. Reprinted with the permission of Cambridge University Press.)*

Although commercial ties did in fact strengthen, very few Americans settled permanently in New Mexico during the 1820s and 1830s. Most of the best lands had already been taken by Indians and Hispanics. And Americans in search of cheap, fertile land did not need to travel that far west; they could find what they were looking for in Texas.

The Texas Frontier   That they would do so, however, was not evident at the time of Mexican independence. Unlike those in New Mexico, indigenous Indians remained the dominant group in Texas in 1821, although the population also included immigrant Indians, Hispanics, Anglos, and mestizos. Of the thirty thousand indigenous people, most were Comanches, but there were also Jumanos, Coahuiltecans, Tonkawas, Karankawas, Apaches, Caddos, and Wichitas. To identify distinctive Indian groups, though, belies the intermarriage and cultural exchange among them. Indians married Indians from other nations, as well as Europeans and African Americans.

Cultural exchange did not prevent intermittent warfare, however, as Indian groups competed with one another for the region's resources. Mounted on horses, the Comanches hunted bison or stole horses, livestock, and crops from their enemies, among whom were the Pawnees, Arapahos, and Cheyennes. Other, smaller Indian groups, such as the Wichitas and Caddos, mostly farmed, growing enough corn, beans, squash, and pumpkin not only to feed themselves but also to trade with the more mobile Comanches. When crops failed, these Indian farmers often turned to bison hunting as well, sometimes bringing them into conflict with the Comanches. But European diseases killed many more Indians than did violence.

Tensions increased around the time of Mexican independence, when the first of another ten thousand Indians began migrating into the region. From the Old Northwest came Shawnees and Kickapoos—former members of Tecumseh's confederacy—who after their defeat during the War of 1812 had headed north to Canada before heading back southward into Kansas, Indian Territory, and then Texas. From the Old Southwest came Cherokees, Creeks, Choctaws, Chickasaws, and Seminoles. As these Indian newcomers competed for land and animals, they came into conflict with established Indian groups, such as the Comanches, who had been there for generations. Many of these immigrant Indians had adopted European clothing and European ideas about land and race. They saw land as a commodity with a market value. Some had intermarried with Anglos, and some owned African American slaves. They often dismissed as "savage" the indigenous Indians who hunted buffalo and wore their skins. But contempt for indigenous Indians did not necessarily mean an affinity for Anglo-Americans, as many of the immigrant Indians deeply resented those who had evicted them from their homelands or who had waged war on them.

Tejanos

Hispanic peoples had been in Texas since the 1500s, establishing missions and presidios, but by 1820 they numbered only five thousand. Most raised livestock on ranches, while others made their living from trading with Indians. Because they were so distant from the Spanish colonial capital in Mexico City, they formed a distinctive identity, seeing themselves as Tejanos (or Texans) rather than as Spaniards. Many intermarried with Indians.

In the years after the War of 1812, Anglo-Americans began entering Texas, where they sought furs, silver, or adventure. They traded manufactured goods—such as guns, ammunition, and kettles—for animal hides, horses, and mules. Although some Anglos settled in Texas, often among Indians, many more Anglos simply traveled along the Santa Fe and Chihuahua trails without settling. These Anglo newcomers largely supplanted the Tejanos as the Indians' trading partners, and the economic fortunes of the region's indigenous and immigrant tribes became increasingly oriented toward the United States and, in particular, the New Orleans market.

American Empresarios

In the 1820s, Americans began settling in Texas under an *empresario* system. The first arrangement was made by Moses Austin, a miner and trader from Missouri, who approached Spanish authorities in Mexico City in January 1821 with a plan to settle the area. The Spanish were interested because they thought of Texas as a buffer between hostile Indians and the United States, and they wanted to see it populated. But they also wanted the newcomers to be assimilated, so they gave Austin an enormous land grant of approximately 200,000 acres along the Brazos River in exchange for his promise to bring three hundred Catholic families—and no slaves—with him. Before Austin could act, though, he died, and Mexico won its independence from Spain in September 1821.

Austin's son, Stephen, took up his father's scheme and pressed the new Mexican government to honor the grant, which it did in 1823, provided that the younger Austin give up his American citizenship and become a Mexican national. By 1825 Stephen Austin had brought in three hundred families (two thousand white people) and, despite the promise of no slaves, four hundred "contract laborers" of African descent. With contracts that ran for ninety-nine years, these African Americans were slaves by another name. Still, Austin's success at luring settlers to Texas encouraged the Mexican government to sign three more contracts granting Austin land in exchange for his bringing nine hundred additional families.

Generally satisfied with the Austin experiment, in 1824 Mexico passed a Colonization Law providing land and tax incentives to future foreign settlers and leaving the details of colonization up to the individual Mexican states. Coahuila y Texas specified that the head of a family could obtain as much as 4,428 acres of grazing land or 177 acres of farming land. The land was cheap, and—unlike land in the United States—could be paid for in installments over six years, with no money due until the fourth year. To be eligible, foreigners had to be upstanding Christians with "good habits," and they had to establish permanent residency. Eager for these new settlers to assimilate into Mexican society, the Coahuila y Texas government provided additional land incentives to those settlers who married Mexican women.

Most U.S. citizens who settled in Mexico did so under the auspices of an *empresario,* or immigration agent, who took responsibility for selecting "moral" colonists, distributing lands, and enforcing regulations. In exchange, he received nearly 25,000 acres of grazing land and 1,000 acres of farming land for every hundred families that he settled. Between 1825 and 1832, approximately twenty-four *empresario* contracts (seventeen of which went to Anglo-Americans) had been signed, with the *empresarios* agreeing to bring eight thousand families total. The land grants were so vast that together they covered almost all of present-day Texas.

During the 1820s, Anglo-Americans emigrated, with their slaves, to Texas, motivated by a combination of push and pull factors. Some were pushed from the United States in large part by the hard times following the Panic of 1819; at the same time, they were drawn by cheap land and, especially, generous terms of credit. Despite Mexican efforts to encourage assimilation with Mexicans of Spanish origin living in Texas, these Americans tended to settle in separate communities and to interact little with the Tejanos. Even more troubling to the Mexican government, the Anglo-Americans outnumbered the Tejanos two to one. Authorities worried that the transplanted Americans would try to make Texas part of the United States.

Texas Politics   In 1826 their fears seemed to materialize when an *empresario* named Haden Edwards called for an independent Texas, which he called the "Fredonia Republic." Other *empresarios,* reasoning that they had more to gain than to lose from peaceful relations with the Mexican government, resisted Edwards's secessionist movement. Austin even sent militia to help put down the rebellion. Although the Fredonia revolt failed, Mexican authorities dreaded what it might foreshadow.

The answer to the secessionist threat, Mexican authorities thought, was to weaken the American presence in Texas. In 1830 they terminated legal immigration from the United States while simultaneously encouraging immigration from Europe and other parts of Mexico as a way of diluting the American influence. They also prohibited American slaves from entering Texas, a provision that brought Texas in line with the rest of Mexico—where slavery had been outlawed the previous year—and that was also meant to repel American slaveholders. Yet these laws did little to discourage Americans and their slaves from coming; soon they controlled most of the Texas coastline and its border with the United States. Mexican authorities repealed the anti-immigration law in 1833, reasoning that it discouraged upstanding settlers but did nothing to stem the influx of those whom they considered undesirable. By 1835 the population of Texas was nearly thirty thousand, with Americans outnumbering Tejanos seven to one.

White Texans divided into two main factions. There were those, like Stephen Austin, who favored staying in Mexico but demanding more autonomy, the legalization of slavery, and free trade with the United States. Others pushed for Texas to secede from Mexico and asked to be annexed to the United States. In 1835 the secessionists overtook a Mexican military installation charged with collecting taxes at Galveston Bay. Austin advocated a peaceful resolution to the crisis, but Mexican authorities nonetheless considered him suspicious and jailed him for eighteen months, an act that helped convert him to the cause of independence. But it would be Sam Houston and Davy Crockett—newly arrived Americans—who would lead the movement.

The Lone Star Republic
With discontent over Texas increasing throughout Mexico, Mexican president General Santa Anna declared himself dictator and marched his army toward Texas. Fearing that Santa Anna would free their slaves, and citing similarities between their own cause and that of the American colonies in the 1770s, Texans staged an armed rebellion. After initial defeats at the Alamo mission in San Antonio and at Goliad in March 1836, the Texans easily won the conflict by the end of the year. They declared themselves the Lone Star Republic and elected Sam Houston as president. The Texas constitution legalized slavery and banned free blacks from living within Texas.

Texas then faced the challenge of nation building, which to its leaders involved Indian removal. When the Indians refused to leave, Mirabeau Lamar, the nation's second president, mobilized the Texas Rangers—mounted non-uniformed militia—to drive them out through terror. Sanctioned by the Texas government, but sometimes acting on their own, the Rangers raided Indian villages, where they robbed, raped, and murdered. Although some Texas officials tried to negotiate with the Indians and Tejanos, it was what one historian has called "ethnic cleansing" that cleared the land of its native settlers to make room for white Americans and their African American slaves.

MIGRATION TO THE FAR WEST

In the following decade, as Texas's future remained uncertain, more and more Americans took the gamble of a lifetime and moved to the Far West, even though California and Utah were part of Mexico. Although some sought religious freedom or to convert others to Christianity, most were looking for fertile farmland.

Western Missionaries

Catholic missionaries—Americans, Europeans, and converted Indians—maintained a strong presence in the Far West even after a Mexican law secularized the California missions in 1833, removing them from ecclesiastical control and using them primarily to organize Indian labor. The missionaries ministered to Catholic immigrants, worked—with some success—to convert Indians, and encouraged specifically Roman Catholic colonies. Missionaries founded schools and colleges, introduced medical services, and even aided in railroad explorations.

In the Pacific Northwest, Catholics vied directly with Protestant missionaries for Indian souls. Although evangelicals focused on the Midwest, a few sought to bring Christianity to the Indians of the Far West. Under the auspices of the American Board of Commissioners for Foreign Missions, two missionary couples—generally credited as being the first white migrants along the Oregon Trail—traveled to the Pacific Northwest in 1836. Narcissa and Marcus Whitman built a meetinghouse for Cayuse Indians in Waiilatpu, near present-day Walla Walla, Washington, while Eliza and Henry Spalding worked to convert the Nez Percé at Lapwai, in what is now Idaho. With their air of cultural superiority, the Whitmans did little to endear themselves to the Cayuses, none of whom converted to Christianity. The Whitmans turned their efforts instead toward the ever-increasing stream of white migrants flowing into Oregon beginning in the 1840s.

The arrival of these migrants escalated tensions with the Cayuses, and when a devastating measles epidemic struck in 1847, the Cayuses saw it as a calculated assault on their people. They retaliated by murdering the Whitmans and twelve other missionaries. After the Whitmans' violent deaths, the Spaldings abandoned their own, more successful mission; blamed Catholics for inciting the massacre; and became farmers in Oregon, not returning to Lapwai for another fifteen years.

Mormons

The Mormons, who had been persecuted in Missouri and Illinois, went west to seek a religious sanctuary. In 1847 Brigham Young led them to their "Promised Land" in the Great Salt Lake valley, still under Mexican control but soon to become part of the unorganized U.S. territory of Utah. As non-Mormons began to settle in Utah, Brigham Young worked to dilute their influence by attracting new Mormon settlers to what he called the state of Deseret. In 1849 Young and his associates set up the Perpetual Emigration Fund, which sponsored "handcart companies" of poor migrants, particularly from Europe, who put all their belongings in small handcarts that they pushed to Utah.

Although Mormons prospered from providing services, such as ferries, and supplies to tens of thousands of California-bound settlers and miners who passed by their settlements, Young discouraged "gentiles" (his term for non-Mormons) from settling in Deseret and advocated boycotts of gentile businesses. When in 1852 the Mormons openly sanctioned polygamy, which some of its followers had practiced for more than a decade, animosity toward them increased throughout the nation. After some young Mormons vandalized federal offices in Utah, President James Buchanan—hoping to divert Americans' attention from the increasingly divisive issue of slavery—dispatched 2,500 federal troops in June 1857 to suppress an alleged Mormon rebellion.

Anxious over their own safety and eager to maintain peaceful relations with neighboring Indians, a group of Mormons joined some Paiutes in attacking a passing wagon train of non-Mormon migrants from Arkansas and Missouri. Approximately 120 men, women, and children died in the so-called Mountain Meadows Massacre in August 1857. In the next two years, the U.S. Army and the Mormons engaged in armed conflict, resulting in much property destruction but no fatalities. As these events indicate, western violence often emerged from complex interactions and alliances which cannot be understood as simply pitting natives against newcomers.

Oregon and California Trails

Not all encounters between natives and newcomers were violent. In the twenty years after 1840, between 250,000 and 500,000 people, many of them children, walked across much of the continent on foot, a trek that took seven months on average. Although they traveled armed for conflict, most of their encounters with Indians were peaceful, if tense.

Overlanders began their journeys at one of the so-called jumping-off points—towns such as Independence, St. Joseph, and Westport Landing—along the Missouri River, where they bought supplies for the 2,000-mile trip still ahead of them. After cramming supplies into wagons already overflowing with household possessions, they set out either in organized wagon trains or on their own. While miners frequently traveled alone or in groups of fortune-seeking young men, farmers—including many women migrating only at their husbands' insistance—often traveled with their relatives, neighbors, church members, and other acquaintances.

They timed their departures to be late enough that they could find forage grass for their oxen and livestock, but not so late that they would encounter the treacherous snows that came early to the Rockies and the Sierra Nevada. Not all were successful. In 1846–1847 the Donner Party took a wrong turn, got caught in a blizzard, and resorted to cannibalism. More fortunate overland migrants trudged alongside their wagons, beginning their days well before dawn, pausing only for a short midday break, and walking until late afternoon. They covered on average 15 miles a day, in weather ranging from freezing cold to blistering heat. In wagon trains composed of families, men generally tended livestock during the day, while women—after an energy-draining day on the trail—set up camp, prepared meals, and tended small children. Trail life was exhausting, both physically and emotionally. Overlanders worried about Indian attack, getting lost, running out of provisions or water, and losing loved ones, who would have to be buried along the trail, in graves never again to be visited. But for most adults, trail life did not prove particularly dangerous, with Indian attacks rare and death rates approximating those of society at large. Children, though, had a greater risk than adults of being crushed by wagon wheels or drowning during river crossings.

Indians were usually peaceful, if cautious. Particularly during the trails' early days, Indians provided migrants with food and information, or they ferried them across rivers; in exchange, migrants offered wool blankets, knives, metal pots, tobacco, ornamental beads, and other items in short supply in Indian societies. When exchanges went bad—when one of the parties misunderstood the other's cultural practices or tried to swindle the other—relationships grew tense, not just between the particular persons involved, but between Indians and migrants more generally. Indians grew suspicious of all white people, just as migrants failed to distinguish different native bands or tribes.

This rare stereocard shows an emigrant train, including two women and possibly a child, dwarfed by the natural landscape in Strawberry Valley, Califonia, in the 1860s. (Library of Congress)

A persistent aggravation among migrants was the theft of their livestock, which they tended to blame on Indians even though white thieves stole livestock, too. Indians who took livestock often did so when whites failed to offer gifts in exchange for grazing rights. One such incident that resulted in human bloodshed, the so-called Mormon Cow Incident (or the Grattan Massacre), forever altered relationships along the Oregon Trail.

In August 1854, a Lakota in present-day Wyoming slaughtered a cow that had strayed from a nearby Mormon camp. When Lakota leaders offered compensation for the cow, U.S. Army Lieutenant John Grattan, intent on making an example of the incident, refused the offer. Tempers flared, Grattan ordered his men to shoot, and after a Lakota chief fell dead, the Indians returned the fire, killing Grattan and all twenty-nine of his men. In retaliation, the following year General William Harney led six hundred soldiers to a village near Ash Hollow, where migrants and Indians had traded peaceably for many years. When Indian leaders refused to surrender any of their people to Harney, the general ordered his men to fire. Thirty minutes later, eighty-seven Indians lay dead, and seventy women and children had been taken prisoner. The event disrupted peaceful exchange along the trail and laid the groundwork for nearly two decades of warfare between the Lakotas and the U.S. Army.

Indian Treaties   Even as the U.S. Army became embroiled in armed conflict with the Lakotas, the Indian Office worked to negotiate treaties aimed to keep Indians—and their intertribal conflicts—from interfering with western migration and commerce. The Fort Laramie Treaty of 1851 (or the Horse Creek Council Treaty) was signed by the United States and eight northern Plains tribes—the Lakotas, Cheyennes, Arapahos, Crows, Assiniboines, Gros-Ventres, Mandans, and Arrickaras—who occupied the Platte River valley through which the three great overland routes westward—the Oregon, California, and Mormon Trails—all passed. Two years later, in 1853, the United States signed a treaty with three southwestern nations, the Comanches, Kiowas, and Apaches, who lived in the vicinity of the Sante Fe Trail. Under the terms of both treaties, the Indians agreed to maintain peace among themselves, to recognize government-delineated tribal boundaries, to allow the United States to construct roads and forts within those boundaries, to refrain from depredations against western migrants, and to issue restitution for any depredations nonetheless committed. In return, they would receive annual allotments from the U.S. government for ten years, to be paid with provisions, domestic animals, and agricultural implements. These allotments could be renewed for another five years at the discretion of the president of the United States.

But these treaties often meant different things to their Indian signatories than to the U.S. officials who brokered them. Contrary to U.S. expectations, Indian chiefs did not believe such treaties to be perpetually binding. Government officials, meanwhile, promised allotments but did little to ensure their timely arrival, often leaving Indians starving and freezing as they waited. The treaties did not mark the end of intratribal warfare, nor did they fully secure the safety of overlanders. But they did represent the U.S. government's continued effort to promote expansion and to protect those citizens who caught the western fever.

Ecological Consequences of Cultural Contact   Armed conflict along the trails took relatively few lives compared to cholera, smallpox, and other maladies. The trails' jumping-off points, where migrants camped in close quarters while preparing for their journeys, bred disease, which migrants carried with them, inadvertently infecting Indians with whom they traded. Fearful of infection, Indians and migrants increasingly shied away from trading relationships.

The disappearance of the buffalo (American bison) from the trails' environs further inflamed tensions. The buffalo not only provided protein to Plains Indians; they also held great spiritual significance. Many Native Americans blamed the migrants for the buffalo's disappearance, even though most overlanders never laid eyes on a buffalo. By the time the overland migration reached its peak in the late 1840s and 1850s, the herds had already been overhunted, in part by Native Americans eager to trade their hides. As traffic picked up on the trail, the surviving buffalo scattered to areas where the grass was safe from the voracious appetites, and trampling feet, of the overlanders' livestock. But on those rare occasions when wagon trains did stumble upon bison herds, men rushed to live out their frontier fantasies—nurtured by the literature they had read—and shot the animals; buffalo chases also provided diversions from the drudgery and anxiety of the trail. Overlanders hunted other animals for sport, too, leaving behind rotting carcasses of antelopes, wolves, bears, and birds—animals that held spiritual significance for many Native Americans.

Overland migrants also caused prairie fires. Indians had long used fire to clear farm land, to stimulate the growth of grasslands, and to create barren zones that would discourage bison from roaming into a rival nation's territory. But now emigrants—more accustomed to cooking over stoves than over open fires—often started fires that got out of control and swept across the prairies, killing animals and the vegetation on which they survived. On rarer occasions, Indians started fires in the hope of capturing the migrants' fleeing livestock. Stories about intentionally lit fires were more prevalent than the events themselves, but they, too, contributed to increasing hostility among Indians and overlanders.

Gold Rush

Nowhere did migrants intrude on Indian life more deeply than near the gold strikes in California. In January 1848, James Wilson Marshall discovered gold in a shallow tributary to the American River near present-day Sacramento, California. During the next year, tens of thousands of "forty-niners" rushed to California, where they practiced what is called placer mining, panning and dredging for gold in the hope of instant riches.

And some did indeed make fortunes. Peter Brown, a black man from Ste. Genevieve, Missouri, wrote his wife in 1851 that "California is the best country in the world to make money. It is also the best place for black folks on the globe." He had earned $300 in two months. Most forty-niners, however, never found enough gold to

MAP 13.5
The California Gold Rush

Gold was discovered at Sutter's Mill in 1848, sparking the California gold rush that took place mostly along the western foothills of the Sierra Nevada mountains.*(Warren A. Beck and Ynez D. Haase, Historical Atlas of California, University of Oklahoma Press, 1974, map 50, p. 407. Copyright © 1974 by the University of Oklahoma Press. Reprinted by permission of the University of Oklahoma Press.)*

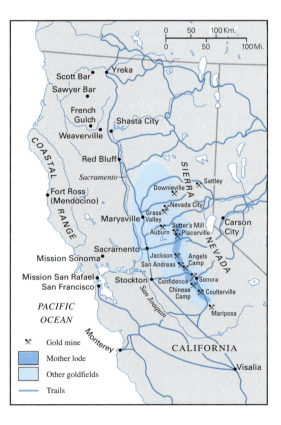

pay their expenses. "The stories you hear frequently in the States," one gold seeker wrote home, "are the most extravagant lies imaginable—the mines are a humbug." With their dreams dashed—and too poor or embarrassed to return home—many forty-niners took wage-paying jobs with large mining companies that used dangerous machinery to cut deep into the earth's surface to reach mineral veins.

The discovery of gold forever changed the face of California. As a remote Mexican province, California had a chain of small settlements surrounded by military forts (presidios) and missions, and it was inhabited mostly by Indians, along with a small number of Mexican rancheros, who raised cattle and sheep on enormous landholdings worked by coerced Indian laborers. With the arrival of forty-niners, who did not have time to grow their own food, came the great California agricultural boom. Wheat became the preferred crop; it required minimal investment, was easily planted, and offered a quick return at the end of a relatively short growing season. In contrast to the Midwest and Oregon, where family farms were the basic unit of production, in California large-scale wheat farming relied largely on bonded Indian laborers. Even as California agriculture thrived overall, the immediate vicinity of mines became barren, when hydraulic mining washed away the surface soil to expose buried lodes.

Mining Settlements   Mining areas experienced a commercial and industrial boom, as enterprising merchants rushed to supply, feed, and clothe the new settlers. Among them was Levi Strauss, a German Jewish immigrant, whose tough mining pants found a ready market among the prospectors. Because men greatly outnumbered women, women's skills (and company) were in great demand. Even as men set up all-male households and performed tasks that bent prevailing notions of gender propriety, women received high fees for cooking, laundering, and sewing. Women also ran boarding houses, hotels, and brothels.

Cities sprang up. In 1848 San Francisco had been a small mission settlement of about 1,000 Mexicans, Anglos, soldiers, friars, and Indians. With the gold rush, it became an instant city, ballooning to 35,000 people in 1850. It was the West Coast gateway to the interior, and ships bringing people and supplies continuously jammed the harbor. A French visitor in that year wrote, "At San Francisco, where fifteen months ago one found only a half-dozen large cabins, one finds today a stock exchange, a theater, churches of all Christian cults, and a large number of quite beautiful homes."

Yet as the Anglo-American, European, Hispanic, Asian, and African American populations swelled, the Indian population experienced devastation. Although California was admitted into the Union as a free state in 1850, its legislature soon passed "An Act for the Government and Protection of Indians" that essentially legalized the enslavement of Indians. The practice of using enslaved Indians in the California mines between 1849 and 1851 ended only when newly arrived miners brutally attacked the Indian workers, believing they degraded white labor and gave an unfair advantage to established miners. Those slaves who survived the violence were sent to work instead as field workers and house servants. Between 1821 and 1860, the Indian population of California fell from 200,000 to 30,000, as Indians died from disease, starvation, and violence. Because masters separated male and female workers, even Indians who survived failed to reproduce in large numbers.

THE POLITICS OF TERRITORIAL EXPANSION

With Americans moving west in numbers that would shift the locus of political power, Democratic and Whig politicians did their best to keep the slavery issue out of the politics of territorial expansion. But they could not. Westward expansion was central to Democratic ideology, which saw the West's fertile and abundant lands as essential for creating a society in which white men could establish independent livelihoods and receive equal rights, freed from the undue influence of established slaveholders or urban elites. Whigs were more suspicious of rapid westward expansion, though they welcomed the commercial opportunities it might bring. Instead, they pushed harder for industrial and commercial development within the nation's current boundaries.

The Texas issue, however, made it impossible for politicians to disentangle westward expansion and slavery. Soon after establishing the Lone Star Republic, Sam Houston approached American authorities to propose annexation as a state. But a new slave state would upset the balance of slave and free states in the Senate which had been maintained since before the time of the Missouri Compromise. Neither the Whigs nor the Democrats, wary of causing sectional divisions within their ranks, were inclined to confront the issue. In the 1830s, Democratic presidents Andrew Jackson and Martin Van Buren—one a strong proponent of slavery, the other a mild opponent—sidestepped the issue. But by the mid-1840s—with cotton cultivation expanding rapidly—some Democratic politicians began to equate the annexation of Texas with the nation's manifest destiny.

Manifest Destiny The belief that American expansion westward and southward was inevitable, just, and divinely ordained dated to the nation's founding but was first labeled "manifest destiny" in 1845, by John L. O'Sullivan, editor of the *United States Magazine and Democratic Review*. O'Sullivan claimed that Texas annexation would be "the fulfillment of our manifest destiny to overspread the continent allotted by Providence for the free development of our yearly multiplying millions." The nation's destiny, he and others believed, was to encompass the continent. Manifest destiny implied that Americans had a God-given right, perhaps even an obligation, to expand their republican and Christian institutions to less fortunate and less civilized peoples. Manifest destiny motivated few Americans to pack their wagons and head westward. It did, however, provide a political rationale for territorial expansion.

Implicit in the idea of manifest destiny was the belief that American Indians and Hispanics, much like people of African descent, were inferior peoples best controlled or conquered. White racial theorists believed that, unlike white people, pure-blooded Indians and blacks were not capable of self-improvement. Nor, according to these racial theorists, were Hispanics, because intermarriage with Indians had left them incapable of improvement. Lansford Hastings, an Ohio native who ventured west and authored *The Emigrants' Guide to Oregon and California* (1845) noted that a *Californio* (a Mexican living in California) was "scarcely a visible grade, in the scale of intelligence, above the barbarous tribes by whom he is surrounded." Hastings hoped that, if enough Anglo-Saxons migrated to California, they could conquer the Mexicans with sheer numbers. And if they did so, they could congratulate themselves for carrying out God's will.

In June 1846, less patient expansionists, including John C. Frémont, staged an armed rebellion against Mexican authorities and declared California an independent republic. Because the U.S. military soon conquered California in its War with Mexico, the "Bear Flag Rebellion"—so named for the symbol on the revolutionaries' flag—was short-lived but further inflamed racial tensions in California.

Fifty-Four Forty or Fight   To the north, Britain and the United States had jointly occupied the disputed Oregon Territory since 1818. Beginning with John Quincy Adams's administration, the United States had tried to fix the boundary at the 49th parallel, but Britain was determined to maintain access to Puget Sound and the Columbia River. As migrants began streaming into Oregon in the early 1840s, expansionists demanded the entire Oregon Country for the United States, up to its northernmost border at latitude 54°40'. Soon "fifty-four forty or fight" became their rallying cry.

President Tyler wanted both Oregon and Texas, but he was obsessed with Texas and pursued the issue tirelessly. He argued that there was little to fear from slavery's expansion, for it would spread the nation's black population more thinly, allowing for the institution's gradual demise. But when word leaked out that Secretary of State John Calhoun had written to the British minister in Washington to justify Texas annexation as a way of protecting slavery—"a political institution essential to the peace, safety, and prosperity of those States in which it exists"—the Senate rejected annexation in 1844 by a vote of 35 to 16.

Polk and the Election of 1844   Worried southern Democrats persuaded their party's 1844 convention to adopt a rule requiring that the presidential nominee receive two-thirds of the convention votes, effectively giving the southern states a veto and allowing them to block the nomination of Martin Van Buren, an opponent of annexation. Instead, the party ran "Young Hickory," House Speaker James K. Polk, an avid expansionist and slaveholding cotton planter from Tennessee. The Democratic platform, designed to appeal to voters across regional lines, called for occupation of the entire Oregon Territory and annexation of Texas. The Whigs, who ran Henry Clay as their nominee, argued that the Democrats' belligerent nationalism would lead the nation into war with Great Britain or Mexico or both. Clay favored expansion through negotiation, whereas many northern Whigs opposed annexation altogether, fearful that it would lead to additional slave states as well as strained relations with vital trading partners.

Polk and the Democrats won the election by 170 electoral votes to 105, though with a margin of just 38,000 out of 2.7 million votes cast. Polk won New York's 36 electoral votes by just 6,000 popular votes. Abolitionist James G. Birney, the Liberty Party candidate, had drawn almost 16,000 votes away from Clay by running on a Free-Soil platform. Without Birney, Clay might have won New York, giving him an edge of 141 to 134 in the electoral college. Abolitionist forces thus unwittingly helped elect a slaveholder as president.

Annexation of Texas   Interpreting Polk's victory as a mandate for annexation, President Tyler proposed that Texas be admitted by joint resolution of Congress. The usual method of annexation, by treaty negotiation, required a two-thirds vote in the Senate—which expansionists clearly did not have, because there were sufficient opponents to slavery who would vote against annexation. Joint resolution required only a simple majority in each house. On

March 1, 1845, the resolution passed the House by 120 to 98 and the Senate by 27 to 25. Three days before leaving office, Tyler signed the measure. Mexico, which had never recognized Texas independence, immediately broke relations with the United States. In October the citizens of Texas ratified annexation, and Texas joined the Union, with a constitution permitting slavery, in December 1845. The nation was on the brink of war with Mexico. That conflict—like none other before it—would lay bare the inextricable relationships among westward expansion, slavery, and sectional discord.

SUMMARY

Encouraged by literary and artistic images of the frontier, easterners often viewed the West as a place of natural abundance, where hard-working individuals could seek security, freedom, and perhaps even fortune. By the millions they poured into the Old Southwest and Old Northwest in the early decades of the nineteenth century. Although the federal government promoted westward expansion—in the form of support for transportation improvements, surveying, cheap land, and protection from Indians—western migrants did not make the decision to head west lightly. Nor did they always find what they were looking for. Some returned home, some moved to new locations, and some—too poor or too embarrassed—stayed in the West, where they reluctantly abandoned their dreams of economic independence. Others found what they were looking for in the West, though often the road to success proved much slower and more circuitous than they had anticipated.

Not everyone who went west did so voluntarily, nor did everyone in the West think of it as an expanding region. African American slaves were moved westward by their owners in enormous numbers in the years between 1820 and 1860. Native Americans saw their lands and their livelihoods constrict, and their environments so altered that their economic and spiritual lives were threatened. Some Indians responded to the white incursion through accommodation and peaceful overtures; others resisted, sometimes forcefully. If their first strategy failed, then they tried another. But the sheer force of numbers favored whites. For Indians in Texas and California, white incursions brought devastation.

Although their belief in Native Americans' inferiority allowed many white Americans to rationalize the Indians' fate, it was white attitudes toward black people and slavery that drove their decisions about where to locate in the West. Those who believed that slavery degraded white labor headed along a northern trajectory, whereas those who dreamed of slave ownership headed southward, where they clashed with yet another group of people whom they deemed racially inferior: Mexicans. When American settlers in Texas achieved their independence from Mexico, legalized slavery, and applied for annexation by the United States, they brought the divisive issue of slavery's westward expansion to the surface of American politics. Although Democratic politicians at first tried to maintain a geographic equilibrium by proposing an ambitious territorial agenda in Oregon as well, it would be Texas annexation that set the stage for military conflict, the addition of vast territories in the Southwest, and reinvigorated sectional conflict.

14

Slavery and America's
Future: The Road to War
1845–1861

THE WAR WITH MEXICO
AND ITS CONSEQUENCES

In the 1840s, territorial expansion surged forward under the leadership of President
James K. Polk of North Carolina. The annexation of Texas just before his inauguration
did not necessarily make war with Mexico inevitable, but through a series of calculated
decisions, Polk brought the conflict on. Mexico broke off relations with the United
States, and during the annexation process, Polk urged Texans to seize all land to the Rio
Grande and claim the river as their southern and western border. Mexico held that the
Nueces River was the border; hence, the stage was set for conflict. Nothing could weaken
Polk's determination to fulfill the nation's manifest destiny to rule the continent. He
wanted Mexico's territory all the way to the Pacific, and all of Oregon Country as well.
He and his expansionist cabinet achieved their goals but were largely unaware of the
price in domestic harmony that expansion would exact.

Oregon   During the 1844 campaign, Polk's supporters had threatened
                war with Great Britain to gain all of Oregon. As president,
however, Polk turned first to diplomacy. Not wanting to fight Mexico and Great Britain
at the same time, he tried to avoid bloodshed in the Northwest, where America and
Britain had since 1819 jointly occupied disputed territory. Dropping the demand for a
boundary at latitude 54°40′, he pressured the British to accept the 49th parallel. In 1846

Great Britain agreed. The Oregon Treaty gave the United States all of present-day Oregon, Washington, and Idaho, and parts of Wyoming and Montana. Thus a new era of land acquisition and conquest had begun under the eleventh president of the United States, the sixth to be a slaveholder and one who, through an agent, secretly bought and sold slaves from the White House.

"Mr. Polk's War" Toward Mexico Polk was more aggressive. In early 1846 he ordered American troops under "Old Rough and Ready," General Zachary Taylor, to march south and defend the contested border of the Rio Grande across from the town of Matamoros, Mexico. Polk especially desired California as the prize in his expansionist strategy, and he attempted to buy from Mexico a huge tract of land extending to the Pacific. When that effort failed, Polk waited for war. Negotiations between troops on the Rio Grande were awkwardly conducted in French because no American officer spoke Spanish and no Mexican spoke English. After a three-week standoff, the tense situation came to a head. On April 24, 1846, Mexican cavalry ambushed a U.S. cavalry unit on the north side of the river; eleven Americans were killed, and sixty-three were taken captive. On April 26, Taylor sent a dispatch overland to Washington, D.C., which took two weeks to arrive, announcing, "Hostilities may now be considered as commenced."

Polk now drafted a message to Congress: Mexico had "passed the boundary of the United States, had invaded our territory and shed American blood on American soil." In the bill accompanying the war message, Polk deceptively declared that "war exists by the act of Mexico itself" and summoned the nation to arms. Two days later, on May 13, the House recognized a state of war with Mexico by a vote of 174 to 14, and the Senate, by 40 to 2, with numerous abstentions. Some antislavery Whigs had tried to oppose the war in Congress but were barely allowed to speak. Because Polk withheld key facts, the full reality of what had happened on the distant Rio Grande was not known. But the theory and practice of manifest destiny had launched the United States into its first major war on foreign territory.

Foreign War and the Popular Imagination The idea of war unleashed great public celebrations. Huge crowds gathered in southern cities, such as Richmond and Louisville, to voice support for the war effort. Twenty thousand Philadelphians and even more New Yorkers rallied in the same spirit. After news came of General Taylor's first two battlefield victories at Palo Alto and Resaca de la Palma, volunteers swarmed recruiting stations. From his home in Lansingburgh, New York, writer Herman Melville remarked that "the people here are all in a state of delirium. . . . A military ardor pervades all ranks. . . . Nothing is talked of but the 'Halls of the Montezumas.' " Publishers rushed books about Mexican geography into print; "Palo Alto" hats and root beer went on sale. And new daily newspapers, now printed on rotary presses, boosted their sales by giving the war a romantic appeal.

Here was an adventurous war of conquest in a far-off, exotic land. Here was the fulfillment of an Anglo-Saxon–Christian destiny to expand and possess the North American continent, and to take civilization to the "semi-Indian" Mexicans. For many, racism fueled the expansionist spirit. In 1846 an Illinois newspaper justified the war on the basis that Mexicans were "reptiles in the path of progressive democracy." For those

CHRONOLOGY

1846 • War with Mexico begins
• Oregon Treaty negotiated
• Wilmot Proviso inflames sectional divisions

1847 • Cass proposes idea of popular sovereignty

1848 • Treaty of Guadalupe Hidalgo gives United States new territory in the Southwest
• Free-Soil Party formed
• Taylor elected president
• Gold discovered in California, which later applies for admission to Union as free state

1850 • Compromise of 1850 passes, containing controversial Fugitive Slave Act

1852 • Stowe publishes *Uncle Tom's Cabin*
• Pierce elected president

1854 • Publication of "Appeal of the Independent Democrats"
• Kansas-Nebraska Act wins approval and ignites controversy
• Republican Party formed
• Return of fugitive Burns to slavery in Virginia

1856 • Bleeding Kansas troubles nation
• Brooks attacks Sumner in Senate chamber
• Buchanan elected president, but Republican Frémont wins most northern states

1857 • *Dred Scott v. Sanford* endorses southern views on black citizenship and slavery in territories
• Economic panic and widespread unemployment begin

1858 • Kansas voters reject Lecompton Constitution
• Lincoln-Douglas debates attract attention
• Douglas contends popular sovereignty prevails over *Dred Scott* decision in territories

1859 • Brown raids Harpers Ferry

1860 • Democratic Party splits in two; southern Democrats demand constitutional guarantee for the territories
• Lincoln elected president in divided, sectional election
• Crittenden Compromise fails
• South Carolina secedes from Union

1861 • Six more Deep South states secede
• Confederacy established at Montgomery, Alabama
• Attack on Fort Sumter begins Civil War
• Four states in the Upper South join the Confederacy

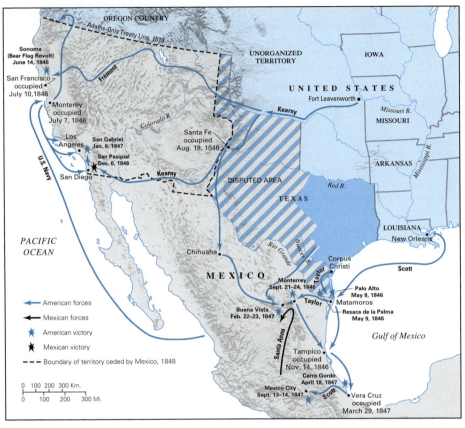

MAP 14.1 The War with Mexico

This map shows the territory disputed between the United States and Mexico. After U.S. gains in northeastern Mexico, in New Mexico, and in California, General Winfield Scott captured Mexico City in the decisive campaign of the war.

who read newspapers, the War with Mexico became the first national event experienced with immediacy. The battles south of the border were reported by war correspondents. From Vera Cruz on the Gulf Coast of Mexico, ships carried news dispatches to New Orleans, whose nine daily newspapers ran a faster steamer out to meet them. With stories set in type before they even reached shore, riders carried the news to the North. Near the end of the war, news traveled by telegraph in only three days from New Orleans to Washington, D.C.

The war spawned an outpouring of poetry, song, drama, travel literature, and lithographs that captured the popular imagination and glorified the conflict. New lyrics to the tune of "Yankee Doodle" proclaimed: "They attacked our men upon our land / and crossed our river too sir / now show them all with sword in hand / what yankee boys can do sir." Most of the war-inspired flowering of the popular arts was patriotic. But not everyone cheered. Abolitionist James Russell Lowell considered the war a "national crime committed in behoof of slavery, our common sin." Ralph Waldo Emerson confided to his journals in 1847, "The United States will conquer Mexico, but it will be as the man swallows arsenic, which brings him down in turn. Mexico will poison us." Even proslavery spokesman John C. Calhoun saw the perils of expansionism. Mexico, he said, was "the forbidden fruit; the penalty of eating it would be to subject our institutions to political death."

Conquest

The troops proved unruly and undisciplined, and their politically ambitious commanders often quarreled among themselves. Nevertheless, early in the war, U.S. forces made significant gains. In May 1846 Polk ordered Colonel Stephen Kearny and a small detachment to invade the remote and thinly populated provinces of New Mexico and California. Taking Santa Fe largely without opposition, Kearny pushed into California, where he joined forces with two U.S. naval units and rebellious American settlers led by Captain John C. Frémont. General Zachary Taylor's forces attacked and occupied Monterrey, which surrendered in September, securing northeastern Mexico.

New Mexico did not prove easy for U.S. forces to subdue, however. In January 1847, in Taos, northwest of Santa Fe, Hispanics and Indians led by Pablo Montoya and Tomas Romero rebelled against the Americans and killed numerous government officials. In what came to be known as the Taos Revolt, some 500 Mexican and Indian insurgents laid siege to a mill in Arroyo Hondo, outside Taos. The U.S. command acted swiftly to suppress the revolt with 300 heavily armed troops. The growing band of insurgents eventually retreated to Taos Pueblo and held out in a thick-walled church. With cannon, the U.S. Army succeeded in killing some 150 and capturing 400 of the rebels. After many arrests, approximately 28 insurgent leaders were hanged in the Taos plaza, ending the bloody resistance to U.S. occupation of lands still claimed by Mexican and Indian peoples.

Before the end of 1846, American forces had also established dominion over California. Because losses on the periphery of their large country had not broken Mexican resistance, General Winfield Scott carried the war to the enemy's heartland. Landing at Veracruz, he led 14,000 men toward Mexico City. This daring invasion proved the decisive campaign of the war. Scott's men, outnumbered and threatened by yellow fever, encountered a series of formidable Mexican defenses, but engineers repeatedly discovered flanking routes around their foes. After a series of hard-fought battles, U.S. troops captured the Mexican capital.

Treaty of Guadalupe Hidalgo

Representatives of both countries signed the Treaty of Guadalupe Hidalgo in February 1848. The United States gained California and New Mexico (including present-day Nevada, Utah, and Arizona, and parts of Colorado and Wyoming), and recognition of the Rio Grande as the southern boundary of Texas. In return, the American government agreed to settle the claims of its citizens (mostly Texans) against Mexico ($3.2 million) and to pay Mexico a mere $15 million. On the day Polk received the treaty from the Senate, a mob in Paris forced Louis Philippe to abdicate the throne of France, and a German writer, Karl Marx, published a pamphlet, *The Communist Manifesto,* in London. The enormous influence of Marx's work would be many years away, but as the 1848 nationalistic revolutions against monarchy spread to Italy, Austria, Hungary, and Germany, republican America seized a western empire.

The costs of the war included the deaths of thirteen thousand Americans (mostly from disease) and fifty thousand Mexicans. Moreover, enmity between Mexico and the United States endured into the twentieth century. The domestic cost to the United States was even higher. Public opinion was sharply divided. Southwesterners were enthusiastic about the war, as were most southern planters; New Englanders strenuously opposed it. Whigs in Congress charged that Polk, a Democrat, had "provoked" an unnecessary war and "usurped the power of Congress." The aged John Quincy Adams denounced the war, and an Illinois Whig named Abraham Lincoln called Polk's justifications the "half insane mumbling of a fever-dream." Abolitionists and a small minority of antislavery Whigs charged that the war was a plot to extend slavery. Congressman Joshua Giddings of Ohio charged that Polk's purpose was "to render slavery secure in Texas" and to extend slavery's dominion over the West.

"Slave Power Conspiracy"

These charges fed northern fear of the "Slave Power." Abolitionists had long warned of a slaveholding oligarchy that intended to dominate the nation through its hold on federal power. Slaveholders had gained control of the South by suppressing dissent. They had forced the gag rule on Congress in 1836 and threatened northern liberties. To many white northerners, even those who saw nothing wrong with slavery, it was the battle over free speech that first made the idea of a Slave Power credible. The War with Mexico deepened such fears. Had this questionable war, asked antislavery northerners, not been launched for vast, new slave territory?

Northern opinion on slavery's expansion began to shift, but the impact of the war on southern opinion was even more dramatic. At first, some southern Whigs attacked the Democratic president for causing the war, and few southern congressmen saw slavery as the paramount issue. Many whites in both North and South feared that large land seizures would bring thousands of nonwhite Mexicans into the United States and upset the racial order. An Indiana politician did not want "any mixed races in our Union, nor men of any color except white, unless they be slaves." And the *Charleston* (South Carolina) *Mercury* asked if the nation expected "to melt into our population eight millions of men, at war with us by race, by language, by religion, manners and laws." Yet, despite their racism and such numerical exaggerations, many statesmen soon saw other prospects in the outcomes of a war of conquest in the Southwest.

Wilmot Proviso

In August 1846, David Wilmot, a Pennsylvania Democrat, proposed an amendment, or proviso, to a military tary appropriations bill: that "neither slavery nor involuntary servitude shall ever exist" in any territory gained from Mexico. Although the proviso never passed both houses of Congress, its repeated introduction by northerners transformed the debate over the expansion of slavery. Southerners suddenly circled their wagons to protect the future of a slave society. Alexander H. Stephens, only recently "no defender of slavery," now declared that slavery was based on the Bible and above moral criticism, and John C. Calhoun took an aggressive stand. The territories, Calhoun insisted, belonged to all the states, and the federal government could do nothing to limit the spread of slavery there. Southern slaveholders had a constitutional right rooted in the Fifth Amendment, Calhoun claimed, to take their slaves (as property) anywhere in the territories.

This position, often called "state sovereignty," which quickly became a test of orthodoxy among southern politicians, was a radical reversal of history. In 1787 the Confederation Congress had discouraged if not fully excluded slavery from the Northwest Territory; Article IV of the U.S. Constitution had authorized Congress to make "all needful rules and regulations" for the territories; and the Missouri Compromise had barred slavery from most of the Louisiana Purchase. Now, however, southern leaders demanded future guarantees for slavery.

In the North, the Wilmot Proviso became a rallying cry for abolitionists. Eventually the legislatures of fourteen northern states endorsed it—and not because all of its supporters were abolitionists. David Wilmot, significantly, was neither an abolitionist nor an antislavery Whig. He denied having any "squeamish sensitiveness upon the subject of slavery" or "morbid sympathy for the slave." Instead, his goal was to defend "the rights of white freemen" and to obtain California "for free white labor." Wilmot's involvement in antislavery controversy is a measure of the remarkable ability of the territorial issue to alarm northerners of many viewpoints.

As Wilmot demonstrated, it was possible, however, to be both a racist and an opponent of slavery. The vast majority of white northerners were not active abolitionists, and their desire to keep the West free from slavery was often matched by their desire to keep blacks from settling there. Fear of the Slave Power was thus building a potent antislavery movement that united abolitionists and antiblack voters. At stake was an abiding version of the American Dream: the free individual's access to social mobility through acquisition of land in the West. This sacred ideal of free labor, and its dread of concentrated power, fueled a new political persuasion in America. A man's ownership and sale of his own labor, wrote British economist Adam Smith, was "the most sacred and inviolable foundation of all property." Slave labor, thousands of northerners had come to believe, would degrade the honest toil of free men and render them unemployable. The West must therefore be kept free of slaves.

The Election of 1848 and Popular Sovereignty

The divisive slavery question now infested national politics. After Polk renounced a second term as president, the Democrats nominated Senator Lewis Cass of Michigan for president and General William Butler of Kentucky for vice president. Cass, a party loyalist who had served in Jackson's cabinet, had devised in 1847 the idea of "popular sovereignty"—letting residents in the western territories decide the question of slavery for themselves. His party's platform declared that Congress lacked the power to interfere with slavery's expansion. The Whigs nominated General Zachary Taylor, a southern slaveholder and war hero; Congressman Millard Fillmore of New York was his running mate. The Whig convention similarly refused to assert that Congress had power over slavery in the territories.

But the issue could not be avoided. Many southern Democrats distrusted Cass and eventually voted for Taylor because he was a slaveholder. Among northerners, concern over slavery led to the formation of a new party. New York Democrats committed to the Wilmot Proviso rebelled against Cass and nominated former president Martin Van Buren. Antislavery Whigs and former supporters of the Liberty Party then joined them to organize the Free-Soil Party, with Van Buren as its candidate (see Table 14.1). This party, which sought to restrict slavery expansion to any western territories and whose

TABLE 14.1 **New Political Parties**

Party	Period of Influence	Area of Influence	Outcome
Liberty Party	1839–1848	North	Merged with other antislavery groups to form Free-Soil Party
Free-Soil Party	1848–1854	North	Merged with Republican Party
Know-Nothings (American Party)	1853–1856	Nationwide	Disappeared, freeing most to join Republican Party
Republican Party	1854–present	North (later nationwide)	Became rival of Democratic Party and won presidency in 1860

slogan was "Free Soil, Free Speech, Free Labor, and Free Men," won almost 300,000 northern votes. For a new third party to win 10 percent of the national vote was unprecedented. Taylor polled 1.4 million votes to Cass's 1.2 million and won the White House, but the results were more ominous than decisive.

American politics had split along sectional lines as never before. Religious denominations, too, severed into northern and southern wings. Many Protestants, North and South, began to fear that God had an appointment with America, either to destroy the national sin of slavery or to help the South defend it as part of his divine order. As the 1850s dawned, the legacies of the War with Mexico and the conflicts of 1848 dominated national life and threatened the nature of the Union itself.

1850: COMPROMISE OR ARMISTICE?

The first sectional battle of the new decade involved California. More than eighty thousand Americans flooded into California during the gold rush of 1849. With Congress unable to agree on a formula to govern the territories, President Taylor urged these settlers to apply directly for admission to the Union. They promptly did so, proposing a state constitution that did not allow for slavery. Because California's admission as a free state would upset the sectional balance of power in the Senate (the ratio of slave to free states was fifteen to fifteen), southern politicians wanted to postpone admission and make California a slave territory, or at least extend the Missouri Compromise line west to the Pacific.

Debate over Slavery in the Territories   Henry Clay, the venerable Whig leader, sensed that the Union was in peril. Twice before—in 1820 and 1833—Clay, the "Great Pacificator," had taken the lead in shaping sectional compromise; now he struggled one last time to preserve the nation. To hushed Senate galleries Clay presented a series of compromise measures in the winter of 1850. At one point he held up what he claimed was a piece of George Washington's coffin as a means of inspiring unity. Over the weeks that followed, he and

Senator Stephen A. Douglas of Illinois, the "Little Giant," steered their compromise package through debate and amendment.

The problems to be solved were numerous and difficult. Would California, or part of it, become a free state? How should the territory acquired from Mexico be organized? Texas, which allowed slavery, claimed large portions of the new land as far west as Santa Fe. Southerners complained that fugitive slaves were not being returned as the Constitution required, and northerners objected to the sale of human beings in the nation's capital. Eight years earlier, in *Prigg v. Pennsylvania* (1842), the Supreme Court had ruled that enforcement of the fugitive slave clause in the Constitution was a federal, not a state, obligation, buttressing long-standing southern desires to bring this issue to a head. The Court further ruled that states could not exact measures, often called "personal liberty laws," banning the seizure and removal of a fugitive. Most troublesome of all, however, was the status of slavery in the territories.

Clay and Douglas hoped to avoid a specific formula, and in Lewis Cass's idea of popular sovereignty they discovered what one historian called a "charm of ambiguity." Ultimately Congress would have to approve statehood for a territory, but "in the meantime," said Cass, it should allow the people living there "to regulate their own concerns in their own way."

Those simple words proved all but unenforceable. When could settlers prohibit slavery? To avoid dissension within their party, northern and southern Democrats explained Cass's statement to their constituents in two incompatible ways. Southerners claimed that neither Congress nor a territorial legislature could bar slavery. Only late in the territorial process, when settlers were ready to draft a state constitution, could they take that step, thus allowing time for slavery to take root. Northerners, however, insisted that Americans living in a territory were entitled to local self-government and thus could outlaw slavery at any time.

The cause of compromise gained a powerful supporter when Senator Daniel Webster committed his prestige and eloquence to Clay's bill. "I wish to speak today," Webster declaimed on March 7 in a scene of high drama, "not as a Massachusetts man, nor as a Northern man, but as an American. I speak today for the preservation of the Union." Abandoning his earlier support for the Wilmot Proviso, Webster urged northerners not to "taunt or reproach" the South with antislavery measures. To southern firebrands he issued a warning that disunion inevitably would cause violence and destruction. For his efforts at compromise, Webster was condemned by many former abolitionist friends in New England who accused him of going over to the "devil."

Only three days earlier, with equal drama, Calhoun had been carried from his sickbed to deliver a speech opposing the compromise. As Calhoun was unable to stand and speak, Senator James Mason of Virginia read his address for him. Grizzled and dying, the South's intellectual defender warned that the "cords which bind these states" were "already greatly weakened." Calhoun did not address the specific measures in the bill; he predicted disunion if southern demands were not met, thereby frightening some into support of compromise.

Compromise of 1850

Yet rising fear and Webster's influence were not enough. After months of labor, Clay and Douglas finally brought their legislative package to a vote, and lost. With Clay sick and absent from Washington, Douglas reintroduced the compromise measures one at a time. Although there was no majority for compromise, Douglas shrewdly realized that different majorities might be created for the separate measures. Because southerners favored some bills and northerners the rest, the small majority for compromise could be achieved on each distinct issue. The strategy worked, and Douglas's resourcefulness alleviated the crisis as the Compromise of 1850 became law. The compromise had five essential measures:

1. California became a free state.
2. The Texas boundary was set at its present limits, and the United States paid Texas $10 million in compensation for the loss of New Mexico Territory.
3. The territories of New Mexico and Utah were organized on a basis of popular sovereignty.
4. The fugitive slave law was strengthened.
5. The slave trade was abolished in the District of Columbia.

Jubilation greeted passage of the compromise; crowds in Washington and other cities celebrated the happy news. "On one glorious night," records a modern historian, "the word went abroad that it was the duty of every patriot to get drunk. Before the next morning many a citizen had proved his patriotism."

In reality, there was less cause for celebration than people hoped. At best, the Compromise of 1850 was an artful evasion. As one historian has argued, the legislation

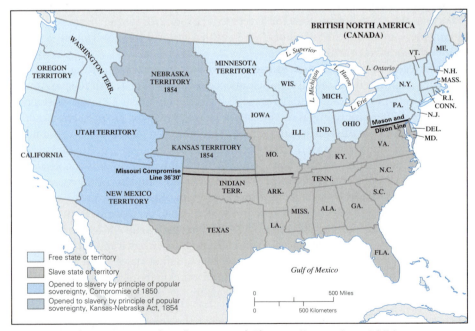

Map 14.2 The Kansas-Nebraska Act and Slavery Expansion, 1854

The vote on the Kansas-Nebraska Act in the House of Representatives (see also Table 14.2 on page 000) demonstrates the sectionalization of American politics due to the slavery question.

was more an "armistice," delaying greater conflict, than a compromise. Douglas had found a way to pass the five proposals without convincing northerners and southerners to agree on fundamentals. The compromise bought time for the nation, but it did not provide a real settlement of the territorial questions.

Furthermore, the compromise had two basic flaws. The first concerned the ambiguity of popular sovereignty. Southerners insisted there would be no prohibition of slavery during the territorial stage, and northerners declared that settlers could bar slavery whenever they wished. The compromise even allowed for the appeal of a territorial legislature's action to the Supreme Court. One witty politician remarked that the legislators had enacted a lawsuit instead of a law.

Fugitive Slave Act   The second flaw lay in the Fugitive Slave Act, which gave new—and controversial—protection to slavery. The law empowered slaveowners to go into court in their own states to present evidence that a slave who owed them service had escaped. The resulting transcript and a description of the fugitive would then serve as legal proof of a person's slave status, even in free states and territories. Specially appointed court officials adjudicated the identity of the person described, not whether he or she was indeed a slave. Penalties made it a felony to harbor fugitives, and the law stated that northern citizens could be summoned to hunt fugitives. The fees paid to U.S. marshals favored slaveholders: $10 if the alleged fugitive was returned to the slaveowner, $5 if not returned.

Abolitionist newspapers quickly attacked the Fugitive Slave Act as a violation of fundamental American rights. Why were alleged fugitives denied a trial by jury? Why were they given no chance to present evidence or cross-examine witnesses? Why did the law give authorities a financial incentive to send suspected fugitives into bondage, and why would northerners now be arrested if they harbored runaways? These arguments convinced some northerners that all free blacks were vulnerable to kidnapping and enslavement. The "free" states were no longer a safe haven for black folk, whatever their origins; an estimated 20,000 fled to Canada in the wake of the Fugitive Slave Act.

Between 1850 and 1854, protests and violent resistance to slave catchers occurred in dozens of northern towns. Sometimes a captured fugitive was broken out of jail or from the clutches of slave agents by abolitionists, as in the 1851 Boston case of Shadrach Minkins, who was spirited by a series of wagons and trains across Massachusetts, up through Vermont, to Montreal, Canada. Also in 1851, a fugitive named Jerry McHenry was freed by an abolitionist mob in Syracuse, New York, and hurried to Canadian freedom. That same year as well, the small black community in Lancaster County, Pennsylvania, rose up in arms to defend four escaped slaves from a federal posse charged with reenslaving them. At this "Christiana riot," the fugitives shot and killed Edward Gorsuch, the Maryland slaveowner who sought the return of his "property." Amid increasing border warfare over fugitive slaves, a headline reporting the Christiana affair screamed, "Civil War, The First Blow Struck!"

Many abolitionists became convinced by their experience of resisting the Fugitive Slave Act that violence was a legitimate means of opposing slavery. In an 1854 column entitled "Is It Right and Wise to Kill a Kidnapper?" Frederick Douglass said that the only way to make the fugitive slave law "dead letter" was to make a "few dead slave catchers."

Uncle Tom's Cabin   At this point, a novel portrayed the humanity and suffering of slaves in a way that touched millions of northerners. Harriet Beecher Stowe, whose New England family had produced many prominent ministers, wrote *Uncle Tom's Cabin* out of deep moral conviction. Her story, serialized in 1851 and published as a book in 1852, conveyed the agonies faced by slave families and described a mother's dash to freedom with her child across the frozen Ohio River. Stowe also portrayed slavery's evil effects on slaveholders, indicting the institution itself more harshly than she indicted the southerners caught in its web. Moreover, Stowe exposed northern racism and complicity with slavery by making the worst slaveholder a man of New England birth and a visiting relative on a plantation a squeamish Vermont woman who could hardly cope with the presence of blacks.

In nine months the book sold over 300,000 copies and by mid-1853 over 1 million. Countless people saw *Uncle Tom's Cabin* performed as a stage play, heard the story in dramatic readings, or read similar novels inspired by it. Stowe brought home the evil of slavery to many who had never given it much thought. Indeed, for generations, the characters in *Uncle Tom's Cabin*—Eliza, Little Eva, Simon Legree, and Uncle Tom himself—entered the American imagination as symbols of slavery and its demise.

The popularity of *Uncle Tom's Cabin* alarmed anxious southern whites. In politics and now in popular literature they saw threats to their way of life. Behind the South's aggressive claims about territorial rights lay the fear that, if nearby areas outlawed slavery, they would be used as bases from which to spread abolitionism into the slave states. To most white southerners, a moral condemnation of slaveholding anywhere meant the same thing everywhere.

To protect slavery in the arena of ideas, southerners needed to counter indictments of the institution as a moral wrong. Accordingly, some fifteen to twenty proslavery novels were published in the 1850s as responses to *Uncle Tom's Cabin.* Most of these paled in comparison to Mrs. Stowe's masterpiece, but southern writers continued to defend their system as more humane than wage labor, and they blamed the slave trade on the "outside interference" of Yankee speculators. In awkward stories, such as J. W. Page's *Uncle Robin in His Cabin and Tom Without One in Boston,* slaves were induced to run away by visiting abolitionists, and then all but starved in northern cities.

The Underground Railroad   In reality, slaveholders were especially disturbed by the 1850s over what was widely called the Underground Railroad. This loose, illegal network of civil disobedience, spiriting runaways to freedom, had never been very organized. Thousands of slaves did escape by these routes, but largely through their own wits and courage, and through the assistance of blacks in some northern cities. Lewis Hayden in Boston, David Ruggles in New York, William Still in Philadelphia, John Parker in Ripley, Ohio, and Jacob Gibbs in Washington, D.C., were only some of the many black abolitionists who managed fugitive slave escapes through their regions.

Moreover, Harriet Tubman, herself an escapee in 1848, returned to her native Maryland and to Virginia at least a dozen times, and through clandestine measures helped possibly as many as three hundred slaves, some of them her own family members, to freedom. Maryland planters were so outraged at her heroic success that they offered a $40,000 reward for her capture.

In Ohio, numerous white abolitionists, often Quakers, joined with blacks as agents of slave liberation at various points along the river border between slavery and freedom. The Underground Railroad also had numerous maritime routes, as coastal slaves escaped aboard ship out of Virginia or the Carolinas, or from New Orleans, and ended up in northern port cities, the Caribbean, or England. Many fugitive slaves from the Lower South and Texas escaped to Mexico, which had abolished slavery in 1829. Some slaves escaped by joining the Seminole communities in Florida, where they fought with them against the U.S. Army in the Seminole Wars of 1835–1842 and 1855–1858.

This constant, dangerous flow of humanity was a testament to human courage and the will for freedom. It never reached the scale believed by some angry slaveholders or that of the countless safe houses and hideaways claimed by hundreds of northern towns and local historical societies today. But, in reality and in legend, the Underground Railroad applied pressure to the institution of slavery and provided slaves with a focus for hope.

Election of 1852 and the Collapse of Compromise

The 1852 election gave southern leaders hope that slavery would be secure under the administration of a new president. Franklin Pierce, a Democrat from New Hampshire, won an easy victory over the Whig presidential nominee, General Winfield Scott. Pierce defended each section's rights as essential to the nation's unity, and southerners hoped that his firm support for the Compromise of 1850 might end the season of crisis. Because Scott's views on the compromise had been unknown and

In Still Life of Harriet Tubman with Bible and Candle, *we see the youthful, calm, determined leader of the Underground Railroad. Appearing gentle, Tubman was in her own way a revolutionary who liberated nearly three hundred of her people.* (© 2000 Louis Psihoyos/Science Faction)

the Free-Soil candidate, John P. Hale of New Hampshire, had openly rejected it, Pierce's victory suggested widespread support for the compromise.

Pierce's victory, however, derived less from his strengths than from the Whig Party's weakness. The Whigs had never achieved much success in presidential politics, and by 1852 sectional discord had rendered it all but dead. President Pierce's embrace of the compromise appalled many northerners. His vigorous enforcement of the Fugitive Slave Act provoked outrage and fear of the Slave Power, especially in the case of the fugitive slave Anthony Burns, who had fled Virginia by stowing away on a ship in 1852. In Boston, thinking he was safe in a city known for abolitionism, Burns began a new life. But in 1854 federal marshals found and placed him under guard in Boston's courthouse. An interracial crowd of abolitionists attacked the courthouse, killing a jailer in an unsuccessful attempt to free Burns, whose case attracted nationwide attention.

Pierce moved decisively to enforce the Fugitive Slave Act. He telegraphed local officials to "incur any expense to insure the execution of the law" and sent marines, cavalry, and artillery to Boston. U.S. troops marched Burns to Boston harbor through streets that his supporters had draped in black and hung with American flags at half-mast. At a cost of $100,000, a single black man was returned to slavery through the power of federal law.

The national will to sustain the future of slavery was now tested at every turn. This demonstration of federal support for slavery radicalized opinion, even among many conservatives. Textile manufacturer Amos A. Lawrence observed that "we went to bed one night old fashioned, conservative, Compromise Union Whigs & waked up stark mad Abolitionists." Juries refused to convict the abolitionists who had stormed the Boston courthouse, and New England states began to pass personal liberty laws designed to impede or block federal enforcement. In such laws, local judges were absolved from enforcing the Fugitive Slave Act, in effect nullifying federal authority. What northerners now saw as evidence of a dominating Slave Power, outraged slaveholders saw as the legal defense of their rights.

Pierce confronted sectional conflict at every turn. His proposal for a transcontinental railroad derailed when congressmen fought over its location, North or South. His attempts to acquire foreign territory stirred more trouble. An annexation treaty with Hawai'i failed because southern senators would not vote for another free state, and efforts to acquire slaveholding Cuba angered northerners. Events in the Pacific also caused division at home over just how far American expansion should extend. With two orchestrated landings in the Bay of Tokyo, in 1853 and 1854, Commodore Matthew Perry established U.S. intentions to trade with Japan, whether that country sought such contact or not. Offended and intrigued, the Japanese were impressed with Perry's steam-powered warships, the first such black smoke–belching, floating machines they had seen. Perry's Treaty of Kanagawa in March 1854 negotiated two ports as coaling stations for American ships. The much sought-after trading arrangements were slow in coming, although this did not stop merchants and bankers from lavishing on Perry a hero's honors when he returned to the United States. In his meetings with the Japanese, the pompous Perry had given his hosts, whom he considered an inferior people, a telegraph system, a quarter-scale railroad train, a bound history of the War with Mexico, and one hundred gallons of Kentucky whiskey.

Soon, back home, another territorial bill threw Congress and the nation into even greater turmoil, and the Compromise of 1850 fell into complete collapse.

SLAVERY EXPANSION AND COLLAPSE OF THE PARTY SYSTEM

The new controversy began in a surprising way. Stephen A. Douglas, one of the architects of the Compromise of 1850, introduced a bill to establish the Kansas and Nebraska Territories. Talented and ambitious for the presidency, Douglas was known for compromise, not sectional quarreling. But he did not view slavery as a fundamental problem, and he was willing to risk some controversy to win economic benefits for Illinois, his home state. A transcontinental railroad would encourage settlement of the Great Plains and stimulate the economy of Illinois, but no company would build such a railroad before Congress organized the territories it would cross. Thus interest in promoting the construction of such a railroad drove Douglas to introduce a bill that inflamed sectional passions.

The Kansas-Nebraska Act The Kansas-Nebraska Act exposed the conflicting interpretations of popular sovereignty. Douglas's bill left "all questions pertaining to slavery in the Territories . . . to the people residing therein." Northerners and southerners, however, still disagreed violently over what territorial settlers could constitutionally do. Moreover, the Kansas and Nebraska Territories lay within the Louisiana Purchase, and the Missouri Compromise prohibited slavery in all that land from latitude 36°30′ north to the Canadian border. If popular sovereignty were to mean anything in Kansas and Nebraska, it had to mean that the Missouri Compromise was no longer in effect and that settlers could establish slavery there.

Southern congressmen, anxious to establish slaveholders' right to take slaves into any territory, pressed Douglas to concede this point. They demanded an explicit repeal of the 36°30' limitation as the price of their support. During a carriage ride with Senator Archibald Dixon of Kentucky, Douglas debated the point at length. Finally he made an impulsive decision: "By God, Sir, you are right. I will incorporate it in my bill, though I know it will raise a hell of a storm."

Perhaps Douglas underestimated the storm because he believed that conditions of climate and soil would keep slavery out of Kansas and Nebraska. Nevertheless, his bill threw open to slavery land from which it had been prohibited for thirty-four years. Opposition from Free-Soilers and antislavery forces was immediate and enduring; many considered this turn of events a betrayal of a sacred trust. The titanic struggle in Congress lasted three and a half months. Douglas won the support of President Pierce and eventually prevailed: the bill became law in May 1854 by a vote that demonstrated the dangerous sectionalization of American politics (Table 14.2).

But the storm was just beginning. Abolitionists charged sinister aggression by the Slave Power, and northern fears of slavery's influence deepened. Opposition to the Fugitive Slave Act grew dramatically; between 1855 and 1859, Connecticut, Rhode Island, Massachusetts, Michigan, Maine, Ohio, and Wisconsin passed personal-liberty laws. These laws enraged southern leaders by providing counsel for alleged fugitives and requiring trial by jury. More important was the devastating impact of the Kansas-Nebraska Act on political parties. The weakened Whig Party broke apart into northern and southern wings that could no longer cooperate nationally. The Democrats survived, but their support in the North fell drastically in the 1854 elections. Northern Democrats lost sixty-six of their ninety-one congressional seats and lost control of all but two free-state legislatures.

TABLE 14.2 The Vote on the Kansas-Nebraska Act

The vote was 113 to 100 in favor.	Aye	Nay
Northern Democrats	44	42
Southern Democrats	57	2
Northern Whigs	0	45
Southern Whigs	12	7
Northern Free-Soilers		4

Birth of the Republican Party

The beneficiary of northern voters' wrath was a new political party. During debate on the Kansas-Nebraska Act, six congressmen had published an "Appeal of the Independent Democrats." Joshua Giddings, Salmon Chase, and Charles Sumner—the principal authors of this protest—attacked Douglas's legislation as a "gross violation of a sacred pledge" (the Missouri Compromise) and a "criminal betrayal of precious rights" that would make free territory a "dreary region of despotism." Their appeal tapped a reservoir of deep concerns in the North, cogently expressed by Illinois's Abraham Lincoln.

Although Lincoln did not personally condemn southerners—"They are just what we would be in their situation"—he exposed the meaning of the Kansas-Nebraska Act. Lincoln argued that the founders, from love of liberty, had banned slavery from the Northwest Territory, kept the word *slavery* out of the Constitution, and treated it overall as a "cancer" on the republic. Rather than encouraging liberty, the Kansas-Nebraska Act put slavery "on the high road to extension and perpetuity," and that constituted a "moral wrong and injustice." America's future, Lincoln warned, was being mortgaged to slavery and all its influences.

Thousands of ordinary white northerners agreed. During the summer and fall of 1854, antislavery Whigs and Democrats, Free-Soilers, and other reformers throughout the Old Northwest met to form the new Republican Party, dedicated to keeping slavery out of the territories. The influence of the Republicans rapidly spread to the East, and they won a stunning victory in the 1854 elections. In their first appearance on the ballot, Republicans captured a majority of northern House seats. Antislavery sentiment had created a new party and caused roughly a quarter of northern Democrats to desert their party.

For the first time, too, a sectional party had gained significant power in the political system. Now the Whigs were gone, and only the Democrats struggled to maintain national membership. The Republicans absorbed the Free-Soil Party and grew rapidly in the North. Indeed, the emergence of the Republican coalition of antislavery interests is the most rapid transformation in party allegiance and voter behavior in American history.

Know-Nothings

Republicans also drew into their coalition a fast-growing nativist movement that called itself the American Party, or Know-Nothings (because its first members kept their purposes secret, answering, "I know nothing" to all questions). This group exploited fear of foreigners and Catholics. Between 1848 and 1860, nearly 3.5 million immigrants entered the United States—proportionally the heaviest inflow of foreigners ever in American history. Democrats courted the votes of these new citizens, but many native-born Anglo-Saxon

Protestants believed that Irish and German Catholics would owe primary allegiance to the pope in Rome and not to the American nation.

In 1854 anti-immigrant fears gave the Know-Nothings spectacular success in some northern states. They triumphed especially in Massachusetts, electing 11 congressmen, a governor, all state officers, all state senators, and all but 2 of 378 state representatives. The temperance movement also gained new strength early in the 1850s with its promises to stamp out the evils associated with liquor and immigrants (a particularly anti-Irish campaign). In this context the Know-Nothings strove to reinforce Protestant morality and to restrict voting and office holding to the native-born. As the Whig Party faded from the scene, the Know-Nothings temporarily filled the void. But, like the Whigs, the Know-Nothings could not keep their northern and southern wings together in the face of the slavery expansion issue, and they dissolved after 1856. The growing Republican coalition wooed the nativists with temperance ordinances and laws postponing suffrage for naturalized citizens (see Table 14.1).

Party Realignment and the Republicans' Appeal With nearly half of the old electorate up for grabs, the demise of the Whig Party ensured a major realignment of the political system. The remaining parties made appeals to various segments of the electorate. Immigration, temperance, homestead bills, the tariff, internal improvements—all played important roles in attracting voters during the 1850s. The Republicans appealed strongly to those interested in the economic development of the West. Commercial agriculture was booming in the Ohio–Mississippi–Great Lakes area, but residents of that region desired more canals, roads, and river and harbor improvements. Because credit was scarce, a homestead program—the idea that western land should be free to individuals who would farm it and make a home on it—attracted many voters. The Republicans seized on these political desires, promising internal improvements and land grants, as well as backing higher tariffs to protect industry.

Partisan ideological appeals became the currency of the realigned political system. As Republicans preached, "Free Soil, Free Labor, Free Men," they captured a self-image of many northerners. These phrases resonated with traditional ideals of equality, liberty, and opportunity under self-government—the heritage of republicanism. Invoking that heritage also undercut charges that the Republican Party was radical and abolitionist.

The northern economy was booming, and thousands of migrants had moved west to establish productive farms and growing communities. Midwesterners multiplied their yields by using new machines, such as mechanical reapers. Railroads were carrying their crops to urban markets. And industry was beginning to perform wonders of production, making available goods that only recently had been beyond the reach of the average person. As northerners surveyed the general growth and prosperity, they thought they saw a reason for it.

Republican Ideology The key to progress appeared, to many people, to be free labor—the dignity of work and the incentive of opportunity. Any hard-working and virtuous man, it was thought, could improve his condition and achieve economic independence by seizing the main chance. Republicans argued that the South, with little industry and slave labor, was backward by comparison. Their arguments captured the spirit of the age in the North.

Traditional republicanism hailed the virtuous common man as the backbone of the country. In Abraham Lincoln, a man of humble origins who had become a successful lawyer and political leader, Republicans had a symbol of that tradition. They portrayed their party as the guardian of economic opportunity, giving individuals a chance to work, acquire land, and attain success. In the words of an Iowa Republican, the United States was thriving because its "door is thrown open to all, and even the poorest and humblest in the land, may, by industry and application, gain a position which will entitle him to the respect . . . of his fellow-men."

At stake in the crises of the 1850s were thus two competing definitions of "liberty": southern planters' claims to protection of their liberty in the possession and transport of their slaves anywhere in the land, and northern workers' and farmers' claims to protection of their liberty to seek a new start on free land, unimpeded by a system that defined labor as slave and black.

Opposition to the extension of slavery had brought the Republicans into being, but party members carefully broadened their appeal by adopting the causes of other groups. Their coalition ideology consisted of many elements: resentment of southern political power, devotion to unionism, antislavery based on free-labor arguments, moral revulsion to slavery, and racial prejudice. As *New York Tribune* editor Horace Greeley wrote in 1856, "It is beaten into my bones that the American people are not yet anti-slavery." Four years later, Greeley again observed that "an Anti-Slavery man per se cannot be elected." But, he added, "a Tariff, River-and-Harbor, Pacific Railroad, Free Homestead man, may succeed although he is Anti-Slavery." As these elements placed their hopes in the Republican Party, they also grew to fear slavery even more.

Southern Democrats

In the South, the disintegration of the Whig Party had left many southerners at loose ends politically; they included a good number of wealthy planters, smaller slaveholders, and urban businessmen. Some gravitated to the American Party, but not for long. In the increasingly tense atmosphere of sectional crisis, these people were highly susceptible to strong states' rights positions and the defense of slavery. The security of their own communities seemed at stake, and in the 1850s, most formerly Whig slaveholders converted to the Democratic Party.

Since Andrew Jackson's day, however, nonslaveholding yeomen had been the heart of the Democratic Party. Democratic politicians, though often slaveowners themselves, lauded the common man and argued that their policies advanced his interests. According to the southern version of republicanism, white citizens in a slave society enjoyed liberty and social equality because black people were enslaved. As Jefferson Davis put it in 1851, in other societies distinctions were drawn "by property, between the rich and the poor." But in the South, slavery elevated every white person's status and allowed the nonslaveholder to "stand upon the broad level of equality with the rich man." To retain the support of ordinary whites, southern Democrats appealed to racism, warning starkly of the main issue: "shall negroes govern white men, or white men govern negroes?"

Southern leaders also portrayed sectional controversies as matters of injustice and insult to the honor of the South. The rights of all southern whites were in jeopardy, they argued, because antislavery and Free-Soil forces threatened an institution protected in

Annexation of Cuba

One of the most contentious issues in antebellum American foreign relations was the annexation of Cuba. As a strategic bulwark against Britain and France in the Western Hemisphere, for its massive sugar wealth, and as a slave society that might reinforce the security of southern slavery, the Spanish-controlled island fired the imagination of manifest destiny. In the early republic, Presidents Thomas Jefferson and James Madison explored acquisition. "I have ever looked on Cuba as the most interesting addition which could . . . be made to our system of states," wrote Jefferson. John Quincy Adams, speaking as secretary of state in 1823, considered Cuba "indispensable to the continuance . . . of the Union."

Until the 1840s, the United States officially supported Spanish rule for stability and the preservation of slavery. Southerners feared a "second Haiti" if Cuba became independent through revolution. The prospect of slave insurrection and the spread of abolitionism throughout the upper Caribbean and the rim of the Deep South drove many southerners and three Democratic administrations to shift course and pursue acquisition of Cuba. Slaveholding politicians viewed Cuba as critical to expansion; human bondage, they believed, had to expand southward and westward, or it might die.

In 1848 President Polk authorized $100 million to purchase Cuba. The Spanish foreign minister, however, told Polk's emissary that his government would rather see Cuba "sunk in the ocean" than sell it to the United States. During the crisis over the Kansas-Nebraska Act in 1854, as President Pierce revived the annexation scheme, some southerners planned to seize Cuba by force. Although the expedition never embarked, its prospect outraged antislavery Republicans eager to halt slavery's expansion and protect their claims for free labor as the basis of America's future.

Yet another aggressive American design on Cuba emerged in the Ostend Manifesto in October 1854. Written after a meeting among the American foreign ministers to Britain, France, and Spain, the document advocated conquest of Cuba if it could not be purchased. The ministers predicted that Cuba "would be Africanized and become a second

Despite the failure of filibustering expeditions, the effort to annex Cuba continued throughout James Buchanan's presidential administration. This cartoon portrays Sam Houston, the famed Texan and proponent of American expansion, rowing the boat for a harpoonist in quest of the whale, Cuba. The dream of appropriating Cuba to the United States died very hard in the antebellum era. *Vanity Fair,* New York, June 1860. (© Bettmann/Corbis)

(Continued)

Annexation of Cuba

St. Domingo, with all its attendant horrors to the white race." But anti-slavery northerners saw schemes of the Slave Power, whose "will is the law of this administration." The Ostend controversy forced temporary abandonment of annexation efforts, but as the fires in Bleeding Kansas subsided in 1858, President Buchanan reignited Cuba fever. A fierce Senate debate over yet another purchase offer in early 1859 ended in bitter division over the extension of slavery's domain.

The failure of Cuban annexation was deeply intertwined with the meaning of the United States as a slaveholding republic. "I want Cuba, and I know that sooner or later we must have it . . . for the planting or spreading of slavery," said Mississippian Albert G. Brown in 1858. Too many northerners, however, understood Brown's intentions. In America's links to the world—in this case only 90 miles from the Florida coast—just as in domestic affairs, the expansion of slavery poisoned the body politic.

the Constitution. The stable, well-ordered South was the true defender of constitutional principles; the rapidly changing North, their destroyer.

Racial fears and traditional political loyalties helped keep the political alliance between yeoman farmers and planters largely intact through the 1850s. Across class lines, white southerners joined together in the interest of community security against what they perceived as the Republican Party's capacity to cause slave unrest in their midst. In the South, no viable party emerged to replace the Whigs, and as in the North, political realignment sharpened sectional identities.

Political leaders of both sections used race in their arguments about opportunity, but northerners and southerners saw different futures. The *Montgomery* (Alabama) *Mail* warned southern whites in 1860 that the Republicans intended "to free the negroes and force amalgamation between them and the children of the poor men of the South. The rich will be able to keep out of the way of the contamination." Republicans warned northern workers that, if slavery entered the territories, the great reservoir of opportunity for ordinary citizens would be poisoned.

Bleeding Kansas   The Kansas-Nebraska Act spawned hatred and violence as land-hungry partisans in the sectional struggle clashed repeatedly in Kansas Territory. Abolitionists and religious groups sent in armed Free-Soil settlers; southerners sent in their reinforcements to establish slavery and prevent "northern hordes" from stealing Kansas away. Conflicts led to vicious bloodshed, and soon the whole nation was talking about "Bleeding Kansas."

Politics in the territory resembled war more than democracy. During elections for a territorial legislature in 1855, thousands of proslavery Missourians—known as Border Ruffians—invaded the polls and ran up a large but fraudulent majority for proslavery candidates. They murdered and intimidated free state settlers. At one rally of such ruffians with other southerners, flags flapped in the breeze with the mottoes "Southern Rights," "Supremacy of the White Race," and "Alabama for Kansas." The resulting legislature legalized slavery, and in response Free-Soilers held an unauthorized convention at which they created their own government and constitution. Kansas was a tinderbox. By the spring of 1856, newspapers screamed for violence. "In a fight, let our motto be 'War to the knife, and knife to the hilt,'" demanded the proslavery *Squatter Sovereign.* Slavery's advocates taunted their adversaries as cowards and likened "abolitionists" to "infidels" worthy only of "total extermination."

In May, a proslavery posse sent to arrest the Free-Soil leaders sacked the Kansas town of Lawrence, killing several people and destroying a hotel with cannon shot. In revenge, John Brown, a radical abolitionist with a band of followers, murdered five proslavery settlers living along Pottawatomie Creek. The victims were taken in the dark of night from the clutches of their families, their heads and limbs hacked to pieces by heavy broadswords, their bodies heaved into dead brush. Brown himself did not wield the swords, but he did fire a single shot into the head of one senseless foe to assure his death. Soon, armed bands of guerrillas roamed the territory, battling over land claims as well as slavery.

These passions brought violence to the U.S. Senate in May 1856, when Charles Sumner of Massachusetts denounced "the Crime against Kansas." Radical in his antislavery views, Sumner bitterly assailed the president, the South, and Senator Andrew P. Butler of South Carolina. Soon thereafter, Butler's cousin, Representative Preston Brooks, approached Sumner at the latter's Senate desk, raised his cane, announced the defense of his kin's honor, and mercilessly beat Sumner on the head. The senator collapsed, bleeding, on the floor while unsympathetic colleagues watched.

Shocked northerners recoiled from what they saw as another case of wanton southern violence and an assault on free speech. William Cullen Bryant, editor of the *New York Evening Post,* asked, "Has it come to this, that we must speak with bated breath in the presence of our southern masters?" As if in reply, the *Richmond Enquirer* denounced "vulgar Abolitionists in the Senate" who "have been suffered to run too long without collars. They must be lashed into submission." Popular opinion in Massachusetts strongly supported Sumner; South Carolina voters reelected Brooks and sent him dozens of commemorative canes.

Election of 1856   The election of 1856 showed how extreme such polarization had become. For Republicans, "Bleeding Sumner" and "Bleeding Kansas" had become rallying cries. When Democrats met to select a nominee, they shied away from prominent leaders whose views on the territorial question would invite controversy. Instead, they chose James Buchanan of Pennsylvania, whose chief virtue was that for the past four years he had been ambassador to Britain, uninvolved in territorial controversies. Superior party organization helped Buchanan win 1.8 million votes and the election, but he owed his victory to southern support. Hence, he was tagged with the label "a northern man with southern principles."

Eleven of sixteen free states voted against Buchanan, and Democrats did not regain ascendancy in those states for decades. The Republican candidate, John C. Frémont, famous as a western explorer, won those eleven free states and 1.3 million votes; Republicans had become the dominant party in the North after only two years of existence. The Know-Nothing candidate, Millard Fillmore, won almost 1 million votes, but this election was that party's last hurrah. The coming battle would pit a sectional Republican Party against an increasingly divided Democratic Party. With huge voter turnouts, as high as 75 to 80 percent in many states, Americans were about to learn that elections really matter.

SLAVERY AND THE NATION'S FUTURE

For years the issue of slavery in the territories had convulsed Congress, and Congress had tried to settle the issue with vague formulas. In 1857 the Supreme Court stepped into the fray, took up this emotionally charged subject, and attempted to silence controversy with a definitive verdict.

Dred Scott Case   A Missouri slave named Dred Scott and his wife, Harriet Robinson Scott, had sued for their freedom. Scott based his claim on the fact that his former owner, an army surgeon, had taken him for several years into Illinois, a free state, and to Fort Snelling in the Minnesota Territory, from which slavery had been barred by the Missouri Compromise. Scott first won and then lost his case as it moved on appeal through the state courts into the federal system and, finally, after eleven years, to the Supreme Court.

The impetus for the lawsuit likely came as much from Harriet as from Dred Scott. They were legally married at Fort Snelling (free territory) in 1836 when Dred was forty and Harriet seventeen. She had already lived as a slave on free soil for at least five years and had given birth to four children, also born on free soil: two sons who died in infancy and two daughters, Eliza and Lizzie, who lived. In all likelihood, the quest to achieve "freedom papers" through a lawsuit—begun in 1846 as two separate cases, one in his name and one in hers—came as much from Harriet's desire to sustain her family and protect her two teenage daughters from potential sale and sexual abuse as from the aging and sickly Dred. Indeed, her legal case for freedom may have been even stronger than Dred's, but their lawyers subsumed her case into his during the long appeal process.

Normally, Supreme Court justices were reluctant to inject themselves into major political issues. An 1851 decision had declared that state courts determined the status of blacks who lived within their jurisdictions. The Supreme Court had only to follow this precedent to avoid ruling on substantive, and very controversial, issues: Was a black person like Dred Scott a citizen of the United States and thus eligible to sue in federal court? Had residence in a free state or territory made him free? Did Congress have the power to prohibit or promote slavery in a territory?

After hesitation, the Supreme Court agreed to hear *Dred Scott v. Sanford* and decided to rule on the Missouri Compromise after all. Two northern justices indicated that they would dissent from the assigned opinion and argue for Scott's freedom and the constitutionality of the Missouri Compromise. Their decision emboldened southerners on the Court, who were growing eager to declare the 1820 geographical restriction on slavery unconstitutional. Southern sympathizers in Washington were pressing for a proslavery verdict, and several justices felt they should simply try to resolve sectional strife once and for all.

In March 1857, Chief Justice Roger B. Taney of Maryland delivered the majority opinion of a divided Court (the vote was 7 to 2). Taney declared that Scott was not a citizen of either the United States or Missouri; that residence in free territory did not make Scott free; and that Congress had no power to bar slavery from any territory. The decision not only overturned a sectional compromise that had been honored for thirty-seven years, it also invalidated the basic ideas of the Wilmot Proviso and popular sovereignty.

The Slave Power seemed to have won a major constitutional victory. African Americans were especially dismayed, for Taney's decision asserted that the founders had never intended for black people to be citizens. At the nation's founding, the chief justice wrote, blacks had been regarded "as beings of an inferior order" with "no rights which the white man was bound to respect." Taney was mistaken, however. African Americans had been citizens in several of the original states and had in fact voted.

Nevertheless, the ruling seemed to shut the door permanently on black hopes for justice. After 1857, African Americans lived in the land of the *Dred Scott* decision. In northern black communities, rage and despair prevailed. Many who were still fugitive slaves sought refuge in Canada; others considered emigration to the Caribbean or even to Africa. Mary Ann Shadd Cary, who was free and the leader of an emigration movement to Canada, advised her fellow blacks, "Your national ship is rotten and sinking, why not leave it?" Another black abolitionist said that the *Dred Scott* decision had made slavery "the supreme law of the land and all descendants of the African race denationalized." In this state of social dislocation and fear, blacks contemplated whether they had any future in the United States.

Northern whites who rejected the decision's content were suspicious of the circumstances that had produced it. Five of the nine justices were southerners; three of the northern justices actively dissented or refused to concur in parts of the decision. The only northerner who supported Taney's opinion, Justice Robert Grier of Pennsylvania, was known to be close to President Buchanan. In fact, Buchanan had secretly brought to bear improper but effective influence.

A storm of angry reaction broke in the North. The decision seemed to confirm every charge against the aggressive Slave Power. "There is such a thing as the slave power," warned the *Cincinnati Daily Commercial*. "It has marched over and annihilated the boundaries of the states. We are now one great homogenous slaveholding community." The *Cincinnati Freeman* asked, "What security have the Germans and the Irish that their children will not, within a hundred years, be reduced to slavery in this land of their adoption?" Poet James Russell Lowell expressed the racial and economic anxieties of poor northern whites when he had his Yankee character Ezekiel Biglow say, in the language of the day,

Wy, it's just ez clear ez figgers,
Clear ez one an' one make two,
Chaps thet make black slaves o' niggers,
Want to make wite slaves o' you.

Abraham Lincoln and the Slave Power

Republican politicians used these fears to strengthen their antislavery coalition. Abraham Lincoln stressed that the territorial question affected every citizen. "The whole nation," he had declared as early as 1854, "is interested that the best use shall be made of these Territories. We want them for homes of free white people. This they cannot be, to any considerable extent, if slavery shall be planted within them." The territories must be reserved, he insisted, "as an outlet for free white people everywhere" so that immigrants could come to America and "find new homes and better their condition in life."

More important, Lincoln warned of slavery's increasing control over the nation. The founders had created a government dedicated to freedom, Lincoln insisted. Admittedly they had recognized slavery's existence, but the public mind, he argued in the "House Divided" speech of 1858, had always rested in the belief that slavery would die either naturally or by legislation. The next step in the unfolding Slave Power conspiracy, Lincoln alleged, would be a Supreme Court decision "declaring that the Constitution does not permit a State to exclude slavery from its limits. . . . We shall lie down pleasantly, dreaming that the people of Missouri are on the verge of making their State free; and we shall awake to the reality instead, that the Supreme Court has made Illinois a slave State." This charge was not hyperbole, for lawsuits soon challenged state laws that freed slaves brought within their borders. Countless northerners heeded Lincoln's warnings, as events convinced them that slaveholders were intent on making slavery a national institution. Southerners, fatefully, never forgot Lincoln's use of the direct words "ultimate extinction."

Politically, Republicans were now locked in conflict with the *Dred Scott* decision. By endorsing the South's doctrine of state sovereignty, the Court had in effect declared that the central position of the Republican Party—no extension of slavery—was unconstitutional. Republicans could only repudiate the decision, appealing to a "higher law," or hope to change the personnel of the Court. They did both and gained politically as fear of the Slave Power grew. But fear also deepened among free blacks. Frederick Douglass continued to try to fashion hope among his people but concluded a speech in the wake of the *Dred Scott* decision bleakly: "I walk by faith, not by sight."

The Lecompton Constitution and Disharmony Among Democrats

For northern Democrats like Stephen Douglas, the Court's decision posed an awful dilemma. Northern voters were alarmed by the prospect that the territories would be opened to slavery. To retain their support, Douglas had to find some way to reassure these voters. Yet, given his presidential ambitions, Douglas could not afford to alienate southern Democrats.

Douglas chose to stand by his principle of popular sovereignty, even if the result angered southerners. In 1857 Kansans voted on a proslavery constitution that had been drafted at Lecompton. It was defeated by more than ten thousand votes in a referendum boycotted by most proslavery voters. The evidence was overwhelming that Kansans did not want slavery, yet President Buchanan tried to force the Lecompton Constitution through Congress in an effort to hastily organize the territory.

Never had the Slave Power's influence over the government seemed more blatant; the Buchanan administration and southerners demanded a proslavery outcome, contrary to the majority will in Kansas. Breaking with the administration, Douglas threw his weight against the Lecompton Constitution. But his action infuriated southern Democrats. After the *Dred Scott* decision, southerners like Senator Albert G. Brown of Mississippi believed that slavery was protected in the territories: "The Constitution as expounded by the Supreme Court awards it. We demand it; we mean to have it." Increasingly, though, many southerners believed that their sectional rights and slavery would be safe only in a separate nation. And northern Democrats, led by Douglas, found it harder to support the territorial protection for slavery that southern Democrats insisted was theirs as a constitutional right. Thus in North and South the issue of slavery in the territories continued to destroy moderation and promote militancy.

DISUNION

It is worth remembering that, in the late 1850s, most Americans were not always caught up daily in the slavery crisis. They were preoccupied with personal affairs, especially coping with the effects of the economic panic that had begun in the spring of 1857. They were worried about widespread unemployment, the plummeting price of wheat, the declining wages at a textile mill, or sons who needed land. In the Midwest, clerks, mechanics, domestics, railroad hands, and lumber camp workers lost jobs by the thousands. Bankers were at a loss for what to do about a weak credit system caused by frenzied western land speculation that began early in the decade. In parts of the South, such as Georgia, the panic intensified class divisions between upcountry yeomen and coastal slaveholding planters. Farmers blamed the tight money policies of Georgia's budding commercial banking system on wealthy planters who controlled the state's Democratic Party.

The panic had been caused by several shortcomings of the unregulated American banking system, by frenzies of speculation in western lands and railroads, and by a weak and overburdened credit system. By 1858 Philadelphia had 40,000 unemployed workers and New York City, nearly 100,000. Fear of bread riots and class warfare gripped many cities in the North. True to form, blame for such economic woe became sectionalized, as southerners saw their system justified by the temporary collapse of industrial prosperity and northerners feared even more the incursions of the Slave Power on an insecure future.

John Brown's Raid on Harpers Ferry   Soon, however, the entire nation's focus would be drawn to a new dimension of the slavery question—armed rebellion, led by the abolitionist who had killed proslavery settlers along Pottawatomie Creek in "Bleeding Kansas." Born in Connecticut in 1800, John Brown had been raised by staunchly religious antislavery parents. Between 1820 and 1855, he engaged in some twenty business ventures, including farming, nearly all of them failures. But Brown had a distinctive vision of abolitionism. He relied on an Old Testament conception of justice— "an eye for an eye"—and he had a puritanical obsession with the wickedness of others, especially southern slaveowners. Brown believed that slavery was an "unjustifiable" state of war conducted by one group of people against another. He also believed that violence in a righteous cause was a holy act, even a rite of purification for those who engaged in it. To Brown, the destruction of slavery in America required revolutionary ideology and revolutionary acts.

On October 16, 1859, Brown led a small band of eighteen whites and blacks in an attack on the federal arsenal at Harpers Ferry, Virginia. Hoping to trigger a slave rebellion, Brown failed miserably and was quickly captured. In a celebrated trial in November and a widely publicized execution in December, in Charles Town, Virginia, Brown became one of the most enduring martyrs, as well as villains, of American history. His attempted insurrection struck fear into the South.

Then it became known that Brown had received financial backing from several prominent abolitionists. When such northern intellectuals as Ralph Waldo Emerson and Henry David Thoreau praised Brown as a holy warrior who "would make the gallows as glorious as the cross," white southerners' outrage intensified. The South almost universally interpreted Brown's attack at Harpers Ferry as an act of midnight terrorism, as the fulfillment of their long-stated dread of "abolition emissaries" who would infiltrate the region to incite slave rebellion.

Perhaps most telling of all was the fact that the pivotal election of 1860 was less than a year away when Brown went so eagerly to the gallows, handing a note to his jailer with the famous prediction "I John Brown am now quite certain that the crimes of this guilty land will never be purged away, but with blood." Most troubling to southerners, perhaps, was their awareness that, though Republican politicians condemned Brown's crimes, they did so in a way that deflected attention onto the still-greater crime of slavery.

Election of 1860

Many Americans believed that the election of 1860 would decide the fate of the Union. The Democratic Party was the only party that was truly national in scope. "One after another," wrote a Mississippi editor, "the links which have bound the North and South together, have been severed . . . [but] the Democratic party looms gradually up . . . and waves the olive branch over the troubled waters of politics." But, fatefully, at its 1860 convention in Charleston, South Carolina, the Democratic Party split.

Stephen Douglas wanted his party's presidential nomination, but he could not afford to alienate northern voters by accepting the southern position on the territories. Southern Democrats, however, insisted on recognition of their rights—as the *Dred Scott* decision had defined them—and they moved to block Douglas's nomination. When Douglas obtained a majority for his version of the platform, delegates from the Deep South walked out of the convention. After efforts at compromise failed, the Democrats presented two nominees: Douglas for the northern wing, and Vice President John C. Breckinridge of Kentucky for the southern.

The Republicans nominated Abraham Lincoln at a rousing convention in Chicago. The choice of Lincoln reflected the growing power of the Midwest, and he was perceived as more moderate on slavery than the early front runner, Senator William H. Seward of New York. A Constitutional Union Party, formed to preserve the nation but strong only in the Upper South, nominated John Bell of Tennessee.

Bell's only issue in the ensuing campaign was the urgency of preserving the Union; Constitutional Unionists hoped to appeal to history, sentiment, and moderation to hold the country together. Douglas desperately sought to unite his northern and southern supporters, while Breckinridge quickly backed away from the appearance of extremism, and his supporters in several states stressed his unionism. Although Lincoln and the Republicans denied any intent to interfere with slavery in the states where it existed, they stood firm against the extension of slavery into the territories.

The election of 1860 was sectional in character, and the only one in American history in which the losers refused to accept the result. Lincoln won, but Douglas, Breckinridge, and Bell together received a majority of the votes. Douglas had broad-based support but won few states. Breckinridge carried nine southern states, all in the Deep South. Bell won pluralities in Virginia, Kentucky, and Tennessee. Lincoln prevailed in the North,

TABLE **14.3 Presidential Vote in 1860 (by State)**

Lincoln (Republican)*	Carried all northern states and all electoral votes except 3 in New Jersey
Breckinridge (Southern Democrat)	Carried all slave states except Virginia, Kentucky, Tennessee, Missouri
Bell (Constitutional Union)	Carried Virginia, Kentucky, Tennessee
Douglas (Northern Democrat)	Carried only Missouri

*Lincoln received only 26,000 votes in the entire South and was not even on the ballot in ten slave states. Breckinridge was not on the ballot in three northern states.

but in the four slave states that ultimately remained loyal to the Union (Missouri, Kentucky, Maryland, and Delaware—the border states) he gained only a plurality, not a majority (see Table 14.3). Lincoln's victory was won in the electoral college. He polled only 40 percent of the total vote and was not even on the ballot in ten slave states.

Opposition to slavery's extension was the core issue for Lincoln and the Republican Party. Moreover, abolitionists and Free-Soil supporters in the North worked to keep the Republicans from compromising on their territorial stand. Meanwhile, in the South, proslavery advocates and secessionists whipped up public opinion and demanded that state conventions assemble to consider secession.

Lincoln made the crucial decision not to soften his party's position on the territories. He wrote of the necessity of maintaining the bond of faith between voter and candidate, and of declining to set "the minority over the majority." Although many conservative Republicans—eastern businessmen and former Whigs who did not feel strongly about slavery—hoped for a compromise, the original and most committed Republicans—old Free-Soilers and antislavery Whigs—held the line on slavery expansion.

In the winter of 1860–1861, Senator John J. Crittenden of Kentucky tried to craft a late-hour compromise. Hoping to don the mantle of Henry Clay and avert disunion, Crittenden proposed that the two sections divide the territories between them at the Missouri Compromise line, 36°30′. But this well-worn and controversial idea did not work. When Lincoln ruled out concessions on the territorial issue, Crittenden's peace-making effort, based on old and discredited measures, collapsed.

Secession and the Confederate States of America   Meanwhile, the Union was being destroyed. On December 20, 1860, South Carolina passed an ordinance of secession amid jubilation and cheering. Secession strategists concentrated their efforts on the most extreme proslavery state, hoping that South Carolina's bold act would induce other states to follow, with each decision building momentum for disunion.

By reclaiming its independence, South Carolina raised the stakes in the sectional confrontation. No longer was secession an unthinkable step; the Union was broken. Secessionists now argued that other states should follow South Carolina and that those who favored compromise could make a better deal outside the Union than in it. Moderates found it difficult to dismiss such arguments, since most of them—even those who felt deep affection for the Union—were committed to defending southern rights and institutions.

Southern extremists soon got their way in the Deep South. Overwhelming their opposition, they called separate state conventions and passed secession ordinances in Mississippi, Florida, Alabama, Georgia, Louisiana, and Texas. By February 1861 these states had joined South Carolina to form a new government in Montgomery, Alabama: the Confederate States of America. The delegates at Montgomery chose Jefferson Davis of Mississippi as their president, and the Confederacy began to function independently of the United States.

This apparent unanimity of action was deceiving. Confused and dissatisfied with the alternatives, many southerners who in 1860 had voted in the U.S. presidential election stayed home a few months later rather than vote for delegates who would decide on secession. Even so, in some state conventions the secession vote was close, and decided by overrepresentation of plantation districts. Four states in the Upper South—Virginia, North Carolina, Tennessee, and Arkansas—flatly rejected secession and did not join the Confederacy until after fighting had begun. In the border states, popular sentiment was deeply divided; minorities in Kentucky and Missouri tried to secede, but these slave states ultimately came under Union control, along with Maryland and Delaware.

Such misgivings were not surprising. Secession posed new and troubling issues for southerners, especially the possibility of war, where it would be fought, and who would die. Analysis of election returns from 1860 and 1861 indicates that slaveholders and nonslaveholders were beginning to part company politically. Heavily slaveholding counties strongly supported secession. But nonslaveholding areas that had favored Breckinridge in the presidential election proved far less willing to support secession: most counties with few slaves took an antisecession position or were staunchly Unionist. With war on the horizon, yeomen were beginning to consider their class interests and to ask themselves how far they would go to support slavery and slaveowners.

As for why the Deep South bolted, we need look no further than the speeches and writings of the secession commissioners sent out by the seven seceded states to try to convince the other slave states to join them. Repeatedly they stressed independence as the only way to preserve white racial security and the slave system against the hostile Republicans. Upon "slavery," said the Alabama commissioner, Stephen Hale, to the Kentucky legislature, rested "not only the wealth and prosperity of the southern people, but their very existence as a political community." Only secession, Hale contended, could sustain the "heaven-ordained superiority of the white over the black race."

Fort Sumter and Outbreak of War The dilemma facing President Lincoln on inauguration day in March 1861 was how to maintain the authority of the federal government without provoking war. Proceeding cautiously, he sought only to hold onto forts in the states that had left the Union, reasoning that in this way he could assert federal sovereignty while waiting for a restoration. But Jefferson Davis, who could not claim to lead a sovereign nation if the Confederate ports were under foreign (that is, U.S.) control, was unwilling to be so patient. A collision soon came.

It arrived in the early morning hours of April 12, 1861, at Fort Sumter in Charleston harbor. A federal garrison there ran low on food, and Lincoln notified the South

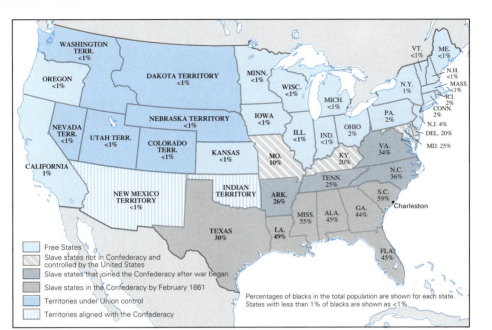

MAP 14.3 The Divided Nation–Slave and Free Areas, 1861

After fighting began, the Upper South joined the Deep South in the Confederacy. How does the nation's pattern of division correspond to the distribution of slavery and the percentage of blacks in the population?

Carolinians that he was sending a ship to resupply the fort. For the Montgomery government, the alternatives were to attack the fort or to acquiesce to Lincoln's authority. After the Confederate cabinet met, the secretary of war ordered local commanders to obtain a surrender or attack the fort. After two days of heavy bombardment, the federal garrison finally surrendered. No one died in battle, though an accident during post-battle ceremonies killed two Union soldiers. Confederates permitted the U.S. troops to sail away on unarmed vessels while Charlestonians celebrated wildly. The Civil War—the bloodiest war in America's history—had begun.

Causation
Historians have long debated the immediate and long-term roots of the Civil War. Some have interpreted it as an "irrepressible conflict," the clash of two civilizations on divergent trajectories of history. Another group saw the war as "needless," the result of a "blundering generation" of irrational politicians and activists who trumped up an avoidable conflict. But the issues dividing Americans in 1861 were fundamental to the future of the republic. The logic of Republican ideology tended in the direction of abolishing slavery, even though Republicans denied any such intention. The logic of southern arguments led to establishing slavery everywhere, though southern leaders, too, denied such a motive.

These positions hardened in American political life during the decade and a half before secession. Lincoln put these facts succinctly. In a postelection letter to his old friend Alexander Stephens of Georgia, soon to be vice president of the Confederacy,

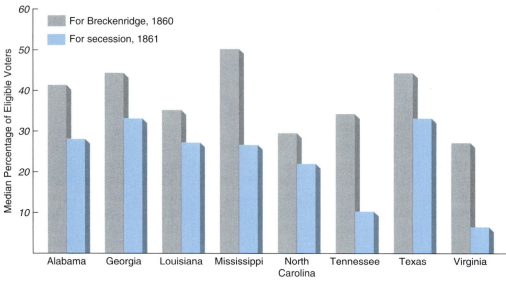

FIGURE **14.1 Voting Returns of Counties with Few Slaveholders, Eight Southern States, 1860 and 1861**

This graph depicts voting in counties whose percentage of slaveholders ranked them among the lower half of the counties in their state. How does voters' support for secession in 1861 compare with support for John Breckinridge, the southern Democratic candidate in 1860? Why was their support for secession so weak? At this time counties with many slaveholders were giving increased support to secession.

Lincoln offered assurance that Republicans would not attack slavery in the states where it existed. But Lincoln continued, "You think slavery is right and ought to be expanded; while we think it is wrong and ought to be restricted. That I suppose is the rub." Frederick Douglass demonstrated that he understood this in a postwar speech in which he declared that the "fight" had not been between "rapacious birds and ferocious beasts, a mere display of brute courage . . . but it was a war between men of thought, as well as of action, and in dead earnest for something beyond the battlefield."

Directly or indirectly, Douglass's "something" had almost everything to do with slavery. Without slavery, there would have been no war. Many Americans still hold to a belief that the war was about states' rights, the theory and practice of the proper relationship of state to federal authority. But the significance of states' rights, then as now, is always in the cause in which it is employed. If secession was an exercise in states' rights—to what end? To borrow from Douglass, it is the meaning within the fight that we must understand.

SUMMARY

Events often seem inevitable after they have occurred. We should never fall into the trap of seeing big events in history only through a lens of inevitability. The events and ideas that Americans clashed over were links in a chain leading to conflict; humans made choices all along the way and to go to war.

The War with Mexico fostered massive land acquisition, which in turn forced an open debate about slavery in the West. The Compromise of 1850 attempted to settle the dispute but only added fuel to the fires of sectional contention, leading to the fateful Kansas-Nebraska Act of 1854, which tore asunder the political party system and gave birth to a genuine antislavery coalition. With Bleeding Kansas and the *Dred Scott* decision by 1857, Americans North and South faced clear and dangerous choices about the future of labor and the meaning of liberty in an ambitious and expanding society. And finally, by 1859, when radical abolitionist John Brown attacked Harpers Ferry to foment a slave insurrection, southerners and northerners came to see each other in conspiratorial terms. Meanwhile, African Americans, slave and free, fled from slave catchers in unprecedented numbers and grew to expect violent if uncertain resolutions to their dreams of freedom in America. No one knew the future, but all knew that the issues and conflicts were real.

Throughout the 1840s and 1850s, many able leaders had worked to avert the outcome of disunion. As late as 1858, even Jefferson Davis had declared, "This great country will continue united," saying that "to the innermost fibers of my heart I love it all, and every part." Secession dismayed northern editors and voters, and it also plunged some planters into depression. Paul Cameron, the largest slaveowner in North Carolina, confessed that he was "very unhappy. I love the Union." Many blacks, however, shared Frederick Douglass's outlook. "The contest must now be decided," he wrote in March 1861, "and decided forever, which of the two, Freedom or Slavery, shall give law to this Republic. Let the conflict come."

Why had war broken out? Why had all efforts to prevent it failed? The emotions bound up in attacking and defending slavery's future were too powerful, and the interests it affected too vital for a final compromise. Advocates of compromise anticipated that the tradition of conciliation and sectional adjustment would yet again save the Union in 1860, but their hopes were dashed.

During the 1850s, every southern victory in territorial expansion increased fear of the Slave Power, and each new expression of Free-Soil sentiment prompted slaveholders to harden their demands. In the profoundest sense, slavery was the root of the war. But as the fighting began, the war's central issue was shrouded in confusion. How would the Civil War affect slavery, its place in the law, and African Americans' place in society? Would the institution survive a short war, but not a long war? As a people and a nation, Americans had reached the most fateful turning point in their history. Answers would now come from the battlefield and from the mobilization of two societies to wage war on a scale they had not imagined.

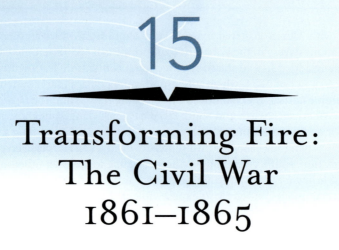

15

Transforming Fire: The Civil War 1861–1865

AMERICA GOES TO WAR, 1861–1862

Few Americans understood what they were getting into when the war began. The onset of hostilities sparked patriotic sentiments, optimistic speeches, and joyous ceremonies in both North and South. Northern communities raised companies of volunteers eager to save the Union and sent them off with fanfare. In the South, confident recruits boasted of whipping the Yankees and returning home before Christmas. Southern women sewed dashing uniforms for men who would soon be lucky to wear drab gray or butter-nut homespun. Americans went to war in 1861 with decidedly romantic notions of what they would experience.

First Battle of Bull Run Through the spring of 1861, both sides scrambled to organize and train their undisciplined armies. On July 21, 1861, the first battle took place outside Manassas Junction, Virginia, near a stream called Bull Run. General Irvin McDowell and 30,000 Union troops attacked General P. G. T. Beauregard's 22,000 southerners. As raw recruits struggled amid the confusion of their first battle, federal forces began to gain ground. Then they ran into a line of Virginia troops under General Thomas Jackson. "There is Jackson standing like a stone wall," shouted one Confederate. "Stonewall" Jackson's line held, and the

CHRONOLOGY

1861 • Battle of Bull Run
  • McClellan organizes Union Army
  • Union blockade begins
  • U.S. Congress passes first confiscation act
  • *Trent affair*

1862 • Union captures Fort Henry and Fort Donelson
  • U.S. Navy captures New Orleans
  • Battle of Shiloh shows the war's destructiveness
  • Confederacy enacts conscription
  • McClellan's Peninsula Campaign fails to take Richmond
  • U.S. Congress passes second confiscation act, initiating emancipation
  • Confederacy mounts offensive in Maryland and Kentucky
  • Battle of Antietam ends Lee's drive into Maryland in September
  • British intervention in the war on Confederate side is averted

1863 • Emancipation Proclamation takes effect
  • U.S. Congress passes National Banking Act
  • Union enacts conscription
  • African American soldiers join Union Army
  • Food riots occur in southern cities
  • Battle of Chancellorsville ends in Confederate victory but Jackson's death
  • Union wins key victories at Vicksburg and Gettysburg
  • Draft riots take place in New York City

1864 • Battles of the Wilderness and Spotsylvania produce heavy casualties on both sides
  • Battle of Cold Harbor continues carnage in Virginia
  • Sherman captures Atlanta
  • Confederacy begins to collapse on home front
  • Lincoln wins reelection, eliminating any Confederate hopes for negotiated end to war
  • Jefferson Davis proposes arming slaves
  • Sherman marches through Georgia to the sea

1865 • Sherman marches through Carolinas
  • U.S. Congress approves Thirteenth Amendment
  • Lee abandons Richmond and Petersburg
  • Lee surrenders at Appomattox Court House
  • Lincoln assassinated
  • Death toll in war reaches 620,000

arrival of 9,000 Confederate reinforcements by train won the day for the South. Union troops fled back to Washington, observed by shocked northern congressmen and spectators who had watched the battle; a few sightseers were actually captured for their folly.

The unexpected rout at Bull Run gave northerners their first hint of the nature of the war to come. Although the United States enjoyed an enormous advantage in resources, victory would not be easy. Pro-Union feeling was growing in western Virginia, and loyalties were divided in the four border slave states—Missouri, Kentucky, Maryland, and Delaware. But the rest of the Upper South—the states of North Carolina, Virginia, Tennessee, and Arkansas—had joined the Confederacy in the wake of the attack on Fort Sumter. Moved by an outpouring of regional loyalty, half a million southerners volunteered to fight—so many that the Confederate government could hardly arm them all. The United States therefore undertook a massive mobilization of troops around Washington, D.C.

Lincoln gave command of the army to General George B. McClellan, an officer who proved to be better at organization and training than at fighting. McClellan put his growing army into camp and devoted the fall and winter of 1861 to readying a formidable force of a quartermillion men whose mission would be to take Richmond, established as the Confederate capital by July 1861. "The vast preparation of the enemy," wrote one southern soldier, produced a "feeling of despondency" in the South for the first time. But southern morale remained high early in the war. Most Americans still possessed a rather romantic conception of the war looming on their horizon.

Grand Strategy   While McClellan prepared, the Union began to implement other parts of its overall strategy, which called for a blockade of southern ports and eventual capture of the Mississippi River. Like a constricting snake, this "Anaconda plan" would strangle the Confederacy. At first the Union Navy had too few ships to patrol 3,550 miles of coastline and block the Confederacy's avenues of supply. Gradually, however, the navy increased the blockade's effectiveness, though it never stopped southern commerce completely.

The Confederate strategy was essentially defensive. A defensive posture was not only consistent with the South's claim of independence, but also reasonable in light of the North's advantage in resources. But Jefferson Davis called the southern strategy an "offensive defensive," taking advantage of opportunities to attack and using its interior lines of transportation to concentrate troops at crucial points. In its war aims, the Confederacy did not need to conquer the North; the Union effort, however, as time would tell, required conquest of the South.

Strategic thinking on both sides slighted the importance of the West, that vast expanse of territory between Virginia and the Mississippi River and beyond. Guerrilla warfare broke out in 1861 in the politically divided state of Missouri, and key locations along the Mississippi and other major western rivers would prove to be crucial prizes in the North's eventual victory. Beyond the Mississippi River, the Confederacy hoped to gain an advantage by negotiating treaties with the Creeks, Choctaws, Chickasaws, Cherokees, Seminoles, and smaller groups of Plains Indians. Meanwhile, the Republican U.S. Congress carved the West into territories in anticipation of state making. For most Indians west of the Mississippi, what began during the Civil War was nearly three decades of offensive warfare against them, an enveloping strategy of conquest, relocation, and slaughter. They, with all Americans, soon knew they were in a war the scale of which few people had ever imagined.

Union Naval Campaign   The last half of 1861 brought no major land battles, but the North made gains by sea. Late in the summer, Union naval forces captured Cape Hatteras and then Hilton Head, one of the Sea Islands off Port Royal, South Carolina. A few months later, similar operations secured vital coastal points in North Carolina, as well as Fort Pulaski, which defended Savannah. Federal naval operations established significant beachheads along the Confederate coastline.

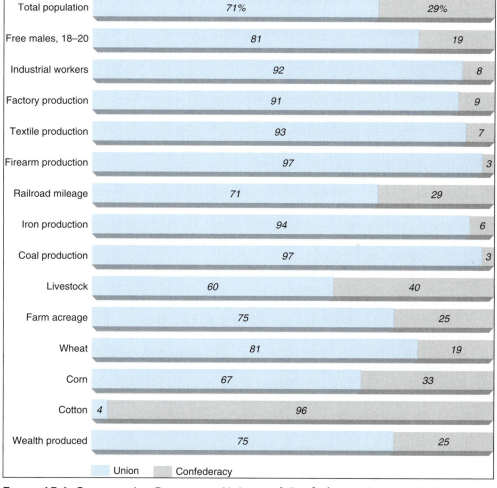

	Union	Confederacy
Total population	71%	29%
Free males, 18–20	81	19
Industrial workers	92	8
Factory production	91	9
Textile production	93	7
Firearm production	97	3
Railroad mileage	71	29
Iron production	94	6
Coal production	97	3
Livestock	60	40
Farm acreage	75	25
Wheat	81	19
Corn	67	33
Cotton	4	96
Wealth produced	75	25

FIGURE 15.1 Comparative Resources, Union and Confederate States, 1861

The North had vastly superior resources. Although the North's advantages in manpower and industrial capacity proved very important, the South still had to be conquered, its society and its will crushed. (*Source:* The Times Atlas of World History. *Used with permission.*)

The coastal victories off South Carolina foreshadowed a revolution in slave society. At the federal gunboats' approach, planters abandoned their land and fled. For a while, Confederate cavalry tried to round up slaves and move them to the interior as well. But thousands of slaves greeted what they hoped to be freedom with rejoicing and broke the hated cotton gins. Some entered their masters' homes and took clothing and furniture, which they conspicuously displayed. A growing stream of runaways poured into Union lines. Unwilling at first to wage a war against slavery, the federal government did not acknowledge the slaves' freedom—though it began to use their labor in the Union cause. This swelling tide of emancipated slaves, defined by many Union officers as "contraband" of war (confiscated enemy property), forced first a bitter and confused debate within the Union Army and government over how to treat the freedmen, and then a forthright attempt to harness their labor and military power.

The coastal incursions worried southerners, but the spring of 1862 brought even stronger evidence of the war's gravity. In March, two ironclad ships—the *Monitor* (a Union warship) and the *Merrimack* (a Union ship seized by the Confederacy)—fought each other for the first time off the coast of Virginia. Their battle, though indecisive, ushered in a new era in naval design. In April, Union ships commanded by Admiral David Farragut smashed through log booms blocking the Mississippi River and fought their way upstream to capture New Orleans. The city at the mouth of the Mississippi, the South's greatest seaport and slave-trading center, was now in federal hands.

War in the Far West

Farther west, three full Confederate regiments were organized, mostly of Cherokees, from Indian Territory, but a Union victory at Elkhorn Tavern, Arkansas, shattered southern control of the region. Thereafter, dissension within Native American groups and a Union victory the following year at Honey Springs, Arkansas, reduced Confederate operations in Indian Territory to guerrilla raids.

In the westernmost campaign of the war, from February to May 1862, some three thousand Confederate and four thousand Union forces fought for control of New Mexico Territory. The military significance of the New Mexico campaign was limited, but the Confederate invasion had grander aims: access to the trade riches of the Santa Fe Trail and possession of gold mines in Colorado and California. If the campaign had endured long enough, the Confederacy would have been much stronger with a western empire. But Colorado and New Mexico Unionists fought for their region, and in a series of battles at Glorieta Pass, 20 miles east of Santa Fe, on March 26 through 28, they blocked the Confederate invasion. By May 1, Confederate forces straggled down the Rio Grande River back into Texas, ending their effort to take New Mexico.

Grant's Tennessee Campaign and the Battle of Shiloh

Meanwhile, in February 1862, land and river forces in northern Tennessee won significant victories for the Union. A Union commander named Ulysses S. Grant saw the strategic importance of Fort Henry and Fort Donelson, the Confederate outposts guarding the Tennessee and Cumberland Rivers. If federal troops could capture these forts, Grant realized, they would open two prime routes into the heartland of the Confederacy. In just ten days he seized the forts, completely cutting off the Confederates and demanding "unconditional surrender" of Fort Donelson. A path into Tennessee, Alabama, and Mississippi now lay open before the Union Army. Grant's achievement of such a surrender from his former West Point roommate, Confederate commander Simon Bolivar Buckner, inspired northern public opinion.

Grant moved on into southern Tennessee and the first of the war's shockingly bloody encounters, the Battle of Shiloh. On April 6, Confederate general Albert Sidney Johnston caught federal troops with their backs to the water awaiting reinforcements along the Tennessee River. The Confederates attacked early in the morning and inflicted heavy damage all day. Close to victory, General Johnston was shot from his horse and killed. Southern forces almost achieved a breakthrough, but Union reinforcements arrived that night. The next day the tide of battle turned, and after ten hours of terrible combat, Grant's men forced the Confederates to withdraw.

Neither side won a decisive victory at Shiloh, yet the losses were staggering, and the Confederates were forced to retreat into northern Mississippi. Northern troops lost 13,000 men (killed, wounded, or captured) out of 63,000; southerners sacrificed 11,000 out of 40,000. Total casualties in this single battle exceeded those in all three of America's previous wars combined. Now both sides were beginning to sense the true nature of the war. "I saw an open field," Grant recalled, "over which Confederates had made repeated charges . . . so covered with dead that it would have been possible to walk across the clearing, in any direction, stepping on dead bodies, without a foot touching the ground." Shiloh utterly changed Grant's thinking about the war. He had hoped that southerners would soon be "heartily tired" of the conflict. After Shiloh, "I gave up all idea of saving the Union except by complete conquest." Memories of the Shiloh battlefield, and many others to come, would haunt the soldiers who survived for the rest of their lives. Herman Melville's "Shiloh, A Requiem" captures the pathos of that spring day when armies learned the truth about war.

> Skimming lightly, wheeling still,
> The swallows fly low
> Over the field in clouded days,
> The forest-field of Shiloh—
> Over the field where April rain
> Solaced the parched ones stretched in pain
> Through the pause of night
> That followed the Sunday fight
> Around the church of Shiloh—
> The church so lone, the log-built one,
> That echoed to many a parting groan
> And natural prayer
> Of dying foemen mingled there—
> Foemen at morn, but friends at eve—
> Fame or country least their care:
> (What like a bullet can undeceive!)
> But now they lie low,
> While over them the swallows skim,
> And all is hushed at Shiloh.

McClellan and the Peninsula Campaign

On the Virginia front, President Lincoln had a different problem. General McClellan was slow to move. Only thirty-six, McClellan had already achieved notable success as an army officer and railroad president. Habitually overestimating the size of enemy forces, he called repeatedly for reinforcements and ignored Lincoln's directions to advance. McClellan advocated war of limited aims that would lead to a quick reunion. He intended neither disruption of slavery nor war on noncombatants. McClellan's conservative vision of the war was practically outdated before he even moved his army into Virginia. Finally he chose to move by a water route, sailing his troops down the Chesapeake, landing them on the peninsula between the York and James Rivers, and advancing on Richmond from the east.

After a bloody but indecisive battle at Fair Oaks on May 31 through June 1, the federal armies moved to within 7 miles of the Confederate capital. They could see the spires on Richmond churches. The Confederate commanding general, Joseph E. Johnston, was badly wounded at Fair Oaks, and President Jefferson Davis placed his chief military adviser, Robert E. Lee, in command. The fifty-five-year-old Lee was an aristocratic Virginian, a lifelong military officer, and a veteran of distinction from the War with Mexico. Although he initially opposed secession, Lee loyally gave his allegiance to his state and became a staunch Confederate nationalist. He soon foiled McClellan's legions.

First, Lee sent Stonewall Jackson's corps of 17,000 northwest into the Shenandoah valley behind Union forces, where they threatened Washington, D.C., and with rapid-strike mobility drew some federal troops away from Richmond to protect their own capital. Further, in mid-June, in an extraordinary four-day ride around the entire Union Army, Confederate cavalry under J. E. B. Stuart, a self-styled Virginia cavalier with red cape and plumed hat, confirmed the exposed position of a major portion of McClellan's army north of the rain-swollen Chickahominy River. Then, in a series of engagements known as the Seven Days Battles, from June 26 through July 1, Lee struck at McClellan's army. Lee never managed to close his pincers around the retreating Union forces, but the daring move of taking the majority of his army northeast and attacking the Union right flank, while leaving only a small force to defend Richmond, forced McClellan (always believing he was outnumbered) to retreat toward the James River.

During the sustained fighting of the Seven Days, the Union forces suffered 20,614 casualties and the Confederates, 15,849. After repeated rebel assaults against entrenched positions on high ground at Malvern Hill, an officer concluded, "It was not war, it was murder." By August 3, McClellan withdrew his army back to the Potomac and the environs of Washington. Richmond remained safe for almost two more years.

Confederate Offensive in Maryland and Kentucky

Buoyed by these results, Jefferson Davis conceived an ambitious plan to turn the tide of the war and gain recognition of the Confederacy by European nations. He ordered a general offensive, sending Lee north into Maryland and Generals Kirby Smith and Braxton Bragg into Kentucky. Calling on residents of Maryland and Kentucky, still slave states, to make a separate peace with his government, Davis also invited northwestern states like Indiana, which sent much of their trade down the Mississippi to New Orleans, to leave the Union. This was a coordinated effort to take the war to the North and to try to force both a military and a political turning point.

In October 1862 in New York City, photographer Mathew Brady opened an exhibition of photographs from the Battle of Antietam. Although few knew it, Brady's vision was very poor, and this photograph of Confederate dead was actually made by his assistants, Alexander Gardner and James F. Gibson. (Library of Congress)

The plan was promising, but in the end the offensive failed. Lee's forces achieved a striking success at the battle of Second Bull Run, August 29 through 30, just southwest of Washington, D.C. On the same killing fields along Bull Run Creek where federal troops had been defeated the previous summer, an entire Union army was sent in retreat back into the federal capital. Thousands of wounded occupied schools and churches, and 2,000 suffered on cots in the rotunda of the U.S. Capitol.

But in the bloodiest day of the entire war, September 17, 1862, McClellan turned Lee back from Sharpsburg, Maryland. In this Battle of Antietam, 5,000 men died, and another 18,000 were wounded. Lee was lucky to escape destruction, for McClellan had intercepted a lost battle order, wrapped around cigars for each Confederate corps commander and inadvertently dropped by a courier. But McClellan moved slowly, failed to use his larger forces in simultaneous attacks, and allowed Lee's stricken army to retreat to safety across the Potomac. In the wake of Antietam, Lincoln removed McClellan from command.

In Kentucky, Generals Smith and Bragg secured Lexington and Frankfort, but their effort to force the Yankees back to the Ohio River was stopped at the Battle of Perryville on October 8. Bragg's army retreated back into Tennessee, where on December 31, 1862, to January 2, 1863, they fought an indecisive but much bloodier battle at Murfreesboro. Casualties exceeded even those of Shiloh, and many lives were sacrificed on a bitter winter landscape.

Confederate leaders had marshaled all their strength for a breakthrough but had failed. Outnumbered and disadvantaged in resources, the South could not continue the offensive. Profoundly disappointed, Davis admitted to a committee of Confederate representatives that southerners were entering "the darkest and most dangerous period we have yet had."

But 1862 also brought painful lessons to the North. Confederate general J. E. B. Stuart executed a daring cavalry raid into Pennsylvania in October. Then, on December 13,

Union general Ambrose Burnside, now in command of the Army of the Potomac, unwisely ordered his soldiers to attack Lee's army, which held fortified positions on high ground at Fredericksburg, Virginia. Lee's men performed so efficiently in killing northerners that Lee was moved to say, "It is well that war is so terrible. We should grow too fond of it." Burnside's repeated assaults up Marye's Heights shocked even the opponents. "The Federals had fallen like the steady dripping of rain from the eaves of a house," remarked Confederate general James Longstreet. And a Union officer observed of the carnage of 1,300 dead and 9,600 wounded Union soldiers, "The whole plain was covered with men, prostrate and dropping. . . . I had never before seen fighting like that . . . the next brigade coming up in succession would do its duty, and melt like snow coming down on warm ground." The scale of carnage now challenged people on both sides to search deeply for the meaning of such a war. The rebellion was far from being suppressed, and people on both home fronts now had to decide just what they would endure to win such an all-out civil war.

WAR TRANSFORMS THE SOUTH

The war caused tremendous disruptions in civilian life and altered southern society beyond all expectations. One of the first traditions to fall was the southern preference for local and limited government. States' rights had been a formative ideology for the Confederacy, but state governments were weak operations. The average citizen, on whom the hand of government had rested lightly, probably knew county authorities best. To withstand the massive power of the North, however, the South needed to centralize; like the colonial revolutionaries, southerners faced a choice of joining together or dying separately. Jefferson Davis quickly saw the necessity of centralization and moved to thwart the separate aims of states.

The Confederacy and Centralization Davis moved promptly to bring all arms, supplies, and troops under his control. But by early 1862 the scope and duration of the conflict required something more. Tens of thousands of Confederate soldiers had volunteered for just one year's service, planning to return home in the spring to plant their crops. More recruits were needed constantly to keep southern armies in the field. However, as one official admitted, "the spirit of volunteering had died out." Finally, faced with a critical shortage of troops, in April 1862 the Confederate government enacted the first national conscription (draft) law in American history. Thus the war forced unprecedented change on states that had seceded out of fear of change.

Davis adopted a firm leadership role toward the Confederate Congress, which raised taxes and later passed a tax-in-kind—paid in farm products. Nearly 4,500 agents dispersed to collect the tax. Where opposition arose, the government suspended the writ of habeas corpus (which prevented individuals from being held without trial) and imposed martial law. Despite Davis's unyielding stance, this tax system proved inadequate for the South's war effort.

To replace the food that men in uniform would have grown, Davis exhorted state governments to require farmers to switch from cash crops to food crops. But the army remained short of food and labor. The War Department resorted to impressing slaves to work on fortifications, and after 1861 the government relied heavily on confiscation of food to feed the troops. Officers swooped down on farms in the line of march and carted away grain, meat, wagons, and draft animals. Such raids caused increased hardship and resentment for women managing farms in the absence of husbands and sons.

Soon the Confederate administration in Richmond gained virtually complete control over the southern economy. The Confederate Congress also gave the central government almost complete control of the railroads. A large bureaucracy sprang up to administer these operations: over 70,000 civilians staffed the Confederate administration. By the war's end, the southern bureaucracy was larger in proportion to population than its northern counterpart.

Confederate Nationalism   Historians have long argued over whether the Confederacy itself was a "rebellion," a "revolution," or the creation of a genuine "nation." Whatever label we apply, Confederates created a culture and an ideology of nationalism. Southerners immediately tried to forge their own national symbols and identity. In flags, songs, language, seals, school readers, and other national characteristics, Confederates created their own story.

In its conservative crusade to preserve states' rights, the social order, and racial slavery, southerners believed that the Confederacy was the true legacy of the American Revolution—a bulwark against centralized power that was in keeping with the war for independence and a bulwark against centralized power. In this view, southern "liberty" was no less a holy cause than that of the patriots of 1776. To southerners, theirs was a continuing revolution against the excesses of Yankee democracy, and George Washington (a Virginian) on horseback formed the center of the official seal of the Confederacy.

Also central to Confederate nationalism was a refurbished defense of slavery as a benign, protective institution. In wartime schoolbooks, children were instructed in the divinely inspired, paternalistic character of slavery. And the idea of the "faithful slave" was key to southerners' nationalist cause. A poem popular among whites captured an old slave's rejection of the Emancipation Proclamation.

Now, Massa, dis is berry fine, dese words
You've spoke to me,
No doubt you mean it kindly, but ole Dinah
Won't be free . . .
Ole Massa's berry good to me—and though I am
His slave,
He treats me like I'se kin to him—and I would
Rather have
A home in Massa's cabin, and eat his black
Bread too,
Dan leave ole Massa's children and go and
Lib wid you.

In the face of defeat and devastation, this and other forms of Confederate nationalism collapsed in the final year of the war. But much of the spirit and substance of

Confederate nationalism would revive in the postwar period in a new ideology of the Lost Cause.

Southern Cities and Industry

Clerks and subordinate officials crowded the towns and cities where Confederate departments set up their offices. Clerks had always been males, but now "government girls" staffed the Confederate bureaucracy. The sudden urban migration that resulted overwhelmed the housing supply and stimulated new construction. The pressure was especially great in Richmond, whose population increased 250 percent. Mobile's population jumped from 29,000 to 41,000; Atlanta, too, began to grow; and 10,000 people poured into war-related industries in little Selma, Alabama.

As the Union blockade disrupted imports of manufactured products, the traditionally agricultural South forged new industries. Many planters shared Davis's hope that industrialization would bring "deliverance, full and unrestricted, from all commercial dependence" on the North or the world. Indeed, beginning almost from scratch, the Confederacy achieved tremendous feats of industrial development. Chief of Ordnance Josiah Gorgas increased the capacity of Richmond's Tredegar Iron Works and other factories to the point that by 1865 his Ordnance Bureau was supplying all Confederate small arms and ammunition. Meanwhile, the government constructed new railroad lines and ironworks, much of the labor for which consisted of slaves relocated from farms and plantations.

Changing Roles of Women

White women, restricted to narrow roles in antebellum society, gained substantial new responsibilities in wartime. The wives and mothers of soldiers now headed households and performed men's work, including raising crops and tending animals. Women in nonslave-owning families cultivated fields themselves, while wealthier women suddenly had to perform as overseers and manage field work. In the cities, white women—who had been largely excluded from the labor force—found a limited number of respectable paying jobs, often in the Confederate bureaucracy, where some found clerks' jobs as "government girls." And female schoolteachers appeared in the South for the first time.

Women experienced both confidence and agony from their new responsibilities. Among them was Janie Smith, a young North Carolinian. Raised in a rural area by prosperous parents, she now faced grim realities as the war reached her farm and troops turned her home into a hospital. "It makes me shudder when I think of the awful sights I witnessed that morning," she wrote to a friend. "Ambulance after ambulance drove up with our wounded. . . . Under every shed and tree, the tables were carried for amputating the limbs. . . . The blood lay in puddles in the grove; the groans of the dying . . . were horrible." But Janie Smith learned to cope with crisis. She ended her account with the proud words "I can dress amputated limbs now and do most anything in the way of nursing wounded soldiers."

Patriotic sacrifice appealed to some women, but others resented their new burdens. A Texas woman who had struggled to discipline slaves pronounced herself "sick of trying to do a man's business." Others grew angry over shortages and resented cooking and unfamiliar contact with lower-class women. Some women grew scornful of the war and demanded that their men return to help provide for their families.

Human Suffering, Hoarding, and Inflation

For millions of ordinary southerners, the war brought privation and suffering. Mass poverty descended for the first time on a large minority of the white population. Many yeoman families had lost their breadwinners to the army. As a South Carolina newspaper put it, "The duties of war have called away from home the sole supports of many, many families. . . . Help must be given, or the poor will suffer." Women on their own sought help from relatives, neighbors, friends, anyone. Sometimes they pleaded their case to the Confederate government. "In the name of humanity," begged one woman, "discharge my husband he is not able to do your government much good and he might do his children some good . . . my poor children have no home nor no Father." To the extent that the South eventually lost the will to fight in the face of defeat, women played a role in demanding an end to the war.

The South was in many places so sparsely populated that the conscription of one skilled craftsman could wreak hardship on the people of an entire county. Often they begged in unison for the exemption or discharge of the local miller, or the neighborhood tanner or wheelwright. Physicians were also in short supply. Most serious, however, was the loss of a blacksmith. As a petition from Alabama explained, "Our Section of County [is] left entirely Destitute of any man that is able to keep in order any kind of Farming Tules."

The blockade of Confederate shipping created shortages of important supplies—salt, sugar, coffee, nails—and speculation and hoarding made the shortages worse. Greedy businessmen cornered the supply of some commodities; prosperous citizens stocked up on food. The *Richmond Enquirer* criticized a planter who purchased so many wagonloads of supplies that his "lawn and paths looked like a wharf covered with a ship's loads." North Carolina's Governor Zebulon Vance worried about "the cry of distress . . . from the poor wives and children of our soldiers. . . . What will become of them?"

Inflation raged out of control, fueled by the Confederate government's heavy borrowing and inadequate taxes, until prices had increased almost 7,000 percent. Inflation particularly imperiled urban dwellers without their own sources of food. As early as 1861 and 1862, newspapers reported that "want and starvation are staring thousands in the face," and troubled officials predicted that "women and children are bound to come to suffering if not starvation." Hoarding continued to cause local conflict, and a rudimentary relief program organized by the Confederacy failed to meet the need.

Inequities of the Confederate Draft

As their fortunes declined, people of once-modest means looked around and found abundant evidence that all classes were not sacrificing equally. The Confederate government enacted policies that decidedly favored the upper class. Until the last year of the war, for example, prosperous southerners could avoid military service by hiring substitutes. Prices for substitutes skyrocketed until it cost a man $5,000 or $6,000 to send someone to the front in his place. Well over fifty thousand upper-class southerners purchased such substitutes. Mary Boykin Chesnut knew of one young aristocrat who "spent a fortune in substitutes. . . . He is at the end of his row now, for all able-bodied men are ordered to the front. I hear he is going as some general's courier."

Anger at such discrimination exploded in October 1862, when the Confederate Congress exempted from military duty anyone who was supervising at least twenty slaves.

"Never did a law meet with more universal odium," observed one representative. "Its influence upon the poor is most calamitous." Protests poured in from every corner of the Confederacy, and North Carolina's legislators formally condemned the law. Its defenders argued, however, that the exemption preserved order and aided food production, and the statute remained on the books.

This "twenty Negro" law is indicative of the racial fears many Confederates felt as the war threatened to overturn southern society. But it also fueled desertion and stimulated new levels of overt Unionism in nonslaveholding regions of the South. In Jones County, Mississippi, an area of piney woods and few slaves or plantations, Newt Knight, a Confederate soldier, led a band of renegades who took over the county, declared their allegiance to the Union, and called their district the "Free State of Jones." They held out for the remainder of the war as an enclave of independent Union sympathizers.

The bitterness of letters to Confederate officials suggests the depth of the dissension and class anger. "If I and my little children suffer [and] die while there Father is in service," threatened one woman, "I invoke God Almighty that our blood rest upon the South." Another woman swore to the secretary of war that, unless help was provided to poverty-stricken wives and mothers, "an allwise god . . . will send down his fury . . . [on] those that are in power." War magnified existing social tensions in the Confederacy, and created a few new ones.

WARTIME NORTHERN ECONOMY AND SOCIETY

With the onset of war, a tidal wave of change rolled over the North as well. Factories and citizens' associations geared up to support the war, and the federal government and its executive branch gained new powers. The energies of an industrializing society were harnessed to serve the cause of the Union. Idealism and greed flourished together, and the northern economy proved its awesome productivity. Unlike the experience in the South, northern farms and factories came through the war unharmed.

Northern Business, Industry, and Agriculture At first the war was a shock to business. Northern firms lost their southern markets, and many companies had to change their products and find new customers in order to remain open. Southern debts became uncollectible, jeopardizing not only northern merchants but also many western banks. In farming regions, families struggled with an aggravated shortage of labor caused by army enlistments. A few enterprises never pulled out of the tailspin caused by the war. Cotton mills lacked cotton; construction declined; shoe manufacturers sold few of the cheap shoes that planters had bought for their slaves.

But certain entrepreneurs, such as wool producers, benefited from shortages of competing products, and soaring demand for war-related goods swept some businesses to new success. To feed the hungry war machine, the federal government pumped unprecedented sums into the economy. The Treasury issued $3.2 billion in bonds and paper money called "greenbacks," and the War Department spent over $360 million in revenues from new taxes, including the nation's first income tax. Government contracts soon totaled more than $1 billion.

Secretary of War Edwin M. Stanton's list of the supplies needed by the Ordnance Department indicates the scope of government demand: "7,892 cannon, 11,787 artillery carriages, 4,022,130 small-arms, . . . 1,022,176,474 cartridges for small-arms, 1,220,555,435 percussion caps, . . . 26,440,054 pounds of gunpowder, . . . and 90,416,295 pounds of lead." Stanton's list covered only weapons; the government also purchased huge quantities of uniforms, boots, food, camp equipment, saddles, ships, and other necessities. War-related spending revived business in many northern states. In 1863 a merchants' magazine examined the effects of the war in Massachusetts: "Seldom, if ever, has the business of Massachusetts been more active or profitable than during the past year. . . . In every department of labor the government has been, directly or indirectly, the chief employer and paymaster." Government contracts saved Massachusetts shoe manufacturers from ruin.

Nothing illustrated the wartime partnership between business and government better than the work of Jay Cooke, a wealthy New York financier. Cooke threw himself into the marketing of government bonds to finance the war effort. With imagination and energy, he convinced both large investors and ordinary citizens to invest enormous sums, in the process earning hefty commissions for himself. But the financier's profit served the Union cause, as the interests of capitalism and government merged in American history's first era of "big government."

War aided some heavy industries in the North as well, especially iron and steel production. Although new railroad construction slowed, the manufacture of rails actually increased with demand for repairs. Of considerable significance for the future was the railroad industry's adoption of a standard gauge (width) for track, which eliminated the unloading and reloading of boxcars, and created a unified transportation system.

The northern economy also grew because of a complementary relationship between agriculture and industry. Mechanization of agriculture had begun before the war. Wartime recruitment and conscription, however, gave western farmers an added incentive to purchase labor-saving machinery. The shift from human labor to machines created new markets for industry and expanded the food supply for the urban industrial work force. The boom in the sale of agricultural tools was tremendous. Cyrus and William McCormick built an industrial empire in Chicago from the sale of their reapers. Between 1862 and 1864, the manufacture of mowers and reapers doubled to 70,000 yearly; by war's end, 375,000 reapers were in use, triple the number in 1861. Thus northern farm families whose breadwinners went to war did not suffer as much as did their counterparts in the South. "We have seen," one magazine observed, "a stout matron whose sons are in the army, cutting hay with her team . . . and she cut seven acres with ease in a day, riding leisurely upon her cutter."

Northern Workers' Militancy   Northern industrial and urban workers did not fare as well. After the initial slump, jobs became plentiful, but inflation ate up much of a worker's paycheck. The price of coffee had tripled; rice and sugar had doubled; and clothing, fuel, and rent had all climbed. Between 1860 and 1864, consumer prices rose at least 76 percent, while daily wages rose only 42 percent. Workers' families consequently suffered a substantial decline in their standard of living.

As their real wages shrank, industrial workers lost job security. To increase production, some employers replaced workers with labor-saving machines. Other employers urged the government to promote immigration to secure cheap labor. Workers responded by forming unions and sometimes by striking. Skilled craftsmen organized to combat the loss of their jobs and status to machines; women and unskilled workers, who were excluded by the craftsmen, formed their own unions. Indeed, thirteen occupational groups—including tailors, coal miners, and railway engineers—formed national unions during the Civil War, and the number of strikes climbed steadily.

Employers reacted with hostility to this new labor independence. Manufacturers viewed labor activism as a threat to their freedom of action and accordingly formed statewide or craft-based associations to cooperate and pool information. These employers shared blacklists of union members and required new workers to sign "yellow dog" contracts (promises not to join a union). To put down strikes, they hired strikebreakers from among blacks, immigrants, and women, and sometimes used federal troops to break the unions' will.

Labor militancy, however, prevented employers neither from making profits nor from profiteering on government contracts. Unscrupulous businessmen took advantage of the suddenly immense demand for army supplies by selling clothing and blankets made of "shoddy"—wool fibers reclaimed from rags or worn cloth. Shoddy goods often came apart in the rain; most of the shoes purchased in the early months of the war were worthless. Contractors sold inferior guns for double the usual price and passed off tainted meat as good. Corruption was so widespread that it led to a year-long investigation by the House of Representatives. These realities of everyday economic life eroded what remained of any romance for war among most Americans.

Economic Nationalism and Government-Business Partnership

Legitimate enterprises also made healthy profits. The output of woolen mills increased so dramatically that dividends in the industry nearly tripled. Some cotton mills made record profits on what they sold, even though they reduced their output. Brokerage houses worked until midnight and earned unheard-of commissions. Railroads carried immense quantities of freight and passengers, increasing their business to the point that railroad stocks skyrocketed in value.

Railroads were also a leading beneficiary of government largesse. With southern representatives absent from Congress, the northern route of the transcontinental railroad quickly prevailed. In 1862 and 1864, Congress chartered two corporations, the Union Pacific Railroad and the Central Pacific Railroad, and assisted them financially in connecting Omaha, Nebraska, with Sacramento, California. For each mile of track laid, the railroads received a loan of from $16,000 to $48,000 in government bonds plus 20 square miles of land along a free 400-foot-wide right of way. Overall, the two corporations gained approximately 20 million acres of land and nearly $60 million in loans.

Other businessmen benefited handsomely from the Morrill Land Grant Act (1862). To promote public education in agriculture, engineering, and military science, Congress granted each state 30,000 acres of federal land for each of its congressional districts. The states could sell the land as long as they used the income for the purposes Congress had intended. The law eventually fostered sixty-nine colleges and universities, but one of its immediate effects was to enrich a few prominent speculators. At the same time, the

Homestead Act of 1862 offered cheap, and sometimes free, land to people who would settle the West and improve their property.

Before the war, there were no adequate national banking, taxation, or currency. Banks operating under state charters issued no fewer than seven thousand different kinds of notes, which were difficult to distinguish from forgeries. During the war, Congress and the Treasury Department established a national banking system empowered to issue national bank notes, and by 1865 most state banks were forced by a prohibitive tax to join the national system. This process created sounder currency, but also inflexibility in the money supply and an eastern-oriented financial structure that, later in the century, pushed farmers in need of credit and cash to revolt.

Republican economic policies expanded the scope of government and bonded people to the nation as never before. Experience with economic nationalism and the marked expansion of presidential power eventually helped buttress public opinion for the controversial cause of slave emancipation.

Yet ostentation coexisted with idealism. In the excitement of wartime moneymaking, an eagerness to display one's wealth flourished in the largest cities. *Harper's Monthly* reported that "the suddenly enriched contractors, speculators, and stock-jobbers . . . are spending money with a profusion never before witnessed in our country. . . . The men button their waistcoats with diamonds . . . and the women powder their hair with gold and silver dust." The *New York Herald* summarized that city's atmosphere: "This war has entirely changed the American character. . . . The individual who makes the most money—no matter how—and spends the most—no matter for what—is considered the greatest man."

The Union Cause   In thousands of self-governing towns and communities, northern citizens felt a personal connection to representative government. Secession threatened to destroy their system, and northerners rallied to its defense. In the first two years of the war, northern morale remained remarkably high for a cause that today may seem abstract—the Union—but at the time meant the preservation of a social and political order that people cherished.

Secular and church leaders supported the cause, and even ministers who preferred to separate politics and pulpit denounced "the iniquity of causeless rebellion." Many churches endorsed the Union cause as God's cause. One Methodist newspaper described the war as a contest between "equalizing, humanizing Christianity" and "disunion, war, selfishness, [and] slavery." Abolitionists campaigned to turn the war into a crusade against slavery. Free black communities and churches both black and white responded to the needs of slaves who flocked to the Union lines, sending clothing, ministers, and teachers to aid the freedpeople. Indeed, northern blacks gave wholehearted support to the war, volunteering by the thousands at first and in spite of the initial rejection they received from the Lincoln administration.

Thus northern society embraced strangely contradictory tendencies. Materialism and greed flourished alongside idealism, religious conviction, and self-sacrifice. In decades to come, Americans would commemorate and build monuments to soldiers' sacrifice and idealism, not to opportunism and sometimes not even to the causes for which they fought, which was a way of forgetting the deeper nature of the conflict.

Northern Women on Home Front and Battlefront

Northern women, like their southern counterparts, took on new roles. Those who stayed home organized over ten thousand soldiers' aid societies, rolled bandages, and raised $3 million to aid injured troops. Women were instrumental in pressing for the first trained ambulance corps in the Union Army, and they formed the backbone of the U.S. Sanitary Commission, a civilian agency officially recognized by the War Department in 1861. The Sanitary Commission provided crucial nutritional and medical aid to soldiers. Although most of its officers were men, the bulk of the volunteers who ran its seven thousand auxiliaries were women. Women organized elaborate "Sanitary Fairs" all across the North to raise money and awareness for soldiers' health and hygiene.

Approximately 3,200 women also served as nurses in frontline hospitals, where they pressed for better care of the wounded. Yet women had to fight for a chance to serve at all; the professionalization of medicine since the Revolution had created a medical system dominated by men, and many male physicians did not want women's aid. Even Clara Barton, famous for her persistence in working in the worst hospitals at the front, was ousted from her post in 1863. But along with Barton, women such as the stern Dorothea Dix, well known for her efforts to reform asylums for the insane, and an Illinois widow, Mary Ann Bickerdyke, who served tirelessly in Sherman's army in the West, established a heroic tradition for Civil War nurses. They also advanced the professionalization of nursing, as several schools of nursing were established in northern cities during or after the war.

Women also wrote popular fiction about the war. In sentimental war poetry, short stories, and novels, and in printed war songs that reached thousands of readers, women produced a commercial literature in illustrated weeklies, monthly periodicals, and special "story papers." In many stories, female characters seek recognition for their loyalty and service to the Union, while others probe the suffering and death of loved ones at the front. One woman writer was Louisa May Alcott, who arrived at her job as a nurse in Washington, D.C., just after the horrific Union defeat at Fredericksburg, in December 1862. From her six weeks' experience (she had to quit because of illness), she later wrote *Hospital Sketches* (1863), a widely selling book in which she described shattered men, "riddled with shot and shell," who had "borne suffering for which we have no name." Alcott provided northern readers a clear-eyed view of the hospitals in which so many of their loved ones agonized and perished.

At its heart, in what one historian has called a "feminized war literature," woman writers explored the relationship between individual and national needs, between home and "the cause." And by 1863 many women found the liberation of slaves an inspiring subject, as Julia Ward Howe did in her immortal "Battle Hymn of the Republic": "As He died to make men holy / Let us die to make men free."

Walt Whitman's War

The poet Walt Whitman also left a record of his experiences as a volunteer nurse in Washington, D.C. As he dressed wounds and tried to comfort suffering and lonely men, Whitman found "the marrow of the tragedy concentrated in those Army Hospitals." But despite "indescribably horrid wounds," he also found inspiration in such suffering and a deepening faith in American democracy. Whitman celebrated the "incredible dauntlessness" and sacrifice of the common soldier who fought for the Union. As he had written in the preface to his great work *Leaves of Grass* (1855), "The genius of the United States is not best or most in its executives or legislatures, but always most in the common people."

Whitman worked this idealization of the common man into his poetry, which also explored homoerotic themes and rejected the lofty meter and rhyme of European verse to strive for a "genuineness" that would appeal to the masses.

In "The Wound Dresser," Whitman meditated unforgettably on the deaths he had witnessed on both sides:

> On, on I go, (open doors of time! open hospital doors!)
> The crush'd head I dress, (poor crazed hand tear not
>   the bandage away,)
> The neck of the cavalry-man with the bullet through
>   and through I examine,
> Hard the breathing rattles, quite glazed already the eye,
>   yet life struggles hard,
> (Come sweet death! be persuaded O beautiful death!
>   In mercy come quickly.)

Whitman mused for millions in the war who suffered the death of a husband, brother, father, or friend. Indeed, the scale of death in this war shocked many Americans into believing that the conflict had to be for purposes larger than themselves.

THE ADVENT OF EMANCIPATION

Despite the sense of loyalty to cause that animated soldiers and civilians on both sides, the governments of the United States and the Confederacy lacked clarity about the purpose of the war. Throughout the first several months of the struggle, both Davis and Lincoln studiously avoided references to slavery. Davis realized that emphasis on the issue could increase class conflict in the South. To avoid identifying the Confederacy only with the interests of slaveholders, he articulated a broader, traditional ideology. Davis told southerners that they were fighting for constitutional liberty: northerners had betrayed the founders' legacy, and southerners had seceded to preserve it. As long as Lincoln also avoided making slavery an issue, Davis's strategy seemed to work.

Lincoln had his own reasons for avoiding slavery. It was crucial at first not to antagonize the Union's border slave states, whose loyalty was tenuous. Also, for many months Lincoln hoped that a pro-Union majority would assert itself in the South. It might be possible, he thought, to coax the South back into the Union and stop the fighting, short of what he later called "the result so fundamental and astounding"—emancipation. Raising the slavery issue would severely undermine both goals. Powerful political considerations also dictated Lincoln's reticence. The Republican Party was a young and unwieldy coalition. Some Republicans burned with moral outrage over slavery; others were frankly racist, dedicated to protecting free whites from the Slave Power and the competition of cheap slave labor. No Republican, or even northern, consensus on what to do about slavery existed early in the war.

Lincoln and Emancipation The president's hesitancy ran counter to some of his personal feelings. Lincoln's compassion, humility, and moral anguish during the war were evident in his speeches and writings. But as a politician, Lincoln distinguished between his own moral convictions and his official acts. His political positions were studied and complex, calculated for maximum advantage.

Many blacks attacked Lincoln furiously during the first year of the war for his refusal to convert the struggle into an "abolition war." When Lincoln countermanded General John C. Frémont's order of liberation for slaves owned by disloyal masters in Missouri in September 1861, the *Anglo-African* declared that the president, by his actions, "hurls back into the hell of slavery thousands . . . rightfully set free." As late as July 1862, Frederick Douglass condemned Lincoln as a "miserable tool of traitors and rebels," and characterized administration policy as reconstruction of "the old union on the old and corrupting basis of compromise, by which slavery shall retain all the power that it ever had." Douglass wanted the old Union destroyed and a new one created in the crucible of a war that would destroy slavery and rewrite the Constitution in the name of human equality. To the black leader's own amazement, within a year, just such a profound result began to take place.

Lincoln first broached the subject of slavery in a substantive way in March 1862, when he proposed that the states consider emancipation on their own. He asked Congress to promise aid to any state that decided to emancipate, appealing especially to border state representatives. What Lincoln proposed was gradual emancipation, with compensation for slaveholders and colonization of the freed slaves outside the United States. To a delegation of free blacks in August 1862 he explained that "it is better for us both . . . to be separated."

Until well into 1864, Lincoln's administration promoted an impractical scheme to colonize blacks in Central America or the Caribbean. Lincoln saw colonization as one option among others in dealing with the impending freedom of America's 4.2 million slaves. He was as yet unconvinced that America had any prospect as a biracial society, and he desperately feared that white northerners might not support a war for black freedom. Led by Frederick Douglass, black abolitionists vehemently opposed these machinations by the Lincoln administration.

Other politicians had much greater plans for a struggle against slavery. A group of Republicans in Congress, known as the Radicals and led by men such as George Julian, Charles Sumner, and Thaddeus Stevens, dedicated themselves to a war for emancipation. They were instrumental in creating a special House-Senate committee on the conduct of the war, which investigated Union reverses, sought to make the war effort more efficient, and prodded the president to take stronger measures against slavery.

Confiscation Acts   In August 1861, at the Radicals' instigation, Congress passed its first confiscation act. Designed to punish the Confederates, the law confiscated all property used for "insurrectionary purposes." Thus, if the South used slaves in a hostile action, those slaves were seized and liberated as "contraband" of war. A second confiscation act (July 1862) went much further: it confiscated the property of anyone who supported the rebellion, even those who merely resided in the South and paid Confederate taxes. Their slaves were declared "forever free of their servitude." These acts stemmed from the logic that, in order to crush the southern rebellion, the government had to use extraordinary powers.

Lincoln refused to adopt that view in the summer of 1862. He stood by his proposal of voluntary gradual emancipation by the states and made no effort at first to enforce the second confiscation act. His stance provoked a public protest from Horace Greeley, editor of the powerful *New York Tribune*. In an open letter to the president entitled

"The Prayer of Twenty Millions," Greeley pleaded with Lincoln to "execute the laws" and declared, "On the face of this wide earth, Mr. President, there is not one . . . intelligent champion of the Union cause who does not feel that all attempts to put down the Rebellion and at the same time uphold its inciting cause are preposterous and futile." Lincoln's reply was an explicit statement of his calculated approach to the question. He disagreed, he said, with all those who would make slavery the paramount issue of the war. "I would save the Union," announced Lincoln. "If I could save the Union without freeing any slave I would do it, and if I could save it by freeing all the slaves I would do it; and if I could save it by freeing some and leaving others alone I would also do that. What I do about slavery, and the colored race, I do because I believe it helps to save the Union." Lincoln closed with a personal disclaimer: "I have here stated my purpose according to my view of official duty; and I intend no modification of my oft-expressed personal wish that all men everywhere could be free."

When he wrote those words, Lincoln had already decided to boldly issue a presidential Emancipation Proclamation. He was waiting, however, for a Union victory so that it would not appear to be an act of desperation. Yet the letter to Greeley was not simply an effort to stall; it was an integral part of Lincoln's approach to the future of slavery, as the text of the Emancipation Proclamation would show. Lincoln was concerned with conditioning public opinion as best he could for the coming social revolution, and he needed to delicately consider international opinion as well.

Emancipation Proclamations   On September 22, 1862, shortly after Union success at the Battle of Antietam, Lincoln issued the first part of his two-part proclamation. Invoking his powers as commander-in-chief of the armed forces, he announced that on January 1, 1863, he would emancipate the slaves in the states "in rebellion." Lincoln made plain that he would judge a state to be in rebellion in January if it lacked legitimate representatives in the U.S. Congress. Thus his September 1862 proclamation was less a declaration of the right of slaves to be free than a threat to southerners: unless they put down their arms and returned to Congress, they would lose their slaves. "Knowing the value that was set on the slaves by the rebels," said Garrison Frazier, a black Georgia minister, "the President thought that his proclamation would stimulate them to lay down their arms . . . and their not doing so has now made the freedom of the slaves a part of the war." Lincoln had little expectation that southerners would give up their effort, but he was careful to offer them the option and compel a reply.

In the fateful January 1, 1863, proclamation, Lincoln declared that "all persons held as slaves" in areas in rebellion "shall be then, thenceforward, and forever free." But he excepted (as areas in rebellion) every Confederate county or city that had fallen under Union control. Those areas, he declared, "are, for the present, left precisely as if this proclamation were not issued." Nor did Lincoln liberate slaves in the border slave states that remained in the Union. "The President has purposely made the proclamation inoperative in all places where . . . the slaves [are] accessible," charged the anti-administration *New York World.* "He has proclaimed emancipation only where he has notoriously no power to execute it." Partisanship aside, even Secretary of State Seward said sarcastically, "We show our sympathy with slavery by emancipating slaves where we cannot reach them and holding them in bondage where we can set them free."

But Lincoln was worried about the constitutionality of his acts, and he anticipated that after the war southerners might sue in court for restoration of their "property." Making the liberation of the slaves "a fit and necessary war measure" raised a variety of legal questions: How long did a war measure remain in force? Did it expire with the suppression of a rebellion? The proclamation did little to clarify the status or citizenship of the freed slaves, although it did open the possibility of military service for blacks. How, indeed, would this change the character and purpose of the war?

Thus the Emancipation Proclamation was an ambiguous document. But if as a legal document it was wanting, as a moral and political document it had great meaning. Because the proclamation defined the war as a war against slavery, Congressional Radicals could applaud it. Yet at the same time it protected Lincoln's position with conservatives, leaving him room to retreat if he chose and forcing no immediate changes on the border slave states. It was a delicate balancing act, but one from which there was no real turning back.

Most important, though, thousands of slaves had already reached Union lines in various sections of the South. They had "voted with their feet" for emancipation, as many said, well before the proclamation. And now, every advance of federal forces into slave society was a liberating step. This Lincoln knew in taking his own initially tentative, and then forthright, steps toward emancipation.

Across the North and in Union-occupied sections of the South, blacks and their white allies celebrated the Emancipation Proclamation with unprecedented fervor. Full of praise songs, these celebrations demonstrated that, whatever the fine print of the proclamation, black folks knew that they had lived to see a new day. At a large "contraband camp" in Washington, D.C., some six hundred black men, women, and children gathered at the superintendent's headquarters on New Year's Eve and sang through the night. In chorus after chorus of "Go Down, Moses" they announced the magnitude of their painful but beautiful exodus. One newly supplied verse concluded with "Go down, Abraham, away down in Dixie's land, tell Jeff Davis to let my people go!"

African American Recruits The need for men soon convinced the administration to recruit northern and southern blacks for the Union Army. By the spring of 1863, African American troops were answering the call of a dozen or more black recruiters barnstorming the cities and towns of the North. Lincoln came to see black soldiers as "the great available and yet unavailed of force for restoring the Union."

African American leaders hoped that military service would secure equal rights for their people. Once the black soldier had fought for the Union, wrote Frederick Douglass, "there is no power on earth which can deny that he has earned the right of citizenship in the United States." If black soldiers turned the tide, asked another man, "would the nation refuse us our rights?"

In June 1864, with thousands of black former slaves in blue uniforms, Lincoln gave his support to a constitutional ban on slavery. On the eve of the Republican national convention, Lincoln called on the party to "put into the platform as the keystone, the amendment of the Constitution abolishing and prohibiting slavery forever." The party promptly called for the Thirteenth Amendment. Republican delegates probably would have adopted such a plank without his urging, but Lincoln demonstrated his commitment by lobbying Congress for quick approval of the measure. The proposed amendment passed in early 1865 and was sent to the states for ratification. The war to save the Union had also become the war to free the slaves.

Who Freed the Slaves?

It has long been debated whether Abraham Lincoln deserved the label (one he never claimed for himself) of "Great Emancipator."

Was Lincoln ultimately a reluctant emancipator, following rather than leading Congress and public opinion? Or did Lincoln give essential presidential leadership to the most transformative and sensitive aspect of the war by going slow on emancipation but, once moving, never backpedaling on black freedom? Once he had realized the total character of the war and decided to prosecute it to the unconditional surrender of the Confederates, Lincoln made the destruction of slavery central to the war's purpose.

Others have argued, however, that the slaves themselves are the central story in the achievement of their own freedom. When they were in proximity to the war zones or had opportunities as traveling laborers, slaves fled for their freedom by the thousands. Some worked as camp laborers for the Union armies, and eventually more than 180,000 black men served in the Union Army and Navy. Sometimes freedom came as a combination of confusion, fear, and joy in the rural hinterlands of the South. Some found freedom as individuals in 1861, and some not until 1865, as members of trains of refugees trekking great distances to reach contraband camps.

However freedom came to individuals, emancipation was a historical confluence of two essential forces: one, a policy directed by and dependent on the military authority of the president in his effort to win the war; and the other, the will and courage necessary for acts of self-emancipation. Wallace Turnage's escape in Mobile Bay in 1864 demonstrates that emancipation could result from both a slave's own extraordinary heroism and the liberating actions of the Union forces. Most blacks comprehended their freedom as both given and taken, but also as their human right. "I now dreaded the gun and handcuffs . . . no more," remembered Turnage of his liberation. "Nor the blowing of horns and running of hounds, nor the threats of death from rebels' authority." He was free in body and mind. "I could now speak my opinion" Turnage concluded, "to men of all grades and colors."

A Confederate Plan of Emancipation

Before the war was over, the Confederacy, too, addressed the issue of emancipation. Jefferson Davis himself offered a proposal for black freedom of a kind. Late in the war he was willing to sacrifice slavery to achieve independence. He proposed that the Confederate government purchase 40,000 slaves to work for the army as laborers, with a promise of freedom at the end of their service. Soon Davis upgraded the idea, calling for the recruitment and arming of slaves as soldiers, who likewise would gain their freedom at war's end. The wives and children of these soldiers, he made plain, must also receive freedom from the states. Davis and his advisers envisioned an "intermediate" status for ex-slaves of "serfage or peonage." Thus, at the bitter end, a few southerners were willing to sacrifice some of the racial, if not class, destiny for which they had launched their revolution.

Bitter debate over Davis's plan resounded through the Confederacy. When the Confederate Congress finally approved slave enlistments in March 1865, owners had to comply only on a "voluntary" basis. In sheer desperation for manpower, General Lee also supported the idea of slave soldiers. Against the reality all around them of slaves fleeing to Union lines, some southern leaders mistakenly hoped that they could still count on the "loyalty" of their bondsmen. Most Confederate slaveholders and editors vehemently opposed the enlistment plan; those who did support it acknowledged that the war had already freed some portion of the slave population. Their aim was to fight to a stalemate, achieve independence, and control the postwar racial order through their limited wartime emancipation schemes. It was too late. As a Mississippi planter wrote to his state's governor, the plan seemed "like a drowning man catching at straws."

By contrast, Lincoln's Emancipation Proclamation stimulated a vital infusion of forces into the Union armies. Before the war was over, 134,000 former slaves (and 52,000 free blacks) had fought for freedom and the Union. Their participation was pivotal in northern victory. As both policy and process, emancipation had profound practical and moral implications for the new nation to be born out of the war.

THE SOLDIERS' WAR

The intricacies of policymaking and social revolutions were far from the minds of most ordinary soldiers. Military service completely altered their lives. Enlistment took young men from their homes and submerged them in large organizations whose military discipline ignored their individuality. Army life meant tedium, physical hardship, and separation from loved ones. Yet the military experience had powerful attractions as well. It molded men on both sides so thoroughly that they came to resemble one another far more than they resembled civilians back home. Many soldiers forged amid war a bond with their fellows and a connection to a noble purpose that they cherished for years afterward.

Union soldiers may have sensed most clearly the massive scale of modern war. Most were young; the average soldier was between eighteen and twenty-one. Many went straight from small towns and farms into large armies supplied by extensive bureaucracies. By late 1861 there were 640,000 volunteers in arms, a stupendous increase over the regular army of 20,000 men.

Hospitals and Camp Life   Soldiers benefited from certain new products, such as canned condensed milk, but blankets, clothing, and arms were often of poor quality. Hospitals were badly managed at first. Rules of hygiene in large camps were scarcely enforced; latrines were poorly made or carelessly used. One investigation turned up "an area of over three acres, encircling the camp as a broad belt, on which is deposited an almost perfect layer of human excrement." Water supplies were unsafe and typhoid epidemics common. About 57,000 men died from dysentery and diarrhea; in fact, 224,000 Union troops died from disease or accidents, far more than the 110,100 who died as a result of battle. Confederate troops were less well supplied, especially in the latter part of the war, and they had no sanitary commission. Still, an extensive network of hospitals, aided by many white female volunteers and black woman slaves, sprang up to aid the sick and wounded.

On both sides, troops quickly learned that soldiering was far from glorious. "The dirt of a camp life knocks all its poetry into a cocked hat," wrote a North Carolina volunteer in 1862. One year later he marveled at his earlier innocence. Fighting had taught him "the realities of a soldier's life. We had no tents after the 6th of August, but slept on the ground, in the woods or open fields. . . . I learned to eat fat bacon raw, and to like it. . . . Without time to wash our clothes or our persons . . . the whole army became lousy more or less with body lice." Union troops "skirmished" against lice by boiling their clothes, but, reported one soldier, "I find some on me in spite of all I can do."

Few had seen violent death before, but war soon exposed them to the blasted bodies of their friends and comrades. "Any one who goes over a battlefield after a battle," wrote one Confederate, "never cares to go over another. . . . It is a sad sight to see the dead and if possible more sad to see the wounded—shot in every possible way you can imagine." Many men died gallantly; there were innumerable striking displays of courage. But often soldiers gave up their lives in mass sacrifice, in tactics that made little sense.

Still, Civil War soldiers developed deep commitments to each other and to their task. As campaigns dragged on, most soldiers who did not desert grew determined to see the struggle through. "We now, like true Soldiers go determined not to yield one inch," wrote a New York corporal. When at last the war was over, "it seemed like breaking up a family to separate," one man observed. Another admitted, "We shook hands all around, and laughed and seemed to make merry, while our hearts were heavy and our eyes ready to shed tears."

The Rifled Musket   Advances in technology made the Civil War particularly deadly. By far the most important were the rifle and the "minie ball." Bullets fired from a smoothbore musket tumbled and wobbled as they flew through the air, and thus were not accurate at distances over eighty yards. Cutting spiraled grooves inside the barrel gave the projectile a spin and much greater accuracy, but rifles remained difficult to load and use until the Frenchman Claude Minie and the American James Burton developed a new kind of bullet. Civil War bullets were lead slugs with a cavity at the bottom that expanded on firing so that the bullet "took" the rifling and flew accurately. With these bullets, rifles were deadly at four hundred yards and useful up to one thousand yards.

This meant, of course, that soldiers assaulting a position defended by riflemen were in greater peril than ever before; the defense thus gained a significant advantage. While artillery now fired from a safe distance, there was no substitute for the infantry assault or the popular turning movements aimed at an enemy's flank. Thus advancing soldiers had to expose themselves repeatedly to accurate rifle fire. Because medical knowledge was rudimentary, even minor wounds often led to amputation and death through infection. Never before in Europe or America had such massive forces pummeled each other with weapons of such destructive power. As losses mounted, many citizens wondered at what Union soldier (and future Supreme Court justice) Oliver Wendell Holmes Jr. called "the butcher's bill."

The Black Soldier's   At the outset of the war, racism in the Union Army was strong.
Fight for Manhood   Most white soldiers wanted nothing to do with black people and regarded them as inferior. "I never came out here for to free the black devils," wrote one soldier, and another objected to fighting beside African Americans, because "We are a too superior race for that." For many, acceptance of black troops grew only because they could do heavy labor and "stop Bullets as well as white

people." A popular song celebrated "Sambo's Right to Be Kilt" as the only justification for black enlistments.

But among some, a change occurred. While recruiting black troops in Virginia in late 1864, Massachusetts soldier Charles Brewster sometimes denigrated the very men he sought to enlist. But he was delighted at the sight of a black cavalry unit because it made the local "secesh" furious, and he praised black soldiers who "fought nobly" and filled hospitals with "their wounded and mangled bodies." White officers who volunteered to lead segregated black units only to gain promotion found that experience altered their opinions. After just one month with black troops, a white captain informed his wife, "I have a more elevated opinion of their abilities than I ever had before. I know that many of them are vastly the superiors of those . . . who would condemn them all to a life of brutal degradation." One general reported that his "colored regiments" possessed "remarkable aptitude for military training," and another observer said, "They fight like fiends."

Black troops created this change through their own dedication. They had a mission to destroy slavery and demonstrate their equality. "When Rebellion is crushed," wrote a black volunteer from Connecticut, "who will be more proud than I to say, 'I was one of the first of the despised race to leave the free North with a rifle on my shoulder, and give the lie to the old story that the black man will not fight.'" Corporal James Henry Gooding of Massachusetts's black Fifty-fourth Regiment explained that his unit intended "to live down all prejudice against its color, by a determination to do well in any position it is put." After an engagement, he was proud that "a regiment of white men gave us three cheers as we were passing them," because "it shows that we did our duty as men should."

Through such experience under fire, the blacks and whites of the Fifty-fourth Massachusetts forged deep bonds. Just before the regiment launched its costly assault on Fort Wagner in Charleston harbor, in July 1863, a black soldier called out to abolitionist Colonel Robert Gould Shaw, who would perish that day, "Colonel, I will stay by you till I die." "And he kept his word," noted a survivor of the attack. "He has never been seen since." Indeed, the heroic assault on Fort Wagner was celebrated for demonstrating the valor of black men. This bloody chapter in the history of American racism proved many things, not least of which that black men had to die in battle to be acknowledged as men.

Such valor emerged despite persistent discrimination. Off-duty black soldiers were sometimes attacked by northern mobs; on duty, they did most of the heavy labor. The Union government, moreover, paid white privates $13 per month plus a clothing allowance of $3.50, whereas black privates earned only $10 per month less $3 for clothing. Outraged by this injustice, several regiments refused to accept any pay whatsoever, and Congress eventually remedied the inequity. In this instance at least, the majority of legislators agreed with a white private that black troops had "proved their title to manhood on many a bloody field fighting freedom's battles."

1863: THE TIDE OF BATTLE TURNS

The fighting in the spring and summer of 1863 did not settle the war, but it began to suggest the outcome. The campaigns began in a deceptively positive way for Confederates, as Lee's army performed brilliantly in battles in central Virginia.

Battle of Chancellorsville   For once, a large Civil War army was not slow and cumbersome, but executed tactics with speed and precision. On May 2 and 3, west of Fredericksburg, Virginia, some 130,000 members of the Union Army of the Potomac bore down on fewer than 60,000 Confederates. Boldly, Lee and Stonewall Jackson divided their forces, ordering 30,000 men under Jackson on a day-long march westward to prepare a flank attack.

This classic turning movement was carried out in the face of great numerical disadvantage. Arriving at their position late in the afternoon, Jackson's seasoned "foot cavalry" found unprepared Union troops laughing, smoking, and playing cards. The Union soldiers had no idea they were under attack until frightened deer and rabbits bounded out of the forest, followed by gray-clad troops. The Confederate attack drove the entire right side of the Union Army back in confusion. Eager to press his advantage, Jackson rode forward with a few officers to study the ground. As they returned at twilight, southern troops mistook them for federals and fired, fatally wounding their commander. The next day, Union forces left in defeat. Chancellorsville was a remarkable southern victory, but costly because of the loss of Stonewall Jackson, who would forever remain a legend in Confederate memory.

Siege of Vicksburg   July brought crushing defeats for the Confederacy in two critical battles—Vicksburg and Gettysburg—that severely damaged Confederate hopes for independence. Vicksburg was a vital western citadel, the last major fortification on the Mississippi River in southern hands (see Map 15.2). After months of searching through swamps and bayous, General Ulysses S. Grant found an advantageous approach to the city. He laid siege to Vicksburg in May, bottling up the defending army of General John Pemberton. If Vicksburg fell, Union forces would control the river, cutting the Confederacy in two and gaining an open path into its interior. To stave off such a result, Jefferson Davis gave command of all other forces in the area to General Joseph E. Johnston and beseeched him to go to Pemberton's aid. Meanwhile, at a council of war in Richmond, General Robert E. Lee proposed a Confederate invasion of the North. Although such an offensive would not relieve Vicksburg directly, it could stun and dismay the North and, if successful, possibly even lead to peace. By invading the North a second time, Lee hoped to take the war out of war-weary Virginia, garner civilian support in Maryland, win a major victory on northern soil, threaten major cities, and thereby force a Union capitulation on his terms.

As Lee's emboldened army advanced through western Maryland and into Pennsylvania, Confederate prospects to the south along the Mississippi darkened. Davis repeatedly wired General Johnston, urging him to concentrate his forces and attack Grant's army. Johnston, however, did little, telegraphing back, "I consider saving Vicksburg hopeless." Grant's men, meanwhile, were supplying themselves from the abundant crops of the Mississippi River valley and could continue their siege indefinitely. Their rich meat-and-vegetable diet became so tiresome, in fact, that one day, as Grant rode by, a private looked up and muttered, "Hardtack," referring to the dry biscuits that were the usual staple of soldiers' diets. Soon a line of soldiers was shouting, "Hardtack! Hardtack!" demanding respite from turkey and sweet potatoes.

**Battle of
Gettysburg**

In such circumstances the fall of Vicksburg was inevitable, and on July 4, 1863, its commander surrendered. The same day, a battle that had been raging for three days concluded at Gettysburg, Pennsylvania. On July 1, Confederate forces hunting for a supply of shoes had collided with part of the Union Army. Heavy fighting on the second day over two steep hills left federal forces in possession of high ground along Cemetery Ridge, running more than a mile south of the town. There they enjoyed the protection of a stone wall and a clear view of their foe across almost a mile of open field.

Undaunted, Lee believed that his reinforced troops could break the Union line, and on July 3 he ordered a direct assault. Full of foreboding, General James Longstreet warned Lee that "no 15,000 men ever arrayed for battle can take that position." But Lee stuck to his plan. Virginians under General George E. Pickett and North Carolinians under General James Pettigrew methodically marched up the slope in a doomed assault known as Pickett's Charge. For a moment, a few hundred Confederates breached the enemy's line, but most fell in heavy slaughter. On July 4 Lee had to withdraw, having suffered almost 4,000 dead and about 24,000 missing and wounded. The Confederate

**MAP 15.1
Battle of Gettysburg**

In the war's greatest battle, fought around a small market town in southern Pennsylvania, Lee's invasion of the North was repulsed. Union forces had the advantage of high ground, shorter lines, and superior numbers. The casualties for the two armies—dead, wounded, and missing—exceeded 50,000 men.

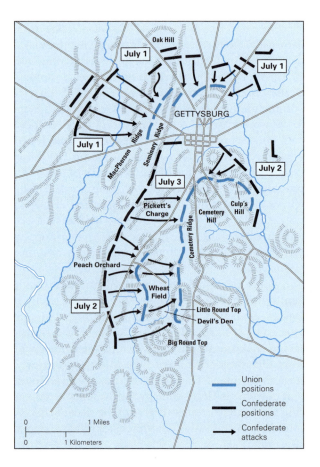

general reported to President Davis that "I am alone to blame" and offered to resign. Davis replied that to find a more capable commander was "an impossibility." The Confederacy had reached what many consider its "high water mark" on that ridge at Gettysburg.

Southern troops displayed unforgettable courage and dedication at Gettysburg, and under General George G. Meade, the Union Army, which suffered 23,000 casualties (nearly one-quarter of the force), exhibited the same bravery in stopping the Confederate invasion. But the results there and at Vicksburg were disastrous for the South. The Confederacy was split in two; west of the Mississippi, General E. Kirby Smith had to operate on his own, virtually independent of Richmond. Moreover, the heartland of Louisiana, Tennessee, and Mississippi lay exposed to invasion. Far to the north, Lee's defeat spelled the end of major southern offensive actions. Too weak to prevail in attack, the Confederacy henceforth would have to conserve its limited resources and rely on a prolonged defense. By refusing to be beaten and by wearing down northern morale, the South might yet win, but its prospects were darker than before.

DISUNITY: SOUTH, NORTH, AND WEST

Both northern and southern governments waged the final two years of the war in the face of increasing opposition at home. Dissatisfactions that had surfaced earlier grew more intense and sometimes violent. The gigantic costs of a civil war that neither side seemed able to win fed the unrest. But protest also arose from fundamental stresses in the social structures of North and South.

Union Occupation Zones   Wherever Union forces invaded they imposed a military occupation consisting roughly of three zones: garrisoned towns, with large numbers of troops in control of civilian and economic life; the Confederate frontier, areas still under southern control but also with some federal military penetration; and "no man's land," the land between the two armies, beyond Confederate authority and under frequent Union patrols.

As many as one hundred southern towns were garrisoned during the war, causing severe disruption to the social landscape. Large regions of Tennessee, Virginia, Louisiana, Mississippi, and Georgia fell under this pattern of occupation and suffered food shortages, crop and property destruction, disease, roadway banditry, guerrilla warfare, summary executions, and the random flow of escaped slaves. After two years of occupation, a southern white woman wrote to a kinsman about their native Clarksville, Tennessee. "You would scarcely know the place," she lamented, "it is nothing but a dirty hole filled . . . with niggers and Yankees."

Disintegration of Confederate Unity   Vastly disadvantaged in industrial capacity, natural resources, and labor, southerners felt the cost of the war more directly and more painfully than northerners. But even more fundamental were the Confederacy's internal problems; the southern class system threatened the Confederate cause.

One ominous development was the planters' increasing opposition to their own government. Along with new taxation, Confederate military authorities also impressed slaves to build fortifications. And when Union forces advanced on plantation areas, Confederate commanders burned stores of cotton that lay in the enemy's path. Many planters bitterly complained about such interference with their agricultural production and financial interests.

Nor were the centralizing policies of the Davis administration popular. The increasing size and power of the Richmond government alarmed planters. In fact, the Confederate constitution had granted substantial powers to the central government, especially in time of war. But many planters took the position articulated by R. B. Rhett, editor of the *Charleston Mercury,* that the Confederate constitution "leaves the States untouched in their Sovereignty, and commits to the Confederate Government only a few simple objects, and a few simple powers to enforce them." Governor Joseph E. Brown of Georgia took a similar states' rights position, occasionally prohibiting supplies and that state's soldiers from leaving its borders.

Years of opposition to the federal government within the Union had frozen southerners in a defensive posture. Now they erected the barrier of states' rights as a defense against change, hiding behind it while their capacity for creative statesmanship atrophied. Planters sought, above all, a guarantee that their plantations and their lives would remain untouched. As secession revolutionized their world and hard war took so many lives, some could never fully commit to the cause.

Confused and embittered planters struck out at Jefferson Davis. Conscription, thundered Governor Brown, was "subversive of [Georgia's] sovereignty, and at war with all the principles for the support of which Georgia entered into this revolution." Searching for ways to frustrate the law, Brown ordered local enrollment officials not to cooperate with the Confederacy. The *Charleston Mercury* told readers that "conscription . . . is . . . the very embodiment of Lincolnism, which our gallant armies are today fighting." In a gesture of stubborn selfishness, Robert Toombs of Georgia, a former U.S. senator, refused to switch from cotton to food crops, defying the wishes of the government, the newspapers, and his neighbors' petitions.

The southern courts ultimately upheld Davis's power to conscript. Davis was deeply devoted to southern independence, but some of his actions earned him the hatred of influential and elite citizens.

Food Riots in Southern Cities

Meanwhile, for ordinary southerners, the dire predictions of hunger and suffering were becoming a reality. Food riots occurred in the spring of 1863 in Atlanta, Macon, Columbus, and Augusta, Georgia, and in Salisbury and High Point, North Carolina. On April 2 a crowd assembled in Richmond to demand relief. A passerby, noticing the excitement, asked a young girl, "Is there some celebration?" "We celebrate our right to live," replied the girl. "We are starving. As soon as enough of us get together we are going to the bakeries and each of us will take a loaf of bread." Soon they did just that, sparking a riot that Davis ordered quelled at gunpoint.

Throughout the rural South, ordinary people resisted more quietly—by refusing to cooperate with conscription, tax collection, and impressments of food. "In all the States impressments are evaded by every means which ingenuity can suggest, and in some openly resisted," wrote a high-ranking commissary officer. Farmers who did provide food for the army refused to accept payment in certificates of credit or government bonds, as required by law. Conscription officers increasingly found no one to draft.

"The disposition to avoid military service is general," observed one of Georgia's senators in 1864. In some areas, tax agents were killed in the line of duty.

Jefferson Davis was ill equipped to deal with such discontent. Austere and private by nature, he failed to communicate with the masses. Often he buried himself in military affairs or administrative details. His class perspective also distanced him from the sufferings of the common people. While his social circle in Richmond dined on duck and oysters, ordinary southerners recovered salt from the drippings on their smokehouse floors and went hungry. Davis failed to reach out to the plain folk and thus lost their support.

Desertions from the Confederate Army

Such discontent was certain to affect the Confederate armies. "What man is there that would stay in the army and no that his family is sufring at home?" an angry citizen wrote anonymously to the secretary of war. Worried about their loved ones and resentful of what they saw as a rich man's war, large numbers of men did indeed leave the armies. Their friends and neighbors gave them support. Mary Chesnut observed a man being dragged back to the army as his wife looked on. "Desert agin, Jake!" she cried openly. "You desert agin, quick as you kin. Come back to your wife and children."

Desertion did not become a serious problem for the Confederacy until mid-1862, and stiffer policing solved the problem that year. But from 1863 on, the number of men on duty fell rapidly. By mid-1863, John A. Campbell, the South's assistant secretary of war, wondered whether "so general a habit" as desertion could be considered a crime. Campbell estimated that 40,000 to 50,000 troops were absent without leave and that 100,000 were evading duty in some way. Furloughs, amnesty proclamations, and appeals to return had little effect; by November 1863, Secretary of War James Seddon admitted that one-third of the army could not be accounted for.

The defeats at Gettysburg and Vicksburg dealt a heavy blow to Confederate morale. When the news reached Josiah Gorgas, the genius of Confederate ordnance operations, he confided to his diary, "Today absolute ruin seems our portion. The Confederacy totters to its destruction." In desperation President Davis and several state governors resorted to threats and racial scare tactics to drive southern whites to further sacrifice. Defeat, Davis warned, would mean "extermination of yourselves, your wives, and children." Governor Charles Clark of Mississippi predicted "elevation of the black race to a position of equality—aye, of superiority, that will make them your masters and rulers."

From this point on, the internal disintegration of the Confederacy quickened. A few newspapers began to call openly for peace. "We are for peace," admitted the *Raleigh* (North Carolina) *Daily Progress,* "because there has been enough of blood and carnage, enough of widows and orphans." Similar proposals were made in several state legislatures, though they were presented as plans for independence on honorable terms. Confederate leaders began to realize that they were losing the support of the common people. It is, indeed, remarkable how long and how effectively the Confederacy sustained a military effort in the face of such internal division.

Antiwar Sentiment, South and North

In North Carolina, a peace movement grew under the leadership of William W. Holden, a popular Democratic politician and editor. Over one hundred public meetings in support of peace negotiations took place during the summer of 1863, and Holden may have had the majority of the people behind him. In Georgia early in 1864, Governor Brown and

Alexander H. Stephens, vice president of the Confederacy, led a similar effort. Ultimately, however, these movements came to naught. The lack of a two-party system threw into question the legitimacy of any criticism of the government; even Holden and Brown could not entirely escape the taint of dishonor and disloyalty.

The results of the 1863 congressional elections strengthened dissent in the Confederacy. Everywhere secessionists and supporters of the administration lost seats to men not identified with the government. In the last years of the war, Davis's support in the Confederate Congress dwindled. Some newspaper editors and a core of courageous, determined soldiers, especially in Lee's Army of Northern Virginia, kept the Confederacy alive in spite of disintegrating popular support.

By 1864 much of the opposition to the war had moved entirely outside the political sphere. Southerners were simply giving up the struggle. Deserters dominated some whole towns and counties. Active dissent was particularly common in upland and mountain regions, where support for the Union had always been genuine. "The condition of things in the mountain districts of North Carolina, South Carolina, Georgia, and Alabama," admitted Assistant Secretary of War Campbell, "menaces the existence of the Confederacy as fatally as either of the armies of the United States." The government was losing the support of its citizens.

Opposition to the war, though less severe, existed in the North as well. Alarm intensified over the growing centralization of government, and by 1863 war-weariness was widespread. Resentment of the draft sparked protest, especially among poor citizens, and the Union Army, too, struggled with a troubling desertion rate. But the Union was so much richer than the South in human resources that none of these problems ever threatened the effectiveness of the government. Fresh recruits were always available, especially after black enlistments in 1863.

Moreover, Lincoln possessed a talent that Davis lacked: he knew how to stay in touch with the ordinary citizen. Through public letters to newspapers and private ones to soldiers' families he reached the common people. The daily carnage, the tortuous political problems, and the ceaseless criticism weighed heavily on him. But this president—a self-educated man of humble origins—was able to communicate his suffering. His moving words helped to contain northern discontent, though they could not remove it.

Peace Democrats   Much of the wartime protest in the North was political in origin. The Democratic Party fought to regain power by blaming Lincoln for the war's death toll, the expansion of federal powers, inflation and the high tariff, and the emancipation of blacks. Appealing to tradition, its leaders called for an end to the war and reunion on the basis of "the Constitution as it is and the Union as it was." The Democrats denounced conscription and martial law, and defended states' rights. They charged repeatedly that Republican policies were designed to flood the North with blacks, depriving white males of their status, their jobs, and their women. In the 1862 congressional elections, the Democrats made a strong comeback, with peace Democrats wielding influence in New York State and majorities in the legislatures of Illinois and Indiana.

Led by outspoken men like Representative Clement L. Vallandigham of Ohio, the peace Democrats became highly visible. Vallandigham criticized Lincoln as a "dictator" who had suspended the writ of habeas corpus without congressional authority and arrested thousands of innocent citizens. He condemned both conscription and emancipation, and urged voters to use their power at the polls to depose "King Abraham." Vallandigham stayed carefully within legal bounds, but his attacks seemed so damaging to the war effort that military authorities arrested him for treason. Lincoln wisely decided against punishment—and martyr's status—for the Ohioan and exiled him to the Confederacy. (Eventually Vallandigham returned to the North through Canada.)

Lincoln believed that antiwar Democrats were linked to secret organizations that harbored traitorous ideas. These societies, he feared, encouraged draft resistance, discouraged enlistment, sabotaged communications, and plotted to aid the Confederacy. Likening such groups to a poisonous snake, Republicans sometimes branded them— and by extension the peace Democrats—as "Copperheads." Although some Confederate agents were active in the North and Canada, they never genuinely threatened the Union war effort.

New York City Draft Riots

More violent opposition to the government arose from ordinary citizens facing the draft, which became law in 1863. Although many soldiers risked their lives willingly out of a

desire to preserve the Union or extend freedom, others openly sought to avoid service. Under the law, a draftee could stay at home by providing a substitute or paying a $300 commutation fee. Many wealthy men chose these options, and in response to popular demand, clubs, cities, and states provided the money for others to escape conscription. In all, 118,000 substitutes were provided and 87,000 commutations paid before Congress ended the commutation system in 1864.

The urban poor and immigrants in strongly Democratic areas were especially hostile to conscription. Federal enrolling officers made up the lists of eligibles, a procedure open to personal favoritism and prejudice. The North's poor viewed the system as discriminatory, and many immigrants suspected (wrongly, on the whole) that they were called in disproportionate numbers. (Approximately 200,000 men born in Germany and 150,000 born in Ireland served in the Union Army.)

As a result, there were scores of disturbances. Enrolling officers received rough treatment in many parts of the North, and riots occurred in New Jersey, Ohio, Indiana, Pennsylvania, Illinois, and Wisconsin. By far the most serious outbreak of violence occurred in New York City in July 1863. The war was unpopular in that Democratic stronghold, and racial, ethnic, and class tensions ran high. Shippers had recently broken a longshoremen's strike by hiring black strikebreakers to work under police protection. Working-class New Yorkers feared an inflow of black labor from the South and regarded blacks as the cause of the war. Poor Irish workers resented being forced to serve in the place of others who could afford to avoid the draft.

Military police officers came under attack first, and then mobs crying, "Down with the rich" looted wealthy homes and stores. But blacks became the special target. The mob rampaged through African American neighborhoods, beating and murdering people in the streets, and burning an orphan asylum. At least seventy-four people died in the violence, which raged out of control for three days. Only the dispatch of army units directly from Gettysburg ended this tragic episode of racism and class resentment.

War Against Indians in the Far West

East and West, over race, land, and culture, America was a deeply divided country. A civil war of another kind raged on the Great Plains and in the Southwest. By 1864 U.S. troops under the command of Colonel John Chivington waged full-scale war against the Sioux, Arapahos, and Cheyennes in order to eradicate Indian title to all of eastern Colorado. Indian chiefs sought peace, but American commanders had orders to "burn villages and kill Cheyennes whenever and wherever found." A Cheyenne chief, Lean Bear, was shot from his horse as he rode toward U.S. troops, holding in his hand papers given him by President Lincoln during a visit to Washington, D.C. Another chief, Black Kettle, was told by the U.S. command that, by moving his people to Sand Creek, Colorado, they would find a safe haven. But on November 29, 1864, 700 cavalrymen, many drunk, attacked the Cheyenne village. With most of the men absent hunting, the slaughter included 105 Cheyenne women and children and 28 men. American soldiers scalped and mutilated their victims, carrying women's body parts on their saddles or hats back to Denver. The Sand Creek Massacre, and the retaliation against white ranches and stagecoaches by Indians in 1865, would live in western historical memory forever.

In New Mexico and Arizona Territories, an authoritarian and brutal commander, General James Carleton, waged war on the Apaches and the Navajos. Both tribes had engaged for generations in raiding the Pueblo and Hispanic peoples of the region to maintain their security and economy. During the Civil War years, Anglo-American farms also became Indian targets. In 1863 the New Mexico Volunteers, commanded in the field by former mountain man Kit Carson, defeated the Mescalero Apaches and forced them onto a reservation at Bosque Redondo in the Pecos River valley.

But the Navajos, who lived in a vast region of canyons and high deserts, resisted. In a "scorched earth" campaign, Carson destroyed the Navajos' livestock, orchards, and crops. On the run, starving and demoralized, the Navajos began to surrender for food in January 1864. Three-quarters of the 12,000 Navajos were rounded up and forced to march 400 miles (the "Long Walk") to the Bosque Redondo Reservation, suffering malnutrition and death along the way. When General William T. Sherman visited the reservation in 1868, he found the Navajos "sunk into a condition of absolute poverty and despair." Permitted to return to a fraction of their homelands later that year, the Navajos carried with them searing memories of the federal government's ruthless policies of both removal and eradication of Indian peoples.

Election of 1864

Back east, war-weariness reached a peak in the summer of 1864, when the Democratic Party nominated the popular general George B. McClellan for president and inserted a peace plank into its platform. The plank, written by Vallandigham, called for an armistice and spoke vaguely about preserving the Union. The Democrats made racist appeals to white insecurity, calling Lincoln "Abe the nigger-lover" and "Abe the widow-maker." Lincoln concluded that it was "exceedingly probable that this Administration will not be reelected." No incumbent president had been reelected since 1832, and no nation had ever held a general election in the midst of all-out civil war. Some Republicans worked to dump Lincoln from their ticket in favor of either Salmon P. Chase or John C. Frémont, although little came of either effort. Even a relatively unified Republican Party, declaring itself for "unconditional surrender" of the Confederacy and a constitutional amendment abolishing slavery, had to contend with the horrible casualty lists and the battlefield stalemate of the summer of 1864.

The fortunes of war soon changed the electoral situation. With the fall of Atlanta and Union victories in the Shenandoah Valley by early September, Lincoln's prospects rose. Decisive in the election was that eighteen states allowed troops to vote at the front; Lincoln won an extraordinary 78 percent of the soldier vote. In taking 55 percent of the total popular vote, Lincoln's reelection—a referendum on the war and emancipation—had a devastating impact on southern morale. Without such a political outcome in 1864, a Union military victory and a redefined nation might never have been possible.

1864–1865: The Final Test of Wills

During the final year of the war, the Confederates could still have won their version of victory if military stalemate and northern antiwar sentiment had forced a negotiated settlement. But events and northern determination prevailed, as Americans endured the bloodiest nightmare in their history.

Northern Diplomatic Strategy

The North's long-term diplomatic strategy succeeded in 1864. From the outset, the North had pursued one paramount goal: to prevent recognition of the Confederacy by European nations. Foreign recognition would belie Lincoln's claim that the United States was fighting an illegal rebellion and would open the way to the financial and military aid that could ensure Confederate independence. Both England and France stood to benefit from a divided and weakened America. Thus, to achieve their goal, Lincoln and Secretary of State Seward needed to avoid both serious military defeats and controversies with the European powers.

Aware that the textile industry employed one-fifth of the British population directly or indirectly, southerners banked on British recognition of the Confederacy. But at the beginning of the war, British mills had a 50 percent surplus of cotton on hand, and they later found new sources of supply in India, Egypt, and Brazil. And throughout the war, some southern cotton continued to reach Europe, despite the Confederacy's embargo on cotton production, an ill-fated policy aimed at securing British support. The British government flirted with recognition of the Confederacy but awaited battlefield demonstrations of southern success. France, though sympathetic to the South, was unwilling to act independently of Britain. Confederate agents managed to purchase valuable arms and supplies in Europe and obtained loans from European financiers, but they never achieved a diplomatic breakthrough.

More than once the Union strategy nearly broke down. An acute crisis occurred in 1861 when the overzealous commander of an American frigate stopped the British steamer *Trent* and removed two Confederate ambassadors, James Mason and John Slidell, sailing to Britain. When they were imprisoned in Boston, northerners cheered, but the British interpreted the capture as a violation of freedom of the seas and demanded the prisoners' release. Lincoln and Seward waited until northern public opinion cooled and then released the two southerners. The incident strained U.S.-British relations.

Then the sale to the Confederacy of warships constructed in England sparked vigorous protest from U.S. ambassador Charles Francis Adams. A few English-built ships, notably the *Alabama,* reached open water to serve the South. Over a period of twenty-two months, without entering a southern port (because of the Union blockade), the *Alabama* destroyed or captured more than sixty U.S. ships, leaving a bitter legal legacy to be settled in the postwar period.

Battlefield Stalemate and a Union Strategy for Victory

On the battlefield, northern victory was far from won in 1864. General Nathaniel Banks's Red River campaign, designed to capture more of Louisiana and Texas, fell apart, and the capture of Mobile Bay in August did not cause the fall of Mobile. Union general William Tecumseh Sherman commented that the North had to "keep the war South until they are not only ruined, exhausted, but humbled in pride and spirit." Sherman soon brought total war to the southern heartland. On the eastern front during the winter of 1863–1864, the two armies in Virginia settled into a stalemate awaiting yet another spring offensive by the North.

Military authorities throughout history have agreed that deep invasion is very risky: the farther an army penetrates enemy territory, the more vulnerable are its own communications and supply lines. Moreover, observed the Prussian expert Karl von Clausewitz, if the invader encounters a "truly national" resistance, his troops will be "everywhere exposed to attacks by an insurgent population." The South's vast size and a determined resistance could yet make a northern victory elusive.

General Grant, by now in command of all the federal armies, decided to test southern will with a strategic innovation of his own: raids on a massive scale. Less tied to tradition and textbook maneuver than most other Union commanders, Grant proposed to use armies to destroy Confederate railroads, thus ruining the enemy's transportation and economy. Abandoning their lines of support, Union troops would live off the land while laying waste all resources useful to the military and to the civilian population of the Confederacy. After General George H. Thomas's troops won the Battle of Chattanooga in November 1863, the heartland of Georgia lay open. Grant entrusted General Sherman with 100,000 men for an invasion deep into the South, toward the rail center of Atlanta.

Fall of Atlanta

Jefferson Davis countered by positioning the army of General Joseph E. Johnston in Sherman's path. Davis's entire political strategy for 1864 was based on demonstrating Confederate military strength and successfully defending Atlanta. Davis hoped that southern resolve would lead to the political defeat of Lincoln and the election of a president who would sue for peace. When General Johnston slowly but steadily fell back toward Atlanta, Davis grew anxious and sought assurances that Atlanta would be held. From a purely military point of view, Johnston maneuvered skillfully. But when Johnston fell silent and continued to retreat, Davis replaced him with the one-legged General John Hood, who knew his job was to fight. "Our all depends on that army at Atlanta," wrote Mary Chesnut. "If that fails us, the game is up."

For southern morale, the game *was* up. Hood attacked but was beaten, and Sherman's army occupied Atlanta on September 2, 1864. The victory buoyed northern spirits and ensured Lincoln's reelection. A government clerk in Richmond wrote, "Our

The Civil War in Britain

So engaged was the British public with America's disunion and war that an unemployed weaver, John Ward, frequently trekked many miles from Britain's Low Moor to Clitheroe just to read newspaper accounts of the strife.

Because of the direct reliance of the British textile industry on southern cotton (cut off by the war), as well as the many ideological and familial ties between the two nations, the American war was significant in Britain's economy and domestic politics. The British aristocracy and most cotton mill owners were solidly pro-Confederate and proslavery, whereas a combination of clergymen, shopkeepers, artisans, and radical politicians worked for the causes of Union and emancipation. Most British workers saw their future at stake in a war for slave emancipation. "Freedom" to the huge British working class (who could not vote) meant basic political and civil rights, as well as the bread and butter of secure jobs in an industrializing economy, now damaged by a "cotton famine" that threw millhands out of work.

English aristocrats saw Americans as untutored, wayward cousins and took satisfaction in America's troubles. Conservatives believed in the superiority of the British system of government and looked askance at America's leveling tendencies. And some aristocratic British Liberals also saw Americans through their class bias and sympathized with the Confederacy's demand for "order" and independence. English racism also intensified in these years, exemplified by the popularity of minstrelsy and the employment of science in the service of racial theory.

The intensity of the British propaganda war over the American conflict is evident in the methods of their debate: public meetings organized by both sides were huge affairs, with cheering and jeering, competing banners, carts and floats, orators and resolutions. In a press war the British argued over when rebellion is justified, whether secession was right or legal, whether slavery was at the heart of the conflict, and especially over the democratic image of America itself. This bitter debate about America's trial became a test of reform in Britain: those eager for a broadened franchise and

Some southern leaders pronounced that cotton was king and would bring Britain to their cause. This British cartoon shows King Cotton brought down in chains by the American eagle, anticipating the cotton famine to follow and the intense debate in Great Britain over the nature and meaning of the American Civil War. (Granger Collection)

(Continued)

The Civil War in Britain

increased democracy were pro-Union, and those who preferred to preserve Britain's class-ridden political system favored the Confederacy.

The nature of the internal British debate was no better symbolized than by the dozens of African Americans who served as pro-Union agents in England. The most popular was William Andrew Jackson, Confederate president Jefferson Davis's former coach-man, who had escaped from Richmond in September 1862. Jackson's articulate presence at British public meetings countered pro-Confederate arguments that the war was not about slavery.

In the end, the British government did not recognize the Confederacy, and by 1864 English cotton lords had found new sources of the crop in Egypt and India. But in this link between America and its English roots at its time of greatest travail, we can see that the Civil War was a transformation of international significance.

---

fondly-cherished visions of peace have vanished like a mirage of the desert." Davis exhorted southerners to fight on and win new victories before the federal elections, but he had to admit that "two-thirds of our men are absent . . . most of them absent without leave." In a desperate diversion, Hood's army marched north to cut Sherman's supply lines and force him to withdraw, but Sherman began to march sixty thousand of his men straight to the sea, planning to live off the land and destroying Confederate resources as he went.

Sherman's March to the Sea   Sherman's army was an unusually formidable force, composed almost entirely of battle-tested veterans and officers who had risen through the ranks from the midwestern states. Before the march began, army doctors weeded out any men who were weak or sick. Weathered, bearded, and tough, the remaining veterans were determined, as one put it, "to Conquer this Rebelien or Die." They believed "the South are to blame for this war" and were ready to make the South pay. Although many harbored racist attitudes, most had come to support emancipation because, as one said, "Slavery stands in the way of putting down the rebellion." Confederate General Johnston later commented, "There has been no such army since the days of Julius Caesar."

As Sherman's men moved across Georgia, they cut a path 50 to 60 miles wide and more than 200 miles long. The totality of the destruction they caused was awesome; indeed, it was Sherman's campaign that later prompted many historians to deem this the first modern "total war." A Georgia woman described the "Burnt Country" this way: "The fields were trampled down and the road was lined with carcasses of horses, hogs, and cattle that the invaders, unable either to consume or to carry with them, had wantonly shot down to starve our people. . . . The stench in some places was unbearable." Such devastation diminished the South's material resources and sapped its will to resist.

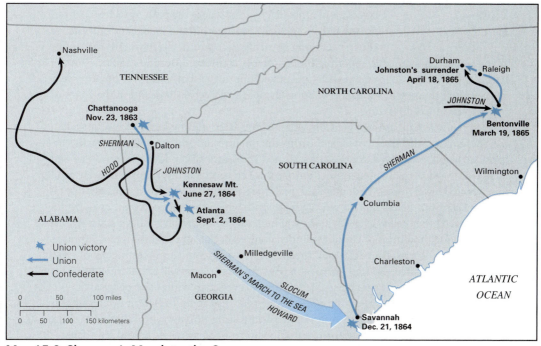

MAP 15.2 Sherman's March to the Sea

The Deep South proved a decisive theater at the end of the war. From Chattanooga, Union forces drove into Georgia, capturing Atlanta. Following the fall of Atlanta, General Sherman embarked on his march of destruction through Georgia to the coast and then northward through the Carolinas.

After reaching Savannah in December, Sherman marched his armies north into the Carolinas. To his soldiers, South Carolina was "the root of secession." They burned and destroyed as they marched, encountering little resistance. The opposing army of General Johnston was small, but Sherman's men should have been prime targets for guerrilla raids and harassing attacks by local defense units. The absence of both led South Carolina's James Chesnut Jr. (a politician and the husband of Mary Chesnut) to write that his state "was shamefully and unnecessarily lost. . . . We had time, opportunity and means to destroy him. But there was wholly wanting the energy and ability required." Southerners had lost the will to continue the struggle.

Sherman's march drew additional human resources to the Union cause. In Georgia alone, as many as nineteen thousand slaves gladly embraced emancipation and followed the marauding Union troops. Others remained on the plantations to await the end of the war, because of either an ingrained wariness of whites or negative experiences with federal soldiers. The destruction of food harmed slaves as well as white rebels, and many blacks lost livestock, clothing, crops, and other valuables to their liberators. In fact, the brutality of Sherman's troops shocked some liberated slaves. "I've seen them cut the hams off of a live pig or ox and go off leavin' the animal groanin'," recalled one man. "The master had 'em kilt then, but it was awful."

Virginia's Bloody Soil

It was awful, too, in Virginia, where the path to victory proved protracted and ghastly. Throughout the spring and summer of 1864, intent on capturing Richmond, Grant hurled his troops at Lee's army and suffered appalling losses: almost eighteen thousand casualties in the Battle of the Wilderness, where skeletons poked out of the shallow graves dug one year before; more than eight thousand at Spotsylvania; and twelve thousand in the space of a few hours at Cold Harbor.

Before the assault at Cold Harbor (which Grant later admitted was a grave mistake), Union troops pinned scraps of paper bearing their names and addresses to their backs, certain they would be mowed down as they rushed Lee's trenches. In four weeks in May and June, Grant lost as many men as were enrolled in Lee's entire army. From early May until July, when Union forces had marched and fought all the way from forests west of Fredericksburg to Petersburg, south of Richmond, which they besieged, the two armies engaged each other nearly every day. The war had reached a horribly modern scale. Wagon trains carrying thousands of Union wounded crawled back toward Washington. "It was as if war," wrote historian Bruce Catton, "the great clumsy machine for maiming people, had at last been perfected. Instead of turning out its grist spasmodically, with long waits between each delivery, it was at last able to produce every day, without any gaps at all."

Undaunted, Grant kept up the pressure, saying, "I propose to fight it out along this line if it takes all summer." Although costly, and testing northern morale to its limits, these battles prepared the way for eventual victory: Lee's army shrank until offensive action was no longer possible, while Grant's army kept replenishing its forces with new recruits. The siege of Petersburg, with the armies facing each other in miles of trenches, lasted throughout the winter of 1864–1865.

Surrender at Appomattox

The end finally came in the spring of 1865. Grant kept battering Lee, who tried but failed to break through the Union line. With the numerical superiority of Grant's army now greater than two to one, Confederate defeat was inevitable. On April 2, Lee abandoned Richmond and Petersburg. On April 9, hemmed in by Union troops, short of rations, and with fewer than thirty thousand men left, he surrendered at Appomattox Court House. Grant treated his rival with respect and paroled the defeated troops, allowing cavalrymen to keep their horses and take them home. The war was over at last. Within weeks, Confederate forces under Johnston surrendered to Sherman in North Carolina, and Davis, who had fled Richmond but wanted the war to continue, was captured in Georgia. The North rejoiced, and most southerners fell into despair, expecting waves of punishment. In the profound relief and stillness of the surrender field at Appomattox, no one could know the harrowing tasks of healing and justice that lay ahead.

With Lee's surrender, Lincoln knew that the Union had been preserved, yet he lived to see but a few days of war's aftermath. On the evening of Good Friday, April 14, he accompanied his wife to Ford's Theatre in Washington to enjoy a popular comedy. There John Wilkes Booth, an embittered southern sympathizer, shot the president in the head at point-blank range. Lincoln died the next day. Twelve days later, troops tracked down and killed Booth. The Union had lost its wartime leader, and millions publicly mourned the martyred chief executive along the route of the funeral train that took his body home to Illinois. Relief at the war's end mingled hauntingly with a renewed sense of loss and anxiety about the future. Millions never forgot where they were and how they felt at the news of Lincoln's assassination.

Financial Tally   Property damage and financial costs were enormous, though difficult to tally. U.S. loans and taxes during the conflict totaled almost $3 billion, and interest on the war debt was $2.8 billion. The Confederacy borrowed over $2 billion but lost far more in the destruction of homes, crops, livestock, and other property. In southern war zones the landscape was desolated. Over wide regions fences and crops were destroyed; houses, barns, and bridges burned; and fields abandoned and left to erode. Union troops had looted factories and put two-thirds of the South's railroad system out of service.

Estimates of the total cost of the war exceed $20 billion—five times the total expenditures of the federal government from its creation until 1861. By 1865 the federal government's spending had soared to twenty times the prewar level and accounted for over 26 percent of the gross national product. Many of these changes were more or less permanent, as wartime measures left the government more deeply involved in manufacturing, banking, and transportation. If southerners had hoped to remove government from the economy, the war had now irrevocably bound them together.

Death Toll   The human costs of the Civil War were especially staggering. The total number of military casualties on both sides exceeded 1 million—a frightful toll for a nation of 31 million people. Approximately 360,000 Union soldiers died, 110,000 of them from wounds suffered in battle. Another 275,175 Union soldiers were wounded but survived. On the Confederate side, an estimated 260,000 lost their lives, and almost as many suffered wounds. More men died in the Civil War than in all other American wars combined until Vietnam. Of an estimated 194,743 northerners in southern prisons, 30,218 died; of 214,865 southerners in northern prisons, 25,976 died. The prison story from the war was one in which neither side could claim pride, and it caused embittered debate for decades over mutual accusations of willful starvation and brutal treatment.

These unprecedented losses (approximately 620,000 total dead) flowed from fundamental strife over the nature of the Union and the liberty of black people. Both sides

The death of President Lincoln caused a vast outpouring of grief in the North. As this Currier & Ives print shows, his funeral train stopped at several cities on its way to Illinois, to allow local services to be held. (Anne S. K. Brown Military Collection, John Hay Library, Brown University)

saw vital interests in the struggle. As Julia Ward Howe wrote in her famous "Battle Hymn," they had heard "the trumpet that shall never call retreat." And so the war took its horrifying course.

SUMMARY

The Civil War altered American society forever. The first great legacy of the war in the lives of its survivors was, therefore, death itself. Although precise figures on enlistments are unavailable, it appears that 700,000 to 800,000 men served in the Confederate armies. Far more, possibly 2.3 million, served in the Union armies. All of these men were taken from home, family, and personal goals; their lives, if they survived, were disrupted in ways that were never repaired. During the war, in both North and South, women, too, took on new roles as they struggled to manage the hardships of the home front, to grieve, and to support the war effort.

Industrialization and economic enterprises grew exponentially in tandem with the war. Ordinary citizens found that their futures were increasingly tied to huge organizations. The character and extent of government power, too, changed markedly. Under Republican leadership, the federal government expanded its power not only to preserve the Union but also to extend freedom. A social revolution and government authority emancipated the slaves, and Lincoln called for "a new birth of freedom" in America. A republic desperately divided against itself had survived, but in new constitutional forms yet to take shape during Reconstruction.

It was unclear at the end of the war how or whether the nation would use its power to protect the rights of the former slaves. Secession was dead, but whether Americans would continue to embrace a centralized nationalism remained to be seen. The war ended decisively after tremendous sacrifice, but it left many unanswered questions: How would white southerners, embittered and impoverished, respond to efforts to reconstruct the nation? How would the country care for the maimed, the orphans, the farming women without men to work their land, and all the dead who had to be found and properly buried? What would be the place of black men and women in American life?

In the West, two civil wars had raged: one between Union and Confederate forces, and the other resulting in a conquest of southwestern Indians by U.S. troops and land-hungry settlers. On the diplomatic front, the Union government had delicately managed to keep Great Britain and other foreign powers out of the war. Dissent flourished in both North and South, playing a crucial role in the ultimate collapse of the Confederacy, and the Union cause was only marginally affected by sabotage and draft riots.

In the Civil War Americans had undergone an epic of destruction and survival—a transformation like nothing else in their history. White southerners had experienced defeat that few other Americans had ever faced. Blacks were moving proudly but anxiously from slavery to freedom. White northerners were, by and large, self-conscious victors in a massive war for the nation's existence and for new definitions of freedom. The war, with all of its drama, sacrifice, and social and political change, would leave a compelling memory in American hearts and minds for generations.

16

Reconstruction:
An Unfinished Revolution:
1865–1877

WARTIME RECONSTRUCTION

Civil wars leave immense challenges of healing, justice, and physical rebuilding. Anticipating that process, reconstruction of the Union was an issue as early as 1863, well before the war ended. Many key questions loomed on the horizon when and if the North succeeded on the battlefield: How would the nation be restored? How would southern states and leaders be treated—as errant brothers or as traitors? What was the constitutional basis for readmission of states to the Union, and where, if anywhere, could American statesmen look for precedence or guidance? More specifically, four vexing problems compelled early thinking and would haunt the Reconstruction era throughout. One, who would rule in the South once it was defeated? Two, who would rule in the federal government—Congress or the president? Three, what were the dimensions of black freedom, and what rights under law would the freedmen enjoy? And four, would Reconstruction be a preservation of the old republic or a second Revolution, a reinvention of a new republic?

**Lincoln's
10 Percent Plan** Abraham Lincoln had never been anti-southern, though he had become the leader of an antislavery war. He lost three brothers-in-law, killed in the war on the Confederate side. His worst fear was that the war would collapse at the end into guerrilla warfare across the South, with surviving bands of Confederates carrying on resistance. Lincoln insisted that his generals give lenient terms to southern soldiers once they surrendered. In his Second Inaugural

Address, delivered only a month before his assassination, Lincoln promised "malice toward none; with charity for all," as Americans strove to "bind up the nation's wounds."

Lincoln planned early for a swift and moderate Reconstruction process. In his "Proclamation of Amnesty and Reconstruction," issued in December 1863, he proposed to replace majority rule with "loyal rule" as a means of reconstructing southern state governments. He proposed pardons to all ex-Confederates except the highest-ranking military and civilian officers. Then, as soon as 10 percent of the voting population in the 1860 general election in a given state had taken an oath to the United States and established a government, the new state would be recognized. Lincoln did not consult Congress in these plans, and "loyal" assemblies (known as "Lincoln governments") were created in Louisiana, Tennessee, and Arkansas in 1864, states largely occupied by Union troops. These governments were weak and dependent on northern armies for survival.

Congress and the Wade-Davis Bill Congress responded with great hostility to Lincoln's moves to readmit southern states in what seemed such a premature manner. Many Radical Republicans, strong proponents of emancipation and of aggressive prosecution of the war against the South, considered the 10 percent plan a "mere mockery" of democracy. Led by Thaddeus Stevens of Pennsylvania in the House and Charles Sumner of Massachusetts in the Senate, congressional Republicans locked horns with Lincoln and proposed a longer and harsher approach to Reconstruction. Stevens advocated a "conquered provinces" theory, arguing that southerners had organized as a foreign nation to make war on the United States and, by secession, had destroyed their status as states. They therefore must be treated as "conquered foreign lands" and returned to the status of "unorganized territories" before any process of readmission could be entertained by Congress.

In July 1864, the Wade-Davis bill, named for its sponsors, Senator Benjamin Wade of Ohio and Congressman Henry W. Davis of Maryland, emerged from Congress with three specific conditions for southern readmission.

1. It demanded a "majority" of white male citizens participating in the creation of a new government.
2. To vote or be a delegate to constitutional conventions, men had to take an "iron-clad" oath (declaring that they had never aided the Confederate war effort).
3. All officers above the rank of lieutenant, and all civil officials in the Confederacy, would be disfranchised and deemed "not a citizen of the United States."

The Confederate states were to be defined as "conquered enemies," said Davis, and the process of readmission was to be harsh and slow. Lincoln, ever the adroit politician, pocket-vetoed the bill and issued a conciliatory proclamation of his own, announcing that he would not be inflexibly committed to any "one plan" of Reconstruction.

This exchange came during Grant's bloody campaign against Lee in Virginia, when the outcome of the war and Lincoln's reelection were still in doubt. On August 5, Radical Republicans issued the "Wade-Davis Manifesto" to newspapers. An unprecedented attack on a sitting president by members of his own party, it accused Lincoln of usurpation of presidential powers and disgraceful leniency toward an eventually conquered South. What emerged in 1864–1865 was a clear debate and a potential constitutional crisis. Lincoln saw Reconstruction as a means of weakening the Confederacy and winning the war; the Radicals saw it as a longer-term transformation of the political and racial order of the country.

CHRONOLOGY

1865 • Johnson begins rapid and lenient Reconstruction
  • White southern governments pass restrictive black codes
  • Congress refuses to seat southern representatives
  • Thirteenth Amendment ratified, abolishing slavery

1866 • Congress passes Civil Rights Act and renewal of Freedmen's Bureau over Johnson's veto
  • Congress approves Fourteenth Amendment
  • In *Ex parte Milligan* the Supreme Court reasserts its influence

1867 • Congress passes First Reconstruction Act and Tenure of Office Act
  • Constitutional conventions called in southern states

1868 • House impeaches and Senate acquits Johnson
  • Most southern states readmitted to Union under Radical plan
  • Fourteenth Amendment ratified
  • Grant elected president

1869 • Congress approves Fifteenth Amendment (ratified in 1870)

1871 • Congress passes second Enforcement Act and Ku Klux Klan Act
  • Treaty with England settles *Alabama* claims

1872 • Amnesty Act frees almost all remaining Confederates from restrictions on holding office
  • Grant reelected

1873 • *Slaughter-House* cases limit power of Fourteenth Amendment
  • Panic of 1873 leads to widespread unemployment and labor strife

1874 • Democrats win majority in House of Representatives

1875 • Several Grant appointees indicted for corruption
  • Congress passes weak Civil Rights Act
  • Democratic Party increases control of southern states with white supremacy campaigns

1876 • *U.S. v. Cruikshank* further weakens Fourteenth Amendment
  • Presidential election disputed

1877 • Congress elects Hayes president

Thirteenth Amendment

In early 1865, Congress and Lincoln joined in two important measures that recognized slavery's centrality to the war. On January 31, with strong administration backing, Congress passed the Thirteenth Amendment, which had two provisions: first, it abolished involuntary servitude everywhere in the United States; second, it declared that Congress shall have the power to enforce this outcome by "appropriate legislation." When the measure passed by 119 to 56, a mere 2 votes more than the necessary two-thirds, rejoicing broke out in Congress. A Republican recorded in his diary, "Members joined in the shouting and kept it up for some minutes. Some embraced one another, others wept like children. I have felt ever since the vote, as if I were in a new country."

But the Thirteenth Amendment had emerged from a long congressional debate and considerable petitioning and public advocacy. One of the first and most remarkable petitions for a constitutional amendment abolishing slavery was submitted early in 1864 by Elizabeth Cady Stanton, Susan B. Anthony, and the Women's Loyal National League. Women throughout the Union accumulated thousands of signatures, even venturing into staunchly pro-Confederate regions of Kentucky and Missouri to secure supporters. It was a long road from the Emancipation Proclamation to the Thirteenth Amendment— through treacherous constitutional theory about individual "property rights," a bedrock of belief that the sacred document ought never to be altered, and partisan politics. But the logic of winning the war by crushing slavery, and of securing a new beginning under law for the nation that so many had died to save, won the day.

Freedmen's Bureau　Potentially as significant, on March 3, 1865, Congress created the Bureau of Refugees, Freedmen, and Abandoned Lands—the Freedmen's Bureau, an unprecedented agency of social uplift necessitated by the ravages of the war. Americans had never engaged in federal aid to citizens on such a scale. With thousands of refugees, white and black, displaced in the South, the government continued what private freedmen's aid societies had started as early as 1862. In the mere four years of its existence, the Freedmen's Bureau supplied food and medical services, built several thousand schools and some colleges, negotiated several hundred thousand employment contracts between freedmen and their former masters, and tried to manage confiscated land.

The Bureau would be a controversial aspect of Reconstruction—within the South, where whites generally hated it, and within the federal government, where politicians divided over its constitutionality. Some Bureau agents were devoted to freedmen's rights, whereas others were opportunists who exploited the chaos of the postwar South. The war had forced into the open an eternal question of republics: what are the social welfare obligations of the state toward its people, and what do people owe their governments in return? Apart from their conquest and displacement of the eastern Indians, Americans were relatively inexperienced at the Freedmen's Bureau's task—social reform through military occupation.

Ruins and Enmity　In 1865, due to the devastation of the war, America was now a land with ruins. Like the countries of Europe, it now seemed an older, more historic landscape. It had torn itself asunder—physically, politically, spiritually. Some of its cities lay in rubble, large stretches of the southern countryside were depopulated and defoliated, and thousands of people, white and black, were refugees. Some of this would in time seem romantic to northern travelers in the post-war South.

Thousands of yeoman farmer-soldiers, some paroled by surrenders and others who had abandoned Confederate ranks earlier, walked home too late in the season to plant a crop in a collapsed economy. Many white refugees faced genuine starvation. Of the approximately 18,300,000 rations distributed across the South in the first three years of the Freedmen's Bureau, 5,230,000 went to whites. In early 1866, in a proud agricultural society, the legislature of South Carolina issued $300,000 in state bonds to purchase corn for the destitute.

In October 1865, just after a five-month imprisonment in Boston, former Confederate Vice President Alexander H. Stephens rode a slow train southward. In Virginia he found "the desolation of the country . . . was horrible to behold." When Stephens reached northern Georgia, his native state, his shock ran over: "War has left a terrible impression. . . . Fences gone, fields all a-waste, houses burnt." A northern journalist visiting Richmond that same fall observed a city "mourning for her sins . . . in dust and ashes." The "burnt district" was a "bed of cinders . . . broken and blackened walls, impassable streets deluged with debris." Above all, every northern traveler encountered a wall of hatred among white southerners for their conquerors. An innkeeper in North Carolina told a journalist that Yankees had killed his sons in the war, burned his house, and stolen his slaves. "They left me one inestimable privilege," he said, "to hate 'em. I git up at half-past four in the morning, and sit up 'til twelve at night, to hate 'em."

THE MEANINGS OF FREEDOM

Black southerners entered into life after slavery with hope and circumspection. A Texas man recalled his father's telling him, even before the war was over, "Our forever was going to be spent living among the Southerners, after they got licked." Freed men and women tried to gain as much as they could from their new circumstances. Often the changes they valued the most were personal—alterations in location, employer, or living arrangements.

The Feel of Freedom   For America's former slaves, Reconstruction had one paramount meaning: a chance to explore freedom. A southern white woman admitted in her diary that the black people "showed a natural and exultant joy at being free." Former slaves remembered singing far into the night after federal troops, who confirmed rumors of their emancipation, reached their plantations. The slaves on a Texas plantation shouted for joy, their leader proclaiming, "We is free—no more whippings and beatings." A few people gave in to the natural desire to do what had been impossible before. One angry grandmother dropped her hoe and ran to confront her mistress. "I'm free!" she yelled. "Yes, I'm free! Ain't got to work for you no more! You can't put me in your pocket now!" Another man recalled that he and others "started on the move," either to search for family members or just to exercise the human right of mobility.

Many freed men and women reacted more cautiously and shrewdly, taking care to test the boundaries of their new condition. "After the war was over," explained one man, "we was afraid to move. Just like terrapins or turtles after emancipation. Just stick our heads out to see how the land lay." As slaves they had learned to expect hostility from white people, and they did not presume it would instantly disappear. Life in freedom might still be a matter of what was possible, not what was right. Many freedpeople evaluated potential employers with shrewd caution. "Most all the Negroes that had good owners stayed with 'em, but the others left. Some of 'em come back and some didn't," explained one man. After considerable wandering in search of better circumstances, a majority of blacks eventually settled as agricultural workers back on their former farms or plantations. But they relocated their houses and did their utmost to control the conditions of their labor.

Reunion of African American Families Throughout the South, former slaves devoted themselves to reuniting their families, separated during slavery by sale or hardship, and during the war by dislocation and the emancipation process. With only shreds of information to guide them, thousands of freedpeople embarked on odysseys in search of a husband, wife, child, or parent. By relying on the black community for help and information, and by placing ads that continued to appear in black newspapers well into the 1880s, some succeeded in their quest, while others searched in vain.

Husbands and wives who had belonged to different masters established homes together for the first time, and, as they had tried under slavery, parents asserted the right to raise their own children. A mother bristled when her old master claimed a right to whip her children. She informed him that "he warn't goin' to brush none of her chilluns no more." The freed men and women were too much at risk to act recklessly, but, as one man put it, they were tired of punishment and "sure didn't take no more foolishment off of white folks."

Blacks' Search for Independence Many black people wanted to minimize contact with whites because, as Reverend Garrison Frazier told General Sherman in January 1865, "There is a prejudice against us . . . that will take years to get over." To avoid contact with overbearing whites who were used to supervising them, blacks abandoned the slave quarters and fanned out to distant corners of the land they worked. "After the war my stepfather come," recalled Annie Young, "and got my mother and we moved out in the piney woods." Others described moving "across the creek" or building a "saplin house . . . back in the woods." Some rural dwellers established small, all-black settlements that still exist along the back roads of the South.

Even once-privileged slaves desired such independence and social separation. One man turned down his master's offer of the overseer's house and moved instead to a shack in "Freetown." He also declined to let the former owner grind his grain for free because it "make him feel like a free man to pay for things just like anyone else."

The Armed Slave, *William Sprang, oil on canvas, c. 1865. This remarkable painting depicts an African American veteran soldier, musket with fixed bayonet leaning against the wall, cigar in hand indicating a new life of safety and leisure, reading a book to demonstrate his embrace of education and freedom. The man's visage leaves the impression of satisfaction and dignity.* (The Civil War Library and Museum, Philadelphia)

Freedpeople's Desire for Land

In addition to a fair employer, what freed men and women most wanted was the ownership of land. Land represented self-sufficiency and a chance to gain compensation for generations of bondage. General Sherman's special Field Order Number 15, issued in February 1865, set aside 400,000 acres of land in the Sea Islands region for the exclusive settlement of freedpeople. Hope swelled among ex-slaves as forty-acre plots, mules, and "possessary titles" were promised to them. But President Johnson ordered them removed in October and the land returned to its original owners under army enforcement. A northern observer noted that slaves freed in the Sea Islands of South Carolina and Georgia made "plain, straight-forward" inquiries as they settled on new land. They wanted to be sure the land "would be theirs after they had improved it." Everywhere, blacks young and old thirsted for homes of their own.

But most members of both political parties opposed genuine land redistribution to the freedmen. Even northern reformers who had administered the Sea Islands during the war showed little sympathy for black aspirations. The former Sea Island slaves wanted to establish small, self-sufficient farms. Northern soldiers, officials, and missionaries of both races brought education and aid to the freedmen but also insisted that they grow cotton. They emphasized profit, cash crops, and the values of competitive capitalism.

"The Yankees preach nothing but cotton, cotton!" complained one Sea Island black. "We wants land," wrote another, but tax officials "make the lots too big, and cut we out." Indeed, the U.S. government eventually sold thousands of acres in the Sea Islands, 90 percent of which went to wealthy investors from the North. At a protest against evictions from a contraband camp in Virginia in 1866, freedman Bayley Wyatt made black desires and claims clear: "We has a right to the land where we are located. For why? I tell you. Our wives, our children, our husbands, has been sold over and over again to purchase the lands we now locates upon; for that reason we have a divine right to the land."

Black Embrace of Education

Ex-slaves everywhere reached out for education. Blacks of all ages hungered for the knowledge in books that had been permitted only to whites. With freedom, they started schools and filled classrooms both day and night. On log seats and dirt floors, freed men and women studied their letters in old almanacs and in discarded dictionaries. Young children brought infants to school with them, and adults attended at night or after "the crops were laid by." Many a teacher had "to make herself heard over three other classes reciting in concert" in a small room. The desire to escape slavery's ignorance was so great that, despite their poverty, many blacks paid tuition, typically $1 or $1.50 a month. These small amounts constituted major portions of a person's agricultural wages and added up to more than $1 million by 1870.

The federal government and northern reformers of both races assisted this pursuit of education. In its brief life the Freedmen's Bureau founded over four thousand schools, and idealistic men and women from the North established others funded by private northern philanthropy. The Yankee schoolmarm—dedicated, selfless, and religious—became an agent of progress in many southern communities. Thus did African Americans seek a break from their past through learning. More than 600,000 were enrolled in elementary school by 1877.

Blacks and their white allies also saw the need for colleges and universities to train teachers, ministers, and professionals for leadership. The American Missionary Association founded seven colleges, including Fisk and Atlanta Universities, between 1866 and 1869. The Freedmen's Bureau helped to establish Howard University in Washington, D.C., and northern religious groups, such as the Methodists, Baptists, and Congregationalists, supported dozens of seminaries and teachers' colleges.

During Reconstruction, African American leaders often were highly educated individuals; many were from the prewar elite of free people of color. Francis Cardozo, who held various offices in South Carolina, had attended universities in Scotland and England. P. B. S. Pinchback, who became lieutenant governor of Louisiana, was the son of a planter who had sent him to school in Cincinnati. Both of the two black senators from Mississippi, Blanche K. Bruce and Hiram Revels, possessed privileged educations. Bruce was the son of a planter who had provided tutoring at home; Revels was the son of free North Carolina blacks who had sent him to Knox College in Illinois. These men and many self-educated former slaves brought to political office not only fervor but education.

Growth of Black Churches

Freed from the restrictions and regulations of slavery, blacks could build their own institutions as they saw fit. The secret churches of slavery came into the open; in countless communities throughout the South, ex-slaves "started a brush arbor." A brush arbor was merely "a sort of . . . shelter with leaves for a roof," but the freed men and women worshiped in it enthusiastically. "Preachin' and shouting sometimes lasted all day," they recalled, for the opportunity to worship together freely meant "glorious times."

Within a few years, independent branches of the Methodist and Baptist denominations had attracted the great majority of black Christians in the South. By 1877 in South Carolina alone, the African Methodist Episcopal (A.M.E.) Church had 1,000 ministers, 44,000 members, and its own school of theology, while the A.M.E. Zion Church had 45,000 members. In the rapid growth of churches, some of which became the wealthiest and most autonomous institutions in black life, the freedpeople demonstrated their most secure claim on freedom and created enduring communities.

Rise of the Sharecropping System

The desire to gain as much independence as possible also shaped the former slaves' economic arrangements. Since most of them lacked money to buy land, they preferred the next best thing: renting the land they worked. But the South had a cash-poor economy with few sources of credit, and few whites would consider renting land to blacks. Most blacks had no means to get cash before the harvest, so other alternatives had to be tried.

Black farmers and white landowners therefore turned to sharecropping, a system in which farmers kept part of their crop and gave the rest to the landowner while living on his property. The landlord or a merchant "furnished" food and supplies, such as draft animals and seed, needed before the harvest, and he received payment from the crop. Although landowners tried to set the laborers' share at a low level, black farmers had some bargaining power, at least at first. Sharecroppers would hold out, or move and try to switch employers from one year to another. As the system matured during the 1870s and 1880s, most sharecroppers worked "on halves"—half for the owner and half for themselves.

The sharecropping system, which materialized as early as 1868 in parts of the South, originated as a desirable compromise between former slaves and white landowners. It eased landowners' problems with cash and credit, and provided them a permanent, dependent labor force; blacks accepted it because it gave them freedom from daily supervision. Instead of working in the hated gangs under a white overseer, as in slavery, they farmed their own plots of land in family groups. But sharecropping later proved to be a disaster. Owners and merchants developed a monopoly of control over the agricultural economy, as sharecroppers found themselves riveted in ever-increasing debt.

The fundamental problem, however, was that southern farmers as a whole still concentrated on cotton. In freedom, black women often chose to stay away from the fields and cotton picking, to concentrate on domestic chores. Given the diminishing incentives of the system, they placed greater value on independent choices about gender roles and family organization than on reaching higher levels of production. By 1878 the South had recovered its prewar share of British cotton purchases. But even as southerners grew more cotton than ever, their reward diminished. Cotton prices began a long decline, as world demand fell off.

Thus southern agriculture slipped deeper and deeper into depression. Black sharecroppers struggled under a growing burden of debt which reduced their independence and bound them to landowners and to furnishing merchants almost as oppressively as slavery had bound them to their masters. Many white farmers became debtors, too; gradually lost their land; and joined the ranks of sharecroppers. By the end of Reconstruction, over one-third of all southern farms were worked by sharecropping tenants, white and black. This economic transformation took place as the nation struggled to put its political house back in order.

JOHNSON'S RECONSTRUCTION PLAN

When Reconstruction began under President Andrew Johnson, many expected his policies to be harsh. Throughout his career in Tennessee he had criticized the wealthy planters and championed the small farmers. When an assassin's bullet thrust Johnson into the presidency, many former slaveowners shared the dismay of a North Carolina woman who wrote, "Think of Andy Johnson [as] the president! What will become of us—'the aristocrats of the South' as we are termed?" Northern Radicals also had reason to believe that Johnson would deal sternly with the South. When one of them suggested the exile or execution of ten or twelve leading rebels to set an example, Johnson replied, "How are you going to pick out so small a number? . . . Treason is a crime; and crime must be punished."

Andrew Johnson of Tennessee Like his martyred predecessor, Johnson followed a path in antebellum politics from obscurity to power. With no formal education, he became a tailor's apprentice. But from 1829, while in his early twenties, he held nearly every office in Tennessee politics: alderman, state representative, congressman, two terms as governor, and U.S. senator by 1857. Although elected as a southern Democrat, Johnson was the only senator from a seceded state who refused to follow his state out of the Union. Lincoln appointed him war governor of Tennessee in 1862; hence his symbolic place on the ticket in the president's bid for reelection in 1864.

Although a Unionist, Johnson's political beliefs made him an old Jacksonian Democrat. And, as they said in the mountainous region of east Tennessee, where Johnson

established a reputation as a stump speaker, "Old Andy never went back on his 'raisin'."
Johnson was also an ardent states' rightist. Before the war, he had supported tax-funded
public schools and homestead legislation, fashioning himself as a champion of the
common man. Although he vehemently opposed secession, Johnson advocated limited
government. He shared none of the Radicals' expansive conception of federal power.
His philosophy toward Reconstruction may be summed up in the slogan he adopted:
"The Constitution as it is, and the Union as it was."

Through 1865 Johnson alone controlled Reconstruction policy, for Congress
recessed shortly before he became president and did not reconvene until December. In
the following eight months, Johnson formed new state governments in the South by
using his power to grant pardons. He advanced Lincoln's leniency by extending even
easier terms to former Confederates.

Johnson's Racial Views

Johnson had owned house slaves, although he had never been
a planter. He accepted emancipation as a result of the war, but
he did not favor black civil and political rights. Johnson
believed that black suffrage could never be imposed on a southern state by the federal
government, and that set him on a collision course with the Radicals. When it came to
race, Johnson was a thoroughgoing white supremacist. He held what one politician
called "unconquerable prejudices against the African race." In perhaps the most bla-
tantly racist official statement ever delivered by an American president, Johnson
declared in his annual message of 1867 that blacks possessed less "capacity for government than any other race of people. No independent government of any form has ever
been successful in their hands; . . . wherever they have been left to their own devices they
have shown a constant tendency to relapse into barbarism."

Such racial views had an enduring effect on Johnson's policies. Where whites were
concerned, however, Johnson seemed to be pursuing changes in class relations. He proposed rules that would keep the wealthy planter class at least temporarily out of power.

Johnson's Pardon Policy

White southerners were required to swear an oath of loyalty
as a condition of gaining amnesty or pardon, but Johnson
barred several categories of people from taking the oath: for-
mer federal officials, high-ranking Confederate officers, and political leaders or grad-
uates of West Point or Annapolis who joined the Confederacy. To this list Johnson
added another important group: all ex-Confederates whose taxable property was
worth more than $20,000. These individuals had to apply personally to the president
for pardon and restoration of their political rights. The president, it seemed, meant to
take revenge on the old planter elite and thereby promote a new leadership of deserv-
ing yeomen.

Johnson appointed provisional governors, who began the Reconstruction process
by calling state constitutional conventions. The delegates chosen for these conventions
had to draft new constitutions that eliminated slavery and invalidated secession. After
ratification of these constitutions, new governments could be elected, and the states
would be restored to the Union with full congressional representation. But only those
southerners who had taken the oath of amnesty and had been eligible to vote on the
day the state seceded could participate in this process. Thus unpardoned whites and
former slaves were not eligible.

Presidential Reconstruction   If Johnson intended to strip former aristocrats of their power, he did not hold to his plan. The old white leadership proved resilient and influential; prominent Confederates won elections and turned up in various appointive offices. Then Johnson started pardoning planters and leading rebels. He hired additional clerks to prepare the necessary documents and then began to issue pardons to large categories of people. By September 1865, hundreds were being issued in a single day. These pardons, plus the rapid return of planters' abandoned lands, restored the old elite to power and quickly gave Johnson an image as the South's champion.

Why did Johnson allow the planters to regain power? Personal vanity may have played a role, as he turned proud planters into pardon seekers. He was also determined to achieve a rapid Reconstruction in order to deny the Radicals any opportunity for the more thorough racial and political changes they desired in the South. And Johnson needed southern support in the 1866 elections; hence, he declared Reconstruction complete only eight months after Appomattox. Thus, in December 1865, many Confederate congressmen traveled to Washington to claim seats in the U.S. Congress. Even Alexander Stephens, vice president of the Confederacy, returned to Capitol Hill as a senator-elect from Georgia.

The election of such prominent rebels troubled many northerners. Some of the state conventions were slow to repudiate secession; others admitted only grudgingly that slavery was dead and wrote new laws to show it.

Black Codes   Furthermore, to define the status of freed men and women and control their labor, some legislatures merely revised large sections of the slave codes by substituting the word *freedmen* for *slaves*. The new black codes compelled former slaves to carry passes, observe a curfew, live in housing provided by a landowner, and give up hope of entering many desirable occupations. Stiff vagrancy laws and restrictive labor contracts bound freedpeople to plantations, and "anti-enticement" laws punished anyone who tried to lure these workers to other employment. State-supported schools and orphanages excluded blacks entirely.

It seemed to northerners that the South was intent on returning African Americans to servility and that Johnson's Reconstruction policy held no one responsible for the terrible war. But memories of the war—not yet even a year over—were still raw and would dominate political behavior for several elections to come. Thus the Republican majority in Congress decided to call a halt to the results of Johnson's plan. On reconvening, the House and Senate considered the credentials of the newly elected southern representatives and decided not to admit them. Instead, they bluntly challenged the president's authority and established a joint committee to study and investigate a new direction for Reconstruction.

THE CONGRESSIONAL RECONSTRUCTION PLAN

Northern congressmen were hardly unified, but they did not doubt their right to shape Reconstruction policy. The Constitution mentioned neither secession nor reunion, but it gave Congress the primary role in the admission of states. Moreover, the Constitution declared that the United States shall guarantee to each state a "republican form of government." This provision, legislators believed, gave them the authority to devise policies for Reconstruction.

The Memphis race riots during Reconstruction. Unarmed blacks are gunned down by well-armed whites in this scene, reinforced by a Congressional investigation. (Library of Congress)

They soon found that other constitutional questions affected their policies. What, for example, had rebellion done to the relationship between southern states and the Union? Lincoln had always believed secession impossible—the Confederate states had engaged in an "insurrection" within the Union in his view. Congressmen who favored vigorous Reconstruction measures argued that the war had broken the Union and that the South was subject to the victor's will. Moderate congressmen held that the states had forfeited their rights through rebellion and thus had come under congressional supervision.

The Radicals

These theories mirrored the diversity of Congress itself. Northern Democrats, weakened by their opposition to the war in its final year, denounced any idea of racial equality and supported Johnson's policies. Conservative Republicans, despite their party loyalty, favored a limited federal role in Reconstruction. The Radical Republicans, led by Thaddeus Stevens, Charles Sumner, and George Julian, wanted to transform the South. Although a minority in their party, they had the advantage of clearly defined goals. They believed it was essential to democratize the South, establish public education, and ensure the rights of the freedpeople. They favored black suffrage, supported some land confiscation and redistribution, and were willing to exclude the South from the Union for several years if necessary to achieve their goals.

Born of the war and its outcome, the Radicals brought a new civic vision to American life; they wanted to create an activist federal government and the beginnings of racial equality. A large group of moderate Republicans, led by Lyman Trumbull, opposed Johnson's leniency but wanted to restrain the Radicals. Trumbull and the moderates were, however, committed to federalizing the enforcement of civil, if not political, rights for the freedmen.

One overwhelming political reality faced all four groups: the 1866 elections. Ironically, Johnson and the Democrats sabotaged the possibility of a conservative coalition. They refused to cooperate with conservative or moderate Republicans and insisted that Reconstruction was over, that the new state governments were legitimate, and that southern representatives should be admitted to Congress. Among the Republicans, the Radicals' influence grew in proportion to Johnson's intransigence and outright provocation.

Congress Versus Johnson

Trying to work with Johnson, Republicans believed a compromise had been reached in the spring of 1866. Under its terms Johnson would agree to two modifications of his program: extension of the Freedmen's Bureau for another year and passage of a civil rights bill to counteract the black codes. This bill would force southern courts to practice equality under the ultimate scrutiny of the federal judiciary. Its provisions applied to public, not private, acts of discrimination. The Civil Rights Bill of 1866 was the first statutory definition of the rights of American citizens and is still on the books today.

Johnson destroyed the compromise, however, by vetoing both bills (they later became law when Congress overrode the president's veto). Denouncing any change in his program, the president condemned Congress's action and revealed his own racism. Because the civil rights bill defined U.S. citizens as native-born persons who were taxed, Johnson claimed that it discriminated against "large numbers of intelligent, worthy, and patriotic foreigners . . . in favor of the negro." The bill, he said, operated "in favor of the colored and against the white race."

All hope of presidential-congressional cooperation was now dead. In 1866 newspapers reported daily violations of blacks' rights in the South and carried alarming accounts of antiblack violence—notably in Memphis and New Orleans, where police aided brutal mobs in their attacks. In Memphis, forty blacks were killed and twelve schools burned by white mobs, and in New Orleans, the toll was thirty-four African Americans dead and two hundred wounded. Such violence convinced Republicans, and the northern public, that more needed to be done. A new Republican plan took the form of the Fourteenth Amendment to the Constitution.

Fourteenth Amendment

Of the five sections of the Fourteenth Amendment, the first would have the greatest legal significance in later years. It conferred citizenship on "all persons born or naturalized in the United States" and prohibited states from abridging their constitutional "privileges and immunities" (see the Appendix for the Constitution and all amendments). It also barred any state from taking a person's life, liberty, or property "without due process of law" and from denying "equal protection of the laws." These resounding phrases have become powerful guarantees of African Americans' civil rights—indeed, of the rights of all citizens, except for Indians, who were not granted citizenship rights until 1924.

Nearly universal agreement emerged among Republicans on the amendment's second and third sections. The fourth declared the Confederate debt null and void, and guaranteed the war debt of the United States. Northerners rejected the notion of paying taxes to reimburse those who had financed a rebellion, and business groups agreed on the necessity of upholding the credit of the U.S. government. The second and third sections barred Confederate leaders from holding state and federal office. Only Congress, by a two-thirds vote of each house, could remove the penalty. The amendment thus guaranteed a degree of punishment for the leaders of the Confederacy.

The second section of the amendment also dealt with representation and embodied the compromises that produced the document. Northerners disagreed about whether blacks should have the right to vote. As a citizen of Indiana wrote to a southern relative, "Although there is a great deal [of] profession among us for the relief of the darkey yet I think much of it is far from being cincere. I guess we want to compel you to do right by them while we are not willing ourselves to do so." Those arched words are indicative not only of how revolutionary Reconstruction had become, but also of how far the public will, North and South, lagged behind the enactments that became new constitutional cornerstones. Many northern states still maintained black disfranchisement laws during Reconstruction.

Emancipation finally ended the three-fifths clause for the purpose of counting blacks, which would increase southern representation. Thus the postwar South stood to gain power in Congress, and if white southerners did not allow blacks to vote, former secessionists would derive the political benefit from emancipation. That was more irony than most northerners could bear. So Republicans determined that, if a southern state did not grant black men the vote, their representation would be reduced proportionally. If they did enfranchise black men, their representation would be increased proportionally. This compromise avoided a direct enactment of black suffrage but would deliver future black southern voters to the Republican Party.

The Fourteenth Amendment specified for the first time that voters were "male" and ignored female citizens, black and white. For this reason it provoked a strong reaction from the women's rights movement. Advocates of women's equality had worked with abolitionists for decades, often subordinating their cause to that of the slaves. During the drafting of the Fourteenth Amendment, however, female activists demanded to be heard. Prominent leaders, such as Elizabeth Cady Stanton and Susan B. Anthony, ended their alliance with abolitionists and fought for women, while others remained committed to the idea that it was "the Negro's hour." Thus the amendment infused new life into the women's rights movement and caused considerable strife among old allies. Many male former abolitionists, white and black, were willing to delay the day of woman suffrage in favor of securing freedmen the right to vote in the South.

The South's and Johnson's Defiance   In 1866, however, the major question in Reconstruction politics was how the public would respond to the congressional initiative. Johnson did his best to block the Fourteenth Amendment in both North and South. Condemning Congress for its refusal to seat southern representatives, the president urged state legislatures in the South to vote against ratification. Every southern legislature except Tennessee's rejected the amendment by a wide margin.

To present his case to northerners, Johnson organized a National Union Convention and took to the stump himself. In an age when active personal campaigning was rare for a president, Johnson boarded a special train for a "swing around the circle" that carried his message into the Northeast, the Midwest, and then back to Washington. In city after city, he criticized the Republicans in a ranting, undignified style. Increasingly, audiences rejected his views, hooting and jeering at him. In this whistle-stop tour, Johnson began to hand out American flags with thirty-six rather than twenty-five stars, declaring the Union already restored. At many towns he likened himself to a "persecuted" Jesus who might now be martyred "upon the cross" for his magnanimity toward the South. And, repeatedly, he labeled the Radicals "traitors" for their efforts to take over Reconstruction.

The elections of 1866 were a resounding victory for Republicans in Congress. Radicals and moderates whom Johnson had denounced won reelection by large margins, and the Republican majority grew to two-thirds of both houses of Congress. The North had spoken clearly: Johnson's official policies of states' rights and white supremacy were prematurely giving the advantage to rebels and traitors. Although the Radicals may have been out ahead of public opinion, most northerners feared Johnson's approach more. Thus Republican congressional leaders won a mandate to pursue their Reconstruction plan.

But Johnson and southern intransigence had brought the plan to an impasse. Nothing could be accomplished as long as the "Johnson governments" existed and the southern electorate remained exclusively white. Republicans resolved to form new state governments in the South and enfranchise the freedmen.

Reconstruction Acts of 1867–1868 After some embittered debate in which Republicans and the remaining Democrats in Congress argued over the meaning and memory of the Civil War itself, the First Reconstruction Act passed in March 1867. This plan, under which the southern states were actually readmitted to the Union, incorporated only a part of the Radical program. Union generals, commanding small garrisons of troops and charged with supervising elections, assumed control in five military districts in the South. Confederate leaders designated in the Fourteenth Amendment were barred from voting until new state constitutions were ratified. The act guaranteed freedmen the right to vote in elections for as well as serve in state constitutional conventions and in subsequent elections. In addition, each southern state was required to ratify the Fourteenth Amendment, to ratify its new constitution by majority vote, and to submit it to Congress for approval.

Thus African Americans gained an opportunity to fight for a better life through the political process, and ex-Confederates were given what they interpreted as a bitter pill to swallow in order to return to the Union. The Second, Third, and Fourth Reconstruction Acts, passed between March 1867 and March 1868, provided the details of operation for voter registration boards, the adoption of constitutions, and the administration of "good faith" oaths on the part of white southerners.

Failure of Land Redistribution In the words of one historian, the Radicals succeeded in "clipping Johnson's wings." But they had hoped Congress could do much more. Thaddeus Stevens, for example, argued that economic opportunity was essential to the freedmen. "If we do not furnish them with homesteads from forfeited and rebel property," Stevens declared, "and hedge them around with protective laws ... we had better left them in bondage." Stevens therefore drew up a plan for extensive confiscation and redistribution of land, but it was never realized.

Racial fears among whites and an American obsession with the sanctity of private property made land redistribution unpopular. Northerners were accustomed to a limited role for government, and the business community staunchly opposed any interference with private-property rights, even for former Confederates. Thus black farmers were forced to seek work in a hostile environment in which landowners opposed their acquisition of land.

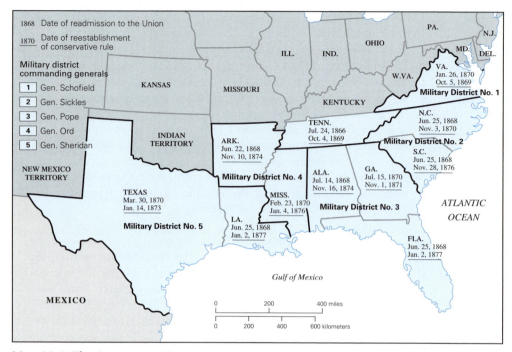

MAP 16.1 The Reconstruction

This map shows the five military districts established when Congress passed the Reconstruction Act of 1867. As the dates within each state indicate, conservative Democratic forces quickly regained control of government in four southern states. So-called Radical Reconstruction was curtailed in most of the others, as factions within the weakened Republican Party began to cooperate with conservative Democrats.

Constitutional Crisis

Congress's quarrels with Andrew Johnson grew still worse. To restrict Johnson's influence and safeguard its plan, Congress passed a number of controversial laws. First, it limited Johnson's power over the army by requiring the president to issue military orders through the General of the Army, Ulysses S. Grant, who could not be dismissed without the Senate's consent. Then Congress passed the Tenure of Office Act, which gave the Senate power to approve changes in the president's cabinet. Designed to protect Secretary of War Stanton, who sympathized with the Radicals, this law violated the tradition that a president controlled appointments to his own cabinet.

All of these measures, as well as each of the Reconstruction Acts, were passed by a two-thirds override of presidential vetoes. The situation led some to believe that the federal government had reached a stage of "congressional tyranny" and others to conclude that Johnson had become an obstacle to the legitimate will of the people in reconstructing the nation on a just and permanent basis.

Johnson took several belligerent steps of his own. He issued orders to military commanders in the South, limiting their powers and increasing the powers of the civil governments he had created in 1865. Then he removed military officers who were conscientiously enforcing Congress's new law, preferring commanders who allowed

TABLE **16.1** **Plans for Reconstruction Compared**

	Johnson's Plan	Radicals' Plan	Fourteenth Amendment	Reconstruction Act of 1867
Voting	Whites only; high-ranking Confederate leaders must seek pardons	Give vote to black males	Southern whites may decide but can lose representation if they deny black suffrage	Black men gain vote; whites barred from office by Fourteenth Amendment cannot vote while new state governments are being formed
Officeholding	Many prominent Confederates regain power	Only loyal white and black males eligible	Confederate leaders barred until Congress votes amnesty	Fourteenth Amendment in effect
Time out of Union	Brief	Several years; until South is thoroughly democratized	Brief	3–5 years after war
Other change in southern society	Little; gain of power by yeomen not realized; emancipation grudgingly accepted, but no black civil or political rights	Expand public education; confiscate land and provide farms for freedmen; expansion of activist federal government	Probably slight, depending on enforcement	Considerable, depending on action of new state governments

disqualified Confederates to vote. Finally, he tried to remove Secretary of War Stanton. With that attempt the confrontation reached its climax.

Impeachment of President Johnson Impeachment is a political procedure provided for in the Constitution as a remedy for crimes or serious abuses of power by presidents, federal judges, and other high government officials. Those who are impeached (judged or politically indicted) in the House are then tried in the Senate. Historically, this power has generally not been used as a means to investigate and judge the private lives of presidents, although in recent times it was used in this manner in the case of President Bill Clinton.

Twice in 1867, the House Judiciary Committee had considered impeachment of Johnson, rejecting the idea once and then recommending it by only a 5-to-4 vote. That recommendation was decisively defeated by the House. After Johnson tried to remove Stanton, however, a third attempt to impeach the president carried easily in early 1868. The indictment concentrated on his violation of the Tenure of Office Act, though many modern scholars regard his efforts to obstruct enforcement of the Reconstruction Act of 1867 as a far more serious offense.

Johnson's trial in the Senate lasted more than three months. The prosecution, led by Radicals, attempted to prove that Johnson was guilty of "high crimes and misdemeanors." But they also argued that the trial was a means to judge Johnson's performance, not a judicial determination of guilt or innocence. The Senate ultimately rejected such reasoning, which could have made removal from office a political weapon against any chief executive who disagreed with Congress. Although a majority of senators voted to convict Johnson, the prosecution fell one vote short of the necessary two-thirds majority. Johnson remained in office, politically weakened and with less than a year left in his term. Some Republicans backed away from impeachment because they had their eyes on the 1868 election and did not want to hurt their prospects of regaining the White House.

Election of 1868 In the 1868 presidential election, Ulysses S. Grant, running as a Republican, defeated Horatio Seymour, a New York Democrat. Grant was not a Radical, but his platform supported congressional Reconstruction and endorsed black suffrage in the South. (Significantly, Republicans stopped short of endorsing black suffrage in the North.) The Democrats, meanwhile, vigorously denounced Reconstruction and preached white supremacy. Indeed, in the 1868 election, the Democrats conducted the most openly racist campaign to that point in American history. Both sides waved the "bloody shirt," accusing each other as the villains of the war's sacrifices. By associating themselves with rebellion and with Johnson's repudiated program, the Democrats went down to defeat in all but eight states, though the popular vote was fairly close. Participating in their first presidential election ever on a wide scale, blacks decisively voted en masse for General Grant.

In office Grant acted as an administrator of Reconstruction but not as its enthusiastic advocate. He vacillated in his dealings with the southern states, sometimes defending Republican regimes and sometimes currying favor with Democrats. On occasion Grant called out federal troops to stop violence or enforce acts of Congress. But he never imposed a true military occupation on the South. Rapid demobilization had reduced a federal army of more than 1 million to 57,000 within a year of the surrender at Appomattox. Thereafter, the number of troops in the South continued to fall, until in 1874 there were only 4,000 in the southern states outside Texas. The later legend of "military rule," so important to southern claims of victimization during Reconstruction, was steeped in myth.

Fifteenth Amendment   In 1869 the Radicals pushed through the Fifteenth Amendment, the final major measure in the constitutional revolution of Reconstruction. This measure forbade states to deny the right to vote "on account of race, color, or previous condition of servitude." Such wording did not guarantee the right to vote. It deliberately left states free to restrict suffrage on other grounds so that northern states could continue to deny suffrage to women and certain groups of men—Chinese immigrants, illiterates, and those too poor to pay poll taxes.

Although several states outside the South refused to ratify, three-fourths of the states approved the measure, and the Fifteenth Amendment became law in 1870. It, too, had been a political compromise, and though African Americans rejoiced all across the land at its enactment, it left open the possibility for states to create countless qualification tests to obstruct voting in the future.

With passage of the Fifteenth Amendment, many Americans, especially supportive northerners, considered Reconstruction essentially completed. "Let us have done with Reconstruction," pleaded the *New York Tribune* in April 1870. "The country is tired and sick of it. . . . Let us have Peace!" But some northerners, like abolitionist Wendell Phillips, worried. "Our day," he warned, "is fast slipping away. Once let public thought float off from the great issue of the war, and it will take . . . more than a generation to bring it back again."

POLITICS AND RECONSTRUCTION IN THE SOUTH

From the start, Reconstruction encountered the resistance of white southerners. In the black codes and in private attitudes, many whites stubbornly opposed emancipation, and the former planter class proved especially unbending because of their tremendous financial loss in slaves. In 1866 a Georgia newspaper frankly observed that "most of the white citizens believe that the institution of slavery was right, and . . . they will believe that the condition, which comes nearest to slavery, that can now be established will be the best." And for many poor whites who had never owned slaves and yet had sacrificed enormously in the war, destitution, plummeting agricultural prices, disease, and the uncertainties of a growing urban industrialization, drove them off land, toward cities, and into hatred of the very idea of black equality.

White Resistance   Fearing loss of control over their slaves, some planters attempted to postpone freedom by denying or misrepresenting events. Former slaves reported that their owners "didn't tell them it was freedom" or "wouldn't let [them] go." Agents of the Freedmen's Bureau reported that "the old system of slavery [is] working with even more rigor than formerly at a few miles distant from any point where U.S. troops are stationed." To hold onto their workers, some landowners claimed control over black children and used guardianship and apprentice laws to bind black families to the plantation.

Whites also blocked blacks from acquiring land. A few planters divided up plots among their slaves, but most condemned the idea of making blacks landowners.

A Georgia woman whose family was known for its support of religious education for slaves was outraged that two property owners planned to "rent their lands to the Negroes!" Such action was, she declared, "injurious to the best interest of the community."

Adamant resistance by whites soon manifested itself in other ways, including violence. In one North Carolina town, a local magistrate clubbed a black man on a public street, and in several states bands of "Regulators" terrorized blacks who displayed any independence. Amid their defeat, many planters believed, as a South Carolinian put it, that blacks "can't be governed except with the whip." And after President Johnson encouraged the South to resist congressional Reconstruction, many white conservatives worked hard to capture the new state governments, while others boycotted the polls in an attempt to defeat Congress's plans.

Black Voters and the Southern Republican Party

Very few black men stayed away from the polls. Enthusiastically and hopefully, they voted Republican. Most agreed with one man who felt he should "stick to the end with the party that freed me." Illiteracy did not prohibit blacks (or uneducated whites) from making intelligent choices. Although Mississippi's William Henry could read only "a little," he testified that he and his friends had no difficulty selecting the Republican ballot. "We stood around and watched," he explained. "We saw D. Sledge vote; he owned half the county. We knowed he voted Democratic so we voted the other ticket so it would be Republican." Women, who could not vote, encouraged their husbands and sons, and preachers exhorted their congregations to use the franchise. Zeal for voting spread through entire black communities.

Thanks to a large black turnout and the restrictions on prominent Confederates, a new southern Republican Party came to power in the constitutional conventions of 1868–1870. Republican delegates consisted of a sizable contingent of blacks (265 out of the total of just over 1,000 delegates throughout the South), some northerners who had moved to the South, and native southern whites who favored change. The new constitutions drafted by this Republican coalition were more democratic than anything previously adopted in the history of the South. They eliminated property qualifications for voting and holding office, and they turned many appointed offices into elective posts. They provided for public schools and institutions to care for the mentally ill, the blind, the deaf, the destitute, and the orphaned.

The conventions broadened women's rights in property holding and divorce. Usually the goal was not to make women equal with men but to provide relief to thousands of suffering debtors. In white families left poverty-stricken by the war and weighed down by debt, it was usually the husband who had contracted the debts. Thus giving women legal control over their own property provided some protection to their families.

Triumph of Republican Governments

Under these new constitutions the southern states elected Republican-controlled governments. For the first time, the ranks of state legislators in 1868 included black southerners. It remained to be seen now how much social change these new governments would foster. Contrary to what white southerners would later claim, the Republican state governments did not disfranchise ex-Confederates as a group. James Lynch, a leading black politician from Mississippi, explained why African Americans shunned the "folly" of disfranchising whites. Unlike northerners who "can leave when it becomes too uncomfortable," landless former slaves "must be in friendly relations with the great body of the whites in the state. Otherwise ... peace can be maintained only by a standing army." Despised and lacking material or social power, southern Republicans strove for acceptance, legitimacy, and safe ways to gain a foothold in a depressed economy.

Far from being vindictive toward the race that had enslaved them, most southern blacks treated leading rebels with generosity and appealed to white southerners to adopt a spirit of fairness. In this way the South's Republican Party condemned itself to defeat if white voters would not cooperate. Within a few years most of the fledgling Republican parties in the southern states would be struggling for survival against violent white hostility. But for a time some propertied whites accepted congressional Reconstruction as a reality.

Industrialization and Mill Towns

Reflecting northern ideals and southern necessity, the Reconstruction governments enthusiastically promoted industry. Accordingly, Reconstruction legislatures encouraged investment with loans, subsidies, and short-term exemptions from taxation. The southern railroad system was rebuilt and expanded, and coal and iron mining made possible Birmingham's steel plants. Between 1860 and 1880, the number of manufacturing establishments in the South nearly doubled.

This emphasis on big business, however, produced higher state debts and taxes, drew money away from schools and other programs, and multiplied possibilities for corruption in state legislatures. The alliance between business and government took firm hold, often at the expense of the needs of common farmers and laborers. It also locked Republicans into a conservative strategy and doomed them to failure in building support among poorer whites.

Poverty remained the lot of vast numbers of southern whites. On a daily basis during the Reconstruction years, they had to subordinate politics to the struggle for livelihood. The war had caused a massive one-time loss of income-producing wealth, such as livestock, and a steep decline in land values. From 1860 to 1880, the South's share of per capita income fell from nearly equal to only 51 percent of the national average. In many regions the old planter class still ruled the best land and access to credit or markets.

As many poor whites and blacks found farming less tenable, they moved to cities and new mill towns. Industrialization did not sweep the South as it did the North, but it certainly laid deep roots. Attracting textile mills to southern towns became a competitive crusade. "Next to God," shouted a North Carolina evangelist, "what this town needs is a cotton mill!" In 1860 the South counted some 10,000 mill workers; by 1880, the number grew to 16,741 and by the end of the century, to 97,559. In thousands of human dramas, poor southerners began the multi-generational journey from farmer to mill worker and other forms of low-income urban wage earner.

Republicans and Racial Equality

Policies appealing to African American voters never went beyond equality before the law. In fact, the whites who controlled the southern Republican Party were reluctant to allow blacks a share of offices proportionate to their electoral strength. Aware of their weakness, black leaders did not push very far for revolutionary economic or social change. In every southern state, they led efforts to establish public schools, although they did not press for integrated facilities. In 1870 South Carolina passed the first comprehensive school law in the South. By 1875, 50 percent of black school-age children in that state were enrolled in school, and approximately one-third of the three thousand teachers were black.

Some African American politicians did fight for civil rights and integration. Many were from cities such as New Orleans or Mobile, where large populations of light-skinned free blacks had existed before the war. Their experience in such communities had made them sensitive to issues of status, and they spoke out for open and equal public accommodations. Laws requiring equal accommodations won passage, but they often went unenforced.

The vexing questions of land reform and enforcement of racial equality, however, all but overwhelmed the Republican governments. Land reform largely failed because in most states whites were in the majority, and former slaveowners controlled the best land and other sources of economic power. Economic progress was uppermost in the minds of most freedpeople. Black southerners needed land, and much land did fall into state hands for nonpayment of taxes. Such land was offered for sale in small lots. But most freedmen had too little cash to bid against investors or speculators. South Carolina established a land commission, but it could help only those with money to buy. Any widespread redistribution of land had to arise from Congress, which never supported such action.

Myth of "Negro Rule" Within a few years, as centrists in both parties met with failure, white hostility to congressional Reconstruction began to dominate. Some conservatives had always wanted to fight Reconstruction through pressure and racist propaganda. They put economic and social pressure on blacks: one black Republican reported that "my neighbors will not employ me, nor sell me a farthing's worth of anything." Charging that the South had been turned over to ignorant blacks, conservatives deplored "black domination," which became a rallying cry for a return to white supremacy.

Such attacks were inflammatory propaganda and part of the growing myth of "Negro rule," which would serve as a central theme in battles over the memory of Reconstruction. African Americans participated in politics but hardly dominated or controlled events. They were a majority in only two out of ten state constitutional writing conventions (transplanted northerners were a majority in one). In the state legislatures, only in the lower house in South Carolina did blacks ever constitute a majority. Sixteen blacks won seats in Congress before Reconstruction was over, but none was ever elected governor. Only eighteen served in a high state office, such as lieutenant governor, treasurer, superintendent of education, or secretary of state.

In all, some four hundred blacks served in political office during the Reconstruction era, a signal achievement by any standard. Although they never dominated the process, they established a rich tradition of government service and civic activism. Elected officials, such as Robert Smalls in South Carolina, labored tirelessly for cheaper land prices, better healthcare, access to schools, and the enforcement of civil rights for their people. For too long the black politicians of Reconstruction were the forgotten heroes of this seedtime of America's long civil rights movement.

Carpetbaggers and Scalawags Conservatives also assailed the allies of black Republicans. Their propaganda denounced whites from the North as "carpetbaggers," greedy crooks planning to pour stolen tax revenues into their sturdy luggage made of carpet material. Immigrants from the North, who held the largest share of Republican offices, were all tarred with this rhetorical brush.

In fact, most northerners who settled in the South had come seeking business opportunities, as schoolteachers, or to find a warmer climate; most never entered politics.

Those who did enter politics generally wanted to democratize the South and to introduce northern ways, such as industry and public education. Carpetbaggers' ideals were tested by hard times and ostracism by white southerners.

In addition to tagging northern interlopers as carpetbaggers, conservatives invented the term *scalawag* to discredit any native white southerner who cooperated with the Republicans. A substantial number of southerners did so, including some wealthy and prominent men. Most scalawags, however, were yeoman farmers, men from mountain areas and nonslaveholding districts who had been Unionists under the Confederacy. They saw that they could benefit from the education and opportunities promoted by Republicans. Sometimes banding together with freedmen, they pursued common class interests and hoped to make headway against the power of long-dominant planters. Such cooperation led to genuine hopes for black-white coalitions, but most of these efforts in the long run floundered in the quicksand of racism.

Tax Policy and Corruption as Political Wedges

Taxation was a major problem for the Reconstruction governments. Republicans wanted to repair the war's destruction, stimulate industry, and support such new ventures as public schools. But the Civil War had destroyed much of the South's tax base. One category of valuable property—slaves—had disappeared entirely. And hundreds of thousands of citizens had lost much of the rest of their property—money, livestock, fences, and buildings—to the war. Thus an increase in taxes (sales, excise, and property) was necessary even to maintain traditional services. Inevitably, Republican tax policies aroused strong opposition, especially among the yeomen.

Corruption was another serious charge levied against the Republicans. Unfortunately, it was often true. Many carpetbaggers and black politicians engaged in fraudulent schemes, sold their votes, or padded expenses, taking part in what scholars recognize was a nationwide surge of corruption in an age ruled by "spoilsmen". Corruption carried no party label, but the Democrats successfully pinned the blame on unqualified blacks and greedy carpetbaggers among southern Republicans.

Ku Klux Klan

All these problems hurt the Republicans, whose leaders also allowed factionalism along racial and class lines to undermine party unity. But in many southern states the deathblow came through violence. The Ku Klux Klan (its members altered the Greek word for "circle," *kuklos*), a secret veterans' club that began in Tennessee in 1866, spread through the South and rapidly evolved into a terrorist organization. Violence against African Americans occurred from the first days of Reconstruction but became far more organized and purposeful after 1867. Klansmen sought to frustrate Reconstruction and keep the freedmen in subjection. Nighttime harassment, whippings, beatings, rapes, and murders became common, as terrorism dominated some counties and regions.

Although the Klan tormented blacks who stood up for their rights as laborers or individuals, its main purpose was political. Lawless nightriders made active Republicans the target of their attacks. Leading white and black Republicans were killed in several states. After freedmen who worked for a South Carolina scalawag started voting, terrorists visited the plantation and, in the words of one victim, "whipped every . . . [black] man they could lay their hands on." Klansmen also attacked Union League clubs—Republican organizations that mobilized the black vote—and schoolteachers who were aiding the freedmen.

Klan violence was not a spontaneous outburst of racism; very specific social forces shaped and directed it. In North Carolina, for example, Alamance and Caswell Counties were the sites of the worst Klan violence. Slim Republican majorities there rested on cooperation between black voters and white yeomen, particularly those whose Unionism or discontent with the Confederacy had turned them against local Democratic officials. Together, these black and white Republicans had ousted officials long entrenched in power. The wealthy and powerful men in Alamance and Caswell who had lost their accustomed political control were the Klan's county officers and local chieftains. They organized a deliberate campaign of terror, recruiting members and planning atrocities. By intimidation and murder, the Klan weakened the Republican coalition and restored a Democratic majority.

Klan violence injured Republicans across the South. One of every ten black leaders who had been delegates to the 1867–1868 state constitutional conventions was attacked, seven fatally. In one judicial district of North Carolina, the Ku Klux Klan was responsible for twelve murders, over seven hundred beatings, and other acts of violence, including rape and arson. A single attack on Alabama Republicans in the town of Eutaw left four blacks dead and fifty-four wounded. In South Carolina, five hundred masked Klansmen lynched eight black prisoners at the Union County jail, and in nearby York County, the Klan committed at least eleven murders and hundreds of whippings. According to historian Eric Foner, the Klan "made it virtually impossible for Republicans to campaign or vote in large parts of Georgia."

Thus a combination of difficult fiscal problems, Republican mistakes, racial hostility, and terror brought down the Republican regimes. In most southern states, Radical Reconstruction lasted only a few years. The most enduring failure of Reconstruction, however, was not political; it was social and economic. Reconstruction failed to alter the South's social structure or its distribution of wealth and power.

RETREAT FROM RECONSTRUCTION

During the 1870s, northerners increasingly lost the political will to sustain Reconstruction in the South, as a vast economic and social transformation occurred in their own region as well as in the West. Radical Republicans like Albion Tourgée, a former Union soldier who moved to North Carolina and was elected a judge, condemned Congress's timidity. Turning the freedman out on his own without protection, said Tourgée, constituted "cheap philanthropy." Indeed, many African Americans believed that, during Reconstruction, the North "threw all the Negroes on the world without any way of getting along." As the North underwent its own transformations and lost interest in the South's dilemmas, Reconstruction collapsed.

Political Implications of Klan Terrorism

In one southern state after another, Democrats regained control, and they threatened to defeat Republicans in the North as well. Whites in the old Confederacy referred to this decline of Reconstruction as "southern redemption," and during the 1870s, "redeemer" Democrats claimed to be the saviors of the South from alleged "black domination" and "carpetbag rule." And for one of only a few times in American history, violence and terror emerged as a tactic in normal politics.

In 1870 and 1871 the violent campaigns of the Ku Klux Klan forced Congress to pass two Enforcement Acts and an anti-Klan law. These laws made actions by individuals against the civil and political rights of others a federal criminal offense for the first time. They also provided for election supervisors and permitted martial law and suspension of the writ of habeas corpus to combat murders, beatings, and threats by the Klan. Federal prosecutors used the laws rather selectively. In 1872 and 1873, Mississippi and the Carolinas saw many prosecutions; but in other states where violence flourished, the laws were virtually ignored. Southern juries sometimes refused to convict Klansmen; out of a total of 3,310 cases, only 1,143 ended in convictions. Although many Klansmen (roughly 2,000 in South Carolina alone) fled their state to avoid prosecution, and the Klan officially disbanded, the threat of violence did not end. Paramilitary organizations known as Rifle Clubs and Red Shirts often took the Klan's place.

Klan terrorism openly defied Congress, yet even on this issue there were ominous signs that the North's commitment to racial justice was fading. Some conservative but influential Republicans opposed the anti-Klan laws. Rejecting other Republicans' arguments that the Thirteenth, Fourteenth, and Fifteenth Amendments had made the federal government the protector of the rights of citizens, these dissenters echoed an old Democratic charge that Congress was infringing on states' rights. Senator Lyman Trumbull of Illinois declared that the states remained "the depositories of the rights of the individual." If Congress could punish crimes like assault or murder, he asked, "what is the need of the State governments?" For years Democrats had complained of "centralization and consolidation"; now some Republicans seemed to agree with them. This opposition foreshadowed a more general revolt within Republican ranks in 1872.

Industrial Expansion and Reconstruction in the North

Both immigration and industrialization surged in the North. Between 1865 and 1873, 3 million immigrants entered the country, most settling in the industrial cities of the North and West. Within only eight years, postwar industrial production increased by 75 percent. For the first time, nonagricultural workers outnumbered farmers, and wage earners outnumbered independent craftsmen. And by 1873 only Britain's industrial output was greater than that of the United States. Government financial policies did much to bring about this rapid growth. Low taxes on investment and high tariffs on manufactured goods aided the growth of a new class of powerful industrialists, especially railroad entrepreneurs.

Railroads became the symbol of and the stimulus for the American age of capital. From 1865 to 1873, 35,000 miles of new track were laid, a total exceeding the entire national rail network of 1860. Railroad building fueled the banking industry and made Wall Street the center of American capitalism. Eastern railroad magnates, such as Thomas Scott of the Pennsylvania Railroad, the largest corporation of its time, created economic empires with the assistance of huge government subsidies of cash and land. Railroad corporations also bought up mining operations, granaries, and lumber companies. In Congress and in every state legislature, big business now employed lobbyists to curry favor with government. Corruption ran rampant, with some congressmen and legislators were paid annual retainers by major companies.

This soaring capitalist-political alliance led as well to an intensified struggle between labor and capital. As captains of industry amassed unprecedented fortunes in an age with no income tax, gross economic inequality polarized American society. The work force, worried a prominent Massachusetts business leader, was in a "transition state . . . living in boarding houses" and becoming a "permanent factory population." In Cincinnati, three large factories employed as many workers as the city's thousands of small shops. In New York or Philadelphia, workers increasingly lived in dark, unhealthy tenement housing. Thousands would list themselves on the census as "common laborer" or "general jobber." Many of the free labor maxims of the Republican Party were now under great duress. Did the individual work ethic guarantee social mobility in America or erode, under the pressure of profit making, into a world of unsafe factories, child labor, and declining wages? In 1868 the Republicans managed to pass an eight-hour workday bill in Congress that applied to federal workers. The "labor question" (see Chapter 18) now preoccupied northerners far more than the "southern" or the "freedmen" question.

Then the Panic of 1873 ushered in over five years of economic contraction. Three million people lost their jobs as class attitudes diverged, especially in large cities. Debtors and the unemployed sought easy-money policies to spur economic expansion (workers and farmers desperately needed cash). Businessmen, disturbed by the widespread strikes and industrial violence that accompanied the panic, fiercely defended property rights and demanded "sound money" policies. The chasm between farmers and workers on the one hand, and wealthy industrialists on the other, grew ever wider.

Liberal Republican Revolt Disenchanted with Reconstruction, a largely northern group calling itself the Liberal Republicans bolted the party in 1872 and nominated Horace Greeley, the famous editor of the *New York Tribune,* for president. The Liberal Republicans were a varied group, including foes of corruption and advocates of a lower tariff. Normally such disparate elements would not cooperate with one another, but two popular and widespread attitudes united them: distaste for federal intervention in the South and an elitist desire to let market forces and the "best men" determine policy and events.

The Democrats also gave their nomination to Greeley in 1872. The combination was not enough to defeat Grant, who won reelection, but it reinforced Grant's desire to avoid confrontation with white southerners. Greeley's campaign for North-South reunion, for "clasping hands across the bloody chasm," was a bit premature to win at the polls but was a harbinger of the future in American politics. Organized Blue-Gray fraternalism (gatherings of Union and Confederate veterans) began as early as 1874. Grant continued to use military force sparingly and in 1875 refused a desperate request from the governor of Mississippi for troops to quell racial and political terrorism in that state.

Dissatisfaction with Grant's administration grew during his second term. Strong-willed but politically naive, Grant made a series of poor appointments. His secretary of war, his private secretary, and officials in the Treasury and Navy Departments were involved in bribery or tax-cheating scandals. Instead of exposing the corruption, Grant defended the culprits. In 1874, as Grant's popularity and his party's prestige declined, the Democrats recaptured the House of Representatives, signaling the end of the Radical Republican vision of Reconstruction.

The Grants' Tour of the World

On May 17, 1877, two weeks after his presidency ended, Ulysses S. Grant and his wife Julia embarked from Philadelphia on a grand tour of the world that would last twenty-six months. Portrayed as a private vacation, the trip was a very public affair. The taint of corruption in Grant's second term could be dissipated only in the air of foreign lands reached by steamship. The small entourage included John Russell Young, a reporter for the *New York Herald* who recorded the journey in the two-volume, illustrated *Around the World with General Grant*. The Grants' expenses were paid by banker friends and by Grant's personal resources, accumulated in gifts.

The Grants spent many months in England attending a bewildering array of banquets, one with Queen Victoria. In Newcastle, thousands of workingmen conducted a massive parade in Grant's honor. He was received as the odd American cousin, simple and great, the conqueror and warrior statesman. In an age that worshiped great men, Grant was viewed as the savior of the American nation, the liberator of slaves, and a celebrity—a measure of the American presence on the world stage.

On the European continent the pattern continued, as every royal or republican head of state hosted the Grants. In Belgium, France, Switzerland, Italy, Russia, Poland, Austria, and Spain, the Grants reveled in princely attentions. In Berlin, Grant met Otto von Bismarck, the chancellor of Germany. The two got along well discussing war, world politics, and the abolition of slavery.

The Grants next went to Egypt, where they rode donkeys into remote villages along the Nile and then traveled by train to the Indian Ocean, where they embarked for India. They encountered British imperialism in full flower in Bombay, and that of the French in Saigon. Northward in Asia, the grand excursion went to China and Japan. In Canton, Grant passed before an assemblage of young men who, according to a reporter, "looked upon the barbarian with . . . contempt in their expression, very much as our young men in

On their tour of the world, Ulysses and Julia Grant sat here with companions and guides in front of the Great Hypostyle Hall at the Temple of Amon-Ra in Karnak at Luxor, Egypt, 1878. The Grants' extraordinary tour included many such photo opportunities, often depicting the plebeian American president's presence in exotic places with unusual people. Whether he liked it or not, Grant was a world celebrity. *(Library of Congress)*

(Continued)

The Grants' Tour of the World

New York would regard Sitting Bull or Red Cloud." In Japan, the Grants had a rare audience with Emperor Mutsuhito in the imperial palace. Grant found Japan "beautiful beyond description," and the receptions there were the most formal of all.

"I am both homesick and dread going home," Grant wrote in April 1879. Sailing across the Pacific, the Grants landed in San Francisco in late June. Why had Grant taken such a prolonged trip? Travel itself had its own rewards, but the tour became an unusual political campaign. Grant sought publicity abroad to convince his countrymen back home that they should reelect him president in 1880. But the strategy failed; Grant had developed no compelling issue or reason why Americans should choose him again. He would spend his final years, however, a war hero and a national symbol. No American president would again establish such personal links to the world until Woodrow Wilson at the end of World War I.

General Amnesty The effect of Democratic gains in Congress was to weaken legislative resolve on southern issues. Congress had already lifted the political disabilities of the Fourteenth Amendment from many former Confederates. In 1872 it had adopted a sweeping Amnesty Act, which pardoned most of the remaining rebels and left only five hundred barred from political office holding. In 1875 Congress passed a Civil Rights Act, partly as a tribute to the recently deceased Charles Sumner, purporting to guarantee black people equal accommodations in public places, such as inns and theaters, but the bill was watered down and contained no effective provisions for enforcement. (The Supreme Court later struck down this law.)

Democrats regained control of four state governments before 1872 and a total of eight by the end of January 1876. In the North, Democrats successfully stressed the failure and scandals of Reconstruction governments. As opinion shifted, many Republicans sensed that their constituents were tiring of southern issues and the legacies of the war. Sectional reconciliation now seemed crucial for commerce. The nation was expanding westward rapidly, and the South was a new frontier for investment.

The West, Race, and Reconstruction Nowhere did the new complexity and violence of American race relations play out so vividly as in the West. As the Fourteenth Amendment and other enactments granted to blacks the beginnings of citizenship, other nonwhite peoples faced continued persecution. Across the West, the federal government pursued a policy of containment against Native Americans. In California, where white farmers and ranchers often forced Indians into captive labor, some civilians practiced a more violent form of "Indian hunting." By 1880, thirty years of such violence left an estimated 4,500 California Indians dead at the hands of white settlers.

In Texas and the Southwest, the rhetoric of national expansion still deemed Mexicans and other mixed-race Hispanics to be debased, "lazy," and incapable of self-government. And in California and other states of the Far West, thousands of Chinese immigrants became the victims of brutal violence. Few whites had objected to the Chinese who did the dangerous work of building railroads through the Rocky Mountains. But when the Chinese began to compete for urban, industrial jobs, great conflict emerged. Anti-coolie clubs appeared in California in the 1870s, seeking laws against Chinese labor, fanning the flames of racism, and organizing vigilante attacks on Chinese workers and the factories that employed them. Western politicians sought white votes by pandering to prejudice, and in 1879 the new California constitution denied the vote to Chinese.

If we view America from coast to coast, and not merely on the North-South axis, the Civil War and Reconstruction years both dismantled racial slavery and fostered a volatile new racial complexity, especially in the West. During the same age when early anthropologists employed elaborate theories of "scientific" racism to determine a hierarchy of racial types, the West was a vast region of racial mixing and conflict. Some African Americans, despite generations of mixture with Native Americans, asserted that they were more like whites than the nomadic, "uncivilized" Indians, while others, like the Creek freedmen of Indian Territory, sought an Indian identity. In Texas, whites, Indians, blacks, and Hispanics had mixed for decades, and by the 1870s forced reconsideration in law and custom of who was white and who was not.

During Reconstruction, America was undergoing what one historian has called a reconstruction of the very idea of race itself. As it did so, tumbling into some of the darkest years of American race relations, the turbulence of the expanding West reinforced the new nationalism and the reconciliation of North and South based on a resurgent white supremacy.

Foreign Expansion   Following the Civil War, pressure for expansion reemerged (see Chapter 22), and in 1867 Secretary of State William H. Seward arranged a vast addition of territory to the national domain through the purchase of Alaska from Russia. Opponents ridiculed Seward's $7.2 million venture, calling Alaska "Frigidia," "the Polar Bear Garden," and "Walrussia." But Seward convinced important congressmen of Alaska's economic potential, and other lawmakers favored the dawning of friendship with Russia.

Also in 1867 the United States took control of the Midway Islands, a thousand miles northwest of Hawai'i. And in 1870 President Grant tried unsuccessfully to annex the Dominican Republic. Seward and his successor, Hamilton Fish, also resolved troubling Civil War grievances against Great Britain. Through diplomacy they arranged a financial settlement of claims on Britain for damage done by the *Alabama* and other cruisers built in England and sold to the Confederacy. They recognized that sectional reconciliation in Reconstruction America would serve new ambitions for world commerce and expansion.

Judicial   Meanwhile, the Supreme Court played its part in the northern
Retreat from   retreat from Reconstruction. During the Civil War, the Court
Reconstruction   had been cautious and inactive. Reaction to the *Dred Scott*
                        decision (1857) had been so vehement, and the Union's wartime emergency so great, that the Court had avoided interference with government actions. The justices breathed a collective sigh of relief, for example, when legal technicalities prevented them from reviewing the case of Clement Vallandigham, a Democratic opponent of Lincoln's war effort who had been convicted by a military tribunal of aiding the enemy. But in 1866 a similar case, *Ex parte Milligan,* reached the Court.

Lambdin P. Milligan of Indiana had plotted to free Confederate prisoners of war and overthrow state governments. For these acts a military court sentenced Milligan, a civilian, to death. Milligan challenged the authority of the military tribunal, claiming that he had a right to a civil trial. The Supreme Court declared that military trials were illegal when civil courts were open and functioning, and its language indicated that the Court intended to reassert its authority.

In the 1870s the Court successfully renewed its challenge to Congress's actions when it narrowed the meaning and effectiveness of the Fourteenth Amendment. The *Slaughter-House* cases (1873) began in 1869, when the Louisiana legislature granted one company a monopoly on the slaughtering of livestock in New Orleans. Rival butchers in the city promptly sued. Their attorney, former Supreme Court justice John A. Campbell, argued that Louisiana had violated the rights of some of its citizens in favor of others. The Fourteenth Amendment, Campbell contended, had revolutionized the constitutional system by bringing individual rights under federal protection. Campbell thus articulated an original goal of the Republican Party: to nationalize civil rights and guard them from state interference.

But in the *Slaughter-House* decision, the Supreme Court dealt a stunning blow to the scope and vitality of the Fourteenth Amendment. Refusing to accept Campbell's argument, the Court declared state citizenship and national citizenship separate. National citizenship involved only matters such as the right to travel freely from state to state, and only such narrow rights, held the Court, were protected by the Fourteenth Amendment.

The Supreme Court also concluded that the butchers who sued had not been deprived of their rights or property in violation of the due-process clause of the amendment. Shrinking from a role as "perpetual censor upon all legislation of the States, on the civil rights of their own citizens," the Court's majority declared that the framers of the recent amendments had not intended to "destroy" the federal system, in which the states exercised "powers for domestic and local government, including the regulation of civil rights." Thus the justices severely limited the amendment's potential for securing and protecting the rights of black citizens—its original intent.

The next day the Court decided *Bradwell v. Illinois,* a case in which Myra Bradwell, a female attorney, had been denied the right to practice law in Illinois because she was a married woman, and hence not considered a free agent. Pointing to the Fourteenth Amendment, Bradwell's attorneys contended that the state had unconstitutionally abridged her "privileges and immunities" as a citizen. The Supreme Court rejected her claim, declaring a woman's "paramount destiny . . . to fulfill the noble and benign offices of wife and mother."

In 1876 the Court weakened the Reconstruction era amendments even further by emasculating the enforcement clause of the Fourteenth Amendment and revealing deficiencies inherent in the Fifteenth Amendment. In *U.S. v. Cruikshank* the Court overruled the conviction under the 1870 Enforcement Act of Louisiana whites who had attacked a meeting of blacks and conspired to deprive them of their rights. The justices ruled that the Fourteenth Amendment did not give the federal government power to act against these whites. The duty of protecting citizens' equal rights, the Court said, "rests alone with the States." Such judicial conservatism had a profound impact down through the next century, blunting the revolutionary potential in the Civil War amendments.

Disputed Election of 1876 and Compromise of 1877   As the 1876 elections approached, most political observers saw that the nation was increasingly focused on economic issues and that the North was no longer willing to pursue the goals of Reconstruction. The results of a disputed presidential election confirmed this fact. Samuel J. Tilden, the Democratic governor of New York, ran strongly in the South and needed only one more electoral vote to triumph over Rutherford B. Hayes, the Republican nominee. Nineteen electoral votes from Louisiana, South Carolina, and Florida (the only southern states not yet under Democratic rule) were disputed; both Democrats and Republicans claimed to have won in those states despite fraud committed by their opponents.

To resolve this unprecedented situation Congress established a fifteen-member electoral commission. Membership on the commission was to be balanced between Democrats and Republicans. Because the Republicans held the majority in Congress, they prevailed, 8 to 7, on every attempt to count the returns, with commission members voting along strict party lines. Hayes would become president if Congress accepted the commission's findings.

Congressional acceptance was not certain. Democrats controlled the House and could filibuster to block action on the vote. Many citizens worried that the nation would slip once again into civil war, as some southerners vowed, "Tilden or Fight!" The crisis was resolved when Democrats acquiesced in the election of Hayes based on a "deal" cut in a Washington hotel between Hayes's supporters and southerners who wanted federal aid to railroads, internal improvements, federal patronage, and removal of troops from southern states. Northern and southern Democrats simply decided not to contest the election of a Republican who was not going to continue Reconstruction policies in the South. Thus Hayes became president, inaugurated privately inside the

MAP 16.2 Presidential Election of 1876 and the Compromise of 1877

In 1876 a combination of solid southern support and Democratic gains in the North gave Samuel Tilden the majority of popular votes, but Rutherford B. Hayes won the disputed election in the electoral college, after a deal satisfied Democratic wishes for an end to Reconstruction.

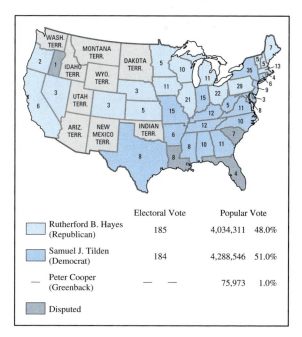

	Electoral Vote	Popular Vote	
Rutherford B. Hayes (Republican)	185	4,034,311	48.0%
Samuel J. Tilden (Democrat)	184	4,288,546	51.0%
Peter Cooper (Greenback)	— —	75,973	1.0%
Disputed			

White House to avoid any threat of violence. Southerners relished their promises of economic aid, and Reconstruction was unmistakably over.

Southern Democrats rejoiced, but African Americans grieved over the betrayal of their hopes for equality. The Civil War had brought emancipation, and Reconstruction had guaranteed their rights under law. But events and attitudes in larger white America were foreboding. In a Fourth of July speech in Washington, D.C., in 1875, Frederick Douglass anticipated this predicament. He reflected anxiously on the American centennial to be celebrated the following year. The nation, Douglass feared, would "lift to the sky its million voices in one grand Centennial hosanna of peace and good will to all the white race . . . from gulf to lakes and from sea to sea." Douglass looked back on fifteen years of unparalleled change for his people and worried about the hold of white supremacy on America's historical memory: "If war among the whites brought peace and liberty to the blacks, what will peace among the whites bring?" Douglass's question would echo down through American political culture for decades.

SUMMARY

Reconstruction left a contradictory record. It was an era of tragic aspirations and failures but also of unprecedented legal, political, and social change. The Union victory brought about an increase in federal power, stronger nationalism, sweeping federal intervention in the southern states, and landmark amendments to the Constitution. But northern commitment to make these changes endure had eroded, and the revolution remained unfinished. The mystic sense of promise for new lives and liberties among the freedpeople, demonstrated in that first Decoration Day in Charleston, had fallen into a new, if temporary, kind of ruin.

The North embraced emancipation, black suffrage, and constitutional alterations strengthening the central government. But it did so to defeat the rebellion and secure the peace. As the pressure of these crises declined, Americans, especially in the North, retreated from Reconstruction. The American people and the courts maintained a preference for state authority and a distrust of federal power. The ideology of free labor dictated that property should be respected and that individuals should be self-reliant. Racism endured and transformed into the even more virulent forms of Klan terror and theories of black degeneration. Concern for the human rights of African Americans was strongest when their plight threatened to undermine the interests of whites, and reform frequently had less appeal than moneymaking in an individualistic, industrializing society.

New challenges to American society and values began to overwhelm the aims of Reconstruction. How would the country develop its immense resources in an increasingly interconnected national economy? Could farmers, industrial workers, immigrants, and capitalists co-exist in harmony? Industrialization not only promised prosperity but also wrought increased exploitation of labor. Moreover, industry increased the nation's power and laid the foundation for an enlarged American role in international affairs. The American imagination again turned to the conquest of new frontiers.

In the wake of the Civil War, Americans faced two profound tasks—the achievement of healing and the dispensing of justice. Both had to occur, but they never developed in historical balance. Making sectional reunion compatible with black freedom and equality overwhelmed the imagination in American political culture, and the nation still faced much of this dilemma more than a century later.

Index